KANSAS TERRITORIAL SETTLERS OF 1860

Who Were Born in Tennessee,

Virginia, North Carolina, and South Carolina

95 - 1054

*A Compilation with Historical Annotations
and Editorial Comment*

By

CLARA HAMLETT ROBERTSON

CLEARFIELD COMPANY
REPRINTS & REMAINDERS

Reprinted for Clearfield Company Inc. by
Genealogical Publishing Co. Inc.
Baltimore, MD 1990

Library of Congress Catalogue Card Number 76-13287
International Standard Book Number 0-8063-0697-1

Made in the United States of America

KANSAS TERRITORIAL SETTLERS OF 1860

WHO WERE BORN IN

TENNESSEE, VIRGINIA, NORTH CAROLINA AND SOUTH CAROLINA

Taken from the W.P.A. index of the eleven-volume hand-written
census books in the Kansas State Historical Society Archives

Together with

MAPS OF KANSAS AND EASTERN COLORADO

Showing the area included in the Kansas Territory

1854-1861

A compilation with historical annotations and editorial comment

by

Clara Hamlett Robertson

In memory of her parents, James Morrison and Maude Clifton Hamlett,
whose forebears came from these four states.

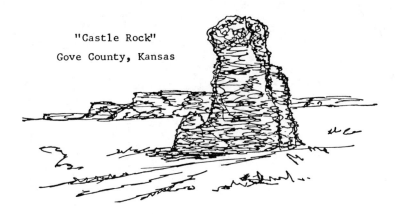

"Castle Rock"
Gove County, Kansas

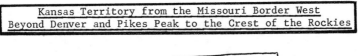

Kansas Territory from the Missouri Border West
Beyond Denver and Pikes Peak to the Crest of the Rockies

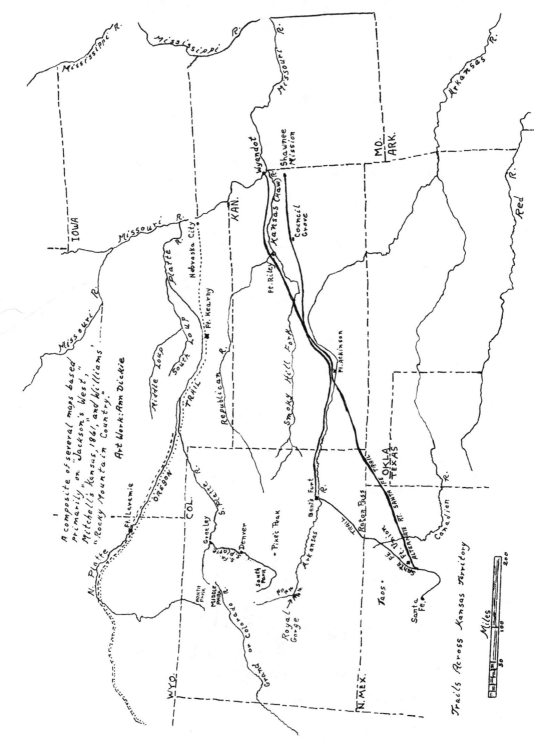

TABLE OF CONTENTS

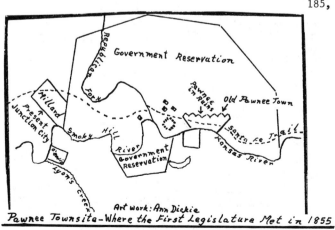

Pawnee Townsite-Where the First Legislature Met in 1855

Art work: Ann Dickie

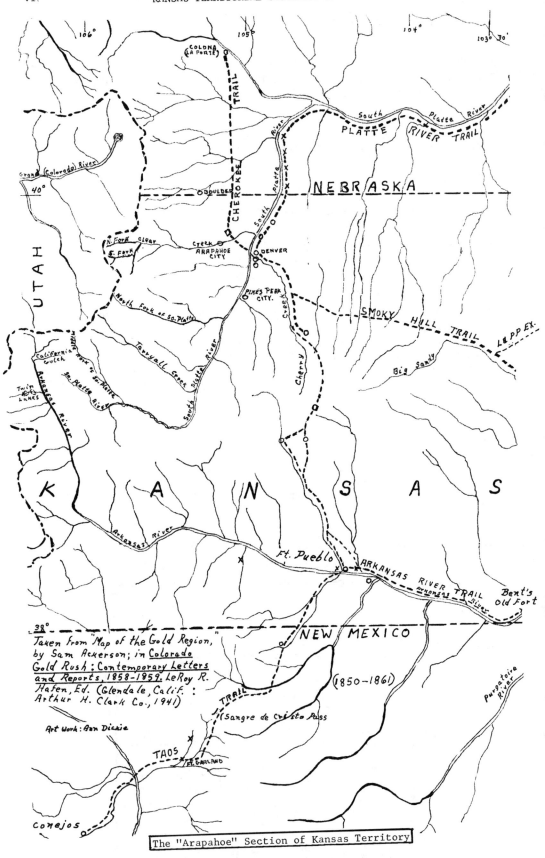

The "Arapahoe" Section of Kansas Territory

List of Maps and Illustrations

Small Maps for Orientation in Locating 1860 Place Names

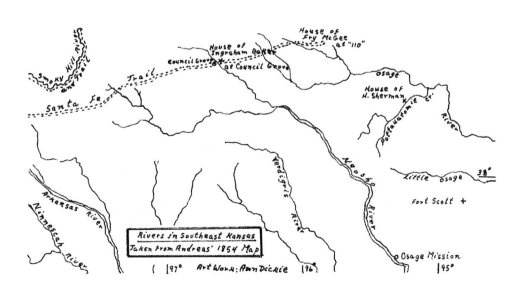

KANSAS TERRITORIAL SETTLERS OF 1860

BORN IN TENNESSEE, VIRGINIA, NORTH CAROLINA AND SOUTH CAROLINA

The Great Seal of the State of Kansas was inspired by the
history of its parent, the Kansas Territory; by the wide-
spread horizons of that vast rising stretch of land, from
the banks of the Missouri with its side-wheeler steamboats
to the snow-capped crests of the Colorado Rockies; by the
nature of the land and of the people who called it home.

FOREWORD

In 1961 Kansas celebrated its 100th year of statehood. It was my good fortune to work in the state from 1960 to 1969 and thus I was able to benefit from the historical review generated during the Centennial year. At one of the festivities the speaker referred poetically to the geologic formation of Kansas, "And God smoothed his hand over Kansas."[1]

This phrase brings visions of the prairies --in early spring green as a golf course, golden with the ripened grain of summer, or brown in fall and winter when the protein-rich grasslands in the Flint Hills are dotted with cattle. Somehow it also brings to mind the sturdy pioneers who were attracted to this good land, their way smoothed by the godliness of their families and neighbors.

I often remarked while living and working in Kansas on the quality of life. Well-established libraries, parks, museums, and historical societies are found in almost all of the counties. The husband of one of my friends had the answer for me. He proudly acknowledged their debt to the past with this: "We had good pioneers."

It was because of my admiration for these Kansas pioneers that I gladly undertook the tabulation of a selected group at the invited suggestion of my East Tennessee Historical Society librarian in Knoxville and with the counsel of the Kansas State Historical Society staff.[2] I chose to tabulate those settlers who were born in Virginia, North Carolina, South Carolina, and Tennessee--states of great interest to me because my own pioneer ancestors had come from the three east coast states where they had lived since colonial days and had journeyed to Middle Tennessee by 1805. I was born there in Clarksville, Montgomery County, about 100 years later.

This present selected group[3] from the Kansas Territorial Census of 1860 gives a glimpse of pioneer life as it was lived in the newly opening west. You will see clues in scanning even one page: large families with sons fifteen or sixteen years old listed as "farmer" along with their fathers; editors, teachers, ministers, gold seekers and gold sackers, quartz millers, wheelwrights, ranchers--all kinds of occupations are listed.

[1] The speaker Fred Seaton was one of the guests honored at the "Kansas Native Sons and Daughters" Centennial banquet January 29, 1961.
[2] Miss Alberta Pantle, Historical Society Librarian (now retired), made the needed arrangements with other helpful personnel in the Memorial Building. Miss Pollyanna Creekmore was my East Tennessee Historical Society contact.
[3] This tabulation is taken from the W.P.A. card index of the eleven-volume hand-written census books in the Kansas State Historical Society Archives. A card file of the K.T. settlers living in the "Colorado" section in 1860 is housed in the Colorado State Historical Society Library.

Discussion of the 1860 Census

The Kansas Territorial Census of 1860 set the population of men, women, and children at 107,206 for that part of the territory which was to become the state of Kansas on January 29, 1861. Congressional representation required 93,560 settlers. The population of the "Arapahoe" area (between the 38th and 40th parallels to the crest of the Rocky Mountains in what is now the midsection of eastern Colorado) was found to be 34,277 settlers, making a total for the Kansas Territory of 141,481 free persons and 2 slaves.

"Thousands and thousands are pouring in from all portions of the Union, but more especially from Missouri, Kentucky, and Tennessee" wrote Mr. Whitehead, a Doniphan County resident in 1854.[1] Perhaps this was true in Doniphan County at that time but by 1860 settlers were coming from many northern states also.

The census, however, does not show where the settlers came from--only where they were born and the place of birth was not always filled in, especially in "Arapahoe" where all information aside from the name was sparse. Thus we have no way of knowing just how complete a picture may be drawn from our tabulations and the statistics derived therefrom. It is probably safe to say that the figures given are generally low.

In the complete census analysis by place of birth, we find that Ohio ranked first with about 11% of the population in Kansas proper as well as in the "Colorado" section (11,617 and 4125) making a total of 15,742. Missouri was a close second, with Illinois and Indiana not far behind. Natives of the Kansas Territory held next place numbering 11,194. All of them were living in "Kansas" except 197 in the "Colorado" section. This was to be expected from the proportion of men, 55%, in Kansas proper and 95% in "Colorado" where there were only 1586 females of all ages.

Almost 11% of the population was foreign born, natives of at least 40 different countries on all of the continents and many of the islands. The greatest majority (90%) of this group of foreign born were natives of the British (including British-American) or the Germanic countries. There were smaller groups from many of the European countries, especially Denmark, France, Switzerland, Belgium, and Sweden.[2]

The Special Index

The official returns cited above show the number of settlers in K. T. from the four states was 9358 and that about one-fourth of the Tennesseans and one-fifth of the Virginians were living in the Colorado section.

[1] Letter to the New York Herald, quoted in the Georgetown (Kentucky) Herald, August 10, 1854. The Kansas Historical Quarterly Vol. XX, 1952-1953.

[2] Population of the U. S. in 1860, pp. 166 & 549.

This special index shows settlers from the four states living in practically all of the census divisions of the territory with the largest group in Kansas proper in Doniphan County where also was the largest group of Virginians (417); largest group of Tennesseans (305) in Bourbon County; South Carolinians in Linn (25); North Carolinians, Linn and Lykins, 109 each. No settlers from the four states were found in Wilson County; Virginians were in every other census area; Tennesseans in all but four; N. C. in all but twelve; S. C. in all but 26. The census area covered 41 "Kansas" counties and 21 "Colorado" census districts, making a total of 62 distinct districts.

A count of this special index shows that only 1796 people were found out of an official total of 1853 from the published returns.

To analyze the place of residence of the Arapahoe settlers from the four states it was necessary to count the number in each census division. Almost as many Virginians were living in South Park (361) as were living in Doniphan County.

Of the 1796 identified Arapahoe settlers from the selected states, the great majority (1328) lived in four of the 21 census divisions, South Park, South Clear Creek, Valley of the Platte, and Denver. More than half (682) of the 1328 were found in one area, South Park, with the three next most populous areas each having less than half as many. This distribution is reflected in the general population shown on page xvii.

The census divisions in the "Colorado" section are difficult to locate by present boundaries. Since the populations fell largely along the rivers and streams, the accompanying maps taken from Colorado Highway Department maps are given with the approximate location of streams superimposed thereon.

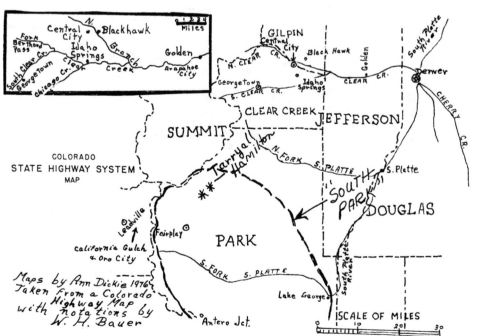

Section of Modern Map of Colorado Showing 1860 Census Districts

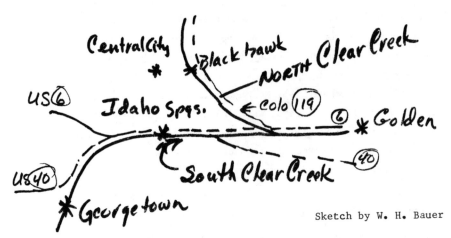

Sketch by W. H. Bauer

1860 Census Districts in the Golden-Central City-Georgetown Area

Central City   South Clear Creek (Idaho Springs to Georgetown)
Golden City (Golden)   Nevada Gulch (Nevada Mining District? Nevadaville?)
Arapahoe: Near Golden, where Clear Creek enters the Plains; prox. 105°15' W.
Long.; appears on Ackerson's "Map of the Gold Region" (page iv) to be on Clear
Creek at a crossroads of trails leading from D'Aubrey's Post and from Denver.

Problem Areas In Using the Indexes

Incomplete Information Given. There are definite advantages, of course, in
examining the original volumes or the microfilm rather than the index cards.
Aside from the obvious one of sidestepping any errors interposed by the indexers, there is much additional information which could not be included on
the W.P.A. index cards for lack of space and in turn is not included in this
special index. A few of the omitted categories are the following:

   Dwelling house and families visited numbered in the order of
      visitation. Family groupings are largely lost in the in-
      dexing process, and especially in this index of the four
      states.
   Value of personal and real property.
   Married within the year; attended school.
   Persons who died within the year ending 1st June 1860 listed
      with full description of person; month of death, cause,
      and number of days ill.
   Description and value of farm, farm implements, machinery,
      & livestock; owner.
   Products: wine, hops, flax, silk cocoons, honey, honey comb, etc.
   Capital investments earning $500 or more annually; raw
      material, including fuel; number of hands employed, male
      and female, with cost of each listed.

Inaccuracies

   The W.P.A. indexers were often unable to decipher the handwriting in the
census books and appended a question mark as the index cards were filled in.
I have made some attempts to check these points in the Historical Society's
records and on the microfilm of the Federal copy, as well as in the 1855 and
1865 census index cards in certain cases. This work resulted in a few
corrections and elimination of some uncertainties, but many unresolved
questions remain.

Kansas 1860 Territorial Census Records: Two Handwritten Sets
(In the National Archives and the Kansas State Historical Society Archives)

Recognition should be made of a problem area in examining the supposed-
ly original census records in the Kansas State Historical Society Archives
in Topeka. The Archives staff has been aware for some time that their
records (eleven handwritten volumes) are not the same (in arrangement,
make-up of pages, handwriting, headings, pagination, and microfilmed order
of county enumerations) as the census records in the National Archives.

This was discovered when references cited in the index were searched
out in the Federal microfilm rather than in the Topeka microfilm. It may be
reasoned that one of these sets of census records is a copy of the original
records, and perhaps both are copies. Names are different—one record may
use an initial while the other spells the word in full, spelling of names
may vary, and occupations may be omitted in one and included on the other
for any one settler. For these reasons it is well to check both microfilm
records.

In such projects, the researcher using my special index should bear in
mind that the volume and page numbers refer to the census books in the
Kansas State Historical Society Archives. These numbers are not helpful
when examining microfilm of the census records in the National Archives,
where county (or census division), township, and post office must be known.

The Historical Society's handwritten census records in eleven bound
volumes vary in size according to the number of pages devoted to each county
enumeration. For example, Atchison occupies 200 pages, Arapahoe 860 pages,
and Brown 69 pages. In addition each volume will include 40 or more pages
devoted to other schedules—value of personal and real property, etc.

The microfilm of these records includes this heading and explanation:

Territorial Census of 1860:

> The 1860 census of Kansas Terr. has been micro-
> filmed exactly as the original was bound into
> volumes so that the existing name index for
> Schedule 1 (enumerations) may be used with the
> film. The arrangement follows no alphabetical
> order. Schedules for the several counties are
> sometimes intermingled and occasionally are
> found in more than one volume.[1]

The Federal handwritten census records are assembled in four volumes
as indicated on the microfilm. Volume (and subsequent paging) differences
between the Federal records and the Topeka eleven volume records are apparent
when comparing the outline below with that found on the following page.

Volume 1   Allen-Doniphan, but including Marion, Otoe, and Hunter
   1A   Arapahoe
   2   Dorn-Leavenworth, but part of Wabaunsee continued after Jackson
   3   Linn-Wyandotte, part of Pottawatomie continued after Wabaunsee

[1]Notation on the box containing Reel #3 of the Topeka microfilm: Vol. 7-8-9:
  pp. 92, 93, 94 of Vol. 9 should have been bound with Jackson Co. in Vol. 5.

Hints For Reconciling the Two Microfilm of the 1860 Census: Federal and Kansas State Historical Society Copies

The Federal microfilm of the 1860 Kansas Territorial Census from the National Archives is divided into seven sections (Catalog numbers 346-352) with the counties listed alphabetically. In contrast, the Historical Society microfilm copy of _their_ original records is placed on four reels with the counties grouped by volumes just as they were in their handwritten original records.

The names of the assistant marshals in charge of the enumeration in each county with the date the work began has been added to the listing below which shows the microfilm arrangement.

Kansas State Historical Society Records, 1860 Census: Volume and microfilm numbers; assistant marshals in charge of the enumeration; date work began.

Reel #1
Census Volume
1	Atchison	William B. Kipp	6/18
	Doniphan	Jas. R. Willis	6/18
2	Bourbon	Chas. Dimon	8/3
	Allen	William Gallahay	6/22
	Dorn	" "	7/21
3	Brown	J. G. Kelsey	7/23
	Nemaha	" " "	6/25
	Marshall	Chas. R. Deming	6/29
	Washington	" " "	8/14

Reel #2
Census Volume
4	Coffey[1]	Jas. W. Junkins	8/13
	Breckinridge[2]	E. Goddard	6/28
	Madison	" "	8/8
	Morris	G. S. Huffaker	7/5
	Dickenson	Sam A. Medary	7/25
	Chase	G. S. Huffaker	7/18
	Butler	" " "	7/28
	Otoe	" " "	8/4
	Hunter	" " "	8/5
	Marion	" " "	8/6
5	Jefferson	W. C. Hicks	9/10
	Jackson	Joseph F. Cummings	7/24
	Wabaunsee	Elford J. Sines	6/19
	Pottawatomie	" " "	7/5
6	Johnson	Pat Cosgrove	6/21
	Douglas	G. A. Reynolds	6/12

Reel #3
Census Volume
7	Linn	Wilson Betts	6/12
	Anderson	S. A. Jones	6/20
8	Lykins	Harry Torney	6/26
	Franklin	G. A. Reynolds	8/15
	Osage	" " "	7/8
9	Shawnee	Joseph F. Cummings	6/18
	Woodson	O. P. Haughawout	6/21
	Greenwood	" " "	7/24
	Godfroy	" " "	7/30
	Wilson	" " "	
	McGee	Chas. Dimon	7/25
	Clay	Sam A. Medary	7/16
	Riley	" " "	6/29
	Davis	" " "	7/25
10	Wyandotte	P. Sidney Port	6/28
	Leavenworth	J.M. Gallagher	6/15

Reel #4
Census Volume
11	Arapahoe	Fox Diefendorf	7/5

[1]Occasionally the spelling Coffee will be seen, even in official census returns. However, this spelling is incorrect as the county was named for A. M. Coffey, member of the first territorial legislature.

[2]The county should be spelled Breckinridge not Breckenridge as seen in the index and census records as well as elsewhere. The county was named for John Cabell Breckinridge, vice-president of the U. S. with President Buchanan, and a native of Kentucky, 1821-1875.

National Archives (Federal) Records, Kansas Territorial Census: Microfilm Catalog Numbers

#346 Allen
     Anderson
     Atchison
     Bourbon
     Breckinridge (Lyon)
#347 Brown
     Chase
     Butler
     Otoe (absorbed)*
     Hunter (absorbed)*
     Clay
     Coffey
     Davis (Geary)
     Dickinson
     Doniphan
     Marion

#348 Arapahoe (E. Colorado)
#349 Dorn (absorbed)*
     Douglas
     Franklin
     Jefferson
#350 Johnson
     Leavenworth

Extinct Counties

Otoe: Butler, Sedgwick,
     Harvey & Marion
Hunter: Cowley, Sumner,
     Sedgwick, Butler
Dorn: Labette & Neosho
Madison: Greenwood, Lyon,
     Chase
Godfroy: Elk & Chautauqua

#351 Linn
     Lykins (Miami)
     McGee (Cherokee)
     Madison*
     Marshall
     Morris
     Nemaha
     Osage
#352 Pottawatomie
     Wabaunsee
     Riley
     Shawnee
     Jackson
     Washington
     Woodson
     Greenwood
     Godfroy*
     Wilson
     Wyandotte

Population Returns, 1860 Kansas Territorial Census

Kansas Area: 41 counties (From the Four States Found in Index)

12,606 Leavenworth (584)	2,609 Wyand. (118)	808 Chase (79)	
8,637 Douglas (659)	2,607 Brown (150)	770 Morris (119	
8,083 Doniphan (489)	2,436 Nemaha (75)	759 Greenw. (38)	
7,729 Atchison (470)	2,400 And. (186)	636 Madison (33)	
6,336 Linn (576)	2,280 Marsh. (165)	437 Butler (30)	
6,101 Bourbon (585)	1,936 Jackson (46)	383 Wash. (16)	
4,980 Lykins (459)	1,529 Potta. (87)	378 Dick. (27)	
4,459 Jefferson (278)	1,501 McGee (205)	238 Otoe (6)	
4,364 Johnson (432)	1,488 Woodson (124)	158 Hunter (11)	
3,513 Shawnee (162)	1,224 Riley (46)	163 Clay (7)	
3,197 Breckinridge (231)	1,163 Davis (45)	88 Dorn (3)	
3,082 Allen (272)	1,113 Osage (49)	74 Marion (13)	
3,030 Franklin (380)	1,023 Wabaun. (24)	27 Wilson-none fnd.	
2,842 Coffey (230)		19 Godfroy (4)	

Total Kansas proper: 107,206; from four states: 7505[1]

"Arapahoe" Area: 21 Census Divisions (From the Four States Found in Index)

10,610 South Park (682)	480 Russell's Gulch (20)
5,966 South Clear Creek (243)	438 Lake Gulch (16)
4,749 Denver (175)	320 Enterprise District (4)
3,714 Valley of the Platte (228)	255 Russell's Gulch and Idahoe (5)
2,036 California Gulch (80)	240 Leavenworth Gulch (18)
1,014 Golden City (44)	160 Eureka Gulch (6)
1,000 Tarryall and South Park (30)	141 Spring Gulch (8)
879 Nevada Gulch (42)	120 Quartz Valley (19)
840 Mountain City (66)	80 Arapahoe City (6)
598 Central City (30)	40 Clear Creek (None found)
597 Missouri City (22)	Total "Arapahoe": 34,277; from four states 1853[1]

The organization of the enumeration procedure for the census was through the 41 counties in Kansas proper with assistant marshals appointed for each county with some serving in more than one of the smaller counties. However, in the largely unorganized western section of the territory in what is now

[1]From The Eighth Census of the United States, 1860, Washington, D. C. 1864, p. 162 Kansas proper, and p. 548 Colorado.

a part of eastern Colorado, only one assistant marshal was appointed. He, in turn, was responsible for the enumeration in the 21 different census divisions established for the procedure. These divisions may be roughly equated with the counties in actuality, but in the present tabulation they appear in the same sequence position as the townships. For example, the interpretation of the heading for the "Colorado" area should be: Arapahoe, census division, post office or general location. This is in contrast to the heading for all the Kansas counties: county, township, post office. The population returns tabulated on page xv show clearly the equating of Kansas counties with "Colorado" census divisions.

The totals of the census returns for the "Arapahoe" section are summarized in the official records of the U. S. Census under Colorado Territory although that territory was not organized until February 28, 1861. Those for Kansas proper are found under Kansas, which is listed with the states although Kansas did not become the 34th state until January 29, 1861. Returns are organized as follows:[1]

Kansas: 106,579 whites; 625 free colored; 2 slaves Total 107,206
Colorado Territory: 34,231   "   46   "   "   --------   "   34,277
                                                                 Indians 2,261

Thus we can see that the total population for the entire Kansas Territory was 141,483, including the whites, the free colored, and slaves, but not the 2,261 Indians. The total 141,483 is not seen in these official returns; however, note part of Andreas' quotation from the Legislative report of the Lecompton session between January 19, 1860 and February 27, 1860.

> . . . The enumeration was known to be imperfect, and as delay
> might arise in the admission of the State under the Wyandotte
> Constitution should the population reported appear less than
> the ratio of representation required for a member of the
> National House of Representatives (93,560), a legislative
> committee on census was chosen. . . The Marshal's return of
> the Federal census, taken June 1, showed a population of
> 109,401 within the limits of the State as defined in the
> Wyandotte Constitution. . . The census of 1860 gave 143,643
> as the total population of which number 34,242 were in the
> vicinity of Pike's Peak. . .[2]

Places of Residence and Post Offices Listed in the 1860 Census

The eastern part of Kansas was beginning to be well settled by 1860 with many towns, villages, and clusters of houses in rural areas. There were also 320 post offices.[3] The number of established communities in "Arapahoe" were few of course in comparison; the names of the 21 census divisions just listed show the existence of some communities, seven of which were post offices.

---

[1] Preliminary Report on the Eighth Census, 1860, Washington, D. C., pp. 130-131.
[2] Andreas, pp. 177-178.
[3] A count of the entries in Kansas Post Offices.

"Colorado" Post Offices In The Kansas Territory 1860-1861

The eleven Colorado Territory counties listed below are those in which the twenty-one already established post offices were located at the time of the creation of the counties by the Colorado Territorial Legislature, November 1, 1861. The county name is given here to aid the reader in locating the general area of the "Arapahoe" addresses appearing in the index.[1] Attention is drawn again to the fact that "Arapahoe" is used in the census enumeration to cover the entire "Colorado" area included in the Kansas Territory. The post offices Tarryall, Arapahoe, Denver City, Golden City, Missouri City, Mountain City (and Nevada Gulch, which may be near Nevada P.O.) appear in the special index of settlers born in the four selected states.

Colorado Counties	Post Offices Established Before the 1860 Census Began and Others Established in 1860 and 1861	
Park	Tarryall	Hamilton, est. 7/26/1860
Clear Creek		Spanish Bar, est. 12/13/1860
Arapahoe	Arapahoe City, Denver, Auraria, Coraville, Jefferson, Montana	
Jefferson	Golden City, Mount Vernon	Golden Gate, est. 9/6/1860
Gilpin	Missouri City, Mountain City	Nevada, est. 1/12/1861
Douglas	Huntsville, est. 3/24/1860	
El Paso	Colorado City, est. 3/24/1860	
Fremont		Canon City, est. 12/8/1860
Huerfano	Fort Wise, est. 3/5/1860	
Lake		Oro City, est. 2/16/1861
Pueblo		Pueblo City, est. 12/13/1860

Note: Boulder, Fort Lupton, Saint Vrain, Colona (Auroria), Julesburg, and Breckinridge are omitted here as they were not in Kansas Territory.

Kansas Territory P. O. in the Colorado Section: Jan. 18, 1859-Feb. 28, 1861

---

[1] Colorado Postal History: The Colorado Post Offices, p. 213.

Arapahoe County In the "Colorado" Section of Kansas Territory

Arapahoe County was established August 30, 1855, by the Kansas territorial legislature, but the organization was not completed for the area was
attached to Marshall County.[1] On March 1, 1859, the vast Arapahoe area was
split into six counties: Arapahoe, Montana, El Paso, Oro, Broderick, and
Fremont.[2] However, only Arapahoe appears in the listing of the post
offices[3] and in the census records.

The territorial Arapahoe (the original bounds in 1855 and the smaller
county in 1859) should not be confused with the Arapahoe County established
by the Colorado territorial legislature described on page xviii under the
discussion of "Colorado" Post Offices. That third Arapahoe County had en-
tirely different bounds lying in a long, narrow, east-west rectangle reach-
ing from the Kansas border to Denver. In comparison, Map II shows the
Arapahoe County of 1859 as a very large rectangle occupying the eastern
third of the "Colorado" section of Kansas Territory. Modern Arapahoe is much
smaller.

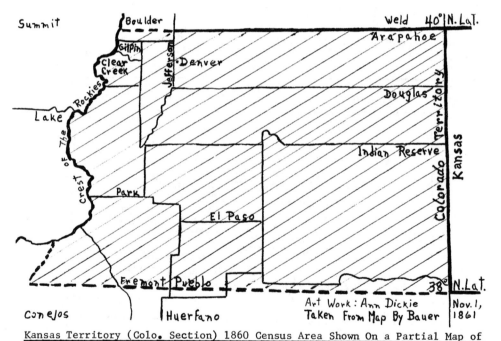

Kansas Territory (Colo. Section) 1860 Census Area Shown On a Partial Map of
Colorado Territory Counties Created Nov. 1, 1861 by the First Legislature

[1] Kansas Historical Collections, Vol. 8, Reprint: "The Establishment of
Counties in Kansas, 1855-1903, With Sixteen Maps," p. 2, Map I, 1855.
[2] Ibid., p. 3, Map II, 1857-59.
[3] Kansas State Historical Society: Kansas Post Offices, "Kansas Post
Offices and First Appointees," p. 158; Colorado Postal History, p. 213.

Arapahoe Census Divisions Used in the Kansas Territorial Census of 1860
With Population Returns and Page References to Handwritten Records[1]

	Pop.	Vol. 11 Page	Micro. page		Pop.
South Park	10,610	1-266	(1-264)	Leavenworth Gulch	240
Cal. Gulch	2,036	267-320	(265-316)	Arapahoe City	80
Denver	4,749	321-440	(317-436)	Idahoe; Russell Gulch	---
Golden City	1,014	441-460	(437-456)	Russell G. and Idahoe	255
Mt. City	840	461-480	(457-476)	South Clear Creek	5,966
Central City	598	481-	(477)	Idahoe (4 pages)	---
Lake Gulch	438	482-489	(478-485)	Tarryall & South Park:	1,000
Russell Gulch	480	490	(486-488	Tarryall, South Park	
Clear Creek	40	493	(489)	Oregon Gulch	
Quartz Valley	120	496-497	(490-491)	Iowa Gulch	
Enterprise Dst.	320	498		Tarryall	
No. Clear Cr.	---	468-491		Tarryall & Fair Play	
Nevada Gulch	879			Valley of the Platte	3,714
Eureka Gulch	160				
Missouri City	597				
Spring Gulch	141			Total population 34,277	

From Nevada Gulch through the end of the tabulation on page 865 (864 in the microfilm) no attempt has been made here to list the pages of each address. Some pages are blank and still numbered. North Clear Creek records are mixed with the Mountain City and subsequent records; there is no clearcut separation, so that identifying the areas separately is difficult if not impossible.

It may be that transportation was not dependable or that it was difficult to find the settlers, especially the miners, to be interviewed on the initial tabulation visit. This explanation may be the cause of the apparently disorganized condition of the census records.

Because the addresses in the Arapahoe area were difficult to locate, I wrote to the Denver Public Library, Western History Department, at the suggestion of the resource personnel of Colorado State Library. The research assistant at the Denver Public Library, after examining a sample page of this special index, wrote a clarifying letter which I shall quote in part:

> The locations given ... are not ... townships.
> They may be either post office or general loca-
> tion of the family (or settler). Colorado did
> not have civil townships which served as agents
> of local government ... Most of the state has
> now been surveyed into numbered Congressional
> townships for purposes of legal description.[2]

With these comments as guidelines, the tabulation heading for place of residence was revised. The initial plan to use "County, township, post office" to describe the settler's place of residence was seen as inadequate for the Arapahoe residents. Therefore, the heading was modified to read:

Kansas: County; Township; Post Office
Arapahoe County: Census Division Not Township

[1] Kansas State Historical Society: 1860 Census, Volume Eleven.
[2] Denver Public Library: Eleanor M. Gehres, Head, Western History Department; Lynn Taylor, research assistant, letters of August 27 and October 3, 1975.

Locating the Boundaries of the 1860 Kansas Counties Included in the Census

The intricacies of multiple boundary and name changes in Kansas counties since territorial days have been discussed in detail by Helen C. Gill in her scholarly Master's thesis which is the primary source of the maps and historical background in this Foreword.[1] The Reprint of the thesis features Maps I, II, and III as large foldouts showing the entire Kansas Territory. [Corresponding maps in Kansas Post Offices have been conveniently telescoped with the "Colorado" area superimposed on the large unorganized section of western Kansas variously labeled as Washington, Peketon, and Marion from 1855 to 1866.] In addition Gill's work includes ten pages of descriptive and expository material with citations to the relevant Kansas laws in the establishment of the counties. Reprint pp. 1-4, 8-9, 12-13, 18-19.

Beginning with Map I, 1855 we see 35 of the census counties of 1860 including the illusive and changeable Marion as well as four county names that were soon changed: Calhoun (Jackson), Richardson (Wabaunsee), Weller (Osage), and Wise (Morris).

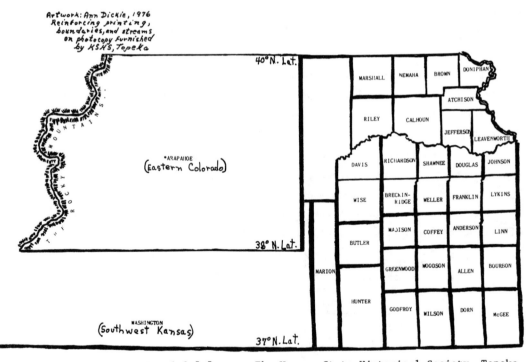

Artwork: Ann Dickie, 1976
Reinforcing printing,
boundaries, and streams
on photocopy furnished
by KSHS, Topeka

40° N. Lat.

(Eastern Colorado)
*ARAPAHOE

38° N. Lat.

(Southwest Kansas)
WASHINGTON

37° N. Lat.

M A P I, 1 8 5 5   The Kansas State Historical Society, Topeka

Arapahoe County is included here as an inset. It was the westernmost county of Kansas Territory, extending to the summit of the Rocky Mountains between the 38th and 40th parallels from the present Kansas border.

[1]"The Establishment of Counties in Kansas, 1855-1903, with Sixteen Maps," Reprint from Kansas Historical Collections, Vol. 8; the page numbers cited in this section refer to this publication, and the map numbers used are exactly those used originally. Maps I, II, III, and IV seen here have been reproduced through the courtesy of the Kansas State Historical Society, Topeka. Maps: Reprint pp. 5-7, 10-11, 14-17, 20-23, and foldouts.

40th Parallel: northern border of K.T. to the crest of the Rockies

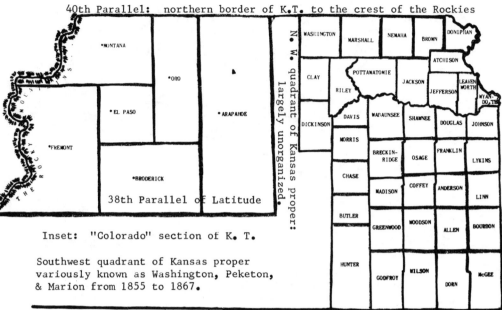

Inset: "Colorado" section of K. T.

Southwest quadrant of Kansas proper
variously known as Washington, Peketon,
& Marion from 1855 to 1867.

MAP II, 1 8 5 7 - 5 9   The Kansas State Historical Society, Topeka

Five 1860 census counties added: Chase, Clay, Dickinson, Wyandotte
and Washington (with newly defined boundaries).[1] Arapahoe boundaries newly defined; Oro, Broderick, El Paso, Montana, and Fremont
created and organized 1859, Reprint p. 3, with no further discussion in the Reprint. Arapahoe, El Paso, and Fremont counties appear
with different boundaries on the first Colorado Territory maps.

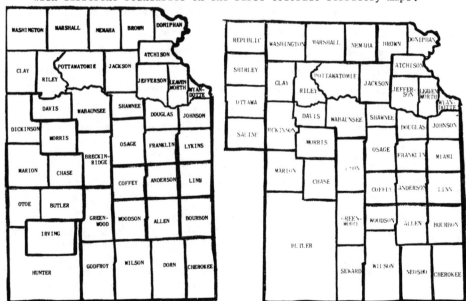

Map III, Eastern Section: 1860, 41 counties   Eastern Part of Map IV
                          The Kansas State Historical Society, Topeka

Map III, 1860: Marion & Otoe added; Madison divided between Breckinridge &
Greenwood; McGee became Cherokee; Irving appears. Map IV, 1861-64: Butler
absorbs Irving, Otoe, & Hunter; name changes: Dorn (Neosho), G(oy
(Steward; later Elk & Chautauqua), Breckinridge (Lyon), & Lykins (Miami).[1]

[1]Reprint discussion: Map II, pp. 2,3,4; Map III, p.4; Map IV, pp. 4, 8.

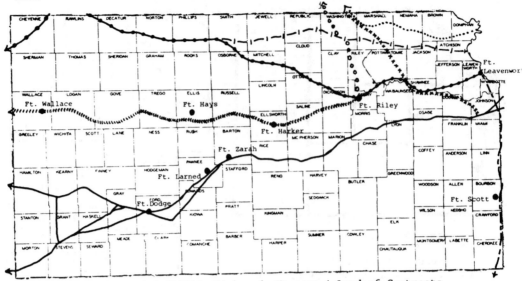

HISTORIC ROADS AND TRAILS, Richmond, <u>Kansas: A Land of Contrasts</u>
(St. Charles, Mo.: Forum Press, 1974)

Santa Fe Trail	▬▬▬	xxxxx	Oregon-California Trail
Smoky Hill Trail	ꞁꞁꞁꞁꞁꞁꞁ	●●●●●	Ft. Riley-Ft. Kearney Road
Parallel Road	—ꞁ—ꞁ—ꞁ—	— ∙— ∙—	Ft. Leavenworth-Ft. Gibson Rd.
Pony Express	●●●●●●●	●◆●◆●◆●	Leavenworth & Pike's Peak Express

<u>Errors and Variations In Spelling Place Names In Special Index</u>

Before leaving the discussion of the individual counties and related
matters, I feel that I must explain and apologize for the variation in the
spelling of certain place names as well as unconscious errors consistently
repeated in the special index. The original handwritten census records con-
tain these variations and errors and thus they are repeated on the W.P.A.
index cards and again in this index. Some errors were discovered during the
final preparation of the manuscript so that only a partial and largely un-
satisfactory effort has been made to correct the index; they have been
corrected in the Foreword however.

To save space and for ease in reference the errors are listed here:

<u>Arapahoe</u>: seen with two "r's" consistently but incorrectly. Arapahoe
County named for the Plains tribe of Indians.

<u>Breckinridge</u>: spelled incorrectly Breckenridge.

<u>Aubry</u>: spelled Aubrey in index as this was thought to be correct; however
early works use Aubry in memory of Francis Xavier Aubry the colorful
Santa Fe Trail scout and guide. The modern and official spelling of
the township in Johnson County is Aubry. However, Aubrey is seen in
many historical and authoritative references as both spellings were
used in Captain Aubry's lifetime.[1]

<u>McGee</u>: spelled McGhee incorrectly. The county was named for Mabillon W.
McGee, a merchant of Westport, Mo., who took a claim near Burlingame
with post office at 110 Crossing in Weller County (Osage). He was
in the territorial legislature in 1855 and was a brother of Fry P.
McGee, of Osage County near Wakarusa whose home was set up as a
voting place in District 7 when the first election districts were
established in 1854.[2]

[1]Letter from Jerry C. Roy, Assistant Reference Librarian, Johnson County
Library, Shawnee Mission, Kansas, dated September 25, 1975.

[2]Map of Eastern Kansas in November, 1854: First Election Districts, Places
of Voting, Andreas, Vol. 1, p. 88.

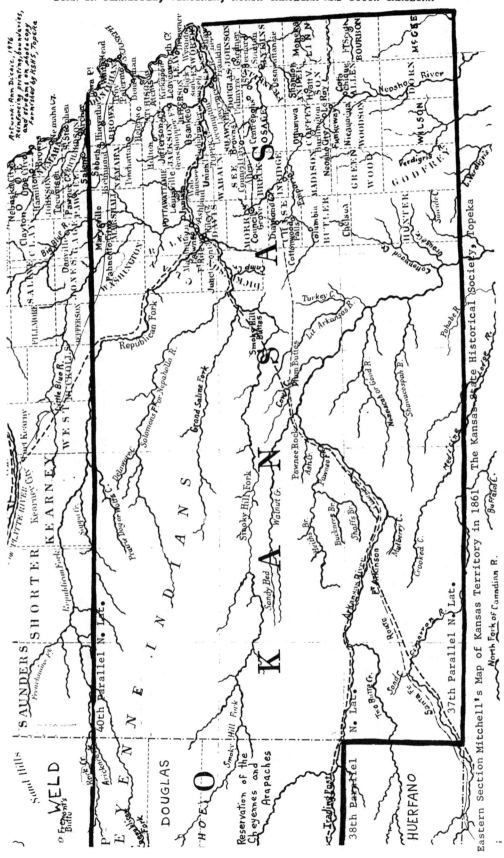

Eastern Section Mitchell's Map of Kansas Territory in 1861 The Kansas State Historical Society, Topeka

The People Who Traveled the Broad Natural Roadway to the Kansas Territory

Dorothy's dream of the Yellow Brick Road to the Land of Oz may well have been inspired by the stories of the sunlit Santa Fe Trail angling across Kansas from northeast to southwest. It is said to have been sixty to one hundred feet wide, worn smooth and hard, and without a bridge its whole length, two-thirds of which lay across the broad face of Kansas. At the height of travel across this and the other famous trails, the nightly campfires of the separate wagon trains were often within sight of each other, lighting up the roads with a yellow or golden glow. The people who had come to the Kansas Territory by this kind of travel are seen in the index, especially when we examine their occupations.

The 1860 census schedule required for the first time that the gainful profession, occupation, or trade of each person, male _and_ female, over 15 years of age should be returned. Previously the schedule had not required this information from the females.[1] As a result we see the farmeress, the woman doctor, or the 15 year old domestic who may be living at the home of a neighbor and earning a livelihood while bearing her full share of the family chores.

The vast majority of employed persons were miners or farmers with most of the miners living in the Colorado section and most of the farmers in Kansas proper. If farmers' wives and farm laborers are counted with the farmers, their number outranks the miners. A partial summary by occupations as well as a summary of the foreign born and the non-whites is given below.

Analysis of Population

	White Native Born			White Foreign Born			Non-White Native Born		Foreign Born		
	Men	Women	Total	Men	Women	Total	Men	Women	Men	Women	Total
Kan.	51,459	43,054	94,513	7,719	4,972	12,691	285	339	1	--	625
Col.	30,213	1,398	31,611	2,478	188	2,666	37	9	-	--	46
	81,672	44,452	126,124	10,197	5,160	15,357	322	348	1	--	671

Selected 1860 Census Returns of Occupations: 41 counties in Kansas Proper
and 21 Census Districts in the "Colorado" Section

	Total Pop.	Men	Women	Lawyers	Dentists	Daguerreo-typists	Bankers	Specu-lators
Kan.	107,204	59,178	48,026	361	14	9	14	25
Col.	34,277	32,691	1,586	89	6	6	11	20
	141,481	91,869	49,612	450	20	15	25	45

	Total Employed	Farmers	Miners	Physi-cians	Teachers	Editors	Mini-sters	Art-ists	Musi-cians
Kan.	31,646	15,572	35	376	328	24	207	12	13
Col.	26,797	195	22,086	116	10	7	11	4	6
	58,443	15,767	22,121	492	338	31	218	16	19

---

[1] _History and Growth of the U. S. Census_, p. 50-51.

Some of the People Who Lived In the Kansas Territory in 1860

A student of Kansas history, tradition, folk lore, and folk heroes might identify many well-known people in this special index. I am not a native Kansan and lack this wide experience in reading Kansas tall tales as well as true stories. I have selected a few settlers that appeal to me because of personal reasons.

The first is J. E. B. Stuart who was to become a beloved cavalry officer in the Confederate Army. The complete listing in the census enumeration reads:

```
Davis Co., Ft. Riley Reserve, Dwelling 723, Family 616   Vol. 9, page 358.
     J. E. B. Stuart  Lieut. U.S.A.  M 27  born in Virginia
            Flora                    F 24   "    " Missouri
            F.                       F  3   "    " Kansas Territory
     Kate Johnson      Servant      BF 49   "    " Maryland
     Lizzie Browzer    Servant      BF 22   "    " Maryland
```

James Ewell Brown Stuart was to die, a young general, within four short tragic years.

I am especially interested in this next choice as my children's great grandmother, Annis Woodson, wife of Archelaus (Archie) Robertson, was born, as was Daniel Woodson, in Albemarle County, Virginia in 1830. She and Daniel Woodson were neighbors and perhaps kinsmen.

The Honorable Daniel Woodson, for whom Woodson County was named, became the first Secretary for the Kansas Territory (June 29, 1854 to April 16, 1857). He served as governor April 17 to June 23, 1855; as secretary and acting governor for four different short periods in 1855, 1856 (two periods), and 1857.

Mr. Woodson was born May 13, 1824 in Albemarle Co., Virginia. Before coming to Kansas in October 1854, he had been a newspaper editor in Lynchburg and Richmond and had married Mrs. America F. (Christian) Palmer of Campbell Co., Virginia. Two of their children, Warren and Elizabeth, were born in Lynchburg, and Mosby was born in Kansas. Daniel Woodson held political offices and farmed in the state, living in Kickapoo Township, Leavenworth County where he was Recorder in the Land Office in 1860 (Census Vol. 10, p. 310). There he held the appointive office, Receiver of Public Moneys, from 1858-1862, retiring to Montgomery County in 1870 where he was living in 1883. (Andreas, Kansas, p. 1577). At that time the son Warren, named for Daniel Woodson's uncle, was a resident of Kickapoo Township in Leavenworth County.

Another Virginian was Charles W. Otey, Clerk of the U. S. District Court at age 29 (Volume 6, page 350 in the 1860 census) when he was living at Lecompton in Douglas County. Earlier in 1856 he had been head clerk in the Register's Department of the Lecompton Land Office, and in 1858 he is referred to as the territorial clerk.

Acknowledgment and Appreciation of Resources

The tabulation of this special index was undertaken as a tribute to my children's father, Judson Hall Robertson. He was a native of Albemarle County, Virginia; but after obtaining his doctorate in Chemistry at the University of Virginia in 1920, he spent his entire professional life until his death at age 70 as Professor of Chemistry at the University of Tennessee in Knoxville. Because his mother's people, the Rothwells and the Whites, had homesteaded in Nebraska in the late 1800's, he was quite interested in the midwest. His father had been a nurseryman and their family had always lived close to the land. Thus the ranches and farms of Kansas and Nebraska challenged his imagination and mine, too, in turn.

The staff of the Kansas State Historical Society Library and Archives has been consistently helpful from the very beginning, and especially during these final weeks before publication. They have assisted me by "long distance" to my home in Henderson, North Carolina, through my friend and research worker, Mrs. James E. (Virginia Speck) Marshall of Topeka. Much of the reference material cited has been brought to my attention by the Historical Society staff members.

Credits

Libraries and Archives: Personnel and Access to Holdings
Kansas State Historical Society, Topeka: The Library of Congress
 Newspaper and Census Division; Library   Kansas State Library, Topeka
Johnson County Public Library, Shawnee Mission, Kansas
Denver Public Library: Western History Department

Use of Maps For Reproduction
Kansas State Historical Society, Topeka   William H. Bauer, New Orleans
State Historical and Natural History Society Library, Denver, Colorado
Perry & Sandy Eberhart, Guide to Colorado Ghost Towns and Mining Camps
Charles Scribner's Sons: "Jackson's West" in Picture Maker of the Old West
Arthur H. Clark, Publisher: details from "Map of the Gold Region" by Sam
 Ackerson in Hafen's Colorado Gold Rush
Hawthorn Books, Inc.: details from Tschirky's map "Early Trails" in Williams'
 Rocky Mountain Country, Erskine Caldwell, Editor, American Folkways Series
Robert W. Richmond's "Historic Roads and Trails" in his Kansas: A Land of
 Contrasts (St. Charles, Mo.: Forum Press, 1974)

Research, Consultation, and Production Assistance including Art Work
Mrs. James E. (Virginia Speck) Marshall, Topeka, Kansas
Mrs. Richard G. (Margaret Candler) Burwell, Henderson, North Carolina
Mrs. Jean Duke, Henderson, North Carolina
Mrs. George (Ann Evans) Dickie, Henderson, North Carolina
Mrs. John (Lelia Chastain) Brigham, Henderson, North Carolina
Mrs. H. W. (Margaret Wilson) Glover, Jr., Henderson, North Carolina

Conclusion

Acknowledging my debt to many others (unnamed) who have been helpful to me, I will conclude my discussion of the index and leave it to undergo the scrutiny of those who may use it in the future. There are errors, I am sure, for which I bear the blame. I hope the information contained in the index itself as well as in the Foreword and Appendix will be helpful to future readers.

Having friends find their forebears in my index has already given me a great deal of pleasure. One of these is Mrs. James E. (Virginia Speck) Marshall who has helped me with crucial research by long distance in Topeka during the last weeks prior to sending my completed manuscript off to the publisher. She found listed her great grandmother, Sarah Ellen Speck who was born in North Carolina. In 1860 at the age of 29, she was living in Mt. Pleasant Township in Atchison County. By searching in the full W.P.A. index in the Historical Society Archives in Topeka, Mrs. Marshall also found listed her great grandfather A. S. Speck, born in Kentucky.

Other friends in Nebraska (cousins of my children through the Rothwell and White lines) found a great deal of information when they looked through my rough manuscript just last spring; it was during my visits with them in Flats (Opal Huffman Streiff) and Ogallala (Odeth Huffman Dykes) for about a week. I was en route home but with a planned stop in Topeka. There I spent four days in the Kansas State Historical Society Library and Archives, rounding out the work on the index that I had completed more than a dozen years ago.

The encouragement that I received from the Kansas State Historical Society personnel and these three personal friends made me hopeful that other family history enthusiasts, genealogists, and even regional historians might find something of value in this special index.

Clara Hamlett Robertson Flannagan
Mrs. Eric Goodyear Flannagan, Sr.

215 Young Avenue
Henderson, North Carolina   27536
October 23, 1975

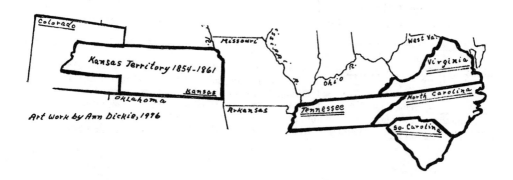

Art Work by Ann Dickie, 1976

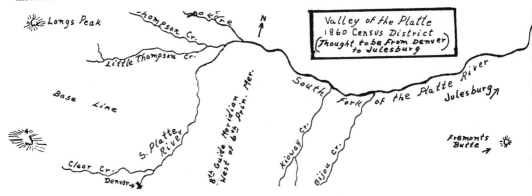

Notes on the Terrain From My Reading

At the forks of Clear Creek, west of Denver, a branch of the railroad was built up the north fork to Black Hawk where began the climb around the hills to Central City on a grade of 135 feet to the mile. South Clear Creek, on the other hand, is nearly level for fifteen miles to the very base of the Continental Divide at Berthoud Pass. (Williams, p. 168)

The upper Arkansas River and California Gulch lie in a clean sunny valley overhung by towering mountains. (Jackson, p. 253)

The large Fairplay section in the northwest part of "South Park" lies in the headwaters of the drainage area of the Middle Fork of the South Fork of the South Platte River. This was a favorite camping ground of the Indians. (Eberhart, p. 121)

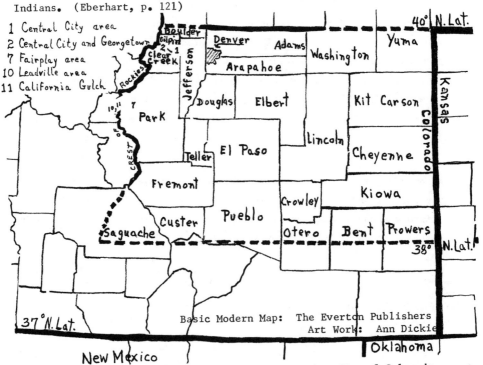

Notations of 1860 Census Place Names on Modern Map of Colorado

South Clear Creek: From Jefferson-Gilpin border west through Idahoe Springs, Georgetown, and Silver Plume.
North Branch of Clear Creek: Quartz Valley, Eureka Gulch, Nevada Gulch, Missouri City, Spring Gulch, Lake Gulch, and Enterprise Mining District in the Central City area. Russell Gulch branches off from the creek toward the west.
Clear Creek from the Gilpin-Jefferson County border east to Denver: Arapahoe City where the creek enters the plains and Golden.
Gregory Gulch Area: Mountain City between Central City and Black Hawk.

Name	Kansas: County; Township; P.O. / Arap. Co.: Census Div. Not Township	Age	Sex	Census Vol.:Page
Abrams, Henry	Arapahoe, South Park	28	M	11:120
Adair, G. R.	Arapahoe, South Clear Creek	29	M	11:704
Adams, Catherine	Douglas, Wakarusa	43	F	6:246
Adams, Eliza	Bourbon, Xenia P.O.	12	F	2:128
Adams, Elizabeth	Atchison, Grasshopper	26	F	1:89
Adams, M.	Douglas, Wakarusa (Farmer)	40	M	6:245
Adams, Nancy	Douglas, Wakarusa	40	F	6:245
Adams, S.	Arapahoe, Denver (Butcher)	51	M	11:421
Adams, Susan	Leavenworth, Ward 4	40	F	10:281
Adamson, E. K.	Leavenworth, Alexandria (Farmer)	38	M	10:440
Adamson, M.	Doniphan, Burr Oak	20	F	1:344
Adamson, Mary A.	Leavenworth, Easton	39	F	10:282
Adamson, Rebecca	Leavenworth, Alexandria	35	F	10:440
Adamson, Samuel	Leavenworth, Easton	40	M	10:282
Addington, Nancy	Anderson, Jackson	37	F	7:209
Adgen, Saml.	Arapahoe, South Park	27	M	11:257
Adkins, E.	Franklin, Peoria	42	F	8:273
Adkins, G.	Arapahoe, Valley of the Platte	23	M	11:841
Agate, M. O.	Arapahoe, South Park	29	M	11:238
Age, W. H.	Arapahoe, Valley of the Platte	29	M	11:841
Agnews, Geo.	Arapahoe, South Park	29	M	11:204
Aiken, Ann	Arapahoe, Denver	24	F	11:354
Aiken, V.	Osage, Ridgeway (Farmer)	24	M	8:343
Aiken, G.	Osage, Ridgeway	15	M	8:343
Aiken, H.	Osage, Ridgeway	22	M	8:343
Aiken, I.	Osage, Ridgeway	13	F	8:343
Aiken, R.	Osage, Ridgeway (Farmer)	22	F	8:343
Akin, Chas.	Arapahoe, South Park	29	M	11:168
Alder, Andrew	Marshall, Guittard	4	M	3:237
Alder, Emily	Marshall, Guittard	14	F	3:236
Alder, Joel	Marshall, Guittard	3	M	3:237
Alder, John	Marshall, Guittard (Farm Laborer)	15	M	3:236
Alder, Joseph	Marshall, Guittard	7	M	3:236
Alder, Margret	Marshall, Guittard	8	F	3:236
Alder, Mary	Marshall, Guittard	10	F	3:236
Alder, Sarah	Marshall, Guittard	12	F	3:236
Alder, Sarah	Marshall, Guittard	40	F	3:236
Alder, Willis	Marshall, Guittard (Farmer)	40	M	3:236
Alder, Willis	Marshall, Guittard	5	M	3:236
Alderson, John B.	Lykins, Wea (Farmer)	44	M	8:116
Alexander, Enoch	Atchison, Shannon (Farmer)	33	M	1:76
Alexander, J.	Linn, Centerville (Farmer)	50	M	7:91
Alexander, Jas.	Jefferson, Grasshopper Falls (Farmer)	51	M	5:7
Alexander, Newman	Atchison, Shannon (Farmer)	39	M	1:76
Alger, P.	Arapahoe, South Park	25	M	11:170
Allen, A.	Franklin, Pottawatomie	61	F	8:243
Allen, A. H.	Atchison, Ward 2	45	M	1:30
Allen, David H.	Madison, Verdigris (Farmer)	22	M	2:244
Allen, E.	Franklin, Pottawatomie	36	F	8:239
Allen, E. J.	Franklin, Pottawatomie	30	F	8:243
Allen, Elizabeth	Jefferson, Grasshopper Falls	29	F	5:12
Allen, I. A.	Franklin, Pottawatomie	60	M	8:243

Non-white races noted: Indian, I; negro, B; mulatto, M: viz.,BM, black male.
Arapahoe is spelled correctly on this page; the incorrect spelling with two
r's is used regrettably in the greater part of this special index.

Name	Kansas: County; Township; P.O. Arap. Co.: Census Div. Not Township	Age	Sex	Census V. Pg.
Allen, Isaac	Bourbon, Fort Scott P.O. (Farmer)	42	M	2:197
Allen, John	Allen, Humboldt P.O.	21	M	2:278
Allen, Jno. R.	Arrapahoe, Eureka Gulch (Miner)	19	M	11:506
Allen, L.	Franklin, Pottawatomie	18	F	8:243
Allen, Margaret	Leavenworth, Delaware	50	F	10:431
Allen, Polly W.	Bourbon, Fort Scott P.O. (Housewife)	39	F	2:197
Allen, Sarah A.	Madison, Hartford	33	F	4:234
Allen, William	Allen, Humboldt P.O.	19	M	2:278
Allen, William	Bourbon, Fort Scott P.O. (Farmer)	21	M	2:190
Allen, William D.	Coffey, Burlington (Farmer	29	M	4:40
Alley, Francis	Marshall, Blue Rapids (Farm Laborer)	22	M	3:201
Ally, Henry	Marshall, Blue Rapids (Farmer)	25	M	3:202
Ally, John	Marshall, Blue Rapids (Farmer)	21	M	3:202
Almyer, W.	Linn, Mound City (Farmer)	36	M	7:112
Amsden, Elizabeth	Woodson, Verdigris (F.W.)	36	F	9:157
Anderson, A. B.	Brown, Claytonville (Farmer)	46	M	3:44
Anderson, Charles	Bourbon, Xenia P.O. (Farmer)	53	M	2:127
Anderson, D. M.	Arrapahoe, Lake Gulch (Miner)	43	M	11:485
Anderson, Danvel	Brown, Claytonville	25	M	3:44
Anderson, David	Brown, Claytonville	14	M	3:44
Anderson, Eliza E.	Bourbon, Turkey Creek P.O.(Housewife)	35	F	2:109
Anderson, Elizabeth	McGhee, Medoc, Missouri P.O.	26	F	9:209
Anderson, Geo.	Linn, Scott (Wagon Maker)	37	M	7:27
Anderson, Isaac	Brown, Claytonville	18	M	3:44
Anderson, James	Nemaha, Rock Creek (Farm Laborer)	23	M	3:82
Anderson, James	Atchison, Grasshopper (Farmer)	35	M	1:96
Anderson, John	McGhee, Osage Mission P.O. (Farmer)	37	M	9:238
Anderson, Mary	Leavenworth, Stranger	27	F	10:462
Anderson, N. A.	Brown, Claytonville	20	F	3:44
Anderson, Rebecca	Linn, Scott	27	F	7:27
Anderson, Robert	Leavenworth, Stranger (Farmer)	30	M	10:462
Andrew, Caswell	Jefferson, Kentucky (Farmer)	41	M	5:77
Andrew, Elizabeth	Jefferson, Kentucky	23	F	5:77
Andrews, Wm. P.	Arrapahoe, South Park	35	M	11:255
Antin, J.W.V.	Arrapahoe, South Park	28	M	11:148
Antrim, Mary	Shawnee, Tecumseh	44	F	9:75
Archas, E.	Doniphan, Wayne	39	F	1:377
Armsted, W.	Arrapahoe, South Clear Creek	29	M	11:763
Armstrong, J. L.	Brown, Claytonville (Farmer)	38	M	3:52
Armstrong, J. W.	Linn, Centerville (Farmer)	46	M	7:97
Armstrong, P. L.	Brown, Claytonville	45	F	3:51
Armstrong, R.	Linn, Paris (Wheelwright)	53	M	7:159
Arnett, Elizabeth	Linn, Scott	27	F	7:27
Arnett, Elizabeth	Bourbon, Fort Scott (Housekeeper)	60	F	2:225
Arnett, J.	Linn, Scott (Farmer)	27	M	7:27
Arrant, Saml.	Anderson, Reeder (Farmer)	32	M	7:262
Arthron, E.	Franklin, Centropolis	56	F	8:208
Asher, Mortiner	Otoe, Otoe (Farmer)	40	M	4:356
Ashmore, M. L.	Greenwood, Eureka (Farmer)	48	M	9:177
Ashmore, Margaret	Greenwood, Eureka	48	F	9:177
Asp, James B.	Coffey, Avon (Farmer)	23	M	4:13
Atkinson, Alfred M.	Bourbon, Turkey Creek P.O. (Farmer)	24	M	2:113
Atkinson, W. M.	Arrapahoe, South Clear Creek (Trader)	42	M	11:740
Austin, M. A.	Franklin, Ottawa	40	F	8:263
Austin, Marien	Leavenworth, Ward 4	32	M	10:276
Austin, W. G.	Arrapahoe, South Park	37	M	11:220
Aviles, A. I.	Arrapahoe, South Park	31	M	11:253
Babb, Jonathan	Lykins, Mound (Farmer)	44	M	8:70
Babb, Mary	Doniphan, White Cloud	30	F	1:443
Babb, Sarah	Leavenworth, Stranger	33	F	10:478
Babb, Wm.	Doniphan, White Cloud (Laborer)	35	M	1:443
Baber, G.	Arrapahoe, South Clear Creek	25	M	11:719

Arapahoe: spelled incorrectly with 2 r's in census and in this index also.

Name	Kansas: County; Township; P.O. Arap. Co.: Census Div. Not Township	Age	Sex	Census V.Pg
Bach, Mary	Morris, Grove	33	F	4:269
Bachelor, Mary	Allen, Humboldt P.O.	24	F	2:285
Bacon, J.	Arrapahoe, South Clear Creek	24	M	11:719
Bagbee, J.	Arrapahoe, South Park (Miner)	71	M	11:28
Baillin, E. J.	Arrapahoe, South Clear Creek	27	M	11:712
Bails, S.	Coffey, California (Farmer)	26	M	4:61
Baker, A. W. D.	Leavenworth, Kickapoo (Druggist)	45	M	10:322
Baker, Elezabeth	Coffey, Ottumwa	55	F	4:49
Baker, G.⁻W.	Franklin, Centropolis (Farmer)	32	M	8:208
Baker, John	Lykins, Indianapolis (Farmer)	31	M	8:59
Baker, Metilda	Greenwood, Eureka	29	F	9:180
Baker, Saml.	Arrapahoe, South Park	36	M	11:189
Baldwin, E. M.	Arrapahoe, Valley of the Platte	28		11:781
Baler, David	Wyandotte, Wyandotte (Farmer)	35	M	10:39
Baler, Jane	Wyandotte, Wyandotte	8	F	10:39
Baler, John	Wyandotte, Wyandotte	12	M	10:39
Baler, Sarah	Wyandotte, Wyandotte	34	F	10:39
Baler, Susan	Wyandotte, Wyandotte	6	F	10:39
Baler, Thomas	Wyandotte, Wyandotte	10	M	10:39
Baley, Josiah	Atchison, Lancaster (Farmer)	63	M	1:114
Ball, S.	Linn, Valley (Farmer)	56	M	7:48
Ballard, James F.	Wabaunsee, Wilmington	2	M	5:282
Ballard, Molly R.	Wabaunsee, Wilmington	3	F	5:282
Balsh, Elizabeth	Shawnee, Auburn	55	F	9:43
Banta, W. S.	Arrapahoe, South Park	24	M	11:163
Barbee, Mary	Linn, Mound City	50	F	7:124
Barbee, Thomas	Linn, Mound City (Farmer)	20	M	7:124
Barber, Levi	Allen, Humboldt P.O. (Farmer)	26	M	2:302
Barkley, E.[1]	Coffey, Ottumwa	1	F	4:54
Barlow, J.	Linn, Paris	44	M	7:139
Barnes, Fulton	Bourbon, Raysville P.O. (Farmer)	24	M	2:159
Barnes, Malivina C.	Bourbon, Raysville P.O. (Housewife)	24	F	2:159
Barnett, Ruben S.	Allen, Humboldt P.O. (Farmer)	40	M	2:278
Barret, Geo. W.	Arrapahoe, Denver	25	M	11:324
Barrett, O. A.	Douglas, Lawrence (Lawyer)	25	M	6:217
Barrett, R.	Linn, Paris (Farmer)	26	M	7:153
Barrow, T. H.	Arrapahoe, South Park	32	M	11:180
Bashel, J. E.	Arrapahoe, Valley of the Platte	29	M	11:821
Basket, J. S.	Arrapahoe, Valley of the Platte	22	M	11:841
Bates, G.	Arrapahoe, Valley of the Platte	40	M	11:804
Bates, Jacob	Arrapahoe, California Gulch	24	M	11:287
Bates, O.	Arrapahoe, South Park (Miner)	20	M	11:76
Bates, S.	Arrapahoe, Russell Gulch (Miner)	27	M	11:517
Baty, Benjamin P.	Bourbon, Fort Scott P.O. (Farmer)	24	M	2:224
Baty, Elizabeth J.	Bourbon, Fort Scott P.O. (Housewife)	27	F	2:224
Baty, William	Bourbon, Fort Scott P.O.	7	M	2:224
Baxter, G.	Arrapahoe, South Clear Creek	36	M	11:712
Baxter, Ruth	McGhee, Brushville P.O. (Housewife)	43	F	9:230
Bayer, M. E.	Arrapahoe, South Clear Creek (Miner)	37	M	11:732
Bayers, Jno.	Arrapahoe, Valley of the Platte	26	M	11:808
Beacon, Henry	Bourbon, Dayton P.O. (Farmer)	26	M	2:124
Bealer, Matilda	Anderson, Walker	37	F	7:234
Bean, Isaac	Arrapahoe, South Park	26	M	11:213
Bean, L. E.	Leavenworth, Easton	42	F	10:289
Bean, Nathan	Arrapahoe, Golden City (Miner)	31	M	11:442
Beard, J.	Douglas, Marion (Farmer)	63	M	6:401
Beard, M.	Arrapahoe, South Park	25	M	11:7
Bearden, Ebenezer	Linn, Paris	32	M	7:146
Beasley, T. M.	Douglas, Lawrence (Teamster)	36	M	6:207

[1] Illegible, possibly Rankley; possibly born in Penn. rather than Tenn.
Arapahoe: spelled incorrectly with 2 r's in census and in this index also.

Name	Kansas: County; Township; P.O. Arap. Co.: Census Div. Not Township	Age	Sex	Census V. Pg
Beauchamp, Letitia Ann	Atchison, Ward 1	35	F	1:11
Beck, Will	Arrapahoe, South Park (Miner)	28	M	11:25
Bedford, J. O.[1]	Arrapahoe, South Clear Creek	30	M	11:730
Beers, N.	Arrapahoe, Valley of the Platte	24		11:788
Beets, James	Lykins, Marysville (Farmer & Hotel Kpr.)	44	M	8:119
Beets, Joseph	Lykins, Marysville (Farmer)	39	M	8:130
Beets, Mary	Lykins, Marysville	25	F	8:122
Bell, Clara	Jefferson, Oskaloosa	13	F	5:130
Bell, Elickander[2]	Madison, Verdigris	32	M	4:245
Bell, Harriet	Jefferson, Oskaloosa	11	F	5:130
Bell, J.	Arrapahoe, Valley of the Platte	29	M	11:846
Bell, Sarah	Jefferson, Oskaloosa	46	F	5:130
Bell, Sarah	Jefferson, Oskaloosa	6	F	5:130
Bemus, J. T.	Arrapahoe, South Clear Creek (Miner)	22	M	11:712
Bennet, M.	Arrapahoe, South Clear Creek	32	M	11:680
Bennett, Ephrian P.	Allen, Humboldt P.O. (Farm Laborer)	18	M	2:292
Bennett, John H.	Allen, Humboldt P.O. (Farmer)	22	M	2:292
Bennett, Joseph M.	Allen, Humboldt P.O.	26	M	2:292
Bennett, William H.	Allen, Humboldt P.O. (Farm Laborer)	21	M	2:292
Benson, A. F.	Arrapahoe, South Clear Creek	24	M	11:693
Beonten, J.	Arrapahoe, South Clear Creek (Miner)	32	M	11:715
Berne, G.	Arrapahoe, Valley of the Platte	29	M	11:808
Bernondy, E.	Arrapahoe, South Park	28	M	11:42
Berry, A.	Doniphan, Center (Farmer)	39	M	1:259
Berry, Martin A.	Bourbon, Fort Scott P.O. (Farmer)	33	M	2:190
Berry, Thos.	Arrapahoe, South Park	36	M	11:257
Bertrand, W. S.	Arrapahoe, Valley of the Platte	27	M	11:793
Berwin, T.	Arrapahoe, Valley of the Platte	28	M	11:856
Beryman, J. E.	Arrapahoe, Valley of the Platte	23	M	11:811
Bigelow, Jas.	Arrapahoe, South Park (Miner)	28	M	11:68
Biggs, Wm.	Arrapahoe, South Park	35	M	11:183
Biles, E.	Doniphan, Iowa Point	40	F	1:446
Biles, L.	Doniphan, Iowa Point	7	F	1:446
Bills, Alfred M. H.	Bourbon, Fort Scott P.O. (Physician)	36	M	2:189
Bingham, S. J.	Arrapahoe, South Park (Miner)	32	M	11:71
Bird, J.	Nemaha, Rock Creek (Farmer)	40	M	3:78
Bird, Sinai	Nemaha, Rock Creek	35	F	3:78
Bishop, Wm. P.	Douglas, Lecompton (Clerk)	21	M	6:352
Bixler, Mary	Butler, Chelsea	32	F	4:342
Black, Joseph H.	Coffey, Ottumwa (Carpenter)	26	M	4:57
Black, Thomas	Lykins, Sugar Creek (Carpenter)	30	M	8:99
Blackford, B.	Arrapahoe, South Park	30	M	11:25
Blackford, F.	Arrapahoe, South Park	39	M	11:151
Blacklidge, E. O.	Arrapahoe, South Park	28	M	11:212
Blackman, G. W.	Arrapahoe, South Park	23	M	11:132
Blackwell, Peter	Allen, Iola P.O. (Farmer)	21	M	2:271
Blady, William M.	Allen, Humboldt P.O. (Farmer)	25	M	2:297
Blair, J. P.	Doniphan, Center (Farmer)	52	M	1:264
Blakely, C.	Doniphan, Iowa Point (Farmer)	42	M	1:431
Blakely, Margarett	Lykins, Marysville	45	F	8:127
Blakely, Martha	Madison, Verdigris	53	F	4:246
Blakely, Samuel	Madison, Verdigris (Farmer)	55	M	4:246
Blantz, Wm.	Arrapahoe, South Clear Creek (Miner)	26	M	11:735
Bliss, J. A.	Arrapahoe, Valley of the Platte	24	M	11:824
Blood, W. T.	Arrapahoe, South Clear Creek	26	M	11:705
Bloomfield, E.	Arrapahoe, South Clear Creek	28	M	11:722

[1]May be J. O. or I. O.

[2]Perhaps Ben or Ball; Elickander or Alexander may be last name.

Arapahoe: spelled incorrectly with 2 r's in census and in this index also.

Name	Kansas: County; Township; P.O. Arap. Co.: Census Div. Not Township	Age	Sex	Census V. Pg.
Bloser, C.	Arrapahoe, South Park	23	M	11:144
Blow, Alfred	Arrapahoe, Golden City (Miner)		M	11:447
Blyard, Catherine	Greenwood, Eureka (Farmer)	41	F	9:179
Boaz, James C.	Bourbon, Fort Scott P.O. (Farmer)	45	M	2:182
Bohanon, W. C.	Arrapahoe, Valley of the Platte	32	M	11:834
Boles, Leonard	Atchison, Mt. Pleasant (Carpenter)	33	M	1:160
Bolton, Emeline	Allen, Humboldt P.O.	12	F	2:293
Bolten, Lafayette	Allen, Humboldt P.O. (Farm Laborer)	18	M	2:292
Bolten, Tabetha	Allen, Humboldt P.O.	38	F	2:292
Bolten, Tennepa	Allen, Humboldt P.O.	9	F	2:293
Bolten, Thomas	Allen, Humboldt P.O.	14	M	2:292
Bond, Henry	Allen, Humboldt P.O. (Farmer)	49	M	2:280
Bonge, W.	Arrapahoe, South Park	33	M	11:107
Booth, S.	Arrapahoe, South Clear Creek	28	M	11:728
Borden, Leon	Leavenworth, Easton (Farmer)	36	M	10:285
Borden, Martha R.	Leavenworth, Easton	35	F	10:282
Borden, Wm.	Leavenworth, Easton	47	M	10:282
Border, George	Linn, Scott	1	M	7:12
Boren, Isaac	Bourbon, Fort Scott P.O. (Farmer)	25	M	2:199
Boren, Jane	Bourbon, Fort Scott P.O.	25	F	2:198
Boren, Nancy	Bourbon, Fort Scott P.O.	10	F	2:199
Boren, William P.	Bourbon, Fort Scott P.O.	8	M	2:199
Borg, Abraham H.	Bourbon, Dayton P.O.	51	M	2:156
Borg, David W.	Bourbon, Dayton P.O.	18	M	2:156
Borg, Jacob H.	Bourbon, Dayton P.O.	15	M	2:156
Borg, Sarah	Bourbon, Dayton P.O. (Housewife)	48	F	2:156
Boring, Mary	Bourbon, Fort Scott P.O. (Housewife)	35	F	2:80
Boring, Rhoda	Bourbon, Fort Scott P.O.	55	F	2:155
Bothwell, John	Atchison, Center (Farmer)	40	M	1:140
Bothwell, Sally	Atchison, Center	30	F	1:140
Botts, S. M.	Arrapahoe, South Clear Creek	31	M	11:763
Bottwood, R. P.	Arrapahoe, South Park	39	M	11:144
Bow..., W.[1]	Arrapahoe, Valley of the Platte	24	M	11:834
Bowling, Ann	Wyandotte, Wyandotte	24	F	10:31
Bowling, George	Wyandotte, Wyandotte (Teamster)	25	M	10:31
Bowman, A. G.	Arrapahoe, South Park	29	M	11:136
Bowman, H. M.	Arrapahoe, South Park	28	M	11:246
Bowman, Jane	Bourbon, Fort Scott P.O. (Housewife)	33	F	2:78
Bowman, T.	Arrapahoe, South Clear Creek	29	M	11:748
Bowser, Catharine	Jefferson, Jefferson	5	F	5:37
Bowser, E.	Atchison, Kappioma	34	F	1:100
Bowser, Elizabeth	Atchison, Kappioma	57	F	1:100
Bowser, Elizabeth	Jefferson, Crooked Creek	29	F	5:37
Bowser, Emily	Morris, Neosho	34	F	4:273
Bowser, George	Jefferson, Jefferson (Laborer)	28	M	5:37
Bowser, Ira	Morris, Neosho (Farmer)	24	M	4:274
Bowser, James	Morris, Neosho (Farmer)	48	M	4:273
Bowser, Napoleon	Jefferson, Jefferson (Farmer)	30	M	5:37
Boyce, O. F.	Arrapahoe, South Park	38	M	11:190
Boyd, A.	Arrapahoe, Central City (Quartz Mnr.)	39	M	11:510
Boyd, J. B.	Arrapahoe, Denver (Drifter)	23		11:416
Boyd, Martha	Leavenworth, Kickapoo	37	F	10:412
Boyd, Thos.	Arrapahoe, South Park	36	M	11:146
Boydston, Martin	Bourbon, Mapleton P.O. (Farmer)	35	M	2:132
Boydston, Sally	Bourbon, Mapleton P.O. (Housewife)	33	F	2:132
Boyer, W. S.	Arrapahoe, Valley of the Platte	29	M	11:816
Boyle, Jas.	Arrapahoe, Denver (Miner)	20	M	11:404
Boyles, S. H.	Arrapahoe, South Park	25	M	11:258

[1]Illegible; may be Bowland.

Arapahoe: spelled incorrectly with 2 r's in census and in this index also.

Name	Kansas: County; Township; P.O. Arap. Co.: Census Div. Not Township	Age	Sex	Census V.: Pg
Boyseton, Chas.	Arrapahoe, South Clear Creek	29	M	11:710
Bradbury, N.	Arrapahoe, South Clear Creek	27	M	11:659
Bradford, R. B.	Arrapahoe, Denver (Merchant)	42	M	11:325
Bradshaw, Ann	Jefferson, Jefferson	20	F	5:29
Bradshaw, Catharine	Jefferson, Jefferson	53	F	5:29
Bradshaw, John	Jefferson, Jefferson (Farm Laborer)	24	M	5:29
Brainerd, J. E.	Arrapahoe, Valley of the Platte	31	M	11:825
Branch, John	Bourbon, Rockford P.O. (Farmer)	26	M	2:101
Branch, Wilson	Bourbon, Rockford P.O. (Farmer)	23	M	2:101
Brandett, Jacob	Arrapahoe, Denver (Farmer)	40	M	11:350
Brandon, W. F.	Arrapahoe, Valley of the Platte	28		11:786
Branner, Ellen W.	Atchison, Kappioma	18	F	1:98
Brannon, William	Lykins, Middle Creek (Farm Hand)	20	M	8:108
Brant, Elvira	Chase, Diamond Creek	19	F	4:326
Braselton, S.	Arrapahoe, Russell Gulch (Miner)	31	M	11:542
Brazelton, J.	Doniphan, Marion	50	F	1:286
Breech, W. E.	Arrapahoe, Valley of the Platte	28	M	11:821
Breedlove, Margaret	Linn, Paris	34	F	7:158
Brenley, Caroline	Douglas, Wakarusa	42	F	6:264
Briggs, Thos. D.	Arrapahoe, South Park	24	M	11:233
Bright, E. F.	Arrapahoe, South Park	37	M	11:237
Bristol, Wm.	Arrapahoe, South Park	28	M	11:241
Briston, N.	Arrapahoe, Central City (Miner)	40	M	11:578
Brizentyne, Susan	Marshall, Blue Rapids	20	F	3:201
Brizentyne, William	Marshall, Blue Rapids (Farmer)	28	M	3:201
Broadwill, T. M.	Arrapahoe, Valley of the Platte	26	M	11:826
Brock, Andrew	Linn, Potosi	14	M	7:55
Brock, Clemens	Bourbon, Fort Scott P.O.	10	M	2:153
Brock, Elisabeth	Leavenworth, Easton	16	F	10:288
Brock, Francis[1]	Leavenworth, Easton	14	F	10:288
Brock, Henry	Linn, Potosi	16	M	7:55
Brock, James	Linn, Potosi (Farmer)	37	M	7:55
Brock, James K. P.	Bourbon, Fort Scott P.O. (Farmer)	20	M	2:153
Brock, Jane	Linn, Potosi	34	F	7:55
Brock, Mary	Atchison, Center (Farmer)	52	F	1:127
Brock, Nancy	Linn, Potosi	12	F	7:55
Brock, Nancy	Bourbon, Fort Scott P.O.	12	F	2:153
Brock, P.	Franklin, Pottawatomie (Farmer)	22	M	8:246
Brock, Prior	Bourbon, Fort Scott P.O. (Farmer)	44	M	2:153
Brock, Sarah	Leavenworth, Easton	9	F	10:288
Brock, Susan C.	Bourbon, Fort Scott P.O.	8	F	2:153
Brock, Tabitha	Bourbon, Fort Scott P.O.	16	F	2:153
Brocket, Elizabeth	Linn, Valley	26	F	7:32
Brofam, J. B.	Arrapahoe, South Park	28	M	11:168
Broner, William	Marshall, Vermillion	30	M	3:213
Broute, C.	Arrapahoe, Denver (Miner)	30	M	11:417
Brown, Daniel	Allen, Iola P.O. (Farmer)	29	M	2:263
Brown, David	Leavenworth, Delaware (Farmer)	40	M	10:434
Brown, Eliza I.	Bourbon, Turkey Creek P.O.	4	F	2:112
Brown, Izar	Allen, Carlisle P.O. (Farmer)	26	M	2:237
Brown, James	Shawnee, Soldier	36	M	9:84
Brown, John	Linn, Mound City (Farmer)	55	M	7:101
Brown, John	Atchison, Lancaster (Farmer)	32	M	1:108
Brown, John W.	Atchison, Walnut (Farmer)	36	M	1:180
Brown, John W.	Bourbon, Turkey Creek P.O. (Farmer)	25	M	2:112
Brown, Joseph N.	Lykins, Marysville (Cabinet Maker)	26	M	8:119
Brown, Margaret	Linn, Mound City	45	F	7:101
Brown, Mary	Shawnee, Soldier	18	F	9:84
Brown, Mary E.	Atchison, Walnut	14	F	1:180

[1]Perhaps spelling should be Frances; 1855 Census lists four unnamed females
    living in home of Rery H. Brock age 40, farmer. Dist. 14, p. 16.
Arapahoe: spelled incorrectly with 2 r's in census and in this index also.

Name	Kansas: County; Township; P.O. Arap. Co.: Census Div. Not Township	Age	Sex	Census V. Pg.
Brown, R.	Arrapahoe, South Park	31	M	11:29
Brown, Rufus	Bourbon, Fort Scott P.O. (Farmer)	20	M	2:199
Brown, Sarah	Jefferson, Kaw	29	F	5:82
Brown, Sarah A.	Atchison, Walnut	15	F	1:180
Brown, Tennessee	Bourbon, Turkey Creek P.O.	3	F	2:112
Brown, Thomas	Leavenworth, Kickapoo (Farmer)	27	M	10:405
Brown, W. D.	Doniphan, Iowa Point (Silversmith)	37	M	1:446
Brown, William	Shawnee, Soldier	7	M	9:84
Brownsdale, P.	Arrapahoe, South Park	26	M	11:258
Brows, William	Bourbon, Fort Scott P.O. (Carpenter)	38	M	2:201
Brueter, Lown[1]	Arrapahoe, Denver (Miner)	28	M	11:390
Bruner, W. C.	Arrapahoe, Valley of the Platte	36	M	11:840
Bryant, Andrew	Bourbon, Fort Scott P.O. (Farmer)	33	M	2:91
Bryant, Marion	Atchison, Mt. Pleasant	4	M	1:145
Bryce, J. S.	Arrapahoe, South Clear Creek (Miner)	16	M	11:683
Bryson, J.	Franklin, Peoria (Farmer)	35	M	8:279
Buckley, James	Leavenworth, Ward 3 (B.maker)	24	M	10:219
Buckner, G.[2]	Arrapahoe, Russell Gulch (Laborer)	40	M	11:552
Buckner, Sarah F.	Bourbon, Fort Scott P.O. (Housewife)	28	F	2:196
Buckner, William G.	Bourbon, Fort Scott P.O. (Farmer)	29	M	2:196
Buford, Elija	Atchison, Mt. Pleasant	34	F	1:145
Buges, James	Linn, Scott (Farmer)	18	M	7:26
Bullinger, Jane	Linn, Mound City	34	F	7:127
Bumanger, M.	Arrapahoe, Denver (Miner)	39	M	11:400
Bumel, Amy A.[3]	Leavenworth, Easton	42		10:296
Bunch, Catherine	Breckenridge, Forest Hill	55	F	4:178
Bunch, Charles	Breckenridge, Forest Hill (Farmer)	61	M	4:178
Bunch, David	Breckenridge, Forest Hill (Farmer)	25	M	4:178
Bunch, James	Linn, Paris (Farmer)	38	M	7:148
Bunch, James C.	Breckenridge, Forest Hill	33	M	4:178
Bunch, Mary	Breckenridge, Forest Hill	18	F	4:179
Bunch, Mary A.	Breckenridge, Forest Hill	34	F	4:178
Bunyan, Elizabeth	Allen, Elizabeth Town P.O.	26	F	2:240
Burk, Catharine	Atchison, Walnut	6	F	1:178
Burk, Marion	Atchison, Walnut (Farmer)	34	M	1:178
Burk, Mary F.	Atchison, Walnut	10	F	1:178
Burk, Perry S.	Atchison, Walnut	8	M	1:178
Burk, Sarah	Atchison, Walnut	30	F	1:178
Burke, Marion	Atchison, Walnut (Farmer)	28	M	1:186
Burke, Mary F.	Atchison, Walnut	9	F	1:186
Burke, Sally	Atchison, Walnut	27	F	1:186
Burket, Mary	Leavenworth, Delaware	20	F	10:420
Burnett, M.	Arrapahoe, Valley of the Platte	36	M	11:801
Burnett, O.	Arrapahoe, South Park	27	M	11:169
Burns, Louisa	Breckenridge, Emporia	42	F	4:195
Burris, J. P.	Arrapahoe, South Park (Miner)	30	M	11:73
Burroughs, T.	Arrapahoe, Valley of the Pltt.(Miner)	27	M	11:825
Burrows, Lucy A.	Leavenworth, Kickapoo	28	F	10:309
Burt, B. S.	Arrapahoe, South Park (Miner)	39	M	11:29
Burt, C.	Arrapahoe, South Park	36	M	11:122
Burt, Geo.	Arrapahoe, South Park	39	M	11:137
Burton, J. A.	Leavenworth, Ward 2 (Clerk Dist.Ct.)	35	M	10:191
Burton, M. P.	Franklin, Peoria	39	F	8:267
Bush, Wm. C.	Arrapahoe, South Park (Saloon)	38	M	11:22
Buskell, S. J.	Arrapahoe, South Clear Creek	28	M	11:737
Busney, W. P.	Franklin, Peoria (Merchant)	45	M	8:267
Butcher, E. N.	Arrapahoe, South Clear Creek	38	M	11:688

[1]Spelling not clear on either name.
[2]Not clearly a "u".
[3]Spelling not clear in original entry.
  Arapahoe: spelled incorrectly with 2 r's in census and in this index also.

Name	Kansas: County; Township; P.O. Arap. Co.: Census Div. Not Township	Age	Sex	Census V. Pg
Butcher, J.	Franklin, Peoria (Carpenter)	24	M	8:269
Buthe, S.	Arrapahoe, California Gulch	39	M	11:309
Butler, James A.	Leavenworth, Easton (Farmer)	34	M	10:293
Butler, Nancy N.	Leavenworth, Easton	33	F	10:293
Butram, H. A.	Johnson, Shawnee	37	F	6:99
Butterly, Wm.	Arrapahoe, South Park	42	M	11:178
Buxton,	McGhee, Crawford Seminary P.O.	40	F	9:220
Buxton, Andrew Mc.	McGhee, Crawford Seminary P.O.	9	M	9:220
Buxton, Catharin B.	McGhee, Crawford Seminary P.O.	7	F	9:220
Buxton, Eliza A.	McGhee, Crawford Seminary P.O.	17	F	9:220
Buxton, Franklin	McGhee, Crawford Seminary P. O.	12	M	9:220
Buxton, John	McGhee, Crawford Seminary P.O.(Farmer)	24	M	9:220
Buxton, Leander	McGhee, Crawford Seminary PO(FrmLbr)	16	M	9:220
Buxton, Mary J.	McGhee, Crawford Seminary P.O.	13	F	9:220
Buxton, Paralla	McGhee, Crawford Seminary P.O.	17	F	9:220
Buxton, Willis A.	McGhee, Crawford Seminary PO (Farmer)	49	M	9:220
Bye, E. B.	Arrapahoe, Denver	33	M	11:388
Byerly, J.	Riley, Henryville-Randolph PO(Farmer)	39	M	9:298
Byler, Alfred	Shawnee, Tecumseh (Farmer)	48	M	9:73
Cabbage, A.	Coffey, Neosho (Farmer)	62	M	4:68
Cable, Hiram	Anderson, Ozark (Farmer)	47	M	7:249
Caffy, Jane	Allen, Humboldt P. O.	53	F	2:282
Cain, Elizabeth	Jefferson, Rock Creek	31	F	5:96
Caldwell, L. V.	Arrapahoe, South Clear Creek	28	M	11:687
Calhoun, Margaret M.	Atchison, Walnut	31	F	1:178
Callaway, Betsy A.	Lykins, Marysville	30	F	8:128
Callender, M.	Arrapahoe, South Park	42	M	11:191
Camking, Robert	McGhee, Medoc,Missouri P.O.(Farmer)	31	M	9:212
Camman, S. P.	Arrapahoe, Valley of the Platte	27	M	11:808
Camp, G. C.	Arrapahoe, South Park	24	M	11:146
Campbell, A.	Johnson, Shawnee	32	F	6:87
Campbell, A.	Johnson, Shawnee (Farmer)	23	M	6:87
Campbell, A.	Johnson, Shawnee	14	M	6:87
Campbell, A. C.	Atchison, Mt. Pleasant (Farmer)	42	M	1:150
Campbell, A. C.	Atchison, Mt. Pleasant (Farmer)	39	M	1:144
Campbell, C.	Johnson, Shawnee	19	F	6:87
Campbell, D.	Johnson, Shawnee(Universal Minst.Ulv.)	40	M	6:87
Campbell, Daniel	Atchison, Center (Farmer)	43	M	1:120
Campbell, E. W.	Coffey, Avon	32	F	4:9
Campbell, Elizabeth	Atchison, Mt. Pleasant	46	F	1:144
Campbell, G. A.	Johnson, Shawnee	12	M	6:87
Campbell, George	Anderson, Town of Garnett	13	M	7:221
Campbell, H. L.	Johnson, Monticello (Farmer)	30	M	6:22
Campbell, J. R.	Coffey, Avon	6	M	4:9
Campbell, J. Y.	Anderson,Town of Garnett(Prob.Judge)	45	M	7:221
Campbell, James	Coffey, Leroy (Farmer)	54	M	4:19
Campbell, Jas.	Johnson, Olathe (Lawyer)	36	M	6:1
Campbell, John H.	Lykins, Osawatomie	16	M	8:51
Campbell, John J.	Breckenridge, Forest Hill (Farmer)	39	M	4:184
Campbell, John W.	Anderson, Town of Garnett	16	M	7:221
Campbell, John W. C.	Atchison, Center	8	M	1:120
Campbell, Joseph C.	Atchison, Center	10	M	1:120
Campbell, Louisa M.	Atchison, Center	17	F	1:120
Campbell, M. M.	Atchison, Center (Agent A.B.S.)	49	M	1:124
Campbell, M. S.	Coffey, Avon	11	M	4:9
Campbell, Martha	Lykins, Osawatomie	53	F	8:51
Campbell, Martha J.	Lykins, Osawatomie	12	F	8:51
Campbell, N.	Johnson, Shawnee	63	F	6:87
Campbell, Nancy	Atchison, Center	46	F	1:120
Campbell, Nathan	Leavenworth, Stranger (Farmer)	37	M	10:462
Campbell, Perlina M.	Atchison, Center	16	F	1:120

Arapahoe: spelled incorrectly with 2 r's in census and in this index also.

Name	Kansas: County; Township; P.O. Arap. Co.: Census Div. Not Township	Age	Sex	Census V. : Pg.
Campbell, Robert W.	Atchison, Mt. Pleasant (Farmer)	39	M	1:150
Campbell, S. B.	Coffey, Avon	8	M	4:9
Campbell, Sarah	Atchison, Mt. Pleasant	70	F	1:144
Campbell, William R.	Lykins, Osawatomie	18	M	8:51
Camran, M.	Doniphan, Wolf River (Farmer)	59	F	1:405
Canaver, Noah	Linn, Paris	36	M	7:144
Canden, Wm.	Arrapahoe, South Park	27	M	11:187
Cannon, E.	Coffey, Neosho	26	F	4:68
Caray, Sarah	Bourbon, Mapleton P.O.	49	F	2:148
Carbre, L.	Johnson, Oxford (Wagonmaker)	27	M	6:104
Carey, Francis M.	Bourbon, Mapleton P.O. (Farmer)	27	M	2:137
Carhinbury, Spencer	Leavenworth, 1st Ward	60	BM	10:91
Carlen, J.	Arrapahoe, South Clear Creek	24	M	11:722
Carner, Saml.	Arrapahoe, Golden City	40	M	11:444
Carpenter, Cynthia	Bourbon, Fort Scott P.O. (Housewife)	45	F	2:95
Carr, Erik	Leavenworth, Stranger (Farmer)	23	M	10:481
Carriger, Angeline	Shawnee, Topeka	39	F	9:32
Carriger, Elizabeth	Linn, Valley	37	F	7:51
Carriger, Elliott	Shawnee, Topeka (Farmer)	44	M	9:32
Carriger, Leonard	Linn, Valley	12	M	7:51
Carriger, Mary	Shawnee, Topeka	17	F	9:32
Carriger, Mary	Linn, Valley	14	F	7:51
Carriger, W.	Linn, Valley (Farmer)	47	M	7:51
Carriger, Mathias	Leavenworth, Easton (Farmer)	26	M	10:295
Carrol, J. O.	Arrapahoe, Valley of the Platte	28		11:776
Carroll, John	Jefferson, Jefferson (Laborer)	18	M	5:36
Carroll, Nathan	Jefferson, Jefferson (Laborer)	49	M	5:36
Carsey, G. W.	Johnson, Shawnee (Farmer)	31	M	6:99
Carson, D.	Douglas, Clinton	66		6:404
Carson, Gideon	Jefferson, Oskaloosa (Merchant)	31	M	5:109
Carson, James F.	Douglas, Clinton	10	M	6:406
Carson, Mary C.	Douglas, Clinton	12	F	6:404
Carson, Sarah	Douglas, Clinton	34	F	6:404
Carson, Sarah	Bourbon, Turkey Creek P.O. (Housewife)	50	F	2:115
Carson, Th. J.	Douglas, Clinton (Farmer)	35	M	6:404
Carter, Amanda A.	Atchison, Walnut	1	F	1:195
Carter, F.	Coffey, Ottumwa	8	F	4:55
Carter, H.	Coffey, Ottumwa (Carpenter)	33	M	4:55
Carter, James	Coffey, Leroy (Physician)	30	M	4:29
Carter, James M.	Atchison, Walnut	14	M	1:195
Carter, Jepe	Allen, Turkey Creek P.O. (Farmer)	31	M	2:304
Carter, John	Atchison, Walnut (Farmer)	22	M	1:195
Carter, John	Linn, Centerville (Laborer)	27	M	7:84
Carter, John	Atchison, Shannon (Farmer)	19	M	1:83
Carter, Mary T.	Atchison, Walnut	8	F	1:195
Carter, R.	Coffey, Ottumwa	3	F	4:55
Carter, Sarah	Atchison, Walnut	30	F	1:195
Carter, Tennessee	Atchison, Walnut	6	F	1:195
Carter, Wm.	Atchison, Mt. Pleasant	44	M	1:166
Carter, Woodford	Atchison, Walnut	11	M	1:195
Cartright, Eliza A.	Bourbon, Fort Scott P.O. (Housewife)	31	F	2:152
Cartshell, Jesse	Bourbon, Mapleton P.O. (Farmer)	33	M	2:134
Cartshell, Joseph	Bourbon, Mapleton P.O.	7	M	2:134
Cartshell, Marinda	Bourbon, Mapleton P.O.	10	F	2:134
Cartshell, Phoebe	Bourbon, Mapleton P.O. (Housewife)	32	F	2:134
Cartshell, Polly	Bourbon, Mapleton P.O.	5	F	2:134
Cartshell, Samuel	Bourbon, Mapleton P.O.	9	M	2:134
Cartwright, Elizabeth	Bourbon, Barnesville P.O.	16	F	2:178
Cartwright, James	Bourbon, Barnesville P.O. (Farmer)	18	M	2:178
Cartwright, Minerva	Bourbon, Barnesville P.O. (Housewife)	40	F	2:178
Cartwright, William	Bourbon, Barnesville P.O.	11	M	2:178

Arapahoe: spelled incorrectly with 2 r's in census and in this index also.

Name	Kansas: County; Township; P.O. Arap. Co.: Census Div. Not Township	Age	Sex	Census V. Pg.
Cary, Wm.	Atchison, Ward 3	18	M	1:48
Caryal, V. H.	Arrapahoe, South Park	37	M	11:258
Casey, E.	Johnson, Monticello	47	F	6:82
Casey, Nancy	Linn, Valley	25	F	7:38
Cash, Celia	Breckenridge, Pike	34	F	4:208
Cash, John	Breckenridge, Pike (Farmer)	32	M	4:208
Cash, Wm.	Breckenridge, Emporia (Farmer)	33	M	4:204
Cashman, G.	Arrapahoe, South Park (Miner)	35	M	11:74
Caskey, Wm. C.	Anderson, Jackson (Farmer)	29	M	7:212
Castle, Andrew	Anderson, Walker (Farmer	41	M	7:241A
Castle, William	Anderson, Walker	17	M	7:241A
Catis, S.	Douglas, Lecompton	17	M	6:369
Catis, Sam[1]	Douglas, Lecompton (Farmer)	48	F	6:369
Cawlfield, David	Jefferson, Jefferson (Farmer)	28	M	5:45
Cawlfield, John	Jefferson, Jefferson (Farmer)	30	M	5:45
Cawlfield, Owen	Jefferson, Jefferson (Farmer)	54	M	5:44
Cayler, T. N.	Arrapahoe, Valley of the Platte	27	M	11:860
Caywood, J.	Linn, Centerville (Farmer)	65	M	7:89
Cermly, Savilla	Douglas, Willow Springs	36	F	6:329
Cermly, Zilphia	Douglas, Willow Springs	18	F	6:329
Chaffin, Anthony	Bourbon, Turkey Creek P.O. (Farmer)	37	M	2:113
Chaffin, Elijah	Bourbon, Turkey Creek P.O. (Farmer)	27	M	2:113
Chaffin, Penelope	Bourbon, Turkey Creek P.O.(Housewife)	30	F	2:113
Chambers, M.	Coffey, Neosho	59	F	4:74
Chambers, Silas	Coffey, Neosho	38	M	4:74
Chamblin, Eliza J.	McGhee, Crawford Seminary P.O.	43	F	9:224
Champlain, R. P.	Arrapahoe, South Park	18	M	11:115
Chandler, Catherine	Lykins, Mound	24	F	8:72
Chandler, Martha	Arrapahoe, Denver	23	F	11:324
Chapell, N.	Nemaha, Grenada	34	F	3:110
Charles, Andrew I.	Bourbon, Xenia P.O.	5	M	2:126
Charles, Anna E.	Bourbon, Xenia P.O.	5	F	2:125
Charles, Arthur F.	Bourbon, Xenia P.O.	8	M	2:126
Charles, Josephas	Bourbon, Xenia P.O.	9	M	2:126
Charles, Martha E.	Bourbon, Xenia P.O.	10	F	2:126
Charles, Mary	Bourbon, Xenia P.O.	12	F	2:126
Charles, Mary S.	Bourbon, Xenia P.O. (Housewife)	26	F	2:125
Charles, Thomas	Bourbon, Xenia P.O. (Farmer)	31	M	2:125
Charles, William	Bourbon, Xenia P.O. (Farmer)	39	M	2:126
Chase, A.	Doniphan, Center (Farmer)	30	M	1:269
Chase, J. E.	Doniphan, Center	5	M	1:269
Chase, John	Marshall, Vermillion	5	M	3:218
Chase, M.	Doniphan, Center	26	F	1:269
Chase, Maria	Marshall, Vermillion	27	F	3:218
Chase, Mina	Marshall, Vermillion	9	F	3:218
Chase, Obediah	Marshall, Vermillion (Farmer)	28	M	3:218
Chase, Sarah J.	Marshall, Vermillion	3	F	3:218
Chase, W. E.	Doniphan, Center	9	F	1:269
Cherry, Geo. W.	Linn, Valley (Farmer)	30	M	7:37
Cherry, J.	Linn, Valley (Farmer)	33	M	7:45
Cherry, Jane	Linn, Valley	32	F	7:45
Chester, ...[2]	McGhee, Medoc, Mo. P.O.(Farm Laborer)	17	M	9:212
Cheumly, M. A.	Doniphan, Washington	16	F	1:329
Chilton, Wm. M.	Arrapahoe, South Park	34	M	11:102
Chistwood, Sarah	Bourbon, Barnesville P.O.	62	F	2:174
Chitting, B. C.	Arrapahoe, South Park	38	M	11:260
Chitwood, Mary	Linn, Town of Paris	32	F	7:134
Chitwood, P.	Linn, Town of Paris (Farmer)	22	M	7:134
Chrisman, John	Clay, Junction City P.O. (Farmer)	32	M	9:268

[1] As recorded in original census.

[2] Possibly Andrew.

Arapahoe: spelled incorrectly with 2 r's in census and in this index also.

Name	Kansas: County; Township; P.O. Arap. Co.: Census Div. Not Township	Age	Sex	Census v. pg.
Christman, Susan	Linn, Mound City	30	F	7:102
Clach, D. R.	Doniphan, Washington (Shingle Maker)	35	M	1:335
Cladin, E. S.	Arrapahoe, Valley of the Platte	28	M	11:859
Clampir, A. J.[1]	Nemaha, Nemaha (Widow)	46	F	3:86
Clampit, William	Nemaha, Nemaha (Farm Laborer)	24	M	3:85
Clark, Alerid	Leavenworth, Alexandria	36	F	10:451
Clark, E. H.	Arrapahoe, South Park	27	M	11:131
Clark, Edward C.	Leavenworth, Alexandria (Farmer)	42	M	10:451
Clark, Elizabeth	Linn, Centerville	24	F	7:94
Clark, Hiram	Coffey, Pottawatomie (Blacksmith)	64	M	4:3
Clark, John	Washington, Washington (Farm Laborer)	37	M	3:261
Clark, Oliver	Madison, Hartford (Farmer)	30	M	4:233
Clark, Samuel	Leavenworth, Alexandria	43	M	10:450
Clarke, Mary	Linn, Valley (Farmer)	32	F	7:34
Clarke, Telman	Linn, Valley	32	M	7:34
Clayet, G.	Arrapahoe, South Clear Creek	39	M	11:689
Claypool, Winnie	Bourbon, Fort Scott P.O. (Housewife)	38	F	2:87
Clayton, F.	Arrapahoe, South Park	38	M	11:150
Clem, Wm.	Arrapahoe, South Park	28	M	11:128
Clemens, Malinda	Douglas, Lawrence	19	F	6:191
Clemens, Solomon	Douglas, Lawrence (Grocer)	25	M	6:191
Clement, Mary	Linn, Valley	25	F	7:43
Clevenga, Amanda	Dickinson, Kansas Falls P.O.(Hsekpr.)	26	F	4:303
Clifford, Maria	Arrapahoe, South Park	29	F	11:158
Clifton, L.	Arrapahoe, Mountain City	32	M	11:473
Cline, Marrion	Jackson, Jefferson	35	F	5:198
Cline, Sam	Woodson, Verdigris (Farmer)	36	M	9:163
Clinton, S. U.	Arrapahoe, South Park	26	M	11:114
Clover, H. A.	Arrapahoe, South Park	34	M	11:168
Coats, P.	Douglas, Eudora (Farmer)	40	M	6:335
Coble, Dempsy	McGhee, Brushville P.O. (Farmer)	32	M	9:232
Cobny, Joanna	Linn, Potosi	12	F	7:71
Cochran, W. W.	Atchison, Ward 3	28	M	1:67
Cochrane, Wm.	Arrapahoe, South Park	37	M	11:154
Coffey, Wm.	Arrapahoe, South Clear Creek	36	M	11:734
Coffman, Danl.	Arrapahoe, South Park	24	M	11:245
Cole, Charles M.	McGhee, Brushville P.O. (Blacksmith)	38	M	9:222
Cole, Easter	McGhee, Brushville P.O. (Servant)	15	F	9:222
Cole, Eliza A.	McGhee, Brushville P.O. (Servant)	20	F	9:222
Cole, Ellen	McGhee, Brushville P.O.	19	F	9:222
Cole, George	McGhee, Brushville P.O.(Farm Laborer)	18	M	9:222
Cole, James	McGhee, Brushville P.O.	7	M	9:222
Cole, Lucinda	McGhee, Brushville P.O.	11	F	9:222
Cole, Masy	McGhee, Brushville P.O.	42	F	9:222
Cole, Patia	Jefferson, Jefferson	32	F	5:39
Cole, Thomas	McGhee, Brushville P.O.	13	M	9:222
Coledo, G.	Arrapahoe, Valley of the Platte	28	M	11:784
Coleston, D.	Johnson, Monticello (Farmer)	35	M	6:82
Colier, I.	Arrapahoe, Valley of the Platte	29	M	11:793
Collins, Earnest	Lykins, Richland	2	M	8:19
Collins, Edna	Atchison, Ward 2 (Seamstress)	43	F	1:39
Collins, J.	Arrapahoe, South Park	28	M	11:162
Collins, Martin	Arrapahoe, South Park	33	M	11:248
Colson, Wm.	Arrapahoe, South Park (Miner)	38	M	11:183
Combs, Welthy	Linn, Centerville	43	F	7:90
Comstock, M.	Arrapahoe, Mountain City (Miner)	28	M	11:550
Conden, Braden W.	Allen, Humboldt P.O. (Farmer)	38	M	2:274
Conger, Mathias	Jefferson, Jefferson (Farmer)	27	M	5:32
Connor, H. G.	Arrapahoe, South Park	34	M	11:179
Conter, T. W.	Atchison, Grasshopper (Farmer)	22	M	1:95

[1]Original entry difficult to decipher, especially the initials.

Arapahoe: spelled incorrectly with 2 r's in census and in this index also.

Name	Kansas: County; Township; P.O. Arap. Co.: Census Div. Not Township	Age	Sex	Census V. Pg.
Conydon, I.	Arrapahoe, South Clear Creek	29	M	11:710
Cook, David	Arrapahoe, Golden City (Miner)	35	M	11:442
Cook, Saml.	Arrapahoe, Golden City (Miner)	33	M	11:442
Cookburg, A. F.	Arrapahoe, Denver (Miner)	29	M	11:399
Cooke, E. Caroline	Arrapahoe, Quartz Valley (Cook)	18	F	11:500
Cooke, J. E. P.	Arrapahoe, Quartz Valley	21	M	11:500
Cooke, W. P.	Arrapahoe, Quartz Valley	45	M	11:500
Cooke, W. T.	Arrapahoe, Quartz Valley	20	M	11:500
Coonrod, Sarah	Bourbon, Fort Scott P.O. (Housewife)	28	F	2:79
Coop, David	Jefferson, Kentucky (Laborer)	46	M	5:67
Cooper, Wm.	Arrapahoe, Denver (Trader)	36	M	11:394
Coopland, Richard E.	Allen, Humboldt P.O.(Farm Laborer)	26	M	2:286
Coots, James	Pottawatomie, Rockingham (Farmer)	25	M	5:289
Copeland, Anna	Bourbon, Fort Scott P.O.(Housewife)	23	F	2:198
Copeland, David	Shawnee, Tecumseh (Farmer)	56	M	9:72
Copeland, Eleanor	Bourbon, Barnesville P.O.(Housewife)	34	F	2:172
Copeland, Emily J.	Allen, Humboldt	22	F	2:298
Copeland, J. H.	Johnson, McCamish (Farmer)	53	M	6:69
Copeland, Jesse	Bourbon, Barnesville P.O. (Farmer)	52	M	2:172
Copeland, Lewis	Bourbon, Fort Scott P.O. (Farmer)	32	M	2:198
Copeland, M.	Johnson, McCamish	56	F	6:69
Copeland, Mary	Shawnee, Tecumseh	45	F	9:72
Copeland, W. K.	Johnson, McCamish (Farmer)	29	M	6:69
Copeland, William D.	Allen, Humboldt P.O. (Farmer)	27	M	2:297
Copengen, Eliza	Doniphan, Iowa Point (Farmer)	31	M	1:426
Copengen, R.	Doniphan, Iowa Point (Farm Hand)	20	M	1:426
Copengen, Wm.	Doniphan, Iowa Point	13	F	1:426
Copings, J.	Doniphan, Marion	33	F	1:292
Copings, Wm.	Doniphan, Iowa Point (Farmer)	19	M	1:425
Coppinger, Elihu	Jefferson, Jefferson (Farmer)	38	M	5:42
Coppinger, Miranda	Jefferson, Jefferson	14	F	5:42
Coppinger, Sarah	Jefferson, Jefferson	32	F	5:42
Coppinger, Thomas	Jefferson, Jefferson	8	M	5:42
Coppinger, William	Jefferson, Jefferson (Farmer)	46	M	5:41
Copple, Sarah	Linn, Paris	34	F	7:148
Copy, Edwin	Arrapahoe, Valley of the Platte	45	M	11:807
Cord, Thos. A.	Arrapahoe, South Park	32	M	11:237
Cordiel, D.	Nemaha, Rock Creek (Laborer)	18	M	3:78
Cordiel, J.	Nemaha, Rock Creek (Farmer)	63	M	3:78
Cordiel, L.	Nemaha, Rock Creek	28	M	3:78
Cordiel, Martha	Nemaha, Rock Creek	31	F	3:78
Cordiel, R. A.	Nemaha, Rock Creek	16	F	3:78
Cordray, H.	Riley, Manhattan-Henryville PO(Frmr.)	54	M	9:297
Cormack, Nancy	Linn, Potosi	36	F	7:55
Cormack, S.	Linn, Potosi (Farmer)	38	M	7:55
Cornish, A.	Arrapahoe, South Park	29	M	11:181
Corser, H.	Arrapahoe, South Clear Creek	29	M	11:760
Cortwood, Anna	Bourbon, Fort Scott P.O. (Housewife)	54	F	2:83
Corwin, H.	Doniphan, Center (Farmer)	32	M	1:256
Coulter, C. E.	Arrapahoe, Valley of the Platte	27	M	11:800
Courtney, Geo. J.	Arrapahoe, Tarryall, South Park	22	M	11:618
Courtney, J. G.	Arrapahoe, South Park	26	M	11:115
Cousalt, Jefferson	Wyandotte, Wyandotte (Laborer)	30	M	10:39
Covert, E.	Arrapahoe, South Park	24	M	11:228
Cowles, D.	Arrapahoe, South Park	26	M	11:209
Cox, Angeline	Jefferson, Rock Creek	30	F	5:87
Cox, E.	Johnson, Monticello	21	F	6:22
Cox, Elizabeth	McGhee, Medoc, Missouri P.O.	29	F	9:213
Cox, J. H.	Doniphan, Marion (Carpenter)	35	M	1:292
Cox, John B.	Breckenridge, Emporia (Farmer)	50	M	4:204
Cox, Mary A.	Coffey, Neosho	22	F	4:71

Arapahoe: spelled incorrectly with 2 r's in census and in this index also.

Name	Kansas: County; Township; P.O. Arap. Co.: Census Div. Not Township	Age	Sex	Census V.:Pg.
Cox, Nancy	McGhee, Medoc, Missouri P.O.	50	F	9:214
Cox, R.	Doniphan, Washington (Domestic)	22	F	1:298
Cox, Ratchel	Coffey, Neosho	17	F	4:71
Coy, Louisa	Arrapahoe, Russell Gulch(Asst.Hskpr)	22	F	11:547
Coyle, Polly	Bourbon, Marmaton P.O. (Housewife)	22	F	2:203
Crabtree, C.	Johnson, Shawnee	37	F	6:29
Crabtree, E.	Linn, Paris	42	F	7:152
Crabtree, N.	Arrapahoe, South Clear Creek (Miner)	27	M	11:682
Crafton, A.	Arrapahoe, Denver (Miner)	24	M	11:399
Crafton, D.	Arrapahoe, Denver (Miner)	27	M	11:399
Crafton, S.[1]	Arrapahoe, South Park	28	M	11:143
Crager, Lydia	Linn, Potosi	30	F	7:68
Craig, I. E.	Doniphan, Iowa Point (Farmer)	28	M	1:418
Craig, W.	Woodson, Verdigris (Me. Minister)	50	M	9:161
Crawford, A.	Linn, Mound City (Teamster)	35	M	7:105
Crawford, Andrew	Leavenworth, 1st Ward (Blacksmith)	36	BM	10:141
Craynton, J.	Arrapahoe, Nevada Gulch (Miner)	21	M	11:519
Crazer, Sarah	Linn, Scott	26	F	7:21
Creach, J.	Davis, Junction City (Farmer)	50	M	9:339
Creek, E.	Linn, Valley (Farmer)	55	F	7:45
Cress, Anna	Morris, Clarks Creek	14	F	4:281
Cress, Eliza	Morris, Clarks Creek	21	F	4:281
Cress, F.	Morris, Grove	22	M	4:265
Cress, Matilda	Morris, Grove	17	F	4:268
Cress, Matilda	Morris, Clarks Creek	18	F	4:281
Cress, Martha	Morris, Clarks Creek	11	F	4:281
Cressey, N. M.	Arrapahoe, South Park	28	M	11:241
Crobarger, Ann	Jefferson, Jefferson	51	F	5:29
Crockett, W. S.[2]	Arrapahoe, Central City (Rancher)	40	M	11:578
Crockett, William	Jefferson, Jefferson (Farmer)	48	M	5:36
Cross, E. H.	Arrapahoe, South Park	26	M	11:215
Cross, Polk	Bourbon, Barnesville P.O.	16	M	2:180
Cross, Virgil	Bourbon, Barnesville P.O.	22	M	2:180
Crosswhite, W. L.	Arrapahoe, Nevada Gulch (Miner)	34	M	11:529
Crow, J. A.	Franklin, Centropolis (Farmer)	20	M	8:216
Crow, W.	Franklin, Centropolis	37	F	8:216
Crow, Wm.	Franklin, Centropolis (Farmer)	42	M	8:216
Crow, William	Jefferson, Oskaloosa (Laborer)	18	M	5:125
Cruekshank, N.[3]	Arrapahoe, South Park	27	M	11:37
Cruise, J. O.	Arrapahoe, Valley of the Platte	22	M	11:843
Crutchfield, Elizabeth	Woodson, Neosho Falls	39	F	9:129
Culern, George A.	Allen, Humboldt P.O.	20	M	2:281
Culern, Osaac J.	Allen, Humboldt P.O. (Farmer)	41	M	2:281
Culern, R. V.	Allen, Humboldt P.O.	30	F	2:281
Culern, Simeon F.	Allen, Humboldt P.O.	39	M	2:281
Cuming, Sarah	Woodson, Belmont	37	F	9:152
Cuningham, Aaron	Breckenridge, Agnes City (Farmer)	35	M	4:148
Cunningham, Jno.	Arrapahoe, Valley of the Platte	25	M	11:834
Cunningham, Lydia	Douglas, Kanwaca	20	F	6:384
Cupper, Geo.	Arrapahoe, South Park	21	M	11:163
Curley, C. S.	Arrapahoe, South Park	26	M	11:201
Curnett, Caperton	Jefferson, Oskaloosa	11	M	5:128
Curnett, Mary	Jefferson, Oskaloosa	26	F	5:128
Curnett, Wm.	Jefferson, Oskaloosa (Farmer)	39	M	5:128
Currey, E.	Nemaha, Richmond	38	F	3:105
Currey, James	Bourbon, Raysville P.O. (Farmer)	52	M	2:159
Currey, Mary A.	Bourbon, Raysville P.O.(Housewife)	23	F	2:159

[1]Original entry looks more like L. Crafton.

[2]Could be W. S. or A. S.

[3]W.P.A. indexer's spelling; original entry appears to be spelled Cruickshank.
 Arapahoe: spelled incorrectly with 2 r's in census and in this index also.

Name	Kansas: County; Township; P.O. Arap. Co.: Census Div. Not Township	Age	Sex	Census V. Pg
Cursac, W. B.	Franklin, Peoria (Farmer)	21	M	8:269
Cursac, J.	Franklin, Peoria (Physician)	54	M	8:269
Cursac, L.	Franklin, Peoria	42?	F	8:269
Curtis, Isabella	Doniphan, Marion	26	F	1:284
Curtis, J. M.	Doniphan, Marion (Farmer)	40	M	1:284
Curtis, M. A.	Doniphan, Marion	47	F	1:284
Curtis, M. A.	Doniphan, Marion	47	F	1:284
Cushenbury, Minnie	Bourbon, Fort Scott P.O.(Housewife)	42	BF	2:210
Cutsinger, Alexander	Allen, Iola P.O.	8	M	2:249
Cutsinger, Charles	Allen, Iola P.O.	48	M	2:249
Cutsinger, Mary J.	Allen, Iola P.O.	25	F	2:249
Cutter, George A.	Coffey, Leroy (Physician)	29	M	4:31
Dagley, J.	Johnson, Monticello (Farmer)	26	M	6:83
Dagley, J.	Johnson, Monticello (Farmer)	64	M	6:83
Dagley, W.	Johnson, Monticello (Farmer)	24	M	6:83
Daily, C. D.	Arrapahoe, Denver (Miner)	22	M	11:417
Daily, Elizabeth	Marshall, Blue Rapids	17	F	3:207
Daily, Mary	Nemaha, Red Vermillion	23	F	3:132
Dalton, John	McGhee, Osage Mission P.O. (Farmer)	49	M	9:242
Dalton, R.	Arrapahoe, South Park	24	M	11:133
Dalton, Riley	Bourbon, Fort Scott P.O. (Farmer)	34	M	2:78
Danham, S. S.	Arrapahoe, South Park	35	M	11:120
Daniels, Alpha A.	Bourbon, Fort Scott P.O. (Housewife)	24	F	2:199
Daniels, Elizer	Linn, Potosi	30	F	7:56
Daniels, Hiram	Linn, Paris (Farmer)	30	M	7:140
Daniels, J.	Arrapahoe, South Park	20	M	11:5
Daniels, Mary	Woodson, Belmont (F. W.)	51	F	9:153
Daniels, W.	Woodson, Verdigris (Farmer)	22	M	9:164
Dark, Saml.	Jefferson, Oskaloosa (Laborer)	12		5:127
Darling, M. O.	Arrapahoe, Denver (Miner)	40	M	11:419
Darmont, G.	Arrapahoe, Valley of the Platte	24	M	11:805
Darn, Chas. P.	Douglas, Lecompton	2	M	6:363
Darnell, Charlotte	Pottawatomie, Rockingham	40	F	5:291
Darnell, J.	Coffey, Burlington (Merchant)	62	M	4:35
Dater, H.	Arrapahoe, South Clear Creek	29	M	11:707
Davenport, Jepthe	Arrapahoe, Russell Gulch	14	F	11:547
Davenport, Mary	Arrapahoe, Russell Gulch	31	F	11:547
Davenport, Mary	Linn, Potosi	3	F	7:76
Davis, A. T.[1]	Otoe, Otoe (Farmer)	22	M	4:353
Davis, Amanda	Leavenworth, Kickapoo	16	F	10:309
Davis, Angeline	Bourbon, Fort Scott P.O.	8	F	2:197
Davis, C. A.	Johnson, Olathe	34	F	6:112
Davis, Cynthia	Bourbon, Fort Scott P.O. (Housewife)	37	F	2:191
Davis, Cynthia A.	Bourbon, Fort Scott P.O.	19	F	2:197
Davis, Daniel	McGhee, Brushville P.O.	8	M	9:232
Davis, Daniel C.	Atchison, Shannon (Farmer)	34	M	1:80
Davis, E.	Johnson, Aubrey	40	F	6:40
Davis, Elizabeth	Leavenworth, Kickapoo (Farmer)	46	F	10:309
Davis, Elizabeth	Lykins, Paola	22	F	8:35
Davis, Elizabeth	Jackson, Franklin	67	F	5:184
Davis, Elizabeth J.	Lykins, Paola	1	F	8:35
Davis, H.	Arrapahoe, South Park	22	M	11:170
Davis, Henry M.	Bourbon, Fort Scott P.O.	16	M	2:191
Davis, D. G.[2]	Johnson, McCamish (Farmr.or U.P.Min)[3]	28	M	6:62
Davis, Henry M.	Bourbon, Fort Scott P.O.	15	M	2:197
Davis, J. M.	Arrapahoe, Russell Gulch (Miner)	22	M	11:552
Davis, James M.	Bourbon, Fort Scott P.O.	14	M	2:197

[1]Census Book entry appears to be clearly A. G.

[2]Appears to be D. T. rather than D. G.

[3]Some confusion because of non-alignment in Census Book.
   Arapahoe: spelled incorrectly with 2 r's in census and in this index also.

Name	Kansas: County; Township; P.O. Arap. Co.: Census Div. Not Township	Age	Sex	Census V.:Pg
Davis, John	Bourbon, Fort Scott P.O. (Farmer)	38	M	2:197
Davis, John	Atchison, Walnut (Farmer)	59	M	1:171
Davis, John A.	Jackson, Franklin (Farmer)	46	M	5:184
Davis, John L.	Anderson, Reeder.	20	M	7:267
Davis, John T.	Bourbon, Fort Scott P.O.	17	M	2:191
Davis, Lucinda	Bourbon, Fort Scott P.O. (Housewife)	34	F	2:197
Davis, Martha	McGhee, Brushville P.O.	5	F	9:232
Davis, Meredy	McGhee, Brushville P.O.	6	M	9:232
Davis, Nathan	Bourbon, Fort Scott P.O.	11	M	2:197
Davis, Nathan	Bourbon, Fort Scott P.O. (Farmer)	41	M	2:191
Davis, Nixon	McGhee, Brushville P.O.	10	M	9:232
Davis, Permina	McGhee, Brushville P.O.	4	F	9:232
Davis, Polly A.	McGhee, Brushville P.O.	29	F	9:232
Davis, Rebecca	Atchison, Shannon	28	F	1:80
Davis, Ridley R.	Atchison, Shannon	10	M	1:80
Davis, Sarah A.	Lykins, Paola	3	F	8:35
Davis, Tabitha	Anderson, Reeder	37	F	7:267
Davis, William	Anderson, Reeder (Farmer)	32	M	7:267
Davis, William J.	Lykins, Paola (Farmer)	23	M	8:35
Dawson, E.	Arrapahoe, South Clear Creek	24	M	11:717
Dawson, W.	Arrapahoe, South Clear Creek	22	M	11:729
Day, Eliza	Allen, Carlisle P.O.	36	F	2:238
Day, James	Brown, Locknow	27	M	3:69
Day, Nancy	Brown, Locknow	30	F	3:69
Day, Samuel	Douglas, Lecompton	32	M	6:358
Deacon, Wm.	Atchison, Shannon	11	M	1:74
Deberch, ? J. F.	Arrapahoe, Denver	42	M	11:385
Decatur, Chas.	Arrapahoe, South Park	34	M	11:131
Defriers, Alexina	Linn, Town of Paris	3	F	7:136
Defriers, Hiram	Linn, Town of Paris (Merchant)	33	M	7:136
Defriers, John M.	Linn, Town of Paris (Saddler)	22	M	7:136
Defriers, Lena	Linn, Town of Paris	4	F	7:136
Defriers, Nancy	Linn, Town of Paris	8	F	7:136
Defriers, Sarah	Linn, Town of Paris	23	F	7:136
Defrierse, Anna	Linn, Potosi	46	F	7:61
Defrierse, Mary	Linn, Potosi	26	F	7:61
Deimrick, G.	Arrapahoe, South Clear Creek	36	M	11:709
Dejarnett, Melody	Bourbon, Dayton P.O. (Housewife)	31	F	2:156
Delany, Caroline	Lykins, Middle Creek	24	F	8:110
Delong, Margaret	Shawnee, Auburn	18	F	9:43
Demarid, ? G.	Arrapahoe, Valley of the Platte	29	M	11:780
Demery, Ezekiel	Bourbon, Fort Scott P.O.(Farm Labr.)	26	BM	2:197
Deming, Wm.	Arrapahoe, South Clear Creek	39	M	11:742
Demock, Jno.	Arrapahoe, Valley of the Platte	24	M	11:819
Denhan, T. R.	Arrapahoe, South Clear Creek	32	M	11:711
Denton, Jefferson	Bourbon, Barnesville P.O.	23	M	2:165
Denton, John	Bourbon, Barnesville P.O.(Frm.Labr.)	27	M	2:165
Denton, Susan A.	Bourbon, Barnesville P.O.	28	F	2:165
Deslebis, John	Woodson, Verdigris (Farmer)	35	M	9:157
Devany, Mahala	Wabaunsee, Wilmington	30	F	5:281
Devany, Saml.	Wabaunsee, Wilmington (Farmer)	40	M	5:281
Dewey, S. M.	Arrapahoe, South Park	26	M	11:103
Dexiter, G. R.	Arrapahoe, South Park	27	M	11:246
Dickard, A. F.	Linn, Centerville (Farmer)	48	M	7:94
Dickard, Mary	Linn, Centerville	22	F	7:94
Dickinson, Alex	Nemaha, Nemaha	28	M	3:88
Dickinson, Lucinda	Nemaha, Nemaha	21	F	3:88
Dicks, Jane	Breckenridge, Agnes City	48	F	4:146
Dillan, D.	Franklin, Centropolis	48	M	8:211
Dillard, S. M.	Arrapahoe, South Park	26	M	11:130
Dillomer, Albert	Arrapahoe, Quartz Valley (Sheriff)	50	M	11:490

Arapahoe: spelled incorrectly with 2 r's in census and in this index also.

Name	Kansas: County; Township; P.O. Arap. Co.: Census Div. Not Township	Age	Sex	Census V. Pg
Dockling, Ann	Pottawatomie, Rockingham	28	F	5:289
Dockling, Hermon	Pottawatomie, Rockingham (Farmer)	30	M	5:289
Dodd, Edward	Arrapahoe, Golden City (Miner)	30	M	11:441
Dodsworth, B.	Arrapahoe, Valley of the Platte	31	M	11:801
Dolan, J.	Arrapahoe, South Park	32	M	11:156
Doland, Aaron	Linn, Mound City (Farmer)	53	M	7:113
Doland, Rebecca₂	Linn, Mound City	47	F	7:113
Dole, Elizabeth²	Madison, Hartford	39	F	4:236
Donahoo, Elizabeth	Jefferson, Grasshopper Falls	50	F	5:12
Donahue, Caroline	Atchison, Center	26	F	1:130
Donahue, Temperance	Lykins, Sugar Creek(Widow & Farmer)	47	F	8:104
Dorcas, W.	Arrapahoe, Valley of the Platte	31	M	11:783
Dorely, Julia	Leavenworth, Kickapoo	16	F	10:406
Dorey, W. C.	Arrapahoe, Denver (Trader)	33	M	11:427
Dorsett, N.	Arrapahoe, Valley of the Platte	27	M	11:811
Dotson, Day¹	McGhee, Medoc, Missouri P.O.(Farmer)	37	M	9:214
Dotson, James	McGhee, Medoc, Missouri P.O.	10	M	9:214
Dotson, Sophona	McGhee, Medoc, Missouri P.O.	13	F	9:214
Dougan, Mariah E.	Atchison, Mt. Pleasant	41	F	1:148
Douglas, W. C.	Arrapahoe, California Gulch			11:313
Dove, Samuel	Atchison, Center (Farmer)	18	M	1:120
Downey, Catharine	Atchison, Walnut	2	F	1:189
Downey, Ezekel	Atchison, Walnut	26	M	1:189
Downing, Martha M.	Bourbon, Fort Scott P.O.(Housewife)	30	F	2:192
Downing, Sarah A.	Lykins, Miami	28	F	8:91
Downing, William	Bourbon, Fort Scott P.O. (Farmer)	33	M	2:192
Downs, Mary E.	Leavenworth, Ward 4	18	F	10:272
Draper, B. S.	Coffey, Leroy (Farmer)	40	M	4:24
Drew, W.	Woodson, Verdigris (Farmer)	23	M	9:157
Driver, Absolom	Bourbon, Fort Scott P.O.(Blacksmith)	32	BM	2:196
Driver, D.	Johnson, Monticello (Farmer)	27	M	6:83
Drum, Alvin	Arrapahoe, South Clear Creek	29	M	11:645
Drum, M.	Franklin, Pottawatomie	24	F	8:238
Drummond, Wm.	Arrapahoe, South Clear Creek	30	M	11:695
Drummonds, P.	Brown, Irving	20	F	3:9
Drummonds, T. J.	Brown, Irving (Farmer)	38	M	3:9
Drury, Peter	Arrapahoe, South Park	24	M	11:245
Drwyer, Wm.	Arrapahoe, South Park	35	M	11:136
Dryer, Wm.	Arrapahoe, South Park (Miner)	38	M	11:37
Dubois, G. B.	Arrapahoe, South Park	26	M	11:131
Dudly, Adran	Leavenworth, Kickapoo	23	M	10:324
Dudly, Matilda	Leavenworth, Kickapoo	18	F	10:324
Duff, Dennis	Allen, Humboldt P.O. (Farmer)	33	M	2:297
Dugan, Mary E.	Lykins, Osawatomie	25	F	8:50
Duke, I. G.	Brown, Claytonville (Farmer)	51	M	3:48
Dumming, A. H.	Doniphan, Wayne (Farmer)	40	M	1:367
Dunham, Z.	Johnson, Shawnee	50	F	6:100
Dunlap, G. E.	Arrapahoe, South Park	35	M	11:165
Dunn, Robt.	Douglas, Palmyra (Wagonmaker)	45	M	6:266
Dunn, S.	Doniphan, Burr Oak	14	F	1:346
Dunnigan, J.	Johnson, Lexington (Farmer)	45	M	6:72
Durand, Henry	Arrapahoe, South Park	30	M	11:246
Dyce, David	Allen, Iola P.O. (Farmer)	28	M	2:269
Dyer, Jane	Jefferson, Jefferson	34	F	5:27
Dyer, Jefferson	Jefferson, Jefferson (Farmer)	40	M	5:27
Dyer, John	Pottawatomie, Shannon (Farmer	29	M	5:301
Dyer, Saml. D.	Pottawatomie, Blue (Farmer)	59	M	5:299
Dyer, W. J.	Doniphan, Burr Oak (Farmer)	25	M	1:345
Dyer, William	Pottawatomie, Shannon (Farmer)	33	M	5:301
Dyker, Henry	Anderson, Monroe	32	M	7:232

¹May be Denj.   ²Born in N. C.

Arapahoe: spelled incorrectly with 2 r's in census and in this index also.

Name	Kansas: County; Township; P.O. Arap. Co.: Census Div. Not Township	Age	Sex	Census V. Pg.
Dyker, John	Anderson, Monrow	27	M	7:232
Dyker, Thomas	Anderson, Walker (Farmer)	23	M	7:234
Dykes, James	Jefferson, Kentucky (Farmer)	26	M	5:65
Earl, Rebeca	Bourbon, Xenia P.O. (Farmer)	41	F	2:129
Easton, Mary E.	Bourbon, Fort Scott P.O.	23	F	2:82
Eddes, Edith	Leavenworth, Stranger	40	BF	10:467
Eddes, Jack	Leavenworth, Stranger	35	BM	10:467
Edwards, Atlantic	Wyandotte, Wyandotte	16	F	10:38
Edwards, B. F.	Leavenworth, Kickapoo (Farmer)	30	M	10:406
Edwards, John	Marshall, Marysville (Workman)	25	M	3:254
Edwards, Mary	Shawnee, Topeka	22	F	9:27
Edwards, Samuel E.	Leavenworth, Kickapoo (Farmer)	53	M	10:406
Edwards, W.	Arrapahoe, Nevada Gulch	29	M	11:531
Edwards, W. J.	Arrapahoe, Nevada Gulch (Miner)	20	M	11:529
Edwards, Wm.	Hunter, Eldorado (Farmer)	30	M	4:361
Ege, S.	Arrapahoe, South Clear Creek	36	M	11:694
Elden, A.	Woodson, Verdigris (Farmer)	39	M	9:157
Eledgr, Mary	Doniphan, Iowa Point	34	F	1:430
Elledge, W.	Johnson, Shawnee (Farmer)	30	M	6:94
Elles, Rolan	Leavenworth, Delaware (Farmer)	31	M	10:424
Elliott, Hamon B.	Breckenridge, Forest Hill (Farmer)	38	M	4:183
Elliott, Jas.	Arrapahoe, Golden City (Trader)	36	M	11:455
Elliott, Jas.	Arrapahoe, Denver	29	M	11:395
Elliott, Jane	Breckenridge, Forest Hill	32	F	4:183
Elliott, Jane	Atchison, Center	47	F	1:135
Elliott, Nancy	Washington, Washington	62	F	3:259
Ellis, Mary C.	Leavenworth, Kickapoo	32	F	10:323
Ellis, W.	Arrapahoe, South Park	22	M	11:97
Ellis, Wm.	Arrapahoe, South Park	28	M	11:167
Ellwell, Mary	Atchison, Ward 3 (Seamstress)	24	F	1:66
Emberly, A. W.	Arrapahoe, South Park	27	M	11:166
England, Joseph	Hunter, Eldorado (Farmer)	53	M	4:361
Engle, Jno.	Arrapahoe, South Park	26	M	11:145
Engler, G. N.	Arrapahoe, Valley of the Platte	24	M	11:820
English, Eliza	Atchison, 1st Ward	40	F	1:11
English, H.	Arrapahoe, South Park	30	M	11:106
English, J. H.	Arrapahoe, Valley of the Platte	28	M	11:811
Ensley, H. A.	Franklin, Pottawatomie	26	M	8:239
Ensley, J. A.	Franklin, Pottawatomie	7	M	8:239
Epps, Charity	Linn, Potosi	33	F	7:73
Epps, Lucetta	Linn, Potosi	13	F	7:73
Epps, Nancy	Linn, Potosi	11	F	7:73
Estes, W. A.	Arrapahoe, Valley of the Platte	30	M	11:805
Ether, Hiram	Bourbon, Fort Scott P.O. (Farmer)	42	M	2:80
Ethridge, Lewis	Bourbon, Turkey Creek P.O. (Farmer)	32	M	2:115
Euback, Stephen G.	Bourbon, Raysville P.O.(Cabinetmaker)	56	M	2:158
Evans, Alphia	Doniphan, Doniphan	27	F	1:391
Evans, Enock	Leavenworth, Kickapoo	29	M	10:323
Evans, Johnathan	Atchison, Mt. Pleasant	32	M	1:167
Evans, Mary	Leavenworth, Easton	23	F	10:282
Evans, Saml.	Arrapahoe, South Park	26	M	11:140
Evens, Wila	Woodson, Liberty (Farmer)	35	M	9:142
Evens, Wm.	Woodson, Liberty (Farmer)	24	M	9:142
Everett, J.	Arrapahoe, South Park	24	M	11:230
Exondine, Francis M.	McGhee, Brushville P.O.(Farm Lbrer)	17	BM	9:217
Exondine, Jane	McGhee, Brushville P.O.	11	BF	9:217
Exondine, Johnston	McGhee, Brushville P.O. (Farmer)	47	BM	9:217
Exondine, Martha A.	McGhee, Brushville P.O. (Servant)	20	BF	9:217
Exondine, Merrell J.	McGhee, Brushville P.O.(Farm Lbrer)	23	BM	9:217
Faddin, W. O.	Arrapahoe, Valley of the Platte	31	M	11:807
Fager, Sarah	Douglas, Palmyra	32	F	6:266

Arapahoe: spelled incorrectly with 2 r's in census and in this index also.

Name	Kansas: County; Township; P.O. Arap. Co.: Census Div. Not Township	Age	Sex	Census V. Pg
Fail, J. H.	Arrapahoe, South Clear Creek	29	M	11:742
Falding, J.	Douglas, Marion (Farmer)	24	M	6:394
Falkerson, E.	Arrapahoe, South Park	28	M	11:157
Falt, Wm.	Arrapahoe, South Park	35	M	11:253
Fanily, Pleasant	Allen, Humboldt P.O.	56	M	2:286
Farrel, Margaret	Leavenworth, Ward 4 (Pupil)	8	F	10:268
Farrell, James D.	Leavenworth, Ward 2	4	M	10:146
Farwell, W.	Arrapahoe, South Park	33	M	11:185
Febrghin, E.	Doniphan, Washington	28	M	1:297
Ferr, James	Linn, Paris (Farmer)	35	M	7:145
Ferrell, Jane	Jefferson, Grasshopper Falls	30	F	5:9
Ferrell, Larkin	Jefferson, Grasshopper Falls (Farmer)	30	M	5:9
Ferris, Y. ? B.	Arrapahoe, Denver (Miner)	35	M	11:414
Fesler, F. H.	Arrapahoe, Valley of the Platte	24	M	11:808
Fester, H. J.	Davis, Junction City	24	F	9:345
Fielder, W.	Arrapahoe, Valley of the Platte	30	M	11:792
Fields, J.	Douglas, Willow Springs (Farmer)	21	F	6:315
Fields, Martha	McGhee, Medoc, Missouri P.O.	31	F	9:215
Fields, Phebe	Douglas, Willow Springs (Farmer)	44	F	6:315
Fields, Thomas	McGhee, Medoc, Missouri P.O. (Farmer)	30	MM	9:215
Finch, Elizabeth	Jefferson, Oskaloosa	27	F	5:132
Fincher, Paulina	Linn, Paris	30	F	7:148
Findley, Wm. C.	Atchison, Mt. Pleasant (Farmer)	28	M	1:163
Finley, G. C.	Arrapahoe, South Park	23	M	11:235
Fisher, Geo.	Arrapahoe, Denver (Horse Doctor)	28	M	11:350
Fisher, Peter	Allen, Carlisle P.O. (Farmer)	59	M	2:242
Fitch, L. U.	Arrapahoe, South Park	37	M	11:24
Fitch, Sam'l	Arrapahoe, South Clear Creek	28	M	11:749
Fite, Caroline	McGhee, Brushville P.O.	28	F	9:226
Fite, James	McGhee, Brushville P.O.	8	M	9:226
Fite, Martha	McGhee, Brushville P.O.	5	F	9:226
Fite, Sarah C.	McGhee, Brushville P.O.	9	F	9:226
Fite, Wesley	McGhee, Brushville P.O. (Farmer)	30	M	9:226
Fleck, R.	Johnson, Olathe	26	F	6:115
Fleischman, J. S.	Arrapahoe, South Park (Miner)	24	M	11:33
Fleming, C.	Arrapahoe, South Park	40	M	11:210
Fleming, S. M.	Arrapahoe, Valley of the Platte	33	M	11:835
Fletcher, George W.	Lykins, Paola	7	M	8:35
Fletcher, Joel J.	Lykins, Paola	11	M	8:35
Fletcher, Louisa N.	Lykins, Paola	17	F	8:35
Fletcher, Moses	Lykins, Paola (Farmer)	45	M	8:35
Fletcher, Saina	Lykins, Paola	19	F	8:35
Fletcher, Sarah C.	Lykins, Paola	3	F	8:35
Fletcher, Thompson N.	Lykins, Paola P.O.	15	M	8:35
Fletcher, William H.	Lykins, Paola P.O.	13	M	8:35
Flinn, William	Linn, Potosi	9	M	7:72
Flint, R.	Arrapahoe, South Park	37	M	11:4
Floyd, Albert	Doniphan, Doniphan	8	M	1:390
Floyd, C.	Arrapahoe, South Park	35	M	11:184
Floyd, James	Doniphan, Doniphan	12	M	1:390
Floyd, S.	Arrapahoe, Denver (Miner)	24	M	11:431
Floyd, Sam	Doniphan, Doniphan	10	M	1:390
Fly, Andrew J.	Bourbon, Turkey Creek P.O. (Farmer)	25	M	2:114
Fly, Elizabeth	Bourbon, Marmaton P.O. (Housewife)	48	F	2:111
Fly, James C.	Bourbon, Marmaton P.O. (Farmer)	4?	M	2:111
Fly, John R.	Bourbon, Marmaton P.O. (Farmer)	49	M	2:111
Fly, Mary	Bourbon, Marmaton P.O. (Housewife)	25	F	2:111
Fly, Wm. M.	Bourbon, Turkey Creek P.O. (Farmer)	24	M	2:112
Folks, Wm.	Arrapahoe, South Park	35	M	11:256
Foot, John	Bourbon, Marmaton P.O.	26	M	2:205
Foote, Richard N.	Bourbon, Marmaton P.O. (Farmer)	44	M	2:106

Arapahoe: spelled incorrectly with 2 r's in census and in this index also.

Name	Kansas: County; Township; P.O. Arap. Co.: Census Div. Not Township	Age	Sex	Census V. Pg.
Foote, Richard N.	Bourbon, Marmaton P.O.	11	M	2:106
Foote, Susan C.	Bourbon, Marmaton P.O.	15	F	2:106
Forbush, M.	Arrapahoe, South Park	35	M	9:159
Ford, L. ?	Arrapahoe, Denver (Miner)	34	M	11:388
Foskit, C.	Arrapahoe, Valley of the Platte	27	M	11:802
Foss, J. F.	Arrapahoe, South Clear Creek	25	M	11:694
Fossett, Frank	Chase, Diamond Creek (Farmer)	35	M	4:326
Foster, Abun	Leavenworth, Stranger (Farmer)	63	M	10:475
Foster, J. W.	Arrapahoe, California Gulch	22	M	11:277
Foster, Jno.	Arrapahoe, Denver (Trader)	29	M	11:427
Foster, Margarett	Arrapahoe, Denver	18	F	11:371
Fowler, E.	Arrapahoe, South Park	49	M	11:163
Fowler, Thos.	Arrapahoe, South Park	35	M	11:219
Fox, A. M.	Johnson, DeSota	27	F	6:20
Fox, N.	Johnson, Lexington	61	F	6:78
Fox, W. S.	Arrapahoe, Val.of the Platte(Teamster)	29	M	11:833
Fox, Wilson	Leavenworth, Delaware (Wheelwright)	45	M	10:416
Frail, Anna[1]	Wyandotte, Wyandotte (Laborer)	40	F	10:46
Francher, E.	Anderson, Jackson (Farmer)	32	M	7:209
Franklin, John J.	Leavenworth, Ward 2 (Teamster)	40	M	10:193
Franklin, Robertson[2]	Leavenworth, Ward 2 (Teamster)	37	M	10:192
Franks, John	Woodson, Neosho Falls (Farmer)	33	M	9:131
Frazier, Sallie	Leavenworth, Fort Leavenworth P.O.	34	BF	10:319
Freeman, Henry	Wyandotte, Wyandotte (Farmer)	24	M	10:6
Freeman, Isaac	Linn, Paris (Lawyer)	22	M	7:148
Freeman, Susan	Linn, Mound City	20	F	7:104
Freeman, W. C.	Linn, Mound City (Engineer)	30	M	7:104
Freeman, B.	Arrapahoe, South Park (Miner)	27	M	11:40
French, W. M. ?	Arrapahoe, South Park	44	M	11:128
Frogge, A.	Doniphan, Iowa Point	32	F	1:426
Frost, A. C.	Arrapahoe, South Clear Creek (Miner)	40	M	11:636
Frost, J.	Arrapahoe, South Park	35	M	11:171
Frost, Martha	Linn, Paris	27	F	7:158
Fry, Malissa	Linn, Scott	32	F	7:25
Fry, Walla	Linn, Scott (Farmer)	32	M	7:25
Fryette, W.	Franklin, Ohio (Farmer)	41	M	8:224
Fuggle, J.	Woodson, Pleasant Grove (Farmer)	29	M	9:168
Fulder, Croket J.	Bourbon, Marmaton P.O. (Farmer)	27	M	2:102
Fuller, Mildred	Breckenridge, Emporia	21	F	4:197
Fuller, Rebecca	Doniphan, Center	29	F	1:246
Fuller, S.	Franklin, Ohio	33	F	8:221
Fuller, S. M.	Linn, Scott (Carpenter)	28	M	7:22
Fulton, Nancy	Shawnee, Soldier	34	F	9:89
Funderbeck, J.	Johnson, Gardner	46	F	6:49
Furgerson, C.	Douglas, Wakarusa	12	M	6:255
Furgerson, L.	Douglas, Wakarusa (Farmer)	34	M	6:255
Furman, W.	Arrapahoe, Valley of the Platte	30	M	11:826
Gable, Abegell	McGhee, Crawford Seminary P.O.	26	F	9:219
Gable, Barnabas	Leavenworth, Delaware (Farmer)	48	M	10:434
Gable, Henry	McGhee, Crawford Seminary P.O.	28	M	9:219
Gable, Mary	Leavenworth, Delaware	41	F	10:434
Gage, J.	Arrapahoe, South Park	26	M	11:142
Gage, John	Shawnee, Tecumseh (Farmer)	50	M	9:66
Gahagan, P.	Arrapahoe, South Park	28	M	11:213
Gainbill, A. M.	Johnson, Aubrey (Farmer)	28	M	6:36
Gale, Saml.	Arrapahoe, South Park	33	M	11:177
Gallatin, P.	Arrapahoe, South Park	20	M	11:255

[1]Anna Frail is listed first as head of the household with the rest of the
    family (all born in Missouri): James, 41; Julia 18; Virginia and
    Missouri twins aged 8; Luther 12, and Eldridge 9.
[2]Census entry reads clearly Robertson Franthlin; Robertson may be last name.
  Arapahoe: spelled incorrectly with 2 r's in census and in this index also.

Name	Kansas: County; Township; P.O. Arap. Co.: Census Div. Not Township	Age	Sex	Census V. Pg.
Galloway, J.	Arrapahoe, Valley of the Platte	24	M	11:800
Ganick, Saml.	Arrapahoe, South Park	26	M	11:220
Gardner, F. H.	Arrapahoe, South Park	28	M	11:148
Garouth, Sarah	Allen, Humboldt P.O.	28	F	2:280
Garrett, Cynthia	Jefferson, Kaw	16	F	5:79
Garrett, S. B.	Davis, Junction City (Reg.Land Office)	38	M	9:335
Garritt, Eleanor	Madison, Verdigris	29	F	4:247
Gates, Peter	Arrapahoe, Denver (Teamster)	18	M	11:396
Gee, Jacob M.	Nemaha, Valley (Farmer)	32	M	3:118
Geer, Fanny	Atchison, Mt. Pleasant	56	F	1:148
Gentry, David	Jefferson, Jefferson (Farmer)	29	M	5:29
Gentry, Henry	Arrapahoe, South Park	26	M	11:129
Gentry, Mary	Jefferson, Jefferson	28	F	5:29
Gentry, O.	Arrapahoe, Valley of the Platte	26	M	11:812
Gertrude, Jno.	Arrapahoe, South Park	25	M	11:147
Gevin, Richard W.	Lykins, Stanton (Farmer)	57	M	8:8
Gibbs, Gideon	Breckenridge, Fremont (Farmer)	27	M	4:168
Gibbs, J. W.	Arrapahoe, South Park	35	M	11:157
Gibbs, Sam'l	Arrapahoe, Valley of the Platte	30	M	11:822
Gibbs, Sarah	Breckenridge, Fremont	19	F	4:168
Gibbs, W.	Arrapahoe, South Park	35	M	11:168
Gibson, Elisha	Breckenridge, Emporia (Farmer)	50	M	4:188
Gibson, James N.	Lykins, Mound (Farmer)	20	M	8:73
Giernsey, A. P.	Arrapahoe, South Park	23	M	11:115
Gifford, R. S.	Arrapahoe, South Park	35	M	11:249
Gill, Caroline	Jefferson, Oskaloosa	15	F	5:125
Gill, Elizabeth	Jefferson, Oskaloosa	19	F	5:125
Gill, Franklin	Jefferson, Oskaloosa	5	M	5:125
Gill, John	Jefferson, Oskaloosa	12	M	5:125
Gill, Mathew	Jefferson, Oskaloosa (Laborer)	18	M	5:125
Gill, Milley	Jefferson, Oskaloosa	49	F	5:125
Gill, Nancy	Arrapahoe, South Clear Creek	24	F	11:626
Gill, S. S.	Arrapahoe, South Clear Creek (Miner)	28	M	11:626
Gill, Sam	Jefferson, Oskaloosa	11	M	5:125
Gill, Saml.	Jefferson, Oskaloosa (Carpenter)	46	M	5:125
Gill, Wm.	Jefferson, Oskaloosa (Farmer)	25	M	5:125
Gillett, G. S.	Arrapahoe, Valley of the Platte	31	M	11:810
Gillett, W. T.	Arrapahoe, South Park (Miner)	22	M	11:34
Gillreth, Evline	Allen, Iola P.O.	5	F	2:271
Gillreth, James L.	Allen, Iola P.O. (Farmer)	39	M	2:271
Gillreth, John	Allen, Iola P.O.	10	M	2:271
Gillreth, Joseph	Allen, Iola P.O.	8	M	2:271
Gillreth, Mary A.	Allen, Iola P.O.	32	F	2:271
Gilmana, T. A.	Doniphan, Iowa Point	34	F	1:427
Gilmore, M.	Doniphan, Iowa Point (Farmer)	45	M	1:431
Gilmore, W.	Arrapahoe, South Clear Creek	32	M	11:722
Gingery, Elizabeth	Douglas, Wakarusa	35	F	6:235
Gingery, J. S.	Douglas, Wakarusa (Farmer)	40	M	6:235
Gingery, James M.	Douglas, Wakarusa	11	M	6:235
Gingery, M.	Douglas, Wakarusa	9	M	6:235
Gingery, Martha	Douglas, Wakarusa	13	F	6:235
Girder, Barbara	McGhee, Brushville P.O.	44	F	9:231
Gladen, C. A.	Doniphan, Washington	26	F	1:300
Glaithout, T. H.	Douglas, Lawrence (Clerk)	24	M	6:184
Glanson, E.	Arrapahoe, South Clear Creek	26	M	11:720
Glenn, Howard	Atchison, Walnut (Farmer)	29	M	1:198
Glenn, Sam'l.	Lykins, Osawatomie (Farmer)	49	M	8:61
Goddard, William	Wyandotte, Wyandotte (Farmer)	39	M	10:2
Godfrey, Alex.	Arrapahoe, Denver (Miner)	20	M	11:410
Goforth, Anna	Linn, Mound City	7	F	7:99
Goforth, James	Linn, Mound City	14	M	7:99

Arapahoe: spelled incorrectly with 2 r's in census and in this index also.

Name	Kansas: County; Township; P.O. Arap. Co.: Census Div. Not Township	Age	Sex	Census V.:Pg.
Goforth, Jeremiah	Linn, Mound City (Farmer)	22	M	7:99
Goforth, Nancy	Linn, Mound City	40	F	7:99
Goforth, Sarah	Linn, Mound City	18	F	7:99
Goforth, Umphry	Linn, Mound City (Farmer)	52	M	7:99
Goldson, Milton	Breckenridge, Pike (Farmer)	48	M	4:213
Gonray, Geo.	Arrapahoe, South Park	27	M	11:186
Good, Rose Ann	Linn, Scott	35	F	7:24
Goodell, S.	Arrapahoe, Valley of the Platte	22	M	11:842
Goodpasture, J. A.	Nemaha, Rock Creek (Merchant)	41	M	3:73
Goodpasture, Mahala	Nemaha, Rock Creek	35	F	3:73
Goodwin, R.	Arrapahoe, South Park (Trader)	48	M	11:3
Goodwin, R.	Doniphan, Washington (Farmer)	26	M	1:302
Goodwin, W.	Linn, Paris (Farmer)	58	M	7:129
Gordon, Didaina	Bourbon, Mapleton P.O. (Housewife)	28	F	2:148
Gore, Sam	Linn, Mound City (Farmer)	55	M	7:110
Goreman, C.	Linn, Valley (Farmer)	24	M	7:50
Gotcher, B.	Doniphan, Burr Oak (Farmer)	61		1:343
Gowers, James M.	Bourbon, Dayton P.O.	18	M	2:148
Gowers, Polly A.	Bourbon, Dayton P.O.	33	F	2:147
Gowers, Zack	Bourbon, Dayton P.O. (Farmer)	43	M	2:147
Gowing, Pleasant	Anderson, Jackson (Farmer)	35	M	7:209
Grace, Wm. P.	Arrapahoe, Denver	23	M	11:384
Grace, Wm. P.	Arrapahoe, California Gulch	35	M	11:300
Gragg, Jacob C.	Atchison, Lancaster (Farmer)	42	M	1:106
Gragg, Jefferson	Atchison, Lancaster (Farmer)	44	M	1:105
Gragg, Lucy	Brown, Locknow	34	F	3:66
Gragg, William	Jefferson, Grasshopper Falls (Farmer)	52	M	5:5
Graham, Cynthia	Bourbon, Raysville P.O. (Housewife)	30	F	2:185
Graham, Margaret C.	Bourbon, Raysville P.O. (Housewife)	25	F	2:185
Graham, Martha	Douglas, Palmyra	8	F	6:274
Gralee, G. A.	Arrapahoe, Tarryall, South Park	23	M	11:620
Grandison, S.	Arrapahoe, Valley of the Platte	31	M	11:793
Grant, S.	Arrapahoe, Denver (Miner)	35	M	11:393
Grass, Jacob	Bourbon, Fort Scott P.O. (Farmer)	27	M	2:200
Grass, Mary J.	Bourbon, Fort Scott P.O.(Housewife)	26	F	2:200
Graton, O.	Arrapahoe, South Park	22	M	11:234
Graves, Emaline	Atchison, Center	20	F	1:127
Graves, Jacob	Atchison, Center (Farmer)	23	M	1:127
Graves, Jane W.	Woodson, Liberty (F. W.)	45	F	9:144
Graves, John	Atchison, Center (Farmer)	29	M	1:127
Gray, B.	Arrapahoe, South Park	36	M	11:20
Gray, V. G.	Arrapahoe, South Park	33	M	11:187
Green, Amanda E.	Allen, Humboldt P.O.	19	F	2:294
Green, Chas.	Arrapahoe, South Park	21	M	11:263
Green, F. M.	Arrapahoe, Denver	12	M	11:374
Green, G. E.	Arrapahoe, Valley of the Platte	36	M	11:363
Green, G. F.	Arrapahoe, Valley of the Platte	24	M	11:834
Green, L. P.	Woodson, Verdigris (Farmer)	50	M	9:165
Green, M. J.	Arrapahoe, South Park (Carpenter)	34	M	11:67
Green, Ruth	Woodson, Verdigris (F. W.)	48	F	9:165
Green, Samuel	Woodson, Verdigris (Farmer)	24	M	9:165
Green, Saml. C.	Arrapahoe, Denver (Recorder)	41	M	11:408
Green, T. C.	Arrapahoe, South Park	30	M	11:131
Gregorie, Henry	Woodson, Belmont (Farmer)	33	M	9:154
Gregorie, Rachall	Woodson, Belmont	57	F	9:154
Griffin, F. R.	Arrapahoe, South Clear Creek	27	M	11:710
Griffin, H. K.	Arrapahoe, South Park	29	M	11:108
Griffin, J. F.	Johnson, Shawnee	7	M	6:28
Griffin, L.	Arrapahoe, South Park	28	M	11:29
Grimsley, Mary	Breckenridge, Americus	31	F	4:216
Grimsley, Wm.	Breckenridge, Americus (Farmer)	51	M	4:216

Arapahoe: spelled incorrectly with 2 r's in census and in this index also.

Name	Kansas: County; Township; P.O. Arap. Co.: Census Div. Not Township	Age	Sex	Census V. Pg.
Grinble, L.	Arrapahoe, South Park (Miner)	21	M	11:76
Grintz, Chas.	Arrapahoe, South Clear Creek (Trader)	34	M	11:699
Griswold, Louisa R.	Allen, Humboldt P.O.	42	F	2:286
Groff, Amanda	Atchison, Walnut	17	F	1:170
Groines, C.	Arrapahoe, South Park	28	M	11:107
Grooms, E.	Doniphan, Washington	53	F	1:338
Grossman, G.	Arrapahoe, South Park	24	M	11:143
Grove, Henry	Lykins, Marysville (Farmer)	30	M	8:124
Grove, R.	Doniphan, Wolf River	39	F	1:405
Grover, A. P.	Johnson, McCamish (Farmer)	34	M	6:60
Grover, E.	Doniphan, Center	26	F	1:247
Grover, M.	Johnson, McCamish	18	F	6:60
Grover, S.	Doniphan, Center (Farmer)	35	M	1:247
Groves, D.	Doniphan, Center (Farmer)	33	M	1:246
Groves, E.	Doniphan, Center (Farmer)	35	M	1:247
Groves, J. ?	Doniphan, Center (Farmer)	25	M	1:247
Guellam, Martin	Leavenworth, Kickapoo (Farmer)	45	M	10:324
Guellam, Polly	Leavenworth, Kickapoo	46	F	10:324
Gulway, H.	Arrapahoe, South Park	39	M	11:219
Gunter, Margaret A.	Bourbon, Barnesville P.O. (Housewife)	41	F	2:180
Gunter, Thomas	Bourbon, Barnesville P.O. (Farmer)	45	M	2:180
Gunter, William C.	Doniphan, Washington (Farmer)	32	M	1:319
Guth, Edward	Arrapahoe, South Park	44	M	11:109
Guthrie, Mary J.	Brown, Claytonville	23		3:41
Guttry, Caroline	Bourbon, Turkey Creek P.O.(Housewife)	22	F	2:114
Guttry, James R.	Bourbon, Turkey Creek P.O. (Farmer)	23	M	2:114
Guttry, John	Bourbon, Marmaton P.O. (Farmer)	25	M	2:111
Hackburn, N.	Arrapahoe, South Clear Creek	25	M	11:710
Hackly, J.	Douglas, Wakarusa	30	M	6:247
Hackway, Jno.	Arrapahoe, Valley of the Platte	23	M	11:810
Hacworth, Jane	Doniphan, Iowa Point	45	F	1:428
Hadden, Polly	Allen, Humboldt P.O.	58	F	2:303
Haddix, Matilda	Jefferson, Kentucky	20	F	5:63
Hadley, C. W.	Arrapahoe, South Park	37	M	11:148
Hadley, Thomas	McGhee, Brushville P.O.	18	M	9:230
Haffner, Debba	Shawnee, Monmouth		F	9:58
Haghes, L. W.	Arrapahoe, South Park	27	M	11:167
Haims, Jefferson	Bourbon, Fort Scott P.O. (Farmer)	26	BM	2:220
Haiter, G.	Arrapahoe, Valley of the Platte	27	M	11:795
Halbert, D.	Douglas, Clinton (Farmer)	37	M	6:417
Hale, Elizabeth	Bourbon, Mapleton P.O.(Housekeeper)	31	F	2:132
Hale, John K.	Bourbon, Fort Scott P.O. (Farmer)	45	M	2:79
Hale, ? S. A.	Arrapahoe, South Clear Creek(Saloon)	29	M	11:736
Hale, Sarah	Bourbon, Fort Scott P.O.(Housewife)	30	F	2:79
Halett, Mary	Arrapahoe, Mountain City	35	F	11:487
Haley, E. R.	Arrapahoe, Valley of the Platte	24	M	11:808
Hall, Caroline L.	Atchison, Kapioma	32	F	1:100
Hall, Geo. R.	Atchison, Kapioma	23	M	1:100
Hall, George W.	Atchison, Kapioma	4	M	1:100
Hall, John A.	Atchison, Kapioma	8	M	1:100
Hall, Landon W.	Atchison, Kapioma	6	M	1:100
Hall, Mary A.	Jefferson, Jefferson	28	F	5:27
Hall, Nancy K.	Bourbon, Xenia P.O. (Housewife)	33	F	2:126
Hall, R.	Doniphan, Center	40	F	1:257
Hall, Sarah J.	Atchison, Kapioma	10	F	1:100
Hall, Wm. H.	Arrapahoe, South Park	28	M	11:247
Halliburten, S.	Arrapahoe, Valley of the Platte	22	M	11:833
Halold, Rachel	Douglas, Clinton	51	F	6:408
Hambright, John	Anderson, Walker (Farmer)	23	M	7:241A
Hamby, Elizabeth	Anderson, Washington	36	F	7:252
Hamil, W.	Arrapahoe, South Park (Miner)	39	M	11:20

Arapahoe: spelled incorrectly with 2 r's in census and in this index also.

Name	Kansas: County; Township; P.O. Arap. Co.: Census Div. Not Township	Age	Sex	Census V.:Pg.
Hamilton, Alex.	Arrapahoe, Denver (Teamster)	20	M	11:396
Hamilton, C. B.[1]	Doniphan, Center (Farmer)	55	M	1:213
Hamilton, Sarah	Linn, Potosi	25	F	7:76
Hamilton, T. M.	Doniphan, Burr Oak	35	M	1:342
Hammond, Doll	Morris, Clarks Creek	4	F	4:279
Hammond, G. N.	Arrapahoe, Valley of the Platte	26	M	11:861
Hammond, G. W.	Arrapahoe, South Park	34	M	11:215
Hammond, J. C.	Linn, Potosi (Farmer)	34	M	7:82
Hammond, James	Morris, Clarks Creek	1	M	4:279
Hammond, Jessee	Morris, Clarks Creek (Farmer)	32	M	4:279
Hammond, John	Morris, Grove (Farmer)	35	M	4:264
Hammond, Jonathan	Morris, Clarks Creek (Farmer)	30	M	4:279
Hammond, Martha	Morris, Clarks Creek	12	F	4:280
Hammond, Mary	Morris, Clarks Creek	37	F	4:279
Hammond, Mary	Linn, Potosi	9	F	7:82
Hammond, Rachel	Morris, Clarks Creek	28	F	4:279
Hammond, Robert	Linn, Potosi	7	M	7:82
Hammond, Rufus	Linn, Potosi (Farmer)	20	M	7:82
Hammond, Sarah	Morris, Clarks Creek	14	F	4:279
Hammond, W. H.	Arrapahoe, Valley of the Platte	21		11:790
Hammond, Wm.	Morris, Clark Creek	10	M	4:280
Hampton, Elizabeth	Shawnee, Williamsport	20	F	9:55
Hanan, G. W. (Geo.)	Arrapahoe, Denver (Miner)	39	M	11:426
Hancock, Sarah	Bourbon, Fort Scott P.O.(Housewife)	20	F	2:81
Hand, Adam	Shawnee, Tecumseh (Farmer)	50	M	9:73
Hand, Almira	Shawnee, Tecumseh	45	F	9:73
Hanley, James L.	Bourbon, Pawnee P.O. (Farmer)	30	M	2:99
Hann, Emily	Linn, Potosi	28	F	7:72
Hann, Joseph	Linn, Potosi	7	M	7:72
Hann, M. L.	Linn, Potosi	29	M	7:72
Hann, Margaret	Linn, Potosi	5	F	7:72
Hann, Martha	Linn, Potosi	10	F	7:72
Hannah, Sarah	Pottawatomie, Shannon	45	F	5:301
Hanon, Jane	Allen, Xenia P.O.	50	F	2:231
Hansbright, John[2]	Franklin, Peoria	30	M	8:270
Hansbright, T. M.[2]	Franklin, Peoria	37	M	8:270
Hantley, Edam	Anderson, Monroe	16	M	7:218
Harboun, James	Doniphan, Burr Oak (Farmer)	25	M	1:355
Hardetty, E.	Anderson, Walker	38	F	7:234
Hardwich, H.	Arrapahoe, South Park	26	M	11:7
Hardwick, C.	Arrapahoe, South Clear Creek	38	M	11:698
Hardy, N. V.	Arrapahoe, Valley of the Platte(Miner)	24	M	11:828
Hargett, M.	Arrapahoe, South Clear Creek	29	M	11:683
Harkins, N.	Arrapahoe, South Park	22	M	11:164
Harksent, J. C.	Arrapahoe, Valley of the Platte	27	M	11:803
Harlin, Martin	Allen, Iola P.O. (Farmer)	48	M	2:266
Harman, Peter	Bourbon, Fort Scott P.O. (Farmer)	47	M	2:191
Harper, Vicent	Leavenworth, Easton	19	M	10:300
Harrington, Geo.	Arrapahoe, South Park	31	M	11:214
Harris, Caroline	Bourbon, Fort Scott P.O.(Housewife)	31	F	2:223
Harris, Catherine	Bourbon, Fort Scott P.O.(Housewife)	23	F	2:95
Harris, Isaac	Bourbon, Fort Scott P.O. (Farmer)	32	M	2:95
Harris, J.	Linn, Paris	50	M	7:144
Harris, Jackson	Wyandotte, Quindaro (Laborer)	65	BM	10:60
Harris, John	Bourbon, Marmaton P.O. (Farmer)	31	M	2:117
Harris, John G.	Bourbon, Fort Scott P.O.(GroceryKpr.)	33	M	2:223
Harris, Margret	Wyandotte, Quindaro	64	BF	10:60
Harris, Mary E.	Bourbon, Fort Scott P.O.	13	F	2:223

[1]Census book citation is to page 213 rather than 273.

[2]Both Hansbright entries almost illegible in original; spelling may be in error.

Arapahoe: spelled incorrectly with 2 r's in census and in this index also.

Name	Kansas: County; Township; P.O. Arap. Co.: Census Div. Not Township	Age	Sex	Census V. Pg.
Harris, N.	Arrapahoe, South Park	37	M	11:165
Harris, Sarah J.	Bourbon, Fort Scott P.O.	11	F	2:223
Harrison, Alex	Leavenworth, Alexandria(FarmerOversr)	24	M	10:446
Harrison, Andrew J.	Leavenworth, Alexandria (Farmer)	23	M	10:446
Harrison, Eliza C.	Leavenworth, Stranger	17	F	10:477
Harrison, Joshua D.	Leavenworth, Alexandria	16	M	10:446
Harrison, Martha	Douglas, Wakarusa	2	M	6:257
Hart, Ashey	Linn, Scott	10	M	7:18
Haryman, Martha	Bourbon, Pawnee P.O. (Housewife)	48	F	2:99
Haskell, William	Jefferson, Jefferson (Farmer)	24	M	5:31
Hauley, Alexander	McGhee, Osage Mission P.O.(Farm Lbr.)	22	M	9:242
Hauley, Elizabeth	McGhee, Osage Mission P.O.	17	F	9:242
Hauley, James	McGhee, Osage Mission P.O.(Farm Lbr.)	19	M	9:242
Hauley, Joseph	McGhee, Osage Mission P.O. (Farmer)	47	M	9:242
Hauley, Mary F.	McGhee, Osage Mission P.O.	14	F	9:242
Havens, J.	Arrapahoe, South Park	38	M	11:252
Hawes, D.	Arrapahoe, South Park	23	M	11:234
Hawkins, Rebecca	Chase, Cottonwood	30	F	4:320
Hawks, Elijah	Nemaha, Richmond	23	M	3:94
Hay, Betsy	Davis, Ft. Riley P.O.	3	F	9:351
Hay, George	Davis, Ft. Riley P.O.	4	M	9:351
Hays, A.	Arrapahoe, Eureka Gulch(Quartz Mill)	40	M	11:512
Hays, Elizabeth	Leavenworth, Alexandria	32	F	10:448
Hays, Settlton	Leavenworth, Alexandria (Farmer)	38	M	10:448
Hazle, B.	Douglas, Clinton	40	M	6:411
Hazle, Margaret	Douglas, Clinton	40	F	6:411
Heath, Charlotte[1]	Leavenworth, Ward 2	2	F	10:153
Heath, Charlotte[2]	Leavenworth, Ward 2	2	F	10:147
Heath, Elizabeth	Leavenworth, Ward 2	7	F	10:153
Heath, James[1]	Leavenworth, Ward 2	4	M	10:147
Heath, James[2]	Leavenworth, Ward 2	4	M	10:153
Haddens, A.	Coffey, Neosho	18	F	4:68
Hedgins, J. W.	Doniphan, Iowa Point (Trader)	37	M	1:451
Helm, Adam	Morris, Grove (Farmer)	41	M	4:269
Helton, H.	Franklin, Centropolis (Farmer)	47	M	8:209
Hendee, H. B.	Arrapahoe, South Park	39	M	11:160
Henderson, C. C.	Douglas, Marion (Farmer)	31	M	6:393
Henderson, Edward	Atchison, Lancaster (Farmer)	37	M	1:110
Henderson, G. W.	Leavenworth, Easton (Farmer)	40	M	10:298
Henderson, H.	Leavenworth, Easton	49	F	10:294
Henderson, Isaac	Atchison, Mt. Pleasant (Farmer)	27	M	1:156
Henderson, James A.	Leavenworth, Easton (Farmer)	31	M	10:294
Henderson, Jane	Douglas, Marion	10	F	6:393
Henderson, Joseph	Leavenworth, Easton (Farmer)	57	M	10:294
Henderson, M.	Douglas, Marion	24	F	6:393
Hendin, Sam'l.	Arrapahoe, Valley of the Platte	22	M	11:816
Hending, J. M.	Douglas, Lawrence	34	M	6:190
Hendricks, Hester A.	Atchison, Shannon (Farmer)	32	F	1:83
Hendricks, J. D.	Atchison, Shannon	10	M	1:83
Hendrix, Enos	Lykins, Paola (Miner)	30	M	8:39
Henley, Edmund	Allen, Humboldt P.O. (Farmer)	31	M	2:291
Henley, Emily	Leavenworth, Stranger	40	F	10:482
Henly, Rebecca	Allen, Humboldt P.O.	49	F	2:291
Henry, H.	Johnson, Olathe (Millwright)	34	M	6:119
Henry, T.	Arrapahoe, South Park	23	M	11:193
Hensley, L. S.	Arrapahoe, South Park (Miner)	26	M	11:35
Hensley, Van Buren	Atchison, Walnut (Farmer)	29	M	1:184

[1]Born either in Penn. or Tenn.

[2]Apparent duplication and confusion in Census Book.

Arapahoe: spelled incorrectly with 2 r's in census and in this index also.

Name	Kansas: County; Township; P.O. Arap. Co.: Census Div. Not Township	Age	Sex	Census V. Pg
Herchford, R. H.	Doniphan, Wayne (Doctor)	27	M	1:363
Herring, C.	Arrapahoe, South Park	28	M	11:121
Herrington, E.	Linn, Potosi	28	F	7:76
Herrington, Elam	Jefferson, Oskaloosa (Minister-Meth.)	34	M	5:117
Hersey, N. P.	Arrapahoe, South Park	26	M	11:120
Hickey, Granville	Atchison, Mt. Pleasant (Farmer)	35	M	1:163
Hickey, Wm.	Nemaha, Valley (Farmer)	38	M	3:119
Hicks, John A.	Lykins, Middle Creek (Farmer)	32	M	8:109
Hicks, Lousia	Wyandotte, Quindaro	18	F	10:63
Hide, Edmond F.	Breckenridge, Agnes City (Farmer)	32	M	4:145
Higginbotham, U.	Riley, Manhattan P.O. (Merchant)	29	M	9:281
High, J.	Doniphan, Washington	44	F	1:314
Highland, Barbara	Jefferson, Grasshopper Falls	24	F	5:13
Highley, M. O.[1]	Doniphan, Center	24	F	1:264
Hildebran, Hallina	Atchison, Ward 2 (Domestic)	18	F	1:29
Hill, David	Lykins, Sugar Creek (Farmer)	48	M	8:97
Hill, H.	Arrapahoe, Lake Gulch (Blacksmith)	42	M	11:481
Hill, M.	Doniphan, Burr Oak	43	F	1:351
Hill, M. J.	Davis, Manhattan P.O.	14	F	9:357
Hill, Margaret	Linn, Paris	4	F	7:153
Hill, Melinda	Breckenridge, Fremont	51	F	4:163
Hill, P.[2]	Bourbon, Dayton P.O. (Housewife)	30	F	2:147
Hill, Thomas J.	Breckenridge, Fremont (Farmer)	52	M	4:163
Hill, W. C.	Doniphan, Burr Oak (Farmer)	42	M	1:351
Hill, W. P.	Wabaunsee, Mission Creek (Farmer)	30	M	5:271
Hilton, W.	Franklin, Centropolis (Farmer)	52	M	8:210
Hilton, W.	Franklin, Centropolis	52	M	8:210
Hinchman, J.	Arrapahoe, South Park	28	M	11:234
Hindman, A.	Arrapahoe, South Park	32	M	11:250
Hinds, J.	Arrapahoe, South Park (Trader)	39	M	11:10
Hinds, J.	Linn, Paris	27	M	7:144
Hiner, Susan	Lykins, Miami	36	F	8:93
Hitchower, John	Bourbon, Fort Scott P.O. (Farmer)	31	M	2:79
Hitter, Elisa	Allen, Humboldt P.O.	20	F	2:293
Hitter, James A.	Allen, Humboldt P.O. (Farmer)	26	M	2:293
Hoag, G.	Arrapahoe, South Park	35	M	11:173
Hobbs, S.	Johnson, Olathe	39	F	6:3
Hobbs, W.	Johnson, Olathe (Farmer)	43	M	6:3
Hodge, T.	Arrapahoe, South Park	25	M	11:134
Hodges, Elisa J.	Leavenworth, Kickapoo	22	F	10:404
Hodges, Eudora K.	Brown, Locknon	9	F	3:62
Hodges, P. M.	Brown, Locknon (Farmer)	36	M	3:62
Hodges, Thomas	Jefferson, Jefferson (Farmer)	48	M	5:43
Hofford, William	Anderson, Washington	18	M	7:254
Hogan, Catherine	Douglas, Marion	4	F	6:394
Hogan, Henry	Arrapahoe, South Park	28	M	11:201
Hogan, William	Lykins, Marysville (Farmer)	54	M	8:124
Hoggatt, John S.	Bourbon, Fort Scott P.O. (Farmer)	29	M	2:81
Hoggett, Lucy A.	Lykins, Miamiville, Osage	19	F	8:85
Hoggett, Martha	Lykins, Miamiville, Osage (Widow)	28	F	8:85
Hogwood, Clement	Bourbon, Fort Scott P.O.	7	M	2:194
Hogwood, Sarah A.	Bourbon, Fort Scott P.O.	30	F	2:194
Hogwood, Sarah P.	Bourbon, Fort Scott P.O.	12	F	2:194
Hogwood, William R.	Bourbon, Fort Scott P.O. (Farmer)	35	M	2:194
Holden, E.	Doniphan, Burr Oak	34	F	1:343
Holding, Penelope	Jefferson, Grasshopper Falls	38	F	5:11
Hollan, George W.	McGhee, Crawford Seminary P.O.	4	M	9:225

[1]May be M. D. rather than M. O.

[2]May be wife of Daniel; listed in same household with children.

Arapahoe: spelled incorrectly with 2 r's in census and in this index also.

Name	Kansas: County; Township; P.O. Arap. Co.: Census Div. Not Township	Age	Sex	Census V. Pg
Hollan, Henry	McGhee, Crawford Seminary P.O.	11	M	9:225
Hollan, Lafayette	McGhee, Crawford Seminary P.O.	13	M	9:225
Hollan, Louisa	McGhee, Crawford Seminary P.O.	10	F	9:225
Hollan, Miranda	McGhee, Crawford Seminary P.O.	6	F	9:225
Hollan, Salathiel	McGhee, Crawford Seminary P.O.(Farmer)	37	M	9:225
Hollan, William E.	McGhee, Crawford Seminary P.O.	9	M	9:225
Holland, Henderson A.	Bourbon, Marmaton P.O. (Farmer)	35	M	2:102
Holland, Louisa A.	Bourbon, Marmaton P.O. (Housewife)	31	F	2:102
Holland, M. C.	Leavenworth, Ward 2(Engine and land)	38	M	10:189
Holland, Sarah	Leavenworth, Ward 2	20	F	10:189
Hollingsworth, J. A.	Linn, Town of Paris (Landlord)	45	M	7:137
Hollingsworth, R. I.	Arrapahoe, Denver	37	M	11:374
Holloway, C.	Arrapahoe, South Park	36	M	11:251
Holloway, C. D. L.	Arrapahoe, Russell Gulch (Miner)	28	M	11:552
Holt, James F.	Bourbon, Turkey Creek P.O. (Farmer)	41	M	2:110
Holt, John H.	Bourbon, Turkey Creek P.O. (Farmer)	52	M	2:109
Holt, S. E. G.	Breckenridge, Forest Hill (Farmer)	38	M	4:173
Holten, W. H.	Arrapahoe, South Clear Creek	35	M	11:722
Howlette, Ch.[1]	Linn, Valley	22	F	7:30
Homer, G.	Arrapahoe, Valley of the Platte	27	M	11:833
Honnewell, C.	Arrapahoe, South Park	34	M	11:244
Hook, William	Bourbon, Fort Scott P.O.(Farm Labr.)	26	M	2:195
Hooper, Clement	Atchison, Center	29	M	1:128
Hooper, James	Atchison, Center (Farmer)	27	M	1:120
Hooper, John	Atchison, Center (Farmer)	25	M	1:120
Hooper, Sarah	Atchison, Center	44	F	1:128
Hoover, J.	Coffey, California (Farmer)	50	M	4:61
Hoover, Jacob	Coffey, California (Farmer)	52	M	4:61
Hopkins, Susan	Shawnee, Tecumseh	40	F	9:73
Hoppen, N.	Doniphan, Wayne	60	F	1:392
Hopper, Joseph	McGhee, Medoc,Mo.P.O.(Farm Laborer)	25	M	9:209
Horaker, S.	Arrapahoe, South Clear Creek	25	M	11:714
Hornens, S. F.	Doniphan, Wayne	59	F	1:392
Horton, Andrew C.	Bourbon, Marmaton P.O. (Farmer)	42	M	2:105
Horton, Mary	Bourbon, Marmaton P.O. (Household)	41	F	2:105
Hously, J. B.	Doniphan, Wayne (Farmer)	56	M	1:371
Hously, S.	Doniphan, Wayne	48	F	1:371
Houston, Eliza	Chase, Cottonwood	13	F	4:321
Houston, Elizabeth	Chase, Cottonwood	11	F	4:321
Houston, George	Chase, Cottonwood (Farmer)	49	M	4:321
Houston, Joseph	Chase, Diamond Creek (Farm Laborer)	21	M	4:326
Houston, Lemenda	Chase, Cottonwood	48	F	4:321
Houston, Martha	Chase, Cottonwood	16	F	4:321
Houston, Robt.	Chase, Cottonwood	19	M	4:321
Houston, S. C.	Johnson, Shawnee (Constable)	24	M	6:25
Houston, Wm. H.	Lykins, Sugar Creek (Farmer)	31	M	8:100
Houston, Wm.	Chase, Cottonwood (Farmer)	24	M	4:321
Howard, Casey	Bourbon, Fort Scott P.O. (Farmer)	39	M	2:75
Howard, G. L.	Arrapahoe, South Park	35?	M	11:148
Howard, H.	Franklin, Ohio City (Farmer)	40?	M	8:227
Howard, Jas.	Arrapahoe, California Gulch	32	M	11:295
Hoyt, Eliza	Leavenworth, Ward 2	28	F	10:155
Hozleman, E. P.	Arrapahoe, South Clear Creek	29	M	11:741
Hudson, M.	Linn, Paris	64	F	7:159
Huff, E.	Franklin, Peoria (Carpenter)	26	M	8:267
Huff, Peter	Allen, Humboldt P.O. (Farmer)	59	M	2:296
Huggins, Benjamin	Leavenworth, Kickapoo (Farmer)	34	M	10:329
Hughes, J. E.	Franklin, Centropolis (Farmer)	32	M	8:204
Hughs, M. J.	Doniphan, Washington	41	F	1:320

[1]Difficult to read; may be Howette.

Arapahoe: spelled incorrectly with 2 r's in census and in this index also.

Name	Kansas: County; Township; P.O. Arap. Co.: Census Div. Not Township	Age	Sex	Census V. Pg.
Humphrey, Eugene[1]	Jefferson, Ozawkie	1	M	5:98
Humphrey, S.	Arrapahoe, South Park	26	M	11:114
Humstead, Berthena	Allen, Humboldt P.O.	17	F	2:298
Humstead, Elisabeth	Allen, Humboldt P.O.	14		2:298
Humstead, Elisabeth	Allen, Humboldt P.O.	41	F	2:298
Humstead, James	Allen, Humboldt P.O.	16	M	2:298
Humstead, James	Allen, Humboldt P.O. (Farmer)	46	M	2:298
Humstead, Minerva	Allen, Humboldt P.O.	8	F	2:298
Humstead, Somerville	Allen, Humboldt P.O.	10	F	2:298
Humstead, Wiley	Allen, Humboldt P.O. (Farmer)	23	M	2:298
Humstead, Winterville	Allen, Humboldt P.O.	12	F	2:298
Hunson, Susan	Leavenworth, Easton	29	F	10:289
Hunt, W.	Arrapahoe, South Park	27	M	11:61
Hupner, L.	Arrapahoe, South Park	28	M	11:113
Hurd, W.	Arrapahoe, South Clear Creek	27	M	11:761
Hutchinson, P.	Douglas, Wakarusa (Farmer)	52	M	6:259
Hutchison, Isaac	Jefferson, Kaw (Blacksmith)	46	M	5:84
Hutson, B.	Doniphan, Wayne (Farmer)	55	M	1:375
Hutson, Mary	Doniphan, Wayne	20	F	1:376
Hutson, S.	Doniphan, Wayne (Farmer)	36	M	1:376
Huxford, George[1]	Lykins, Paola (Laborer)	23	M	8:39
Hyder, David	Arrapahoe, Golden City (Laborer)	28	M	11:582
Hyolt, Lucinda	McGhee, Crawford Seminary P.O.	34	F	9:219
Iamp, J. H.	Arrapahoe, California Gulch	23	M	11:297
Igoe, H. I.	Arrapahoe, South Park	35	M	11:111
Inburgh, O. B.	Arrapahoe, South Park	34	M	11:258
Ingraham, Elizabeth	Bourbon, Barnesville P.O.(Housewife)	41	F	2:173
Ingram, Miller	Bourbon, Pawnee P.O. (Farmer)	59	M	2:96
Ingram, Rebecca	Bourbon, Pawnee P.O. (Housewife)	59	F	2:96
Irvin, ? Charlotte	Arrapahoe, Arrapahoe City	40	F	11:587
Irvin, Wm.	Leavenworth, Easton (Farmer)	21	M	10:286
Irving, Elzabeth	Marshall, Vermillion	27	F	3:218
Irving, James	Marshall, Vermillion (Farm Laborer)	29	M	3:218
Irving, William	Marshall, Vermillion	7/12	M	3:218
Irwin, W. H.	Arrapahoe, South Clear Creek	39	M	11:749
Isaacs, C. N.	Arrapahoe, South Park	26	M	11:138
Isiah, Moses	Bourbon, Barnesville P.O.	14	M	2:174
Isley, Nancy J.	McGhee, Brushville P.O.	31	F	9:217
Jacet, Chas.	Douglas, Palmyra	56	M	6:277
Jacet, Ellen	Douglas, Palmyra	29	F	6:277
Jacet, Eve	Douglas, Palmyra	54	F	6:277
Jacet, G.	Douglas, Palmyra (Farmer)	32	M	6:277
Jacet, Selina	Douglas, Palmyra	14	F	6:277
Jackson, A.	Arrapahoe, Valley of the Platte(Miner)	24	M	11:799
Jackson, A.	Arrapahoe, Valley of the Platte	28	M	11:847
Jackson, B.	Douglas, Willow Springs	54	M	6:313
Jackson, Chas.	Doniphan, Iowa Point (Farmer)	30	M	1:423
Jackson, Jacob	Arrapahoe, Golden City(Liquor Dealer)	38	M	11:455
Jackson, Jane	McGhee, Brushville P.O.	24	F	9:231
Jackson, L.	Arrapahoe, South Park	23	M	11:235
Jackson, L.	Doniphan, Iowa Point (Farmer)	31	M	1:423
Jackson, P.	Arrapahoe, Valley of the Platte	26	M	11:847
Jackson, Sarah[2]	Douglas, Willow Springs	31	F	6:318
Jackson, Thomas J.	McGhee, Brushville P.O. (Farmer)	25	M	9:231
James, A.	Linn, Mound City	33	F	7:119
James, Allen	Linn, Valley (Farmer)	45	M	7:41
James, E.	Doniphan, Doniphan	56	F	1:385
James, Elizabeth	Linn, Valley	42	F	7:41

[1]Place of birth listed as unknown in both original entries.

[2]Duplicate entry also on p. 328 of same Census Book.

Arapahoe: spelled incorrectly with 2 r's in census and in this index also.

Name	Kansas: County; Township; P.O. Arap. Co.: Census Div. Not Township	Age	Sex	Census Vol.:Pg.
Janes, Martha	Anderson, Jackson	21	F	7:210
Janeway, Albert	Bourbon, Fort Scott P.O.	12	M	2:199
Janeway, Catherine	Bourbon, Fort Scott P.O.(Housewife)	59	F	2:198
Janeway, Daniel	Bourbon, Fort Scott P.O.	20	M	2:199
Janeway, John	Bourbon, Fort Scott P.O. (Farmer)	59	M	2:198
Janeway, Sarah F.	Bourbon, Fort Scott P.O.	10	F	2:199
Janey, John	Anderson, Washington	19	M	7:256
Jeffers, Basheba	Jefferson, Jefferson	45	F	5:38
Jeffers, S. J.	Doniphan, Iowa Point	95	F	1:427
Jennegan, Wm.	Arrapahoe, South Park	32	M	11:252
Jesse, Eliza J.	Breckenridge, Forest Hill	24	F	4:171
Jesse, John C.	Breckenridge, Forest Hill	6	M	4:171
Jesse, Margaret	Breckenridge, Forest Hill	4	F	4:171
Jesse, Wm.	Breckenridge, Fremont	7	M	4:171
Jewett, S. M.	Arrapahoe, South Park	34	M	11:103
Johns, Mary	Dickinson, Kansas Falls P.O.	35	F	4:303
Johns, T. H.	Dickinson, Kansas Falls P.O. (Farmer)	40	M	4:303
Johnson, Abijah	Douglas, Marion (Farmer)	23	M	6:394
Johnson, Anne	Leavenworth, Ward 2	25	BF	10:159
Johnson, B. Y.	Arrapahoe, California Gulch	38	M	11:270
Johnson, C.	Pottawatomie, Vienna	30	F	5:250
Johnson, David	Wyandotte, Wyandotte (Farmer)	44	M	10:2
Johnson, E. J.	Doniphan, Iowa Point	4	F	1:427
Johnson, H. C.	Arrapahoe, South Park	26	M	11:160
Johnson, L.	Doniphan, Iowa Point	26	F	1:427
Johnson, Mary	Leavenworth, Ward 4	14	F	10:268
Johnson, Mary J.[1]	Atchison, Walnut	37	F	1:187
Johnson, Nancy	Jefferson, Kentucky	22	F	5:64
Johnson, P.	Doniphan, Iowa Point (Farmer)	26	M	1:427
Johnson, Rolin	Doniphan, Highland	12	M	1:414
Johnson, S. A.	Doniphan, Iowa Point	4	F	1:427
Johnson, Sarah	Lykins, Osage	51	F	8:84
Johnson, Telitha C.	Lykins, Richland	35	F	8:17
Johnson, Thomas W.	Atchison, Walnut (Farmer)	41	M	1:187
Johnston, Eliza	Anderson, Washington	25	F	7:251
Johnston, John	Anderson, Washington (Farmer)	62	M	7:252
Johnston, Margaret	Anderson, Washington	54	F	7:252
Jones, A. S.[2]	Arrapahoe, Valley of the Platte	31	M	11:800
Jones, Alexander C.	Bourbon, Pawnee P.O. (Farmer)	31	M	2:99
Jones, Andrew J.	Wyandotte, Wyandotte	8	M	10:41
Jones, Archie	Leavenworth, Alexandria	45	M	10:449
Jones, Carlton	Arrapahoe, South Park	29	M	11:248
Jones, Caroline	Wyandotte, Wyandotte	11	F	10:41
Jones, Cassel	Wyandotte, Quindaro (Laborer)	30	M	10:59
Jones, Chas.	Arrapahoe, Denver (Miner)	31	M	11:395
Jones, E.	Doniphan, Wayne (Farmer)	40	M	1:366
Jones, Elizabeth	Leavenworth, Kickapoo	43	F	10:405
Jones, Emanuel G.	Bourbon, Pawnee P.O.	10	M	2:99
Jones, J. H.	Leavenworth, 1st Ward (Saloon)	22	M	10:137
Jones, J. W.	Doniphan, Iowa Point	30	F	1:426
Jones, Jas.	Arrapahoe, Denver (Miner)	29	M	11:425
Jones, James R.	Leavenworth, Kickapoo (Farmer)	43	M	10:405
Jones, Jane	Bourbon, Pawnee P.O. (Housewife)	34	F	2:99
Jones, Jesse	Coffey, Burlington (Farmer)	22	M	4:41
Jones, Jonathan	Wyandotte, Quindaro (Laborer)	27	M	10:59
Jones, Jonas	Jefferson, Kentucky (Farmer)	24	M	5:72
Jones, Lucind	Douglas, Palmyra, Prairie City	33	F	6:298

[1] Original entry looks more like age 32 than 37.

[2] May be A. P. rather than A. S.

Arapahoe: spelled incorrectly with 2 r's in census and in this index also.

Name	Kansas: County; Township; P.O. Arap. Co.: Census Div. Not Township	Age	Sex	Vol. Pg.
Jones, Lucinda	Woodson, Verdigris (Farmer)	18	F	9:160
Jones, M. C.[1]	Johnson, McCamish	37	F	6:69
Jones, Mary C.	Bourbon, Pawnee P.O.	12	F	2:99
Jones, Matilda	Wyandotte, Wyandotte	31	F	10:41
Jones, Matilda	Wyandotte, Quindaro	25	F	10:59
Jones, Pleasant W.	Bourbon, Pawnee P.O.	6	M	2:99
Jones, Rachael	Lykins, Middle Creek	41	F	8:106
Jones, S. F.	Arrapahoe, Denver (Miner)	28	M	11:414
Jones, Wm.	Shawnee, Williamsport (Farm Laborer)	35	M	9:55
Jordan, J. M.	Arrapahoe, South Park (Miner)	22	M	11:42
Jordon, M. E.	Arrapahoe, South Clear Creek	33	M	11:715
Joy, Zera	Johnson, Olathe (Farmer)	47	M	6:118
Judkin, J. S.	Arrapahoe, South Park	26	M	11:255
Judkins, Chas.	Arrapahoe, Golden City (Laborer)	18	M	11:583
Judkins, Ellan	Arrapahoe, Golden City	14	F	11:582
Judkins, Wm.	Arrapahoe, Golden City (Laborer)	15	M	11:583
Julian, Thomas B.	Bourbon, Mapleton P.O. (Farm Laborer)	16	M	2:148
Julian, Thomas K.	Bourbon, Mapleton P.O. (Farmer)	44	M	2:148
Juster, Henry	Leavenworth, Ward 2 (Boatman)	26	M	10:179
Juster, John	Leavenworth, Ward 2	13	M	10:179
Juster, Mary	Leavenworth, Ward 2	46	F	10:179
Justice, A.	Johnson, Shawnee (Farmer)	54	M	6:33
Justice, S.	Johnson, Shawnee	50	F	6:33
Justice, Wm.	Douglas, Kanwaca (Farmer)[2]		M	6:384
Kain, J. H.	Arrapahoe, South Park	22	M	11:122
Kallent, J.	Arrapahoe, South Park	28	M	11:210
Katzemstein, O.	Arrapahoe, South Park	24	M	11:234
Kauffman, O. S.	Arrapahoe, South Park	35	M	11:206
Kavanaugh, Wm.	Arrapahoe, South Park	27	M	11:6
Keasling, James W.	Bourbon, Xenia P.O. (Farmer)	32	M	2:140
Keasling, ... [3]	Bourbon, Xenia P.O. (Housewife)	25	F	2:140
Kee, J. A.	Woodson, Pleasant Grove (Farmer)	34	M	9:167
Kee, Lucinda	Woodson, Pleasant Grove (Farmer's wife)	23	F	9:167
Kee, Nancy	Woodson, Pleasant Grove	30	F	9:167
Kee, William	Woodson, Pleasant Grove (Farmer)	33	M	9:167
Keens, Betsy	Nemaha, Nemaha	50	F	3:86
Keeser, M.	Johnson, Shawnee	19	F	6:30
Kehler, W.	Arrapahoe, Valley of the Platte	22		11:781
Kelch, Thos.	Arrapahoe, Valley of the Platte	27	M	11:820
Kelley, Mary	Madison, Hartford	48	F	4:233
Kelley, Reuben	Madison, Hartford (Farmer)	48	M	4:233
Kelly, Aaron	Arrapahoe, South Park (Miner)	24	M	11:58
Kelly, H.	Douglas, Marion (Farmer)	35	M	6:401
Kelly, Mary E.	Allen, Humboldt P.O. (Farmer)	29	F	2:291
Kelly, Nancy	Allen, Humboldt P.O.	28	F	2:278
Kelly, Pamelia	Madison, Verdigris	23	F	4:246
Kelsey, Sarah	Leavenworth, Easton	44	F	10:283
Kelsey, W.	Leavenworth, Easton	45	M	10:283
Kelso, Mary	Bourbon, Fort Scott P.O. (Housewife)	44	F	2:221
Kenneda, Mary	Woodson, Neosho Falls (F. W.)	22	F	9:130
Kennedy, Franklin	Woodson, Neosho Falls (Farmer)	18	M	9:128
Kennedy, Hiram	Jefferson, Kaw (Farmer)	24	M	5:90
Kennedy, Nancy	Woodson, Neosho Falls	39	F	9:128
Kennedy, Rachel	Coffey, California	47	F	4:58
Kennott, J. M.	Arrapahoe, South Park	24	M	11:221
Kent, Chas.	Arrapahoe, Golden City (Miner)	35	M	11:441
Kepley, Jane	Bourbon, Dayton P.O. (Housewife)	30	F	2:149

[1] Indexer's error; should be Susan rather than M. C.

[2] His age is given as 33? suggesting actual age not known.

[3] First name illegible; may be Thusmithea.

Arapahoe: spelled incorrectly with 2 r's in census and in this index also.

Name	Kansas: County; Township; P.O. Arap. Co.: Census Div. Not Township	Age	Sex	Census V. Pg.
Key, G. F.	Atchison, Walnut (Farmer)	30	M	1:190
Kilgore, R. M.	Arrapahoe, South Park	24	M	11:114
Killebrew, Elius P.	McGhee, Brushville P.O.	26	M	9:230
Killick, W.	Arrapahoe, Valley of the Platte	28	M	11:843
Kimbly, Maria	Bourbon, Marmaton P.O. (Housewife)	43	F	2:116
Kimbro, H. W.	Arrapahoe, California Gulch	23	M	11:302
Kimbro, W. M.	Arrapahoe, Denver	23	M	11:382
Kimmerman, Jo	Greenwood, Eureka (Farmer)	48	M	9:179
Kimmerman, Susan	Greenwood, Eureka	44	F	9:179
Kincade, Caroline C.	Leavenworth, Kickapoo	41	F	10:343
Kincade, Luther	Leavenworth, Kickapoo	19	M	10:343
Kines, Sam'l.	Arrapahoe, Valley of the Platte	27		11:782
King, George	McGhee, Crawford Seminary P.O.	6	M	9:225
King, H. C.	Atchison, Walnut	15	M	1:172
King, I.	Osage, Ridgeway	19	F	8:343
King, John	McGhee, Crawford Seminary P.O.(Farmer)	45	M	9:225
King, John	McGhee, Crawford Seminary P.O.	14	M	9:225
King, Laura	McGhee, Crawford Sem. P.O. (Servant)	16	F	9:225
King, Marcus	McGhee, Crawford Seminary P.O.(Farmer)	19	M	9:225
King, Martha J.	Atchison, Walnut	12	F	1:172
King, Mary	Doniphan, Burr Oak	46	F	1:344
King, Pilsey	McGhee, Crawford Seminary P.O.	8	F	9:225
King, Richard M.	Atchison, Walnut (Farmer)	23	M	1:172
King, S.	Doniphan, Burr Oak (Farmer)	49	M	1:344
King, S.	Atchison, Walnut (Farmer)	17	M	1:172
King, Sarah	McGhee, Crawford Seminary P.O.	40	F	9:225
King, Tobias	McGhee, Crawford Seminary P.O.	10	M	9:225
King, Wellington B.	Atchison, Walnut (Farmer)	20	M	1:172
Kinkade, Rachel	Jefferson, Kentucky (Seamstress)	36	F	5:73
Kinkade, William A.	McGhee, Crawford Seminary P.O.(Farmer)	24	M	9:224
Kinner, L. T.	Arrapahoe, South Park	25	M	11:179
Kip, G. F.[1]	Arrapahoe, South Park	38	M	11:126
Kirby, Sarah.	Bourbon, Turkey Creek P.O.(Housewife)	20	F	2:107
Kirby, William H.	Bourbon, Turkey Creek P.O. (Farmer)	45	M	2:107
Kirkendall, S.	Davis, Manhattan P.O. (Farmer)	42	M	9:357
Kirkland, Fanny	Lykins, Osawatomie	25	F	8:58
Kirkland, John R.	Lykins, Osawatomie (Farmer)	51	M	8:65
Kisbarbey, Phebe	McGhee, Brushville P.O.	28	F	9:218
Kisell, J. S.	Arrapahoe, South Park	26	M	11:118
Kline, Frank	Arrapahoe, South Clear Creek	29	M	11:689
Kloble, T.	Arrapahoe, South Clear Creek	30	M	11:714
Klock, E.	Arrapahoe, South Park	31	M	11:244
Knapp, D.	Arrapahoe, Denver (Miner)	29	M	11:398
Knight, Anna E.	Anderson, Town of Greeley	26	F	7:242
Knight, Benj.	Anderson, Town of Greeley (Farmer)	31	M	7:242
Knight, N. G.	Arrapahoe, South Clear Creek	29	M	11:763
Knought, S. E.	Osage, Ridgeway	26	F	8:357
Kookegey, H. E.	Arrapahoe, South Clear Creek	26	M	11:685
Koones, Margaret	Breckenridge, Agnes City	33	F	4:148
Kress, P.	Riley, Manhattan-Henryville	50	F	9:311
Kurthrale, S. M.	Arrapahoe, South Clear Creek	27	M	11:718
Kurtz, Lewis	Riley, Manhattan P.O. (Merchant)	34	M	9:281
Kurtz, M. A.	Riley, Manhattan P.O.	30	F	9:281
Lacey, W.	Arrapahoe, Valley of the Platte	31	M	11:794
Lacy, Elizabeth	Leavenworth, Kickapoo	40	F	10:412
Lacy, Johnathan	Leavenworth, Kickapoo (Farmer)	45	M	10:412
Lamar, Eliza	Jefferson, Jefferson	52	F	5:28
Lamar, John	Jefferson, Jefferson	14	M	5:28

[1]May not be G. F.; writing almost illegible.

Arapahoe: spelled incorrectly with 2 r's in census and in this index also.

Name	Kansas: County; Township; P.O. Arap. Co.: Census Div. Not Township	Age	Sex	Census V. Pg.
Lamar, Louisa	Jefferson, Jefferson	19	F	5:28
Lamar, Mariah	Jefferson, Jefferson	38	F	5:28
Lamar, Napoleon	Jefferson, Jefferson (Farm Laborer)	32	M	5:28
Lamar, Samuel	Jefferson, Jefferson	12	M	5:28
Lamar, Thomas	Jefferson, Jefferson (Farmer)	57	M	5:28
Lamb, Eli	Linn, Potosi (Farmer)	17	M	7:83
Lamb, Elizabeth	Linn, Potosi	42	F	7:82
Lamb, Wm.	Arrapahoe, Valley of the Platte	26	M	11:857
Lamb, William	Linn, Potosi (Farmer)	20	M	7:83
Lambart, J. H.	Arrapahoe, South Park	37	M	11:192
Lamberson, A. P.	Arrapahoe, South Park	25	M	11:141
Lamer, G.	Arrapahoe, Valley of the Platte	29	M	11:860
Land, E.	Johnson, Shawnee	37	F	6:28
Lane, A.	Morris, Grove (Farmer)	28	M	4:270
Lane, A. E. [1]	Morris, Grove	25	F	4:268
Lane, Elizabeth	Morris, Grove	26	F	4:270
Lane, John	Marshall, Vermillion (Farmer)	57	M	3:216
Lane, Lucinda	Morris, Grove	38	F	4:267
Lane, Mary	Marshall, Vermillion	22	F	3:216
Lane, Wm.	Morris, Grove (Farmer)	36	M	4:267
Laney, A. B.	Arrapahoe, South Clear Creek	34	M	11:687
Langley, J.	Osage, Ridgeway (Farmer)	25	M	8:349
Langley, O.	Arrapahoe, South Park	33	M	11:172
Lape, John	Jefferson, Oskaloosa (Laborer)	25	M	5:127
Large, Abraham	McGhee, Medoc, Missouri P.O. (Farmer)	23	M	9:215
Large, W. L.	Leavenworth, Kickapoo (Farmer)	51	M	10:340
Larne, S.	Greenwood, Eureka (Farmer)	27	M	9:184
Laster, Abner	Atchison, Mt. Pleasant	40	M	1:165
Latts, O.	Arrapahoe, South Park	37	M	11:182
Laughlin, Sarah E.	Linn, Paris	24	F	7:139
Lewellin, Martha	Anderson, Jackson		F	7:209
Laws, O. S.	Johnson, McCamish (Physician)	33	M	6:65
Leach, Eliza J.	Coffey, Leroy	34	F	4:25
Leander, J.	Arrapahoe, South Park	35	M	11:164
Leaney, Charles S.	Atchison, Grasshopper (Loafer)	24	M	1:93
Leaver, Elizabeth	McGhee, Medoc, Mo. P.O.	34	F	9:214
Leaver, Jackson	McGhee, Medoc, Mo. P.O. (Farmer)	34	M	9:214
Leaver, Marinda	McGhee, Medoc, Mo. P.O.	10	F	9:214
Leaver, Rebecca	McGhee, Medoc, Mo. P.O.	7	F	9:214
Leaverton, Francis	Jefferson, Oskaloosa	44	M	5:125
Lebow, Caroline	Lykins, Marysville	38	F	8:123
Lebow, Wm. H.	Lykins, Marysville (Farmer)	43	M	8:123
Lebring, W.	Arrapahoe, Valley of the Platte	22	M	11:860
Lee, C. E.	Doniphan, Iowa Point	34	M	1:447
Lee, J.	Doniphan, Iowa Point (Doctor)	36	M	1:447
Lemon, Mary	Linn, Scott	31	F	7:18
Lemons, David	Jefferson, Ozawkie (Teamster)	42	M	5:99
Lemons, John	McGhee, Osage Mission P.O. (Farmer)	49	M	9:238
Lemons, S. A.	Doniphan, Washington	26	F	1:317
Lenager, Martha J.	Lykins, Marysville	21	F	8:122
Leonard, J. P.	Arrapahoe, South Park	27	M	11:190
Leslie, Lafayette	Atchison, Walnut (Farmer)	25	M	1:196
Lester, Josephine	Atchison, Walnut	15	F	1:196
Levy, William	Nemaha, Rock Creek (Farm hand)	21	M	3:74
Lewis, Ann M.	Linn, Scott	50	F	7:27
Lewis, C.	Doniphan, Wolf River (Farmer)	35	M	1:405
Lewis J.	Arrapahoe, South Park	31	M	11:175

[1] May not be A. E.; writing almost illegible.

Arapahoe: spelled incorrectly with 2 r's in census and in this index also.

Name	Kansas: County; Township; P.O. Arap. Co.: Census Div. Not Township	Age	Sex	Census V. Pg.
Lewis, J. M.	Douglas, Lawrence (Physician)	30	M	6:208
Lewis, Jesse	Linn, Scott (Teacher)	19	M	7:27
Lewis, Larkin	Linn, Town of Paris (Farmer)	54	M	7:134
Lewis, Markes	Linn, Scott	13	M	7:27
Lewis, T. D.	Arrapahoe, South Park	34	M	11:167
Lewis, Z.	Linn, Scott (Farmer)	51	M	7:27
Lichbree, Edward	Wyandotte, Wyandotte	6	M	10:43
Lichbree, Elizabeth	Wyandotte, Wyandotte	4	F	10:43
Lichbree, Henry	Wyandotte, Wyandotte	18	M	10:42
Lichbree, Lucinda	Wyandotte, Wyandotte	14	F	10:42
Lichbree, Mary	Wyandotte, Wyandotte	4	F	10:43
Lichbree, Mary	Wyandotte, Wyandotte	36	F	10:42
Lichbree, Paine	Wyandotte, Wyandotte	12	M	10:43
Lichbree, Patton	Wyandotte, Wyandotte	16	M	10:43
Lichbree, Wm.	Wyandotte, Wyandotte (Farmer)	40	M	10:42
Lightbody, S....[1]	Arrapahoe, Valley of the Platte	32	M	11:804
Lighter, S. S.	Arrapahoe, Denver (Miner)	34	M	11:425
Lightner, E. G.	Arrapahoe, South Park	24	M	11:107
Lillie, Ellender	Lykins, Richland	33	F	8:14
Lilly, E. S.	Arrapahoe, South Clear Creek	24	M	11:762
Lilern, D. H.	Arrapahoe, South Park	38	M	11:187
Lindsay, Demsey	McGhee, Osage Mission P.O.	16	M	9:242
Lindsay, Eli	McGhee, Osage Mission P.O.	14	M	9:242
Lindsay, Felix	McGhee, Osage Mission P.O.	7	M	9:242
Lindsay, John	McGhee, Osage Mission P.O.	19	M	9:242
Lindsay, Samuel	McGhee, Osage Mission P.O.	13	M	9:242
Lindsay, Warren	McGhee, Osage Mission P.O.	10	M	9:242
Lindsay, William	McGhee, Osage Mission P.O.	22	M	9:242
Lintner, S. P.	Arrapahoe, South Park	28	M	11:140
Linville, Ann A.	Leavenworth, Easton	38	F	10:293
Linville, Granville	Leavenworth, Easton (Farmer)	53	M	10:293
Lishback, J. H.	Arrapahoe, South Park	41	M	11:127
Litcomb, A. W.	Arrapahoe, South Park	38	M	11:191
Littacur, Moses	Marshall, Blue Rapids (Farmer)	40	M	3:201
Livesey, Robert	McGhee, Osage Mission P.O. (Farmer)	35	M	9:237
Leab, Matilda	Douglas, Lecompton	45	M	6:349
Loback, C.	Arrapahoe, South Park (Miner)	27	M	11:28
Lom, D. C.	Anderson, Walker (Farmer)	33	M	7:234
Longbottom, Nancy	Atchison, Mt. Pleasant (Domestic)	28	F	1:156
Longhmiller, Wm.	Leavenworth, Easton (Merchant)	54	M	10:282
Longly, Elisabeth	Leavenworth, Easton	24	F	10:297
Longly, Silas	Leavenworth, Easton (Farmer)	34	M	10:297
Lord, J. C. R.	Arrapahoe, South Park	32	M	11:43
Lory, G.	Coffey, Neosho (Farmer)	44	M	4:68
Lory, Susan	Coffey, Neosho	37	F	4:68
Love, Jno.	Arrapahoe, South Park	41	M	11:127
Lovelace, Charles	Wyandotte, Wyandotte (Lumberman)	29	M	10:3
Loveless, James	Bourbon, Fort Scott P.O. (Farmer)	28	M	2:183
Loveless, Martha	Bourbon, Fort Scott P.O.(Housewife)	52	F	2:183
Loveless, Mary	Bourbon, Fort Scott P.O. (Housewife)	30	F	2:183
Loveless, Yayock	Bourbon, Fort Scott P.O. (Farmer)	50	M	2:183
Lovell, W.	Arrapahoe, Valley of the Platte	32	M	11:809
Low, Abraham M.	Atchison, Mt. Pleasant (Grocer)	51	M	1:150
Low, Albert W.	Atchison, Mt. Pleasant (Farmer)	20	M	1:150
Low, James B.[2]	Atchison, Mt. Pleasant (Gold Seeker)	22	M	1:150
Low, S.	Atchison, Mt. Pleasant	46	M	1:150
Low, William	Bourbon, Barnesville P.O. (Farmer)	30	M	2:165
Lowe, A. L.	Arrapahoe, South Park	28	M	11:97
Lowman, Wm.	Douglas, Lawrence (Merchant)	30	M	6:208
Lowrance, Joseph B.	Lykins, Paola (Cumberland clergyman)	37	M	8:36

[1]Looks like Sml in original. [2]See Part II, A. C. Harrison, gold sacker.

Arapahoe: spelled incorrectly with 2 r's in census and in this index also.

Name	Kansas: County; Township; P.O. Arap. Co.: Census Div. Not Township	Age	Sex	Census V. Pg
Lowry, Chas.	Arrapahoe, Valley of the Platte	30		11:789
Loyal, G. F.	Arrapahoe, Valley of the Platte	22		11:790
Luce, Margaret	Leavenworth, Ward 3	50	F	10:229
Luits, Henry	Bourbon, Xenia P.O. (Farmer)	37	M	2:127
Lull, E. W.[1]	Arrapahoe, Valley of the Platte	39	M	11:820
Lumps, J.	Arrapahoe, Central City (Miner)	25	M	11:574
Luse, J.	Arrapahoe, South Clear Creek	29	M	11:714
Lyle, Almeda L.	Arrapahoe, Eureka Gulch (Housekeeper)	28	F	11:506
Lyman, H.	Arrapahoe, Valley of the Platte	25	M	11:858
Lynch, H. G.	Chase, Falls (Wagon maker)	32	M	4:322
Lynihan, James	Atchison, Kapioma	4	M	1:97
McAdams, A. A.	Doniphan, Center	22	F	1:260
McAdder, Wm.	Arrapahoe, South Park	28	M	11:257
McAllister, W. H.	Arrapahoe, California Gulch	28	M	11:294
McAlmon, C.	Arrapahoe, South Park	26	M	11:184
McAtoon, W. I.	Arrapahoe, South Clear Creek	29	M	11:762
McGlain, W.	Arrapahoe, South Clear Creek (Miner)	26	M	11:699
McBride, Elizabeth A.	Atchison, Center	30	F	1:121
McBride, Floretta	Atchison, Center	7	F	1:121
McBride, Isaac	Atchison, Center	10	F	1:129
McBride, Jeneva	Atchison, Center	13	F	1:121
McBride, John A.	Atchison, Center	8	M	1:129
McBride, Joseph	Atchison, Mt. Pleasant (Farmer)	40	M	1:146
McBride, Kate	Atchison, Center	9	F	1:121
McBride, Malinda	Atchison, Mt. Pleasant	36	F	1:146
McBride, Mary	Atchison, Center	32	F	1:129
McBride, Nancy	Atchison, Mt. Pleasant	14	F	1:146
McBride, Nanny Cooley	Atchison, Mt. Pleasant	2	F	1:146
McBride, Pemelia	Atchison, Center	12	F	1:129
McBride, Priscilla S.	Atchison, Mt. Pleasant	19	F	1:146
McBride, Sarah E.	Atchison, Center	7	F	1:129
McBride, Sarah E.	Atchison, Center	11	F	1:121
McBride, T. C.	Atchison, Center (Farmer)	33	M	1:129
McBride, Thomas	Atchison, Mt. Pleasant	12	M	1:146
McBride, Wm. C.	Atchison, Mt. Pleasant (Farmer)	17	M	1:146
McCaffrey, W. D.	Arrapahoe, South Park	32	M	11:179
McCallie, Elizabeth	Linn, Town of Paris	38	F	7:136
McCallie, Ellen	Linn, Town of Paris	10	F	7:136
McCallie, Henry	Linn, Town of Paris	13	M	7:136
McCallie, J. J.	Linn, Town of Paris	12	M	7:136
McCallie, Nancy L.	Linn, Town of Paris	9	F	7:136
McCallie, Pinka	Linn, Town of Paris	4	F	7:136
McCallie, William	Linn, Town of Paris	15	M	7:136
McCamish, W. H.	Johnson, Union (Farmer)	22	M	6:14
McCammish, R.	Johnson, McCamish (Farmer)	24	M	6:61
McCarne, S.	Doniphan, Marion (Farmer)	24	M	1:285
McCarty, C. D.	Arrapahoe, South Park	29	M	11:158
McCarty, D.	Arrapahoe, Mountain City (Miner)	51	M	11:466
McCarty, Rany	Bourbon, Turkey Creek P.O.(Housewife)	39	F	2:115
McCarty, Wm.	Jefferson, Oskaloosa (Merchant)	49	M	5:121
McClathohy, Cynthia	Wyandotte, Wyandotte	34		10:38
McClathohy, F. F.	Wyandotte, Wyandotte (Farmer)	48	M	10:38
McClathohy, John	Wyandotte, Wyandotte	13	M	10:38
McClathohy, Threrasa R.	Wyandotte, Wyandotte	11	F	10:38
McClelland, Angeline	Arrapahoe, Denver	29	F	11:341
McClemcey, Nancy	Bourbon, Turkey Creek P.O.(Housewife)	44	F	2:107
McClenny, John	Jefferson, Grasshopper Falls (Farmer)	34	M	5:12
McClung, Jas.	Lykins, Wea (Farmer)	35	M	8:116
McClung, Sarah	Lykins, Wea	37	F	8:116

[1]Some question about whether he was born in Tennessee.

Arapahoe: spelled incorrectly with 2 r's in census and in this index also.

Name	Kansas: County; Township; P.O. Arap. Co.: Census Div. Not Township	Age	Sex	Census V. Pg.
McClure, H. C.	Arrapahoe, Tarryall, South Park	27	M	11:598
McClure, Jno.	Arrapahoe, South Park	20	M	11:250
McColl, H. H.	Franklin, Ohio (Farmer)	25	M	8:226
McColm, Thos.	Coffey, Avon	16	M	4:6
McColumn, George W.	Coffey, Leroy	13	M	4:25
McColumn, James	Coffey, Leroy	4	M	4:25
McColumn, John W.	Coffey, Leroy	11	M	4:25
McColumn, Martha J.	Coffey, Leroy	9	F	4:25
McColumn, Nancy	Coffey, Leroy	6	F	4:25
McColumn, Thomas	Coffey, Leroy (Farmer)	16	M	4:25
McCone, Wm.	Douglas, Palmyra (Farmer)	49	M	6:296
McCray, Sarah	Leavenworth, Ward 4	42	F	10:276
McCray, W. M.	Leavenworth, Ward 4 (Farmer)	50	M	10:276
McCraary, Benj.	Leavenworth, Stranger (Farmer)	49	M	10:476
McCully, Aelisah	Bourbon, Fort Scott P.O.	6	F	2:94
McCully, Angelica	Bourbon, Fort Scott P.O.	4	F	2:94
McCully, Eakin	Bourbon, Fort Scott P.O.	2	M	2:94
McCully, Elizabeth	Bourbon, Fort Scott P.O. (Housewife)	26	F	2:94
McCully, Jane	Bourbon, Fort Scott P.O.(Housekeeper)	50	F	2:94
McCully, Joseph	Bourbon, Fort Scott P.O. (Farmer)	48	M	2:94
McCully, Magnolia	Bourbon, Fort Scott P.O.	10	F	2:94
McCully, Rebecca	Bourbon, Fort Scott P.O.	24	F	2:94
McCully, Rosamond	Bourbon, Fort Scott P.O.	32	F	2:94
McCurdy, E. R.	Wabaunsee, Zeandale (Farmer)	41	M	5:235
McCutcheon, Samuel	Shawnee, Monmouth (Farmer)	50	M	9:64
McDaniel, Anna	Lykins, Marysville	38	F	8:130
McDaniel, C.	Linn, Centerville (Farmer)	35	M	7:96
McDaniel, Gressa J.	Lykins, Marysville	22	F	8:131
McDaniel, Joseph P.	Lykins, Marysville	16	M	8:131
McDaniel, Levisa J.	McGhee, Brushville P.O. (Servant)	16	IF	9:227
McDaniel, Lucinda	McGhee, Brushville P.O.	36	IF	9:227
McDaniel, M.	Linn, Paris (Farmer)	33	M	7:142
McDaniel, Margaret	McGhee, Brushville P.O. (Servant)	17	IF	9:227
McDaniel, Mary	Linn, Centerville	34	F	7:96
McDaniel, Mary J.	Lykins, Marysville	17	F	8:130
McDaniel, Nancy	Linn, Paris	32	F	7:142
McDaniel, Narcasa S.	Lykins, Lykins	4	F	8:131
McDonald, Columbus	Linn, Centerville	13	M	7:95
McDonald, S. N.	Arrapahoe, South Park	38	M	11:187
McDonald, Sarah	Linn, Centerville	11	F	7:95
McDonald, Susannah	Chase, Diamond Creek	61	F	4:326
McDonald, W.	Arrapahoe, South Park	29	M	11:27
McElroy, J.	Arrapahoe, South Clear Creek	36	M	11:714
McFadden, Andrew H.	Lykins, Wea (Farmer)	42	M	8:116
McFarland, B. M.	Franklin, Centropolis (Farmer)	26	M	8:212
McFarland, Unity J.	Lykins, Paola	22	F	8:40
McGill, Elizabeth	Nemaha, Capioma	44	F	3:107
McGill, T. L.	Doniphan, Washington (Butcher)	31	M	1:295
McGinnis, W. H.	Arrapahoe, South Clear Creek	34	M	11:738
McGinnis, W. W.	Arrapahoe, South Clear Creek	23	M	11:728
McGoin, James	Woodson, Verdigris (Farmer)	22	M	9:155
McGuire, Margaret	Brown, Walnut Creek	39	F	3:28
McHaley, I. N.	Arrapahoe, South Clear Creek	29	M	11:711
McIlvaine, G. W.	Arrapahoe, South Park	55	M	11:142
McIntire, O. S.	Arrapahoe, South Park	25	M	11:124
McIntyre, J. B.	Davis, Ft. Riley Reserve(Lieut.U.S.A.)	26	M	9:358
McKenzie, Jno.	Arrapahoe, Valley of the Platte	32		11:789
McKibbin, Elizabeth	Bourbon, Marmaton P.O. (Housewife)	29	F	2:207
McKinkey, G.	Leavenworth, Ward 2 (Carpenter)	30	M	10:171
McKinney, E. A.	Johnson, Oxford	21	F	6:107
McKinstry, J. B.	Linn, Mound City (Farmer)	33	M	7:116

Arapahoe: spelled incorrectly with 2 r's in census and in this index also.

Name	Kansas: County; Township; P.O. Arap. Co.: Census Div. Not Township	Age	Sex	Census V. : Pg
McKinstry, Nathan	Linn, Mound City (Farmer)	27	M	7:116
McKonkey, G.	Leavenworth, Ward 3	29	M	10:206
McKown, D. M.	Johnson, Oxford	39	F	6:105
McLane, I.[1]	Franklin, Prairie (Farmer)	42	M	8:268
McLaughlin, Vilotta	Lykins, Sugar Creek (Widow)	37	F	8:98
McMechan, Thos.	Arrapahoe, South Park	35	M	11:188
McMutru, Sarah	Greenwood, Eureka	33	F	9:180
McMutru, William	Greenwood, Eureka (Farmer)	33	M	9:180
McQuigg, James R. P.	Allen, Geneva P.O. (Farmer)	24	M	2:255
McQuigg, Robert J.	Allen, Geneva P.O. (Farmer)	29	M	2:254
McQuown, Thomas	Leavenworth, Easton (Farmer)	35	M	10:292
McRea, Jas.	Arrapahoe, South Park	30	M	11:247
Macy, Margaret	Madison, Verdigris	23	F	4:247
Madden, Barbara	Leavenworth, Delaware	42	F	10:430
Maddox, Desey	Leavenworth, Delaware	62	F	10:431
Mahony, Mary	Leavenworth, 1st Ward	40	F	10:90
Maiden, Nathan J.	Lykins, Sugar Creek (Farmer)	45	M	8:97
Majors, Allen	Arrapahoe, Denver (Miner)	25	M	11:409
Majors, Nancy	Linn, Valley	30	F	7:42
Majors, P.	Linn, Valley (Farmer)	36	M	7:42
Maler, Mary	McGhee, Crawford Seminary P.O.	35	F	9:228
Malin, G.	Arrapahoe, South Clear Creek	27	M	11:749
Manford, John	Bourbon, Fort Scott P.O. (Farmer)	21	BM	2:196
Manlovy, Rachael	Coffey, Leroy	42	F	4:18
Mann, J.	Arrapahoe, South Park	30	M	11:253
Mansfield, B.	Arrapahoe, South Park	26	M	11:115
Mansfield, L.	Doniphan, Center	42	F	1:270
Maple, S. L.	Arrapahoe, South Park	36	M	11:185
Margraff, Mary J.	Leavenworth, Ward 4	22	F	10:264
Mark, L.	Douglas, Lecompton	45	F	6:356
Marsh, R. M.	Arrapahoe, South Park	23	M	11:1
Marshall, E. T.	Arrapahoe, Valley of the Platte	28	M	11:861
Marshall, Mary	Nemaha, Nemaha	30	F	3:88
Marshall, R.	Nemaha, Nemaha (Farmer)	35	M	3:88
Martin, Christina	Leavenworth, Ward 2	25	F	10:155
Martin, Clay	Arrapahoe, South Park	40	M	11:131
Martin, E.	Arrapahoe, Lake Gulch (Miner)	50	M	11:482
Martin, J.	Linn, Valley (Farmer)	33	M	7:36
Martin, John	Shawnee, Tecumseh (Lawyer)	26	M	9:68
Martin, Mary	Arrapahoe, South Park	25	F	11:65
Martindale, C.	Coffey, Ottumwa	29	F	4:49
Mask, J. S.[2]	Johnson, Aubrey (Farmer)	23	M	6:40
Masner, Hiram	Lykins, Stanton (Farmer)	47	M	8:9
Masner, Margarette	Lykins, Stanton	32	F	8:9
Mason, Mary	Linn, Paris	38	F	7:153
Massey, A. H. D.	Atchison, Walnut	6	M	1:190
Massey, Cassander L.	Atchison, Walnut	16	F	1:190
Massey, Charles E.	Atchison, Walnut	20	M	1:190
Massey, Marsilla	Atchison, Walnut	12	F	1:190
Massey, Matilda J.	Atchison, Walnut	18	F	1:190
Massey, Milly	Bourbon, Fort Scott P.O.(Housekeeper)	44	F	2:87
Massey, Polly A.	Atchison, Walnut	40	F	1:190
Massey, Ricd. W.	Lykins, Stanton (Attorney)	36	M	8:11
Massey, W. L.	Atchison, Walnut	50	M	1:190
Massey, Wm. M.	Atchison, Walnut	22	M	1:190
Massick, J. W.	Arrapahoe, Valley of the Platte	30	M	11:795
Matheny, Chas.	Douglas, Willow Springs (Farmer)	50	M	6:323

[1] Initial may not be I; almost illegible.

[2] Initials may not be J. S.; entry almost illegible.

Arapahoe: spelled incorrectly with 2 r's in census and in this index also.

Name	Kansas: County; Township; P.O. Arap. Co.: Census Div. Not Township	Age	Sex	Census V. Pg.
Mathews, E.[1]	Arrapahoe, South Clear Creek	31	M	11:699
Mathews, Joseph	Brown, Irving (Farmer)	62	M	3:10
Mattox, Frances	Linn, Valley	45	F	7:45
Maxwell, Alma	Allen, Humboldt P.O.	35	F	2:299
Maxwell, L.	Doniphan, Iowa Point	20	F	1:422
Maxwell, R.	Linn, Potosi (Farmer)	27	M	7:57
Mayberry, Caroline	Allen, Humboldt P.O.	40	F	2:277
Mayers, Francis	Anderson, Washington (Farmer)	25	M	7:251
Mayo, Alfred H.	Lykins, Marysville	12	M	8:124
Mayo, Edw. W. P.	Lykins, Marysville (Farmer)	41	M	8:124
Mayo, Emeline B.	Lykins, Marysville	24	F	8:124
Mayo, Ferdinand J.	Lykins, Marysville	14	M	8:124
Mayo, Jacob T.	Lykins, Marysville	5	M	8:124
Mayo, James P.	Lykins, Marysville	16	M	8:124
Mayo, P. B.	Lykins, Marysville	8	M	8:124
Mays, Jackson	Linn, Centerville (Farmer)	25	M	7:96
Meadows, J. N.	Arrapahoe, South Park	29	M	11:179
Mealer, Robt.	Doniphan, Doniphan (Farmer)	30	M	1:389
Mears, Isaac	Allen, Iola P.O. (Miller)	39	M	2:267
Mears, Mary	Allen, Iola P.O.	29	F	2:267
Medhurst, G.	Arrapahoe, South Park	24	M	11:243
Medlen, John	McGhee, Medoc, Missouri P.O.(Farmer)	30	M	9:207
Medlen, William	McGhee, Medoc, Missouri P.O.(Farmer)	25	M	9:208
Medlen, Wilson	McGhee, Medoc, Missouri P.O.(Farmer)	23	M	9:208
Medler, A.	Arrapahoe, South Park	36	M	11:143
Medlin, J.	Linn, Scott (Miller)	49	M	7:21
Meech, Allen	Linn, Valley	10	M	7:51
Meech, J. R.	Arrapahoe, South Park	34	M	11:165
Meech, Margaret	Linn, Valley	8	F	7:51
Meek, E. S.	Arrapahoe, South Park	26	M	11:129
Meek, Susan	Doniphan, Burr Oak	35	F	1:349
Mellinger, Lousia	Leavenworth, Kickapoo	23	F	10:405
Meltose, W.	Linn, Scott (Farmer)	43	M	7:19
Menerief, J.	Arrapahoe, South Clear Creek	21	M	11:713
Meredith, J.	Arrapahoe, Denver (Miner)	26	M	11:430
Merrill, C. W.	Arrapahoe, California Gulch	21	M	11:312
Merrill, James F.	McGhee, Brushville P.O.	4	M	9:226
Merrill, John	McGhee, Brushville P.O. (Farmer)	25	M	9:226
Merrill, Nellie	McGhee, Brushville P.O.	60	F	9:226
Merrith, A. E.	Doniphan, Center (Farmhand)	22	M	1:272
Merrith, Nezekiah	Doniphan, Center (Farm laborer)	18	M	1:272
Merrith, Lew	Doniphan, Center (Farmer)	39	M	1:272
Merrith, R. W.	Doniphan, Center (Farmer)	24	M	1:272
Meselle, M.	Leavenworth, Alexandria	29	M	10:441
Michaels, Jane	Doniphan, Wayne	29	F	1:392
Micker, J. W.	Arrapahoe, South Clear Creek	31	M	11:728
Middleton, W.	Linn, Paris	50	F	7:140
Migdgett, James	Nemaha, Valley	37	M	3:121
Mik, J. L.	Arrapahoe, California Gulch	28	M	11:291
Mik, R.	Arrapahoe, California Gulch	24	M	11:291
Milam, Harriet	Jackson, Franklin	25	F	5:182
Mill, W.	Arrapahoe, South Clear Creek	36	M	11:704
Miller, A.	Johnson, Shawnee	11	F	6:96
Miller, A. C.	Doniphan, Wolf River (Farmer)	55	F	1:398
Miller, C.	Doniphan, Burr Oak	37	F	1:342
Miller, C.	Johnson, Shawnee	15	F	6:96
Miller, David	Breckenridge, Agnes City (Farmer)	53	M	4:147
Miller, E.	Johnson, Olathe	32	F	6:112

[1] Matthew rather than Matthews in original entry.
  Arapahoe: spelled incorrectly with 2 r's in census and in this index also.

Name	Kansas: County; Township; P.O. Arap. Co.: Census Div. Not Township	Age	Sex	Census V. Pg.
Miller, E.	Johnson, Shawnee	9	F	6:96
Miller, G.	Johnson, Shawnee (Farmer)	14	M	6:96
Miller, Geo. W.	Linn, Valley	6	M	7:37
Miller, Harriet	McGhee, Osage Mission P.O.	29	F	9:234
Miller, J.	Linn, Valley (Farmer)	54	M	7:46
Miller, Jonathan	McGhee, Osage Mission P.O. (Farmer)	35	M	9:234
Miller, Louisa C.	Bourbon, Barnesville P.O. (Housewife)	23	F	2:165
Miller, Marshall	Linn, Valley	4	M	7:37
Miller, Mary J.	Atchison, Shannon	19	F	1:80
Miller, Nancy	Brown, Claytonville	50	F	3:45
Miller, O.	Johnson, Shawnee	4	M	6:96
Miller, S. R.	Arrapahoe, South Clear Creek (Miner)	22	M	11:762
Mills, Robert	Bourbon, Marmaton P.O. (Carpenter)	26	M	2:206
Millsap, Amanda	Nemaha, Valley	16	F	3:122
Millsap, Baxter	Nemaha, Valley	13	M	3:122
Millsap, George	Nemaha, Valley	11	M	3:120
Minton, J. W.	Anderson, Ozark (Farmer)	28	M	7:250
Misier, F. J.	Doniphan, Center (Farmer)	20	M	1:246
Mitchel, Mary	Jackson, Douglas	75	F	5:174
Mitchel, Moses	Jackson, Douglas (Farmer)	35	M	5:174
Mitchell, A. J.	Breckenridge, Forest Hill (Farmer)	46	M	4:183
Mitchell, Catherine	Breckenridge, Forest Hill	22	F	4:183
Mitchell, Ellen D.	Bourbon, Marmaton P.O. (Housewife)	51	F	2:102
Mitchell, Henry	Jackson, Douglas (Farmer)	28	M	5:175
Mitchell, Jacob	Breckenridge, Forest Hill (Farmer)	22	M	4:183
Mitchell, M.	Douglas, Wakarusa	30	F	6:245
Mitchell, Mary A.	Breckenridge, Forest Hill	48	F	4:183
Mitchell, Robert	Jackson, Douglas (Farmer)	40	M	5:174
Mize, Burril B.	Leavenworth, Kickapoo (Farmer)	49	M	10:339
Mobley, Susan	Riley, Ogden P.O.	26	F	9:290
Mois, S. A.	Coffey, Ottumwa	23	F	4:55
Monroe, G. A.	Arrapahoe, South Park	43	M	11:41
Monson, H.	Douglas, Clinton (Laborer)	24	M	6:425
Montague, A.	Arrapahoe, South Park	23	M	11:212
Montague, H.	Arrapahoe, South Park	28	M	11:147
Montague, Martha	Doniphan, Center	25	F	1:262
Montgomery, John	Breckenridge, Agnes City (Farmer)	25	M	4:148
Moore, D.	Doniphan, Center (Farmer)	50	M	1:247
Moore, Elez.	Douglas, Clinton	27	F	6:419
Moore, George	Linn, Scott (Farmer)	46	M	7:22
Moore, J.	Douglas, Clinton (Farmer)	33	M	6:419
Moore, J. S.[1]	Atchison, Walnut (Farmer)	23	M	1:190
Moore, Jeremiah	Brown, Claytonville	14	M	3:54
Moore, Jno. L.	Arrapahoe, South Clear Creek (Miner)	35	M	11:739
Moore, M.	Franklin, Ottawa	56	F	8:253
Moore, Mary	Doniphan, White Cloud	34	F	1:441
Moore, Meloia	Linn, Scott	49	F	7:22
Moore, Rebecca	Breckenridge, Americus	20	F	4:220
Moore, Richard	Bourbon, Barnesville P.O. (Farmer)	38	M	2:184
Moore, S.	Arrapahoe, Valley of the Platte	26	M	11:834
Moore, William	Brown, Claytonville (Farmer)	17	M	3:54
Morahan, James	Shawnee, Auburn (Farmer)	32	M	9:38
Morahan, Mary	Shawnee, Auburn	32	F	9:38
Morahan, Nancy	Shawnee, Auburn	15	F	9:38
More, Mary	Allen, Humboldt P.O.	38	F	2:303
Morehead, W.	Arrapahoe, Valley of the Platte	28	M	11:816
Morgan, Caroline	Bourbon, Fort Scott P.O. (Housewife)	29	F	2:155
Morgan, John P.	Bourbon, Fort Scott P.O. (Farmer)	24	M	2:200

[1]Perhaps J. T. rather than J. S.

Arapahoe: spelled incorrectly with 2 r's in census and in this index also.

Name	Kansas: County; Township; P.O. Arap. Co.: Census Div. Not Township	Age	Sex	Census V. Pg
Morgan, Larnia	Bourbon, Fort Scott P.O.(Housewife)	45	F	2:200
Morgan, Levi	Bourbon, Fort Scott P.O.	10	M	2:155
Morgan, Margarett	Lykins, Miami	50	F	8:90
Morgan, Martha	Coffey, Pottawatomie	33	F	4:4
Morgan, May	Arrapahoe, Denver	23	F	11:319
Morgan, Susannah	Bourbon, Fort Scott P.O.	22	F	2:200
Morgan, Theodocia	Bourbon, Fort Scott P.O.	4	F	2:155
Morgan, Thompson	Bourbon, Fort Scott P.O.	20	M	2:200
Morgan, W.	Arrapahoe, South Clear Creek	31	M	11:751
Morgan, William R.	Bourbon, Fort Scott P.O. (Farmer)	27	M	2:210
Morgan, William R.	Bourbon, Fort Scott P.O. (Farmer)	33	M	2:155
Morris, Anna	McGhee, Crawford Seminary P.O.	38	F	9:233
Morris, Elisa M.	Allen, Geneva P.O.	47	F	2:251
Morris, Enoch	McGhee, Crawford Sem.P.O.(Farm Labr.)	20	M	9:233
Morris, Gallant	McGhee, Crawford Sem.P.O.(Farm Labr.)	20	M	9:233
Morris, George	McGhee, Crawford Seminary P.O.(Farmer)	43	M	9:233
Morris, S. W.	Arrapahoe, Mountain City	22	M	11:458
Morris, William	Bourbon, Raysville P.O.	28	M	2:185
Morrison, H.	Douglas, Clinton (Laborer)	24	M	6:420
Morrison, Margaret	Marshall, Vermillion	35	F	3:225
Morrow, Comfort	Coffey, Avon	42	F	4:11
Morrow, John D.	McGhee, Crawford Seminary P.O.(Trader)	40	M	9:225
Morrow, Samuel	Linn, Mound City (Farmer)	35	M	7:124
Mortimer, W.	Arrapahoe, Valley of the Platte	26	M	11:863
Mortland, S.	Arrapahoe, South Clear Creek	28	M	11:738
Morton, A. I.	Arrapahoe, South Park	27	M	11:204
Mosely, W.	Arrapahoe, South Park	28	M	11:205
Mosher, E. P.	Arrapahoe, South Park	26	M	11:174
Mosier, S.	Doniphan, Center	70	F	1:247
Mosker, E. F.[1]	Arrapahoe, South Clear Creek (Miner)	37	M	11:696
Moslever, C.[1]	Arrapahoe, South Park	27	M	11:142
Muller, F.	Arrapahoe, South Clear Creek (Miner)	17	M	11:682
Munford, Mary J.	Leavenworth, Kickapoo	28	F	10:309
Munrite, E. E.	Doniphan, Center	8	M	1:269
Munrite, F. A.	Doniphan, Center	7	M	1:269
Munrite, J. R.	Doniphan, Center	3	F	1:269
Munrite, L.	Doniphan, Center	39	F	1:269
Murran, Geo.	Arrapahoe, South Clear Creek	25	M	11:704
Murdoch, A. R.	Arrapahoe, South Park	23	M	11:227
Murner, Benjamin	Arrapahoe, Denver (Teamster)	28	M	11:374
Murphy, B. F.	Doniphan, Center (Laborer)	34	M	1:251
Murphy, Ben F.	Doniphan, Center (Carpenter)	27	M	1:266
Murphy, Eli	Doniphan, Center (Teacher)	36	M	1:266
Murray, Mary A.	Shawnee, Monmouth	15	F	9:59
Murray, Wm.	Shawnee, Monmouth (Farmer)	37	M	9:59
Mury, James	Linn, Paris (Farmer)	40	M	7:141
Myers, B.	Johnson, Shawnee (Grocer)	17	M	6:25
Myers, Catharine	Atchison, Walnut	23	F	1:175
Myers, Ellen	Davis, Junction City P.O.	37	F	9:337
Myrick, A.	Doniphan, Center (Domestic)	21	F	1:269
Myrick, Elizabeth	Bourbon, Mapleton P.O.	18	F	2:138
Myrick, Fredrick D.	Bourbon, Mapleton P.O. (Farmer)	22	M	2:138
Myrick, James	Bourbon, Mapleton P.O.	12	M	2:138
Myrick, Matthew C.	Bourbon, Mapleton P.O.	16	M	2:138
Myrick, Newton G.	Bourbon, Mapleton P.O.	14	M	2:138
Myrick, Randolph	Bourbon, Mapleton P.O.	20	M	2:138
Nail, Julia	Linn, Centerville	16	F	7:95
Nail, T. J.	Franklin, Pottawatomie (Farmer)	24	M	8:241
Neal, Eliza	Bourbon, Mapleton P.O.(Housewife)	24	F	2:138

[1]Initial may not be "C"; handwriting very poor.

Arapahoe: spelled incorrectly with 2 r's in census and in this index also.

Name	Kansas: County; Township; P.O. Arap. Co.: Census Div. Not Township	Age	Sex	Census V: Pg.
Neal, H. J.	Doniphan, Highland (Farmer)	58	M	1:413
Neal, John T.	Bourbon, Barnesville P.O. (Merchant)	29	M	2:177
Neel, M. A.	Doniphan, Highland	43	F	1:414
Nelson, Elizabeth	Bourbon, Fort Scott P.O.(Housewife)	27	F	2:213
Nelson, Francis	Linn, Paris	38	F	7:140
New, C.	Johnson, Lexington	12	F	6:72
Newland, G.	Arrapahoe, Valley of the Platte	24	M	11:840
Newley, C. P.	Arrapahoe, Idahoe (Miner)	26	M	11:594
Newman, Alex	Nemaha, Rock Creek (Laborer)	60	M	3:76
Newman, L. C.	Allen, Iola P.O.	30	M	2:250
Newman, Rosanna	Allen, Iola P.O.	27	F	2:250
Nodingway, Wm.	Arrapahoe, Valley of the Platte	27		11:784
Noland, S. R.	Arrapahoe, South Clear Creek	27	M	11:715
Nomack, Lucinda	Atchison, Walnut	53	F	1:182
Norman, Jno.	Arrapahoe, South Park	39	M	11:179
Norman, Wm.	Arrapahoe, Golden City (Merchant)	35	M	11:449
Norris, Thos.	Allen, Iola P.O. (Farmer)	34	M	2:235
North, A. D.	Arrapahoe, South Park	35	M	11:128
Norton, Sophia	Anderson, Washington	53	F	7:253
Norway, W. H.	Arrapahoe, California Gulch (Miner)		M	11:310
Oakes, J. P.	Arrapahoe, South Clear Creek (Miner)	29	M	11:748
O'Dell, G.	Arrapahoe, South Clear Creek (Miner)	36	M	11:670
Odell, G. M.	Arrapahoe, South Park	28	M	11:178
Odell, Samuel	Bourbon, Barnesville P.O.(Blacksmith)	36	M	2:176
Oden, Sarah	Jackson, Jefferson	48	F	5:210
Odom, James D.	Bourbon, Fort Scott P.O. (Farmer)	32	M	2:91
Ogden, Mahala	Breckenridge, Americus	36	F	4:222
Ogden, Mahala	Brown, Locknow	36	F	3:64
Ogle, Henry	Jefferson, Oskaloosa (Farmer)	32	M	5:127
Ohlsen, E. R.	Arrapahoe, Central City (Farmer)	24	M	11:577
Oldham, Charles	Wyandotte, Wyandotte	21	M	10:42
Oldham, G. H.	Wyandotte, Wyandotte (Farmer)	44	M	10:42
Oldham, Sarah	Wyandotte, Wyandotte	42	F	10:42
Oliphint, James M.	Lykins, Stanton (Farmer)	35	M	8:8
Oliver, Francis	Marshall, Blue Rapids	40	F	3:212
Oliver, G. H.	Arrapahoe, South Clear Creek	26	M	11:715
Oliver, Lucinda	Woodson, Liberty (F. W.)	24	F	9:144
Oliver, Wm.	Woodson, Liberty (Farmer)	26	M	9:143
Olney, Martin	Arrapahoe, South Clear Creek (Miner)	45	M	11:642
Omby, Irwin	Linn, Valley (Farmer)	29	M	7:45
Omer, W. F.	Arrapahoe, South Clear Creek	25	M	11:699
Orander, Amelia	Shawnee, Soldier	18	F	9:86
Orander, Basheba	Shawnee, Soldier	14	F	9:86
Orander, John	Shawnee, Soldier (Farmer)	50	M	9:86
Orander, Margaret	Shawnee, Soldier	45	F	9:86
Orander, Marion	Shawnee, Soldier	12	M	9:86
Orander, Martha	Shawnee, Soldier	16	F	9:86
Orander, Michael	Shawnee, Soldier	10	M	9:86
Order, Wm.	Arrapahoe, South Park	39	M	11:186
Ornkite, J. H.	Arrapahoe, Valley of the Platte	33	M	11:825
Orr, S.	Franklin, Pottawatomie (Farmer)	20	M	8:238
Orr, W.	Franklin, Pottawatomie (Farmer)	22	M	8:238
Orth, W. P.	Arrapahoe, South Clear Creek	23	M	11:704
Osborn, Mary	Bourbon, Raysville P.O.(Housewife)	36	F	2:158
Osborn, Mary	Bourbon, Dayton P.O. (Housewife)	36	F	2:124
Osburn, Amanda	Woodson, Pleasant Grove(Farmer'sWife)	39	F	9:169
Osburn, James	Woodson, Pleasant Grove (Farmer)	55	M	9:170
Overley, John	Coffey, Neosho	19	M	4:72
Overley, Richard	Coffey, Neosho	13	M	4:72
Overley, Sarah	Coffey, Neosho	16	F	4:72
Owen, Alexander	Jefferson, Jefferson	32	M	5:47

Arapahoe: spelled incorrectly with 2 r's in census and in this index also.

Name	Kansas: County; Township; P.O. Arap. Co.: Census Div. Not Township	Age	Sex	Census V.: Pg
Owen, Mahala	Allen, Humboldt P.O.	49	F	2:274
Owen, Martha	Allen, Humboldt P.O.	17	F	2:274
Owens, Albert	Leavenworth, Stranger	7	M	10:477
Owens, J.	Johnson, Monticello (Farmer)	47	M	6:83
Owens, John	Leavenworth, Easton (Grocer)	28	M	10:284
Oxley, J. P.	Arrapahoe, South Park	33	M	11:180
Ozias, J.	Arrapahoe, South Clear Creek	37	M	11:738
Page, E. M.	Arrapahoe, Valley of the Platte	29		11:788
Page, G.	Arrapahoe, South Clear Creek	38	M	11:718
Pain, Elisabeth	Leavenworth, Easton	30	F	10:304
Pain, Seiedah	Anderson, Jackson	34	F	7:207
Pain, William	Anderson, Jackson (Farmer)	38	M	7:207
Palkingham, B. S.	Arrapahoe, South Park	25	M	11:179
Palmer, Edward	Doniphan, Marion	18	M	1:290
Palmer, M.	Doniphan, Marion	17	F	1:290
Palmer, M.	Doniphan, Marion	12	F	1:290
Pamplin, Lucinda	Linn, Paris	58	F	7:129
Pardon, J.[1]	Arrapahoe, South Clear Creek	22	M	11:716
Parker, Eliza J.	Bourbon, Fort Scott P.O.(Housewife)	22	F	2:194
Parker, Elizabeth	Bourbon, Fort Scott P.O.(Housewife)	52	F	2:193
Parker, James	Bourbon, Fort Scott P.O. (Farmer)	46	M	2:193
Parker, M. D.	Arrapahoe, South Park	35	M	11:128
Parker, P. M.	Arrapahoe, Denver	20	M	11:388
Parkhurst, C.	Linn, Valley (Farmer)	42	M	7:31
Parks, Eli	Arrapahoe, South Clear Creek	28	M	11:684
Parks, Elizabeth	Linn, Mound City	53	F	7:125
Parkweather, Jno.	Arrapahoe, South Park	37	M	11:223
Parsons, Elizabeth	Allen, Iola P.O.	48	F	2:235
Partner, O.	Arrapahoe, South Park	26	M	11:183
Pasley, Charles	Lykins, Marysville (Blacksmith)	42	M	8:121
Pate, Bola	Atchison, Grasshopper	17	F	1:92
Pate, John A.	Atchison, Grasshopper	15	M	1:92
Pate, Juanita	Atchison, Grasshopper	22	F	1:92
Pate, M.	Doniphan, Washington (Engineer)	50	M	1:312
Pate, Mary Jane	Atchison, Grasshopper	13	F	1:92
Pate, Mary	Atchison, Grasshopper	49	F	1:92
Pate, Wm.	Atchison, Grasshopper	19	M	1:92
Pate, Wm. M.	Atchison, Grasshopper (Farmer)	35	M	1:91
Patrich, William	Doniphan, Washington (Teamster)	35	M	1:293
Pattero, Malissa	McGhee, Brushville P.O.	40	F	9:227
Patterson, Ephraim A.	Bourbon, Fort Scott P.O. (Farmer)	31	M	2:94
Patterson, Maria	Leavenworth, Kickapoo	29	F	10:406
Patton, Eddy	Morris, Clarks Creek	28	F	4:279
Patton, Edith	Lykins, Marysville	30	F	8:131
Patton, Elora	Lykins, Marysville	3	F	8:131
Patton, Isabel	Morris, Clarks Creek	10	F	4:279
Patton, Jane	Lykins, Marysville	1	F	8:131
Patton, Martha	Lykins, Marysville	5	F	8:131
Patton, Martha	Morris, Clarks Creek	12	F	4:279
Patton, Mary	Morris, Clarks Creek	6	F	4:279
Patton, Mary J.	Lykins, Marysville	4	F	8:131
Patton, R.	Doniphan, Iowa Point	55	F	1:450
Patton, Tracy	Morris, Clarks Creek	2	F	4:279
Patton, William	Lykins, Marysville (Laborer)	35	M	8:131
Patton, Wm.	Morris, Clarks Creek (Farmer)	30	M	4:279
Patty, Sarah J.	Shawnee, Tecumseh	29	F	9:69
Paugh, L. R.[2]	Arrapahoe, Denver (Carpenter)	23	M	11:356
Paul, Esther	Anderson, Washington	42	F	7:255

[1]Perhaps it is Porden rather than Pardon; writing not clear.

[2]Could be Pangle; Census Book entry difficult to read.

Arapahoe: spelled incorrectly with 2 r's in census and in this index also.

Name	Kansas: County; Township; P.O. Arap. Co.: Census Div. Not Township	Age	Sex	Census V : Pg
Paul, John W.	Anderson, Washington (Farmer)	42	M	7:255
Payne, Colbey	Leavenworth, Easton (Farmer)	37	M	10:294
Payne, Elija Ann	Atchison, Mt. Pleasant	18	F	1:149
Payne, Henry R.	Marshall, Vermillion (Farmer)	35	M	3:230
Payne, John	McGhee, Osage Mission P.O. (Farmer)	47	M	9:240
Payne, Sarah	Breckenridge, Forest Hill	42	F	4:183
Payne, Thomas	Breckenridge, Forest Hill	20	M	4:183
Payne, Wm.	Breckenridge, Forest Hill (Farmer)	25	M	4:183
Peak, J.	Johnson, Oxford (Farmer)	33	M	6:102
Pearse, C. F.	Arrapahoe, California Gulch	29	M	11:305
Pearsell, F.	Douglas, Palmyra (Farmer)	35	M	6:297
Peason, M. A.	Douglas, Wakarusa	19	F	6:233
Peason, T.	Douglas, Wakarusa (Farmer)	54	M	6:245
Pedde, W. H.	Arrapahoe, South Clear Creek	29	M	11:662
Peels, E.	Arrapahoe, California Gulch (Miner)		M	11:310
Pellott, J. M.	Douglas, Lecompton	30	M	6:350
Pemberton, M.	Linn, Mound City	26	F	7:99
Penore, C.	Arrapahoe, South Clear Creek	22	M	11:738
Perce, A. S.	Linn, Paris	29	M	7:144
Perdue, David	Marshall, Blue Rapids (Farmer)	31	M	3:206
Perkins, G. M.	Arrapahoe, Eureka Gulch (Miner)	27	M	11:506
Perkins, G. W.	Franklin, Centropolis (Farmer)	52	M	8:215
Perry, E. C.	Arrapahoe, South Park	33	M	11:166
Perry, James [1]	Jefferson, Kaw	13		5:83
Perry, V.	Arrapahoe, South Park	38	M	11:139
Peters, O.	Arrapahoe, South Park	35	M	11:184
Peterson, N.	Arrapahoe, South Park	31	M	11:134
Pettels, Thos.	Arrapahoe, Denver (Laborer)	50	M	11:319
Phoenix, A. J.	Anderson, Monroe (Farmer)	36	M	7:216
Philips, Henry	McGhee, Crawford Seminary P.O.(Farmer)	45	M	9:233
Philips, M. M.	Arrapahoe, Leavenworth Gulch (Miner)	31	M	11:555
Phillips, Arron	Dickinson, Kansas Falls P.O.(Laborer)	23	M	4:307
Phillips, Fanny	Woodson, Belmont	36	F	9:152
Phillips, Lucinda	Woodson, Belmont	33	F	9:152
Phipps, Thos.	Arrapahoe, South Park	24	M	11:110
Phy, A.	Johnson, Lexington (Farmer)	40	M	6:78
Pickens, Amanda	Atchison, Kapioma	22	F	1:99
Pickens, J. H.	Atchison, Kapioma (Farmer)	29	M	1:99
Pickerel, James	McGhee, Medoc, Missouri P.O.(Farmer)	45	M	9:215
Pickerel, Thomas	McGhee, Brushville P.O. (Farmer)	42	M	9:217
Pickering, J. B.	Woodson, Liberty (Farmer)	41	M	9:144
Pierce, Abigal A.	Atchison, Center	22	F	1:137
Pierce, Anna	Atchison, Center	44	F	1:137
Pierce, Charles E.	Atchison, Center	3	M	1:137
Pierce, F.	Woodson, Neosho Falls (Farmer)	39	M	9:131
Pierce, Geo. R.	Atchison, Center	10	M	1:137
Pierce, Joseph J.	Atchison, Center	5	M	1:137
Pierce, Wm. E.	Atchison, Center	7	M	1:137
Pillip, L. S.	Arrapahoe, South Clear Creek	27	M	11:687
Pillsbury, Wm.	Arrapahoe, South Park	29	M	11:146
Pinkerton, Jas. H.	Arrapahoe, Golden City (Farmer)	28	M	11:586
Pinkerton, N. J.	Wabaunsee, Zeandale	27	F	5:235
Pinkhard, Elizabeth	Breckenridge, Forest Hill	35	F	4:182
Pinkney, O.	Arrapahoe, South Park	28	M	11:243
Pintard, W. C.	Arrapahoe, Valley of the Platte	24	M	11:804
Pitcher, Elizabeth	Jefferson, Jefferson	50	F	5:30

[1] Census book gives James Perry age 13, born in Tennessee in same family as
Eveline Perry age 32, born in Ill.; index cards show birthplaces reversed.

Arapahoe: spelled incorrectly with 2 r's in census and in this index also.

Name	Kansas: County; Township; P.O. Arap. Co.: Census Div. Not Township	Age	Sex	Census V. Pg
Pitcher, Wm.	Arrapahoe, South Park	30	M	11:128
Pitman, John	Marshall, Blue Rapids (Farmer)	26	M	3:200
Pittengill, Chas. C.[1]	Arrapahoe, Valley of the Platte	28	M	11:823
Pittman, S. B.	Leavenworth, Easton	28	M	10:288
Plasterer, P.	Arrapahoe, South Park	26	M	11:136
Platt, G. M.	Arrapahoe, South Park	28	M	11:214
Pliss, S.	Nemaha, Valley	20	F	3:122
Plumer, Rachel	Douglas, Marion	59	F	6:398
Plunkett, L.	Arrapahoe, South Park	46	M	11:241
Polk, C. T.	Arrapahoe, South Clear Creek	28	M	11:767
Polk, James K.	Atchison, Kapioma (Farmer)	21	M	1:100
Polk, Martha L.	Atchison, Kapioma	17	F	1:100
Polk, Wm. S.	Atchison, Kapioma	14	M	1:100
Pollard, J.	Johnson, Shawnee (Farmer)	30	M	6:87
Polleny, Catharine	Doniphan, Washington	20	F	1:296
Pollock, Elizabeth	McGhee, Brushville P.O.	23	F	9:226
Pollock, James H.	McGhee, Brushville P.O. (Farmer)	24	M	9:226
Pomeroy, Wm.	Arrapahoe, Valley of the Platte	30	M	11:800
Porter, S. B.	Johnson, Aubrey (Farmer)	38	M	6:40
Poteel, A. G.	Anderson, Washington (Farmer)	36	M	7:253
Potter, Matilda	Bourbon, Fort Scott P.O.(Housewife)	30	F	2:90
Potts, Mary Jane	Arrapahoe, Golden City	22	F	11:582
Powell, C. F.	Arrapahoe, South Park	25	M	11:123
Power, E.	Arrapahoe, South Clear Creek	56	M	11:714
Poyner, Calvin	Bourbon, Fort Scott P.O.	20	M	2:192
Poyner, James	Bourbon, Fort Scott P.O.	23	M	2:192
Poyner, John G.	Bourbon, Fort Scott P.O.	14	M	2:193
Poyner, Nancy	Bourbon, Fort Scott P.O.	17	F	2:192
Poyner, William C.	Bourbon, Fort Scott P.O. (Farmer)	43	M	2:192
Poyner, William W.	Bourbon, Fort Scott P.O.	18	M	2:192
Prather, O.	Arrapahoe, Valley of the Platte			11:778
Prather, R. M.	Atchison, Mt. Pleasant (Farmer)	47	M	1:167
Prayer, Mary	Linn, Valley	44	F	7:51
Prayer, W.	Linn, Valley (Farmer)	46	M	7:51
Presbury, S. C.	Arrapahoe, South Park	28	M	11:231
Price, Elizabeth	Anderson, Ozark	44	F	7:249
Price, S. D.	Arrapahoe, California Gulch	52	M	11:312
Price, Sarah A.	McGhee, Osage Mission P.O.	37	F	9:240
Price, Watson	Arrapahoe, South Park (Carpenter)	44	M	11:40
Prichard, A.	Doniphan, Center	38	F	1:269
Prichard, D.	Doniphan, Center (Farmer)	61	M	1:269
Prichard, Eli	Doniphan, Iowa Point (Farm Hand)	22	M	1:425
Prichard, J.	Doniphan, Iowa Point (Farmer)	45	M	1:425
Prichard, L.	Doniphan, Iowa Point (Farmer)	37	M	1:418
Prince, R.	Arrapahoe, South Park	26	M	11:176
Privit, Wm.	Doniphan, Center (Farmer)	23	M	1:258
Puett, Ann	Anderson, Monroe	4	F	7:215
Purcell, Perry	Chase, Bazaar (Farm Laborer)	21	M	4:332
Purcill, Mary	Arrapahoe, South Park	32	F	11:163
Purdy, E.	Arrapahoe, South Park	29	M	11:244
Purdy, F.	Arrapahoe, South Park	22	M	11:122
Pyde, Ann	Jefferson, Oskaloosa	48	F	5:122
Quackenbush, Jas.	Arrapahoe, South Clear Creek (Miner)	38	M	11:636
Quiett, Elsie	Madison, Hartford (Farmer)	52	F	4:235
Quiett, Esther	Atchison, Center	57	F	1:136
Quiett, Susan	Madison, Hartford	44	F	4:235
Quiett, Wm.	Jefferson, Ozawkie (Farmer)	26	M	5:105
Quigman, Geo. W.	Arrapahoe, South Park	26	M	11:187
Quinly, Elizabeth A.	Bourbon, Fort Scott P.O.(Housewife)	22	F	2:212

[1]Perhaps not Chas. C.; census entry difficult to read.

Arapahoe: spelled incorrectly with 2 r's in census and in this index also.

Name	Kansas: County; Township; P.O. Arap. Co.: Census Div. Not Township	Age	Sex	Census. V. Pg
Race, Margaret	Allen, Iola P.O.	26	F	2:264
Race, Nancy A.	Allen, Iola P.O.	30	F	2:264
Race, William	Allen, Iola P.O.	36	M	2:264
Ragan, Aramenta	Lykins, Marysville	40	F	8:126
Ragan, Dennis	Nemaha, Red Vermillion (Farmer)	27	M	3:133
Ragan, Jas.	Lykins, Marysville (Farmer)	39	M	8:126
Ragan, Keziah	Lykins, Marysville	12	F	8:127
Ragan, Mary F.	Lykins, Marysville	15	F	8:127
Ragan, William	Lykins, Marysville	10	M	8:127
Ragsdale, Emily	Doniphan, Iowa Point (Servant)		B F	1:446
Ragsdale, Kesiah	Doniphan, Iowa Point (Servant)	40	B F	1:446
Ragsdale, M. E.	Doniphan, Iowa Point	13	F	1:446
Ragsdall, S.	Arrapahoe, South Clear Creek	36	M	11:728
Rainwater, Amaida J.	Breckenridge, Americus	14	F	4:225
Rainwater, G. W.	Breckenridge, Americus (Farmer)	22	M	4:224
Rainwater, Hannah N.	Breckenridge, Americus	13	F	4:225
Rainwater, Jacob	Breckenridge, Americus	15	M	4:225
Rainwater, John R.	Breckenridge, Americus (Farmer)	28	M	4:225
Rainwater, Mary A.	Breckenridge, Americus	48	F	4:225
Rainwater, Wm.	Breckenridge, Americus (F. Laborer)	16	M	4:225
Ralston, Daniel I.	Bourbon, Turkey Creek P.O. (Farmer)	42	M	2:112
Ralston, Malinda	Bourbon, Turkey Creek P.O.(Housewife)	27	F	2:112
Ramay, Eric	Leavenworth, Ward 3	24	F	10:223
Ramey, L.	Johnson, Gardner	4	F	6:50
Ramey, M. E.	Johnson, Gardner	6	F	6:50
Ramey, W.	Johnson, Gardner (Farmer)	29	M	6:50
Ramsey, Rachel	Brown, Irving	16	F	3:9
Ramsey, Sarah	Atchison, Center	22	F	1:129
Ramsey, Thos.	Arrapahoe, South Park	28	M	11:193
Randal, S. R.	Arrapahoe, Valley of the Platte	20	M	11:805
Randall, C. M.	Arrapahoe, South Clear Creek	31	M	11:712
Randolph, Lucy	Allen, Humboldt P.O.	21	F	2:279
Randolph, N.	Johnson, Olathe	43	F	6:115
Ransom, Margaret	Wyandotte, Wyandotte	27	F	10:37
Ransom, Wm.	Wyandotte, Wyandotte (Farmer)	32	M	10:37
Ransom, W.	Johnson, Olathe (Prison: Larceny)	30	M	6:9
Rapp, Wm.	Arrapahoe, South Park	35	M	11:120
Rawson, H. V.	Arrapahoe, South Park	34	M	11:139
Ray, Azanah	Allen, Iola P.O. (Farmer)	21	M	2:248
Ray, Eliza	Bourbon, Fort Scott P.O.(Housewife)	24	F	2:152
Ray, James F.	Bourbon, Fort Scott P.O. (Farmer)	24	M	2:152
Ray, Rhoda	Linn, Scott	38	F	7:27
Ray, S.	Linn, Scott (Farmer)	41	M	7:27
Raynes, E.	Arrapahoe, Valley of the Platte	28	M	11:806
Reaves, E.	Arrapahoe, South Clear Creek (Miner)	36	M	11:712
Record, Margaret	Bourbon, Fort Scott P.O.(Housewife)	20	F	2:82
Rector, Wm.	Arrapahoe, South Park	25	M	11:241
Redcliffe, Wm.	Arrapahoe, South Park	24	M	11:191
Redfern, Polly A.	Lykins, Marysville	36	F	8:131
Reed, D. C.	Arrapahoe, Mountain City(QuartzMiller)	45	M	11:464
Reed, J.	Douglas, Marion (Farmer)	23	M	6:395
Reed, L.	Douglas, Marion (Farmer)	33	M	6:395
Reese, A. J.	Arrapahoe, Valley of the Platte	31	M	11:816
Reese, C. J.	Linn, Valley (Farmer)	36	M	7:47
Reese, E.	Douglas, Lecompton	6	F	6:358
Reese, J. N.	Arrapahoe, Arrapahoe City (Farmer)	31	M	11:588
Reeve, E. A. E.	Chase, Toledo	1	F	4:339
Reeve, Hannah	Chase, Toledo	34	F	4:339
Reeve, Mark	Chase, Toledo	3	M	4:339
Reeve, Martha	Chase, Toledo	5	F	4:339
Reeve, Roxana	Chase, Toledo	7	F	4:339

Arapahoe: spelled incorrectly with 2 r's in census and in this index also.

Name	Kansas: County; Township; P.O. Arap. Co.: Census Div. Not Township	Age	Sex	Census V.: Pg.
Reeve, Sarah	Chase, Toledo	10	F	4:339
Reeves, E. P.	Arrapahoe, South Park	26	M	11:125
Regan, Moses	Coffey, Burlington (Farmer)	70	M	4:37
Rehver, H. N.	Arrapahoe, South Clear Creek	30	M	11:706
Renfrew, M. G.	Johnson, Olathe	30	F	6:115
Renfro, James	Morris, Marion (Farmer)	34	M	4:367
Renfrow, Richard	Bourbon, Fort Scott P.O. (Farmer)	22	M	2:93
Renneeker, A.	Arrapahoe, South Park	28	M	11:185
Reno, J. A.	Doniphan, Burr Oak	36	F	1:344
Reupe, Mary S.	Leavenworth, Kickapoo	30	F	10:333
Reyerson, H. I.	Arrapahoe, South Park	29	M	11:213
Reynolds, Almira	Allen, Iola P.O.	29	F	2:249
Reynolds, Mary	Bourbon, Fort Scott P.O.(Housewife)	37	F	2:79
Reynolds, T.	Davis, Junction City P.O. (Farmer)	61	M	9:338
Reynolds, T. H.	Arrapahoe, South Park	33	M	11:213
Reynolds, Willie	Allen, Iola P.O. (Farmer)	30	M	2:249
Reynolds, William L.	Bourbon, Fort Scott P.O.	14	M	2:79
Rhia, Spinten F.	Leavenworth, Easton (Farmer)	42	M	10:296
Rhotun, Mack	Bourbon, Turkey Creek P.O.	19	M	2:113
Rhotun, Martha	Bourbon, Turkey Creek P.O.	16	F	2:113
Rice, C. R.	Johnson, Shawnee (Minister)	27	M	6:24
Rice, Dolena	Bourbon, Fort Scott P.O. (Housewife)	47	F	2:211
Rice, E.	Franklin, Peoria City P.O.	23	F	8:271
Rice, G. A.	Franklin, Peoria City P.O. (Farmer)	29	M	8:271
Rice, Henderson	Lykins, Mound (Farmer)	35	M	8:72
Rice, James M.	Lykins, Mound	11	M	8:72
Rice, Mary E.	Lykins, Mound	13	F	8:72
Rice, W.	Franklin, Peoria (Farmer)	25	M	8:271
Rich, James	Coffey, Avon (Farmer)	35	M	4:8
Richer, Elizabeth	Greenwood, Eureka	50	F	9:180
Richer, Peter	Greenwood, Eureka (Farmer)	51	M	9:180
Richie, Obediah	Jefferson, Ozawkie (Farmer)	46	M	5:105
Richmond, James M.	Allen, Humboldt P.O.(Blacksmith)	36	M	2:300
Richmond, Martha	Allen, Humboldt P.O.	40	F	2:300
Ricker, Peter	Marshall, Marysville (Farmer)	36	M	3:240
Rickner, Margaret	McGhee, Crawford Seminary P.O.	28	F	9:224
Riddle, Sarah J.	Douglas, Kanwaca	20	F	6:384
Rider, Missouri	Lykins, Richland	28	F	8:21
Rider, William E.	Lykins, Richland (Saw & Grist Miller)	35	M	8:21
Ridgeway, G. W.	Arrapahoe, South Park	39	M	11:232
Rigeons, Dorcas	Morris, Clarks Creek	3	F	4:279
Rigeons, Sarah	Morris, Clarks Creek	48	F	4:279
Riggs, K.	Franklin, Centropolis	23	F	8:216
Riley, R.	Arrapahoe, South Clear Creek (Miner)	28	M	11:625
Rinehart, James	Atchison, Kapioma (Laborer)	28	M	1:100
Rinker, Washington	Breckenridge, Emporia (Farmer)	56	M	4:190
Risley, P.	Arrapahoe, South Park	32	M	11:171
Ritz, David	Wyandotte, Wyandotte (Laborer)	20	M	10:41
Roach, Mary	Leavenworth, Kickapoo	18	F	10:344
Roach, Sarah A.	Atchison, Grasshopper	27	F	1:90
Roark, Saul	Bourbon, Fort Scott P.O. (Farmer)	35	M	2:215
Robbins, P. V. R.	Arrapahoe, South Clear Creek	29	M	11:690
Robbins, S. T.	Arrapahoe, South Park	35	M	11:177
Roberts, Joseph	Allen (Farmer)	37	M	2:234
Roberts, Josetick	Lykins, Miami (Farmer)	38	M	8:94
Roberts, Mary A.	Lykins, Miami	35	F	8:94
Roberts, Mat	Nemaha, Rock Creek (Farmer)	49	M	3:80
Roberts, S.	Doniphan, Washington	50	F	1:297
Roberts, Salina	Butler, Chelsea	44	F	4:350
Robertson, D.	Linn, Valley	48	F	7:39

Arapahoe: spelled incorrectly with 2 r's in census and in this index also.

Name	Kansas: County; Township; P.O. Arap. Co.: Census Div. Not Township	Age	Sex	Census V.:Pg.
Robertson, Ellen	Linn, Scott	27	F	7:13
Robins, Caroline	Morris, Grove	36	F	4:264
Robinson, B.	Arrapahoe, South Park	25	M	11:144
Robinson, E.	Arrapahoe, South Clear Creek	24	M	11:738
Robinson, J. M.	Leavenworth, Kickapoo (Laborer)	26	BM	10:327
Robinson, M. H.	Leavenworth, Ward 2 (Barber)	34	BM	10:175
Robison, Harriet	Bourbon, Marmaton P.O. (Housewife)	26	F	2:116
Robison, S. H.	Linn, Valley (Farmer)	30	M	7:32
Rochill, E.	Johnson, McCamish	41	F	6:60
Rochill, H.	Johnson, McCamish	9	M	6:60
Rochill, H.	Johnson, McCamish	11	M	6:60
Rochill, J.	Johnson, McCamish (Farmer)	45	M	6:60
Rockhold, Sarah R.	Leavenworth, 1st Ward	2	F	10:112
Rockhold, Sophina	Leavenworth, 1st Ward(Artfcl.Flowers)	30	F	10:112
Rockport, T.	Arrapahoe, South Park	28	M	11:204
Rodgers, Jno. W.	Jefferson, Grasshopper Falls(Farmer)	28	M	5:9
Roe, Martha	Doniphan, Burr Oak	51	F	1:356
Roger, Mary	Linn, Scott	38	F	7:23
Rogers, B. S.	Arrapahoe, South Clear Creek	32	M	11:722
Rogers, Dianna	Woodson, Belmont (F. W.)	33	F	9:151
Rogers, J.	Woodson, Belmont (Farmer)	33	M	9:151
Rogers, Thomas	Woodson, Belmont (Farmer)	24	M	9:151
Rojer, Mitilda E.	McGhee, Brushville P.O.	38	F	9:221
Rojer, William	McGhee, Brushville P.O. (Farmer)	46	M	9:221
Romins, George	Bourbon, Fort Scott P.O. (Farmer)	45	M	2:78
Romins, Martha E.	Bourbon, Fort Scott P.O.	15	F	2:78
Romins, Mary C.	Bourbon, Fort Scott P.O.	17	F	2:78
Romins, Minerva	Bourbon, Fort Scott P.O.(Housewife)	37	F	2:78
Root, Nancy	Nemaha, Valley	45	F	3:119
Roper, L. M.	Atchison, 1st Ward	31	M	1:18
Rosebury, James	Bourbon, Xenia P.O. (Farmer)	37	M	2:128
Rossett, O.	Arrapahoe, South Park	35	M	11:184
Round, L.	Arrapahoe, South Park	28	M	11:176
Rounds, C. C.	Arrapahoe, Golden City (Miner)	28	M	11:453
Routh, John	Leavenworth, Easton (Carpenter)	47	M	10:284
Rowe, P.	Arrapahoe, South Park	28	M	11:195
Rowe, Wm.	Arrapahoe, South Clear Creek (Miner)	21	M	11:655
Rowell, H. C.	Arrapahoe, South Park	28	M	11:121
Rowen, Isabella	Leavenworth, Stranger (Farmer)	66	F	10:466
Rowen, John	Leavenworth, Stranger (Farmer)	30	M	10:466
Rowen, Nathaniel	Leavenworth, Stranger(Farmer & Phys.)	22	M	10:466
Rowland, Finis E.	Lykins, Marysville (Farmer)	38	M	8:131
Rowland, Geo.	Arrapahoe, South Park	26	M	11:258
Rowland, Zerilla	Lykins, Marysville	24	F	8:131
Royas, William	Bourbon, Turkey Creek P.O.(Farmer)	30	M	2:109
Ruble, Elizabeth	Leavenworth, Delaware	32	F	10:433
Ruble, Thomas	Leavenworth, Delaware (Farmer)	39	M	10:433
Rubling, Mary	Atchison, Ward 3 (Seamstress)	20	F	1:66
Rucker, Susan	Bourbon, Rockford P.O.(Housekeeper)	38	F	2:101
Ruckle, Wm.	Arrapahoe, South Park	34	BM	11:125
Rudd, William B.	Lykins, Mound (Farmer)	25	M	8:71
Rudd, Wyley A.	Lykins, Mound	23	M	8:71
Ruffian, Ellender	McGhee, Crawford Seminary P.O.	33	F	9:224
Ruffian, James H.	McGhee, Crawford Seminary P.O.	6	M	9:224
Ruffian, Malsena D.	McGhee, Crawford Seminary P.O.	10	F	9:224
Ruffian, Thomas W.	McGhee, Crawford Seminary P.O.(Farmer)	32	M	9:224
Ruffian, William D.	McGhee, Crawford Seminary P.O.	8	M	9:224
Runnels, E. J.	Johnson, Shawnee	14	F	6:87
Runnels, S.	Johnson, Shawnee	50	F	6:87
Runnels, S.	Johnson, Shawnee (Farmer)	54	M	6:87
Runnels, W. D.	Johnson, Shawnee	13	M	6:87

Arapahoe: spelled incorrectly with 2 r's in census and in this index also.

Name	Kansas: County; Township; P.O. Arap. Co.: Census Div. Not Township	Age	Sex	Census V. : Pg.
Runsey, G. B.	Arrapahoe, South Clear Creek	39	M	11:728
Runyon, P.	Arrapahoe, South Park	43	M	11:170
Rupel, Temperance	Leavenworth, Kickapoo	49	F	10:333
Rupell, Mary E.	Leavenworth, Alexandria	24	F	10:447
Ruppelyea, J.	Doniphan, Marion (Farmer)	60	M	1:287
Russell, Halden	Arrapahoe, South Park	28	M	11:127
Russell, N. P.	Arrapahoe, Val.of the Plte (Freighter)	36	M	11:843
Russell, Sam'l.	Arrapahoe, South Clear Creek	28	M	11:734
Rust, James	McGhee, Crawford Seminary P.O.	13	M	9:220
Rust, John	McGhee, Crawford Sem.P.O.(Farm Labr.)	15	M	9:220
Rust, Josphine	McGhee, Crawford Seminary P.O.	8	F	9:220
Rust, Margaret A.	McGhee, Crawford Seminary P.O.	6	F	9:220
Rust, Marion	McGhee, Crawford Seminary P.O.	10	M	9:220
Rust, Mary	Arrapahoe, Denver (Seamstress)	24	F	11:422
Rust, Mary	McGhee, Crawford Seminary P.O.	38	F	9:220
Rust, Vinson G.	McGhee, Crawford Seminary P.O.(Farmer)	42	M	9:220
Rutledge, G.	Arrapahoe, Valley of the Platte	28	M	11:793
Rutledge, John	Atchison, Mt. Pleasant (Farmer)	47	M	1:149
Rutledge, J.	Linn, Valley	33	M	7:31
Rutlidge, John	Allen, Iola P.O. (Farmer)	44	M	2:234
Rutlidge, Mary	Allen, Iola P.O.	48	F	2:235
Rutter, H. C.	Arrapahoe, South Park	28	M	11:199
Ryan, J.	Doniphan, Wolf River (Farmer)	40	M	1:408
Rye, Jno.	Arrapahoe, Valley of the Plte(Mechnc)	30	M	11:858
Ryhwm, B.	Doniphan, Washington (Carpenter)	43	M	1:320
Sackett, G. W.	Arrapahoe, South Clear Creek	32	M	11:748
Sage, Susan	Lykins, Sugar Creek	24	F	8:104
Sakely, Camsada	Linn, Centerville	18	F	7:90
Sakely, James	Linn, Centerville (Farmer)	16	M	7:90
Sakely, Thomas	Linn, Centerville (Farmer)	45	M	7:90
Sales, C.	Arrapahoe, South Clear Creek (Miner)	23	M	11:727
Saling, Susan	Lykins, Osawatomie	30	F	8:56
Salisman, Elizabeth	Dorn, Osage Catholic Mission P.O.	41	F	2:353
Sallers, F.	Doniphan, Burr Oak	32	M	1:347
Sallers, J.	Doniphan, Burr Oak (Farmer)	30	M	1:347
Sallers, M.	Doniphan, Burr Oak	65	F	1:347
Sallers, M. L.	Doniphan, Burr Oak (Farmer)	36	M	1:347
Sallers, S.[1]	Doniphan, Burr Oak (Farmer)	45	M	1:347
Sambeth, Henry	Linn, Valley (Carpenter	46	M	7:53
Sambeth, John	Linn, Valley	14	M	7:53
Sambeth, Julia	Linn, Valley	11	F	7:53
Samberth, R.	Linn, Scott (Farmer)	34	M	7:22
Sameburner, P. C.	Arrapahoe, Denver (Recorder)	54	M	11:408
Sampless, John	Jefferson, Kentucky (Farmer)	50	M	5:75
Sampless, Ruth	Jefferson, Kentucky (Weaver)	38	F	5:75
Sampson, A.	Arrapahoe, South Park	28	M	11:134
Samuels, Wm.	Arrapahoe, South Park	33	M	11:185
Sanderlin, E. I.	Arrapahoe, Denver (Barber)	29	BM	11:344
Sanders, Mary	Jefferson, Kentucky	50	F	5:70
Sandlin, Giles	Anderson, Jackson (Farmer)	25	M	7:207
Sanger, O.	Arrapahoe, South Park	35	M	11:226
Sawnigan, P. E.	Arrapahoe, South Park	29	M	11:201
Sayton, A. J.	Arrapahoe, South Park	29	M	11:240
Scagg, Nancy	Bourbon, Fort Scott P.O.(Housewife)	44	F	2:81
Scott, C.	Johnson, Shawnee	30	F	6:87
Scott, Eleaner	Jefferson, Oskaloosa(Spinner&Weaver)	48	F	5:127
Scott, Julian	Linn, Scott (Farmer)	27	M	7:12
Scott, Samuel	Linn, Scott (Farmer)	22	M	7:10

[1]Looks like Saberts.

Arapahoe: spelled incorrectly with 2 r's in census and in this index also.

Name	Kansas: County; Township; P.O. Arap. Co.: Census Div. Not Township	Age	Sex	Census V. Pg
Scott, Sarah	Clay, Junction City P.O.	32	F	9:269
Scott, Thomas	Linn, Scott (Farmer)	25	M	7:12
Scraity, Udolph[1]	Arrapahoe, Denver (Miner)	36	M	11:422
Scrimp, E.	Franklin, Centropolis	29	F	8:208
Scrivener, Eliza	Linn, Potosi	32	F	7:76
Scrivener, J.	Linn, Potosi (Farmer)	53	M	7:76
Scully, Levi	Allen, Humboldt P.O.	21	M	2:278
Seals, J.	Johnson, Shawnee (Farmer)	34	M	6:26
Seals, S. M.	Johnson, Shawnee	23	F	6:26
Seits, John	Lykins, Sugar Creek (Farmer)	40	M	8:101
Seits, Lodema	Lykins, Sugar Creek	11	F	8:101
Seits, Martha T.	Lykins, Sugar Creek	10	F	8:101
Seits, Thomas F.	Lykins, Sugar Creek	14	M	8:101
Sellers, Andrew	Arrapahoe, Leavenworth Gulch(Carpntr.)	32	M	11:554
Semore, Cha.	Linn, Valley (Farmer)	33	M	7:47
Semore, Sarah	Linn, Valley	21	F	7:47
Semple, H. D.	Arrapahoe, South Park	28	M	11:188
Seribner, Mary A.	Arrapahoe, South Park	29	F	11:140
Sevest, Mary A.	McGhee, Medoc, Missouri P.O.	28	F	9:212
Sevier, John	Brown, Walnut Creek (Farmer)	59	M	3:32
Sevier, Mary	Linn, Scott	26	F	7:25
Sevier, Wm.	Linn, Scott	1	M	7:25
Shackleford, W.	Arrapahoe, Valley of the Platte	24	M	11:817
Shankel, Phebe	Bourbon, Fort Scott P.O.(Housewife)	37	F	2:91
Shannon, Wm.	Arrapahoe, South Clear Creek (Miner)	29	M	11:734
Shards, B. T.[2]	Arrapahoe, Valley of the Platte	30	M	11:810
Sharp, A.	Doniphan, Center (Farmer)	43	M	1:246
Sharp, Abegal	Chase, Bazaar	13	F	4:332
Sharp, Anderson	Morris, Neosho (Farmer)	51	M	4:277
Sharp, Andrew	Chase, Bazaar (Farm Laborer)	18	M	4:332
Sharp, Calvin	Chase, Bazaar	16	M	4:332
Sharp, Caperton	Chase, Bazaar	7	M	4:332
Sharp, Elezabeth	Morris, Neosho	47	F	4:277
Sharp, Gordon	Chase, Bazaar (Farm Laborer)	22	M	4:332
Sharp, J.	Doniphan, Washington (Merchant)	33	M	1:302
Sharp, James	Morris, Neosho (Farmer)	28	M	4:277
Sharp, James	Doniphan, Center	23	M	1:246
Sharp, John	Morris, Marion (Farmer)	30	M	4:367
Sharp, John	Chase, Bazaar	23	M	4:332
Sharp, John	Chase, Bazaar (Farming)	48	M	4:332
Sharp, John	Morris, Neosho (Farmer)	26	M	4:277
Sharp, Lyda	Chase, Bazaar	14	F	4:332
Sharp, M.	Doniphan, Center	43	F	1:246
Sharp, Moranda	Chase, Bazaar	11	F	4:332
Sharp, Nancy	Chase, Bazaar	45	F	4:332
Sharp, Nancy	Chase, Bazaar	6	F	4:332
Sharp, Polly	Chase, Bazaar	19	F	4:332
Sharp, R.	Chase, Bazaar	9	F	4:332
Sharp, S. J.	Doniphan, Center	18	F	1:246
Sharp, W.	Leavenworth, Kickapoo	36	M	10:406
Sharper, John	Arrapahoe, South Park	42	M	11:9
Shaw, Nancy E.	Allen, Iola P.O.	15	F	2:257
Shaw, R.	Arrapahoe, South Park	28	M	11:231
Shaw, S.	Douglas, Kanwaca	40	F	6:391
Shaw, Thomas	Douglas, Kanwaca	14	M	6:391
Shaw, Wm.	Douglas, Kanwaca	12	M	6:391
Shaw, William	Allen, Iola P.O.(Farm Laborer)	16	M	2:257
Sheep, Campbell	Doniphan, Iowa Point	4	M	1:455

[1]Perhaps Seraity, W. Dolph; very poor handwriting.
[2]Perhaps should be Shanks rather than Shards.
  Arapahoe: spelled incorrectly with 2 r's in census and in this index also.

Name	Kansas: County; Township; P.O. Arap. Co.: Census Div. Not Township	Age	Sex	Census V. Pg.
Sheep, H. H.	Doniphan, Iowa Point (Farmer)	24	M	1:455
Sheep, R.	Doniphan, Iowa Point	26	F	1:455
Sheffield, Fanny[1]	Doniphan, Columbus City		F	1:360
Shelton, A.	Woodson, Eureka (Farmer)	35	M	9:181
Shelton, John	Woodson, Eureka	12	M	9:181
Shelton, S.	Doniphan, Washington (Farmer)	30?	M	1:337
Shepherd, J.	Arrapahoe, South Park	39	M	11:63
Shepherd, J.	Franklin, Ottawa (Farmer)	48	M	8:260
Shepherd, S.	Douglas, Lecompton	22	F	6:356
Shepley, Joana	Lykins, Miami (Farmer)	54	F	8:93
Sherbume, G.	Arrapahoe, South Park	28	M	11:105
Shi, Anna	McGhee, Osage Mission P.O.(Servant)	17	F	9:238
Shi, Prisecilla	McGhee, Osage Mission P.O.	38	F	9:238
Shields, Jane	Anderson, Reeder	46	F	7:259
Shipley, Amand M.	Lykins, Miami	16	F	8:87
Shipley, James	Lykins, Miami (Laborer)	23	M	8:87
Shipley, Jno. F.	Lykins, Miami (Laborer)	27	M	8:87
Shipley, Raleigh	Lykins, Miami	24	M	8:87
Shipley, Thomas	Lykins, Miami (Farmer)	53	M	8:87
Shiply, Sarah	Butler, Chelsea	41	F	4:348
Shipman, Louisa	Bourbon, Raysville P.O.(Housewife)	30	F	2:168
Shivers, Sarah[2]	McGhee, Medoc, Mo. P.O.	30	F	9:214
Shoberd, B. R.[2]	Douglas, Marion (Farmer)	34	M	6:396
Shoberd, C.	Douglas, Marion (Farmer)	65	M	6:396
Shoberd, Elezabeth	Douglas, Marion	4	F	6:396
Shoberd, H.	Douglas, Marion	25	F	6:396
Shoberd, J.	Douglas, Marion (Farmer)	28	F	6:396
Shoberd, Jo.	Douglas, Marion	20	F	6:396
Shoberd, Mary	Douglas, Marion	21	F	6:396
Shoberd, Mary	Douglas, Marion	16	F	6:396
Shoberd, Mary	Douglas, Marion	55	F	6:396
Shoberd, S.	Douglas, Marion	8	F	6:396
Shoberd, Susanna	Douglas, Marion	6	F	6:396
Shoberd, Susanna	Douglas, Marion	24	F	6:396
Shores, C.[3]	Franklin, Centropolis	32		8:219
Shrewsbury, Georgiana	Atchison, 1st Ward	25	F	1:5
Shrink, ...	McGhee, Fort Scott P.O.	50	F	9:242A
Silvers, M. E.	Arrapahoe, South Park	37	M	11:179
Simmerivelle, Susan	Shawnee, Auburn	27	F	9:41
Simmons, Benjamin W.	McGhee, Osage Mission P.O. (Farmer)	35	M	9:235
Simmons, Joseph	McGhee, Osage Mission P.O. (Farmer)	41	M	9:239
Simmons, Tabitha A.	McGhee, Osage Mission P.O.	33	F	9:239
Simpson, Geo. W.	Arrapahoe, California Gulch(HotelKpr)	33	M	11:312
Simpson, L. D.	Arrapahoe, Leavenworth Gulch	9	M	11:557
Simpson, W. C.	Arrapahoe, Central City (Hotel)	39	M	11:576
Sims, John	Bourbon, Fort Scott P.O.	14	M	2:194
Sipes, Thos. F.	Arrapahoe, South Park	27	M	11:252
Skeggs, G. W.	Arrapahoe, Valley of the Platte	26	M	11:841
Skeen, William	Bourbon, Fort Scott P.O. (Farmer)	30	M	2:80
Sligall, William	McGhee, Crawford Sem.P.O.(Farm Labr.)	23	M	9:228
Slturdwood, D.	Jefferson, Kentucky (Farmer)	46	M	5:72
Small, Chas. P.	Arrapahoe, Valley of the Platte	29	M	11:861
Smith, A.	Arrapahoe, Lake Gulch (Quartz Miner)	29	M	11:483
Smith, Abran	Arrapahoe, Denver (Miner)	20	M	11:408

[1]Age is recorded on index card as 46?; figures are not clear in census entry; may be 16.

[2]May not be B. R.; initials difficult to read.

[3]Original looks more like Shires than Shores.

Arapahoe: spelled incorrectly with 2 r's in census and in this index also.

Name	Kansas: County; Township; P.O. Arap. Co.: Census Div. Not Township	Age	Sex	Census V. : Pg.
Smith, Anna	Leavenworth, 1st Ward	14	F	10:103
Smith, Anna	Douglas, Willow Springs	46	F	6:329
Smith, Arsena	Bourbon, Xenia P.O. (Housewife)	31	F	2:128
Smith, Benj. R.	Allen, Geneva P.O. (Farmer)	36	M	2:246
Smith, C. N.	Arrapahoe, Denver (Miner)	26	M	11:412
Smith, Charles	Bourbon, Fort Scott P.O. (Farmer)	33	M	2:183
Smith, Clark	Arrapahoe, Denver (Miner)	24	M	11:412
Smith, Daniel	Douglas, Willow Springs (Farmer)	58	M	6:329
Smith, David	Arrapahoe, Denver (Miner)	22	M	11:408
Smith, E. C.	Coffey, Ottumwa	32	F	4:53
Smith, E. R.	Arrapahoe, Valley of the Platte	28	M	11:863
Smith, E. W.	Doniphan, Wolf River (Farmer)	74	M	1:403
Smith, Eliza J.	Bourbon, Marmaton P.O.	6	F	2:105
Smith, Elizabeth	Leavenworth, Delaware	34	F	10:434
Smith, Enoch	Arrapahoe, Denver (Miner)	50	M	11:408
Smith, Frances M.	Bourbon, Mapleton P.O. (Farmer)	31	M	2:132
Smith, Isaac	Jefferson, Oskaloosa (Blacksmith)	42	M	5:118
Smith, J.	Arrapahoe, Nevada Gulch	6	M	11:531
Smith, J. S.	Doniphan, Wayne (Farmer)	47	M	1:367
Smith, J. W.	Doniphan, Iowa Point (M. Carpenter)	30	M	1:447
Smith, Jas.	Linn, Paris (Farmer)	67	M	7:132
Smith, James P.	Bourbon, Rockford P.O.	9	M	2:104
Smith, Jas. R.	Lykins, Osawatomie (Brick Maker)	35	M	8:57
Smith, Jemima	Marshall, Blue Rapids	37	F	3:212
Smith, Jennie	Arrapahoe, Denver	23	F	11:412
Smith, Jno.	Arrapahoe, Denver (Laborer)	24	M	11:408
Smith, John	Anderson, Washington (Farmer)	25	M	7:256
Smith, Lizzie	Arrapahoe, Denver	45	F	11:408
Smith, M.	Doniphan, Burr Oak	26	F	1:347
Smith, M.	Johnson, DeSota	34	F	6:20
Smith, Martha	Bourbon, Dayton P.O.	66	F	2:147
Smith, Nelson	Jefferson, Kentucky (Farmer)	33	M	5:69
Smith, Pleasant	Bourbon, Fort Scott P.O. (Farmer)	36	M	2:78
Smith, S. J.	Franklin, Centropolis	18	F	8:216
Smith, Sarah	Bourbon, Rockford P.O. (Housewife)	33	F	2:104
Smith, T.	Arrapahoe, South Park	34	M	11:171
Smith, Thomas	Marshall, Blue Rapids (Farmer)	40	M	3:212
Smith, Thomas	Bourbon, Rockford P.O.	32	M	2:104
Smith, W. F.	Franklin, Centropolis	7/12	M	8:216
Smith, Wight	Arrapahoe, Denver (Miner)	10	M	11:408
Smith, Wm.	Douglas, Willow Springs (Farmer)	24	M	6:328
Smith, Wm.	Douglas, Willow Springs (Farmer)	26	M	6:312
Smith, William H.	Bourbon, Marmaton P.O.	7	M	2:105
Smith, Wm. M.	Atchison, Center (Farmer)	26	M	1:135
Smith, Wm. O.	Lykins, Wea (Carpenter)	23	M	8:117
Smoly, S.	Franklin, Peoria	35	F	8:270
Smothers, P.	Greenwood, Eureka (Farmer)	40	M	9:180
Smothers, Polly	Greenwood, Eureka	55	F	9:180
Smyth, A. B.	Arrapahoe, Golden City (Miner)	31	M	11:446
Smyth, J. R.	Arrapahoe, South Park	26	M	11:2
Snivet, Thos.	Arrapahoe, Valley of the Platte	26	M	11:806
Snodgrass, Sarah	McGhee, Fort Scott P.O.	53	F	9:206
Snody, Margaret C.	Leavenworth, Easton	24	F	10:298
Snody, Thomas A.	Leavenworth, Easton (Farmer)	34	M	10:298
Sombeth, Hardy M.	Linn, Scott (Farmer)	18	M	7:22
Sombeth, James	Linn, Scott (Farmer)	20	M	7:22
Sombeth, Louisa	Linn, Scott	16	F	7:22
Sombeth, Thomas	Linn, Scott (Farmer)	22	M	7:22
Sombeth, W.	Linn, Scott (Carpenter)	56	M	7:22
Soule, G.	Arrapahoe, South Park	38	M	11:252
Sournsberry, W.	Arrapahoe, South Clear Creek	23	M	11:697

Arapahoe: spelled incorrectly with 2 r's in census and in this index also.

Name	Kansas: County; Township; P.O. Arap. Co.: Census Div. Not Township	Age	Sex	Census V. Pg.
South, Caroline	Anderson, Walker	20	F	7:239
South, R. B.	Arrapahoe, South Park	57	M	11:2
South, Sarah	Anderson, Walker	30	F	7:239
Sparkman, C.	Linn, Scott (Farmer)	32	M	7:27
Sparkman, Elizabeth	Linn, Paris	36	F	7:129
Sparkman, Margaret	Linn, Scott	24	F	7:27
Sparkman, Temple	Linn, Paris (Farmer)	21	M	7:129
Sparks, Anne	Leavenworth, Alexandria	20	F	10:445
Spears, Amanda	Leavenworth, Delaware	12	F	10:425
Spears, Amanda	Leavenworth, Delaware	51	F	10:425
Spears, Andrew J.	Leavenworth, Delaware	16	M	10:425
Spears, B.	Arrapahoe, Mountain City (Miner)	34	M	11:464
Spears, Burrell	Leavenworth, Delaware	24	M	10:425
Spears, James	Leavenworth, Delaware (Farmer)	28	M	10:425
Spears, Sarah E.	Leavenworth, Delaware	18	F	10:425
Spears, Wm.	Leavenworth, Delaware (Farm Hand)	26	M	10:425
Speass, J.	Doniphan, Burr Oak (Farmer)	27	M	1:343
Speatley, J. N.	Leavenworth, Ward 2 (Clerk)	22	M	10:145
Speck, E.	Arrapahoe, South Clear Creek	29	M	11:696
Spiles, L. W.	Arrapahoe, Missouri City (Miner)	35	M	11:524
Spivey, Temple	Chase, Diamond Creek (Farming)	26	M	4:326
Sploon, J.	Linn, Valley (Farmer)	47	M	7:52
Spotts, Wm.	Arrapahoe, South Park	30	M	11:109
Spowl, F.	Doniphan, Wayne (Farmer)	30	M	1:392
Sprague, S.	Franklin, Ottawa	13	F	8:259
Springer, Letta	Doniphan, Wolf River	27	F	1:409
Springer, Mary E.	Anderson, Town of Garnett	45	F	7:223
Springer, Sarah	Coffey, Pottawatomie	38	F	4:3
Sprolling, O.	Douglas, Clinton (Farmer)	34	M	6:411
Spunk, J.	Arrapahoe, South Park (Miner)	45	M	11:5
Stacey, E. F.	Arrapahoe, South Park	21	M	11:208
Stamly, M.	Osage, Ridgeway	36	F	8:362
Stanfield, David	Allen, Humboldt P.O. (Merchant)	43	M	2:279
Stanfield, Elizabeth	Coffey, Burlington	56	F	4:34
Stanfield, William	Coffey, Burlington (Merchant)	56	M	4:34
Stanfield, William E.	Coffey, Pottawatomie (Farmer)	28	M	4:4
Stanley, Clotilda	Woodson, Eureka (F. W.)	46	F	9:174
Stanley, H.	Nemaha, Granada (Farmer)	33	M	3:114
Stanbury, Chas. W.	Lykins, Paola (Shoemaker)	32	M	8:33
Stansbury, Mary D.	Lykins, Paola	41	F	8:33
Stanton, Ada	Douglas, Lecompton	10	F	6:371
Stanton, H.	Douglas, Lecompton	20	F	6:371
Stanton, L.	Douglas, Lecompton	13	M	6:371
Starnes, Charles	Leavenworth, Delaware (Farmer)	47	M	10:431
Starnes, G. W.	Leavenworth, Delaware (Farmer)	32	M	10:432
Stary, J. N.[1]	Arrapahoe, Leavenworth Gulch (Miner)	23	M	11:557
Stather, W.	Arrapahoe, Valley of the Platte	25	M	11:812
Stauder, J.	Arrapahoe, South Park	47	M	11:106
Staunchford, Wm.	Jefferson, Oskaloosa (Mason)	39	M	5:119
Staunton, J.	Arrapahoe, South Park (Miner)	38	M	11:25
Stearnes, James	Brown, Walnut Creek (Farmer)	61	M	3:18
Stedman, E.	Arrapahoe, South Park	22	M	11:184
Stedman, M.	Arrapahoe, South Park	32	M	11:217
Steele, H.	Arrapahoe, South Park	28	M	11:208
Stephens, B. F.	Leavenworth, Easton (Carpenter)	20	M	10:292
Stephens, William	Bourbon, Marmaton P.O. (Farmer)	35	M	2:102
Stepp, Nance	Bourbon, Fort Scott P.O. (Housewife)	39	F	2:220
Steth, Jordon	Bourbon, Mapleton P.O. (Farmer)	26	M	2:134

Omission: Smyth, Jno.; Arrapahoe, Golden City (Miner) 30 M, 11:446.

[1]Original looks more like Starr than Stary.

Arapahoe: spelled incorrectly with 2 r's in census and in this index also.

Name	Kansas: County; Township; P.O. Arap. Co.: Census Div. Not Township	Age	Sex	Census V. Pg.
Steth, Lucetta	Bourbon, Mapleton P.O.	7	F	2:134
Steth, Sarah	Bourbon, Mapleton P.O.(Housewife)	26	F	2:134
Stevenson, Esther	Anderson, Washington	51	F	7:256
Stevenson, S. A.	Arrapahoe, South Clear Creek (Miner)	34	M	11:633
Stevenson, T.	Arrapahoe, Russell Gulch(Carpenter)	20	M	11:544
Stewart, Joseph	Jefferson, Jefferson (Laborer)	22	M	5:28
Stewart, Sarah	Bourbon, Fort Scott P.O.(Housewife)	55	F	2:153
Stewart, William	Bourbon, Mapleton P.O. (Farmer)	30	M	2:142
Stickney, Jas.	Arrapahoe, South Park	34	M	11:247
Stile, J. W.	Franklin, Centropolis (Editor)	24	M	8:205
Stile, Ma	Franklin, Centropolis	22	F	8:205
Stiles, Charles	McGhee, Brushville P.O. (Farmer)	25	M	9:230
Still, A. T.	Douglas, Centropolis (Physician)	35	M	6:265
Still, John M.	Douglas, Palmyra (Farmer)	24	M	6:281
Stilts, Irene	Leavenworth, Kickapoo	36	F	10:331
Stinson, Amanda	Linn, Paris	44	F	7:158
Stock, J.	Arrapahoe, South Park	36	M	11:250
Stock, W.	Arrapahoe, Valley of the Platte	32		11:788
Stock, Wm. M.	Arrapahoe, South Park	26	M	11:221
Stoker, Elias	Lykins, Sugar Creek (Farmer)	34	M	8:97
Stokes, Carolina	Jackson, Franklin	40	F	5:182
Stokes, Thos. H.	Jackson, Franklin (Farmer)	50	M	5:181
Stokes, William	Jackson, Franklin (Farmer)	28	M	5:182
Stone, Andrew	Arrapahoe, South Park	33	M	11:92
Stone, Matilda	Bourbon, Raysville P.O.	39	M	2:168
Stone, Polly	Brown, Claytonville	30	F	3:53
Stone, Thomas	Atchison, Lancaster (Farmer)	44	M	1:112
Stonington, F.	Arrapahoe, South Park	35	M	11:236
Storm, J.	Arrapahoe, Mountain City (Lumberman)	62	M	11:461
Storrs, Wm. M.	Arrapahoe, South Park	26	M	11:224
Story, H. G.	Arrapahoe, South Park	33	M	11:259
Stout, M. J.	Doniphan, Iowa Point	34	F	1:446
Stover, T.	Arrapahoe, South Clear Creek	29	M	11:720
Stout, Maurenis	Linn, Scott	39	F	7:8
Straight, Hester	Leavenworth, Kickapoo	34	F	10:323
Strang, H.	Arrapahoe, South Park	26	M	11:219
Stratton, J.	Arrapahoe, South Clear Creek	30	M	11:697
Strayler, Eli	Arrapahoe, South Park	17	M	11:3
Stringfellow, Harry F.	Atchison, Ward 2	2	M	1:39
Strong, Mary	Arrapahoe, South Park (Hotel)	38	F	11:1
Stroud, Catharine	Coffey, Leroy	12	F	4:21
Stroud, Mary J.	Coffey, Leroy	14	F	4:21
Stroud, Peter	Coffey, Leroy (Farmer)	18	M	4:21
Stroud, Robert F.	Coffey, Leroy	9	M	4:21
Stroud, Sarah	Coffey, Leroy	15	F	4:21
Stuart, Clara A.	Bourbon, Dayton P.O. (Housewife)	24	F	2:123
Stubbfield, Wesley	Coffey, Pottawatomie (Farmer)	48	M	4:1
Stublefield, Nancy	Anderson, Ozark	29	F	7:249
Stublefield, W. P.	Anderson, Ozark (Merchant)	32	M	7:249
Studer, Doet	Arrapahoe, South Park	31	M	11:248
Stukesberry, Alpha	Jefferson, Jefferson	11	F	5:42
Stukesberry, Eda	Jefferson, Jefferson	59	F	5:42
Stukesberry, George	Jefferson, Jefferson (Farmer)	28	M	5:42
Stukesberry, Jane	Jefferson, Jefferson	24	F	5:29
Stukesberry, Melinda	Jefferson, Jefferson	19	F	5:42
Stukesberry, Nancy	Jefferson, Jefferson	13	F	5:42
Stukesberry, Volina	Jefferson, Jefferson	24	F	5:42
Sturdevant, Thos.	Arrapahoe, Valley of the Platte	21	M	11:816
Stutton, J.	Doniphan, Center (Farmer)	35	M	1:269
Stutton, M. M.	Doniphan, Center	12	F	1:269
Stutton, R. A.	Doniphan, Center	34	F	1:269

Arapahoe: spelled incorrectly with 2 r's in census and in this index also.

Name	Kansas: County; Township; P.O. Arap. Co.: Census Div. Not Township	Age	Sex	Census V. Pg.
Stutton, R. M.	Doniphan, Center	4	F	1:269
Stultz, Joseph	Atchison, Walnut (Carpt.)	29	M	1:192
Sulivan, E.	Johnson, Gardner	11	F	6:52
Sulliger, W. H.	Arrapahoe, South Clear Creek	38	M	11:721
Sumpner, E. J.	Arrapahoe, South Clear Creek	36	M	11:722
Sumpter, Thos. S.	Atchison, Mt. Pleasant (Farmer)	28	M	1:147
Sunett, James H.	Leavenworth, Stranger (Farmer)	40	M	10:464
Surrette, Elisha	Leavenworth, Kickapoo (Farmer)	37	M	10:405
Sutton, Harriet A.	Anderson, Walker	22	F	7:236
Sutton, M. S.	Arrapahoe, South Park	34	M	11:255
Sutton, Nancy	Anderson, Walker	34	F	7:236
Swagerty, Andrew	Linn, Mound City (Farmer)	40	M	7:116
Swagerty, Mary	Linn, Mound City	41	F	7:116
Swagerty, Rachel	Linn, Mound City	43	F	7:117
Swan, W. C.	Arrapahoe, Valley of the Platte	31	M	11:808
Swatzel, D. or I. F.	Wyandotte, Wyandotte (Farmer)	27	M	10:41
Swatzel, E. V.[1]	Wyandotte, Wyandotte (Laborer)	28	M	10:41
Swift, Jno.	Arrapahoe, South Park	35	M	11:139
Tacket, Betsey	Douglas, Clinton	24	F	6:412
Tacket, Wm.	Douglas, Clinton (Laborer)	30	M	6:412
Talburson, Jno.	Arrapahoe, South Park	34	M	
Tarry, B.	Douglas, Wakarusa (Engineer)	37	M	6:249
Tate, Gushom[2]	Butler, Chelsea (Farmer)	29	M	4:348
Tayler, Cincinatti	Allen, Iola P.O.	37	F	2:273
Taylor, J. A.	Franklin, Pottawatomie (Farmer)	28	M	8:239
Taylor, J. M.	Doniphan, Washington (Merchant)	25	M	1:302
Taylor, James F.	Lykins, Osawatomie (Farmer)	33	M	8:55
Taylor, Jane	Linn, Scott	36	F	7:12
Taylor, Jesse B.	Jefferson, Jefferson (Farmer)	30	M	5:26
Taylor, Levi	Morris, Neosho (Farmer)	34	M	4:278
Taylor, M. T.	Franklin, Pottawatomie	30	F	8:239
Taylor, Rosa[3]	McGhee, Medoc, Mo. P.O.	42	F	9:215
Taylor, Tempy	Jefferson, Jefferson	30	F	5:26
Tedford, A. H.	Franklin, Pottawatomie (Farmer)	26	M	8:238
Tedford, M. M.	Franklin, Pottawatomie	74	F	8:238
Teneyck, A.	Arrapahoe, South Park	42	M	11:110
Tenison, Elizabeth J.	Bourbon, Marmaton P.O. (Housewife)	21	F	2:106
Tenison, John W.	Bourbon, Turkey Creek P.O. (Farmer)	33	M	2:107
Tenison, Sarah	Bourbon, Marmaton P.O. (Housewife)	35	F	2:106
Tenison, Raidiford	Bourbon, Marmaton P.O.(Preacher M.E.)	55	M	2:106
Tenny, J. B.	Arrapahoe, Denver (Recorder)	46	M	11:402
Terrill, Minerva	Douglas, Wakarusa	27	F	6:255
Terry, C.	Arrapahoe, Valley of the Platte			11:778
Terry, John B.	Atchison, Mt. Pleasant (Farmer)	45	M	1:167
Theobold, T. F.	Arrapahoe, Valley of the Platte	30	M	11:811
Thomas, C.	Johnson, Shawnee (Farmer)	38	M	6:100
Thomas, Catherine	Jefferson, Oskaloosa	36	F	5:126
Thomas, E.	Nemaha, Home	45	F	3:130
Thomas, J. A.	Arrapahoe, South Park	39	M	11:202
Thomas, W. T.	Arrapahoe, South Park	38	M	11:102
Thomas, Wm.	Arrapahoe, South Park	23	M	11:209
Thomes, T. P.	Arrapahoe, South Park	40	M	11:2
Thompson, Elizabeth	Woodson, Pleasant Grove	45	F	9:169
Thompson, H. A.	Doniphan, Center	22	F	1:246
Thompson, L.	Doniphan, Center	30	F	1:246
Thompson, N.	Arrapahoe, South Park	35	M	11:144

[1] Could be E. W. or E. N. rather than E. V.
[2] Original plainly Gershom.
[3] Looks more like Roller.

Arapahoe: spelled incorrectly with 2 r's in census and in this index also.

Name	Kansas: County; Township; P.O. Arap. Co.: Census Div. Not Township	Age	Sex	Census V. Pg
Thompson, Nancy	Lykins, Marysville	40	F	8:130
Thompson, Sam'l M.	Lykins, Marysville (Carpenter)	59	M	8:130
Thomson, H. C.	Breckenridge, Waterloo	14	M	4:151
Thompson, Jane	Breckenridge, Waterloo	30	F	4:151
Thomson, Matthew	Breckenridge, Waterloo (Farmer)	17	M	4:151
Thornburg, John	Leavenworth, Easton (Farmer)	30	M	10:292
Thornburg, Pleasant	Leavenworth, Easton (Farmer)	28	M	10:292
Thornhill, A. B.	Atchison, Lancaster (Farmer)	36	M	1:105
Thornton, G. B.	Arrapahoe, Valley of the Platte	26	M	11:816
Thornburg, John	Leavenworth, Easton (Farmer)	30	M	10:301
Thornton, Thos.	Arrapahoe, South Park	29	M	11:146
Threewit, Elizabeth	Lykins, Paola (Farmer)	53	F	8:41
Threewit, Frances	Lykins, Paola	24	F	8:41
Threewit, Louis	Lykins, Paola	15	M	8:41
Threewit, Marcus	Lykins, Paola	10	M	8:41
Threewit, Nancy	Lykins, Paola	22	F	8:41
Threewit, Sarah	Lykins, Paola	19	F	8:41
Threewit, William	Lykins, Paola	18	M	8:41
Thrift, J. D.	Arrapahoe, South Clear Creek (Miner)	21	M	11:728
Thronburgh, Mary	McGhee, Brushville P.O.	35	F	9:218
Tiffius, S.	Arrapahoe, Valley of the Platte	27	M	11:804
Tiphane, Robt.[1]	Arrapahoe, South Park	28	M	11:154
Tipton, H. B.	Arrapahoe, South Park	26	M	11:263
Tipton, Marion	Atchison, Lancaster (Farmer)	35	M	1:106
Tittle, Diadaura	Bourbon, Mapleton P.O.(Housewife)	52	F	2:132
Tittle, Susan	Bourbon, Mapleton P.O.(Housewife)	25	F	2:132
Tittle, David	Bourbon, Mapleton P.O. (Farmer)	28	M	2:132
Tittle, Thomas C.	Bourbon, Mapleton P.O.(Farm Laborer)	26	M	2:132
Todd, Amanda	Arrapahoe, Nevada Gulch	26	F	11:527
Todd, Benjamine	McGhee, Crawford Seminary P.O.(Farmer)	44	M	9:228
Todd, Elisa	Allen, Iola P.O.	28	F	2:258
Todd, James A.	Allen, Iola P.O. (Farmer)	35	M	2:258
Todd, Jno. W.	Arrapahoe, Nevada Gulch	6	M	11:527
Todd, Legrande	McGhee, Crawford Sem.P.O.(FarmLabr.)	17	M	9:228
Todd, M.	Arrapahoe, Nevada Gulch (Teamster)	38	M	11:527
Todd, Sarah A.	McGhee, Crawford Seminary P.O.	33	F	9:228
Todd, Susan	Allen, Iola P.O.	36	F	2:259
Todd, Wm.	Arrapahoe, Nevada Gulch	4	M	11:527
Todd, William P.	McGhee, Crawford Sem.P.O.(FarmLabr.)	22	M	9:228
Todhunter, R.	Douglas, Lecompton	60	F	6:370
Toler, M.	Johnson, Monticello(Teacher)	24	F	6:83
Tomlinson, T. C.	Douglas, Willow Springs (Farmer)	49	M	6:294
Toncey, Geo.	Arrapahoe, South Park	20	M	11:212
Towns, James	Otoe, Otoe (Farmer)	25	BM	4:353
Tracy, Jno. V.	Arrapahoe, California Gulch	42	M	11:298
Trail, Robert	Bourbon, Fort Scott P.O.(FarmLabr.)	19	M	2:78
Trammel, Archabald	Lykins, Sugar Creek (Farmer)	31	M	8:99
Trapp, F.	Jefferson, Oskaloosa(Wagon Maker)	52	M	5:119
Trible, A.	Doniphan, Burr Oak (Farmer)	54	F	1:348
Tristam, C. V.	Arrapahoe, Denver (Mechanic)	22	M	11:411
Trott, R.	Arrapahoe, Valley of the Platte	31	M	11:807
Trusty, Josiah	McGhee, Brushville P.O. (Farmer)	20	M	9:221
Tryle, E.	Johnson, Olathe	12	M	6:9
Tryle, R. B.	Johnson, Olathe	9	M	6:9
Tuckett, H.	Douglas, Clinton (Farmer)	48	M	6:420
Tulley, Jno.	Arrapahoe, South Clear Creek	19	M	11:649
Turman, J. D.	Johnson, Shawnee (Farmer)	36	M	6:101
Turner, Elizabeth	Atchison, Walnut	26	F	1:178
Turner, Geo.	Arrapahoe, California Gulch	38	M	11:311

[1] Census entry difficult to read; may be Liphano.

Arapahoe: spelled incorrectly with 2 r's in census and in this index also.

Name	Kansas: County; Township; P.O. Arap. Co.: Census Div. Not Township	Age	Sex	Census V. : Pg.
Turner, George	Linn, Mound City (Farmer)	17	M	7:102
Turner, Geo. W.	Atchison, Walnut	4	M	1:178
Turner, John F.	Atchison, Walnut	6	M	1:178
Turner, Lydia	McGhee, Brushville P.O.	25	BF	9:217
Turner, Lydia	Leavenworth, Easton	20	F	10:299
Turner, Rosanna	Linn, Potosi	25	F	7:72
Turner, Wm. M.	Atchison, Walnut	10	M	1:178
Tyler, H.	Arrapahoe, Valley of the Platte	27	M	11:861
Underwood, M.	Anderson, Washington (Farmer)	19	M	7:256
Updegraff, W.	Arrapahoe, South Park	31	M	11:142
Usler, F. E.	Arrapahoe, Valley of the Platte	24	M	11:806
Vail, Danial	Wyandotte, Wyandotte (Farmer)	38	M	10:42
Vail, Hannah	Wyandotte, Wyandotte	4	F	10:42
Vail, Isaac	Shawnee, Tecumseh	13	M	9:75
Vail, James T.	Wyandotte, Wyandotte	11	M	10:42
Vail, Joseph	Wyandotte, Wyandotte	8	M	10:42
Vail, Mary J.	Wyandotte, Wyandotte	10	F	10:42
Vail, Zacheriah	Wyandotte, Wyandotte	9	M	10:42
Vanato, Henry	Arrapahoe, South Park	36	M	11:118
Vanbebber, J. C.	Linn, Valley (Farmer)	31	M	7:42
Vanbebber, Sarah	Linn, Valley	30	F	7:42
Vance, M. B.	Arrapahoe, South Park	36	M	11:189
Van Duzen, Mary	Arrapahoe, South Park	45	F	11:5
Van Duzen, Wm.	Arrapahoe, South Park (Miner)	22	M	11:5
Van Horn, Danl.	Arrapahoe, South Park	28	M	11:246
Van Horn, Malinda	Lykins, Osawatomie (Farmer)	43	F	8:65
Vanranken, E.	Johnson, DeSota	53?	F	6:21
Vanscoyee, Wm. R.	Anderson, Jackson	31	M	7:208
Van Siew, John	Jefferson, Grasshopper Falls	4	M	5:10
Van Siew, Julia	Jefferson, Grasshopper Falls	2	F	5:10
Vanzant, L.	Douglas, Lecompton	5	F	6:372
Vanzant, M.	Douglas, Lecompton	9	F	6:372
Vanzant, R.	Douglas, Lecompton	7	F	6:372
Varble, Catherine	Bourbon, Marmaton P.O.(Housewife)	35	F	2:206
Vaughan, Barbara	Douglas, Palmyra	28	F	6:266
Vaughn, William	McGhee, Medoc, Missouri P.O.(Farmer)	22	M	9:215
Veach, E.	Linn, Mound City (Farmer)	65	M	7:125
Veach, Holland	Atchison, Mt. Pleasant	18	M	1:152
Velpean, C.	Arrapahoe, South Park	28	M	11:241
Vermillion, Edward	Bourbon, Dayton P.O. (Farmer)	29	M	2:150
Vermillon, Harman W.	Bourbon, Dayton P.O. (Farmer)	38	M	2:150
Vermilion, Hiram	Bourbon, Raysville P.O.		M	2:159
Vermilion, Octava B.	Bourbon, Raysville P.O.(Housewife)	25	F	2:159
Vernon, C. M.	Arrapahoe, South Park	24	M	11:214
Vernon, Willis	Arrapahoe, South Park	28	M	11:186
Vickers, Amanda	McGhee, Fort Scott P.O.	25	F	9:210
Vickers, William	McGhee, Fort Scott P.O.	24	M	9:210
Viele, G.	Arrapahoe, Valley of the Platte	27	M	11:825
Vigrow, C. T.	Arrapahoe, South Park	30	M	11:246
Vines, H.	Johnson, Monticello	33	F	6:83
Vines, J.	Johnson, Monticello (Farmer)	41	M	6:83
Vosgett, H.	Arrapahoe, South Park	26	M	11:141
Waddell, C.	Arrapahoe, South Clear Creek	28	M	11:764
Wade, Elizabeth	Atchison, Walnut	41	F	1:188
Walker, Elizabeth	Marshall, Guittard	48	F	3:237
Walker, George	Marshall, Guittard (Farmer)	49	M	3:237
Walker, H.	Linn, Paris	41	F	7:130
Walker, John	Linn, Paris (Farmer)	42	M	7:130
Wallace, Berena	Bourbon, Fort Scott P.O.	29	BF	2:227

Arapahoe: spelled incorrectly with 2 r's in census and in this index also.

Name	Kansas: County; Township; P.O. Arap. Co.: Census Div. Not Township	Age	Sex	Census V.: Pg.
Wallace, E. R.	Arrapahoe, South Clear Creek	28	M	11:709
Wallace, M.	Johnson, Olathe	37	F	6:117
Walls, Nancy	Marshall, Vermillion	40	F	3:218
Walter, Jennie	Arrapahoe, Denver	27	F	11:333
Walton, James H.	Bourbon, Fort Scott P.O. (Farmer)	33	M	2:155
Walton, Morris	Shawnee, Auburn (Farmer)	46	M	9:49
Ward, Angeline	Lykins, Marysville	14	F	8:126
Ward, Benj.	Lykins, Marysville	17	M	8:126
Ward, Emely	Lykins, Marysville	12	F	8:126
Ward, Geo.	Doniphan, Center (Farmer)	38	M	1:270
Ward, J. B.	Arrapahoe, California Gulch	23	M	11:280
Ward, James	Lykins, Marysville	3	M	8:126
Ward, John	Lykins, Marysville	21	M	8:126
Ward, Judith	Doniphan, Center	55	F	1:270
Ward, Julia	Lykins, Marysville	7	F	8:126
Ward, Lucinda	Linn, Valley (Farmer)	38	F	7:34
Ward, Melinda	Jefferson, Ozawkie	51	F	5:101
Ward, Peter	Arrapahoe, California Gulch	27	M	11:280
Ward, Robert	Jefferson, Ozawkie (Farmer)	51	M	5:101
Ward, Sarah	Doniphan, Center (Domestic)	36	F	1:270
Ward, Texana	Lykins, Marysville	9	F	8:126
Warden, Abijah H.	Linn, Potosi (Teacher)	24	M	7:59
Warren, Elizabeth	Douglas, Willow Springs	46	F	6:322
Warren, Lydia A.	Linn, Valley	51	F	7:33
Wasterson, Elizabeth[1]	Douglas, Palmyra	31	F	6:271
Water, Edmund	Atchison, Mt. Pleasant	10	M	1:166
Waters, Agnes	Marshall, Guittard (Domestic)	23	F	3:237
Waters, Anthony	Marshall, Guittard (Farmer)	49	M	3:237
Waters, Elizabeth[1]	Marshall, Guittard	12	F	3:237
Waters, Elizabeth[1]	Marshall, Guittard	50	F	3:237
Waters, Ellen	Marshall, Guittard (Domestic)	25	F	3:237
Waters, George	Marshall, Guittard (Farm Laborer)	21	M	3:237
Waters, Harvey	Marshall, Guittard	6	M	3:237
Waters, Henry	Marshall, Guittard (Farm Laborer)	15	M	3:237
Waters, James	Marshall, Guittard	9	M	3:237
Waters, John	Marshall, Guittard (Farm Laborer)	16	M	3:237
Waters, Mahala	Marshall, Guittard (Domestic)	28	F	3:237
Waters, William	Marshall, Guittard (Farm Laborer)	18	M	3:237
Watts, James	McGhee, Osage Mission P.O.(Farmer)	41	M	9:237
Weaver, Lucinda	Shawnee, Tecumseh	30	F	9:74
Webb, Benjamin J.	Allen, Humboldt P.O. (Farmer)	42	M	2:285
Webb, E.	Arrapahoe, South Clear Creek	29	M	11:761
Weeks, Stephen	Arrapahoe, Golden City (Miner)		M	11:447
Weer, A. W.	Johnson, Shawnee (Farmer)	38	M	6:29
Weer, David	Wyandotte, Wyandotte (Farmer)	45	M	10:7
Weer, J.	Johnson, Shawnee (Farmer)	47	M	6:94
Weer, Nancy	Wyandotte, Wyandotte	38	F	10:7
Weer, S.	Johnson, Shawnee (Farmer)	49	M	6:94
Welborn, Charles	Wyandotte, Quindaro	5	M	10:60
Welbraham, F.	Arrapahoe, South Park	35	M	11:226
Welch, James	Woodson, Verdigris	25	M	9:165
Welch, Margaret	Woodson, Verdigris	24	M	9:165
Welch, Nancy	Leavenworth, Easton	26	F	10:302
Weld, Julius M.	Atchison, 1st Ward	30	F	1:10
Welkens, Mary	Linn, Valley	36	F	7:30
Welles, T. E.	Arrapahoe, South Park	35	M	11:201
Wellingham, L.	Arrapahoe, South Clear Creek		M	11:658

[1]Interpreted as El̲ezabeth by the W.P.A. indexer, but original entry looks
  more like Eli̲zabeth in each case.
  Arapahoe: spelled incorrectly with 2 r's in census and in this index also.

Name	Kansas: County; Township; P.O. Arap. Co.: Census Div. Not Township	Age	Sex	Census V.:Pg.
Wells, Albert	Douglas, Willow Springs	5	M	6:328
Wells, Alvin C.	Bourbon, Xenia P.O. (Farmer)	43	M	2:128
Wells, Elizabeth[1]	Douglas, Willow Springs	23	F	6:328
Wells, Kaziah	Bourbon, Turkey Creek P.O.(Housewife)	29	F	2:114
Wells, Margaret	Breckenridge, Waterloo	28	F	4:153
Wells, Mary	Douglas, Willow Springs	8	F	6:328
Wells, Mary A.	Lykins, Marysville	33	F	8:127
Wells, Matilda	Bourbon, Turkey Creek P.O.(Housewife)	26	F	2:107
Wells, Sam	Arrapahoe, Denver (Miner)	29	M	11:429
Wells, Wm.	Douglas, Willow Springs	5	M	6:328
Wennoys, J. H.	Arrapahoe, Valley of the Platte	30		11:788
Wentens, Ann[2]	Leavenworth, Ward 4	9	F	10:268
West, G. N.	Arrapahoe, South Park	26	M	11:29
West, Jas.	Arrapahoe, Tarryall South Park	36	M	11:614
Weston, D.	Franklin, Centropolis	50	F	8:207
Weston, G. C.	Arrapahoe, South Park	27	M	11:229
Weston, R. D.	Arrapahoe, South Park	22	M	11:173
Whaler, A. F.	Arrapahoe, South Park (Miner)	22	M	11:194
Wharton, J.	Arrapahoe, South Clear Creek	38	M	11:713
Wheeler, Eliza	Atchison, Grasshopper	11	F	1:85
Wheeler, Elizabeth	Atchison, Grasshopper	38	F	1:85
Wheeler, G. W.	Atchison, Grasshopper	52	M	1:85
Wheeler, John	Atchison, Grasshopper	8	M	1:85
Wheeler, Wm.	Atchison, Grasshopper	10	M	1:85
Whetstone, Martha E.	McGhee, Fort Scott P.O.	33	F	9:210
Whitaker, Joseph	Lykins, Osage (Farmer)	41	M	8:80
White, A.	Douglas, Clinton (Farmer)	59	M	6:406
White, D.	Doniphan, Wolf River	16	F	1:404
White, Edw. W.	Lykins, Paola (Attorney)	36	M	8:28
White, Elizabeth M.	Lykins, Paola	21	F	8:28
White, Hugh	Doniphan, Wolf River	5	M	1:405
White, I.	Doniphan, Wolf River	12	M	1:404
White, J.	Arrapahoe, South Park	29	M	11:175
White, J. W.	Arrapahoe, Nevada Gulch (Miner)	45	M	11:531
White, Jackson	Anderson, Walker	20	M	7:236
White, James L. D.	Lykins, Paola	5	M	8:28
White, Julius S.	Anderson, Walker (Farmer)	20	M	7:236
White, Lawson	Anderson, Walker	18	M	7:236
White, Louisa	Doniphan, Wolf River	7	F	1:405
White, Mary J.	Lykins, Marysville	17	F	8:127
White, Nancy	Butler, Chelsea (Farmer)	43	F	4:349
White, Polly	Douglas, Clinton	58	F	6:406
White, T. A.	Doniphan, Wolf River	9	F	1:404
White, W.	Johnson, Shawnee (Farmer)	50	M	6:98
White, Wiley	Doniphan, Wolf River	13	M	1:404
Whiteside, Henry	Pottawatomie, Shannon (Farmer)	54	M	5:301
Whitfield, J. W.	Leavenworth, Kickapoo(RegisterLandOff.)	42	M	10:324
Whitfield, John A.	Leavenworth, Kickapoo	5	M	10:324
Whitfield, John F.	Leavenworth, Kickapoo	18	M	10:324
Whitfield, Sarah B.	Leavenworth, Kickapoo	32	F	10:324
Whitman, C.	Arrapahoe, South Clear Creek	27	M	11:723
Whitney, O.	Arrapahoe, South Park	39	M	11:172
Wicklip, M.	Doniphan, Iowa Point	40	F	1:452
Wieher, Tawdy	Linn, Potosi (Farmer)	26	M	7:57
Wiffely, Barbara	Leavenworth, Easton	30	F	10:297
Wiggins, Rachel A.	McGhee, Crawford Seminary P.O.	29	F	9:228

[1] Original entry clearly Elizabeth; W.P.A. indexer gives Elezabeth.

[2] Spelling of Wentens uncertain; handwriting not clear.

Arapahoe: spelled incorrectly with 2 r's in census and in this index also.

Name	Kansas: County; Township; P.O. Arap. Co.: Census Div. Not Township	Age	Sex	Census V. Pg.
Wilbuforce, Emily	Arrapahoe, South Park	55	F	11:5
Wilbuforce, Geo.	Arrapahoe, South Park	30	M	11:5
Wilburn, Richard	Leavenworth, Delaware (Farmer)	35	M	10:419
Wiley, E. A.	Johnson, McCamish	42	F	6:63
Wiley, Thos. A.	Arrapahoe, California Gulch	28	M	11:307
Wilhart, Silas M.	Pottawatomie, Shannon (Farmer)	27	M	5:302
Wilhoit, Catharn	Brown, Irving	17	F	3:10
Wilhoit, J. W.	Brown, Irving (Farmer)	39	M	3:10
Wilkins, Ellendor	Breckenridge, Americus	40	F	4:221
Wilkins, John	Breckenridge, Americus (Farmer)	45	M	4:221
Williard, Elias	Bourbon, Mapleton P.O. (Farmer)	58	M	2:137
Williams, A.	Johnson, Shawnee (Farmer)	51	M	6:33
Williams, Andien[1]	Greenwood, Eureka (Farmer)	35	M	9:179
Williams, Benjamin	Shawnee, Tecumseh (Farmer)	35	M	9:78
Williams, Celishia C.	Atchison, Walnut	28	F	1:179
Williams, David	Shawnee, Tecumseh (Farmer)	48	M	9:78
Williams, Edward	Woodson, Verdigris (Farmer)	48	M	9:158
Williams, Emiline[1]	Greenwood, Eureka	14	F	9:179
Williams, F. M.	Atchison, Walnut (M.E. South)	35	M	1:179
Williams, Henry T.	Lykins, Marysville (Carpenter)	25	M	8:131
Williams, J.	Riley, Manhattan P.O. (Farmer)	25	M	9:296
Williams, J.	Johnson, Shawnee (Farmer)	26	M	6:87
Williams, Jane	Woodson, Verdigris (F. W.)	41	F	9:158
Williams, John R.	Linn, Valley (Farmer)	52	M	7:34
Williams, Joseph[1]	Greenwood, Eureka (Farmer)	15	M	9:179
Williams, M. M.	Johnson, Olathe	37	F	6:114
Williams, Margaret E.	Bourbon, Fort Scott P.O.	42	F	2:221
Williams, Mary	Lykins, Marysville	20	F	8:131
Williams, Melvina	Linn, Valley	23	F	7:52
Williams, Minerva	Coffey, Avon	24	F	4:7
Williams, R. M.	Johnson, Shawnee (Farmer)	28	M	6:87
Williams, Rebecca	Lykins, Mound	47	F	8:68
Williams, S.	Linn, Scott (Farmer)	39	M	7:20
Williams, Sarah[1]	Greenwood, Eureka	28	F	9:179
Williams, Sarah	Chase, Diamond Creek	24	F	4:326
Williams, Stephen	Riley, Manhattan P.O. (Farmer)	23	M	9:296
Williams, Stephen B.	Arrapahoe, Golden City (Laborer)	30	M	11:584
Williams, Thomas[1]	Greenwood, Eureka (Farmer)	18	M	9:179
Williams, W.	Arrapahoe, Denver	32	M	11:386
Williamson, J.	Arrapahoe, South Park	26	M	11:100
Willis, Francis	Brown, Claytonville	5	F	3:54
Willis, L. A.	Brown, Claytonville	6	F	3:54
Willis, M. C.	Brown, Claytonville (Farmer)	30	M	3:54
Willis, Sarah	Atchison, Lancaster	34	F	1:104
Wills, George	Leavenworth, Kickapoo (Farmer)	66	M	10:406
Willson, Amos	Marshall, Guittard	7	M	3:237
Willson, Betsy	Marshall, Guittard	10	F	3:237
Willson, John	Marshall, Guittard (Farmer)	33	M	3:237
Willson, Lucia	Marshall, Guittard	30	F	3:237
Wilson, A. M.	Franklin, Peoria (Minister)	57	M	8:271
Wilson, Elizabeth	Marshall, Guittard	10	F	3:237
Wilson, Frances	Linn, Scott,	35	F	7:23
Wilson, John	Marshall, Guittard	3	M	3:237
Wilson, Lee	Linn, Valley (Farmer)	28	M	7:47
Wilson, Mary K.	Atchison, Lancaster	28	F	1:108
Wilson, Sarah	Marshall, Guittard	29	F	3:237
Wilson, T. A.	Franklin, Peoria	55	F	8:271

[1]Could be Willamy, Willams, or Wiliams; very poor handwriting on all entries.

Arapahoe: spelled incorrectly with 2 r's in census and in this index also.

Name	Kansas: County; Township; P.O. Arap. Co.: Census Div. Not Township	Age	Sex	Census V. Pg.
Wilson, Wm.	Otoe, Otoe (Farmer)	40	M	4:355
Winfield, J. S.	Arrapahoe, Valley of the Platte	31		11:781
Winn, Jas. M.	Lykins, Miami (Laborer)	19	M	8:94
Wise, Elizabeth	Allen, Carlisle P.O.	47	F	2:238
Wisley, I. A.	Arrapahoe, Denver (Carpenter)	28		11:332
Witel, Abram	Douglas, Palmyra	17	M	6:297
Witel, Elezabeth	Douglas, Palmyra	53	F	6:297
Witel, James	Douglas, Palmyra (Farmer)	68	M	6:297
Witha, Andrew F.	Allen, Humboldt P.O.(Farm Laborer)	18	M	2:293
Witha, Benjamin	Allen, Humboldt P.O.(Farm Laborer)	15	M	2:293
Witha, Mary A.	Allen, Humboldt P.O.	52	F	2:293
Witha, Thomas N.	Allen, Humboldt P.O.(Farm Laborer)	24	M	2:293
Witha, William A.	Allen, Humboldt P.O. (Farmer)	52	M	2:293
Wittan, Emily	Allen, Humboldt P.O.	25	F	2:295
Wittan, William N.	Allen, Humboldt P.O. (Farmer)	28	M	2:295
Wolf, Nathan	Bourbon, Fort Scott P.O. (Farmer)	36	M	2:192
Wood, R.	Douglas, Clinton	53	F	6:404
Woodcock, Henry	Brown, Claytonville	51	M	3:46
Woods, Adeline	Bourbon, Turkey Creek P.O.(Housewife)	23	F	2:113
Woods, G.	Johnson, McCamish (Farmer)	30	M	6:70
Woods, Michael	Bourbon, Fort Scott P.O.	1	M	2:225
Woody, Nancy	Linn, Paris	42	F	7:159
Woolff, S.	Arrapahoe, South Clear Creek (Miner)	38	M	11:723
Woolheater, George	Jackson, Jefferson (Farmer)	37	M	5:207
Word, L.	Franklin, Ohio (Farmer)	45	M	8:233
Work, R. C.	Arrapahoe, Central City (Rancher)	25	M	11:578
Workman, Annah Lacy	Atchison, Mt. Pleasant	39	F	1:162
Workman, Diana	Bourbon, Fort Scott P.O.(Housewife)	36	F	2:77
Workman, Henderson	Shawnee, Soldier (Farmer)	22	M	9:86
Workman, Isaac	Butler, Chelsea (Farmer)	32	M	4:343
Workman, Jacob	Bourbon, Fort Scott P.O. (Farmer)	33	M	2:77
Workman, John	Atchison, Mount Pleasant (Farmer)	35	M	1:142
Workman, L.	Arrapahoe, South Park	18	M	11:108
Workman, Martha A.	Bourbon, Fort Scott P.O.(Housewife)	20	F	2:82
Workmen, Stephen	Anderson,Town of Greeley(Day Laborer)	45	M	7:242
Worley, Henry	Hunter, Eldorado (Farmer)	30	M	4:361
Wormington, T. W.	Woodson, Pleasant Grove (Farmer)	30	M	9:167
Wortdyke, J.	Arrapahoe, South Clear Creek	33	M	11:742
Wortman, N.	Franklin, Centropolis	52	F	8:214
Wright, A. J.	Arrapahoe, Central City(QuartzMiller)	27	M	11:516
Wright, Ann	Breckenridge, Cahola (Farmer)	60	F	4:230
Wright, B. F.	Arrapahoe, Central City(QuartzMiller)	30	M	11:516
Wright, David	Arrapahoe, Central City (Engineer)	38	M	11:516
Wright, Geo. W.	Arrapahoe, Central City(QuartzMiller)	28	M	11:516
Wright, H. D.	Arrapahoe, South Park	34	M	11:168
Wright, Jas.	Arrapahoe, Central City(QuartzMiller)	35	M	11:516
Wright, Mary J.	Leavenworth, Alexandria	32	F	10:453
Wright, T. B.	Arrapahoe, Denver (Lawyer)	29	M	11:429
Wyate, George[1]	Nemaha, Rock Creek (Farmer)	48	M	3:75
Wyatt, Thomas	Bourbon, Dayton P.O.	60	M	2:156
Wylie, Fannie	Atchison, Kapioma	20	F	1:97
Wyman, J. N.	Arrapahoe, Valley of the Platte	24	M	11:807
Yandle, Priscilla	Anderson, Monroe	44	F	7:215
Yandle, Tabitha	Anderson, Monroe	17	F	7:215
Yates, Thomas	Leavenworth, Delaware	45	M	10:312
Yeakley, Elijah	Breckenridge, Americus (Farmer)	35	M	4:217
Yeakley, Wm. P.	Breckenridge, Americus (Farmer)	32	M	4:217
Yoakum, W. C.	Leavenworth, Easton (Carpenter)	47	M	10:292

[1]Original census looks more like Wyatt.

Arapahoe: spelled incorrectly with 2 r's in census and in this index also.

Name	Kansas: County; Township; P.O. Arap. Co.: Census Div. Not Township	Age	Sex	Census V. Pg.
York, T.	Arrapahoe, South Park	26	M	11:217
Young, F. W.	Arrapahoe, Denver	23	M	11:382
Young, George N.	Allen, Humboldt P.O. (Farmer)	30	M	2:280
Young, Jane	Doniphan, Iowa Point	33	F	1:433
Young, N.	Arrapahoe, South Clear Creek (Miner)	52	M	11:626
Young, Sarah	Allen, Humboldt P.O.	21	F	2:280
Young, T. M.	Arrapahoe, California Gulch	23	M	11:302
Young, W. J.	Atchison, Walnut (Farmer)	43	M	1:182
Youngblood, Nancy	Bourbon, Fort Scott P.O.(Housewife)	34	F	2:213
Zack, Jonathan	Bourbon, Fort Scott P.O. (Farmer)	34	M	2:87
Zimmerman, Mary[1]	Douglas, Lawrence	26	F	6:191

Addendum

Smyth, Jno.	Arapahoe, Golden City (Miner)	30	M	11:446

[1]Birthplace given as Holsten; possibly the Holston River area in Tennessee, but more probably the duchy belonging to Denmark at the time, later part of Schleswig-Holstein.

Arapahoe: spelled incorrectly with 2 r's in census and in this index also.

Jerry Crippen, Hill City, Kansas
With Tennesseans on the Smoky Hill Trail across Kansas,
heading for Colorado
I believe it was 1966 ... or was it 1866?

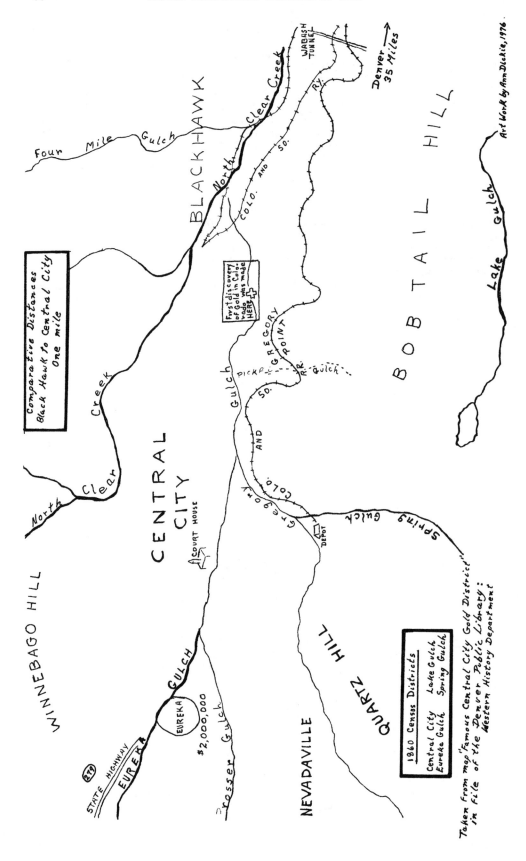

1860 Census Districts

Central City   Lake Gulch
Eureka Gulch   Spring Gulch

Taken from map "Famous Central City Gold District" in file of the Denver Public Library; Western History Department

Name	Kansas: County; Township; P.O. Arap. Co.: Census Div. Not Township	Age	Sex	Census V. Pg.
Aaron, (Haray?), H.	Arrapahoe, Eureka Gulch (Miner)	55	M	11:507
Abott, Boedicia	Atchison, Ward 3 (Domestic)	14	F	1:60
Abott, E.	Doniphan, Center, Troy	45	F	1:256
Abott, John	" " "	45	M	1:256
Aberman, G.	Arrapahoe, Valley of the Platte	50	M	11:825
Abger, E. C.	Franklin, Ohio, Ohio City	1	M	8:231
Abraham, R. H.	Breckinridge, Fremont (Farmer)	31	M	4:164
Absher, Abram	Brown, Clayton., Robinson (Farmer)	61	M	3:42
Absher, Alex.	" " " (Farmer)	19	M	3:42
Abshire, Eliza	Jackson, Franklin, Holton	40	F	5:185
Abshire, Thomas J.	" " " (Farmer)	45	M	5:185
Adams, A. A.	Frank., Ottawa, Hickory Cr. (Farmer)	21	M	8:261
Adams, A. L. M.	Arrapahoe, Spring Gulch (Storage)	32	M	11:538
Adams, Calvin NC	Doug., Wakarusa, Lawrence (Farmer)	43	M	6:246
Adams, Clara F.	Arrapahoe, Spring Gulch	38	F	11:538
Adams, J.	Frank., Ottawa, Hickory Cr. (Farmer)	19	M	8:261
Adams, J. NC	Johnson, Spring Hill (Farmer)	38	M	6:44
Adams, J. M.	Franklin, Ottawa, Hickory Creek	12	M	8:261
Adams, J. W. W.	Arrapahoe, South Clear Creek	36	M	11:710
Adams, Jesse	Nem., Rock Cr., Central City (Farmer)	60	M	3:78
Adams, M.	Franklin, Ottawa, Hickory Creek	17	F	8:261
Adams, M. J.	" " " "	15	F	8:261
Adams, O.	" " " "	8		8:261
Adams, Orris S.	Arrapahoe, South Park	37	M	11:217
Adams, W. M.	" " "	32	M	11:221
Addickks, Jno. D.	" " "	33	M	11:213
Addington, Margaret	Anderson, Jackson, Garnett	26	F	7:212
Addington, Nancy	" " "	27	F	7:210
Addleman, Catherine NC	Linn, Town of Paris	26	F	7:138
Addleman, J. NC	" " " (Laborer)	30	M	7:138
Adkins, Manuel	Bourbon, Barnesville P.O. (Farmer)	44	M	2:166
Agell, C. C.	Doniphan, Iowa Point (Farmer)	30	M	1:451
Agnew, A.	Frank., Ohio, Ohio City	39	F	8:229
Agnew, J. R.	" " " " (Farmer)	19	M	8:229
Agnew, M.	" " " "	14	M	8:229
Agnew, W. H.	" " " " (Farmer)	48	M	8:229
Aid, John	Atchison, Shannon, Atch. (Farmer)	40	M	1:73
Aiken, H. NC	Osage, Ridgeway, Superior	44	M	8:343
Aiken, I. NC	Osage, Ridgeway, Superior (Farmer)	54	F	8:343
Albin, Debora	Douglas, Clinton	45	F	6:421
Albin, M.	" " (Farmer)	50	M	6:421
Alder, Conrad	Lykins, Mound, Osawatomie (Farmer)	45	M	8:71
Alder, Ida	Douglas, Willow Springs, McKinney	2	F	6:295
Alderman, Henry	Anderson, Monroe, Garnett (Farmer)	60	M	7:230
Alderson, Carey F.	Atchison, Ward 3	7	F	1:64
Alderson, David T.	Atchison, Lancaster	12	M	1:113
Alderson, Elgin F.	Atchison, Ward 3	39	M	1:64
Alderson, Elizabeth T.	Atchison, Lancaster	20	F	1:113
Alderson, Ellen F.	" "	15	F	1:113
Alderson, Harriett	" "	44	F	1:113
Alderson, Harriet Ann	" "	2	F	1:113
Alderson, Irwing	Atchison, Ward 3 (Student)	15	M	1:64
Alderson, John	Atchison, Lancaster (Farmer)	48	M	1:113
Alderson, John A.	" "	9	M	1:113
Alderson, L. A.	Atchison, Ward 3 (B. F. Clergyman)	48	M	1:64
Alderson, Mary Cornelia	" " "	12	F	1:64

All settlers listed in Part II were born in Virginia except those with the
adscripts NC or SC; i.e., person born in North Carolina or South Carolina.
Non-white races noted: Indian, I; negro, B; mulatto, M: viz., BM, black male.
Arapahoe: spelled incorrectly with 2 r's in census and in this index also.

Name	Kansas: County; Township; P.O. Arap. Co.: Census Div. Not Township	Age	Sex	Census V. Pg.
Alderson, Mary C.	Atchison, Lancaster	7	F	1:113
Alderson, Sophrona L.	" "	18	F	1:113
Alderson, Walter W.	Atchison, Ward 3	4	M	1:64
Alderson, Wm. A.	Atchison, Lancaster	14	M	1:113
Alderson, Caisey F.	Atchison, Ward 3	6	M	1:55
Alderson, Irwin	" "	17	M	1:55
Alderson, Mary C.	" "	10	F	1:55
Alexander, Catharine	Jefferson, Grasshopper Falls	48	F	5:7
Alexander, John SC	Nemaha, Rock Cr., Albany (Farmer)	27	M	3:76
Alford, Catharine SC	Leavenworth, Ward 4	55	F	10:273
Alford, J. A.	Brown, Irving, White Cloud (Farmer)	32	M	3:2
Allen, Catherine	Lykins, Sugar Cr., West Point, Mo.	38	F	8:96
Allen, Chas. B.	Potta., Blue, Manhattan (Farmer)	23	M	5:297
Allen, Elizabeth NC	Woodson, Pleasant Grove (F. W.)	51	F	9:170
Allen, F. T.	Arrapahoe; Tarryall, S. P.; Tarryall	20	M	11:613
Allen, J.	Potta., Vienna, Louisville (Farmer)	30	M	5:245
Allen, Jacob P.	Leavenworth, Easton	8	M	10:305
Allen, James P.	" "	7	M	10:305
Allen, Joseph	Arrapahoe, Central City (Miner)	35	M	11:574
Allen, M.	Pottawatomie, Vienna, Louisville	27	F	5:245
Allen, M. B.	Douglas, Kanwaca, Lawrence	6	F	6:374
Allen, Mary	Woodson, Pleasant Grove	5	F	9:170
Allen, Rebecca J. NC	Lykins, Paola	40	F	8:36
Allen, T. C. NC	Breck., Pike, Plymouth (Farmer)	25	M	4:210
Allen, Thos.	Arrapahoe, California Gulch		M	11:310
Allen, W. A.	Pottawatomie, Vienna, Louisville	5	M	5:245
Allen, Walter NC	Jefferson, Oskaloosa (Attorney-at-law)	26	M	5:109
Allen, William F.	Potta., Blue, Manhattan (Farmer)	25	M	5:297
Allerton, A. H.	Arrapahoe, South Park	27	M	11:145
Alley, G. W. SC	Arrapahoe, Nevada Gulch (Miner)	28	M	11:583
Allibaugh, N.	Arrapahoe, Mountain City (Grocery)	36	M	11:459
Allison, C.	Doniphan; Center, Lafayette; Troy	17	F	1:249
Allison, Chet	" " " "	9	M	1:249
Allison, Fanny	" " " "	15	F	1:249
Allison, John	" " " "	7	M	1:249
Allison, Mary	" " " "	19	F	1:249
Allison, P. B.	" " " " (Merchant)	39	M	1:249
Allison, S.	Franklin, Ottawa, Prairie City	18	F	8:253
Allison, W.	Doniphan; Center, Lafayette; Troy	39	F	1:249
Allman, T. [1]	Frank., Prairie, Peoria City(Farmer)	20	M	8:268
Alney, B.	Linn, Potosi (Farmer)	30	M	7:77
Alney, Jane	" "	4	F	7:78
Alney, John	" "	8	M	7:78
Alney, Mary	" "	6	F	7:78
Alney, Nancy	" "	2	F	7:78
Alney, W.	" "	70	F	7:78
Amill, John	Atchison, Ward 3 (Clerk)	30	M	1:51
Ammon, W.	Arrapahoe, Valley of the Platte	29	M	11:821
Amsell, E. H.	Arrapahoe, South Clear Creek	33	M	11:728
Amsick, S. E.	Arrapahoe, South Park	39	M	11:220
Amsbrough, N.	Doniphan, Marion, Palermo	56	F	1:277
Anderson, Anna	McGhee, Medoc, Missouri P.O.	53	F	9:209
Anderson, Anna	Bourbon, Xenia P.O. (Housewife)	49	F	2:127
Anderson, Barbara	Bourbon, Turkey Creek P.O.(Housewife)	60	F	2:108
Anderson, Elizabeth	Bourbon, Xenia P.O.	15	F	2:127
Anderson, Elizabeth	Bourbon, Turkey Creek P.O.(Housewife)	48	F	2:108
Anderson, Elizabeth W.	Lykins, Richland, Paola	38	F	8:14
Anderson, Geo. W.	Shawnee, Topeka (Merchant)	26	M	9:8
Anderson, J. J.	Doniphan, Marion, Palermo (Farmer)	32	M	1:281

[1]Perhaps born in La. or Ia. rather than Va.

Arapahoe: spelled incorrectly with 2 r's in census and in this index also.

Name	Kansas: County; Township; P.O. Arap. Co.: Census Div. Not Township	Age	Sex	Census V. Pg.
Anderson, J. P.	Arrapahoe, South Park	29	M	11:194
Anderson, James[NC]	Allen, Xenia P.O.	25	M	2:229
Anderson, James	Leav., Alexandria, Easton (Farmer)	43	M	10:446
Anderson, James[NC]	Bourbon, Turkey Creek P.O. (Farmer)	48	M	2:108
Anderson, John R.	Bourbon, Xenia P.O.	20	M	2:127
Anderson, Lousia	Leavenworth, Alexandria, Easton	26	F	10:446
Anderson, M. A.	Doniphan, Marion, Palermo	9	F	1:281
Anderson, Margaret	Bourbon, Xenia P.O.	11	F	2:127
Anderson, Martha[1,NC]	Leavenworth, Kickapoo	58	F	10:335
Anderson, Mary	Bourbon, Xenia P.O.	80	F	2:127
Anderson, Oliver	Doniphan, Marion, Palermo	32	F	1:287
Anderson, S.	" " " (Farmer)	30	M	1:277
Anderson, S. R.	Nem., Capioma, Pleas.Sp.(Physician)	36	M	3:109
Anderson, Sarah	Douglas, Wakarusa, Lawrence	62	F	6:241
Anderson, Watson G.[NC]	Allen, Iola P.O.	44	M	2:259
Andrews, Danl.	Arrapahoe, Denver	50	M	11:350
Andrews, Sarah	Douglas, Palmyra, McKinney	24	F	6:305
Andricks, Jaco	Bourbon, Fort Scott P.O. (Farmer)	77	M	2:219
Angel, Harrison[NC]	Allen, Humboldt P.O. (Farmer)	17	M	2:297
Angel, James[NC]	" " " (Farmer)	56	M	2:297
Angel, James A.[NC]	" " " (Farmer)	22	M	2:297
Angel, Lowell[NC]	" " "	55	F	2:297
Angel, Mathias[NC]	" " "	14	M	2:297
Angel, William[NC]	" " " (Farmer)	25	M	2:297
Annett, F. L.	Johnson, Gardner	22	F	6:49
Anthony, A.	Doug., Wakarusa, Lawrence(HackDriver)	25	M	6:229
Archer, George[SC]	Wyandotte, Wyandotte (Laborer)	46	M	10:3
Ard, Mary	Allen, Humboldt P.O.	43	F	2:303
Argnbright, P.	Johnson, Lexington (Farmer)	45	M	6:71
Arlington, Wm.	Arrapahoe, South Park	34	M	11:138
Armor, Mary V.	Atchison, Mt. Pleasant	29	F	1:157
Armstrong, J.	Frank., Peoria, Stanton (Farmer)	73	M	8:278
Armstrong, M. H.	Doniphan, White Cloud	21	F	1:438
Armstrong, Malinda[NC]	Linn, Centerville, Hawks Wing	48	F	7:97
Armstrong, Mary J.	Leavenworth, Fort Leavenworth	24	F	10:320
Arney, Salin B.	Anderson, Washington, Garnett	42	F	7:255
Arney, Saml.	And., Washington, Garnett(Postmaster)	21	M	7:255
Arney, Wm. E.	" " "	13	M	7:255
Arnold, D.	Doniphan, Iowa Point (Farmer)	31	M	1:433
Arnold, J. M.	Johnson, Monticello (Farmer)	34	M	6:84
Arnold, Jas.	Arrapahoe, South Park	29	M	11:246
Arnold, M. E.	Franklin, Ohio, Ohio City	2	F	8:228
Arnold, Mary	Arrapahoe, South Park	31	M	11:246
Arnold, W.	Arrapahoe, Valley of the Platte	28		11:781
Arnott, C.	Doniphan, Burr Oak, Whitehead	54	F	1:341
Arnott, James	" " " (Farmer)	60	M	1:341
Asbury, Thomas	Leavenworth, Ward 4 (Plasterer)	63	M	10:274
Ashbrook, H. T.	Arrapahoe, South Park (Miner)	20	M	11:66
Ashly, Mary M.	Linn, Paris (Farmer)	18	F	7:129
Atha, Calvin	Jefferson, Oskaloosa (Blacksmith)	24	M	5:118
Atkinrow, Isaac M.	Leavenworth, Kickapoo (Farmer)	38	M	10:413
Atkinrow, Charity	" "	35	F	10:413
Atkins, C. T.	Arrapahoe, South Park	56	M	11:126
Atkinson, Catherine	Bourbon, Turkey Creek P.O.(Housewife)	23	F	2:113
Atkinson, Nancy	Morris, Clarks Creek, Council Grove	45	F	4:280
Audmen, Wm.[1,NC]	Leavenworth, Kickapoo (Farmer)	59	M	10:335
Austin, Belfield P.	Atchison, Lancaster	3	M	1:110

[1]Name clearly Anderson in census record; W.P.A. indexer shows Audmen (which
   see) for members of the same household, dwelling No. 2313.
Arapahoe: spelled incorrectly with 2 r's in census and in this index also.

Name	Kansas: County; Township; P.O. Arap. Co.: Census Div. Not Township	Age	Sex	Census V.	Census Pg.
Austin, John	Atchison, Lancaster (Wheelwright)	33	M	1:110	
Austin, L.	Franklin, Centropolis, Prairie City	20	F	8:220	
Austin, Louise Jane	Atchison, Lancaster	22	F	1:110	
Austin, Wm. Franklin	"	5	M	1:110	
Avery, Jno.	Arrapahoe, Valley of the Platte	24	M	11:803	
Ayres, J.	Johnson, Aubrey (Carpenter)	28	M	6:37	
Ayres, M.	" "	53	F	6:37	
Babb, Luanna[NC]	Lykins, Mound, Osawatomie	45	F	8:70	
Babber, Rebecca[NC]	Linn, Centerville, Oakwood	23	F	7:92	
Backmaster, Geo.	Arrapahoe, Denver (Saloon)	27	M	11:376	
Badger, O. C.	Arrapahoe, South Park (Miner)	39	M	11:63	
Bailey, A.	Arrapahoe, Leavenworth Gulch (Miner)	23	M	11:556	
Bailey, Alexander	Breckenridge, Forest Hill (Farmer)	44	M	4:183	
Bailey, Charles E.	Lykins, Middle Creek, Jonesville	6	M	8:110	
Bailey, F.	Arrapahoe, Golden City (Miner)	30	M	11:586	
Bailey, Jas.	Arrapahoe, Missouri City (Miner)	20	M	11:564	
Bailey, Jerome P.	Arrapahoe, Arrapahoe City (Miner)	18	M	11:587	
Bailey, Joh[NC]	Jackson, Holton (Laborer)	23	M	5:178	
Bailey, L.	Doniphan, Center, Troy	40	F	1:268	
Bailey, L. T.	Arrapahoe, South Park (Miner)	30	M	11:45	
Bailey, Mary	Arrapahoe, Golden City	25	F	11:586	
Bailey, R.	Arrapahoe, Leavenworth Gulch (Miner)	27	M	11:556	
Bailey, Wm. [SC]	Atchison, Walnut, Sumner (Farmer)	66	M	1:184	
Baily, Washington	Mars., Blue Rapids, Irving (Farmer)	45	M	3:208	
Baine, B. F.	Arrapahoe, Arrapahoe City (Laborer)	34	M	11:587	
Bainter, D.	Arrapahoe, South Clear Creek	22	M	11:744	
Baird, John	Allen, Geneva P.O. (Farmer)	30	M	2:255	
Bairr, R.	Davis, Ft. Riley-Ashland P.O.	4	M	9:347	
Bairr, R.	" " " " "	2	F	9:347	
Baker, A. I.	Breckenridge, Agnes City (Lawyer)	36	M	4:146	
Baker, Celena	Anderson, Town of Greeley, Garnett	35	F	7:242	
Baker, E.	Frank.; Potta.; Walker, Anderson Co.	44	F	8:243	
Baker, Francis[NC]	Jefferson, Ozawkie (Farm Laborer)	27	M	5:99	
Baker, J.	Franklin, Potta.; Walker (Farmer)	48	M	8:243	
Baker, Jesse	And., Town of Greeley, Garnett(Farmer)	35	M	7:242	
Baker, John[NC]	Cof., Ottumwa, Burlington (Farmer)	54	M	4:49	
Baker, John F.[NC]	Leavenworth, Kickapoo	18	M	10:330	
Baker, John T.[NC]	Allen, Humboldt P.O. (Painter)	34	M	2:277	
Baker, Mahala	Lykins, Sugar Creek, West Point, Mo.	27	F	8:100	
Baker, Martin A.[NC]	Leavenworth, Kickapoo	16	M	10:330	
Baker, Mary[NC]	" "	51	F	10:330	
Baker, S.	Franklin, Centropolis, Minneola	33	F	8:207	
Baker, Susan	Atchison, Walnut, Sumner	6	F	1:183	
Baker, Susan E.[NC]	Leavenworth, Kickapoo	15	F	10:330	
Baker, T. J.	Wyandotte, Wyandotte (Postmaster)	27	M	10:44	
Baker, W. H.[NC]	Leavenworth, Kickapoo	19	M	10:330	
Baker, William	Lyk.; Sug.Cr.,West Pt.,Mo.(Farmer)	30	M	8:100	
Balb, Elizabeth	Green., Eureka, Pleasant Gr.	30	F	9:184	
Balb, James	" " " " (Farmer)	35	M	9:184	
Baldwin, C. F.	Arrapahoe, South Park	33	M	11:93	
Baldwin, Hannah[NC]	Linn, Mound City	35	F	7:111	
Baldwin, M. A.	Doniphan, Center, Troy	25	F	1:272	
Baldwin, M. N.	Arrapahoe, South Park	37	M	11:221	
Baldwin, Robert[NC]	Linn, Mound City (Farmer)	41	M	7:111	
Baldwin, Sam	" " "	27	M	7:110	
Baldwin, Wm.	Arrapahoe, South Park	23	M	11:236	
Baldwin, Wm.	Doniphan, Center, Troy (Farm Hand)	16	M	1:272	
Bales, R.	Linn, Potosi	60	F	7:72	
Baley, Rebecca[NC]	Atchison, Lancaster	59	F	1:114	
Balfour, John[NC]	Linn, Scott, Brooklyn (Physician)	43	M	7:15	
Ball, Ann	Franklin, Centropolis, Minneola	Inf.	F	8:204	

Arrapahoe: spelled incorrectly with 2 r's in census and in this index also.

Name	Kansas: County; Township; P.O. Arap. Co.: Census Div. Not Township	Age	Sex	Census V. : Pg.
Ball, Eliza	Linn, Valley, Blooming Grove	45	F	7:48
Ball, L. E.	Franklin, Centropolis, Minneola	3	F	8:204
Ball, T.	" " "	2	M	8:204
Ballard, C. W.	Coffey, Avon, Burlington (Farmer)	43	M	4:11
Ballard, Richard	Marshall, Marysville (Merchant)	29	M	3:251
Ballard, W. B.	Franklin, Centropolis, Minneola	3	M	8:209
Balling, Margaret	Madison, Verdigris, Madison Centre	31	F	4:246
Balson, M.	Arrapahoe, South Park	28	M	11:79
Bancroft, E. F.NC	Arrapahoe, South Park (Miner)	33	M	11:45
Bangess, BryantNC	Bourbon, Fort Scott P.O. (Farmer)	36	M	2:92
Banguess, Eli P.NC	Anderson, Garnett P.O. (Farmer)	32	M	7:213
Banningarter, J.SC	Arrapahoe; Tarryall,South Park(Miner)	29	M	11:604
Barbee, J.	Linn, Mound City (Farmer)	54	M	7:124
Barber, M. A.	Douglas, Lawrence	25	F	6:211
Barber, Sm.	Arrapahoe, Valley of the Platte	23	M	11:856
Barby, G. W.	Doniphan, Center, Troy (Carpenter)	43	M	1:243
Barclaw, Patsey	Douglas, Palmyra, McKinney	48	F	6:307
Barker, EnochNC	Anderson, Walker, Garnett (Farmer)	35	M	7:248
Barker, JamesNC	Anderson, Monroe, Garnett	50	M	7:219
Barkes, A. E.	Doniphan, Wayne, Doniphan	22	F	1:368
Barkes, C.	" " " (Farmer)	32	M	1:368
Barkley, Isaac	Brown, Claytonville (Farmer)	35	M	3:54
Barlow, T. S.	Arrapahoe, South Park	28	M	11:127
Barnard, CalvinNC	Lykins, Osawatomie (Farmer)	40	M	8:55
Barnard, Lucinda S.NC	" "	40	F	8:55
Barnell?, Geo.	Arrapahoe, South Clear Creek	26	M	11:751
Barnes, F.	Frank.; Centrop., Minneola(Chairmaker)	43	M	8:201
Barnes, George W.	Nem.,Grenada, Pleas.Sp. (Farmer)	64	M	3:112
Barnes, K.	Franklin, Centropolis Minneola	33	F	8:201
Barnes, Lydia	Breckenridge, Fremont	51	F	4:164
Barnes, S.SC	Johnson, Shawnee (Farmer)	54	M	6:32
Barnes, S.NC	" " (Farmer)	54	M	6:26
Barnet, Nancy J.	Arrapahoe, Central City(Seamstress)	26	F	11:574
Barnett, W. B.	Brown, Irving, Hiawatha (Farmer)	36	M	3:17
Barr, Gatera	Leavenworth, Stranger, Leav. City	50	F	10:479
Barr, H.	Arrapahoe, South Park	22	M	11:149
Barr, Jackson R.	Allen, Humboldt P.O. (Farmer)	35	M	2:284
Barr, Mary A.	" " "	28	F	2:284
Barr, Samuel	Bourbon, Marmaton P.O. (Farmer)	54	M	2:105
Barr, Uticus	Leav., Stranger, Leav.City (Farmer)	48	M	10:479
Barret, M. E.NC	Johnson, Shawnee	29	F	6:30
Barret, Martha A.	Wyandotte, Wyandotte	50	F	10:20
Barret, William	" Wyand.(Meth. Clergyman)	55	M	10:20
Barrett, Elezabeth	Douglas, Palmyra, Baldwin	52	F	6:284
Barrett, John	Doug., Palmyra, Baldwin (Farmer)	53	M	6:284
Barrett, S. T.	Arrapahoe, Valley of the Platte	29	M	11:832
Barringer, P. W.	Douglas, Willow Springs (Farmer)	52	M	3:316
Barror, Alfred	Anderson, Washington, Garnett	4	M	7:256
Barror, Catherine	" " "	12	F	7:256
Barror, Eliza	" " "	16	F	7:256
Barror, Elizabeth	" " "	16	F	7:256
Barror, Jemima	" " "	8	F	7:256
Barror, M.	" " "	14	M	7:256
Barror, Mary	" " "	35	F	7:256
Barror, Rebecca	" " "	2	F	7:256
Barror, Ryly	" " "	40	M	7:256
Barror, Solomon	" " "	10	M	7:256
Barror, William	" " "	6	M	7:256
Barry, Morgan V.	Lykins, Stanton (Farmer)	25	M	8:2
Barry, WilliamNC	Allen, Iola P.O. (Farmer)	49	M	2:271
Bartlett, R.	John., Oxford, N.Santa Fe,Mo.(Farmer)	25	M	6:109

Arapahoe: spelled incorrectly with 2 r's in census and in this index also.

Name	Kansas: County; Township; P.O. Arap. Co.: Census Div. Not Township	Age	Sex	Census V. Pg.
Barton, F.	John., Oxford, N.Santa Fe, Mo.	54	F	6:108
Barton, George	Douglas, Palmyra, Baldwin (Farmer)	29	M	6:302
Barton, J. G.	Johnson, Olathe (Physician)	28	M	6:4
Barton, Jeremiah	Douglas, Palmyra, Baldwin	6	M	6:302
Barton, Nancy	" " "	24	F	6:302
Barton, T. F.	Franklin, Centropolis, Minneola	2	M	8:214
Barton, W. G.	Arrapahoe, South Park (Miner)	33	M	11:42
Basey, John J.	Jackson, Franklin, Holton (Farmer)	45	M	5:185
Bashaw, Thomas H.	Allen, Humboldt P.O. (Farmer)	66	M	2:295
Bassow, J. W.	Arrapahoe, Denver	34	M	11:384
Batchelor, S. J.	Arrapahoe, South Park (Miner)	34	M	11:57
Bates, Mary J.	Coffey, Avon, Burlington	36	F	4:9
Batleson, Benj.	Douglas, Lecompton (Farmer)	45	M	6:369
Batriff, Elizabeth[NC]	Breckenridge, Forest Hill	34	F	4:176
Batson, Elisabeth	Leavenworth, Easton	65	F	10:298
Batson, Wm.	" " (Farmer)	63	M	10:297
Batson, Wm. T.	Jackson, Douglas, Holton (Farmer)	31	M	5:173
Battle, Geo.	Arrapahoe, South Clear Creek	23	M	11:706
Baty, W.	Johnson, Monticello (Blacksmith)	60	M	6:86
Baugh, B.[SC]	Linn, Potosi, Rovella (Farmer)	51	M	7:59
Baugh, Cassia[SC]	" " "	8	F	7:58
Baugh, Elizabeth[SC]	" " "	50	F	7:59
Baugh, John[SC]	" " " (Farmer)	18	M	7:58
Baugh, John[SC]	" " " (Farmer)	45	M	7:58
Baugh, Louisa[SC]	" " "	6	F	7:58
Baugh, Manerva[SC]	" " "	40	F	7:58
Baugh, Margaret[SC]	" " "	11	F	7:58
Baugh, Martha[SC]	" " "	14	F	7:58
Baugh, Sarah[SC]	" " "	16	F	7:58
Baugh, Virginia[SC]	" " "	10	F	7:58
Baugher, J.	Arrapahoe, South Clear Creek	25	M	11:729
Baxter, J. M.	" " " "	24	M	11:762
Baxter, L.	" " " "	33	M	11:136
Baxter, Mary	Bourbon, Fort Scott P.O.(Housewife)	56	F	2:190
Baxter, Mary J.	Breckenridge, Emporia	18	F	4:197
Bay, J. I.	Arrapahoe, South Park	44	M	11:185
Bayless, Roena[NC]	Atchison, Mt. Pleasant	65	F	1:148
Bayne, Alex	Jefferson, Ky., Oskaloosa (Farmer)	47	M	5:69
Bayne, Mahala	Bourbon, Xenia P.O. (Housewife)	23	F	2:125
Beal, H. B.	Coffey, Neosho, Burlington (Farmer)	41	M	4:70
Beal, Philip	" " "	13	M	4:70
Beam, J. H.	Arrapahoe, Mountain City (Doctor)	28	M	11:462
Beam, Wm.	Arrapahoe, South Park	28	M	11:235
Bear, G. W.	Franklin, Ohio, Ohio City	7	M	8:229
Bear, J.	" " " "	5	M	8:229
Bear, Jacob A. B.	Lykins, Paola	23	M	8:25
Bear, M. F.	Franklin, Ohio, Ohio City	8	F	8:229
Beard, James	Coffey, Leroy, Burlington (Farmer)	35	M	4:24
Beaser, Samuel	Bourbon, Fort Scott P.O.(Preacher M.E)	40	M	2:90
Beath, R.	Woodson, Neosho Falls (Farmer)	31	M	9:135
Beavers, W.	Linn, Paris	36	M	7:144
Beck, Alfro P.[NC]	Allen, Humboldt P.O.	3	M	2:295
Beck, Amanda[NC]	" " "	5	F	2:295
Beck, Elisa[NC]	" " "	46	F	2:295
Beck, Elisabeth[NC]	" " "	10	F	2:295
Beck, Henry[NC]	" " "	7	M	2:295
Beck, Israel[NC]	" " " (Farm Laborer)	15	M	2:295
Beck, John[NC]	" " " (Farmer)	23	M	2:295
Beck, John H.[NC]	" " " (Farmer)	51	M	2:295
Beck, Mary[NC]	" " "	17	F	2:295
Beck, Phillip[NC]	" " " (Farm Laborer)	19	M	2:295

Arapahoe: spelled incorrectly with 2 r's in census and in this index also.

Name	Kansas: County; Township; P.O. Arap. Co.: Census Div. Not Township	Age	Sex	Census V.	Census Pg.
Beck, William[NC]	Bourbon, Xenia P.O. (Farmer)	23	M	2:129	
Beck, William[NC]	Allen, Humboldt P.O.(Farm Laborer)	12	M	2:295	
Becket, H.	Doniphan, White Cloud (Farmer)	30	M	1:443	
Beckett, James	Doniphan, White Cloud (Confectioner)	44	M	1:439	
Beckly, Wooly	Lykins, Osawatomie (Farmer)	42	M	8:57	
Beckner, Elizabeth[NC]	Leavenworth, Easton	32	F	10:297	
Becwell, J. B.	Linn, Potosi, Rovella (Carpenter)	40	M	7:59	
Bedell, W.	Arrapahoe, South Clear Creek	26	M	11:692	
Bee, Abner	Linn, Potosi	4	F	7:71	
Bee, Elias	" "	9	M	7:71	
Bee, Joseph[NC]	" " (Farmer)	24	M	7:71	
Bee, Ruth	" "	15	F	7:71	
Bee, Sarah	" " (Farmer)	76	M	7:71	
Beebe, H.	Doniphan, Center, Troy	4	F	1:262	
Beebe, John	" " "	8	M	1:262	
Beland, Amanda	Jefferson, Grasshopper Falls	22	F	5:4	
Beland, Laura	" " "	6	F	5:4	
Belanny, J.	Frank., Centrop.., Minneola (Farmer)	28	M	8:208	
Bell, J. C.[NC]	Arrapahoe, Russell Gulch (Miner)	33	M	11:590	
Bendle, Reshaw	Douglas, Wakarusa, Lawrence	55	M	6:257	
Benedict, B. C.	Arrapahoe, South Clear Creek (Miner)	24	M	11:628	
Beninght, S. D.	Doniphan, Center, Troy (Clerk)	28	M	1:243	
Benjamin, C. C.	Arrapahoe, Valley of the Platte	30	M	11:805	
Benjamin, D.	Arrapahoe, South Park	43	M	11:198	
Benjamin, E. E.	Franklin, Ottawa, Hickory Creek	18	F	8:264	
Benjamin, Geo.	Arrapahoe, South Park	39	M	11:231	
Benjamin, S.	" " " (Miner)	26	M	11:18	
Bennett, E.[1]	Franklin, Peoria, Stanton	3	F	8:284	
Bennett, Owen[NC]	Doniphan, Wolf River, Walnut Grove	12	M	1:400	
Bennett, Samuel[NC]	Wyandotte, Wyandotte (Laborer)	49	M	10:41	
Benson, Benniah[NC]	Breckenridge, Americus (Farmer)	31	M	4:217	
Benson, Calvin	Mars., Vermillion, Bar.Mills,(Farmer)	31	M	3:214	
Benson, Danl.[NC]	Breck., Pike, Plymouth (Farmer)	55	M	4:207	
Benson, Eleza	Mars., Vermil., Barrett Mills	24	F	3:214	
Benson, James C.	" " " " (Farmer)	21	F	3:214	
Benson, Margaret[NC]	Breckenridge, Americus	27	F	4:217	
Bentley, James	Nem., Richmond, Seneca(Expr. Rider)	30	M	3:94	
Bentley, W.	Johnson, Lexington (Farmer)	34	M	6:75	
Bently, Elizabeth[NC]	Woodson, Verdigris, Belmont (F. W.)	15	F	9:159	
Bently, Jas.	" " " (Farmer)	61	M	9:159	
Benton, Nancy	Marshall, Vermillion, Barrett Mills	20	F	3:225	
Benton, T.	Arrapahoe, South Park	21	M	11:143	
Berkley, W.	Atchison, Ward 3 (Painter)	24	M	1:44	
Berkshire, A.	Johnson, Spring Hill (Farmer)	50	M	6:43	
Berkshire, A.	" " "	16	F	6:44	
Berkshire, E. A.	" " "	48	F	6:44	
Berkshire, James	Lykins, Wea, Paola (Engineer)	28	M	8:112	
Berkshire, M. A.	Johnson, Spring Hill	4	F	6:44	
Bernard, W.	Arrapahoe, South Park (Miner)	17	M	11:81	
Bernett, Henry[NC]	Allen, Humboldt P.O. (Farmer)	45	M	2:291	
Bernis (Bemis?) A. E.	Franklin, Peoria, Stanton	2	F	8:285	
Beroven, V.	Doniphan, Washington, Elwood	61	F	1:335	
Berry, B. A.	Franklin, Centropolis, Minneola	3	F	8:213	
Berry, B. K.	Doniphan, Doniphan (Farmer)	44	M	1:387	
Berry, Chas.	Arrapahoe, Central Park (Farmer)	67	M	11:580	
Berry, D.	Doniphan, Doniphan (F. Hand)	20	M	1:387	
Berry, M. C.	Franklin, Centropolis, Minneola	5	F	8:213	
Berry, Marg	Doniphan, Doniphan	43	F	1:387	

[1]W.P.A. indexer questioned state of birth; possibly born in Virginia.

Arapahoe: spelled incorrectly with 2 r's in census and in this index also.

Name	Kansas: County; Township; P.O. Arap. Co.: Census Div. Not Township	Age	Sex	Census V. Pg.
Berry, Robt.	Doniphan, Doniphan	16	M	1:387
Berry, Wm.	Arrapahoe, South Park	29	M	11:112
Berryman, Wm. B.	Shawnee, Topeka (Farmer)	51	M	9:21
Best, John W.	And., Jackson, Garnett (Farmer)	30	M	7:205
Best, Sarah^{NC}	Jefferson, Jefferson, Crooked Cr.	25	F	5:39
Bethel, Buford	Mars., Vermillion, Bar. Mills(Farmer)	37	M	3:217
Betters, Elisabeth^{NC}	Leavenworth, Ward 3	65	BF	10:220
Beverlee, Jno.	Arrapahoe, Nevada Gulch (Store-house)	50	M	11:519
Bible, H. J.	Breckenridge, Fremont (Farmer)	23	M	4:162
Billard, C.	Arrapahoe, South Park	35	M	11:130
Binkley, Elizabeth	Lyk., Sugar Cr., N.Lanc. (Widow)	62	F	8:99
Binkley, James	" " " " (Farm Hand)	62	M	8:99
Binkley, James^{NC}	Atchison, Mt. Pleasant (Farmer)	30	M	1:163
Bird, Elizabeth	Morris, Neosho, Council Grove	63	F	4:273
Bird, H. A.^{NC}	Arrapahoe, South Park	32	M	11:132
Birlis, Nathan^{NC}	Hunter, Eldor., Chelsea(FarmLaborer)	21	M	4:360
Bishop, J. H.	Nem., Red Vermil., America (Merchant)	38	M	3:132
Bishop, M. S.^{NC}	" " " "	27	F	3:132
Bishop, Sophrona^{NC}	" " " "	10	F	3:132
Bishop, Thomas C.	Leavenworth, Easton (Farmer)	67	M	10:300
Bixby, M. B.	Arrapahoe, South Park (Miner)	27	M	11:32
Black, Elizabeth	Morris, Neosho, Council Grove	32	F	4:278
Black, George	" " "	3	M	4:278
Black, J.	Frank., Ottawa, Hickory Cr. (Farmer)	47	M	8:264
Black, James	Morris, Neosho, Council Grove	11	M	4:278
Black, John	" " " "	14	M	4:278
Black, Martha	" " " "	21	F	4:278
Black, Priscilla	" " " "	9	F	4:278
Black, Samuel	" " " "	7	M	4:278
Black, Sarah	" " " "	23	F	4:278
Black, Wm.	" " " "	5	M	4:278
Blacker, R. A.	Chase, Toledo (Farmer	51	M	4:336
Blackshier, J. R.	Chase, Cottonwood Cot.Falls (Farming)	26	M	4:319
Blackwood, Harry	Lykins, Paola (Clerk)	23	M	8:24
Blackwood, James	Arrapahoe, Denver	44	M	11:319
Blackwood, Sam	Leavenworth, 1st Ward (Teamster)	50	BM	10:98
Blair, Kate	Arrapahoe, Denver (Spinster)	18	F	11:393
Blair, Mary	Bourbon, Fort Scott P.O.(Housewife)	32	F	2:155
Blair, W.	Arrapahoe, South Park	26	M	11:232
Blake, George	Brown, Locknon, Powhattan (Farmer)	66	M	3:68
Blake, I. H. (J.H.?)^{NC}	Olathe, Olathe (Clerk)	37	M	6:4
Blake, J. V.	Arrapahoe, South Park	34	M	11:196
Blake, Thos. A.^{NC}	Jeff., Grasshopper Falls (Farmer)	39	M	5:8
Blakely, Wm. ^{NC}	Arrapahoe, South Clear Creek	46	M	11:753
Blakeman, C.	Arrapa., Leavenworth Gulch (Miner)	26	M	11:557
Blanton, Mary	Douglas, Wakarusa, Lawrence	19	F	6:238
Blanton, Mary	" " "	49	F	6:238
Blare, William P.	Lykins, Middle Cr., Paola (Farmer)	47	M	8:109
Blassingham, J. N.^{SC}	Arrapahoe, Central City (Miner)	26	M	11:576
Bledraw, Elizabeth^{SC}	Douglas, Willow Springs (Farmer)	43	F	6:323
Block, D.	Arrapahoe, South Park	33	M	11:199
Block, S. H.	Arrapahoe, South Clear Creek	27	M	11:699
Bloomer, E. S.	Arrapahoe, South Park	35	M	11:159
Bloss, C. G.	Arrapahoe, Valley of the Platte	24	M	11:856
Blunt, Jacob C.^{NC}	Bourbon, Fort Scott P.O. (Farmer)	40	M	2:95
Bobb, Martha	Wood., Verdigris, Pleasant Gr. (F.W.)	40	F	9:163
Bobertson, Elizabeth	Leavenworth, Alexandria, Easton	26	F	10:445
Boggs, H. L.	Johnson, Olathe (Farmer)	28	M	6:121
Boles, Levi J.^{NC}	Atchison, Mt. Pleasant (Merchant)	38	M	1:160
Bollis, J. W.^{NC}	Arrapahoe, Nevada Gulch	24	M	11:530
Bond, Mary J.^{NC}	Douglas, Eudora	14	F	6:341

Arapahoe: spelled incorrectly with 2 r's in census and in this index also.

Name	Kansas: County; Township; P.O. Arap. Co.: Census Div. Not Township	Age	Sex	Census v. Pg.
Bond, Robt. NC	Douglas, Eudora	16	M	6:341
Bond, Sarah NC	" "	35	F	6:341
Bonngerton, Max.	Arrapahoe, Russell Gulch (Miner)	37	M	11:543
Booth, A. NC	Allen, Humboldt P.O. (Farmer)	26	M	2:295
Booth, Harriet NC	" " "	25	F	2:295
Boots, A.	Doniphan, Doniphan (Carpenter)	33	M	1:386
Bowen, John SC	Atchison, Ward 1 (Blacksmith)	38	M	1:11
Boykin, C. NC	Johnson, Shawnee	27	F	6:25
Boykin, W. A. NC	" " (Carpenter)	41	M	6:25
Boykin, W. W. NC	" "	10	M	6:25
Brackett, O.	Arrapahoe, South Park	35	M	11:121
Bradford, Ann	Mars., Vermil., Bar. Mills (Domestic)	16	F	3:227
Bradford, George	" " " "	10	M	3:227
Bradford, James	" " " "	12	M	3:227
Bradford, John	" " " " (FarmLaborer)	20	M	3:227
Bradford, Joseph	" " " "	7	M	3:228
Bradford, M. T.	Arrapahoe, South Park	22	M	11:193
Bradford, Martha	Marshall, Vermillion, Barrett Mills	6	F	3:228
Bradford, Mary	" " " "	14	F	3:227
Bradford, Sarah	" " Bar.M.(Domestic)	18	F	3:227
Bradford, William	" " " "	8	M	3:227
Bradley, George	Jackson, Franklin, Holton (Farmer)	45	M	5:182
Bradley, Mary SC	McGhee, Fort Scott P.O.	42	F	9:211
Bradley, Sophia	Otoe, Otoe, Chelsea	59	F	4:352
Bradly, Nancy	Linn, Centerville, Hawks Wing	29	F	7:97
Bradshaw, James	Breckenridge, Waterloo(Farm Laborer)	58	M	4:154
Bradshaw, Lewis	Jeff., Jeff., Crooked Cr. (Farmer)	49	M	5:29
Brady, C.	Doniphan, Iowa Point	5	F	1:418
Brady, Elizabeth	Lykins, Wea, Squiresville	22	F	8:115
Brady, Ezra T.	" " " (Farmer)	34	M	8:115
Brady, J. B.	Doniphan, Center, Troy (Merchant)	25	M	1:241
Brady, Jno.	Doniphan, Iowa Point	9	M	1:418
Braggle, Agilla NC	Woodson, Pleasant Grove (F. W.)	36or56?	F	9:166
Brainfield, Emily	Wyandotte, Wyandotte	54	F	10:41
Brainfield, Jordon	" " (Grocer)	44	M	10:41
Bramhall, D.	Arrapahoe, South Park	28	M	11:175
Branard, John	Linn, Potosi (Farmer)	60	M	7:72
Branch, Henry C.	Leavenworth, Easton (Farmer)	33	M	10:294
Branch, W.	Arrapahoe, South Park	35	M	11:175
Branson, J. C. NC	Chase, Falls (Farm Laborer)	25	M	4:330
Branson, Jesse G. NC	Breckenridge, Forest Hill (Farmer)	24	M	4:179
Branson, Ruth NC	Breckenridge, Emporia	56	F	4:194
Brantly, Benjamin NC	Bourbon, Fort Scott P.O. (Farmer)	67	M	2:219
Brassfield, C. NC	Johnson, Monticello (Farmer)	53	M	6:85
Brassfield, D. NC	Johnson, Olathe (Farmer)	42	M	6:120
Brassfield, M.	Johnson, Monticello	40	F	6:85
Bratcher, J. NC	Linn, Potosi, Rovella (Farmer)	58	M	7:62
Bratton, James	Lyk., Marysville, Spr.Hill (Farmer)	28	M	8:128
Bratton, Sabina	" " " "(Widow&Farmer)	56	F	8:128
Brazil, Sarah	Dorn, Turkey Creek P.O.	32	F	2:356
Bready, J. W.	Arrapahoe, Tarryall South Park	23	M	11:610
Brett, L.	Arrapahoe, South Park	22	M	11:184
Brewer, Andrew NC	Nem., Clear Cr., Ash Point (Farmer)	42	M	3:91
Brewer, Eunice NC	" " " " "	38	F	3:91
Brewer, M. NC	Douglas, Kanwaca, Lawrence	52	F	6:392
Brewster, Jno.	Arrapahoe, Golden City (Miner)	28	M	11:443
Briant, Sarah	Lykins, Osawatomie, Indianapolis	66	F	8:64
Briant, Sarah E.	Lykins, Stanton	8	F	8:11
Briant, William C.	" " (Shoemaker)	32	M	8:11
Briant, William C.	" "	8/12		8:12
Bridges, A. M.	Arrapahoe, Quartz Valley (Laborer)	26	M	11:496

Arapahoe: spelled incorrectly with 2 r's in census and in this index also.

Name	Kansas: County; Township; P.O. Arap. Co.: Census Div. Not Township	Age	Sex	Census V. Pg.
Brien, Hannah	Leavenworth, 3rd Ward	27	F	10:213
Brient, Barnet E.	Lykins, Stanton (Grocer)	34	M	8:11
Briger, Charles	Linn, Centerville, Keokuk	7	M	7:84
Briger, John	" " "	11	M	7:84
Briger, Josiah	" " " (Merchant)	38	M	7:84
Briger, Margaret	" " "	36	F	7:84
Briger, Sarah	" " "	9	F	7:84
Briggs, A.	Frank., Ottawa, Prairie City	5	F	8:256
Briggs, E.	" " " "	8	M	8:256
Briggs, Eliza	Doniphan, White Cloud	34	F	1:438
Briggs, G. O.NC	Arrapahoe, South Clear Creek (Miner)	26	M	11:759
Briggs, J.	Linn, Potosi, Rovella (Farmer)	28	M	7:57
Bright, A.	Linn, Town of Paris (Teamster)	45	M	7:138
Briles, A.NC	Coffey, Neosho, Burlington (Farmer)	43	M	4:71
Briles, B.NC	Woodson, Liberty, Leroy (Farmer)	35	M	9:145
Briles, CharlesNC	Coffey, Neosho, Burlington	22	M	4:71
Briles, CordeliaNC	Woodson, Liberty, Leroy	8	F	9:145
Briles, Dorcas NC	" " "	36	F	9:145
Briles, HarrisonNC	Coffey, Neosho, Burlington	9	M	4:71
Briles, JamesNC	Woodson, Liberty, Leroy	10	M	9:145
Briles, JohnNC	Coffey, Neosho, Burlington	16	M	4:71
Briles, Leonidus NC	Woodson, Liberty, Leroy	4	M	9:145
Briles, LouisaNC	Coffey, Neosho, Burlington	14	F	4:71
Briles, MaryNC	Woodson, Liberty, Leroy	16	F	9:145
Briles, Nancy C. NC	Coffey, Neosho, Burlington	4	F	4:71
Briles, Noch M. NC	" " "	20	M	4:71
Briles, Robert NC	" " "	11	M	4:71
Briles, SarahNC	" " "	43	F	4:71
Briles, SarahNC	Woodson, Liberty, Leroy	3	F	9:145
Briles, Sarah R. NC	Coffey, Neosho, Burlington	18	F	4:71
Briles, Z. B. NC	" " "	6	M	4:71
Brill, S. R.	Johnson, Monticello	22	F	6:22
Brillow, E.	Arrapahoe, South Clear Creek	28	M	11:717
Bristol, A.	Arrapahoe, South Park	26	M	11:181
Broadway, Geo.	" " "	29	M	11:43
Brock, RebeccaNC	Leavenworth, Easton	32	F	10:288
Brockett, T.SC	Linn, Valley, Blooming Gr.(Physician)	67	M	7:33
Broffer, E.1	Frank., Ottawa, Prair.City,Doug.Co.	4	F	8:257
Broffer, M.1	" " " " " (Farmer)	19	M	8:257
Broffer, T.1	" " " " "	19	M	8:257
Bronse, N. R.	Arrapahoe, South Clear Creek	29	M	11:705
Brook, James	Jefferson, Ky., Oskaloosa (Farmer)	38	M	5:75
Brook, Mary A.	" " "	31	F	5:75
Brooks, Warrick	Allen, Iola P.O. (Carpenter)	27	M	2:261
Brotherton, W. C.	Arrapahoe, Valley of the Platte	26	M	11:827
Brough, George	Anderson, Walker, Garnett (Miller)	35	M	7:245
Browman, B. F.	Don., Wash., Wathena (M.E.Minister)	37	M	1:329
Brown, A.	Leavenworth, 1st Ward (Grocer)	50	M	10:141
Brown, Amanda	" " "	50	F	10:141
Brown, C.	Johnson, Lexington (Farmer)	23	M	6:77
Brown, C.	Arrapahoe, Mountain City (Washer)	35	MF	11:471
Brown, Charles	Jefferson, Oskaloosa	8	M	5:113
Brown, ElmiraNC	Linn, Mound City	31	F	7:120
Brown, Emily J.	Leavenworth, Fort Leavenworth P.O.	15	F	10:320
Brown, Fanny	Linn, Potosi, Rovella (Teacher)	22	F	7:55
Brown, Geo. NC	Arrapahoe, Denver (Miner)	28	M	11:420
Brown, Geo. NC	" " (Miner)	43	M	11:414
Brown, George R.	Breckenridge, Waterloo (Farmer)	78	M	4:153
Brown, Hannah M. NC	Bourbon, Xenia P.O. (Housewife)	29	F	2:129

1Birth state could be Pa. or La. rather than Va.

Arapahoe: spelled incorrectly with 2 r's in census and in this index also.

Name	Kansas: County; Township; P.O. Arap. Co.: Census Div. Not Township	Age	Sex	Census V. Pg.
Brown, Harrison	Linn, Potosi, Rovella (Teacher	25	M	7:55
Brown, J. B.NC	Arrapahoe, South Park (Miner)	44	M	11:3
Brown, James	Linn, Mound City	4	M	7:102
Brown, James H.	Leavenworth, Fort Leavenworth P.O.	2	M	10:320
Brown, James W.	Leavenworth, 1st Ward (Livery stable)	32	M	10:141
Brown, John	Jefferson, Oskaloosa	13	M	5:113
Brown, Julia	Leavenworth, 1st Ward	23	F	10:141
Brown, Lucy	" " "	28	F	10:141
Brown, Martha A.	Bourbon, Fort Scott P.O. (Housewife)	30	F	2:200
Brown, Mary	Atchison, Walnut, Sumner	51	F	1:178
Brown, Mary	Leavenworth, Alexandria, Easton	45	F	10:442
Brown, Mary	Jefferson, Oskaloosa (Housekeeper)	49	F	5:113
Brown, Mary A.NC	Jefferson, Kaw, Kaw City	22	F	5:85
Brown, MatildaNC	Bourbon, Xenia P.O.	11	F	2:129
Brown, S.	Johnson, Monticello	18	F	6:22
Brown, Sarah	Jackson, Douglas, Grasshopper Falls	32	F	5:168
Brown, Sarah	Linn, Potosi, Rovella	48	F	7:55
Brown, SimpsonNC	Bourbon, Xenia P.O. (Farmer)	37	M	2:129
Brown, T.SC	Johnson, Shawnee (Farmer)	41	M	6:100
Brown, W.	Johnson, Lexington (Farmer)	54	M	6:77
Brown, Wm.	Linn, Potosi, Rovella (Farmer)	24	M	7:55
Browne, W. B.	Arrapahoe, Quartz Valley (Laborer)	31	M	11:493
Brownele, H. E.	Doniphan, Center, Troy	29	F	1:248
Brownele, W.	" " " (Farmer)	29	M	1:248
Brownell, A. E.	" " "	40	F	1:247
Brownell, L.	" " "	12	F	1:247
Brownell, W.	" " " (Farmer)	39	M	1:247
Brownlee, C.	Franklin, Centropolis, Minneola	4	F	8:209
Brownlee, D. P.	Arrapahoe, Quartz Valley (Chopper)	31	M	11:495
Brownlee, W.	Franklin, Centropolis, Minneola	6	M	8:209
Bruce, Charles	Wash., Wash., Marysville (Farmer)	48	M	3:266
Bruce, Charles	Marshall, Blue Rapids (Farmer)	42	M	3:198
Bruce, Francis	" " "	13	M	3:198
Bruce, James	Wash., Wash., Marysv.(Farm Laborer)	17	M	3:266
Bruce, James	Marshall, Blue Rapids (Farm Laborer)	17	M	3:198
Bruce, James E.	Leav., Delaware, Del. City (Farmer)	28	M	10:421
Bruce, Manha	Washington, Wash., Marysville	13	F	3:266
Bruce, Martha	Marshall, Blue Rapids	41	F	3:198
Bruce, Mary	Washington, Wash., Marysville	41	F	3:266
Brughter, Jno.	Arrapahoe, Missouri City(QuartzMiller)	22	M	11:569
Brumly, Martha	Doniphan, Wolf River, Walnut Grove	33	F	1:406
Brushear, Mary	Lykins, Osage, Osawatomie	49	F	8:81
Bryan, Wm. H.	Atchison, Ward 1 (Wagon maker)	29	M	1:19
Bryson, C.NC	Franklin, Peoria, Stanton	8	F	8:280
Buchanan, GeorgeNC	Bourbon, Fort Scott P.O. (Farmer)	22	M	2:223
Buchanan, John W.NC	" " " " (Constable)	29	M	2:223
Buchanan, S.	Franklin, Peoria, Peoria City	57	F	8:273
Buck, A.	Coffey, Avon, Burlington	33	F	4:9
Buck, E.	Arrapahoe, South Park	20	M	11:171
Bucket, Augustus	Wyandotte, Wyandotte	20	M	10:40
Bucket, Elisabeth	" "	26	F	10:40
Bucket, Emeline	" "	13	F	10:40
Bucket, Emily	" "	18	F	10:40
Bucket, Henry	" "	15	M	10:40
Bucket, Henry	" "	18	M	10:40
Bucket, Jane	" "	14	F	10:40
Bucket, John	" " (Farmer)	42	M	10:40
Bucket, John	" "	11	M	10:40
Bucket, Joshua	" " (Farmer)	37	M	10:40
Bucket, Lousia	" "	40	F	10:40
Bucket, Polly	" "	42	F	10:40

Arapahoe: spelled incorrectly with 2 r's in census and in this index also.

Name	Kansas: County; Township; P.O. Arap. Co.: Census Div. Not Township	Age	Sex	Census V. : Pg.
Bucket, Rebecca	Wyandotte, Wyandotte	18	F	10:40
Bucket, Rebecca	" "	9	F	10:40
Bucket, Sally	" "	12	F	10:40
Bucket, Wm.	" "	16	M	10:40
Bucket, Wm.	" " (Farmer)	40	M	10:40
Buckley, Mary NC	Jefferson, Jefferson, Winchester	27	F	5:42
Buckley, Smith NC	" " " (Farmer)	32	M	5:42
Buckner, S. A. NC	Otoe, Otoe, Chelsea	41	BF	4:353
Buffington, Wm.	Atchison, Walnut, Sumner (Pastor)	33	M	1:177
Buford, Wm.	Arrapahoe, Denver (Merchant)	35	M	11:340
Bulkley, C.	Arrapahoe, Nevada Gulch (Miner)	20	M	11:526
Bullin, Jno.	Arrapahoe, South Park	29	M	11:222
Bullinger, P.	Linn, Mound City (Farmer)	38	M	7:127
Bunch, Benj.	Linn, Paris (Farmer)	45	M	7:155
Bunch, David	" "	34	M	7:155
Bundrum, Martha NC	Breck., Emporia (Boarding House)	52	F	4:198
Bundy, Henrietta NC	Coffey, Avon, Burlington	23	F	4:6
Bundy, Mary NC	Lykins, Stanton (Farmer)	48	F	8:7
Buneger, W.	Arrapahoe, Valley of the Platte	29	M	11:857
Buntly, Minerva	Douglas, Palmyra, Baldwin	30	F	6:281
Burgis, Sarah A.	Leavenworth, Stranger, Leav. City	77	F	10:478
Burgis, William	" " " "	84	M	10:478
Burgoyne, C.	Riley, Ogden-Manhattan P.O.	35	M	9:293
Burgoyne, Sarah	Jefferson, Oskaloosa	4	F	5:113
Burke, Mary	Wyandotte, Wyandotte	1	F	10:20
Burket, John	Leavenworth, Delaware (Farmer)	42	M	10:420
Burket, Melvina NC	" "	40	F	10:420
Burky, Nannie P.	Bourbon, Fort Scott P.O.	7	F	2:90
Burky, Rebecca A.	" " " " (Housewife)	42	F	2:90
Burky, Robert O.	" " " " (Preacher)	38	M	2:90
Burnell, William	Leav., Stranger, Leav.City(Farmhand)	16	M	10:468
Burnet, Priscilla NC	Atchison, Mt. Pleasant	55	F	1:152
Burnet, Richard	" " " (Farmer)	68	M	1:152
Burnett, Anna	Jackson, Franklin, Holton	37	F	5:191
Burnett, Benjamin	" " " (Farmer)	36	M	5:190
Burnett, Clay	" " "	13	M	5:190
Burnett, Eliza	" " "	10	F	5:191
Burnett, Lucinda	" " "	11	F	5:191
Burnett, Mary	" " "	6	F	5:191
Burnett, Melinda	" " "	9	F	5:190
Burnett, Obadiah	" " " (Farmer)	36	M	5:191
Burnett, Preston	" " "	13	M	5:191
Burnett, William	" " " (Laborer)	16	M	5:191
Burnett, Winfield	" " "	8	M	5:191
Burnham, C. C.	Arrapahoe, South Park	38	M	11:240
Burns (Brims?), Ames	Wyandotte, Wyandotte (Seamstress)	57	M	10:28
Burns, Caleb	Lykins, Osawatomie (Farmer)	52	M	8:66
Burns, Clarita SC	Bourbon, Turkey Creek P.O.	52	F	2:120
Burns, Jno.	Arrap., California Gulch (Trader)	35	M	11:311
Burns, Sydney	Lykins, Osawatomie	52	F	8:66
Burnside, Asenath NC	Breckenridge, Pike, Plymouth	68	F	4:214
Burnt, James	Douglas, Lecompton (Clerk)	36	M	6:350
Burr, B. L.	Arrapahoe, South Park	35	M	11:140
Burres, B. L.	Leavenworth, 1st Ward (Grocer)	25	M	10:130
Burres, Margaret	" "	22	F	10:130
Burris, B. NC	Jeff., Ozawkie (Weaver & spinner)	49	F	5:103
Burris, Dan NC	Shawnee, Topeka (Farmer)	60	M	9:14
Burris, J.	Arrapahoe, South Park	46	M	11:209
Burris, Lydia SC	Jefferson, Ozawkie	70	F	5:103
Burton, D.	Frank., Peoria, Peoria City (Farmer)	47	M	8:267
Burton, Margaret E.	Allen, Geneva P.O.	29	F	2:251

Arapahoe: spelled incorrectly with 2 r's in census and in this index also.

Name	Kansas: County; Township; P.O. Arap. Co.: Census Div. Not Township	Age	Sex	Census V.: Pg.
Burton, Mary F.	Douglas, Willow Springs, McKinney	21	F	6:312
Busbank, J. B.	Arrapahoe, Valley of the Platte	23	M	11:826
Bush, A. V.	Doniphan, Doniphan	3	F	1:383
Butcher, E. O.	Arrapahoe, South Park	26	M	11:228
Buswell, M. A.	Franklin, Centropolis, Prairie City	23	F	8:220
Butler, Elizabeth	Jefferson, Oskaloosa	49	F	5:126
Butler, Elizabeth[SC]	Allen, Elizabeth Town P.O.	60	F	2:239
Butler, H. L.	Johnson; Oxford; New Santa Fe, Mo.	35	F	6:103
Butler, Isaac[SC]	Allen, Elizabeth Town P.O. (Farmer)	60	M	2:239
Butler, Madison	Arrapahoe, South Park (Miner)	30	M	11:15
Butler, O. S.	Arrapahoe, South Park	25	M	11:209
Butler, William	Allen, Iola P.O. (Farmer)	35	M	2:258
Butt, William T.	Breckenridge, Waterloo (Farmer)	38	M	4:152
Buxton, John	McGhee, Crawford Sem.P.O.(Wagon maker)	68	M	9:220
Cabbill, G. S.	Arrapahoe, Valley of the Platte	23	M	11:810
Cabels, J. E.	Johnson, Lexington	33	F	6:71
Cable, Ben	Doniphan, Iowa Point (Carpenter)	25	M	1:449
Cable, Elizabeth[NC]	Anderson, Ozark, Garnett	45	F	7:250
Cable, J.	Doniphan, Iowa Point (Carpenter)	23	M	1:449
Cade, Margaret	Leavenworth, Kickapoo	45	F	10:410
Cadwalder, H.	Arrapahoe; Tarryall, S.P.; Fair Play	22	M	11:616
Caffity, Sarah	Doniphan, Marion, Palermo	48	F	1:292
Cahill, E. F.	Arrapahoe, South Clear Creek	36	M	11:754
Cain, Isabell[NC]	Jefferson, Grasshopper Falls	16	F	5:11
Cain, Mary[NC]	" " "	18	F	5:23
Cain, William[NC]	" " " (Laborer)	20	M	5:11
Caldwell, Adam	Leav., Stranger, Leav.City(Farmhand)	21	M	10:461
Caldwell, C.	Arrapahoe, South Park	27	M	11:197
Caldwell, E.[NC]	Douglas, Lecompton	47	F	6:358
Caldwell, Elizabeth	Jefferson, Ky., Oskaloosa (Weaver)	48	F	5:74
Caldwell, R.	Arrapahoe, South Park	42	M	11:124
Callaway, Annie B.	Shawnee, Topeka	3	F	9:1
Callaway, Chas. L.	" "	8	M	9:1
Callaway, Charles M.	" " (P. E. Minister)	32	M	9:1
Callaway, Davidson K.	" "	5	M	9:1
Calpus, W.	Arrapahoe, South Clear Creek	39	M	11:698
Calvar, C.	Cof., Ottumwa, Burlington (Farmer)	27	M	4:53
Calvin, Mary	Arrapahoe, Denver (Laborer)	28	F	11:317
Calwell, Sarah	Coffey, Leroy, Burlington	40	F	4:27
Cameron, Jas.	Lyk.; Sug. Cr.; W. Pt., Mo.(Farmer)	76	M	8:97
Cameron, James	Brown, Claytonv., Robinson (Farmer)	46	M	3:41
Campbell, A.[NC]	Johnson, Shawnee (Farmer)	56	M	6:87
Campbell, Anna[NC]	Shawnee, Tecumseh	64	F	9:78
Campbell, D.[SC]	Davis, Ft. Riley Reserve (Servant)	45	BF	9:359
Campbell, George W.[NC]	Bourbon, Pawnee P.O.	16	M	2:96
Campbell, Isaac	Shawnee, Tecumseh (Mason)	26	M	9:65
Campbell, J. C.	Douglas, Eudora (Farmer)	36	M	6:340
Campbell, James	Leavenworth, Alexandria, Easton	4	M	10:454
Campbell, Margaret	Anderson, Town of Garnett	45	F	7:221
Campbell, Mary	Lykins, Richland, Paola	49	F	8:14
Campbell, R.[NC]	Nemaha, Granada	57	F	3:114
Campbell, S. F.	Arrapahoe, South Clear Creek	37	M	11:692
Campbell, S. W.	Bourbon, Barnesville P.O. (Farmer)	63	M	2:177
Campbell, Sarah F.	Leavenworth, Alexandria, Easton	17	F	10:453
Campbell, Thomas	" " " (Farmer)	53	M	10:454
Campbell, U. M.(W.M.?)	Arrapahoe, South Clear Creek	26	M	11:748
Campbell, Wm.	Arrapahoe, Mountain City (Merchant	23	M	11:457
Campbell, Wm.	Chase, Diam.Cr., Cot.Falls (Laborer)	76	M	4:324
Campbell, William[NC]	Bourbon, Pawnee P.O. (Farmer)	38	M	2:96
Cannon, Phebe	Arrapahoe, Nevada Gulch	51	F	11:520
Canterberry, A. D.	Doniphan, Washington, Wathena	15	M	1:301

Arapahoe: spelled incorrectly with 2 r's in census and in this index also.

Name	Kansas: County; Township; P.O. Arap. Co.: Census Div. Not Township	Age	Sex	Census V. : Pg
Canterberry, Andrew	Doniphan, Washington, Wathena	7	M	1:301
Canterberry, E.	" " "	8	F	1:301
Canterberry, James	" " "	5	M	1:301
Canterberry, Jane	" " "	33	F	1:301
Canterberry, John	" " " (Farmer)	37	M	1:301
Canterberry, M. M.	" " "	11	M	1:301
Canterberry, Zudre	" " "	13	M	1:301
Capes, J.	Arrapahoe, South Park	26	M	11:258
Carcel, H. S.	Doug., Willow Spr., Brooklyn(Farmer)	34	M	6:322
Carl, J.	Doug., Wakarusa, Lawrence	18	F	6:230
Carl, James	" " " (Farmer)	26	M	6:232
Carl, Julia	" " "	16	F	6:232
Carl, Rebecca	" " "	69	F	6:232
Carl, Wm.	" " " (Farmer)	30	M	6:230
Carlile, McKenzie	Leav., Stranger, Leav. City (Farmer)	42	M	10:480
Carlisle, Alexander SC	Atch., Grassh., Kennek. (Mechanic)	26	M	1:95
Carlisle, Nancy	Jefferson, Kentucky, Oskaloosa	62	F	5:70
Carmichael, M. A. NC	Arrapahoe, California Gulch (Miner)	32	M	11:297
Carmon, Geo. NC	Wood., Verdigris, Belmont (Farmer)	22	M	8:162
Carney, Daniel S. NC	Breck., Pike, Plymouth (Farmer)	30	M	4:207
Carney, Wm. J. NC	Breckenridge, Emporia	32	M	4:200
Carpenter, H.	Linn, Valley, Blooming Gr. (Farmer)	34	M	7:38
Carpenter, P.	Arrapahoe, South Park	29	M	11:150
Carpenter, Robert	Nemaha, Rock Creek (Laborer)	77	M	3:80
Carpenter, S. M. SC	Johnson, Olathe (Farmer)	50	M	6:119
Carpenter, Susan	And., Monroe, Garnett (Housekeeper)	27	F	7:228
Carr, Caroline P. SC	Atchison, Ward 2	27	F	1:33
Carr, Guss SC	" " "	6	M	1:33
Carr, Harry W. SC	" " "	4	M	1:33
Carr, John	Leavenworth, Easton (Laborer)	28	M	10:282
Carr, Joseph P. SC	Atchison, Ward 2 (Lawyer)	28	M	1:33
Carr, L.	Douglas, Kanwaca, Lawrence	13	F	6:385
Carrol, Edward	Leavenworth, 1st Ward (Clerk)	19	M	10:134
Carroll, J. R.	Linn, Paris (Farmer)	36	M	7:149
Carry, Sarah	Nemaha, Richmond, Seneca	46	F	3:95
Carson, A.	Franklin, Centropolis, Minneola	9	M	8:212
Carson, A. G.	" " "	12	M	8:212
Carson, E. A.	Frank.; Potta.; Scipio, Anderson Co.	3	F	8:239
Carson, E. J.	" " " " "	7	F	8:239
Carson, Elisha NC	Lykins, Stanton (Farmer)	56	M	8:12
Carson, M. E. SC	Frank.; Potta.; Scipio, Anderson Co.	38	F	8:238
Carson, M. S. SC	" " " " "	40	M	8:238
Carson, S. M.	" " " " "	5	F	8:239
Carson, W.	Franklin, Centropolis, Minneola	7	M	8:212
Carson, W. M.	" " "	10	M	8:212
Carson, William	Cof., Ottumwa, Burlington (Farmer)	30	M	4:55
Cartee, Floyd	Shawnee, Topeka,(Laborer)	27	M	9:10
Carter, A.	Douglas, Palmyra, Lawrence	71	F	6:267
Carter, Amanda	Jefferson, Oskaloosa	23	F	5:132
Carter, Elizabeth	Douglas, Palmyra, Lawrence	27	F	6:267
Carter, F.	" " " (Farmer)	30	M	6:267
Carter, G. O.	Arrapahoe, South Park	27	M	11:104
Carter, Hannah	Leavenworth, Ward 3	40	F	10:218
Carter, J. H. NC	Franklin, Ohio, Ohio City (Farmer)	26	M	8:234
Carter, J. V. NC	Breckenridge, Pike, Plymouth	27	M	4:214
Carter, John	Marshall, Marysville (Farm Laborer)	22	M	3:247
Carter, John P.	Leavenworth, Ward 3 (Carpenter)	42	M	10:218
Carter, M. S.	Coffey, Leroy	26	F	4:29
Carter, R. NC	Franklin, Ohio, Ohio City	32	F	8:234
Cartwright, Elizabeth	Coffey, Leroy P. O.	25	F	4:28
Carver, Jane	McGhee, Brushville P.O.	53	F	9:227

Arapahoe: spelled incorrectly with 2 r's in census and in this index also.

Name	Kansas: County; Township; P.O. Arap. Co.: Census Div. Not Township	Age	Sex	Census V.	Pg.
Casebolt, Arthur	Bourbon, Barnesville P.O.	6	M	2:171	
Casebolt, Barbara	" " " (Housewife)	43	F	2:171	
Casebolt, Elizabeth	" " "	8	F	2:171	
Casebolt, Fompsey	" " "	17	F	2:171	
Casebolt, George	" " "	14	M	2:171	
Casebolt, John	" " "	15	M	2:171	
Casebolt, Josiah	" " " (Blacksmith)	43	M	2:171	
Casebolt, William	" " "	11	M	2:171	
Casebrier, Elizabeth	Jefferson, Oskaloosa	77	F	5:120	
Casey, I. (or J.?)SC	Johnson, Monticello (Farmer)	50	M	6:82	
Cash, ElizabethNC	Breckenridge, Emporia	25	F	4:204	
Caskier, E.	Douglas, Clinton	7	F	6:414	
Caskier, James	" " (Laborer)	45	M	6:414	
Caskier, M.	" "	9	F	6:414	
Caskier, M. A.	" "	38	F	6:414	
Casner, P.	Coffey, Leroy (Hardware Mcht.)	23	M	4:29	
Cassell, H. SC	Frank., Potta., Scipio (Farmer)	28	M	8:238	
Cassell, M. A. SC	" " "	24	F	8:238	
Caster, George	Jefferson, Oskaloosa (Teamster)	23	M	5:122	
Caster, John	Leavenworth, Ward 2	60	BM	10:159	
Castle, MelissaNC	Anderson, Walker	48	F	7:241A	
Castor, John	Leavenworth, 1st Ward	45	BM	10:137	
Caswell, Jno.	Arrapahoe, South Park	50	M	11:247	
Cavass, H. C.NC	Doug., Pal., Baldwin(Shoe & B.Dealer)	50	M	6:284	
Cavass, MaryNC	Douglas, Palmyra, Baldwin	52	F	6:284	
Cavell, F. C.NC	Arrapahoe; Tarryall; Fair Play	29	M	11:616	
Cazort, James J.NC	Wyandotte, Wyandotte (Farmer)	44	M	10:42	
Chalmer, John	Mars., B.Rap.,Merrimac (Day Laborer)	22	M	3:212	
Chambers, Jane1	Osage, Ridgeway, Burlingame	3	F	8:334	
Chambers, John D. SC	Bourbon, Fort Scott P.O. (Farmer)	31	M	2:90	
Chamnoss, LennathaNC	Breckenridge, Emporia	23	F	4:194	
Chamnoss, MiltonNC	" " (Farmer)	37	M	4:194	
Chance, M.	Doniphan, Wayne, Doniphan	26	F	1:376	
Chapman, Christopher	Jeff., Ky., Oska.(Master H. Carpenter)	30	M	5:63	
Chapman, J. M.	Arrapahoe, Valley of the Platte	28	M	11:804	
Chapman, John	Arrapahoe, Denver (Farmer)	30	M	11:343	
Chapman, Mary	Jefferson, Kentucky, Oskaloosa	2	F	5:63	
Chapman, Nancy	Jefferson, Kentucky, Oskaloosa	28	F	5:63	
Chapman, Rebecca	Arrapahoe, Denver	22	F	11:343	
Chapman, Susanah	Jefferson, Kentucky, Oskaloosa	24	F	5:63	
Chapple, E.	Doniphan, Center, Troy	25	F	1:262	
Chapple, E. A.	" " "	7	F	1:262	
Chapple, M. M.	" " "	5	F	1:262	
Chapple, M. W.	" " "	3	M	1:262	
Chapson, Ann	Doniphan, Iowa Point	58	F	1:458	
Charles, Betsy	Doniphan, Center, Troy	1	F	1:263	
Charles, Mary	" " "	3	F	1:263	
Charles, Robt.	" " "	5	M	1:263	
Charles, Thos.	" " "	7	M	1:263	
Chase, B. F.	Arrap., Mountain City (Mechanic?)	40	M	11:468	
Chase, Cilus	Shawnee, Topeka	23	F	9:14	
Chase, Joseph	" " (Plasterer)	28	M	9:14	
Chase, W. H.	Arrapahoe, Mountain City (Miner)	39?	M	11:468	
Chatwood, James NC	Leav., Delaware, Del. City (Farmer)	28	M	10:423	
Cheatwood, JoelNC	Leav., Delaware, Delaware City	28	M	10:423	
Chevingston, Martha	Arrapahoe, Denver	48	F	11:354	
Childers, Allen	Shawnee, Topeka (Brickmaker)	29	M	9:13	
Childers, Amanda J.	Lykins; Middle Cr.; Jonesville, Mo.	8	F	8:105	
Childers, Harriett	" " " . " "	29	F	8:105	

1W.P.A. indexer gave state of birth as Va.?

Arapahoe: spelled incorrectly with 2 r's in census and in this index also.

Name	Kansas: County; Township; P.O. Arap. Co.: Census Div. Not Township	Age	Sex	Census V. Pg.
Childers, James	Lykins; Middle Cr.; Jonesville,Mo.	3	M	8:105
Childers, Nathan	" " " " (Farmer)	38	M	8:105
Childers, Polly A.	" " " "	1	F	8:105
Childers, Sarah	Shawnee, Topeka	32	F	9:13
Childers, Sarah C.	Lykins, Middle Creek, Jonesville,Mo.	6	F	8:105
Childers, Spencer	Shawnee, Topeka (Plasterer)	37	M	9:14
Childers, Spencer	" "	11	M	9:13
Childes, H.	Woodson, Pleasant Grove (Farmer)	22	M	9:169
Childs, Caroline[NC]	Lykins, Stanton	37	F	8:10
Chinn, Richard	Jackson, Douglas, Holton (Farmer)	40	M	5:173
Choplin, Hannah	Arrapahoe, Denver	32	F	11:342
Chouse, Soloman[NC]	McGhee, Crawford SeminaryP.O(Farmer)	28	M	9:225
Chouteau, Anna E.	Atchison, Ward 3	20	F	1:52
Christian, Franklin	Allen, Carlisle P.O. (Farmer)	30	M	2:242
Christian, Geo. W.[NC]	Arrapahoe, South Park (Miner)	40	M	11:16
Christian, Jas. M.[NC]	" " " (Miner)	46	M	11:16
Christian, W. H.	Douglas, Lecompton (Farmer)	32	M	6:369
Christian, Wm. H.	Arrapahoe, South Park (Miner)	26	M	11:44
Chronic, E.	Doniphan, Doniphan	38	F	1:386
Church, Caleb	Arrapahoe, South Park (Miner)	22	M	11:37
Churchill, Sophia	Leavenworth, Ward 2	23	F	10:162
Claibourne, M. H.	Cof., Ottumwa, Burlington (Farmer)	53	M	4:54
Clair, W.	Anderson, Monroe, Garnett (Farmer)	40	M	7:219
Clark, Albert W.	Bourbon, Mapleton P.O. (Farmer)	31	M	2:137
Clark, Alice O.	" " "	5	F	2:137
Clark, Almira I.	" " "	9	F	2:137
Clark, Balzura	" " "	3	F	2:137
Clark, C. I.	Arrapahoe, Denver (Book Store)	17	M	11:334
Clark, C. M.[NC]	Arrap., Mountain City (Carpenter)	47	M	11:459
Clark, Catharine	Coffey, Pottawatomie, Burlington	43	F	4:3
Clark, Eliza	Bourbon, Barnesville P.O.(Housewife)	42	F	2:176
Clark, Francis P.	Bourbon, Mapleton P.O.	6	M	2:137
Clark, William	Bourbon, Barnesville P.O.	20	M	2:177
Clarke, Benjamin N.[SC]	Leavenworth, Delaware, Delaware City	14	M	10:421
Clarke, George W.[SC]	" " " "	11	M	10:421
Clarke, John P.[SC]	" " " "	3	M	10:421
Clarke, Kate[SC]	" " " "	5	F	10:421
Clarke, Latitia N.	Leavenworth, 1st Ward	41	F	10:136
Clarke, Minerva A.[SC]	Leav., Delaware, Del. City	10	F	10:421
Clarke, W. S.[SC]	" " " " (Farmer)	38	M	10:421
Clarkson, Elizabeth	Lykins, Paola	39	F	8:39
Clay, J.	John.; Oxf.; N.Santa Fe,Mo.(Farmer)	59	M	6:107
Clay, John	Linn, Mound City (Farmer)	58	M	7:115
Clayton, B.	Arrapahoe, South Park (Miner)	28	M	11:74
Clemmans, J.	Johnson, Olathe (Carpenter)	70	M	6:4
Cleveland, C. P.	Arrapahoe, Valley of the Platte	29	M	11:842
Cleveland, W. F.[NC]	Arrapahoe, Leavenworth Gulch (Miner)	35	M	11:555
Clever, Easter	Linn, Mound City (Farmer)	27	M	7:116
Clever, Mary	" " "	23	F	7:116
Clewell, A. F.[NC]	Arrap.;Tarry.,S.P.;Fair Play(Lawyer)	26	M	11:616
Clewell, B. F.[NC]	Arrapahoe, California Gulch	19	M	11:293
Clewell, F.[NC]	" " " " (Miner)	29	M	11:293
Clifford, Wm.	Arrapahoe, South Park	29	M	11:182
Cline, Elizabeth Mrs.	Atchison, Ward 1	54	F	1:16
Cline, Hezekiah	Bourbon, Fort Scott P.O. (Farmer)	43	M	2:193
Cline, J. M.	Franklin, Centropolis, Minneola	5	M	8:211
Cline, Wm.	Atchison, Ward 1 (Teamster)	30	M	1:19
Cline, Henry	Atchison, Mount Pleasant (Farmer)	50	M	1:143
Clinton, Mary[NC]	Shawnee, Soldier, Indianola	25	F	9:83
Clinton, Wm. A.	Arrapahoe, South Park	34	M	11:192
Cloud, M. M.	Arrapahoe, Denver	31	M	11:364

Arapahoe: spelled incorrectly with 2 r's in census and in this index also.

Name	Kansas: County; Township; P.O. Arap. Co.: Census Div. Not Township	Age	Sex	Census V. Pg.
Clute, C. C.SC	Leavenworth, Ward 2	28	F	10:189
Cobb, G.NC	Arrapahoe, South Park (Miner)	20	M	11:11
Cobell, P. C.	Douglas, Lecompton (Lawyer)	26	M	6:350
Cochrane, John	Jefferson, Oskaloosa (Potter)	26	M	5:117
Cochrane, Joseph	" " (Attorney)	27	M	5:117
Cochrane, William	" " (Potter)	29	M	5:117
Cocker, Thompson	Leavenworth, Easton (Farmer)	43	M	10:304
Cockerill, Mortimer	Potta., Blue, Manhattan (Farmer)	35	M	5:300
Coe, J. F.	Arrapahoe, South Park	24	M	11:195
Coffel, A. M.1	Frank., Peor., Peor. City	3	F	8:269
Coffel, C.1	" " " "	5	F	8:269
Coffel, E. C.	" " " "	72	F	8:269
Coffel, J.	" " " " (Farmer)47 or 49?		M	8:269
Coffin, John M.NC	Lykins, Mound, Osawatomie (Farmer)	34	M	8:70
Coffin, Martha D.NC	" " "	7	F	8:70
Coffman, Edgar	Jefferson, Kaw, Kaw City (Laborer)	24	M	5:83
Coffman, Elias	Jeff., Grasshopper Falls (Farmer)	62	M	5:10
Coffman, G.	Douglas, Kanwaca, Lawrence (Farmer)	35	M	6:386
Coffman, Jeremiah	Jefferson, Kaw, Kaw City	13	M	5:83
Coffman, John	" " " " (Farmer)	27	M	5:83
Coffman, Martha	" " " "	14	F	5:83
Coffman, Mary	" " " "	52	F	5:83
Coffman, Saml.	" " " " (Farmer)	58	M	5:83
Coffman, William	" " " "	11	M	5:83
Cofield, J. B.NC	Arrap., Nevada Gulch (Quartz Miller)	44	M	11:504
Coger, D.	Johnson, Monticello (Laborer)	21	M	6:86
Cogher, Henry	Bourbon, Fort Scott P.O.(FarmLaborer)	23	M	2:199
Cogar, LuranSC	Leavenworth, Delaware	30	F	10:437
Cohoon, BarnabasNC	Atch., Grasshopper, Kennekuk (Farmer)	43	M	1:89
Cohoon, Jacob,A.NC	" " "	18	M	1:89
Cohoon, LucyNC	" " "	39	F	1:89
Cohoon, SusanNC	" " "	15	F	1:89
Cohoon, Wm. B.NC	" " "	20	M	1:89
Cole, CarolineNC	Douglas, Palmyra, Prairie	36	F	6:296
Cole, Rebecca	Allen, Humboldt P.O.	37	F	2:301
Colier, Alx.	Douglas, Lecompton	1	M	6:359
Colier, T. W.	Atchison, Ward 3	14	M	1:55
Collen, S.NC	Johnson, Lexington	41	F	6:74
Collen, W.	" " (Shoemaker)	48	M	6:74
Collier, G. W.	Arrapahoe, Valley of the Platte	24	M	11:809
Collier, Jackson	Morris, Grove, Council Gr. (Farmer)	26	M	4:272
Collier, Joseph	Mor., Neosho, Council Gr. (Farming)	28	M	4:273
Collier, Sally	" " "	24	F	4:273
Collin, Samuel K.	Allen, Iola P.O. (Physician)	46	M	2:270
Collins, AngelineNC	McGhee, Osage Mission P.O.	22	F	9:240
Collins, D.	Frank., Centrop., Minneola (Farmer)	43	M	8:211
Collins, Demetreus	Atchison, Ward 2 (Saloon Keeper)	24	M	1:43
Collins, E.NC	Doniphan, Iowa Point (Farmer)	40	M	1:435
Collins, ElizabethNC	McGhee, Osage Mission P.O.	42	F	9:240
Collins, G. W. P.	Franklin, Centropolis, Minneola	4	M	8:211
Collins, J.	Frank., Potta., Shermanville (Farmer)	59	M	8:246
Collins, J.	Franklin, Centropolis, Minneola	4	M	8:211
Collins, J.	" " " (Farmer)45		M	8:211
Collins, J.	" " "	8	M	8:211
Collins, J. J.	Don., Wolf R., Walnut Gr. (Farmer)	60	M	1:406
Collins, James NC	McGhee, Osage Mission P.O. (Farmer)	48	M	9:240
Collins, John C.	Bourbon, Mapleton P.O.	15	M	2:148
Collins, Martha	" " "	8	M	2:148

1State of birth could be Va., Ia., or La.

Arapahoe: spelled incorrectly with 2 r's in census and in this index also.

Name	Kansas: County; Township; P.O. Arap. Co.: Census Div. Not Township	Age	Sex	Census V.: Pg.
Collins, Miles NC	Brown, Claytonv., Robinson. (Farmer)	36	M	3:42
Collins, N.	Arrapahoe, South Park	23	M	11:11
Collins, R. J.	Franklin, Centropolis, Minneola	6	F	8:211
Collins, S. G.	" " "	9	F	8:211
Collins, S.	Franklin, Potta., Shermanville	49	F	8:246
Collins, Sophia	Leavenworth, Ward 3	46	F	10:210
Colt, Wm.	Arrapahoe, South Park	29	M	11:237
Colviler, J.	Nemaha, Red Vermillion, America	36	M	3:133
Combs, Keziah NC	Bourbon, Fort Scott P.O.(Housewife)	22	F	2:153
Comstock, Daniel	Jeff., Grasshopper Falls(Wagon Maker)	62	M	5:23
Concil, Levi	Arrapahoe, South Park	21	M	11:127
Conell, Susan	Douglas, Palmyra, McKinney	39	F	6:305
Conell, T. NC	" " " (Farmer)	44	M	6:305
Conger, Miranda	Marshall, Vermillion, Barrett Mills	21	F	3:224
Conkling, A. C.	Arrapahoe, South Park	34	M	11:154
Conn, William	Wyandotte, Wyandotte	27	BM	10:9
Connell, Elizabeth	Atchison, Ward 3	17	F	1:57
Connelly, J. M. SC	Arrapahoe, Nevada Gulch (Miner)	22	M	11:533
Conner, Charles	Lykins, Sugar Cr., West Point, Mo.	9	M	8:101
Conner, J. H. SC	Atchison, Walnut, Sumner (Farmer)	28	M	1:190
Conner, Wm. SC	" " "	14	M	1:190
Connet, C. S.	Franklin, Centropolis, Minneola	5	M	8:215
Connet, E. J.	" " "	22	F	8:215
Connet, G. W. P.	" " "	3	M	8:215
Connor, John	Leavenworth, Ward 2	6	M	10:188
Conrey, Helan	Lykins, Osage, Osawatomie	42	F	8:81
Conway, E. J.	Arrapahoe, Valley of the Platte	28	M	11:810
Conway, Jas.	Riley, Ogden P.O.	6	M	9:290
Conway, John	" " "	3	M	9:290
Conway, Jno. SC	Arrapahoe, California Gulch	30	M	11:309
Conway, Thos.	Riley, Ogden P.O.	5	M	9:290
Coock, Clarasa	Lykins, Miami, Paola	30	F	8:90
Cook, Annie	Washington, Washington, Marysville	45	F	3:263
Cook, Catharine	Leavenworth, Kickapoo	27	F	10:413
Cook, Daton NC	Breck., Pike, Plymouth (Farmer)	35	M	4:207
Cook, Elizabeth[1],C	Atchison, Center, Parkee	22	F	1:125
Cook, Franklin	Wyandotte, Quindaro (Carpenter)	46	M	10:57
Cook, John H.	Leavenworth, Kickapoo (Farmer)	42	M	10:413
Cook, M.	Linn, Mound City	18	F	7:104
Cook, Thomas NC	Atchison, Lancaster (Farmer)	26	M	1:108
Cook, Wm.	Atchison, Walnut, Sumner (Farmer)	30	M	1:181
Cooley, C. E.	Arrapahoe, Denver (Speculator)	25	M	11:336
Cooper, D. NC	Woodson, Verdigris (Farmer)	69	M	9:158
Cooper, Elizabeth	Pottawatomie, Rockingham, Elden	19	F	5:293
Cooper, G. B.	Breckenridge, Emporia (Painter)	27	M	4:199
Cooper, J. F.	Davis, Kansas Falls P.O.(Att.-at-Law)	24	M	9:331
Cooper, Nancy NC	Woodson, Verdigris (F.W.)	50	F	9:158
Cooper, R.	Arrapahoe, South Clear Creek (Miner)	19	M	11:625
Cooper, Sarah NC	Woodson, Belmont	41	F	9:151
Cooper, Silas NC	" " (Farmer)	43	M	9:151
Cooper, W. P.	Arrapahoe, Denver (Miner)	40/46?	M	11:358
Copenberger, Peter	Lykins, Paola (Farmer)	40	M	8:42
Copenlan, S.	Brown, Walnut Cr., Hamlin (Farmer)	29	M	3:22
Copland, L. NC	Doniphan, Iowa Point (Farmer)	29	M	1:419
Copp, David H.	Jeff., Grasshopper Falls (Farmer)	49	M	5:17
Copple, Philip NC	Linn, Paris (Constable)	44	M	7:148
Corbell, T.	Arrapahoe, South Clear Creek	34	M	11:729
Corder, Geo. W.	Jackson, Franklin, Holton (Farmer)	39	M	5:182
Cordray, Jane NC	Riley, Manhattan-Henryville P.O.	56	F	9:297

[1]Original entry is Carolina as birth state.
  Arapahoe: spelled incorrectly with 2 r's in census and in this index also.

Name	Kansas: County; Township; P.O. Arap. Co.: Census Div. Not Township	Age	Sex	Census V. Pg.
Corey, J.	Riley, Ogden P.O.	12	M	9:292
Cork, J.	Franklin, Centropolis, Minneola	8	M	8:203
Corkell, Jas.	Arrap., Tarryall S.P. (Miner) 23or25		M	11:601
Cornatzer, S. M.NC	Johnson, Shawnee (Farmer)	26	M	6:94
Corrol, Jas.	Frank.,Ohio,Sac&Fox Agency (Farmer)	40	M	8:225
Corry, L.NC	Franklin, Ottawa, Prairie City	60	F	8:256
Coseley, G. W.	Doug., Kanwaca, Lawrence (Farmer)	55	M	6:376
Coseley, H. A.	" " " (Farmer)	33	M	6:376
Coulter, Ida	Atchison, Ward 3	15	F	1:55
Cowen, ElizaNC	Leavenworth, Kickapoo	40	F	10:414
Cowen, John M.	Allen, Iola P.O. (Farmer)	50	M	2:247
Cox, A. A.?NC	Johnson, Olathe (Clerk)	29	M	6:2
Cox, AsenathNC	Breckenridge, Pike, Plymouth	35	F	4:210
Cox, DelilahNC	Jefferson, Oskaloosa	56	F	5:116
Cox, Elizabeth	Breckenridge, Pike, Plymouth	31	F	4:208
Cox, James	Leavenworth, Delaware (Farmhand)	26	M	10:435
Cox, John	Mars., Vermil., Bar. Mills (Farmer)	50	M	3:226
Cox, Moses H.	Don., Washington, Elwood (Farmer)	41	M	1:338
Cox, O.	Arrapahoe, South Park	26	M	11:181
Cox, RatchelNC	Coffey, Neosho, Burlington	31	F	4:73
Cox, Rebecca	Marshall, Vermillion, Barrett Mills	45	F	3:226
Cox, RichardSC	McGhee, Osage Mission P.O. (Farmer)	52	M	9:236
Cox, Salathiel	Lykins; Miamiville, Osage; Osawat.	39	M	8:85
Cox, Samuel	Shawnee, Topeka (Farmer)	48	M	9:21
Cox, Silas NC	Breck., Pike, Plymouth (Farmer)	36	M	4:210
Cox, ThomasNC	McGhee, Medoc, Missouri P.O.(Farmer)	57	M	9:214
Cox, Virginia	Doniphan, Marion, Palermo	24	F	1:292
Coy, G. W.	Douglas, Willow Springs, McKinney	25	M	6:312
Coy, L.	" " " "	18	F	6:312
Coy, M.	" " " "	51	F	6:312
Coy, V.	" " " "	25	M	6:312
Coyne, A. M.	Arrapahoe, South Park	33	M	11:201
Cozzens, E.	Arrapahoe, South Park (Trader)	31	M	11:241
Cozzens, J. F.	Arrapahoe, Valley of the Platte(Miner)	29	M	11:835
Crabtree, N. W.	Johnson, Shawnee (Miller)	41	M	6:29
Craig, Henry	Mor., Grove, Council Gr. (Minister)	30	M	4:272
Craig, Jno.	Arrapahoe, Mountain City (Baker)	40	M	11:458
Craig, M. M.NC	Arrapahoe, Denver	27	M	11:330
Craig, M. W. NC	Arrapahoe, California Gulch	27	M	11:306
Craig, Mary	Bourbon, Xenia P.O.	60	F	2:129
Craig, W. T.	Arrapahoe, Valley of the Platte	31	M	11:835
Craighill, Henry	Doniphan, Wayne, Doniphan	23	BM	1:376
Craighill, S. J.	" " " (Farmer)	35	M	1:376
Cramer, Jno. C.	Arrapahoe, California Gulch	30	M	11:277
Cramer, R. W.	Arrapahoe, South Park	30	M	11:155
Crane, Geo.	Arrapahoe, Central City (Carpenter)	45	M	11:510
Crawford, Anna	Chase, Toledo	34	F	4:339
Crawford, B. F.NC	Arrapahoe, South Clear Creek		M	11:658
Crawford, Eliza	Arrapahoe, South Park	30	F	11:68
Creach, EdithNC	Davis, Junction City, Kansas Falls	50	F	9:339
Creasy, Frederick	Leavenworth, 1st Ward (Teamster)	40	BM	10:97
Creed, S.	Doug., Kanwaca, Lawrence (Farmer)	30	M	6:386
Creighamer, Josiah	Madison, Hartford (Farmer)	30	M	4:235
Creighton, B. C.NC	Arrapahoe, Valley of the Platte	36	M	11:849
Cress, George	Mor.,Clarks Cr.,Council Gr.(Farming)	40	M	4:281
Cress, Nancy	" " " "	35	F	4:281
Cressy, J. N.	Arrapahoe, Mountain City (Miner)	34	M	11:468
Crest, L. F.	Johnson, Olathe (Farmer)	25	M	6:113
Crippen, A. C.	Arrapahoe, South Park	29	M	11:225
Critchfield, MaryNC	McGhee, Brushville P.O.	26	F	9:217
Crittenden, Henry	Woodson, Neosho Falls (Farmer)	60	M	9:127

Arapahoe: spelled incorrectly with 2 r's in census and in this index also.

Name	Kansas: County; Township; P.O. Arap. Co.: Census Div. Not Township	Age	Sex	Census V.:Pg.
Crobarger, Francis	Jeff., Jeff., Crooked Cr. (Farmer)	46	M	5:29
Crocket, P.	Douglas, Lecompton (Farmer)	56	M	6:362
Crocket, S.	" " (Farmer)	24	M	6:362
Crockett, Jack	Arrapahoe, Tarryall South Park	28	M	11:612
Croley, D.	Arrapahoe, Mountain City (Carpenter)	26	M	11:474
Cronenhold, F. M.	Arrapahoe, South Park	39	M	11:188
Crook, Burton NC	Dickinson, Kansas Falls P.O.	6	M	4:307
Crook, Enoch NC	" " " "	12	M	4:307
Crook, J. C. NC	" " " " (Farmer)	42	M	4:307
Crook, Jane NC	" " " "	45	F	4:307
Crook, Jessy NC	" " " "	10	M	4:307
Crook, Joseph NC	" " " "	13	M	4:307
Crook, Julianna NC	" " " "	8	F	4:307
Crook, Marion NC	" " " " "(Farm Hand)	18	M	4:307
Crook, Nancy NC	" " " "	14	F	4:307
Crook, Newton NC	" " " " "(Farm Hand)	21	M	4:307
Crook, Wm. NC	" " " "	15	M	4:307
Cross, B. NC	Johnson, Gardner	40	F	6:56
Cross, Casandra NC	Bourbon, Barnesville P.O.(Housewife)	52	F	2:180
Cross, Levi	Coffey, Burlington (Farmer)	36	M	4:42
Cross, Lewis NC	Bourbon, Barnesville P.O. (Farmer)	51	M	2:180
Cross, Sarah J. NC	Coffey, Burlington	24	F	4:42
Crothaes,? H.	Leavenworth, Ward 4 (Farmer)	42	F	10:249
Crow, A. M.	Franklin, Centropolis, Minneola	4	F	8:216
Crow, J. M.	" " " (Farmer)	15	M	8:216
Crow, J. P.	" " "	12	M	8:216
Crow, S. W.	" " "	8	M	8:216
Crow, William F.	Allen, Iola P.O.	24	M	2:265
Crow, Wm. H.	Franklin, Centropolis, Minneola	10	M	8:216
Crowder, L.	Doniphan, Iowa Point	71	F	1:436
Crowle, Jacob	Arrapahoe, Missouri City (Miner)	28	M	11:561
Crowley, J. C.	Arrapahoe, South Park	33	M	11:29
Crune, W. E.	Frank., Centropolis, Minneola(Farmer)	49	M	8:202
Crusan, Mary J.	Douglas, Willow Springs	47	F	6:313
Crusan, Susan C.	" " "	11	F	6:313
Crusan, Wm. R.	" " "	7	M	6:313
Cuberly, Aaron C.	Shawnee, Monmouth, Tecumseh (Farmer)	40	M	9:57
Cuberly, Elenor	" " "	67	F	9:57
Cuberly, Joseph	" " " (Blacksmith)	67	M	9:57
Cudny, E.	Wood.,Verdigris,Pleas.Gr. (Farmer)	25	M	9:164
Cuennbo, Mary?	Leavenworth, Ward 2	36	F	10:172
Culberson, Andrew NC	Lyk., Mound, Osawatomie (Farmer)	52	M	8:72
Culberson, Larkin NC	" " "	11	M	8:72
Culberson, Martha A. NC	" " "	16	F	8:72
Culberson, Martha A. NC	" " "	51	F	8:72
Culberson, Samuel NC	" " "	14	M	8:72
Culern, Nancy NC	Allen, Humboldt P.O.	39	F	2:281
Cullent, Mik	Arrapahoe, South Clear Creek	26	M	11:744
Cumins, Allen	Doniphan, Wolf River, Walnut Gr.	11	M	1:408
Cumins, Gaston	" " " " "	10	M	1:408
Cumins, J.	" " " " (Farmer)	38	M	1:408
Cumins, Woodson	" " " "	15	M	1:408
Cummings, Charles	Atch., Shannon, Atchison (Farmer)	60	M	1:75
Cummings, Elizabeth	" " "	38	F	1:75
Cummings, Jessee W. NC	Bourbon, Fort Scott P.O. (Farmer)	40	M	2:209
Cummings, Nancy Ellen	Atchison, Shannon, Atchison	10	F	1:75
Cummings, Peter	" " "	24	M	1:75
Cummings, Sarah	" " "	60	F	1:75
Cuningham, M.	Johnson, Lexington (Teacher)	20	F	6:71
Cuningham, M. A.	" "	60	F	6:71
Cuningham, J.	" " (Saddler)	65	M	6:71

Arapahoe: spelled incorrectly with 2 r's in census and in this index also.

Name	Kansas: County; Township; P.O. Arap. Co.: Census Div. Not Township	Age	Sex	Census V. : Pg.
Cunningham, J. A. SC	Frank., Potta., Scipio (Carpenter)	53	M	8:239
Curry, G.	Potta., Vienna, Louisville	12	M	5:247
Curry, Geo.	" " " (Farmer)	48	M	5:247
Curry, J.	" " " (Farmer)	17	M	5:247
Curry, John	Douglas, Willow Springs	29	M	6:313
Curry, L.	Potta., Vienna, Louisville (Farmer)	21	M	5:247
Curry, Leroy	Jefferson, Oskaloosa (Mason)	35	M	5:123
Curry, M.	Pottawatomie, Vienna, Louisville	42	F	5:247
Curry, M.	" " "	19	F	5:247
Curry, P.	" " "	18	F	5:247
Curry, Wm.	Douglas, Willow Springs	33	M	6:313
Curtis, P.	Franklin, Prairie, Peoria	38	F	8:268
Cypherd, C. B.	Linn, Paris (Laborer)	18	M	7:142
Daggett, Wm. NC	Arrapahoe, South Park	26	M	11:132
Dagley, M. NC	Johnson, Monticello	64	F	6:83
Dallas, Nancy	Douglas, Palmyra, McKinney	39	F	6:306
Dalton, D.	Arrapahoe, Lake Gulch (Barkeeper)	24	M	11:482
Danche, Alex	Arrapahoe, California Gulch	33	M	11:303
Danforth, Eliza	Arrapahoe, South Park (Washer)	36	F	11:5
Danforth, J.	" " " (Miner)	37	M	11:5
Daniels, Amanda	Woodson, Verdigris, Pleas.Gr.(F.W.)	35	F	9:165
Daniels, C.	Johnson; Oxford; New Santa Fe,Mo.	6	M	6:105
Daniels, Catharine	Coffey, Avon, Burlington	65	F	4:8
Daniels, D.	Johnson; Oxford; New Santa Fe, Mo.	23	F	6:105
Daniels, Henry	Wood., Verdigris, Pleas.Gr.(Farmer)	35	M	9:165
Daniels, James	" " " " (Farmer)	38	M	9:165
Daniels, Mary	" " " "	37	F	9:165
Daniels, Nancy NC	Linn, Mound City	65	F	7:119
Daniels, Sarah NC	Linn, Paris	28	F	7:140
Daniels, T.	Arrapahoe, South Clear Creek	27	M	11:709
Daniels, T. NC	John.;Oxf.;N.Santa Fe,Mo. (Farmer)	30	M	6:105
Daniels, Thomas E.	Leavenworth, Kickapoo (Farmer)	29	M	10:336
Danihoe, Ellen	Wyandotte, Wyandotte	8	F	10:10
Danihoe, John	" "	10	M	10:10
Danlap, T.	Arrapahoe, South Park	29	M	11:125
Darn, M. E.	Douglas, Lecompton	3or5?	F	6:363
Darn, M.? J.	" "	23	F	6:363
Darnell, James NC	Potta., Rockingham, Elden (Farmer)	45	M	5:291
Darnell, Polly	Coffey, Burlington	54	F	4:35
Darnell, William H.	Coffey, Leroy (Carpenter)	53	M	4:32
Davson, Hiram[1]	Marshall, Marysville (Farmer)	29	M	3:240
Davson, Mary[1]	" "	29	F	3:240
Davenport, V. F.	Atchison, Ward 2	25	F	1:30
Davidson, F. NC	Arrapahoe, South Clear Creek	38	M	11:754
Davidson, J.	Johnson, Gardner (Farmer)	52	M	6:53
Davidson, John C.	Doug., Willow Sp., Brooklyn (Farmer)	51	M	6:321
Davidson, S.	Douglas, Wakarusa, Lawrence	39	F	6:255
Davies, Loucinda	Atchison, Walnut, Sumner	24	F	1:177
Davis, A.	Johnson, Gardner (Farmer)	19	M	6:16
Davis, A.	Coffey, Leroy (Cabinet Maker)	30	M	4:33
Davis, Abel	Coffey, Avon, Burlington (Farmer)	34	M	4:9
Davis, Alben C.	Bourbon, Barnesville P.O. (Farmer)	72	M	2:170
Davis, Andrew J.	Bourbon, Rockford P.O.	14	M	2:100
Davis, Anna	Coffey, Avon, Burlington	32	F	4:9
Davis, B.	Johnson, Gardner	1/12	F	6:51
Davis, Charlotte	Jackson, Franklin, Holton	46	F	5:184
Davis, D.	Johnson, Gardner	23	F	6:15
Davis, D. K.	Coffey, Leroy (Farmer)	27	M	4:28
Davis, Deborah	" "	34	F	4:30

[1]There is a Hiram Dawson in 1855 census; Dist. 3, p. 5.

Arapahoe: spelled incorrectly with 2 r's in census and in this index also.

Name	Kansas: County; Township; P.O. / Arap. Co.: Census Div. Not Township	Age	Sex	Census V. : Pg.
Davis, Delilah	Breckenridge, Pike, Plymouth	37	F	4:213
Davis, Diwrnal	Lykins, Richland, Paola (Farmer)	26	M	8:17
Davis, E.	Johnson, Gardner	17	F	6:51
Davis, Edith	Coffey, Leroy	27	F	4:33
Davis, Eli H.NC	Bourbon, Dayton P.O. (Farm Laborer)	19	M	2:149
Davis, Elias L.	Lykins, Wea, Paola (Farmer)	43	M	8:117
Davis, Elisha	Bourbon, Rockford P.O.	9	M	2:100
Davis, Eliza	Coffey, Leroy	15	F	4:30
Davis, F.	Don., Washington, Elwood (Teamster)	25	M	1:337
Davis, George W.	Bourbon, Rockford P.O.	12	M	2:100
Davis, H.	Johnson, Gardner	12	M	6:51
Davis, J.	Arrapahoe, Central City (Miner)	49	M	11:516
Davis, J.	Davis, Ft. Riley P.O. (Laborer)	22	M	9:350
Davis, J.	Johnson, Gardner (Landlord)	53	M	6:16
Davis, J. B.NC	Franklin, Centropolis, Minneola	35	M	8:205
Davis, James M.	Coffey, Leroy	6	M	4:33
Davis, John	Don., Washington, Elwood (Laborer)	22	M	1:337
Davis, John	Coffey, Avon, Burlington (Farmer)	60	M	4:6
Davis, Josna	Coffey, Leroy	5	M	4:33
Davis, Isaac	Coffey, Avon, Burlington (Merchant)	32	M	4:9
Davis, K.	Johnson, Gardner	39	F	6:51
Davis, L.	" "	9	F	6:51
Davis, Love	Coffey, Leroy	18	F	4:30
Davis, M.	Johnson, Gardner	3	M	6:51
Davis, M.	" "	7	F	6:51
Davis, M.	" "	15	F	6:16
Davis, M.	Doniphan, Washington, Elwood	20	F	1:337
Davis, Margaret	Shawnee, Topeka	26	F	9:13
Davis, Margaret	Bourbon, Rockford P.O. (Housekeeper)	55	F	2:100
Davis, MatildaSC	Leavenworth, Ward 4	36	F	10:273
Davis, Moses	Bourbon, Rockford P.O.	17	M	2:100
Davis, Pamelia	Coffey, Avon, Burlington	56	F	4:6
Davis, R.	Johnson, Gardner	18	F	6:51
Davis, S.	" "	50	F	6:16
Davis, S. A.	Coffey, Leroy (Hotel Keeper)	40	M	4:30
Davis, S. D.	Coffey, Avon, Burlington (Farmer)	32	M	4:17
Davis, S. J.	Johnson, Gardner	13	F	6:16
Davis, SimonNC	Chase, Bazaar (Farmer)	67	M	4:334
Davis, T.	Johnson, Gardner (Farmer)	42	M	6:51
Davis, T. B.	" " (Farmer)	17	M	6:16
Davis, T. C.	" " (Farmer)	15	M	6:51
Davis, WilliamNC	Mars.,Vermillion,Bar. Mills (Farmer)	35	M	3:231
Davison, George	Shaw., Soldier, Indianola (Retired)	78	M	9:86
Dawe, Mary	Doniphan, Center, Troy		F	1:262
Dawson, Alice	Shawnee, Topeka	8	F	9:27
Dawson, Daniel	Shawnee, Topeka (Farmer)	40	M	9:27
Dawson, Flora	" "	10	F	9:27
Dawson, Frank	" " (Farmer)	35	M	9:27
Dawson, George	" " (Farmer)	30	M	9:20
Dawson, John R.	Linn, Paris, Potosi (Carpenter)	30	M	7:139
Dawson, Mary	Shawnee, Topeka	35	F	9:27
Dawson, Olive	" "	12	F	9:27
Dawson, Sam'l	Arrapahoe, Valley of the Platte	29	M	11:806
Day, G. W.	Arrapahoe, South Park	28	M	11:88
Day, George	Douglas, Eudora (Farmer)	63	M	6:342
Day, Hugh	Atch., Walnut, Sumner (Carpenter)	55	M	1:188
Day, PhillipsNC	Brown, Locknow, Powhattan	60	M	3:69
Day, R.NC	Arrapahoe, Quartz Valley (Miner)	25	M	11:493
Day, Thomas J.	Allen, Carlisle P.O. (Farmer)	39	M	2:238
Day, Travis	Lykins, Mound, Osawatomie	74	M	8:73
Davis, L. C.	Johnson, Gardner	15	M	6:51

Arapahoe: spelled incorrectly with 2 r's in census and in this index also.

Name	Kansas: County; Township; P.O. Arap. Co.: Census Div. Not Township	Age	Sex	Census V.:Pg.
Daylory, J. J.[1]	Cof.,Cal.,Burlington (Wagon Maker)	31	M	4:66
Dean, J. D.	Arrapahoe, South Park	28	M	11:178
Deaner, Jesse	Jack., Doug., Grasshpr. Falls(Farmer)	39	M	5:167
Deaner, Mary	" " " "	36	F	5:167
Dearborn, Jno.	Arrapahoe, South Park	32	M	11:131
Dearing, Lewis	Jeff., Kaw, Kaw City (Wagon Maker)	31	M	5:85
Decker, Moses	Doug., Palmyra, Black Jack (Farmer)	80	M	6:278
Deckerson, R. A.	Doniphan, Iowa Point (Teacher)	22	F	1:426
Dedlingbee, G. W.	Doniphan, Doniphan (Farmer)	34	M	1:383
Defrierse, A. B.[NC]	Linn, Potosi, Rovella (Farmer)	51		7:61
DeHaran, D.	Arrapahoe, South Park (Miner)	26	M	11:42
Dehart, Sarah[NC]	Leavenworth, Ward 2	31	F	10:179
Delahunt, M. C.	Johnson, Lexington	19	F	6:72
DeLashmitt, John	Mor.,Grove, Counc.Gr. (Stock Dealer)	29	M	4:265
DeLong, Susan	Lykins, Indianapolis (Domestic)	30	F	8:59
Delp, J. W.?	Douglas, Palmyra, Black Jack	21	M	6:277
Denham, Susan J.	Madison, Elmendaro	39	F	4:238
Denis, Alisan[NC]	Anderson, Jackson, Garnett (Farmer)	27	M	7:210
Dennis, Esther[NC]	" " "	23	F	7:210
Dennis, M. A.	Nemaha, Valley	69	F	3:120
Dennis, Rebecca[NC]	Anderson, Jackson, Garnett	54	F	7:210
Dennis, Solomon[NC]	" " "	22	M	7:210
Dennis, William[NC]	" " " (Farmer)	55	M	7:210
Dennison, C. F.[NC]	Arrapahoe, South Park (Farmer)	38	M	11:15
Dennison, F. A.	Riley, Manhattan P.O.	30	F	9:307
Denny, D. J.[NC]	Arrapahoe, Missouri City (Miner)	24	M	11:558
Densenberg, A.[NC]	Arrapahoe, Denver (Miner)	22	M	11:432
Denton, Mary[SC]	Bourbon, Barnesville P.O.	48	F	2:165
Denton, W.	Arrapahoe, Valley of the Platte	19		11:782
Deraccan, S.[NC]	Butler, Chelsea (Farmer)	56	M	4:347
Derr,? Thos. J.	Arrapahoe, Nevada Gulch (Miner)	29	M	11:518
Deskhard, Bradley	Leavenworth, Ward 4	3	M	10:242
Deskhard, J. B.	" " " (Clerk)	28	M	10:242
Devanport, A.[NC]	Johnson, Olathe	59	F	6:120
Deskhard, Lousia	Leavenworth, Ward 4	24	F	10:242
Deskhard, Mary	Leavenworth, Ward 4	5/12	F	10:242
Devanport, M.[NC]	Johnson, Olathe (Farmer)	63	M	6:120
Devenney, A. S.	" " (Lawyer)	26	M	6:2
Deveraux, J.	Arrapahoe, South Park	29	M	11:177
Devol, A. N.	" " "	40	M	11:188
Dewitt, W. F.[SC]	Johnson, Aubrey (Farmer)	52	M	6:36
Dewvatt, Mary	Doniphan, Iowa Point	56	F	1:418
Dickenson, Benj.	Brown, Claytonv., Robinson	8	M	3:41
Dickenson, Boyd	" " "	23	M	3:41
Dickenson, Dan'l	" " "	11	M	3:41
Dickenson, E.	" " "	13	F	3:41
Dickenson, James	" " "(Teacher C.S.)	29	M	3:59
Dickenson, John	" " "(Teacher)	50	M	3:41
Dickenson, L.	" " "	46	F	3:41
Dickenson, Larimer	" " "	2	F	3:59
Dickenson, Louisa	" " "	15	F	3:41
Dickenson, Martin	" " "	6	M	3:59
Dickenson, Martin	" " "	21	M	3:41
Dickenson, Mary	" " "	8	F	3:59
Dickenson, Rebecca	" " "	19	F	3:41
Dickenson, Samuel	" " "	25	M	3:41
Dickenson, Susan	" " "	17	F	3:41
Dickenson, Thomas	" " "	4	M	3:59
Dickenson, Virginia	" " "	6	F	3:41

[1]The name Daylong appears in the 1865 census, Anderson,Ozark,Eliz.Town, 1:11.
Arapahoe: spelled incorrectly with 2 r's in census and in this index also.

Name	Kansas: County; Township; P.O. Arap. Co.: Census Div. Not Township	Age	Sex	Census V. Pg.
Dickinson, Anna[NC]	Leavenworth, Alexandria, Easton	41	F	1:451
Dicks, Ezekiel[NC]	Breckenridge, Agnes City (Farmer)	58	M	4:146
Dicks, M.	Coffey, Ottumwa, Burlington	2	M	4:55
Dickson, D. M.	Nem., Red Vermillion, America (Clerk)	32	M	3:133
Dickson, M. F.	" " " "	22	F	3:133
Diddle, F. N.[NC]	Arrapahoe, South Clear Creek (Rancher)	45	M	11:635
Diefendorf, N.	Arrapahoe, California Gulch	27	M	11:283
Dike, Joseph	Nemaha, Rock Cr., Albany (Farmer)	50	M	3:76
Dillin, H. A.[SC]	Doniphan, Washington, Wathena	24	F	1:302
Dingman, Wm.	Arrapahoe, South Park	34	M	11:147
Dingus, H.	Linn, Mound City (Farmer)	29	M	7:123
Dinwiddie, Geo.[SC]	Arrapahoe, South Clear Creek (Miner)	45	M	11:633
Diriss, Ann[1]	McGhee; Medoc, Missouri P.O.	46	F	9:208
Diviss, John L.[1]	" " " " (Farmer)	66	M	9:208
Dix, Nathan[NC]	Morris, Grove, Council Gr.(Laborer)	26	M	4:270
Dixon, Adison D.	Atchison, 1st Ward (Artist)	30	M	1:19
Dixon, Joseph	Atchison, Ward 2 (Merchant)	43	M	1:4
Dixon, Martha T.	Atchison, 1st Ward	22	F	1:19
Dixon, Samuel	" " " (Merchant)	37	M	1:9
Dobyns, Henry	Linn, Paris (Farmer)	43	M	7:152
Dockson, J.	Arrapahoe, South Park	28	M	11:228
Dodd, J. P.	" " "	34	M	11:90
Dole, Elizabeth[NC]	Madison, Hartford	39	F	4:236
Doler, Caroline	Lykins, Paola	22	F	8:43
Donly, Jas. P.	Arrapahoe, Enterprise Dist. (Miner)	50	M	11:492
Donnegan, Saml.	Arrapahoe, South Park	24	M	11:223
Dony, N.?	Frank., Ottawa, Hickory Cr.(Farmer)	35	M	8:266
Dooley, J.	Don., Wolf R., Walnut Gr. (Farmer)	59	M	1:411
Doolittle, Wm.	Arrapahoe, South Park (Trader)	57	M	11:63
Dooly, J.	Doniphan, Iowa Point (Farmer)	39	M	1:419
Dooly, Louis	" " "	15	M	1:419
Dooly, M.	" " "	13	M	1:419
Dooly, M.	" " "	33	F	1:419
Dooly, Mary	Nemaha, Home, Centralia	2	F	3:131
Doran, Wm. P.	Arrapahoe, South Park	28	M	11:40
Dorby, W.	Arrapahoe, Valley of the Platte	24	M	11:832
Dorn, Abram	Arrapahoe, Denver (Miner)	45	M	11:428
Doron, Henry	Allen, Carlisle P.O. (Farmer)	56	M	2:238
Doron, Susannah[NC]	" " "	50	F	2:238
Doroughty, D.	Doniphan, Iowa Point (Farmer)	39	M	1:426
Dorset, James[NC]	Anderson, Jackson, Garnett (Farmer)	40	M	7:211
Dorsey, Ann	Lykins, Paola	39	F	8:40
Dorsey, James H.	" "	22	M	8:40
Dorsey, John	" " (Farmer)	50	M	8:40
Dotson, H.	Doniphan, Center, Troy (Farmer)	66	M	1:266
Dotson, Louisa[NC]	McGhee, Medoc, Missouri P.O.	32	F	9:214
Doty, Daniel N.[NC]	Allen, Humboldt P.O.	14	M	2:276
Doty, John[NC]	Allen, Humboldt P.O. (Farmer)	41	M	2:276
Doty, Sophia[NC]	Allen, Humboldt P.O.	44	F	2:276
Dougherty, Sarah[NC]	Coffey, Burlington (Farmer)	73	F	4:44
Douglas, Barbary	Morris, Clarks Creek, Council Grove	18	F	4:282
Douglas, G. H. (G.M.?)	Chase, Bazaar (Millwright)	35	M	4:333
Douglas, John	Mor.,Clarks Cr.,Counc.Gr. (Merchant)	44	M	4:282
Douglas, Susan	" " " " " (Farming)	44	F	4:282
Douglas, Wm.	" " " " "	14	M	4:282
Douglass, E.	Frank., Ohio, Sac & Fox Agency	33	F	8:224
Douglass, G.	" " " " " " (Farmer)	36	M	8:224
Douglass, M. F.	" " " " " "	11	F	8:224
Douglass, W. H.	" " " " " "	14	M	8:224

[1]Surnames almost illegible; Diriss and Diviss may both be actually Davis.
Arapahoe: spelled incorrectly with 2 r's in census and in this index also.

Name	Kansas: County; Township; P.O. Arap. Co.: Census Div. Not Township	Age	Sex	V.	Census Pg.
Dounahor, Andrew	Butler, Chelsea (Farmer)	25	M		4:351
Dounahor, David	" " (Farmer)	33	M		4:351
Dounahor, Prudence	" "	30	F		4:351
Dounahor, Wm.	" "	12	M		4:351
Dowel, John A.	Brown, Claytonville (Farmer)	30	M		3:37
Dower, Elizabeth	Douglas, Kanwaca, Lawrence	26	F		6:391
Downer, Sam'l	Arrapahoe, Valley of the Platte	24	M		11:826
Downes, W.	Frank., Ottawa,Pra.City(Brickmaker)	37	M		8:256
Downie, Saml.	Arrapahoe, Denver (Trader)	26	M		11:416
Downing, Mary	Morris,Neosho,Council Gr. (Farming)	68	F		4:277
Downs, R. S.	Arrapahoe, South Park	38	M		11:258
Downs, W. R.SC	Arrapahoe, Nevada Gulch (Miner)	24	M		11:533
Doyles, MatildiaNC	Brown, Irving, Hiawatha	23	F		3:10
Drake, Adelade	Bourbon, Fort Scott P.O. (Housewife)	22	F		2:225
Drake, Amy	Wyandotte, Quindaro	28	BF		10:55
Drake, JohnNC	Leav., Alexandria, Easton (Farmer)	66	M		10:440
Drake, Martha	Leav., Stranger, Leav. City	48	F		10:482
Drake, Wm. M.	" " " " (Farmer)	48	M		10:482
Drew, S.	Arrapahoe, South Clear Creek	28	M		11:755
Drew, W. M.	Arrapahoe, South Park	33	M		11:237
Driemin, Aley	Shawnee, Williamsport	24	F		9:52
Driver, RachaelNC	Bourbon, Fort Scott P.O. (Housewife)	30	BF		2:196
Drubert, Barbara1	Leavenworth, Ward 3	6/12	F		10:230
Drubert, Elisa	" " "	6	F		10:230
Drubert, Kate1	" " "	2	F		10:230
Druggs, Elizabeth	Douglas, Eudora, Lawrence	34or54?	F		6:335
Druggs, StevenNC	" " " (Farmer)	53	M		6:335
Drum, J. A.	Frank., Potta., Scipio, Anderson Co.	3	M		8:238
Drum, T. S.	Arrapahoe, South Park	28	M		11:117
Drum, W. A.SC	Frank.; Potta.; Scipio, Anderson Co.	49	F		8:239
Drummond, Chas.	Arrapahoe, Denver (Miner)	34	M		11:421
Drummond, Geo.	" " (Miner)	22	M		11:413
Drummond, Jas.	" " (Miner)	30	M		11:421
Drummond, Jno. H.	Lyk.,Marysv.,Sp.Hill (P.E. Clergyman)	45	M		8:129
Drummond, Thos.	Arrapahoe, Denver (Miner)	28	M		11:421
Dudley, Julian	Allen, Iola P.O.	30	F		2:259
Dudley, Rowena	Allen, Humboldt P.O.	28	F		2:275
Dudley, William	Allen, Iola P.O. (Farmer)	69	M		2:259
Duff, G.NC	Johnson, Spring Hill	36	F		6:12
Duffield, E.	Doug., Kanwaca, Lawrence (Farmer)	40	M		6:391
Duffield, M.	" " "	58	F		6:391
Dunavan, A.	Linn, Centerville (Farmer)	65	M		7:89
Dunavan, Jane	" "	55	F		7:89
Dunbar, AbigaleNC	Lykins, Osawatomie	3	F		8:56
Dunbar, James M.NC	" " (Farmer)	28	M		8:56
Dunbar, LouisaNC	" "	23	F		8:56
Duncan, C. S.?	Douglas, Lawrence (Merchant)	38	M		6:190
Duncan, Charles H.	Lykins, Marysville, Lyons	12	M		8:122
Duncan, E. S.	Arrapahoe, South Park (Miner)	36	M		11:57
Duncan, Elizabeth	Douglas, Lawrence (Merchant)	24	F		6:184
Duncan, Francis V.	Lykins, Marysville, Lyons	9	F		8:122
Duncan, Jas. H.	" " " (Farmer)	33	M		8:122
Duncan, Mary	" " "	34	F		8:122
Duncan, M. J.	Brown, Claytonville, Robinson	33	F		3:48
Duncan, R. R.	Leavenworth, Easton (Farmer)	28	M		10:303
Duncan, Saml. S.	Arrapahoe, South Park	24	M		11:245
Duncan, Thomas M.	Lykins, Marysville, Lyons	7	M		8:122
Dunham, Henry B.	Arrapahoe, South Park (Miner)	34	M		11:49
Duning, Mary T.	Atchison, Ward 3	35	F		1:46

[1]State of birth may be La. or Ia. rather than Va.

Arapahoe: spelled incorrectly with 2 r's in census and in this index also.

Name	Kansas: County; Township; P.O. Arap. Co.: Census Div. Not Township	Age	Sex	Census V. Pg.
Dunlap, Elizabeth[NC]	Linn, Mound City	33	F	7:110
Dunlap, J.? A.	Morris, Grove, Council Grove	31	F	4:268
Dunley, L.	Franklin, Centropolis, Minneola	30	F	8:210
Dunn, J.	Johnson, Aubrey (Carpenter)	50	M	6:38
Dunn, Lewis C.	Brown, Irving (Farmer)	44	M	3:1
Dunn, R. P.	Johnson, Shawnee (Laborer)	21	M	6:100
Dunn, S.	Johnson, Aubrey	40	F	6:38
Dunnigan, M.[SC]	Johnson, Lexington	48	F	6:72
Durand, Saml. P.	Potta., Blue, Manhattan (Teamster)	30	M	5:299
Dwight, C. H.	Arrapahoe, South Park	37	M	11:203
Dyche, E.	Osage, Ridgeway, Superior (Farmer)	27	M	8:361
Dyche, L.	" " "	3	M	8:361
Dyer, Drisilla	Potta.,Shannon,Henryville-Manhattan	20	F	5:301
Dyer, Luke[NC]	Bourbon, Turkey Creek P.O. (Farmer)	60	M	2:120
Dyer, Margaret P.	Pottawatomie, Blue, Manhattan	23	F	5:299
Dyer, Mary J.	Potta., Shannon, Henryville-Manhattan	22	F	5:301
Dyer, Olive[NC]	Bourbon, Turkey Creek P.O.(Housewife)	54	F	2:120
Enyc?, Wm.	Don., Burr Oak, Whitehead (Farmer)	26	M	1:343
Dyke, George P.	Leavenworth, Ward 4 (Carpenter)	38	M	10:276
Eagle, I.?	Doug.,Lecom.,B.Sp. (Hotel Keeper)	32	M	6:366
Earl, A. R.	Atchison, Walnut, Sumner (M. D.)	38	M	1:175
Earl, C.[SC]	Wabaunsee, Zeandale	39	F	5:237
Earl, E.	Johnson, Union, Hibbard (Miller)	45	M	6:13
Earl, Polly	Marshall, Blue Rapids (Domestic)	27	F	3:202
Earle, E. C.	Arrapahoe, South Park	30	M	11:129
Earle, Wm.	" " "	20	M	11:234
Easley, J. C.[NC]	Johnson, Spring Hill (Farmer)	29	M	6:45
Easter, Sarah	Wabaunsee, Wilmington	38	F	5:281
Eaton, Sam	Leavenworth, Ward 4	24	M	10:276
Edens, Enoch	Morris, Neosho, Council Gr.(Farmer)	33	M	4:275
Edens, Louisa	" " " "	23	F	4:275
Edgar, Russ	Arrapahoe, South Park (Miner)	34	M	11:54
Edgarton, W.	Arrapahoe, Valley of the Platte	36	M	11:859
Edgington, J. A.[1]	Frank.; Potta.; Walker,Anderson Co.	3	M	8:245
Edmonson, Anna A.	Allen, Iola P.O.	20	F	2:269
Edson, E. D.	Arrapahoe, South Park	26	M	11:208
Edwards, Edward[NC]	Breckenridge, Emporia (Farmer)	40	M	4:187
Edwards, F.[NC]	Lyk., Marysv., Paola (Widow; farmer)	54	F	8:124
Edwards, Isbella	Lykins, Paola	7	F	8:40
Edwards, Martha J.	" "	35	F	8:40
Edwards, Phillip	Breckenridge, Fremont (Farmer)	28	M	4:167
Edwards, Sarah F.	Lykins, Paola	4	F	8:40
Eikenberry, Peter	Breck., Pike, Plymouth (Farmer)	53	M	4:212
Eisenhart?, Emmanuel	Jackson, Jefferson, Holton (Farmer)	27	M	5:194
Eiler, Jacob	Atchison, Walnut, Sumner (Farmer)	50	M	1:180
Eiler, Margaret	" " "	40	F	1:180
Elisa, Elizabeth[NC]	Jefferson, Rock Creek, Mt. Florence	29	F	5:91
Elledge, S. C.	Johnson, Shawnee	21	F	6:94
Ellingwood, F.	Arrapahoe, South Park	30	M	11:250
Elliott, Archibald[SC]	Atchison, Center, Pardee (Farmer)	53	M	1:135
Elliott, Orpha[NC]	Lykins, Stanton	74	F	8:7
Elliott, Stephen J.[NC]	Jackson, Douglas, Holton (Farmer)	30	M	5:170
Ellis, Charles A.	Lykins, Osawatomie	7	M	8:56
Ellis, Dorkus[SC]	Bourbon, Marmaton P.O. (Housewife)	43	F	2:116
Ellis, John P.	Lykins, Osawatomie (Farmer)	35	M	8:56
Ellis, Lucinda	" "	26	F	8:56
Ellis, M. C.	Johnson, Gardner	24	F	6:57
Ellis, Mildred M.	Lykins, Wea, Paola	34	F	8:112
Ellis, William J.	Lykins, Osawatomie (Laborer)	26	M	8:56

[1] Spelling of Edgington is questionable; state of birth may be Ia. or La. rather than Va.

Arapahoe: spelled incorrectly with 2 r's in census and in this index also.

Name	Kansas: County; Township; P.O. Arap. Co.: Census Div. Not Township	Age	Sex	Census V. Pg.
Ellis, May	Arrapahoe, Central City	33	F	11:571
Ellis, Pleasant P.NC	Bourbon, Marmaton P.O. (Farmer)	33	M	2:116
Ellis, T.	Arrapahoe, Nevada Gulch (Miner)	27	M	11:518
Ellis, V. R.	Johnson, Gardner (Farmer)	27	M	6:57
Ellison, Amanda S.	Atchison, Mt. Pleasant	10	F	1:157
Ellison, Charles W.	" " "	8	M	1:157
Ellison, L. L.	" " " (Farmer)	44	M	1:157
Ellison, Martha J.	" " "	15	F	1:157
Ellison, Nancy	" " "	35	F	1:157
Ellison, Olevi	" " "	13	F	1:157
Ellison, Overton A.	" " "	17	M	1:157
Elmaker, F.	Arrapahoe, South Clear Cr.(Teamster)	23	M	11:730
Elwood, J.	" " " " "	34	M	11:731
Elwanger, R.	Arrapahoe, South Park	31	M	11:22
Elwood, H. H.	Arrapahoe, Russell Gulch (Miner)	29	M	11:542
Elwood, Hugh	Arrapahoe, Nevada Gulch (Miner)	28	M	11:531
Ely, George Jr.	Marshall, Vermillion, Barrett Mills	4	M	3:223
Embre, W. E.	Arrapahoe, Missouri City. (Miner)	22	M	11:564
Emersons, Louisa	Pottawatomie, St. George, Elden	21	F	5:265
Emery, NaomieNC	Leavenworth, Kickapoo	64	F	10:332
Emory, H.	Arrapahoe, Idahoe (Miner)	24	M	11:595
Endicott, LizeyNC	Leavenworth, Stranger, Leav. City	48	F	10:476
Endicott, Abner	Bourbon, Fort Scott P.O.(FarmLaborer)	23	M	2:93
Endicott, Gabriel	" " " " (Farmer)	59	M	2:93
Engerman, M. C.	Douglas, Wakarusa, Lawrence	24	F	6:258
Engle, SilasNC	Woodson, Belmont	4	M	9:150
English, W. W.	Arrapahoe, South Park	35	M	11:128
Enshenger, C.[1]	Douglas, Lawrence	45	F	6:214
Ensley, J.NC	Frank.;Potta.;Scipio,And.Co. (Farmer)	26	M	8:239
Ensley, J. M.	" " " " "	3	M	8:239
Ensminger, H. T.	Arrapahoe, South Park	25	M	11:210
Epps, R.NC	Linn, Potosi (Farmer)	34	M	7:73
Erwin, M.	Johnson, Shawnee	29	F	6:99
Erwin, S.	Johnson, Olathe (Blacksmith)	32	M	6:4
Eskridge, C. V.	Breckenridge, Emporia	25	M	4:199
Estes, S.NC	John.;Oxf.;N.Santa Fe, Mo.(Farmer)	26	M	6:108
Estis, T. J.NC	Riley, Ogden P.O. (Laborer)	25	M	9:291
Estus, A.NC	Franklin, Peoria, Peoria City	35	F	8:272
Etheridge, AlmaNC	Bourbon, Turkey Creek P.O.(Housewife)	64	M	2:114
Etheridge, BurwellNC	" " " " (Farmer)	60	M	2:114
Etherton, Lewis	Nemaha, Richmond, Seneca (Farmer)	60	M	3:98
Etherton, Polly	Doniphan, Wolf River, Walnut Grove	37	F	1:405
Eubanks, A. E.	Franklin, Prairie, Stanton	14	F	8:283
Eubanks, G.	" " " (Farmer)	50	M	8:283
Eubanks, MariaNC	Riley, Manhattan P.O.	37	F	9:306
Evans, Fanny	Douglas, Lecompton	31	F	6:353
Evans, N. R.	Arrapahoe, California Gulch	34	M	11:300
Evans, P.	Doniphan, Doniphan (Farmer)	40	M	1:391
Evans, Ripley	Arrapahoe, South Park (Miner)	37	M	11:1
Evins, Felix C.NC	Linn, Paris	14	M	7:133
Evins, JohnNC	" "	10	M	7:133
Evins, John B.NC	" "	8	M	7:133
Ewing, ElizabethNC	Linn, Scott, Brooklyn	53	F	7:13
Eye, Bery	Brown, Irving, White Cloud (Farmer)	24	M	3:2
Fackler, John M.	Leavenworth, Ward 2 (Physician)	44	M	10:194
Fackler, Wiley B.	" " "	19	M	10:194
Fagg, Rebecca	Anderson, Jackson, Garnett	42	F	7:209
Failing, W. R.?	Arrapahoe, South Park	36	M	11:2
Fair, Marlington	Arrapahoe, Denver	22	M	11:330

[1] Looks more like Enslinger in original entry.

Arapahoe: spelled incorrectly with 2 r's in census and in this index also.

Name	Kansas: County; Township; P.O. Arap. Co.: Census Div. Not Township	Age	Sex	Census V. : Pg.
Falcher, Wm. F.	Leavenworth, Ward 2 (Blacksmith)	37	M	10:167
Fale, Mary[1],[NC?]	Douglas, Kanwaca, Lawrence	5	F	6:392
Fale, Patrick[1],[NC?]	" " "	3	M	6:392
Fall, G. W.	Arrapahoe, Denver	38	M	11:342
Falwell, Ephriam	Atch., Shannon, Atchison (Farmer)	46	M	1:74
Farfield, J.	Arrapahoe, South Park	35	M	11:191
Farmer, Wm.	Wyandotte, Quindaro	81	M	10:52
Farnsworth, D. M.	Atchison, Ward 2 (Laborer)	28	M	1:1
Farnsworth, Samuel	Leavenworth, 1st Ward	60	M	10:102
Farr, Mary[NC]	Jefferson, Jefferson, Crooked Creek	24	F	5:27
Farrell, Thos.	Arrapahoe, South Park	24	M	11:249
Farrill, H. L.	Doniphan, White Cloud	23	F	1:443
Faucett, I. G. (J.G.?)	Douglas, Lawrence (Laborer)	28	M	6:212
Faukner, Jefferson[NC]	Jeff., Jeff., Winchester (Farmer)	42	M	5:41
Faukner, Lucinda[NC]	" " "	36	F	5:41
Fawinthay, J. C.	Douglas, Palmyra, Prairie City	62	M	6:269
Fease, Margaret	Jackson, Douglas, Holton	34	F	5:174
Feazel, Pleasant	Madison, Elmendaro (Farmer)	63	M	4:242
Fekes, Elmira	Linn, Scott, Brooklyn	5	F	7:28
Felix, G.	Arrapahoe, South Park (Miner)	37	M	11:74
Fenman, O. S.	" " "	33	M	11:123
Fennal, Samuel	Leavenworth, Ward 2 (Stone mason)	64	M	10:183
Fenniss, J.	Don., Wolf R., Walnut Gr. (Farmer)	30	M	1:407
Fenton, Geo.	Linn, Mound City (C. Maker)	29	M	7:106
Ferdinand, J.	Doniphan, White Cloud (Miller)	28	M	1:442
Fergason, P. C.	Don., Marion, Palermo (Physician)	46	M	1:281
Fergurson, W.[NC]	Cof., Ottumwa, Burlington (Farmer)	36	M	4:50
Ferguson, A. M.[NC]	Don., Wash., Elwood (Merchant)	32	M	1:313
Ferguson, H.	Johnson, Shawnee	22	F	6:87
Ferguson, O.	Arrapahoe, South Park	26	M	11:132
Ferguson, S. Ellen	Doniphan, Washington, Elwood	22	F	1:313
Ferrald, Susan[NC]	Linn, Potosi, Rovella	38	F	7:58
Farrel, Ann	Leavenworth, Ward 3	4	F	10:219
Ferris, F. J.	Franklin, Centropolis, Minneola	11	F	8:204
Few, Ann C.	Leavenworth, Ward 3	28	F	10:230
Few, O. D.	Arrapahoe, Valley of the Platte	29	M	11:846
Few, Samuel F.	Leavenworth, Ward 3	42	M	10:230
Ficklin, I. E.	Arrapahoe, Denver (Express Agent)	20	M	11:328
Field, H. C.	Leavenworth, Ward 2 (Clerk)	25	M	10:151
Fields, Wm.	Doniphan, Center, Troy (Farmer)	59	M	1:242
Fieldsman, Elliot	Shawnee, Soldier, Indianola	5	M	9:85
Fieldsman, Francis	" " "	30	F	9:85
Figer, David	Atch., Shannon, Atchison (Farmer)	61	M	1:71
Figer, Eliza	" " "	60	F	1:71
Filkins, J. R.	Arrapahoe, South Park	35	M	11:127
Finch, H. W. G.	Johnson, Shawnee (Farmer)	51	M	6:98
Finch, R. S.	" " (Farmer)	45	M	6:98
Fincher, Levi[NC]	Linn, Paris (Farmer)	30	M	7:148
Findley, Sarah[NC]	Leavenworth, Kickapoo	36	F	10:414
Finley, James A.	Douglas, Lawrence (Druggist)	31	M	6:181
Fips, David M.[NC]	Bourbon, Dayton P.O. (Farmer)	23	M	2:157
Fish, John F.	Shawnee, Auburn (Farmer)	25	M	9:47
Fisher, A.	Frank.,Ottawa,Prairie City (Farmer)	21	M	8:256
Fisher, A. S.	" " " "	14	M	8:256
Fisher, Adam	Leavenworth, Ward 2 (Hotel)	41	M	10:163
Fisher, Aloisa	Lykins, Marysville, Lyons	12	F	8:131
Fisher, Althias	" " "	15	F	8:131
Fisher, B.	Johnson, Spring Hill	11	F	6:47

[1]State of birth possibly S. C.
Arapahoe: spelled incorrectly with 2 r's in census and in this index also.

Name	Kansas: County; Township; P.O. Arap. Co.: Census Div. Not Township	Age	Sex	Census V.	Pg.
Fisher, Charles W.	Leavenworth, Delaware	9	M	10:435	
Fisher, E.	Frank.; Ottawa; Prairie City,Doug.Co.	48	F	8:256	
Fisher, Edwin	Lykins, Marysville, Lyons	16	M	8:131	
Fisher, Eliza	" ' " "	24	F	8:131	
Fisher, Elizabeth P.	Lykins, Paola	19	F	8:27	
Fisher, F.	Johnson, Spring Hill	12	M	6:47	
Fisher, G. S.	Frank.;Ottawa;Prairie City,Doug. Co.	10	M	8:256	
Fisher, G. W.	Leavenworth, Delaware (Farmer)	44	M	10:435	
Fisher, George	Lykins, Marysville, Lyons (Farmer)	37	M	8:131	
Fisher, H.	Frank.,Ottawa,Prairie City (Farmer)	23	M	8:256	
Fisher, J.	Johnson, Spring Hill (Farmer)	15	M	6:47	
Fisher, J.	Frank.;Ottawa, Prairie City (Farmer)	19	M	8:256	
Fisher, J.	" " " "(Blacksmith)	45	M	8:256	
Fisher, J. M.	Johnson, Spring Hill	31	F	6:47	
Fisher, John W.	Lykins, Paola (Druggist)	29	M	8:27	
Fisher, L.	Johnson, Spring Hill	1	F	6:47	
Fisher, Louisa	Lykins, Marysville, Lyons	12	F	8:131	
Fisher, Lungerburn	" " ■	14	M	8:131	
Fisher, M.	Johnson, Spring Hill	3	M	6:47	
Fisher, P.	" " "	7	M	6:47	
Fisher, S.	Franklin; Ottawa; Prair.City,Doug.Co.	16	F	8:256	
Fisher, Sarah C.	Leavenworth, Delaware	12	F	10:435	
Fisher, T. H.	Johnson, Spring Hill (Farmer)	17	M	6:47	
Fisher, W.	Arrapahoe, Valley of the Platte	22	M	11:862	
Fitch, L.	Arrapahoe, South Park	34	M	11:105	
Fitch, R. H.	Doniphan, Iowa Point (Carpenter)	28	M	1:422	
Fittsyne, P.	Arrap.,Mt.City, Mountain (Engineer)	26	M	11:459	
Fitzpatrick, Sarah	Breckenridge, Waterloo	28	F	4:153	
Fix, D.	Douglas, Kanwaca, Lawrence	42	F	6:388	
Flanagan, Elizabeth	Lykins, Stanton	34	F	8:2	
Flaniot, G. S.NC	Arrapahoe, South Park (Miner)	33	M	11:16	
Flay, S.	Doniphan, Washington, Wathena	19	F	1:326	
Fleak, E.	Franklin, Centropolis, Minneola	22	F	8:211	
Fleck, H.	Johnson, Olathe (Farmer)	27	M	6:115	
Fleck, J.	" " (Farmer)	29	M	6:115	
Fleming, Bethany·SC	Linn, Paris	54	M	7:158	
Fleming, J. P.	Arrapahoe, South Park	24	M	11:4	
Fleming, Jas. F.	Lykins, Paola (Farmer)	43	M	8:27	
Flesher, James E.	Allen, Iola P.O. (Farmer)	25	M	2:270	
Flesher, William	Allen, Iola P.O. (Farmer)	31	M	2:260	
Fleshman, Emily	Shawnee, Soldier, Indianola	40	F	9:88	
Fleshman, Perry	" " " (Farmer)	45	M	9:88	
Fletcher, Denry?	Doug., Willow Sp., Brooklyn (Farmer)	44	M	6:322	
Fletcher, E. R.	Arrapahoe, Valley of the Platte(Miner)	27	M	11:806	
Fletcher, J. H.	Arrapahoe, South Park	34	M	11:189	
Fletcher, Polly	Atchison, Center, Pardee	66	F	1:119	
Fletcher, Thomas	" " " (Farmer)	57	M	1:119	
Fletcher, V. C.	Arrapahoe, South Park	29	M	11:128	
Flim, Royal NC	Allen, Xenia P.O.	60	M	2:232	
Flinn, D. W.	Doniphan, Iowa Point (M. Carpenter)	32	M	1:422	
Flinn, L.NC	Linn, Potosi (Farmer)	35	M	7:72	
Flinn, M. A.	Doniphan, Iowa Point	30	F	1:422	
Flinn, M. B.	" " " (Carpenter)	50	M	1:422	
Flinn, M. E.	" "	8	F	1:422	
Flint, J.	Arrapahoe, South Park	36	M	11:156	
Flong, R. V.	Leavenworth, 1st Ward (Brickmason)	45	M	10:132	
Flood, Lucy NC	Doniphan, Washington, Wathena	60	F	1:305	
Floory, Jonathan	Linn, Centerville, Keokuk (Farmer)	50	M	7:83	
Flory, M. M.	Mor.,Grove,Council Gr. (House Joiner)	26	M	4:265	
Flower, Jane NC	Wyandotte, Wyandotte	26	F	10:15	
Foard, J. F.	Leavenworth, Ward 2 (Shoe Merchant)	24	M	10:148	

Arapahoe: spelled incorrectly with 2 r's in census and in this index also.

Name	Kansas: County; Township; P.O. Arap. Co.: Census Div. Not Township	Age	Sex	Census V. Pg.
Foner, H.	Linn, Valley, Blooming Grove	63	F	7:34
Font?, Roberta Virginia	Bourbon, Fort Scott P.O.	21	F	2:223
Foote, D.	Arrapahoe, Nevada Gulch (Miner)	29	M	11:531
Foraley, Jane	Doniphan, White Cloud	22	F	1:438
Forbes, Ann	Doniphan, Wayne, Doniphan	35	F	1:374
Forbes, F. J.	" " " (Farmer)	40	M	1:374
Forbes, R.	" " "	11	F	1:374
Forbes, Thomas	" " "	9	M	1:374
Ford, A.	Johnson, Monticello (Farmer)	38	M	6:22
Forester, A. J.	Arrapahoe, South Park	29	M	11:180
Forgunen, Crittenden	Allen, Iola	87	M	2:273
Foristor, R.	Arrapahoe, South Park	29	M	11:89
Fortune, Thomas	Atchison, Mt. Pleasant	63	M	1:150
Fortune, Thomas L.	" " " (Merchant)	35	M	1:149
Fortus, Adam[1]	Doniphan, Wayne, Doniphan	14	M	1:371
Fortus, C.[1]	" " "	38	F	1:371
Fortus, L.[1]	" " "	6	M	1:371
Fortus, L. T.[1]	" " "	11	F	1:371
Fortus, T. J.[1]	" " " (Farmer)	42	M	1:371
Fortus, V. C.[1]	" " "	13	F	1:371
Forsyth, John[NC]	McGhee, Crawford Seminary P.O.(Farmer)	30	M	9:225
Foster, C.	Wabaunsee, Wabaunsee (Farmer)	32	M	5:233
Foster, Elloner	Leavenworth, Stranger, Leavenworth	46	F	10:475
Foster, Isaac	Atchison, 1st Ward	49	M	1:14
Foster, James	Wash., Mill Cr., Marysville (Farmer)	24	M	3:267
Foster, Jno. [SC]	Arrapahoe, South Clear Creek (Miner)	37	M	11:633
Foster, Jno.	Arrapahoe; Tarryall, South Park	29	M	11:614
Foster, Wm. B.	Arrapahoe, Denver (Trader)	28	M	11:371
Fosto, A. B.[2]	Doniphan, Wayne, Doniphan (Farmer)	30	M	1:369
Fosto, Lucinda	" " "	29	F	1:369
Fountain, G.	Arrapahoe, Valley of the Platte	23	M	11:808
Fouts, John [NC]	Linn, Paris (Farmer)	45	M	7:147
Fouts, Lawrena	" "	40	F	7:148
Fowler, Femta [NC]	Breckenridge, Emporia	25	F	4:187
Fowler, Harvey[NC]	" " (Farmer)	30	M	4:187
Fowler, Isaac[NC]	Jefferson, Oskaloosa (Farmer)	90	M	5:128
Fowler, John [NC]	Breckenridge, Emporia (Farmer)	60	M	4:186
Fowler, Milly[NC]	" "	50	F	4:186
Fox, E.	Doniphan, Iowa Point (Carpenter)	50	F	1:422
Fox, Mary C.	Leavenworth, Delaware	28	F	10:416
Fracker, E. A.	Arrapahoe, Valley of the Platte	24	M	11:825
France, Andrew	Atch., Walnut, Sumner (Farmer)	55	M	1:194
France, Elizabeth	" " "	39	F	1:194
France, F. J.	Leavenworth, Delaware (Farmer)	29	M	10:419
Francis, Nancy	Jefferson, Ozawkie	30	F	5:102
Francis, William	" " (Farmer)	39	M	5:102
Frank, Andrew J.	And., Town Greeley, Garnett (Farmer)	40	M	7:243
Frank, Anna E.	" " " "	14	F	7:243
Frank, Jacob	" " " "	18	M	7:243
Frank, James	" " " "	16	M	7:243
Frank, Michael[NC]	Bourbon, Barnesville P.O. (Farmer)	53	M	2:169
Frank, Rebecca[NC]	" " (Housewife)	44	F	2:169
Frank, Sophia	Anderson, Town of Greeley, Garnett	40	F	7:243
Frank, Wm.[NC]	Arrapahoe, South Park	38	M	11:231
Franklin, Emily[SC]	Leavenworth, 1st Ward (Servant)	27	BF	10:104
Franklin, Lousia[NC]	Leavenworth, Ward 2	36	F	10:193
Franklin, Sam	Leavenworth, 1st Ward (Cook)	31	BM	10:104
Franks, Abraham	Wyandotte, Wyandotte (Farmer)	53	M	10:39

[1]Spelling may be Foster; difficult to decipher.

[2]May be Fristo or Foster; see Fortus, also in Doniphan County.

Arapahoe: spelled incorrectly with 2 r's in census and in this index also.

Name	Kansas: County; Township; P.O. Arap. Co.: Census Div. Not Township	Age	Sex	Census V.	Pg.
Fraser, George E.	Leavenworth, 1st Ward	16	M	10:140	
Fraser, Mary E.	" " "	34	F	10:140	
Fraser, Robinson	" " " (Clerk)	40	M	10:140	
Fraser, Samuel	" " "	14	M	10:140	
Fraser, Wm. M.	" " "	12	M	10:140	
Frawbridge, David	Breckenridge, Emporia (Farmer)	40	M	4:186	
Frawbridge, Jesse	" " (Carpenter)	28	M	4:186	
Frazier, B. G.	Arrapahoe, South Park	29	M	11:211	
Frazier, Cyrus	Leav., Stranger, Leav.City (Farmhand)	23	M	10:468	
Frazier, Edmund NC	" " " " (Farmhand)	35	M	10:468	
Fredrick, J.	Arrapahoe, South Clear Creek	23	M	11:735	
Fredericks, Paulina NC	Breckenridge, Emporia	26	F	4:196	
Freeborn, W.	Arrapahoe; Tarryall, South Park	33	M	11:614	
Freeh, Barney	Jeff., Jeff., Crooked Cr. (Laborer)	40	M	5:26	
Freeland, James P.	Brown, Claytonv., Robinson (Farmer)	26	M	3:43	
Freeman, Andrew J. NC	Dickinson, Kansas Falls P.O.	10	M	4:306	
Freeman, Caloin NC	" " " "	11	M	4:306	
Freeman, George W. NC	" " " " (Farmer)	40	M	4:306	
Freeman, J.	Linn, Paris (Farmer)	32	F	7:142	
Freeman, John NC	Wyandotte, Quindaro (Farmer)	47	M	10:65	
Freeman, Louisa	Linn, Paris	10	F	7:142	
Freeman, Mary	" "	14	F	7:142	
French, H. R.	Johnson, Lexington	4	M	6:73	
French, J. B.	" " (Farmer)	31	M	6:78	
French, J. F.	" " (Farmer)	32	M	6:73	
French, Jacob	Arrapahoe, South Park (Miner)	36	M	11:191	
French, W.	Johnson, Lexington	2	M	6:73	
Friend, M. D.	Arrapahoe, Central City (Carpenter)	23	M	11:580	
Frill, Wm. NC	Anderson, Monroe, Garnett	34	M	7:215	
Frishman, Jacob	Atch., Shannon, Atchison (Farmer)	78	M	1:69	
Frishman, Sarah	" " "	73	F	1:69	
Fritzer, Henry	Douglas, Lawrence	22	M	6:189	
Fritzett, J.	Arrapahoe, Valley of the Platte	30	M	11:841	
Frome, Henry	Doniphan, Wolf River, Walnut Grove	7	M	1:397	
Frost, B.	Johnson, Shawnee	14	M	6:89	
Frost, E.	Arrapahoe, South Park	25	M	11:142	
Frost, G.	Johnson, Shawnee (Farmer)	16	M	6:89	
Frost, J.	" " (Farmer)	23	M	6:89	
Frost, M.	" "	8	F	6:89	
Frost, N.	" "	40	F	6:89	
Frost, P.	" "	7	M	6:89	
Frost, P.	" " (Farmer)	20	M	6:89	
Frost, W.	" " (Farmer)	44	M	6:89	
Frost, W. R.	Arrapahoe, South Park	46	M	11:3	
Fulton, Lena (Tena?)	Shawnee, Soldier, Indianola	68	M	9:89	
Fulton, Lousa	" " "	32	F	9:89	
Fulton, Polla	" " " (Farmer)	48	M	9:89	
Funderbeck, E. L. SC	Johnson, Gardner (Farmer)	46	M	6:49	
Funk, I. W.	Arrapahoe, Central City (Miner)	24	M	11:509	
Funk, J.	Frank.,Ohio,Sac&Fox Agency (Farmer)	54	M	8:224	
Furguson, B. F. NC	Johnson, Spring Hill	10	M	6:47	
Furguson, David NC	Leavenworth, 1st Ward (Washer)	47	BM	10:100	
Furguson, E. S. NC	Johnson, Spring Hill	12	F	6:47	
Furguson, G. W. NC	" " " (Farmer)	33	M	6:47	
Furguson, Lydia	Leavenworth, 1st Ward	49	F	10:100	
Furguson, N. (or W.?) NC	Johnson, Spring Hill	33	F	6:47	
Furroughs, J.	Davis, Junction City P.O. (Farmer)	79	M	9:337	
Furse, Martha	Linn, Paris	45	F	7:149	
Furthey, Mary	Coffey, Leroy	55	F	4:31	
Gadus, R. NC	Douglas, Willow Springs (Farmer)	24	M	6:329	
Gaines, J. D. NC	Arrapahoe, South Clear Creek (Miner)	25	M	11:644	

Arapahoe: spelled incorrectly with 2 r's in census and in this index also.

Name	Kansas: County; Township; P.O. Arap. Co.: Census Div. Not Township	Age	Sex	Census V. Pg.
Gaines, Wm.[NC]	Arrapahoe, South Clear Creek (Miner)	30	M	11:644
Gains, H.	Arrapahoe, South Park	41	M	11:200
Gains, S.	Doniphan, Marion, Palermo	70	F	1:281
Gains, W.	" " " (Farmer)	72	M	1:281
Gale, G. M.	Leavenworth, Ward 2 (Baker)	30	M	10:171
Gale, Rebecca	Chase, Toledo	35	F	4:338
Gall, Davie	Brown, Irving, Padonia (Farmer)	30	M	3:7
Gallusha, J. J.[NC]	Arrapahoe, California Gulch	36	M	11:293
Gandy, A. P.	Chase, Falls,Cotton.Falls(Chairmaker)	35	M	4:322
Ganes, Mary	Doniphan, Burr Oak, Whitehead	30	F	1:351
Gant, Jno. O.[NC]	Arrapahoe, Golden City	19	M	11:583
Gardiner, Eliza[NC]	Jefferson, Kentucky, Oskaloosa	38	F	5:76
Gardner, A. D.	Leavenworth, 1st Ward (Clerk)	30	M	10:137
Gardner, James	Jefferson, Jefferson, Crooked Creek	76	M	5:38
Gardner, T.	Arrapahoe, South Park	28	M	11:217
Gardner, W. R.	Brown, Walnut Creek, Hamlin	33	M	3:28
Garland, H.[NC]	Arrapahoe, South Park	30	M	11:255
Garnett, G. W.	Arrapahoe, Spring Gulch (Miner)	21	M	11:538
Garr, G.[NC]	Frank.,Centrop.,Minneola (Farmer)	45	M	8:213
Garret, Marshall	Wyandotte, Wyandotte	27	M	10:32
Garrett, Alonzo A.	Pottowatomie, Blue, Manhattan (Farmer)	36	M	5:296
Garrett, John [SC]	Coffey, Ottumwa, Burlington (Farmer)	35	M	4:49
Garrett, Sarah	Douglas, Lecompton	37	F	6:350
Garris, S. E.	Arrapahoe, South Clear Creek	33	M	11:715
Garvin, Nancy [NC]	Lykins; Sugar Cr.; West Point, Mo.	70	F	8:103
Garvin, William	" " " " " "	74	M	8:103
Gaskins, Cassanda	Hunter, Eldorado, Chelsea	65	BF	4:359
Gay, A.	Doniphan, Center, Troy (Farmer)	45	M	1:248
Gay, Enoch	" " " (Farmer)	16	M	1:248
Gay, J. N.	" " " (Farmer)	20	M	1:248
Gay, J. R.	" " " (Farmer)	19	M	1:248
Gay, M. J. (or M.T.?)	" " "	45	F	1:248
Gaylord, J.	Arrapahoe, Valley of the Platte	21	M	11:803
Gaylord, J. H.	Arrapahoe, South Clear Creek	31	M	11:714
Gearhart, W.	Arrapahoe, Valley of the Platte	23	M	11:820
Geffin, J. M.	Johnson, Olathe (Editor)	26	M	6:4
Gelder, T.	Arrapahoe, South Clear Creek	36	M	11:748
Gent, William	Bourbon, Fort Scott P.O. (Farmer)	51	M	2:209
Gentry, M.	Johnson, DeSota, Lexington	57	F	6:19
George, C. O.	Arrapahoe, South Park	27	M	11:116
George, Mary	Doniphan, Burr Oak, Whitehead	55	F	1:349
George, R.	" " " " (Farmer)	55	M	1:349
Gevens, A.	Johnson, Olathe	22	F	6:2
Gevens, C.	" "	51	F	6:2
Gevens, C.	" "	24	F	6:2
Gevens, E.	" "	18	F	6:2
Gibson, B.[NC]	Chase, Toledo (Farmer)	40	M	4:337
Gibson, Huldy[NC]	Arrapahoe, Golden City	44	F	11:439
Gibson, Isabel[NC]	Chase, Toledo	33	F	4:337
Gibson, Robt.[NC]	" "	10	M	4:337
Gibson, Wm.[NC]	" "	14	M	4:337
Gieer, M.[SC]	Doniphan, Marion, Palermo	47	F	1:292
Gideon, John A.[NC]	McGhee, Crawford Seminary P.O.	44	M	9:233
Giesy, Adaline	Coffey, Avon, Burlington	44	F	4:8
Gifford, C.	Arrapahoe, South Clear Creek	32	M	11:698
Gift, Peter	Marshall, Marysville (Blacksmith)	41	M	3:251
Gilbert, Sophia	Atchison, Shannon, Atchison	33	F	1:75
Gilchrist, L. S.	Arrapahoe, South Park	35	M	11:122
Gilkerson, John	Allen, Carlisle P.O. (Farmer)	39	M	2:242
Gilkerson, Mary E.	" " "	35	F	2:242
Gill, Henry T.	Atchison, Kapioma, Muscotan(Farmer)	45	M	1:102

Arapahoe: spelled incorrectly with 2 r's in census and in this index also.

Name	Kansas: County; Township; P.O. Arap. Co.: Census Div. Not Township	Age	Sex	Census V. : Pg.
Gill, Wm.	Arrapahoe, California Gulch	28	M	11:293
Gillum, Elizabeth	Morris, Neosho, Council Grove	14	F	4:274
Gillum, Henry	" " " " (Farmer)	40	M	4:274
Gillum, Wm.	" " "	13	M	4:274
Gilmore, Jane NC	Doniphan, Iowa Point	39	F	1:431
Gilmore, Samuel G.NC	Dorn, Turkey Creek P.O. (Merchant)	37	M	2:356
Gilpin, Prudence	Shawnee, Topeka	33	F	9:23
Gilstrap, Julia NC	Linn, Potosi, Rovella	46	F	7:54
Gilstrap, Lewis NC	" " " (Farmer)	61	M	7:54
Gimble, Geo.	Arrapahoe, South Park	28	M	11:129
Gird, Margaret	Leavenworth, Kickapoo	46	F	10:334
Girenstreet, Saphrona	Linn, Valley, Blooming Grove	25	F	7:44
Gish, Richard NC	Atchison, Center, Pardee (Farmer)	49	M	1:120
Gish, Wm.	" " " (Farmer)	56	M	1:119
Giss, Lawrence	Arrapahoe, Golden City (Miner)	23	M	11:448
Gist, Patience	Leav., Stranger, Leav. City (Servant)	40	BF	10:477
Given, Amanda	Leavenworth, 1st Ward	27	F	10:118
Given, Thomas	" " " (Blacksmith)	38	M	10:118
Given, Wm.	Arrapahoe, South Park	32	M	11:129
Given, Wm.	" " " (Miner)	26	M	11:41
Givvens, G.	Arrapahoe, California Gulch	30	M	11:292
Glaze, H.	Doniphan, Marion, Palermo (Farmer)	41	M	1:286
Glenn, Robt. Y.	Breckenridge, Emporia (Merchant)	31	M	4:196
Gloden, Mary	Doniphan, Burr Oak, Whitehead	65	F	1:340
Glome, M. J.	Don.; Center, Lafayette; Troy	22	F	1:249
Glome, P. C.	" " " "(Painter)	23	M	1:249
Glover, O.	Franklin, Ohio, Ohio City	2	M	8:231
God, John	Linn, Centerville, Keokuk (Farmer)	57	M	7:84
Godard, Ann E.	Atchison, Walnut, Sumner	?	F	1:173
Godley, W. N.	Linn, Centerville, Keokuk (Farmer)	38	M	7:84
Godsy, Henry S. NC	Lykins, Paola (Carpenter)	30	M	8:31
Goe, S. S.	Arrapahoe, Valley of the Platte	22	M	11:792
Goer, Emaline	Atchison, Shannon, Atchison	22	F	1:75
Goer, Green L.	" " " (Farmer)	28	M	1:75
Goer, Noah G.?	" " " (Farmer)	26	M	1:75
Goethe, A. S.	Arrapahoe, South Clear Creek (Hotel)	37	M	11:644
Goingis, R.	Wood., Liberty, Neosho Falls (Farmer)	42	M	9:143
Goldsbery, James	Mars., Vermil., Bar. Mills (Farming)	40	M	3:222
Goldsbery, Permellia	" " " "	75	F	3:222
Good, Amay	Atchison, 1st Ward	18	F	1:24
Good, J. J.	" " " (Gunsmith)	34	M	1:24
Good, Peter	Bourbon, Marmaton P.O. (Farmer)	26	M	2:206
Goodale, I.	Franklin, Ohio, Sac & Fox Agency	40	F	8:222
Goodale, S.	" " " "	15	M	8:222
Goodlett, S. R.	Arrapahoe, Valley of the Platte	25	M	11:833
Goodow, NewtonNC	Lykins, Mound, Osawatomie (Farmer)	42	M	8:69
Goodrich, A.	Arrapahoe, South Park	25	M	11:243
Goodrick, Benj.	Lykins, Stanton (Farmer)	56	M	8:5
Goodrick, Daniel	" " (Farmer)	46	M	8:3
Goodwin, Cyrus	Linn, Paris	40	M	7:144
Goodwin, SusanahNC	Coffey, Leroy, Burlington	79	F	4:27
Gord, B.	Arrapahoe, Lake Gulch (Miner)	25	M	11:483
Gorden, J.	Johnson, Shawnee (Farmer)	32	M	6:92
Gordon, PolinaNC	Jefferson, Grasshopper Falls	51	F	5:2
Gorton, H. W.	Arrapahoe, South Park	24	M	11:16
Goss, Jos.NC	Linn, Valley, Blooming Gr. (Farmer)	58	M	7:40
Gossin, Henrietta	Leavenworth, Ward 2	7	F	10:164
Gossin, Louisa	" " "	5	F	10:164
Gossin, Wm.	" " "	2	M	10:164
Gotcher, E. NC	Doniphan, Burr Oak, Whitehead	37	F	1:343
Gotten, Daniel	Chase, Toledo (Farmer)	30	M	4:337

Arapahoe: spelled incorrectly with 2 r's in census and in this index also.

Name	Kansas: County; Township; P.O. Arap. Co.: Census Div. Not Township	Age	Sex	Census V. Pg.
Grace, Elizabeth[NC]	Marshall, Marysville	50	F	3:241
Grace, John	" " (Farm Laborer)	55	M	3:241
Graham, C.	Douglas, Palmyra, Prairie City	14	M	6:260
Graham, Columbus	" " " "	13	M	6:269
Graham, E.[SC]	Linn, Scott, Brooklyn (Farmer)	72	M	7:19
Graham, Eda	Douglas, Palmyra, Prairie City	47	F	6:269
Graham, Elezabeth	Marshall, Vermillion, Barrett Mills	52	F	3:230
Graham, G. H.	Arrapahoe, South Park	27	M	11:229
Graham, J. D.[NC]	Arra., California Gulch (Blacksmith)		M	11:310
Graham, Jane	Douglas, Palmyra, Prairie City	11	F	6:269
Graham, John	Douglas, Kanwaca, Lawrence (Farmer)	56	M	6:386
Graham, Joseph	Mars., Vermil., Bar.M.(Farm Laborer)	22	M	3:228
Graham, Thomas	Doug., Palmyra, Prairie City (Farmer)	49	M	6:269
Graner, D.	Linn, Valley, Blooming Gr. (Farmer)	39	M	7:49
Granslopp, S. T.	Doniphan, Center, Troy (Laborer)	22	M	1:251
Grant, Martin	Arrapahoe, Denver (Butcher)	30	M	11:420
Grass, James	Linn, Valley, Blooming Gr.(Physician)	37	M	7:30
Grassmuck, O.	Arrapahoe, South Park	24	M	11:235
Graves, D. P.	Linn, Mound City (Farmer)	30	M	7:103
Graves, W.	" " " (Merchant)	25	M	7:103
Gray, Benjamin W.[SC]	Bourbon; Wheeling, Mo. P.O.(Farmer)	46	M	2:85
Gray, E.	Arrapahoe, South Park (Miner)	42	M	11:59
Gray, E. M.	Leavenworth, 1st Ward	70	M	10:128
Gray, H. E. A.	" " "	50	F	10:127
Gray, Joseph	" " "	80	M	10:128
Grayson, N.	Arrapahoe, South Park	18	M	11:115
Greely, F.	Douglas, Clinton	55	F	6:405
Green, Andrew	McGhee, Crawford Sem.P.O.(Carpenter)	48	M	9:223
Green, C.	Douglas, Lecompton (Mason)	36	M	6:359
Green, G. P.	Arrapahoe, Valley of the Platte	29	M	11:784
Green, H. F.	Leavenworth, Ward 3 (Lawyer)	34	M	10:222
Green, Jane	Leavenworth, 1st Ward	30	BF	10:117
Green, S.	Johnson, Lexington	19	F	6:71
Green, T. P.	Arrapahoe, South Park (Miner)	28	M	11:48
Green, V.	Johnson, McCamish, Hibbard	21	F	6:61
Green, Virginia[1]	Wyandotte, Wyandotte	20	F	10:38
Greenlee, Gruman	Arrap., Calif. Gulch (Blacksmith)	37	M	11:277
Greeson, Nancy[NC]	Breckenridge, Emporia	29	F	4:191
Greeson, Reuber[NC]	" " (Farmer)	30	M	4:191
Gregg, Susan	Leavenworth, Easton	21	F	10:303
Gregory, Mary	Linn, Potosi	28	F	7:82
Gregory, Wm. H.[SC]	Arrapahoe, Missouri City (Miner)	35	M	11:569
Grey, J.	John.;Oxford;N.Santa Fe,Mo. (Farmer)	33	M	6:109
Grey, L.	" " " "	21	F	6:109
Gridner, J.[NC]	Arrapahoe, South Clear Creek	38	M	11:755
Griffin, Ellen[SC]	Arrapahoe, Missouri City	7	F	11:540
Griffin, L.[NC]	Doniphan, Center, Troy (Farmer)	63	M	1:273
Griffin, Mathias[SC]	Arrapahoe, Missouri City	27	M	11:540
Griffith, James	Jefferson, Ozawkie (Farmer)	32	M	5:103
Griffith, Margaret	Bourbon, Marmaton P.O. (Housewife)	36	F	2:208
Griffith, Vrial[2]	Don., Burr Oak, Whitehead (Farmer)	48	M	1:346
Griffith, Wm.	Arrapahoe, South Park	20	M	11:126
Grimes, James	Mars., Vermil., Bar. Mills (Farmer)	40	M	3:233
Grimes, Jane	" " " "	11	F	3:233
Grimes, John	" " " "	9	M	3:233
Grimes, Susan	" " " "	32	F	3:233
Grimes, Thomas	" " " "	6	M	3:233
Grimshaw, N. K.	Arrapahoe, South Park	25	M	11:135

[1]W.P.A. indexer listed state of birth as Va.?
[2]Spelled Uriah in 1855 census.

Arapahoe: spelled incorrectly with 2 r's in census and in this index also.

Name	Kansas: County; Township; P.O. Arap. Co.: Census Div. Not Township	Age	Sex	Census V. Pg.
Grise, G.	Arrapahoe, South Clear Creek	27	M	11:694
Griswold, A.	Arrapahoe, South Park	30	M	11:235
Groat, J. B.	" " "	36	M	11:1
Groff, Hiram[1,C]	Atchison, Walnut, Sumner (Farmer)	26	M	1:170
Groff, John[1,C]	" " " (Farmer)	28	M	1:170
Grooms, A.	Don., Washington, Elwood (Farmer)	55	M	1:338
Grooms, E.[NC]	Doniphan, Center, Troy	38	F	1:264
Grooms, M.	Doniphan, Washington, Elwood	30	F	1:338
Grove, Martha	Lykins, Marysville, Paola	23	F	8:124
Grovenor, J.	Arrapahoe, Valley of the Platte	30	M	11:809
Grua?, David[NC]	Arrapahoe, Denver (Miner)	28	M	11:429
Grubb, W. H.	Arrapahoe, Nevada Gulch (Carpenter)	42	M	11:503
Grumbey, John	Doniphan, White Cloud (Shoemaker)	46	M	1:438
Grumbey, L.	" " "	19	F	1:438
Guernsay, J. H.	Arrapahoe, South Clear Creek	28	M	11:729
Gunner, Benjamin	Bourbon, Turkey Creek P.O. (Farmer)	30	M	2:111
Gunter, Henry[NC]	Jackson, Holton (Mason)	35	M	5:178
Gutman, Joseph	Arrapahoe, South Park	30	M	11:189
Gwen, Harriet	Leavenworth, 1st Ward	26	BF	10:110
Gye, Benj.	Brown, Irving, White Cloud (Farmer)	24	M	3:2
Haas, Sarah	Leavenworth, 1st Ward	29	F	10:120
Hacworth, A.	Doniphan, Iowa Point (Farmer)	45	M	1:428
Haddix, Ellen	Jefferson, Kentucky, Oskaloosa	31	F	5:64
Haddix, Lydia[NC]	" " "	58	F	5:64
Haderal, W.	Doniphan, Wayne, Doniphan (Servant)	52	BF	1:373
Hadicks, E.[NC]	Doniphan, Burr Oak, Whitehead (Farmer)	43	M	1:345
Hadine, H. C.	Arrapahoe, South Park	24	M	11:89
Hadley, J.[NC]	Johnson, Monticello (Clerk)	19	M	6:83
Hadley, J. M.[NC]	" " (Farmer)	25	M	6:83
Hadley, Jane[NC]	Breckenridge, Pike, Plymouth (Farmer)	52	F	4:208
Hadley, Mary[NC]	" " "	23	F	4:214
Hadley, Mary A.[NC]	Breckenridge, Emporia	24	F	4:198
Hadly, Barman[SC]	Wyandotte, Wyandotte (Laborer)	25	M	10:38
Hagadon, H. G.	Arrapahoe, South Park (Miner)	39	M	11:20
Haggard, Harriett	Lykins, Sugar Creek, New Lancaster	54	F	8:99
Hainens?, B. P.	Arrapahoe, Central City (Hotel)	36	M	11:579
Hainens?, Rachel	" " "	35	F	11:579
Hains, S.	Franklin, Centropolis, Minneola	11	F	8:202
Hair, A.	Riley, Manhattan	26	F	9:309
Haiskell, Charles S.	Lykins, Paola	15	M	8:40
Haiskell, Wm. A.	" " (Farmer)	52	M	8:40
Halan, Mary	Doniphan, Washington, Wathena	42	F	1:340
Hale, Jacob[NC]	Coffey, Neosho, Burlington (Farmer)	58	M	4:74
Haley, Martha	Leavenworth, Kickapoo	28	F	10:412
Hall, Adam	Atchison, Mt. Pleasant (Blacksmith)	25	M	1:160
Hall, Alex.	Arrapahoe, South Clear Creek (Miner)	40	M	11:625
Hall, Banks	Douglas, Palmyra, Baldwin (Farmer)	51	M	6:283
Hall, Cyrus	Wash.,Mill Cr.,Marys.(Farm Laborer)	15	M	3:267
Hall, Elizabeth[NC]	Allen, Elizabeth Town P.O.	54	F	2:235
Hall, Geo. (or Theo?)	Arrapahoe, Lake Gulch	17	M	11:488
Hall, Jefferson	Jeff., Jefferson, Crooked Cr.(Farmer)	28	M	5:27
Hall, John	" " "(Laborer)	31	M	5:27
Hall, Joshua	Leavenworth, Easton (Farmer)	34	M	10:305
Hall, Syntha	" "	60	F	10:305
Hall, W. T.	Arrapahoe, Valley of the Platte	28	M	11:843
Hall, William[NC]	Allen, Xenia P.O. (Farmer)	45	M	2:232
Haller, W. H.	Arrapahoe, South Park	32	M	11:230
Halsey, Robert	Coffey, Burlington (Farmer)	31	M	4:43
Halstead, A.[NC]	Johnson, Gardner	63	F	6:56

[1]Birth place listed as Carolina.

Arapahoe: spelled incorrectly with 2 r's in census and in this index also.

Name	Kansas: County; Township; P.O. Arap. Co.: Census Div. Not Township	Age	Sex	Census V.: Pg.
Halstead, A. NC	Johnson, Gardner (Farmer)	65	M	6:56
Halsted, F.	Arrapahoe, South Park	33	M	11:204
Hamby, W. N. NC	And.,Washington, Garnett (Meth.Min.)	45	M	7:252
Hamilton, D. F.	Arrapahoe, Central City (Miner)	22	M	11:571
Hamilton, E.	Doniphan, Center, Troy	56	F	1:273
Hamilton, J. M.	Shawnee, Topeka (Merchant)	45	M	9:5
Hamilton, Matilda	Leavenworth, Ward 4	45	F	10:254
Hamilton, Matilda NC	Bourbon, Fort Scott P.O.(Housewife)	46	F	2:182
Hamilton, T. 1	Osage, Ridgeway, Superior (Farmer)	28	M	8:346
Hammond, Ellen	Linn, Potosi	25	F	7:82
Hammond, J. H.	Johnson, Gardner (Laborer)	37	M	6:58
Hampson, Cath.	Doniphan, Wolf River, Walnut Grove	30	F	1:407
Hampson, E. NC	" " " " "(Farmer)	33	M	1:407
Hand, E. Mills SC	Shawnee, Tecumseh (Farmer)	76	M	9:73
Handley, G.	Arrapahoe, South Park	34	M	11:157
Hanfro, George	Anderson, Walker, Garnett (Miller)	34	M	7:245
Hanley, Charles	Leav., Stranger, Leav.City (Farmer)	66	M	10:481
Hanley, Jackson	" " " " (Farmer)	33	M	10:482
Hanley, Nancy	" " " "	63	F	10:481
Hanley, Ranson	" " " " (Farmer)	37	M	10:482
Hann, C. P. NC	Linn, Potosi (Farmer)	47	M	7:72
Hann, Harrison NC	" " (Farmer)	16	M	7:72
Hann, John NC	" " (Farmer)	32	M	7:73
Hann, Mary NC	" "	30	F	7:72
Hann, Virgil NC	" " (Farmer)	19	M	7:72
Hanon, James SC	Allen, Xenia P.O. (Farmer)	66	M	2:231
Hanover, E.	Pottawatomie, Vienna, Louisville	35	F	5:250
Hanson, J. H.	Arrapahoe, Valley of the Platte	23	M	11:808
Hanson, N. O.	Doniphan, Wayne, Doniphan	56	F	1:373
Hanson, Seth	Arrapahoe, Denver (Miner)	36	M	11:411
Haray (Aaron?), H.	Arrapahoe, Eureka Gulch (Miner)	55	M	11:507
Harbor, A.	Franklin, Centropolis, Minneola	24	M	8:201
Harbor, J.	" " "(Brickmason)	22	M	8:201
Hardesty, F.	" "	19	M	8:211
Hardin, H. S. SC	Arrapahoe, Missouri City (Miner)	22	M	11:569
Harding, Keziah	Lykins, Richland, Gardner	55	F	8:22
Harding, Wm.	Arrapahoe, South Park	32	M	11:66
Hardson, Lucinda	Allen, Humboldt P.O.	32	F	2:284
Hardy, A.	Doniphan, Marion, Palermo (Laborer)	33	M	1:291
Hardy, Charles	" " " (Merchant)	32	M	1:291
Hardy, S. E.	" " " (Merchant)	38	M	1:291
Hariland, S. C.	Arrapahoe, South Park	35	M	11:222
Harman, Emeline	Jefferson, Grasshopper Falls	25	F	5:10
Harman, Noah H.	" " " (Farmer)	30	M	5:10
Harman, Webster	" " "	5	M	5:10
Harmon, Jacob	Arrapahoe, Denver (Doctor)	56	M	11:352
Harmon, T.	Arrapahoe, South Park (Miner)	36	M	11:186
Harmon, T.	Arrapahoe, Valley of the Platte	27	M	11:821
Harner, M. A. NC	Johnson, Lexington	31	F	6:75
Harper, Branson NC	Breckenridge, Emporia (Carpenter)	34	M	4:186
Harper, John	Butler, Chelsea, Eureka (Farmer)	55	M	4:346
Harper, John	Allen, Xenia P.O.	23	M	2:229
Harper, M. A.	Doniphan, Columbus City, Whitehead	42	F	1:359
Harper, S.	Linn, Potosi, Rovella (Farmer)	48	M	7:56
Harer, Wm. H.	Arrapahoe, South Park	28	M	11:125
Harrell, W. B.	Morris, Grove, Council Gr. (Farmer)	55	M	4:272
Harren, Wm.	Arrapahoe, South Park	27	M	11:188
Harris, Aaron	Doniphan, Doniphan (Carpenter)	26	M	1:383
Harris, Adelate	Linn, Scott, Twin Springs	8	F	7:8

1State of birth could be Ia. or La. rather than Va.
  Arapahoe: spelled incorrectly with 2 r's in census and in this index also.

Name	Kansas: County; Township; P.O. Arap. Co.: Census Div. Not Township	Age	Sex	Census V. Pg.
Harris, Angeline	Linn, Scott, Twin Springs	11	F	7:8
Harris, Ann	Davis, Ft. Riley P.O.	18	F	9:348
Harris, Barbara	Linn, Scott, Twin Springs	13	F	7:8
Harris, C. NC	Arrapahoe, Valley of the Platte(Miner)			11:778
Harris, C. S.	Franklin, Centropolis, Minneola	3	M	8:203
Harris, Elizabeth	Lykins, Osawatomie	38	F	8:55
Harris, G. K.	Davis, Ft. Riley P.O. (Farmer)	61	M	9:348
Harris, George	Mars.,Vermil.,Bar.M. (Farm Laborer)	18	M	3:222
Harris, Henry	Linn, Scott, Twin Springs (Farmer)	17	M	7:8
Harris, Henry P. C.	Leav.,Kickapoo (Physician & Farmer)	33	M	10:414
Harris, Jane NC	Coffey, Ottumwa, Burlington	43	F	4:57
Harris, John	Linn, Scott, Twin Springs (Farmer)	19	M	7:8
Harris, Louisa	" " " "	48	F	7:8
Harris, Mary	Davis, Ft. Riley P.O.	57	F	9:348
Harris, Mary E.	Douglas, Willow Springs, McKinney	36	F	6:295
Harris, Rebecca	Linn, Scott, Twin Springs	15	F	7:8
Harris, S. SC	Johnson, Monticello (Physician)	25	M	6:83
Harris, Susan	Marshall, Vermillion, Barrett Mills	40	F	3:222
Harris, Verginia	Wyandotte, Wyandotte	27	F	10:12
Harris, W.	Linn, Scott, Twin Springs (Farmer)	56	M	7:8
Harris, W. NC	Coffey, Ottumwa, Burlington	20	F	4:53
Harrison, A. C.	Arrapahoe, Denver (Teacher)	33	M	11:320
Harrison, A. C.[2]	Atchison, 1st Ward (Gold sacker)[2]	39	M	1:20
Harrison, Mrs. Ann	" " "	57	F	1:20
Harrison, B. F.	" " " (Lumberman)	37	M	1:20
Harrison, J. M.[1]	Frank.;Potta.;Walker, Anderson Co.	5	M	8:242
Harrison, M.[1]	Osage, Ridgeway, Burlingame	1	F	8:338
Harrison, Richard	Atchison, 1st Ward (Lumberman)	36	M	1:20
Harsgrove, Sarah NC	Linn, Valley, Blooming Grove	58	F	7:39
Harsgrove, W. SC	" " " " (Farmer)	59	M	7:39
Harshy, M.	Frank.;Potta.;Scipio, Anderson Co.	3	M	8:239
Harshy, M.	" " " " "	33	F	8:239
Hart, A.	Arrapahoe, Denver (Barber)	40	MM	11:379
Hart, John	Jeff., Jefferson, Crooked Cr.(Farmer)	62	M	5:28
Hart, Martha NC	Allen, Iola P.O.	44	F	2:270
Hart, Martha NC	" " "	14	F	2:270
Hartford, Harry C.	Atchison, Ward 3	24	M	1:33
Hartford, Junius	Atchison, Ward 2 (Lawyer)	28	M	1:33
Hartley, William	Bourbon, Fort Scott P.O. (Farmer)	30	M	2:78
Harvey, J. M.	Riley, Randolph,Ft.Riley P.O.(Farmer)	25	M	9:301
Harvey, M. H.	Johnson, Shawnee	51	F	6:94
Harvey, Nancy NC	Bourbon, Fort Scott P.O.	16	F	2:153
Harvey, S. D.(or L.B.?) NC	Johnson, Shawnee (Farmer)	56	M	6:94
Harvey, William J.	Don., Washington, Whitehead (Farmer)	56	M	1:299
Haskell, C. H.	Arrapahoe, California Gulch	40	M	11:286
Hastings, John NC	Jackson, Douglas, Holton (Farmer)	55	M	5:170
Hastings, O.	Arrapahoe, South Park	28	M	11:142
Hastings, W.	Frank., Peoria, Peoria City (Farmer)	41	M	8:275
Hastings, Edith NC	Allen, Humboldt P.O.	52	F	2:289
Haswell, J. G.	Arrapahoe, South Park (Saloon)	25	M	11:44
Hatch, F.	Franklin, Ohio, Ohio City	3	M	8:233
Hatton, Mary	Jefferson, Kentucky, Oskaloosa	50	F	5:71
Haukins, Alice	Wyandotte, Quindaro	20	F	10:59
Haunay, Emily	Bourbon, Barnesville P.O.(Housewife)	26	F	2:175
Haunay, George	" " " (Farmer)	39	M	2:175
Haur, J.	Johnson, Olathe (Farmer)	58	M	6:116

[1]Birth state could be Pa. or Ia. rather than Va.

[2]See Jas. B. Low, "gold seeker", Part I, address Atchison Co., Mt. Pleasant
   Township and P.O., age 22, Vol. 1, p. 150.

Arapahoe: spelled incorrectly with 2 r's in census and in this index also.

Name	Kansas: County; Township; P.O. Arap. Co.: Census Div. Not Township	Age	Sex	Census V.: Pg.
Haur, J. F.	Johnson, Olathe (Farmer)	23	M	6:116
Haur, L.	" "	56	F	6:116
Haur, V.	" "	21	F	6:116
Haverhill, T. T.	Arrapahoe, Denver (Lawyer)	28	M	11:411
Haverty, M.	Johnson, Olathe (Farmer)	21	M	6:5
Hawk, A.	Linn, Valley, Blooming Gr. (Farmer)	22	M	7:38
Hawk, Chas.	" " " "	6	M	7:38
Hawk, Eliza	" " " "	9	F	7:38
Hawk, Harriett	" " " "	11	F	7:38
Hawk, Mary	" " " "	13	F	7:38
Hawk, Mary	" " " "	31	F	7:38
Hawk, N. M.	" " " "(Farmer)	41	M	7:38
Hawk, Sarah	" " " "	17	F	7:38
Hawkins, John[NC]	Chase, Cottonwood, C. Falls(Farming)	42	M	4:32
Hawkins, Martha E.	Bourbon, Fort Scott P.O.(Housewife)	28	F	2:182
Hawkins, Warren R.[SC]	Bourbon, Marmaton P.O. (Farmer)	49	M	2:207
Hawkins, William	Coffey, Potta., Burlington (Farmer)	53	M	4:2
Hawley, Frances H.	Leavenworth, Easton (Farmer)	75	M	10:299
Haworth, Nancy[NC]	Breckenridge, Fremont	37	F	4:165
Haws, F. T.	Arrapahoe, South Park (Miner)	34	M	11:70
Hay, Asa B.	Leavenworth, 1st Ward (Clerk)	30	M	10:137
Hayne, Geo.[NC]	Arrapahoe, Valley of the Platte(Miner)	27	M	11:836
Haynes, William[NC]	Jeff., Rock Cr., Mt.Florence (Farmer)	20	M	5:88
Hays, J.	Riley, Manhattan-Henryv.P.O. (Farmer)	32	M	9:297
Hays, Mary E.	Atchison, Walnut, Sumner	40	F	1:184
Hays, Robert	Potta.,Shannon,Henryv.-Man.(Farmer)	32	M	5:301
Hays, Saml.	" " " " (Farmer)	28	M	5:301
Hays, Wm. M.	Atchison, Walnut, Sumner (Farmer)	62	M	1:184
Hazelton, T. M.	Arrapahoe;Tarryall,S.P.; Iowa Gulch	27	M	11:607
Hearn, B.	Arrapahoe, South Clear Creek		M	11:658
Heatherly, Jane[SC]	Atchison, Walnut, Sumner	59	F	1:169
Heberlin, H.	Osage, Ridgeway, Burlingame (Farmer)	49	M	8:362
Hazlip, John	Lykins, Osawatomie (Farmer)	25	M	8:57
Heddens, N.	Coffey, Neosho, Burlington (Farmer)	20	M	4:68
Hedges, Joseph	Arrapahoe, Nevada Gulch (Miller)	38	M	11:504
Hefelbower, Ezran	Lykins, Wea, Squiresville (Farmer)	30	M	8:115
Hefelbower, Margaret E.	" " "	23	F	8:114
Heimici?, Mary	Clay, Junction City P.O.	14	F	9:270
Helelinda, Elizabeth	Wyandotte, Wyandotte	50	F	10:27
Helfelbower, Daniel F.	Lykins, Wea, Squiresville (Farmer)	31	M	8:114
Helfelbower, David H.	" " " (Farmer)	24	M	8:115
Helfelbower, Mary E.	" " "	24	F	8:115
Helm, Chas.	Douglas, Clinton	12	M	6:405
Helm, Charles	Leavenworth, 1st Ward	25	M	10:123
Helm, Joanna	Douglas, Clinton	10	F	6:405
Helm, Martha	" "	41	F	6:405
Helm, Mary	" "	18	F	6:405
Helm, Thomas	" "	14	M	6:405
Helm, W.	" " (Farmer)	45	M	6:405
Helm, W. B.	" "	16	M	6:405
Hemphill, E.	Arrapahoe, South Clear Creek	33	M	11:741
Henders, P. M.	Arrapahoe, Nevada Gulch	40	M	11:527
Henderson, A.	Arrapahoe, South Park	29	M	11:38
Henderson, Elvina	Leavenworth, Alexandria, Easton	49	F	10:453
Henderson, John	Jeff., Jeff., Crooked Cr. (Carpenter)	22	M	5:38
Henderson, John H.	Leav., Alexandria, Easton (Farmer)	60	M	10:453
Henderson, Nathaniel[NC]	Leavenworth, Kickapoo (Farmer)	39	M	10:414
Henderson, Rose	Bourbon, Mapleton P.O. (Housewife)	38	F	2:146
Henderson, Sarah E.[NC]	Atchison, Mt. Pleasant	19	F	1:156
Henderson, Wm.[NC]	Atchison, Lancaster (Farmer)	70	M	1:111
Henderson, Wm. M.	Leavenworth, Alexandria, Easton	25	M	10:453

Arapahoe: spelled incorrectly with 2 r's in census and in this index also.

Name	Kansas: County; Township; P.O. Arap. Co.: Census Div. Not Township	Age	Sex	Census v.·pg.
Hendley, T.	Arrapahoe, Golden City (Teamster)	26	M	11:582
Hendrick, A. E.	Leavenworth, Kickapoo (Farmer)	52	M	10:330
Hendrick, Sarah	" "	52	F	10:330
Hendricks, David NC	Bourbon, Turkey Creek P.O. (Farmer)	48	M	2:110
Hendricks, J.	Franklin, Ohio, Ohio City (Merchant)	54	M	8:229
Hendricks, Jno.	Arrapahoe, California Gulch	41	M	11:311
Hendricks, S. P.	Johnson, Olathe (Farmer)	45	M	16:112
Henley, Franklin NC	Coffey, Neosho, Burlington	11	M	4:75
Henley, Frederick NC	" " " (Farmer)	35	M	4:75
Henley, J. R. NC	" " "	7	M	4:75
Henley, Jacob E. NC	" " " (Farmer)	28	M	4:75
Henley, Jane NC	" " "	27	F	4:75
Henley, Margaret NC	" " "	3	F	4:75
Henley, Maria NC	" " "	4	F	4:75
Henley, Nancy NC	" " "	28	F	4:75
Henning, S. P.	Arrapahoe, South Park	29	M	11:128
Henry, Alphens NC	Coffey, Neosho, Burlington	23	M	4:74
Henry, J. L. SC	Douglas, Clinton (Farmer)	59	M	6:417
Henry, J. P.	Arrapahoe, Central City (Merchant)	23	M	11:574
Henry, Joseph	Breckenridge, Americus (Farmer)	52	M	4:219
Henry, Mary	Leavenworth, 1st Ward	70	F	10:126
Henry, Sarah J.	Bourbon, Xenia P.O. (Housewife)	29	F	2:129
Henshaw, Andrew NC	Breckenridge, Emporia (Farmer)	31	M	4:192
Hensley, E.	Leavenworth, Ward 2	50	M	10:146
Hensly, Abraham D.	Madison, Verdigris, Madison Centre	12	M	4:245
Hensly, Delilah	" " " "	40	F	4:245
Hensly, Jonatha	" " " "(Farmer)	48	M	4:245
Hensly, Jonathan E.	" " " "	2	F	4:245
Hensly, Marion D.	" " " "	6	F	4:245
Hensly, Mary M.	" " " "	9	F	4:245
Hensley, William SC	Lyk.;Sugar Cr.;West Pt.,Mo. (Farmer)	59	M	8:96
Henson, Allen NC	Atchison, Walnut, Sumner (Farmer)	55	M	1:174
Henson, Jame Ann	Lykins, Stanton	37	F	8:12
Herbert, W. W. SC	Davis, Kansas Falls P.O.(Lawyer-Editor	32	M	9:331
Hermon, David	Wyandotte, Quindaro (Millwright)	73	M	10:55
Herndon, P. M.	Arrapahoe, Nevada Gulch (Carpenter)	42	M	11:502
Herndon, Thomas	Atchison, Mt. Pleasant (Farmer)	66	M	1:146
Herr, L.	Franklin, Ohio, Sac and Fox Agency	30	F	8:222
Herrington, Lousia NC	Jefferson, Oskaloosa	26	F	5:117
Herron, John NC	Jeff., Jeff., Crooked Cr. (Laborer)	56	M	5:39
Hershaw, Nathan NC	Douglas, Eudora	21	M	6:340
Hershaw, M. (or N.?) NC	" " (Farmer)	26	M	6:340
Herzlemoore, Thomas	Leavenworth, Kickapoo (Laborer)	24	M	10:323
Hester, D.	Franklin, Peoria, Stanton	10	M	8:280
Hester, E.	" " "	18	F	8:280
Hester, E.	" " "	2	M	8:280
Hester, F.	" " "	15	F	8:280
Hester, H.	" " "	4	M	8:280
Hester, J.	" " "	13	M	8:280
Hester, W.	" " "	6	M	8:280
Hewket, E. NC	Johnson, Lexington	25	F	6:75
Hewket, S. C. NC	" " (Farmer)	27	M	6:75
Hiatt, B. H. NC	Leavenworth, Alexandria,Easton(Farmer)	34	M	10:449
Hiatt, Edith NC	Coffey, Burlington	40	F	4:41
Hiatt, Enos NC	Breckenridge, Emporia (Farmer)	46	M	4:192
Hiatt, Joel NC	Leavenworth, Kickapoo (Farmer)	54	M	10:341
Hiatt, Matilda NC	" "	49	F	10:341
Hiatt, Nathen NC	Anderson, Monroe, Garnett (Farmer)	49	M	7:219
Hiatt, Sabina NC	Breckenridge, Emporia	43	F	4:203
Hick, S. S.	Douglas, Lawrence (Blacksmith)	40	M	6:202
Hickanbottom, Joseph	Atchison, Center, Pardee (Farmer)	21	M	1:138

Arapahoe: spelled incorrectly with 2 r's in census and in this index also.

Name	Kansas: County; Township; P.O. Arap. Co.: Census Div. Not Township	Age	Sex	Census V.:Pg.
Hicks, D.	Arrapahoe, California Gulch (Miner)	25	M	11:281
Hicks, Linza NC	Linn, Liberty, Centerville (Farmer)	20	M	7:3
Hicks, M.	Linn, Mound City (Farmer)	35	M	7:112
Hicks, T. E.	Breckenridge, Emporia (Farmer)	39	M	4:195
Higginbotham, C. D.	Riley, Manhattan P.O.	28	F	9:281
Higginbothan, C. E.	" " "	18	F	9:282
Higginbottom, Cyrus	Shawnee, Soldier, Indianola (Clerk)	24	M	9:83
Higgins, H. G.	Arrapahoe, South Park	37	M	11:217
Higgins, Thomas	Doni., Marion, Palermo (Lumberman)	40	M	1:279
High, W. H. NC	Doni., Wash., Elwood (Millwright)	40	M	1:310
Highley, Albert A.	Lykins, Paola	16	M	8:26
Highley, Emily S.	" "	20	F	8:26
Highley, Hyrennus	" "	18	M	8:26
Highley, Maria J.	" "	8	F	8:26
Highley, Mary E.	" "	38	F	8:26
Highley, Robt. B.	" " (Justice of the Peace)	51	M	8:26
Higginbottom, Francis A.	Leavenworth, Ward 2	8	F	10:190
Higginbottom, S. C.	" " "	29	F	10:190
Higginbottom, Thomas E.	" " "	7	M	10:190
Higins, S.	Don., Burr Oak, Whitehead (Farmer)	54	M	1:342
Higler, Enoch	Coffey, Ottumwa, Burlington (Farmer)	33	M	4:52
Hill, Martha	Lyk.; Sugar Cr.; West P., Mo.	48	F	8:97
Hill, N. NC	Linn, Potosi (Merchant)	56	M	7:66
Hill, Rebecca	Leavenworth, Ward 2	50	F	10:192
Hill, Sarah	Lykins, Marysville, Lyons	17	F	8:122
Hill, Sophia	" " "	41	F	8:122
Hiller, W. N. NC	Arrapahoe, South Clear Creek (Miner)	27	M	11:764
Hinchman, S. N.	" " " "	24	M	11:710
Hindburch, H. O.	" " " "	25	M	11:711
Hindman, Richard SC	Shawnee, Soldier, Indianola (Farmer)	22	M	9:87
Hinshaw, Jemima NC	Chase, Falls, Cottonwood Falls	3	F	4:330
Hinshaw, Martin NC	" " " " (Farming)	33	M	4:330
Hinshaw, Rachel NC	" " " "	31	F	4:330
Hinton, Guy	Bourbon, Rockford P.O. (Farmer)	50	M	2:97
Hinton, M. H.	Johnson, Shawnee	21	F	6:92
Hinton, R.	" " (Farmer)	25	M	6:92
Hite, Alex	Jack., Doug., Grasshopper F.(Farmer)	50	M	5:167
Hixon, Mahala E.	Bourbon, Dayton P.O. (Housewife)	27	F	2:156
Hobbs, E. C.	Brown, Irving, Hiawatha (Farmer)	33	M	3:16
Hobson, Th.? NC	Linn, Paris (Miller)	48	M	7:153
Hodgeman, H.	Arrapahoe, Denver	45	M	11:349
Hodges, Jesse M.	Lykins, Wea, Squiresville (Farmer)	36	M	8:114
Hodges, Lawson M.	Bourbon, Barnesville P.O. (Farmer)	42	M	2:180
Hodgiss, J. B. NC	Chase, Falls, Cottonwood Falls	25	M	4:330
Hodgiss, Mary NC	" " " "	25	F	4:330
Hodgson, Fanny	Linn, Paris	50	F	7:151
Hodgson, Lydia	" "	77	F	7:152
Hodson, Rosina	Linn, Scott, Twin Springs	24	F	7:6
Hoffman, Althea	Bourbon, Turkey Creek P.O.	14	F	2:108
Hoffman, Amy	" " " "(Housewife)	31	F	2:108
Hoffman, John A.	" " " "(Farmer)	37	M	2:108
Hoffman, Josanna	" " " "	11	F	2:108
Hoffman, Mary J.	" " " "	7	F	2:108
Hoffman, Rachael	Doniphan, Doniphan	46	F	1:387
Hoffman, T.	John.;Oxford; N.Santa Fe,Mo. (Farmer)	31	M	6:102
Hoffman, Ursula A.	Bourbon, Turkey Creek P.O.	5	F	2:108
Holbert, T.	Linn, Centerv., Hawks Wing (Farmer)	26	M	7:97
Holborn, Iola	Allen, Iola P.O.	28	F	2:260
Holbrook, Simeon NC	Allen, Xenia P.O. (Farmer)	42	M	2:229
Holby, C. NC	Arrapahoe, Mountain City (Saloon)	27	M	11:461
Holcomb, Elizabeth NC	Linn, Potosi, Rovella	28	F	7:58

Arapahoe: spelled incorrectly with 2 r's in census and in this index also.

Name	Kansas: County; Township; P.O. Arap. Co.: Census Div. Not Township	Age	Sex	Census V. Pg.
Holcomb, J. NC	Linn, Potosi, Rovella (Farmer)	30	M	7:58
Holcomb, Nancy NC	" " "	10	F	7:58
Holder, Augustin R. NC	Lykins, Middle Creek, Paola (Farmer)	35	M	8:107
Holder, Jonathan M.NC	" " " "	5	M	8:107
Holder, Joseph N.NC	" " " "	29	M	8:107
Holder, Nancy A.NC	" " " "	7	F	8:107
Holder, Rebecca P.NC	" " " "	30	F	8:107
Holiday, N.NC	Franklin, Pottawat., Shermanville	30	F	8:249
Hollan, Mary NC	McGhee, Crawford Seminary P.O.	44	F	9:225
Holland, Elizabeth	Linn, Scott, Brooklyn (Farmer)	38	F	7:27
Holland, JamesNC	Doniphan, Iowa Point (Farmer)	27	M	1:457
Holland, Jno. C.NC	Arrapahoe, California Gulch	24	M	11:298
Holland, U. P.NC	Doniphan, Iowa Point	23	M	1:457
Holliday, E.NC	Franklin, Pottawat., Shermanville	63	F	8:247
Hollinsworth, Elias	Brown, Locknow, Powhattan (Farmer)	20	M	3:63
Hollinsworth, Phoeba	" " "	26	F	3:63
Holly, NancySC	Madison, Hartford	64	F	4:234
Holmes, D.	Arrapahoe, Denver	12	M	11:366
Holmes, D.	Johnson, Spring Hill (Wagonmaker)	45	M	6:42
Holmes, David G.	Lyk., Wea, Squiresville (Wagonmaker)	42	M	8:113
Holmes, Jackson	Breckenridge, Pike, Plymouth (Farmer)	43	M	4:212
Holmes, Rebecca	Coffey, Ottumwa, Burlington	40	F	4:52
Holmes, W.	Arrapahoe, Valley of the Platte	31		11:782
Holmes, W.	Arrapahoe, South Park	29	M	11:170
Holren, Thomas	Lykins, Wea, Squiresville	43	M	8:114
Holt, E.NC	Doniphan, Iowa Point (Farmer)	44	F	1:458
Holt, G.	Arrapahoe, South Park	29	M	11:135
Holyfield, David NC	Breckenridge, Waterloo (Farmer)	32	M	4:158
Holyfield, Elizabeth NC	" "	36	F	4:158
Holyfield, George W. NC	" "	15	M	4:158
Holyfield, James T. NC	" "	8	M	4:158
Holyfield, Rufus W. NC	" "	13	M	4:158
Holyfield, Samuel W. NC	" "	11	M	4:158
Holzer, Thos.	Arrapahoe, South Park	41	M	11:129
Honeycutt, H.NC	Arrapahoe, Nevada Gulch (Miner)	54	M	11:531
Hood, Isabella NC	Allen, Iola P.O.	34	F	2:270
Hood, Rufus NC	" " " (Farmer)	36	M	2:270
Hood, Samuel NC	" " "	65	M	2:267
Hooker, Eliza	Linn, Mound City (Farmer)	51	F	7:116
Hooker, James	" " " (Farmer)	25	M	7:116
Hookrods, H. P.	Arrapahoe, Valley of the Platte	27	M	11:772
Hookrods, Malissa D.	Atchison, 1st Ward	16	F	1:24
Hookrods, Thomas	" " "	24	M	1:24
Hoover, S.NC	Coffey, California, Burlington	49	F	4:60
Hope, B. F.	Arrapahoe, Quartz Valley (Miner)	20	M	11:494
Hope, Jno.	" " " (Miner)	31	M	11:494
Hopkins, A. H.	Arrapahoe, California Gulch	25	M	11:281
Hopkins, EliSC	Shawnee, Tecumseh (Farmer)	35	M	9:73
Hopkins, W.NC	Arrapahoe, South Park	32	M	11:17
Hoppess, Jas.	Lykins, Paola (Farmer)	27	M	8:41
Horey, Kate	Atchison, Ward 2	23	F	1:34
Horn, Susannah NC	Atchison, Mt. Pleasant	29	F	1:153
Hornens, Jane	Doniphan, Wayne, Geary City (Farmer)	73	F	1:392
Horner, M.	Franklin, Pottawat., Shermanville	32	F	8:246
Hors, Elezabeth	Marshall, Vermillion, Barrett Mills	33	F	3:234
Horsses, P. A.	Don., Wolf River, Walnut Gr.(Farmer)	48	M	1:408
Horton, Emily	Leavenworth, Easton	25	F	10:285
Hosic, D. C.	Coffey, Leroy (Farmer)	31	M	4:32
Hoskins, Benj.	Jefferson, Oskaloosa (Farmer)	58	M	5:122
Hoskins, Frances NC	Linn, Paris	71	F	7:155
Hoskins, James	Jefferson, Oskaloosa (Laborer)	20	M	5:123

Arapahoe: spelled incorrectly with 2 r's in census and in this index also.

Name	Kansas: County; Township; P.O. Arap. Co.: Census Div. Not Township	Age	Sex	Census V.:Pg.
Hoskins, Miner	Jefferson, Oskaloosa (Laborer)	16	M	5:123
Hoskins, Sam NC	Linn, Paris (Farmer)	73	M	7:155
Hottle, Frances	Atchison, Walnut, Sumner	47	F	1:175
Houck, Dewett	Marion, Marion, Cottonwood	4	M	4:362
Houck, Hammon	Mar.,Marion,Cot.F. (HouseCarpenter)	62	M	4:362
Houck, Lucinda	" " " "	39	F	4:362
Houck, Peter	" " " " (Wagon maker)	37	M	4:362
Houck, Philip	" " " "	13	M	4:362
Houck, Victoria	" " " "	10	F	4:362
Houshe, Rebecca B.	Leavenworth, Ward 3	28	F	10:221
Houts, Mary E.	Leavenworth, Easton	26	F	10:303
Hover, Andrew NC	Breckenridge, Waterloo (Farmer)	55	M	4:154
Hover, Andrew NC	" " (Farmer)	55	M	4:154
Hover, David NC	" "	15	M	4:154
Hover, Margaret NC	" "	22	F	4:154
Hover, Nancy NC	" "	57	F	4:154
Hover, Nancy J. NC	" "	13	F	4:154
Hover, Susan NC	" "	16	F	4:154
Howard, D. D. NC	Leavenworth, Alexandria,Easton(Farmer)	35	M	10:446
Howard, Drusilla	" " "	33	F	10:446
Howe, A. B.	Arrapahoe, Denver	33	M	11:322
Howel, A.	Doniphan, Washington, Elwood	15	F	1:322
Howel, Augustus	Chase, Diam. Cr.,Cot. Falls (Farming)	29	M	4:323
Howel, E.	Doniphan, Washington, Elwood	40	F	1:322
Howel, R.	" " (Farmer)	40	M	1:322
Howell, John NC	Bourbon, Xenia P.O. (Farmer)	32	M	2:141
Howerton, Samuel E.	Coffey, Burlington (Farmer)	29	M	4:40
Howsh, Flarissa NC	Linn, Scott, Brooklyn	54	F	7:14
Hoy, C. P.	Johnson, Monticello (Laborer)	24	M	6:81
Hoy, S. P.	" " (Laborer)	23	M	6:81
Hubbard, Abigail E.	Atchison, Shannon, Atchison	10	F	1:74
Hubbard, C. W.	" " " (Farmer)	46	M	1:74
Hubbard, Caroline NC	Allen, Humboldt P.O.	35	F	2:274
Hubbard, Christopher C.	Atchison, Shannon, Atchison	18	M	1:74
Hubbard, Clinton J.	" " " (Farmer)	20	M	1:74
Hubbard, Gusland C.	Atchison, 1st Ward (Surveyor)	59	M	1:15
Hubbard, John F.	Atchison, Shannon, Atchison	12	M	1:74
Hubbard, Mary J.	" " "	14	F	1:74
Hubbard, Millie	Jackson, Franklin, Holton	50	F	5:182
Hubbard, Paul	" " " (Farmer)	30	M	5:182
Hubbard, Rebecca	Atchison, Shannon, Atchison	49	F	1:74
Hubbard, Samuel J. NC	Allen, Humboldt P.O. (Farmer)	36	M	2:274
Huckstep,? E.	Arrapahoe, Leavenworth Gulch (Miner)	55	M	11:554
Hud, A.	Doniphan, Center, Troy (Lawyer)	37	M	1:241
Huddleston, Daniel	Bourbon, Fort Scott P.O. (Farmer)	58	M	2:84
Huddleston, E. NC	Douglas, Clinton (Farmer)	46	M	6:408
Huddleston, Mary NC	" "	52	F	6:408
Hudnal, H. H.	Doniphan, Doniphan (Doctor)	47	M	1:386
Hudnall, Martha	" "	60	F	1:382
Hudnall, W. M.	" " (Farmer)	55	M	1:382
Hudson, B. D. NC	Arrapahoe, South Park (Miner)	34	M	11:55
Hudson, Robert NC	Anderson, Walker, Garnett (Farmer)	42	M	7:240
Hudson, T.	Doniphan, Iowa Point	63	F	1:452
Huff, E. R.	Nemaha, Valley, Seneca (Farmer)	69	F	3:122
Huff, M. NC	Linn, Scott, Brooklyn	50	F	7:15
Huff, P. P.	Osage, Ridgeway, Superior (Farmer)	45	M	8:360
Huffman, Alice NC	Lykins, Miami, New Lancaster	44	F	8:88
Huffman, Elizabeth NC	Lykins, Richland, Gardner	48	F	8:22
Huffman, Yost	Bourbon, Fort Scott P.O. (Farmer)	55	M	2:84
Hughes, F.	Franklin, Centropolis, Minneola	6	M	8:204
Hughes, J.	" " "	9	M	8:204

Arapahoe: spelled incorrectly with 2 r's in census and in this index also.

Name	Kansas: County; Township; P.O. Arap. Co.: Census Div. Not Township	Age	Sex	Census V.:Pg
Hughes, L. A.	Franklin, Centropolis, Minneola	8	F	8:204
Hughes, R.	Douglas, Palmyra, Black Jack	45	F	6:277
Huld, E. S.	Arrapahoe; Tarryall, South Park	36	M	11:611
Hull, S.	Wabaunsee, Zeandale	24	F	5:237
Hull, Sam'l.	Arrapahoe, South Clear Creek	29	M	11:713
Humboldt, S. T.	Arrapahoe, South Park	35	M	11:198
Hummer, James	Lyk.,Marysv.,Lyons (Bapt.Clergyman)	37	M	8:120
Humphrey, David	Breckenridge, Americus	12	M	4:226
Humphrey, Edward	Leavenworth, 1st Ward	35	M	10:141
Humphrey, Elizabeth	Breckenridge, Americus	4	F	4:226
Humphrey, Evlina W.	Breckenridge, Emporia	30	F	4:188
Humphrey, Martha V.	Breckenridge, Americus	10	F	4:226
Humphrey, Wm.	" "	9	M	4:226
Hundle, D.	Douglas, Wakarusa, Lawrence	61	F	6:237
Hunley, Charles	Leavenworth, Kickapoo (Farmer)	35	M	10:333
Hunnian, Amasiah	Atchison, 1st Ward	30	M	1:5
Hunnian, John	" " " (Carpenter)	40	M	1:5
Hunt, Asail[NC]	Lykins, Indianapolis (Farmer)	30	M	8:60
Hunt, C.	Arrapahoe, Valley of the Platte	29	M	11:777
Hunt, E.[NC]	Arrapahoe, Central City (Butcher)	39	M	11:514
Hunt, Elena A.	Leavenworth, 1st Ward	13	F	10:116
Hunt, Felix G.[NC]	Breckenridge, Pike, Plymouth (Farmer)	37	M	4:209
Hunt, Jonathan[NC]	Atch.,Grasshop.,Kennekuk (Landlord)	50	M	1:86
Hunt, P. H.[NC]	Breckenridge, Emporia (Silversmith)	30	M	4:201
Hunt, Rebekah J.[NC]	Breckenridge, Pike, Plymouth	24	F	4:209
Hunt, S. M.[SC]	Johnson, Monticello (Laborer)	50	M	6:80
Hunt, Susan	Breckenridge, Emporia	27	F	4:201
Hunt, William	Lykins, Indianapolis (Laborer)	53	M	8:60
Hunt, William H.[NC]	Bourbon, Fort Scott P.O. (Landlord)	33	M	2:223
Hunter, Charles S.	Leav., Stranger, Leav.City (Farmer)	33	M	10:474
Hunter, Roonclas?	" " " " (Farmer)	24	M	10:474
Hunter, Samuel S.	" " " " (Carpenter)	28	M	10:474
Huntoon, G. O.	Arrapahoe,Valley of the Platte(Miner)	30	M	11:827
Hurd, N.	Linn, Centerville (Farmer)	52	M	7:89
Hurst, Robt.	Breckenridge, Emporia (Merchant)	29	M	4:203
Hurst, Thomas	" " (Clerk)	20	M	4:203
Hutchinson, H. J.	Johnson, Olathe	1	F	6:2
Hutchinson, J.	" " (Farmer)	30	M	6:1
Hutchinson, J. H.	Arrapahoe, South Park	21	M	11:215
Hutchinson, Jno.	Arrapahoe, California Gulch	21	M	11:281
Hutchinson, L. A.	Johnson, Olathe	3	F	6:2
Hutchinson, L. E.	" "	5	F	6:2
Hutchinson, N.	" "	26	F	6:1
Hutchinson, N.?[NC]	Doniphan, Burr Oak, Whitehead	52	F	1:357
Hutton, Sarah	Lykins, Mound, Osawatomie	23	F	8:71
Hylop, W. E.	Arrapahoe, Valley of the Platte	22	M	11:819
Hymer, Edison[1,NC]	Nemaha, Valley, Seneca		M	3:126
Hyolt, Abidney H.[NC]	McGhee, Crawford Sem. P.O. (Farmer)	37	M	9:219
Iddings, J. M.[NC]	Arrapahoe, Denver (Merchant)	30	M	11:355
Iliff, W.	Johnson, Gardner (Blacksmith)	38	M	6:16
Ingalls, I.	Arrapahoe, South Clear Creek	21	M	11:696
Ingels, Cusander	Atchison, Shannon, Atchison	46	F	1:76
Ingels, G. B.	Doniphan, Center, Troy	26	M	1:264
Ingle, John	Douglas, Willow Springs	48	M	6:327
Ingle, John	Doug., Willow Sp.,Brooklyn (Farmer)	57	M	6:319
Ingraham, Sarah	Arrapahoe, Golden City	20	F	11:586
Ingraham, T. J.	Johnson, Shawnee (Farmer)	52	M	6:93
Ingrame, Hannah	Atchison, Ward 2 (Domestic)	50	B F	1:37
Irwin, Isaac	Linn, Paris (Farmer)	33	M	7:141
Irwin, Phoebe A.	Allen, Humboldt P.O.	34	F	2:287

[1] Age was listed as unknown.

Arapahoe: spelled incorrectly with 2 r's in census and in this index also.

Name	Kansas: County; Township; P.O. Arap. Co.: Census Div. Not Township	Age	Sex	Census V . Pg.
Irwin, Riley	Linn, Paris	9	M	7:141
Irwin, Temperance	" "	35	F	7:141
Isaacs, Amos[NC]	Atchison, Mt. Pleasant (Farmer)	38	M	1:164
Isaacs, Jesse[NC]	" " " (Farmer)	62	M	1:164
Isaacs, O.	Arrapahoe, South Park	25	M	11:123
Isaacs, Jesse[NC]	Atchison, Mt. Pleasant (Farmer)	60	M	1:153
Isaacs, Mary[NC]	" " "	55	F	1:153
Isley, Jacob[NC]	McGhee, Brushville P.O. (Farmer)	34	M	9:217
Israel, J. P.[NC]	Arrapahoe, South Clear Creek (Miner)	32?	M	11:592
Ives, S. T.[NC]	Arrapahoe, Denver (Carpenter)	30	M	11:412
Ives, T. I.[NC]	" " (Carpenter)	31	M	11:412
Jack, John	Brown, Irving, Hiawatha (Farmer)	30	M	3:9
Jacks, M.[NC]	Don., Burr Oak, Whitehead (Farmer)	54	F	1:346
Jackson, Allen H.[NC]	Arrapahoe, South Park (Miner)	21	M	11:14
Jackson, C.	Johnson, Aubrey	37	F	6:37
Jackson, C.	Doniphan, Iowa Point	26	F	1:423
Jackson, Cynthia[NC]	Lykins, Osawatomie, Indianapolis	63	F	8:61
Jackson, E.	Johnson, Aubrey	13	M	6:37
Jackson, J.	Arrapahoe, Valley of the Platte	36	M	11:776
Jackson, J. G.?	Johnson, Aubrey (Farmer)	39	M	6:37
Jackson, J. H.	" "	4	M	6:37
Jackson, J. K.[NC]	Arrapahoe, South Park (Miner)	28	M	11:14
Jackson, Jesse[NC]	Lyk.,Sug. Cr., N. Lancaster (Farmer)	49	M	8:98
Jackson, John[SC]	Leavenworth, Ward 2 (Blacksmith)	26	M	10:185
Jackson, L.	Johnson, Aubrey	15	F	6:37
Jackson, M. E.	" "	16	F	6:37
Jackson, M. J.	" "	6	M	6:37
Jackson, N. L.	" "	1	M	6:37
Jackson, R. A.?	" "	10	F	6:37
Jackson, S.	Don., Washington, Elwood (Teamster)	34	M	1:324
Jackson, Thomas[NC]	Lyk.,Osawat.,Indianapolis (Farmer)	67	M	8:61
Jackson, Thomas[NC]	Allen, Humboldt P.O. (Farmer)	55	M	2:299
Jacobs, Ferdnand[SC]	Marshall, Marysville (Master Mason)	23	M	3:252
Jacoby, Margaret A.	Breckenridge, Waterloo	26	F	4:152
Jambor, B.[SC]	Johnson, Shawnee	46	M	6:95
Jambor, G.[SC]	" "	15	M	6:95
Jambor, J.[SC]	" " (Farmer)	21	M	6:95
Jambor, T.[SC]	" " (Farmer)	25	M	6:95
James, George	Doniphan, Doniphan (Laborer)	22	M	1:385
James, Hannah	Linn, Potosi	52	F	7:83
James, James W.	McGhee, Fort Scott P.O. (Farmer)	24	M	9:206
James, Mary	Douglas, Wakarusa, Lawrence	48	F	6:234
James, Paul	" " "	32	M	6:234
James, Phebe[NC]	Linn, Mound City	58	F	7:118
James, S. T.	Arrapahoe, South Park	31	M	11:21
James, Temperance	Linn, Potosi	30	F	7:73
James, Vincent N.	Atch., Center, Pardee (C.M.E. South)	32	M	1:140
Jamison, Allen	Greenwood, Eureka	14	M	9:177
Jamison, Mary	" "	18	F	9:177
Jamison, Sarah	" "	12	F	9:177
Janes, Joseph B.	Atch., Kapioma, Muscotah (Laborer)	43	M	1:100
Jarred, John	Lyk.; Miami; West Pt. Mo. (Farmer)	51	M	8:95
Jarrell, Alfred[NC]	Atchison, Center, Pardee	23	M	1:124
Jarrell, H. P.	Arrapahoe, Valley of the Platte	30	M	11:794
Jarrott, H.[NC]	Doniphan, Wayne, Doniphan (Farmer)	32	M	1:373
Jarvell, Sanford[NC]	Atchison, Center, Pardee (Farmer)	26	M	1:120
Javins, H.	Frank., Centrop., Minneola (Farmer)	42	M	8:202
Javins, J. F.	" " " (Farmer)	39	M	8:202
Javins, W.	" " "	74	F	8:202
Jeffers, John	Jeff., Jeff., Crooked Cr. (Farmer)	55	M	5:38
Jellison, J.	Don., Wolf River, Walnut Gr. (Farmer)	63	M	1:404

Arapahoe: spelled incorrectly with 2 r's in census and in this index also.

Name	Kansas: County; Township; P.O. Arap. Co.: Census Div. Not Township	Age	Sex	Census V. Pg.
Jenkins, E.	Franklin, Ohio, Ohio City	11	M	8:230
Jenkins, E. S.	" " " "	4	M	8:232
Jenkins, G. T.	" " " "	14	M	8:232
Jenkins, J. B.	Arrapahoe, Denver (Painter)	25	M	11:359
Jenkins, J. W.?	Douglas, Lawrence (Lawyer)	24	M	6:217
Jenkins, M. E.	Franklin, Ohio, Ohio City	12	F	8:232
Jenkins, M. J.	" " " "	10	F	8:232
Jenkins, M. J.	" " " "	12	F	8:230
Jenkins, P.	" " " "	5	F	8:230
Jenkins, R. E. [NC]	Doniphan, Burr Oak, Whitehead	29	F	1:344
Jenkins, S. E.	Franklin, Ohio, Ohio City	8	F	8:232
Jennings, J. R. [1]	Franklin, Ottawa, Hickory Creek	11	M	8:266
Jennings, S. E. [1]	" " " "	5	F	8:266
Jenny, G. W.	Arrapahoe, Lake Gulch (Miner)	22	M	11:485
Jerdon, Eliza	Lykins, Marysville, Lyons	33	F	8:122
Jerdon, George W.	" " "	10	M	8:122
Jerdon, Jas. L.	" " " (Farmer)	35	M	8:122
Jerdon, James M.	" " "	8	M	8:122
Jesse, David	Breckenridge, Forest Hill (Farmer)	33	M	4:171
Jesse, S.	Doniphan, Iowa Point (Farmer)	40	M	1:454
Jessee, W.	Douglas, Clinton (Farmer)	51	M	6:406
Jessell, Thos. [NC]	Arrapahoe, Denver (Mechanic)	18	M	11:427
Jessie, David	Douglas, Clinton	18	M	6:406
Jessee, H.	" "	10	F	6:406
Jessie, H.	" "	12	F	6:406
Jessie, M.	" "	16	F	6:406
Jessie, Nancy	" "	50	F	6:406
Jessup, Rosanna [NC]	Bourbon, Raysville P.O. (Housekeeper)	61	F	2:168
Jewett, Jno. R.	Arrapahoe, South Park	31	M	11:245
Johnesee, Ellz M. [NC]	Allen, Xenia P.O. (Farmer)	35	M	2:229
Johns, Lucy [NC]	Linn, Liberty, Centerville	40	F	7:3
Johnson, Ann	Leav., 1st Ward (Washer & ironer)	27	BF	10:98
Johnson, B.	Arrapahoe, California Gulch (Miner)	31	M	11:296
Johnson, Benedict	Atchison, Walnut, Sumner (Farmer)	45	M	1:187
Johnson, Clarinda	Shawnee, Auburn	24	F	9:37
Johnson, Emily	Leavenworth, Kickapoo	53	F	10:340
Johnson, F. [NC]	Davis, Ft. Riley Reserve (Servant)	21	BF	9:358
Johnson, J.	Riley, Manhattan P.O. (Farmer)	50	M	9:310
Johnson, J.	Arrapahoe, South Park	29	M	11:184
Johnson, J. J. [2]	Franklin, Peoria, Stanton	5	M	8:285
Johnson, James [NC]	Woodson, Neosho Falls (Farmer)	39	M	9:132
Johnson, Jas. B.	Arrapahoe, Nevada Gulch (Quartz Mill)	25	M	11:521
Johnson, James M.	Leavenworth, Ward 2 (Saloon)	33	M	10:162
Johnson, John [2]	Leavenworth, 1st Ward (Cook)	37		10:98
Johnson, John G.	Atch., Shannon, Atchison (Farmer)	26	M	1:79
Johnson, Joseph	Lykins, Osage, Osawatomie (Farmer)	51	M	8:84
Johnson, K.	Franklin, Centropolis, Minneola	9	M	8:215
Johnson, Louisa	Lykins, Osawatomie	35	F	8:56
Johnson, M. T. [2]	Franklin, Peoria, Stanton	3	F	8:285
Johnson, Mary	Lykins, Osage, Osawatomie (Farmer)	49	F	8:80
Johnson, Mary	Bourbon, Rockford P.O. (Housewife)	38	F	2:97
Johnson, Mary Ann	Atchison, Shannon, Atchison	27	F	1:79
Johnson, S. D.	Arrapahoe, South Clear Creek	27	M	11:647
Johnson, Thomas [NC]	Breckenridge, Emporia	22	M	4:190
Johnson, Varilla H.	Atchison, Shannon, Atchison	2	F	1:79
Johnson, William [NC]	Leav., Stranger, Leav.City(Farmhand)	28	M	10:474
Johnson, William	Bourbon, Fort Scott P.O.	43	M	2:226

[1]State of birth difficult to decipher; could be Ia. or Va.
[2]State of birth given as Va.? by W.P.A. indexer.
Arapahoe: spelled incorrectly with 2 r's in census and in this index also.

Name	Kansas: County; Township; P.O. Arap. Co.: Census Div. Not Township	Age	Sex	Census V. Pg.
Johnston, Asa [NC]	Arrapahoe, South Park (Ranch)	67	M	11:9
Johnston, W. A. [NC]	Anderson, Town of Garnett (Lawyer)	29	M	7:224
Jolly, Alias [NC]	Lykins, Osage, Osawatomie (Farmer)	49	M	8:83
Jones, A. [SC]	Douglas, Lecompton (Farmer)	41	M	6:372
Jones, A. S.	Woodson, Pleasant Grove (Farmer)	31	M	9:168
Jones, Albert	Arrapahoe, South Park (Miller)	42	M	11:16
Jones, Albert [NC]	Lykins, Mound, Osawatomie (Farmer)	32	M	8:70
Jones, Alex	Arrapahoe, Golden City (Miner	27	M	11:456
Jones, Allen	Wyandodtte, Wyandotte (Laborer)	40	M	10:41
Jones, Alphens [NC]	Douglas, Clinton	17	M	6:417
Jones, Amanda	" "	15	F	6:417
Jones, Clayton	Douglas, Willow Springs	8	M	6:318
Jones, Edward	Bourbon, Marmaton P.O. (Merchant)	38	M	2:205
Jones, Emily H.	Douglas, Willow Springs	30	F	6:317
Jones, J.	Doniphan, Iowa Point (Farmer)	50	M	1:421
Jones, J.	Linn, Centerville, Keokuk (Farmer)	42	M	7:85
Jones, J. B.	Johnson, McCamish, Hibbard (Farmer)	46	M	6:69
Jones, James	Woodson, Pleasant Grove (Farmer)	24	M	9:169
Jones, Jas.	Arrapahoe, Golden City (Miner)	26	M	11:456
Jones, James	Douglas, Clinton	12	M	6:417
Jones, James	Jeff., Kaw, Kaw City (Atty.-at-law)	32	M	5:85
Jones, John [NC]	Hunter, Eldorado, Chelsea (Farmer)	36	M	4:358
Jones, Lavina	Linn, Mound City	18	F	7:114
Jones, Lewis [NC]	Lykins, Mound, Osawatomie (Farmer)	27	M	8:70
Jones, Lucy	Douglas, Willow Springs	28	F	6:318
Jones, M. T. (or M.J.?)	Douglas, Clinton	9	F	6:417
Jones, Malinda	Atchison, Center, Pardee	35	F	1:121
Jones, Martha [NC]	Shawnee, Tecumseh	34	F	9:78
Jones, Martha	Douglas, Clinton	9	F	6:417
Jones, Martha R.	Leavenworth, Alexandria, Easton	37	F	10:449
Jones, Mary	Woodson, Pleasant Grove	76	F	9:169
Jones, Mary [NC]	Wyandotte, Quindaro	61	F	10:59
Jones, Mary	Douglas, Clinton	44	F	6:417
Jones, Mary [NC]	Lykins, Mound, Osawatomie	13	F	8:70
Jones, Mary [NC]	" " "	23	F	8:70
Jones, Matitia [NC]	" " "	11	F	8:70
Jones, Millicent [NC]	" " "	49	F	8:70
Jones, Milton [NC]	" " "	8	M	8:70
Jones, N.	Arrapahoe, South Park	25	M	11:170
Jones, P.	Doniphan, Iowa Point	40	M	1:421
Jones, Robert [NC]	Lykins, Mound, Osawatomie	4	M	8:70
Jones, Saml. T.	Arrapahoe, Denver (Miner)	26	M	11:409
Jones, Simon [NC]	Lykins, Mound, Osawatomie (Farmer)	49	M	8:70
Jones, Thos.	Arrapahoe, Denver (Miner)	28	M	11:419
Jones, Thos. M.	Douglas, Clinton	7	M	6:417
Jones, Thomas N. [NC]	Lykins, Mound, Osawatomie	19	M	8:70
Jones, Vincint [NC]	Jeff., Kentucky, Oskaloosa (Farmer)	66	M	5:72
Jones, Virginia	Douglas, Clinton	11	F	6:417
Jones, W. B.	Douglas, Willow Springs (Farmer)	29	M	6:318
Jones, Wesley	Bourbon, Barnesville P.O. (Farmer)	37	M	2:171
Jones, Wm.	Arrapahoe, South Park	46	M	11:126
Jones, Wm.	Douglas, Palmyra, Lawrence (Farmer)	25	M	6:268
Jones, William	Woodson, Pleasant Grove	10	M	9:169
Jones, William [NC]	Lykins, Mound, Osawatomie	5	M	8:70
Jones, William J.	Lyk.;Mid.Cr.; Jonesville,Mo.(Farmer)	48	M	8:106
Jones, Wm. K. [NC]	Breckenridge, Forest Hill (Farmer)	59	M	4:184
Jordan, Robert [NC]	Allen, Humboldt P.O. (Shoemaker)	31	M	2:299
Jorden, Clarisa A.	Lykins, Marysville, Paola	5	F	8:126

[1]State of birth given as Va.? by W.P.A. indexer.
Arapahoe: spelled incorrectly with 2 r's in census and in this index also.

Name	Kansas: County; Township; P.O. / Arap. Co.: Census Div. Not Township	Age	Sex	Census V.: Pg.
Jorden, Jeremiah	Lykins, Marysville, Lyons	14	M	8:126
Jorden, Morris D.	" " "	18	M	8:126
Jorden, Nancy A.	" " "	7	F	8:126
Jorden, Wm. M.	" " " (Farmer)	60	M	8:126
Jordon, Charles	Shawnee, Tecumseh (Meth. Clergyman)	69	M	9:71
Jordon, S. R.	Leavenworth, 1st Ward (Barber)	29	BM	10:137
Jount, Rhoda	Shawnee, Topeka	29	F	9:28
Joy, E.[1]	Arrapahoe, Valley of the Platte	21	M	11:821
Jsenhart?, Emmanuel	Jackson, Jefferson, Holton (Farmer)	27	M	5:194
Judkins, Rebecca[NC]	Arrap., Golden City (Boarding House)	38	M	11:582
Julian, Elizabeth[NC]	Bourbon, Dayton P.O. (Housewife)	44	F	2:149
Julian, Joseph[NC]	" " "	10	M	2:149
Julian, Joseph P.[NC]	" " " (Farmer)	40	M	2:149
Julian, Lewis M.[NC]	" " "	20	M	2:149
Julian, Lobias B.[NC]	" " "	8	M	2:149
Julian, Martha[NC]	" " "	18	F	2:149
Julian, Mary E.[NC]	" " "	5	F	2:149
Julian, Milton P.[NC]	" " "	12	M	2:149
Julian, Sally[NC]	" " "	15	F	2:149
Julien, L.[NC]	Linn, Mound City (Farmer)	27	M	7:120
Julien, Robert[NC]	" " " (Farmer)	71	M	7:120
Julien, Robert B.[NC]	Bourbon, Xenia P.O. (Farm Laborer)	21	M	2:129
Jump, Ed.	Arrapahoe, Denver	28	M	11:322
Jump, J. F.[NC]	Arrapahoe, South Clear Creek (Miner)	25	M	11:767
Junkins, James W.[SC]	And., Jackson, Garnett (Carpenter)	33	M	7:205
Jurd, Edward B.[NC]	Lykins, Stanton (Merchant)	37	M	8:11
Justice, Jane	Douglas, Kanwaca, Lawrence	30	F	6:384
Justice, M. R.	Linn, Paris, Potosi-Paris (Domestic)	19	F	7:138
Justice, Martha	Douglas, Kanwaca, Lawrence	10	F	6:384
Isenhart, Emmanuel	Jackson, Jefferson, Holton (Farmer)	27	M	5:195
Kane, M. T.	Doniphan, Marion, Palermo	53	F	1:290
Kany, R.	Don., Washington, Wathena (Engineer)	22	M	1:340
Kaw, T. C.	Arrapahoe, Denver (Miner)	43	M	11:419
Kay, Francis[NC]	Arrapahoe, South Clear Creek (Miner)	21	M	11:635
Kayo, John	Leavenworth, Ward 2	7	M	10:188
Kays, Alfred[NC]	Breck., Pike, Plymouth (Farmer)	29	M	4:209
Keasling, Joseph	Bourbon, Xenia P.O. (Farmer)	56	M	2:127
Keasling, Mary	" " " (Housewife)	53	F	2:127
Keath, Louisa[NC]	Allen, Humboldt P.O.	20	F	2:283
Keeler, Catherine	Linn, Mound City	32	F	7:110
Keeler, Henrietta	" " "	10	F	7:110
Keeler, Mary	" " "	11	F	7:110
Keeler, N.	Arrapahoe, South Park	25	M	11:134
Keeler, William	Linn, Mound City (Farmer)	35	M	7:110
Keeney, Thos.	Lykins, Marysville, Lyons (Farmer)	28	M	8:12
Keesecker, S.	Woodson, Neosho Falls (Farmer)	63	M	9:141
Kefoever, Caroline	Marshall, Marysville	14	F	3:243
Kefoever, William	" " (Farmer)	35	M	3:243
Kehler, Jno. H.	Arrapahoe, Mountain City (Sheriff)	31	M	11:469
Kehler, W. W.	" " "	16	M	11:469
Keith, Martha	Lykins, Osawatomie	14	F	8:57
Keith, Permelia	" "	11	F	8:57
Keith, William	" " (Farmer)	38	M	8:57
Keller, Cornelius	Douglas, Wakarusa, Lawrence	14	M	6:258
Keller, George	" " " (Farmer)	42	M	6:258
Keller, H. B.	" " "	16	M	6:258
Keller, H. H.	Arrapahoe, Denver (Merchant)	27	M	11:349

[1]Initial not clear; could be E, Ei, I, or J.
 Arapahoe: spelled incorrectly with 2 r's in census and in this index also.

Name	Kansas: County; Township; P.O. Arap. Co.: Census Div. Not Township	Age	Sex	Census V.:Pg.
Keller, Mary C.	Leav., Stranger, Leavenworth City	40	F	10:473
Keller, Rebecca	Douglas, Wakarusa, Lawrence	46	F	6:258
Keller, Wm. D.	" " "	13	M	6:258
Kelley, D.	Arrapahoe, Denver	25	M	11:383
Kelling, C.	Arrapahoe, South Park	28	M	11:116
Kellogg, C. S.	" " " (Miner)	37	M	11:11
Kellogg, W. P.[NC]	" " " (Miner)	35	M	11:34
Kelly, Culbert H.[NC]	Allen, Humboldt P.O. (Farmer)	43	M	2:278
Kelly, Elinor	Leavenworth, Ward 3	56	F	10:216
Kelly, Francis[NC]	Linn, Valley, Blooming Gr. (Farmer)	31	M	7:44
Kelly, H. S.	Arrapahoe; Tarryall, South Park(Miner)	22	M	11:610
Kelly, J. A.	Douglas, Kanwaca, Lawrence (Farmer)	33	M	6:374
Kelly, Jane	Leav., Delaware, Del. City (Farmer)	42	F	10:422
Kelly, Thomas T.[NC]	Leavenworth, Easton (Farmer)	45	M	10:293
Kelsey, J. M.[SC]	Frank.; Potta.;Scipio (Carpenter)	32	M	8:237
Kelsey, M.[SC]	" " "	59	F	8:237
Kelsey, M. A.	" " "	3	F	8:237
Kelsey, T.[SC]	" " " (Farmer)	26	M	8:237
Kelsey, T.[SC]	" " " (Farmer)	60	M	8:237
Kelso, William[SC]	Brown, Claytonv., Robinson (Farmer)	35	M	3:49
Kemp, Elizabeth	Douglas, Marion, Lawrence	9	F	6:398
Kemp, T. D.?[1]	" " " (Farmer)	39	M	6:398
Kemp, William	Wyandotte, Wyandotte	19	M	10:15
Kemper, Lucy Ann	Brown, Claytonville, Robinson	40	F	3:49
Kemper, V. N.	" " "	9	F	3:49
Kempston, R.	Arrapahoe, South Park	32	M	11:214
Kemyer, H.	Douglas, Wakarusa, Lawrence	28	F	6:257
Kenary, Ann	Wyandotte, Quindaro	8	F	10:59
Kenary, John	" "	9	M	10:59
Kendall, James P.	Douglas, Willow Springs (Farmer)	65	M	6:313
Kendall, Phebe	" " "	57	F	6:313
Kendall, Wm.	" " " (Farmer)	44	M	6:328
Kennedy, Edward[NC]	Jeff., Kaw City (Physician)	28	M	5:90
Kennesaw, J.	Arrapahoe, Leavenworth Gulch (Miner)	38	M	11:556
Kents, Mary A.	Atchison, Ward 3	32	F	1:47
Keply, Ephriam[NC]	Bourbon, Dayton P.O. (Farmer)	34	M	2:149
Kerkman, Elizabeth	Wood., Neosho Falls	28	F	9:134
Kerkman, Elisha[NC]	" " " (Farmer)	25	M	9:134
Kertz, Alexander	Marshall, Marysville (Day Laborer)	20	M	3:252
Kessinger, Sarah	Douglas, Willow Springs	35	F	6:318
Ketner, Caroline	Leavenworth, 1st Ward	45	F	10:135
Keyer, E.	Arrapahoe, South Park	35	M	11:173
Keys, Joseph[NC]	Breck., Pike, Plymouth (Farmer)	56	M	4:210
Keys, Lucinda[NC]	" " "	52	F	4:210
Killiam, H.[SC]	Arrapahoe, Leavenworth Gulch (Miner)	26	M	11:555
Killick, Thomas[SC]	Leav., Kickapoo (General Agent)	27	M	10:327
Kimball, M.	Johnson, DeSota, Lexington	25	F	6:19
Kimberlan, Wm.	Arrapahoe, Mountain City (Lawyer)	29	M	11:472
King, Abraham	Atchison, Walnut, Sumner (Farmer)	53	M	1:172
King, Ann E.	" " "	25	F	1:172
King, J. H.[NC]	Arrapahoe, Golden City (Trader)	42	M	11:583
King, Louisa[NC]	Coffey, Burlington	22	F	4:43
King, Mahala	Atchison, Walnut, Sumner	43	F	1:172
Kingor, Nancy[NC]	Hunter, Eldorado, Chelsea	10	F	4:360
Kingor, Oda[NC]	" " "	9	M	4:360
Kingor, Rebecca[NC]	" " "	38	F	4:360
Kingston, Catharine	Allen, Humboldt P.O.	23	F	2:298
Kinison, Alonzo	Linn, Potosi (Farmer)	18	M	7:78
Kinison, Clara	" "	4	F	7:78

[1]W.P.A. indexer gave state of birth as Va.?

Arapahoe: spelled incorrectly with 2 r's in census and in this index also.

Name	Kansas: County; Township; P.O. Arap. Co.: Census Div. Not Township	Age	Sex	Census V.: Pg.
Kinison, Cordelia	Linn, Potosi (Teacher)	21	M	7:78
Kinison, Emily	" "	12	F	7:78
Kinison, George	" "	8	M	7:78
Kinison, Hannah	" "	47	F	7:78
Kinison, Isaac	" " (Farmer)	45	M	7:78
Kinison, Wallace	" " (Farmer)	15	M	7:78
Kinison, William	" " (Farmer)	16	M	7:78
Kinkaid, Elizabeth	Lykins, Stanton (Domestic)	20	F	8:11
Kinley, R. NC	Arrapahoe, South Park (Miner)	22	M	11:78
Kinly, H.[1]	Atchison, Mt. Pleasant (Gold Seeker)	40	M	1:151
Kinney, J. A.	Coffey, Leroy, Burlington (Farmer)	30	M	4:26
Kinsey, S.	John.; Oxford; New Santa Fe, Mo.	40	F	6:106
Kinsly, P.	Johnson, McCamish, Hibbard	35	F	6:67
Kirby, Kirny NC	Bourbon, Turkey Creek P.O. (Farmer)	45	M	2:107
Kirby, Pleasant	Jeff., Kentucky, Oscaloosa (Farmer)	57	M	5:78
Kirch, William	Marshall, Marysville (Farmer)	24	M	3:243
Kirk, J. N.SC	Arrapahoe, Leavenworth Gulch (Miner)	23	M	11:555
Kirk, Joseph	Brown, Walnut Creek, Hamlin (Farmer)	30	M	3:22
Kirk, Lewis	" " " "	67	M	3:22
Kirk, Margaret	" " " "	60	F	3:22
Kirk, Martha[2],SC	Bourbon, Barnesville P.O. (Farmer)	75	M	2:174
Kirk, Winny NC	" " " (Housewife)	38	F	2:174
Kirkham, C.	Frank., Centrop., Minneola (Farmer)	16	M	8:214
Kirkham, E.	" " " (Farmer)	20	M	8:214
Kirkham, E. V.	" " "	7	F	8:214
Kirkham, F. M.	" " "	4	M	8:214
Kirkham, M.	" " " (Farmer)	18	F	8:214
Kirkham, M. A.	" " "	10	M	8:214
Kirkham, S. W.	" " "	14	M	8:214
Kirkham, T. T.	" " "	12	M	8:214
Kisbarbey, Joel	McGhee, Brushville P.O. (Farmer)	24	M	9:218
Kishler, Crimora	Arrapahoe, Denver	23	F	11:318
Kisling, Jacob	Breck., Forest Hill (Carpenter)	46	M	4:180
Kitchen, Catharine	Leavenworth, Delaware	53	F	10:422
Kitchen, George W.	Leavenworth, Easton	26	M	10:283
Kitchen, Henry	Leav., Delaware, Del. City (Farmer)	60	M	10:422
Kleinhaus, Mary	Jefferson, Kaw, Kaw City	17	F	5:82
Klinstock, S. C.NC	Arrapahoe, South Park (Miner)	23	M	11:63
Knight, C.	Arrapahoe, South Clear Creek	32	M	11:708
Knight, Mary	Marshall, Marysville	35	F	3:246
Knison, Mary	Atchison, Ward 3	5	F	1:55
Knof, M.	Franklin, Centropolis, Minneola	47	F	8:202
Knopf, Wm.	Johnson, Olathe (Farmer)	29	M	6:118
Knott, Ira J.	Allen, Humboldt P.O.	20	F	2:290
Knott, Isaac	" " " (Farmer)	40	M	2:290
Knott, Mary E.	" " "	18	F	2:290
Knott, Sarah	" " "	16	F	2:290
Knowton, J.	Arrapahoe, Denver (Miner)	31	M	11:404
Knox, C.	Potta., Vienna, Louisville (Farmer)	50	M	5:253
Knox, M.	" " "	48	F	5:253
Knox, R.	" " " (Farmer)	22	M	5:253
Knox, W.	" " " (Farmer)	24	M	5:253
Kohn, H. L.	Arrapahoe, South Park	24	M	11:113
Koome, Johnathan	" " "	27	M	11:192
Korman, C.NC	" " "	36	M	11:8
Kreglom, A.	" " "	35	M	11:138
Krelsneger, Geo.	Douglas, Palmyra, Black Jack	43	M	6:276
Krtsinger, Martha E.	" " " "	20	F	6:289

[1]See A. C. Harrison, gold sacker, in this same section and James B. Low,
   gold seeker, in Part I, both living in Atchison County also.
[2]Looks like Charlter (instead of Martha) which could be a man's name.
 Arapahoe: spelled incorrectly with 2 r's in census and in this index also.

Name	Kansas: County; Township; P.O. Arap. Co.: Census Div. Not Township	Age	Sex	Census V. : Pg.
Krtsinger, S.	Douglas, Palmyra, Black Jack (Farmer)	44	M	6:289
Kuhn, Lewis W. NC	Madison, Elmendaro	30	M	4:238
Kury, Jno.	Arrapahoe, Valley of the Platte	30	M	11:858
Kusner, E.	Doniphan, Center, Troy	1	F	1:274
Kusner, Ezra	" " "	9	M	1:274
Kusner, J.	" " " (Laborer)	30	M	1:274
Kusner, May	" " "	22	F	1:274
Kusner, Silas	" " "	13	M	1:274
Kusner, Thomas	" " "	7	M	1:274
Kuth, Christian	Allen, Geneva P.O.	38	F	2:243
Kyle, James C.	Leavenworth, Ward 2 (Engineer)	30	M	10:162
Kyton, A.	Don., Iowa Point (Mail Contractor)	34	M	1:450
Kyton, J. G.	Don., Washington, Whitehead (Farmer)	48	M	1:298
Kyton, S.	" " "	40	F	1:298
Kyton, S. N.	" " "	19	M	1:298
Kyton, W.	" " "	17	M	1:298
Lacy, Betsey	Douglas, Kanwaca, Lawrence	68	F	6:381
Lacy, Elizabeth SC	" " "	35	F	6:379
Lacy, Jas. NC	Arrapahoe, Denver (Miner)	22	M	11:349
LaFountain, E. S.	" " (Bar-Keeper)	15	M	11:357
LaFountaine, M.	Arrapahoe, South Clear Creek (Miner)	45	M	11:628
LaFountaine, S. B.	" " " " (Miner)	36	M	11:628
Laha, Nancy	Douglas, Kanwaca, Lawrence	25	F	6:385
Laird, Ann	Lykins, Stanton	87	F	8:8
Laird, Joseph NC	" "	58	M	8:8
Laird, Saml. NC	" "	47	M	8:7
Lairzon, J. T. NC	Arrapahoe, California Gulch	28	M	11:297
Laison, W. H. NC	" " "	30	M	11:298
Lake, Catherine	Allen, Iola P.O.	65	F	2:250
Lamb, Hannah NC	Linn, Potosi	21	F	7:72
Lamb, Wm. NC	Dickinson, Kansas Falls P.O.(Farmer)	53	M	4:305
Lambdin, Amelia	Butler, Chelsea	11	F	4:342
Lambdin, George	" "	17	M	4:342
Lambdin, James	" "	21	M	4:342
Lambdin, John	" " (Machinist)	25	M	4:342
Lambdin, Milton	" " (Farmer)	27	M	4:341
Lambert, H. A.	Johnson, Lexington	41	M	6:78
Lamont, A.	Arrapahoe, Denver	23	M	11:319
Lamp, Harry	Cof., Leroy, Burlington (Engineer)	30	M	4:21
Lancaster, B.	Doug., Wakarusa, Lawrence (Laborer)	45	M	6:237
Lancaster, B. F. NC	Leavenworth, Ward 2 (Laborer)	24	M	10:178
Lancaster, S. S.	Arrapahoe, Denver (Cook)	28	B M	11:359
Landen, S. P.	Arrapahoe, South Park (Miner)	36	M	11:62
Landers, W.	Leavenworth, Delaware	45	M	10:312
Landis, Mary	Leavenworth, Ward 3	35	F	10:206
Landis, W. C.	Arrapahoe, Valley of the Platte	29	M	11:840
Landrume, Priscilla	Atchison, Lancaster	50	F	1:118
Lane, George W. M.	Leavenworth, Ward 4 (Lawyer)	30	M	10:268
Lane, J. NC	Marshall, Vermillion, Barrett Mills	44	F	3:216
Lane, M.	Coffey, California, Burlington	40?-70?	F	4:61
Lane, Susan	Arrapahoe, Mountain City	52	F	11:458
Lang, Mary	Breckenridge, Emporia	49	F	4:188
Langdon, Artemetia	Marshall, Vermillion, Barrett Mills	63	F	3:214
Langdon, Joseph	" " " (Farmer)	60	M	3:214
Langley, John	Breckenridge, Waterloo (Farmer)	38	M	4:154
Langley, Lidda NC	Leavenworth, Easton	26	F	10:288
Langley, Milton H. NC	" " (Farmer)	37	M	10:288
Lanham, Abraham	Leavenworth, 1st Ward (Sawyer)	30	M	10:92
Laningham, A. W.	Doniphan, Wolf River, Walnut Grove	7	M	1:398

See p. 160: omissions, Sarah Lock, W. Pitter, I. Prest, Jno & M. Rush.
Arapahoe: spelled incorrectly with 2 r's in census and in this index also.

Name	Kansas: County; Township; P.O. Arap. Co.: Census Div. Not Township	Sex	Census V.: Pg.
Laningham, Charity	Doniphan, Wolf River, Walnut Grove 9	M	1:398
Laningham, J.	" " " " (Domestic)34	F	1:398
Lannum, L. P.	Arrapahoe, South Park 26	M	11:234
Lanters, John	Anderson, Walker, Garnett (Farmer) 58	M	7:241
Larusa, Sarah NC	Douglas, Lawrence 59	F	6:214
Large, David	Jack., Doug., Grassh.Falls (Farmer) 49	M	5:168
Large, Jane	Leavenworth, Alexandria, Easton 51	F	10:443
Large, John	" " " (Farmer) 55	M	10:443
Large, Mary	Jackson, Douglas, Grasshopper Falls 48	F	5:168
Lasater, W.	Arrapahoe, South Park 28	M	11:185
Lasey, T. A. SC	Atchison, Mt. Pleasant (M. D.) 23	M	1:150
Laster, Alex P. NC	" " " 75	M	1:166
Laster, J. NC	Arrapahoe, Valley of the Platte(Miner) ?		11:778
Laster, Morris NC	Atchison, Mt. Pleasant (Farmer) 50	M	1:166
Lathan, J. SC	Frank.;Potta.;Scipio,And.Co.(Farmer) 36	M	8:238
Lathan, M. SC	" " " " " 60	F	8:238
Lathan, M. SC	" " " " " (Farmer) 25	M	8:237
Lathan, M. SC	" " " " " 28	F	8:237
Lathan, M. K. SC	" " " " " 40	F	8:238
Laughlin, H. M.	Doug., Wakarusa, Lawrence (Farmer) 21	M	6:232
Laurance, Eli NC	Allen, Iola P.O. (Farmer) 48	M	2:265
Law, M.	Osage, Ridgeway, Burlingame 31	M	8:362
Lawes (Lowe?), B.?	Don., Wash., Wathena (Shoemaker) 31	M	1:340
Lawman, Jas.	Arrapahoe, South Park 44	M	11:137
Lawrence, Francis	Linn, Centerville, Oakwood 59	F	7:95
Lawrence, Jacob NC	Arrapahoe, Denver (Miner) 50	M	11:414
Lawrence, Sylva NC	Linn, Mound City 58	F	7:108
Lawry, Melvin	Jeff., Jeff., Hickory Pt. (Farmer) 35	M	5:45
Laws, J. T. NC	Arrapahoe, Lake Gulch (Miner) 30	M	11:522
Lawson, James SC	Douglas, Willow Springs, Willow Spr. 35	M	6:327
Lawson, James NC	Doug., Willow Sp., Brooklyn (Farmer) 58	M	6:319
Lawson, Jane NC	Douglas, Willow Springs, Willow Spr. 32	F	6:327
Lawson, Jane NC	Douglas, Willow Springs, Brooklyn 52	F	6:319
Layton, America	Jefferson, Jefferson, Crooked Creek 20	F	5:31
Layton, George N.	Leavenworth, 1st Ward 40	BM	10:137
Leadham, C.	Arrapahoe, Enterprise Dist. (Miner) 21	M	11:492
Lears, E. O.	Arrapahoe, South Park 33	M	11:171
Lease, T.	Doniphan, White Cloud (Laborer) 34	M	1:440
Leaverton, Noah NC	Jefferson, Oskaloosa (Farmer) 64	M	5:125
Lee, Anna Marie	Leavenworth, 1st Ward 24	BF	10:110
Lee, Bridget	McGee, Brushville P.O. 14	F	9:222
Lee, Emily	Leavenworth, 1st Ward 28	BF	10:110
Lee, Jerry	" " 26	BM	10:110
Lee, Nancy	McGee, Brushville P.O. 5	F	9:222
Lee, Priscilla	Leavenworth, 1st Ward (Washer) 44	BF	10:110
Lee, Wm. S.	Arrapahoe, California Gulch 50	M	11:294
Leech, W. P.	Woodson, Pleasant Grove (Teacher) 21	M	9:169
Leffingwell, H.	Arrapahoe, South Park 27	M	11:80
Leggert, S. J.	" " " 31	M	11:156
Lehmkuhl, May	Jefferson, Ozawkie 25	F	5:106
Lenon, W.	Don., Washington, Elwood (Clerk) 20	M	1:313
Leonard, Joseph M.	Breckenridge, Pike, Plymouth 21	M	4:210
Leonard, K.	Arrapahoe, South Park 29	M	11:134
Lesh, Elizabeth	Jefferson, Kentucky, Oskaloosa 31	F	5:63
Lester, C.	Arrapahoe, South Park 22	M	11:228
Leterman, Jonas	Bourbon, Dayton P.O. (Farmer) 45	M	2:149
Leterman, Mary	" " " (Housewife) 39	F	2:149
Levy, T.	Arrapahoe, Mountain City (Miner) 26	M	11:463
Lewellen, Emeline	Bourbon, Turkey Creek P.O.(Housewife) 26	F	2:110
Lewellen, Hannah	Butler, Chelsea 8	F	4:343
Lewellen, Samuel	Bourbon, Turkey Creek P.O. (Farmer) 27	M	2:110

Arapahoe: spelled incorrectly with 2 r's in census and in this index also.

Name	Kansas: County; Township; P.O. Arap. Co.: Census Div. Not Township	Age	Sex	Census V.:Pg.
Lewellen, Susanna	Butler, Chelsea	27	F	4:343
Lewin, C.	Doniphan, Iowa Point (Banker)	23	M	1:446
Lewis, Absalom SC	Shawnee, Tecumseh (Merchant)	31	M	9:65
Lewis, Catherine NC	Allen, Iola P.O.	57	F	2:266
Lewis, Columbus NC	" " " (Farm laborer)	16	M	2:266
Lewis, Eliza NC	" " "	24	F	2:266
Lewis, George NC	" " " (Farm laborer)	15	M	2:266
Lewis, Henry	Arrapahoe, South Clear Cr.(Carpenter)	26	M	11:641
Lewis, Irvin G. NC	Allen, Iola P.O. (Farmer)	28	M	2:266
Lewis, J. NC	Doniphan, Iowa Point (Farmer)	68	M	1:431
Lewis, John NC	Jefferson, Oskaloosa (Farmer)	24	M	5:131
Lewis, L. 1	Franklin, Ohio, Sac & Fox Agency	22	M	8:221
Lewis, Margaret J. NC	Allen, Iola P.O.	2	F	2:266
Lewis, Martha E. NC	" " "	1	F	2:266
Lewis, Mary NC	" " "	24	F	2:266
Lewis, Nancy	Doniphan, Center, Troy	46	F	1:265
Lewis, Sarah	Atchison, Ward 3	30	F	1:54
Lewis, W. D.	Arrapahoe, South Park	34	M	11:160
Lichtities, Louisa	Doniphan, Center, Troy	44	F	1:273
Lichtities, William	" " " (Farmer)	46	M	1:273
Lickner, W. P.	Arrapahoe, South Clear Creek	38	M	11:716
Lidington, Wm.	Doniphan, Doniphan (Farmer)	31	M	1:388
Life, John	Mars., Guittard, Marys. (Farmer)	33	M	3:235
Liggett, J. D. SC	Leav., Ward 3 (Cong. Minister)	38	M	10:226
Lightfoot, G.	Doniphan, Center, Troy (Farmer)	72	M	1:253
Lightfoot, Goodrich	" " " (Farmer)	22	M	1:253
Lilly, A.	Johnson, Olathe (Farmer)	34	M	6:121
Lilly, C. A.	" "	9	F	6:121
Lilly, D. H.	" "	11	M	6:121
Lilly, E. C.	" "	7	F	6:121
Lilly, J. A.	" "	12	M	6:121
Lilly, J. H.	" "	5	M	6:121
Lilly, N.	" "	32	F	6:121
Lilly, P. E.	" "	4	F	6:121
Lilton, J. H.	Arrapahoe, South Park	37	M	11:203
Limeberry, Abram NC	Chase, Falls, Cotton.Falls (Farmer)	44	M	4:330
Limeberry, Deviet NC	" " " "	6	M	4:330
Limeberry, Jemima NC	" " " "	43	F	4:330
Limeberry, Rachel NC	" " " "	14	F	4:330
Limeberry, Velma NC	" " " "	4	F	4:330
Limerick, James	Potta., Rockingham, Elden (Farmer)	44	M	5:289
Linch, John T.? I.	Douglas, Palmyra, McKinney	32	M	6:305
Linch, L.	" " "	23	F	6:305
Lincoln, N.	Arrapahoe, South Park	29	M	11:172
Linden, E. NC	" " "	36	M	11:123
Lindenmuller, G.	" " "	37	M	11:221
Lindley, Jno.	" " "	23	M	11:117
Lindley, L. A.	" " "	27	M	11:129
Lindsay, Edward NC	McGee, Osage Mission P.O. (Farmer)	45	M	9:242
Lindsay, I. C. NC	Davis, Junct.City, Kansas F.(Farmer)	30	M	9:339
Lindsay, Nancy NC	McGee, Osage Mission P.O.	45	F	9:242
Lindsay, T.	Johnson, Spring Hill (Farmer)	56	M	6:43
Lindsley, L. A.	Doniphan, Marion, Palermo		F	1:277
Linebaugh, Eliza	And.,Town Greeley,Garnett(Shoemaker)	40	F	7:242
Linkenanger, C. A.	Osage, Ridgeway, Superior (Farmer)	30	M	8:344
Linsley, Elmer	Atchison, Ward 2 (Boss Mason)	47	M	1:31
Liptrap, Leander	" 1st Ward (Farmer)	16	M	1:20
Lisher, H.	Nemaha, Richmond, Seneca (Farmer)	24	M	3:105
Litchfield, A. Y.	Arrapahoe, Central City	23	M	11:580

1 Born in Va.? Omitted: Sarah Lock; Bourbon, Mapleton P.O.; 15 F, 2:148.
Arapahoe: spelled incorrectly with 2 r's in census and in this index also.

Name	Kansas: County; Township; P.O. Arap. Co.: Census Div. Not Township	Age	Sex	Census V.:Pg.
Litchfield, . . .	Arrapahoe, Denver (Lawyer)	25	M	11:351
Little, H. P.	Arrapahoe, South Park	30	M	11:192
Little, W.SC	Arrapahoe, Mountain City (Miner)	19	M	11:550
Littlejohn, Frances	Lykins, Osawatomie (Farmer)	43	F	8:67
Littlejohn, H. P.	Arrapahoe, South Park (Miner)	36	M	11:63
Littlepage, J.	Linn, Valley, Blooming Gr. (Farmer)	43	M	7:49
Livinghan, C. C.	Doniphan, Wolf River, Walnut Grove	10	F	1:398
Livingstone, H.	Arrapahoe, South Park	20	M	11:200
Lixon, R. F.	" " "	38	M	11:253
Lizenbe, CharlesSC	McGee, Crawford Seminary P.O.(Farmer)	58	M	9:228
Lock, James A.	Bourbon, Mapleton P.O. (Farmer)	41	M	2:148
Lock, Mary L.	" " "	7	F	2:148
Lock, Nancy	" " "	14	F	2:148
Lock, Rhoda C.	" " "	5	F	2:148
Lock, Squire M.	" " "	10	M	2:148
Lock, William	" " "	17	M	2:148
Locke, A. G.	Arrapahoe, South Park	26	M	11:127
Locker, G.	Arrapahoe, Valley of the Platte	30	M	11:820
Lockhart, David W.	Lyk., Mound, Osawatomie (Farmer)	41	M	8:71
Lockhart, John	Leavenworth, 1st Ward (Miller)	38	M	10:89
Lockhart, Margaret E.	Leavenworth, 1st Ward	12	F	10:89
Lockhart, Mary	" " "	35	F	10:89
Lockland, Jno. L.	Arrapahoe, Denver	55	M	11:327
Lodge, Adolphus	Linn, Scott, Twin Springs	9	M	7:8
Lodge, Ellen	" " " "	26	F	7:8
Loen, John W.	Leavenworth, Delaware (Bricklayer)	43	M	10:433
Logan, L. A.	Franklin, Centropolis, Minneola	5	F	8:208
Logan, PermeliaNC	Linn, Mound City	50	F	7:115
Logan, Rachael	Coffey, Avon, Burlington	28	F	4:14
Lom, Mary C.	Anderson, Walker, Garnett	29	F	7:234
Loman, Thomas	Bourbon, Fort Scott P.O. (Farmer)	39	M	2:155
Lombard, Sam'l.	Arrapahoe, Valley of the Platte	28	M	11:819
Long, B.NC	Linn, Scott (Farmer)	21	M	7:21
Long, Diana	Jefferson, Grasshopper Falls	22	F	5:11
Long, Ellen	Leavenworth, Ward 3	4	F	10:210
Long, EnosNC	Linn, Scott (Farmer)	23	M	7:21
Long, G.	Arrapahoe, Mountain City (Slave)	50	BM	11:462
Long, G. M.	Linn, Potosi (Farmer)	26	M	7:70
Long, JohnNC	Linn, Scott (Farmer)	18	M	7:21
Long, M.	Linn, Valley, Blooming Gr. (Farmer)	46	M	7:46
Long, MaryNC	Linn, Scott	51	F	7:21
Long, W. M.NC	" " (Farmer)	52	M	7:21
Long, WilliamNC	" " (Farmer)	15	M	7:21
Long, William	Bourbon, Mapleton P.O.	75	M	2:142
Longerbone, C. E.	Brown, Walnut Creek, Hamlin(Teacher)	28	F	3:33
Longworth, C.	Arrapahoe, Valley of the Platte	31	M	11:802
Lope, G. W.NC	Arrapahoe, South Clear Creek	29	M	11:651
Lord, E. H.	Arrapahoe, South Park	29	M	11:43
Loring, H.NC	Arrapahoe, South Clear Creek	25	M	11:653
Lornsburg, L. A.	Arrapahoe, South Park	28	M	11:122
Lotis, G.	Arrapahoe, South Park	34	M	11:249
Letty, Wm.SC	Linn, Mound City (Farmer)	37	M	7:113
Louis, C.NC	Don., Burr Oak, Whitehead (Farmer)	40	F	1:344
Louis, Jno. C.	Arrapahoe, California Gulch (Miner)	27	M	11:267
Louis, RebeccaNC	Atchison, Kapioma, Muscotah	28	F	1:98
Louis, S.	Doniphan, Washington, Elwood	21	F	1:317
Lovesay, R.	Arrapahoe, Russell Gulch (Miner)	42	M	11:486
Lowe, E. M.	Leavenworth, Ward 2 (Lawyer)	27	M	10:146
Lowe, Jennetta	Shawnee, Tecumseh	51	F	9:74
Lowe, Reuben	" " (Farmer)	45	M	9:74
Lowe, T.	Arrapahoe, South Clear Creek	36	M	11:754

Arapahoe: spelled incorrectly with 2 r's in census and in this index also.

Name	Kansas: County; Township; P.O. Arap. Co.: Census Div. Not Township	Age	Sex	Census V. Pg.
Lowman, Ephraim	Jeff., Grasshopper Falls (Carpenter)	57	M	5:2
Lowry, C. W.	Arrapahoe, South Park	31	M	11:130
Lowry, F.	Douglas, Lawrence (Ferryman)	20	M	6:219
Lowry, James B.	Anderson, Reeder, Garnett (Lawyer)	39	M	7:258
Lucas, Hetty	Bourbon, Fort Scott P.O.	35	BF	2:220
Lucas, Phillip	" " " "	70	BM	2:220
Luck, E. NC	Cof., Calif., Burlington (Farmer)	30	M	4:63
Lucus, J. NC	Arrapahoe, South Park (Saloon)	33	M	11:18
Luman, J.	Douglas, Kanwaca, Lawrence (Farmer)	50	M	6:389
Luman, Jane	" " "	48	F	6:389
Lumbkins, John	Coffey, Neosho, Burlington	19	M	4:75
Lumbkins, Sarah E.	" " "	15	F	4:75
Lumbkins, Th.	" " " (Farmer)	69	M	4:75
Lumbkins, Wood	" " "	20	M	4:75
Lunsey, Celia	Douglas, Wakarusa, Lawrence	8	F	6:247
Lunsey, Eda	" " "	10	F	6:247
Lunsey, Maria	" " "	30	F	6:247
Lust, J. C.	Linn, Centerville, Oakwood (Farmer)	38	M	7:92
Luther, J.	Arrapahoe, South Park	34	M	11:215
Lyder, C.	Arrapahoe, Valley of the Platte	37	M	11:838
Lyder, Sanders	Wyandotte, Quindaro (Carpenter)	49	M	10:57
Lyeett, David	Arrapahoe, Denver	24	M	11:404
Lykins, Caroline SC	Douglas, Lawrence	22	F	6:182
Lykins, Elizabeth SC	" "	14	F	6:182
Lykins, Joseph W.	Lykins, Paola (Druggist)	58	M	8:24
Lyles, David	Arrapahoe, Lake Gulch (Butcher)	49	M	11:484
Lyman, J.	Linn, Mound City (Editor)	50	M	7:104
Lynch, D.	Arrapahoe, Denver (Miner)	26	M	11:404
Lynch, F. C. NC	Doni., Wayne, Geary City (Farmer)	64	M	1:378
Lynch, J. T.	Doug., Palmyra, McKinney (C. Maker)	32	M	6:304
Lynd, Elezabeth SC	Washington, Washington, Marysville	33	F	3:262
Lynde, N. H.	Arrapahoe, South Park	27	M	11:176
Lynn, Ruth	Brown, Locknon, Powhattan	32	F	3:67
Lynns, A. B.	Doniphan, Doniphan (Merchant)	29	M	1:382
Lynns, E. C.	" "	22	F	1:382
Lyon, B.	Doniphan, Wayne, Doniphan (Farmer)	49	M	1:375
Lyon, Henry L.	Lyk., Marysville, Lyons (Merchant)	34	M	8:118
Lyon, Isaac	Arrapahoe, South Park	41	M	11:109
Lyon, J.	Doniphan, Wayne, Doniphan	13	M	1:375
Lyon, J. R.	" " "	8	M	1:375
Lyon, James	Leav., Alexandria, Easton (Farmer)	48	M	10:449
Lyon, James R.	Doniphan, Wayne, Doniphan	10	M	1:375
Lyon, Marlow	" " "	5	M	1:375
Lyon, S. A.	" " "	37	M	1:375
Merkle (Markle?), H.	Arrapahoe, Mountain City	23	M	11:462
McArkle, W.	" " " (Freighter)	42	M	11:462
McArkle, W.	" " "	3	M	11:462
McBride, J. W.	Arrapahoe, Valley of the Platte	29	M	11:834
McBride, Sarah	Atchison, Center, Pardee	76	F	1:129
McBride, Wm.	Arrapahoe, Central City (Carpenter)	26	M	11:577
McBrien, R. M. NC	Arrapahoe, Lake Gulch (Miner)	40	M	11:483
McCafe, Jas.	Arrapahoe; Tarryall, South Park (Miner)	35	M	11:601
McCahan, M.	Arrapahoe, South Clear Creek	32	M	11:737
McCalester, Ann	Leavenworth, Alexandria, Easton	20	F	10:442
McCallen, J. SC	Arrap., Mt. City, N.Clear Cr.(Miner)	34	M	11:464
McCamish, M. J.	Johnson, Union, Hibbard	19	F	6:14
McCarty, Kate	Leavenworth, Ward 4	4	F	10:256
McCarty, Pantha A. NC	Shawnee, Topeka	28	F	9:28
McCauley, Oile	Leavenworth, Ward 4	47	M	10:262
McCaw, Ann SC	Breckenridge, Americus	55	F	4:225
McCaw, James SC	" " (Miller)		M	4:226

Arapahoe: spelled incorrectly with 2 r's in census and in this index also.

Name	Kansas: County; Township; P.O. Arap. Co.: Census Div. Not Township	Age	Sex	Census V.:Pg.
McCaw, John M. SC	Breckenridge, Americus (Farmer)	71	M	4:225
McCaw, Martha SC	" " (Housework)	36	F	4:225
McCaw, Samuel SC	" " (Miller)		M	4:226
McCelland, L.	Franklin, Centropolis, Minneola	60	F	8:202
McCelling, C. M.	Doniphan, Center, Troy (Domestic)	21	F	1:243
McClain, William	Mars., Blue Rapids, Merrimac (Farmer)	45	M	3:212
McCleary, Jas.	Arrapahoe, California Gulch	27	M	11:312
McClemcey, Robert NC	Bourbon, Turkey Creek P.O. (Farmer)	57	M	2:107
McClennan, T.	Arrapahoe, South Clear Creek	31	M	11:712
McClintoc, Joseph	Atchison, Walnut, Sumner (Farmer)	58	M	1:189
McClosky, E. R.	Arrapahoe, South Clear Creek	25	M	11:717
McClure, Myra	Atchison, Ward 2	39	F	1:41
McComas, C.	Arrapahoe, South Park	24	M	11:171
McComes, Americus	Leavenworth, Alexandria, Easton	26	M	10:453
McCormick, A. T.	Wabaunsee, Zeandale (Farmer)	37	M	5:237
McCormick, H. W.	" " (Farmer)	37	M	5:235
McCormick, J. M.	" " (Farmer)	33	M	5:235
McCoy, Mary	Jackson, Holton	35	F	5:178
McCubben, August NC	Atchison, Ward 2	30	M	1:43
McCuben, Elizabeth NC	Atchison, Ward 3	68	F	1:47
McCulloch, T. H.? NC	Don., Columbus C., Whitehead (Farmer)	54	M	1:360
McCullom, Alexander	Bourbon, Wheeling, Mo. P.O. (Farmer)	52	M	2:86
McCollom, Mary	" " " (Housewife)	45	F	2:86
McCullough, Eli A. NC	Leavenworth, Kickapoo P.O. (Farmer)	46	M	10:407
McCullough, Nancy	Leavenworth, Ward 2	39	F	10:168
McCune, James	Breckenridge, Fremont (Farmer)	57	M	4:163
McDaniel, Duncan SC	McGee, Brushville P.O. (Farmer)	47	M	9:227
McDaniel, Elizabeth E. NC	Atchison, Walnut, Sumner	23	F	1:172
McDaniel, Frances NC	Atchison, Walnut, Sumner	60	M	1:173
McDaniel, James NC	Lykins, Marysville, Lyons (Laborer)	26	M	8:131
McDaniel, Jesse NC	Anderson, Monroe, Garnett (Farmer)	22	M	7:217
McDaniel, Jesse G. NC	Lykins, Marysville, Lyons (Farmer)	36	M	8:130
McDaniel, John NC	Anderson, Monroe, Garnett (Farmer)	34	M	7:220
McDaniel, Mackha SC	McGee, Brushville P.O.	73	F	9:227
McDaniel, Mary NC	Anderson, Monroe, Barnett	32	F	7:220
McDaniel, Nancy A. SC	McGee, Brushville P.O. (Servant)	18	F	9:227
McDaniel, Samuel NC	Anderson, Monroe, Garnett (Farmer)	44	M	7:217
McDaniel, Sarah NC	" " "	44	F	7:217
McDaniel, Susana NC	Lykins, Marysville, Lyons	56	F	8:131
McDaniel, Wm. G. NC	" " " (Farmer)	60	M	8:131
McDermot, John	Mars., Blue Rapids, Irving (Farmer)	24	M	3:210
McDill, John SC	Chase, Cottonwood, C.Falls (Carpenter)	40	M	4:319
McDonald, B.	Arrapahoe, California Gulch	27	M	11:282
McDonald, J. SC	Linn, Centerville, Oakwood (Farmer)	37	M	7:94
McDonald, Juda	" " "	38	F	7:95
McDougal, E.	Johnson, Monticello (Farmer)	45	M	6:81
McDougall, Josiah	Bour., Marmaton P.O. (Grocery Keeper)	47	M	2:205
McDow, Elmira B. SC	Anderson, Walker, Garnett	41	F	7:240
McDowell, J. B.	Arrapahoe, Golden City (Miner)	32	M	11:451
McDowell, J. H.	Leavenworth, Ward 4 (Lawyer)	35	M	10:281
McDowell, R. B.	Arrapahoe, Golden City (Miner)	21	M	11:451
McDowold, E. B.	Arrapahoe, Valley of the Platte	33	M	11:823
Mace, Wm.	Douglas, Lecompton (Farmer)	32	M	6:371
Mace, Wm.	" "	9	M	6:371
McEvers, Mary	Arrapahoe, Denver	24	F	11:319
McEwen, A.	Arrapahoe, Enterprise District (Miner)	28	M	11:492
McEwen, Eliza	Lykins, Paola	24	F	8:40
McEwen, Thomas	Leavenworth, Alexandria, Easton	35	M	10:452
Macey, William NC	Mars., Guittard, Marysville (Farmer)	30	M	3:235
McFarland, C.	Franklin, Centropolis, Minneola	24	F	8:204
McFarland, E. NC	Johnson, Shawnee	28	F	6:25

Arapahoe: spelled incorrectly with 2 r's in census and in this index also.

Name	Kansas: County; Township; P.O. Arap. Co.: Census Div. Not Township	Age	Sex	Census V. : Pg.
McFarland, William	Allen, Humboldt P.O. (Farmer)	30	M	2:283
McGalorth, J. M.[NC]	Doniphan, Center, Troy (Farmer)	38	M	1:260
McGee, Oliva	Douglas, Wakarusa, Lawrence	21	F	6:232
McGee, Rebecca	" " " " (Farmer)	16	F	6:231
McGhee, Catherine	Bourbon, Fort Scott P.O. (Housewife)	52	F	2:154
McGhee, James H.	Bourbon, Barnesville P.O. (Farmer)	30	M	2:174
McGhee, John	Bourbon, Fort Scott P.O. (Farmer)	56	M	2:154
McGill, Jas.[NC]	Arrapahoe, California Gulch (Miner)	25	M	11:266
McGinnis, J. E.	Madison, Hartford (Physician)	54	M	4:234
McGiven, E.	Arrapahoe, South Clear Creek	39	M	11:729
McGlothlin, Martha	Jefferson, Oskaloosa	83	F	5:111
McGranaham, John F.	Leav., Stranger, Leav.City (Farmer)	52	M	10:478
McGrath, Jas.[NC]	Arrapahoe, South Park (Carpenter)	27	M	11:5
McGrimes, S.	Arrapahoe, Valley of the Platte	28	M	11:818
McGuire, Anna	Shawnee, Tecumseh	38	F	9:80
McGuire, John	" " (Farmer)	43	M	9:80
McIlvaine, Geo.	Arrapahoe, South Park	35	M	11:216
McKane, A. J.[SC]	Anderson, Walker, Garnett (Sewing)	45	M	7:237
McKenny, J.	Douglas, Clinton (Laborer)	50	M	6:420
McKenny, Mary	Douglas, Clinton	43	F	6:420
McKenzie, S. D.[1]	Franklin, Peoria, Peoria City	4	F	8:269
McKinley, J.	Franklin, Peoria, Peoria C.(Carpenter)	26	M	8:275
McKinney, S. J.	Arrapahoe, Valley of the Platte	32		11:785
McKinny, L.	Douglas, Lecompton	32	M	6:371
McKinzie, Alfred G.[SC]	Lyk., Miamiw-Osage, Osawat.(Grocer)	28	M	8:85
Macloy?, T. R.	Arrapahoe, South Clear Creek	33	M	11:728
McKnight, James	Leavenworth, Ft. Leav.P.O.(Teamster)	27	M	10:315
McKonkey, Maria	Leavenworth, Ward 3, Leavenworth	26	F	10:206
McKoon, J. A.	Leavenworth, Ward 2, Leav.(Druggist)	45	M	10:150
McLane, George	Marshall, Blue Rapids, Merrimac	40	M	3:212
McLaughlin, M. M.	Nemaha, Home, Centralia	30	F	3:130
McLendry, A.	Arrapahoe, California Gulch	25	M	11:282
McMaines, Theresa	Anderson, Reeder, Garnett	6	F	7:263
McMana, John	Jeff., Kentucky, Oskaloosa (Farmer)	28	M	5:77
McMarland, R.	Franklin, Centropolis, Minneola	33	F	8:210
McMillan, H. R.	Arrapahoe, South Clear Creek	33	M	11:629
McMillan, M. D.	" " " "	52	M	11:629
McMillen, Sarah	Linn, Potosi, Rovella	47	F	7:58
McMore, Barbara J.	Allen, Humboldt P.O.	31	F	2:291
McNally, J.	Arrapahoe, South Park	29	M	11:90
McNarnee, H.	Johnson, Monticello (Carpenter)	25	M	6:83
McNutt, S.	Franklin, Peoria, Stanton	53	F	8:276
McPhatter, A. W.[NC]	Arrapahoe, Denver (Carpenter)	25	M	11:358
McPherson, F.	Atchison, Center, Pardee	54	F	1:131
McReynolds, M.	Wabaunsee, Wabaunsee	40	F	5:233
McRaynolds, R.	" " (Farmer)	46	M	5:233
McTaggot, Wm.	Arrapahoe, South Park	41	M	11:112
McTalfer (McTalafer)David M.	Leavenworth, Kickapoo(FarmHand)	26	M	10:340
McVey, Ann[NC]	Jackson, Franklin, Holton	28	F	5:183
McWhiet, C.? T.	Arrapahoe, Golden City (Trader)	31	M	11:581
Macy, Joanna	Madison, Hartford	29	F	4:237
Macy, Samuel R.	Madison, Verdigris, Madison Centre	58	M	4:247
Madden, Mary M.[NC]	Douglas, Lawrence	27	F	6:220
Maddoe, Delia	Leavenworth, 1st Ward (Washer)	75	BF	10:90
Maddoe, Edmund	" " " (Blacksmith)	27	BM	10:90
Maddox, J. W.	Breck.,Forest Hill (Meth.Clergyman)	51	M	4:174
Maddox, Susan C.	" " "	27	F	4:174
Madox, John P.	Lykins, Paola (Constable)	26	M	8:36

[1]Birth state could be Ia. or La. rather than Va.
    Arapahoe: spelled incorrectly with 2 r's in census and in this index also.

Name	Kansas: County; Township; P.O. Arap. Co.: Census Div. Not Township	Age	Sex	Census V. : Pg.
Mageath, John	Anderson, Reeder, Garnett	2	M	7:266
Mageath, James	" " "	9/12	M	7:266
Mageath, Mary	" " "	6	F	7:266
Magill, D.	Douglas,Wakarusa,Lawrence(Laborer)	37	M	6:253
Magill, Ella[1],SC	Marshall, Maryland	24	F	3:254
Magill, Loyal[1],SC	Marshall, Marysville	7	M	3:254
Magruder, Thos.	Arrapahoe, South Park (Miner)	19	M	11:58
Maher, Virginia	Leavenworth, Ward 2	30	F	10:186
Mahon, William	Cof.,Leroy,Burling.(Justice of Peace)	61	M	4:19
Mahoney, John	Leavenworth, 1st Ward	6	M	10:94
Mahoney, Kate	" " "	3	F	10:94
Maiden, Eliza[NC]	Lykins; Sugar Creek; West Point,Mo.	43	F	8:97
Main, Anna	Bourbon, Dayton P.O.	15	F	2:124
Main, Cary Z.	Bourbon, Xenia P.O. (Housewife)	17	F	2:139
Main, Catherine	Doniphan, Center, Troy	14	F	1:263
Main, Cowley F.	Bourbon, Dayton P.O.	22	M	2:124
Main, E.	Doniphan, Center, Troy	42	F	1:263
Main, G. B.	" " " (Farmer)	46	M	1:263
Main, G.	" " "	13	M	1:263
Main, Henry	Bourbon, Dayton P.O. (Farm Laborer)	23	M	2:124
Main, J. G.	Doniphan, Center, Troy	16	M	1:263
Main, J. M.	" " " (Farm Hand)	19	M	1:263
Main, Jackson	Bourbon, Xenia P.O. (Farmer)	27	M	2:139
Main, Jane	Doniphan, Center, Troy	9	F	1:263
Main, Jefferson	Bourbon, Dayton P.O.	18	M	2:124
Main, John	Doniphan, Center, Troy	8	M	1:263
Main, John	" " "	8	M	1:263
Main, John	Bourbon, Dayton P.O. (Farmer)	42	M	2:124
Main, Morgan	Doniphan, Center, Troy	2	M	1:263
Main, R.	" " "	11	F	1:263
Maise, George W.	Potta., St.George, Elden (Farmer)	28	M	5:265
Maker, Lennia	Atchison, Grasshopper, Kennekuk	26	F	1:87
Malone, Jasper[NC]	Linn, Liberty, Centerville	4	M	7:3
Malone, Julia A.[NC]	Bourbon, Fort Scott P.O. (Housewife)	30	F	2:223
Malone, Wm.	Arrapahoe, Russell Gulch (Miner)	26	M	11:543
Maloney, John	Doniphan, Washington, Wathena (D.L.)	27	M	1:340
Malony, George	Woodson, Greenfield, Pleasant Grove	7	M	9:171
Manford, Sarah[NC]	Bourbon, Fort Scott P.O. (Housewife)	47	BF	2:196
Manlove, David[NC]	" " " "(School Teacher)	64	M	2:220
Mann, B. A.	Doniphan, Center, Troy (Domestic)	23	F	1:263
Mann, E.	" " "	37	F	1:263
Mann, E. F.	Doniphan, Washington, Whitehead	4	F	1:299
Mann, E. J.	Doniphan, Center, Troy	14	F	1:263
Mann, H. P.	" " "	1	M	1:263
Mann, Harriett	" " "	10	F	1:263
Mann, J.	Doniphan, Washington,Whitehead(Farmer)	31	M	1:299
Mann, J. A.	" " "	29	F	1:299
Mann, J. B.	Doniphan, Center, Troy	4	M	1:263
Mann, L. M.	Doniphan, Washington, Whitehead	6	F	1:299
Mann, M. S.	Doniphan, Center, Troy	6	F	1:263
Mann, S. D.	Linn, Valley, Blooming Gr.(Physician)	30	M	7:30
Mann, Thos.	Arrapahoe, Denver	40	M	11:317
Mann, Virginia	Doniphan, Washington, Whitehead	8	F	1:299
Mann, W.	Doniphan, Center, Troy	12	M	1:263
Mann, Wm. L.	" " " (Farmer)	20	M	1:263
Manning, W.	Arrapahoe, Valley of the Platte	27	M	11:804
Manpin, Alexander	Bourbon, Fort Scott P.O.	9	M	2:95
Manpin, Martha	" " " " (Housewife)	28	F	2:95

[1]See P. Magill, 1855 Census, Dist. 16, p. 20, age 30.
Arapahoe: spelled incorrectly with 2 r's in census and in this index also.

Name	Kansas: County; Township; P.O. Arap. Co.: Census Div. Not Township	Age	Sex	Census V. Pg.
Manpin, Mary	Bourbon, Fort Scott P.O.	7	F	2:95
Manpin, Samuel	" " " "	10	M	2:95
Manpin, Silas	" " " " (Farmer)	36	M	2:95
Manpin, Wesley	" " " "	5	M	2:95
March, G. C.	Arrapahoe, South Clear Creek	30	M	11:720
Marcum, Rebecca	Brown, Walnut Creek, Hamlin	60	F	3:21
Marcum, Joseph	" " " " (Farmer)	66	M	3:21
Mareman, B. D.	Doniphan, Iowa Point (Lawyer)	40	M	1:437
Margfield, I.SC	Johnson, Monticello (Farmer)	28	M	6:82
Mark, A.NC	Douglas, Lecompton (Farmer)	60	M	6:356
Markham, Cynthia	Doniphan, Iowa Point	59	F	1:447
Markham, J. E.	" " " (Laborer)	24	M	1:447
Markham, J. H.	" " " (Laborer)	19	M	1:447
Markham, John A.	Brown, Claytonville (Farmer)	27	M	3:37
Markham, John	Brown, Walnut Creek, Hamlin	5	M	3:20
Markham, Mary	Doniphan, Iowa Point	23	F	1:447
Markham, Nancy	Brown, Claytonville	27	F	3:37
Markham, S. B.	Doniphan, Iowa Point (Laborer)	22	M	1:447
Markham, W. A.	" " " (Lawyer?)	31	M	1:447
Marks, Charles	Linn, Centerville, Keokuk	10	M	7:83
Marks, D.	Frank., Centrop.,Minneola (Laborer)	22	M	8:205
Marks, Vincent	Atchison, Ward 2 (Laborer)	60	BM	1:36
Marlow, T.SC	Doniphan, Iowa Point (M. Carpenter)	38	M	1:452
Marshal, Geo.	Arrapahoe, South Park (Miner)	32	M	11:55
Marshal, L.	" " "	23	M	11:228
Marshall, AquillaNC	Leavenworth, Ft. Leav. P.O. (Waiter)	23	M	10:313
Marshall, Francis	Marshall, Marysville (Merchant)	44	M	3:251
Marshall, Jennie	Leavenworth, 1st Ward	24	F	10:124
Marshall, Jno.	Arrapahoe, South Park	29	M	11:189
Marshall, Mary Ann	Jeff., Jefferson, Crooked Creek	30	F	5:29
Marshall, ThomasNC	" " " " (Farmer)	25	M	5:29
Marten, NancyNC	Allen, Elizabeth Town P.O.	40	F	2:233
Martin, A.	Linn, Mound City (Farmer)	29	M	7:123
Martin, A.	Bourbon, Barnesville P.O.	15	M	2:170
Martin, Bennet A.	Shawnee, Tecumseh (Farmer)	44	M	9:69
Martin, C.	Arrapahoe, South Park	37	M	11:168
Martin, C. M.	" " " (Miner)	25	M	11:65
Martin, Charles E.	Lykins, Middle Creek, Paola	12	M	8:109
Martin, Edna	" " " "	17	F	8:109
Martin, ElizabethNC	Bourbon, Fort Scott P.O.(Housewife)	26	F	2:75
Martin, George	Jack.,Doug.,Grasshop.Falls (Farmer)	50	M	9:94
Martin, Hannah M.	Lykins, Middle Creek, Paola	15	F	8:109
Martin, Harry	Bourbon, Barnesville P.O.	18	M	2:170
Martin, Hellen	Lykins, Middle Creek, Paola	39	F	8:109
Martin, Hiram S.NC	Allen, Elizabeth Town P.O.	14	M	2:233
Martin, J. G.NC	Davis,Ft.Riley Res.(Brevt.Maj.USA)	41	M	9:359
Martin, James H.NC	Allen, Elizabeth Town P.O.	12	M	2:233
Martin, JaneNC	" " " "	21	F	2:233
Martin, JohnNC	" " " " (Farmer)	45	M	2:233
Martin, John	Bourbon, Barnesville P.O.	11	M	2:170
Martin, Joseph	Mars., Guittard, Marysville (Farmer)	26	M	3:235
Martin, Lucretia	Doniphan, Washington, Whitehead	33	F	1:296
Martin, Margaret	Bourbon, Barnesville P.O.	17	F	2:170
Martin, Martha M.NC	Allen, Elizabeth Town P.O.	7	F	2:233
Martin, Mary	Atchison, Mt. Pleasant	56	F	1:158
Martin, Mary	Atchison, Center, Pardee	56	F	1:136
Martin, Mildred	Lykins, Middle Creek, Paola	13	M	8:109
Martin, Mildred S.NC	Allen, Elizabeth Town P.O.	18	F	2:233
Martin, Peter	Leavenworth, Ward 2	22	M	10:162
Martin, Rebecca	Linn, Mound City	30	F	7:101
Martin, SarahNC	Allen, Elizabeth Town P.O.	44	F	2:233

Arapahoe: spelled incorrectly with 2 r's in census and in this index also.

Name	Kansas: County; Township; P.O. / Arap. Co.: Census Div. Not Township	Sex	Age	Census V: Pg.
Martin, Sarah D. NC	Allen, Elizabeth Town P.O.	10	F	2:233
Martin, Sarah E.	Bourbon, Barnesville P.O.	7	F	2:170
Martin, T. W.	Arrapahoe, Valley of the Platte	30	M	11:841
Martin, Wm. NC	Douglas, Marion (Farmer)	31	M	6:401
Martin, William	Lykins, Middle Creek, Paola (Farmer)	42	M	8:109
Martin, William Y. NC	Allen, Elizabeth Town P.O.	23	M	2:233
Martindale, Lucinda	Brown, Claytonville, Robinson	21	F	3:42
Martin, Joseph	Bourbon, Fort Scott P.O. (Farmer)	58	M	2:191
Marvin, Joseph	" " " " (Farmer)	58	M	2:191
. . . ., Mary [1]	Don., Washington, Wathena (Servant)	55	BF	1:306
Mason, A. W.	Leav., Alexandria, Easton (Farmer)	49	M	10:453
Mason, B.	Arrap., Mo. City (Boarding House)	43	M	11:524
Mason, D. SC	Jefferson, Oskaloosa	65	F	5:113
Mason, J.	Arrapahoe, Valley of the Platte(Miner)	24	M	11:848
Mason, Mary	Arrapahoe, Missouri City	36	F	11:524
Mason, Obedia	Leavenworth, Alexandria, Easton	75	M	10:454
Mason, Paulene	Arrapahoe, Nevada Gulch	28	M	11:525
Mason, Wm.	Arrapahoe, Valley of the Platte(Miner)	30	M	11:853
Massell, E. M.	Wyandotte, Wyandotte (Farmer)	36	M	10:5
Massey, Catherine L.	Lykins; Sugar Creek; West Point, Mo.	25	F	8:96
Massey, R.	Arrapahoe, South Park	26	M	11:115
Massey, Sally E.	Lykins, Stanton	28	F	8:11
Massle, S.B.(or S.R.?) [2]	Arrapahoe, Valley of the Platte	23	M	11:827
Masters, Mary	Atchison, Ward 3	50	F	1:66
Mateny, R. B.	Doug., Willow Spr.,Brooklyn (Farmer)	38	M	6:322
Mathens, Catharine	Leavenworth, Alexandria, Easton	45	F	10:441
Mathery, Georgianna	Linn, Paris	5	F	7:150
Mathery, J.	" " (Farmer)	30	M	7:150
Mathery, Julia	" "	28	F	7:150
Mathery, Susan	" "	7	F	7:150
Mathews, M.	Arrapahoe, South Park	20	M	11:24
Mathews, Nancy NC	Brown, Irving, Hiawatha	46	F	3:10
Mathews, T. NC	Davis, Junction City P.O. (Farmer)	67	M	9:341
Mathewus, Sally NC	Brown, Irving, Hiawatha	25	F	3:10
Mathias, E. N.	Leavenworth, 1st Ward	23	F	10:107
Mathney, Mary NC	Doniphan, Doniphan	39	F	1:385
Matlock, C.	Doniphan, Iowa Point	21	F	1:447
Matlock, J. B.	" . " " (M. Carpenter)	30	M	1:447
Matney, Wm., Jr.	Shaw., Monmouth, Tecumseh (Farmer)	30	M	9:57
Matoney, Charles	" " " (Farmer)	38	M	9:61
Maxwell, John	Brown, Claytonv.,Robinson (Farmer)	35	M	3:59
Maxwell, M.	" " "	23	F	3:59
Maxwell, Nancy J. NC	Lykins, Wea, Paola	21	F	8:118
Maxwell, Sarah	Lykins, Wea, Squiresville	71	F	8:113
May, Anna	Jefferson, Grasshopper Falls	8	F	5:10
May, D.	Davis, Junction City (Carpenter)	40	M	9:334
May, Elizabeth	Lykins, Stanton			8:7
May, George	Jeff., Grasshopper Falls (Laborer)	16	M	5:10
May, Isaac	" " " (Laborer)	18	M	5:10
May, James	" " " (Laborer)	17	M	5:10
May, Jasper	" " " (Laborer)	19	M	5:10
May, Jepe	Lykins, Stanton (Farmer)	42	M	8:7
May, Joseph	Jefferson, Grasshopper Falls	5	M	5:10
May, Martha	" " "	21	F	5:10
May, Nancy NC	Bourbon, Barnesville P.O. (Housewife)	42	F	2:179
May, Rachel	Jefferson, Grasshopper Falls	10	F	5:10
May, Salathiel	" " " (Farmer)	24	M	5:10

[1]Listed only as Mary, living in household of Jno. Stewart.

[2]Surname could be Mussey or Muscle rather than Massle.

Arapahoe: spelled incorrectly with 2 r's in census and in this index also.

Name	Kansas: County; Township; P.O. Arap. Co.: Census Div. Not Township	Age	Sex	Census V. Pg.
May, Signey	Lykins, Stanton	41		8:7
May, William	" " (Farm Laborer)	22	M	8:7
Mayer, A. H.	Arrapahoe, Denver	32	M	11:375
Mayhew, P. NC	Linn, Mound City (Farmer)	58	F	7:113
Maynard, Elizabeth	Linn, Potosi	46	F	7:80
Mead, Thos. W.	Arrapahoe, Valley of the Platte	31	M	11:822
Meadows, Wm.	Atchison, Walnut, Sumner (Farmer)	21	M	1:177
Means, B.	Douglas, Lawrence (Student of Mdc.)	33	M	6:206
Means, James NC	Anderson, Reeder, Garnett (Farmer)	47	M	7:257
Means, Mary	Douglas, Lawrence	26	F	6:206
Mecher, W. D.	Franklin, Centropolis, Minneola	25	M	8:210
Medlen, Abraham SC	McGee; Medoc, Mo. P.O. (Farmer)	66	M	9:208
Medlin, Cynthia SC	" " " "	63	F	9:208
Medlen, Francis M. SC	" " " " (Farmer)	31	M	9:213
Medley, Jobez	Chase, Bazaar (Farming)	44	M	4:332
Medlin, L. SC	Linn, Potosi (Farmer)	30	M	7:80
Meigan, Catherine	Douglas, Lawrence	3	F	6:203
Melbun, T. O.	Arrapahoe, South Clear Creek	31	M	11:763
Melone, Borella NC	Linn, Liberty, Centerville	14	F	7:2
Melone, Louisa NC	" " "	24	F	7:2
Melone, Nashville NC	" " " (Farmer)	30	M	7:2
Melvin, Mary NC	Doniphan, Burr Oak, Whitehead	24	F	1:345
Mendenhall, F. NC	Johnson, Lexington	55	F	6:75
Mendenhall, J. NC	" " (Farmer)	60	M	6:75
Mendenhall, Sarah	Leavenworth, Alexandria, Easton	30	F	10:458
Mendenhall, Sarah A.	Lykins, Osawatomie	48	F	8:54
Meridith, J. M.	Brown, Walnut Creek, Carson (Farmer)	42	M	3:25
Merifield, Ann	Arrapahoe, Missouri City	23	M	11:524
Merkle, Jno. W.	Arrap., Idahoe, Russell Gulch (Miner)	23	M	11:589
Merrett, M.	Franklin, Ohio, Ohio City	35	F	8:231
Merrill, W. SC	Don., Washington, Whitehead (Farmer)	66	M	1:325
Merrith, A. H.	Arrapahoe, South Park	26	M	11:231
Merrith, E. NC	Doniphan, Center, Troy (Farmer)	66	M	1:272
Merrith, Sarah	" " "	59	F	1:272
Merwin, N.	Arrapahoe, South Park	46	M	11:115
Messick, Clarissa	Coffey, Pottawatomie, Burlington	27	F	4:1
Messen (Morgan?), E.	Doniphan, Iowa Point (Farmer)	27	M	1:431
Mezzen (Metzen?), G.	" " " (Farmer)	31	M	1:431
Metuey, D.	Johnson, Shawnee (Grocer)	23	M	6:25
Metuey, E.	" "	18	F	6:25
Metuey, G.	" " (Farmer)	27	M	6:25
Metuey, S.	" "	18	F	6:25
Micely (Nicely?), Wm.	Shawnee, Topeka (Merchant)	21	M	9:8
Middleton, H.	Arrapahoe, South Park	27	M	11:113
Middleton, John	Allen, Iola P.O. (Farmer)	68	M	2:247
Middleton, Martha	Bourbon, Fort Scott P.O. (Housewife)	24	F	2:217
Middlitzer, George	Leavenworth, Ward 2, Leavenworth	10	M	10:184
Might, John NC	Leav., Alexandria, Easton (Farmer)	35	M	10:443
Milan, Margaret	McGee, Brushville P.O.	20	F	9:222
Miles, F. E.	Doniphan, Center, Troy	44	F	1:257
Milhaer, E.	Johnson, Olathe	56	F	6:112
Milhaer, G.	" " (Farmer)	22	M	6:112
Milhaer, T.	" " (Farmer)	28	M	6:112
Miller, Augustus NC	Lykins, Stanton (Farmer)	33	M	8:3
Miller, B. J.	Johnson, Monticello (Laborer)	22	M	6:80
Miller, Benjamin	Atchison, Ward 3 (Carpt.)	18	M	1:57
Miller, David NC	Lykins, Stanton (Farmer)	56	M	8:3
Miller, Franklin R.	Leavenworth, Easton	26	M	10:285
Miller, G. W.	Arrapahoe, South Park	21	M	11:128
Miller, Haddassa	Atchison, Ward 3 (Dressmaker)	35	F	1:57
Miller, Harriet	Lykins; Sugar Creek; West Point, Mo.	34	F	8:101

Arapahoe: spelled incorrectly with 2 r's in census and in this index also.

Name	Kansas: County; Township; P.O. Arap. Co.: Census Div. Not Township	Age	Sex	Census V.:Pg.
Miller, John	Chase, Cottonwood, C. Falls (Farmer)	43	M	4:321
Miller, John A.	Lykins; Sugar Creek; West Point, Mo.	14	M	8:101
Miller, Lydia NC	Lykins, Stanton	56	F	8:3
Miller, Maria H.	Breckenridge, Fremont	28	F	4:164
Miller, Mary	Lykins; Sugar Creek; West Point, Mo.	9	F	8:101
Miller, P.	Coffey, Leroy, Burlington (Farmer)	25	M	4:24
Miller, Racheal N. SC	Shawnee, Topeka	30	F	9:34
Miller, Solomon R.	Atchison, Ward 3 (Bootmaker)	44	M	1:60
Miller, Thomas	Bourbon, Mapleton P.O. (Farmer)	28	M	2:132
Miller, W.	Johnson, Olathe (Farmer)	41	M	6:112
Miller, Wilber NC	Allen, Humboldt P.O. (Farmer)	56	M	2:301
Miller, William	Bourbon, Raysville P.O. (Farmer)	60	M	2:168
Miller, Wm. H.	Lykins;Sugar Creek;W.Point,Mo.(Farmer)	37	M	8:101
Millison, Mahala	Morris, Grove, Council Grove	20	F	4:265
Mills, Anne	Doniphan, Wayne, Doniphan	24	F	1:365
Mills, Cathern	Brown, Irving, Hiawatha	59	F	3:7
Mills, J. C.	Arrapahoe; Tarryall, South Park	23	M	11:610
Mills, M. SC	Davis, Ft.Riley Res. (Surgeon,USA)	48	M	9:359
Mills, Sarah NC	Linn, Potosi	54	F	7:82
Mills, T.	Arrapahoe, South Park	24	M	11:169
Mills, W. R.	Doniphan, Center, Troy (Farmer)	41	M	1:273
Millsap, R.	Nemaha, Valley, Seneca	35	F	3:122
Millsap, Wm.	" " " (Farmer)	49	M	3:122
Milton, John NC	Linn, Scott, Brooklyn (Farmer)	57	M	7:20
Mindenhall, Chas. C.	Leav., Delaware, Easton (Farmer)	37	M	10:457
Mineas, Wm.?	Don., Washington, Elwood (Laborer)	25	M	1:331
Mintum, O. P.	Arrapahoe, South Park	25	M	11:122
Mitchel, Sarah A.	Leavenworth, Delaware	23	F	10:435
Mitchell, A. M.	Johnson, Spring Hill	25	F	6:46
Mitchell, E.	Arrapahoe, South Park	29	M	11:225
Mitchell, J.	Doniphan, Highland (Farmer)	24	M	1:413
Mitchell, Jas.	Arrapahoe, South Park (Miner)	27	M	11:69
Mitchell, John A.	Jackson, Douglas, Holton (Farmer)	35	M	5:172
Mitchell, T. W. NC	Arrap.,Mt.City,N.Clear Cr.(Teamster)	40	M	11:464
Mitchell, Sarah	Jackson, Douglas, Holton	35	F	5:172
Mitchell, Wm.	Arrapahoe, South Park (Miner)	37	M	11:66
Mobley, Mary NC	Riley, Ogden P.O.	66	F	9:291
Mock, G.	Doniphan, White Cloud (Lawyer)	24	M	1:442
Mock, G. W.	" " " (Lawyer)	19	M	1:442
Mock, K.?	" " "	61	F	1:442
Mock, L.	" " "	3	M	1:441
Mock, M. A.	" " "	5	F	1:441
Mock, M. S.	" " " (Lawyer)	21	M	1:442
Mock, Martha	" " "	7	F	1:441
Mock, S. A.	" " "	27	F	1:441
Mock, W. H.	" " " (Miller)	30	M	1:441
Mock, Wm.	" " " (Lumberman)	60	M	1:442
Modie, J. W.	" Iowa Point (Blacksmith)	52	M	1:447
Modlin, E. NC	Cof.,Ottumwa,Burlington (Carpenter)	62	M	4:56
Moffat, S NC	Ril.,Henryv.-Rand. P.O.(Blacksmith)	36	M	9:298
Moffit, Catherine	Woodson, Liberty, Leroy (F. W.)	50	F	9:144
Molery, R.	Don., Washington, Elwood (Gardener)	29	M	1:336
Moley, Cyrus	Doniphan, Center, Troy	10	M	1:253
Miley, C. F.	" " "	11	M	1:253
Moley, J. W.	" " "(Farm Laborer)	20	M	1:253
Moley, L. M.	" " "	2	M	1:253
Moley, M.	" " "	26	F	1:253
Moley, M. M.	" " "	17	F	1:253
Moley, Nancy	" " "	14	F	1:253
Moley, V.	" " " (Farmer)	49	M	1:253
Molin, Esther	Washington, Washington, Marysville	10	F	3:263

Arapahoe: spelled incorrectly with 2 r's in census and in this index also.

Name	Kansas: County; Township; P.O. Arap. Co.: Census Div. Not Township	Age	Sex	Census V:Pg.
Molin, Martha	Washington, Washington, Marysville	8	F	3:263
Monnich, Elizabeth	Jeff.,Ky., Oskaloosa (Seamstress)	23	F	5:71
Monnich, Wm.	Jeff., " " (Millwright)	25	M	5:71
Monroe, Eliza	Linn, Centerville, Oakwood	40	F	7:93
Moody, Andrew NC	Woodson, Neosho Falls (Teacher)	40	M	9:136
Moody, Benjamine NC	" " " (Farmer)	25	M	9:136
Moody, Gelly A. NC	" " " (F.W.)	63	F	9:136
Moody, Joll?) NC	" " " (Farmer)	62	M	9:136
Moody, Martha NC	" " "	36	F	9:136
Moody, Mary M. NC	" " " (F.W.)	23	F	9:136
Moon, Elizabeth NC	Brown, Claytonville	59	F	3:53
Moon, John NC	Breckenridge, Pike, Plymouth (Farmer)	47	M	4:214
Moon, Joseph NC	Breckenridge, Emporia (Farmer)	51	M	4:206
Moon, Lavina NC	Breckenridge, Pike, Plymouth	46	F	4:214
Moon, Lydia NC	Breckenridge, Emporia	47	F	4:206
Moon, Mavilla NC	Breckenridge, Pike, Plymouth	24	F	4:215
Moor, Levi	Marshall, Marysville (Workman)	26	M	3:254
Moor, Noah W.	Bourbon, Fort Scott P.O.	35	M	2:195
Moore, A. SC	Franklin, Peoria, Peoria City	49	M	8:270
Moore, Alexander	Marshall, Blue Rapids	3	M	3:200
Moore, B.	Jefferson, Kentucky, Oskaloosa	9	F	5:71
Moore, B. B.	Leavenworth, Alex.,Easton (Farmer)	40	M	10:442
Moore, Benj.	Douglas, Lecompton (Farmer)	26	M	6:363
Moore, Creswell	Lyk.,Marysville,Lyons (Physician)	35	M	8:120
Moore, Elizabeth	Marshall, Marysville	28	F	3:243
Moore, Ellen	" "	5	F	3:243
Moore, Francis	Marshall, Blue Rapids	7	M	3:200
Moore, G. W.	Arrapahoe, California Gulch	23	M	11:282
Moore, George	Jeff., Kentucky, Oskaloosa (Farmer)	35	M	5:71
Moore, J. NC	Douglas, Clinton (Farmer)	46	M	6:409
Moore, James	Marshall, Blue Rapids (Farm Laborer)	19	M	3:200
Moore, James W.	Atchison, Walnut, Sumner (Farmer)	59	M	1:187
Moore, John NC	Coffey, Burlington (Farmer)	48	M	4:42
Moore, John	Marshall, Blue Rapids	10	M	3:200
Moore, John B. NC	Breckenridge, Americus	23	M	4:220
Moore, Malvina	Jefferson, Kentucky, Oskaloosa	31	F	5:71
Moore, Martha	Marshall, Blue Rapids	14	F	3:200
Moore, Mary	" " "	16	F	3:200
Moore, Mary NC	Coffey, Burlington	48	F	4:42
Moore, Mary	Jefferson, Kentucky, Oskaloosa	11	F	5:71
Moore, Mary	Marshall, Blue Rapids	38	F	3:200
Moore, Mary F.	Leavenworth, Alexandria, Easton	9	F	10:442
Moore, Morris NC	Breckenridge, Americus (Farmer)	26	M	4:220
Moore, Peter P.	Bourbon, Barnesville P.O. (Farmer)	29	M	2:175
Moore, Prudence	Linn, Potosi	70	F	7:77
Moore, S. D. NC	Atchison, Center, Pardee (M. D.)	53	M	1:132
Moore, Stephen Jr.	Marshall, Blue Rapids	12	M	3:200
Moore, Susan C.	Leavenworth, Alexandria	9	F	10:442
Moore, Theodore	Jefferson, Kentucky, Oskaloosa	13	M	5:71
Moore, W. NC	Frank., Ottawa,Prair.City(Minister)	55	M	8:253
Moore, William	Mars., Blue Rapids (Farm Laborer)	21	M	3:200
Moore, Wm. B.	Doug., Palmyra, Baldwin (Carpenter)	22	M	6:282
Moorman, Mary	Jefferson, Oskaloosa	54	F	5:119
Morall, Albert SC	Marshall, Marysville	25	M	3:252
More, David NC	Allen, Humboldt P.O. (Farmer)	44	M	2:303
More, Joseph NC	Chase, Bazaar (Farm Laborer)	22	M	4:334
More, Peter	Bourbon, Barnesville P.O. (Farmer)	29	M	2:180
Morel, G.	Arrapahoe, South Park	39	M	11:196
Moren, R. W.	Arrapahoe, South Clear Creek (Miner)	29	M	11:685
Morettz, Christana	Morris, Neosho, Council Grove	50	F	4:273
Morey, Elizabeth J.	Breckenridge, Waterloo	35	F	4:152

Arapahoe: spelled incorrectly with 2 r's in census and in this index also.

Name	Kansas: County; Township; P.O. Arap. Co.: Census Div. Not Township	Age	Sex	Census V. Pg.
Morgan, B.	Arrapahoe, South Park	20	M	11:133
Morgan, Elizabeth	Breckenridge, Americus	34	F	4:223
Morgan, Francis	Bourbon, Fort Scott P.O. (Farmer)	50	M	2:200
Morgan, Pleasant	Breckenridge, Americus (Farmer)	52	M	4:223
Morgan, Roland	Jeff.,Rock Cr.,Mt.Florence (Farmer)	50	M	5:94
Morgan, Sam'l.	Linn, Valley, Blooming Gr. (Farmer)	49	M	7:40
Morgan, Starling SC	Lykins, Miami, Paola (Farmer)	60	M	8:90
Moriden, S. T.	Arrapahoe, South Park	26	M	11:122
Morris, A.	Doniphan, Washington, Elwood(Brick M.)	38	M	1:309
Morris, Cyrus	Anderson, Walker, Garnett (Farmer)	35	M	7:233
Morris, David	" " " (Farmer)	62	M	7:233
Morris, Elizabeth NC	Bourbon, Raysville P.O. (Housewife)	53	F	2:185
Morris, H.	Arrapahoe, South Park	39	M	11:132
Morris, Jacob	Bourbon, Raysville P.O. (Farmer)	55	M	2:185
Morris, Jeremiah NC	Arrapahoe, Golden City (Farmer)	44	M	11:586
Morris, Julia	Doniphan, Washington, Elwood	24	F	1:309
Morris, M.	" " "	20	F	1:334
Morris, M. A.	Chase, Falls, Cottonwood Falls	52	M	4:322
Morris, Manuel	Don., Washington, Elwood (Laborer)	25	M	1:334
Morris, Matilda	Anderson, Walker, Garnett	36	F	7:233
Morris, N. D.	Arrapahoe, Denver (Tailor)	28	M	11:351
Morris, Polly	Anderson, Walker, Garnett	58	F	7:233
Morris, W. NC	Cof., Neosho, Burlington (Farmer)	69	M	4:75
Morrison, J. NC	Arrapahoe, South Park	41	M	11:4
Morrow, A. NC	Coff., Neosho, Burlington (Farmer)	50	M	4:72
Morrow, D. NC	Don., Burr Oak, Whitehead (Farmer)	40	M	1:343
Morrow, Richard NC	Bourbon, Fort Scott P.O. (Farmer)	57	M	2:210
Morrow, Susan	Linn, Mound City	31	F	7:124
Morten, Joseph	Coffey, Leroy, Burlington (Farmer)	25	M	4:26
Morton, W. H.	Arrapahoe, South Park	26	M	11:248
Mosely, L.	" " "	35	M	11:121
Mosely, Mary	Coffey, Neosho, Burlington	31	F	4:69
Moser, Nancy A. E. NC	Breckenridge, Americus	27	F	4:217
Moshn, L. NC	Arrapahoe, South Park	30	M	11:6
Mosier, Sarah	Morris, Grove, Council Grove	30	F	4:263
Moss, W. NC	Arrapahoe, Lake Gulch (Miner)	23	M	11:522
Mott, Geo.	Arrapahoe, South Park	32	M	11:35
Motto, Wm.	" " "	35	M	11:181
Mount, Elizabeth	Jefferson, Oskaloosa	35	F	5:117
Mous, Sarah F.	Leavenworth, Alexandria, Easton	24	F	10:442
Moyer, Lydia	Bourbon, Xenia P.O. (Housewife)	55	F	2:140
Moyers, John	Leavenworth, Ward 2 (Farmer)	68	M	10:175
Muchman, Elizabeth	Greenwood, Eureka	16	F	9:177
Muchman, Mary	" " (Farmer)	44	F	9:177
Muchmon, George	" "	12	M	9:177
Muchmon, John	" "	4	M	9:177
Muchmon, Mary	" "	18	F	9:177
Muchmott, Nancy	" "	19	F	9:177
Muelux, Margaret	Woodson,Verdigris,Pleasant Gr. (F.W.)	30	F	9:163
Mullen, Nancy NC	Allen, Humboldt P.O.	25	F	2:283
Mullen, Susan	Lykins, Stanton	45	F	8:4
Mulliken, G. F.	Arrapahoe, South Park	37	M	11:256
Mullinix, N.	Johnson, Olathe (Farmer)	44	M	6:116
Mullis, A. J.	Doniphan, Center	9	F	1:274
Mullis, James	" "	6	M	1:274
Mullis, Samuel	" "	16	M	1:274
Mullis, Thomas	" "	10	M	1:274
Mullis, William	" " (Farmer)	38	M	1:274
Munger, C.	Arrapahoe, South Park	36	M	11:200
Munger, Jas.	" " "	31	M	11:200
Munsell, H. P.	" " "	39	M	11:132

Arapahoe: spelled incorrectly with 2 r's in census and in this index also.

Name	Kansas: County; Township; P.O. Arap. Co.: Census Div. Not Township	Age	Sex	Census V.	Census Pg.
Munson, G.	Arrapahoe, South Park	29	M	11:125	
Munson, N. S.	" " "	26	M	11:123	
Murden, WilliamSC	Coffey, Leroy, Burlington	61	M	4:24	
Murdock, Benton	Breckenridge, Forest Hill	18	M	4:172	
Murdock, Catherine	" " "	43	F	4:172	
Murdock, H. H.	Arrapahoe; Tarryall, South Park	19	M	11:610	
Murdock, JoshuaNC	Chase, Falls, Cottonwood Falls	14	M	4:330	
Murdock, Josiah NC	" " " "	7	M	4:330	
Murdock, Leora	Breckenridge, Forest Hill	20	F	4:172	
Murdock, Marshall	" " "	22	M	4:172	
Murdock, Roland	" " "	16	M	4:172	
Murdock, Samuel NC	Chase, Falls,Cot. Falls (Farming)	44	M	4:330	
Murdock, Susan NC	" " " "	43	F	4:330	
Murdock, W.	Potta., Vienna, Louisville (Farmer)	25	M	5:250	
Murdock, Wm. NC	Chase, Falls, Cottonwood Falls	12	M	4:330	
Murphy, A. B.	Arrapahoe, Central City (Miner)	43	M	11:574	
Murphy, B.	Franklin, Centropolis, Minneola	5	M	8:206	
Murphy, B. S.	" " " (Grocer)	32	M	8:202	
Murphy, Hannah	Atchison, Mt. Pleasant	5	F	1:150	
Murphy, Howard	Doniphan, Center, Troy	4	M	1:251	
Murphy, Jim	Arrap., Nevada Gulch (Quartz Miller)	31	M	11:505	
Murphy, M.	Johnson, Monticello	41	F	6:81	
Murphy, Margaret	Atchison, Mt. Pleasant	7	F	1:150	
Murphy, Mary	Dickinson, Kansas P.O.	46	F	4:306	
Murphy, N. M.	Johnson, Monticello (Farmer)	40	M	6:81	
Murphy, Rebecca	Doniphan, Center, Troy	31	F	1:251	
Murphy, Thomas	Dickinson, Kansas Falls P.O.(Farmer)	50	M	4:306	
Murphy, V. D.	Frank.,Centro.,Minneola (Brick Layer)	35	M	8:206	
Murry, Emmilla	Linn, Paris	60	F	7:149	
Murry, Samuel	Mar.,Marion,Cotton.Falls (Shoemaker)	50	M	4:362	
Musgrave, G.	Arrapahoe, Valley of the Platte	25	M	11:863	
Muzum, G. R.	Doniphan, Iowa Point (Doctor)	30	M	1:430	
Myckoff, Charlott	Pottawatomie, Vienna, Louisville	14	F	5:247	
Myckoff, Chas.	" " "	12	M	5:247	
Myckoff, G.	" " " (Farmer)	18	M	5:247	
Myckoff, N.	" " " (Farmer)	73	M	5:247	
Myckoff, S.	" " "	27	F	5:247	
Myckoff, W.	" " " (Farmer)	30	M	5:247	
Myers, Albert	Arrapahoe, South Park	33	M	11:69	
Myers, FrankNC	Brown, Walnut Creek, Hamlin	28	M	3:32	
Myers, George	Leavenworth, Kickapoo (Farmer)	35	M	10:413	
Myers, John L.	Breck., Agnes City (Wagon Maker)	30	M	4:149	
Myers, S.	Doniphan, Marion, Palermo	37	F	1:281	
Myers, L. S.	Arrapahoe, South Park	20	M	11:21	
Myers, SarahNC	Leavenworth, Delaware	73	F	10:431	
Myers, Samuel NC	Brown, Walnut Creek, Hamlin	26	M	3:32	
Myres, George	Wash., Wash., Marysville (Farmer)	58	M	3:264	
Myres, J. H.	Coffey, Leroy (Physician)	32	M	4:30	
Myres, Sarah	Washington, Washington, Marysville	47	F	3:264	
Myrick, E. F.	Arrapahoe, South Clear Creek	31	M	11:699	
Myrick, H.	Johnson, Gardner (Farmer)	39	M	6:15	
Myrick, S. B.	Johnson, Olathe (Clerk)	25	M	6:7	
Myrick, WilliamNC	Bourbon, Mapleton P.O. (Farmer)	59	M	2:138	
Nall, J.NC	Johnson, Shawnee (Farmer)	27	M	6:91	
Nall, T.NC	" " (Farmer)	33	M	6:91	
Nard, Washington	Leavenworth, 1st Ward (Cook)	30	BM	10:136	
Nayler, Henry	Atchison, Center, Pardee (Farmer)	55	M	1:128	
Neal, K.	Franklin, Centropolis, Minneola	65	F	8:203	
Nealy, J. A.	Arrapahoe, Valley of the Platte	24	M	11:819	
Nede, M.NC	Doniphan, Burr Oak, Whitehead	30	F	1:343	
Negley, A.	Arrapahoe, South Park (Miner)	26	M	11:60	

Arapahoe: spelled incorrectly with 2 r's in census and in this index also.

Name	Kansas: County; Township; P.O. Arap. Co.: Census Div. Not Township	Age	Sex	Census V. Pg.
Nellis,	Arrapahoe, South Park	29	M	11:171
Nelson, J. M.	Johnson, Shawnee (Farmer)	29	M	6:92
Nese, C.	Doniphan, Wayne, Doniphan	50	F	1:393
Nese, S.	" " " (Farmer)	55	M	1:393
Nese, Wm.	" " " (Laborer)	25	M	1:393
Newell, Amos	Arrapahoe, South Park	27	M	11:137
Newell, Elizabeth	Linn, Paris	38	F	7:146
Newland, D.	Frank., Peoria, Peoria City (Farmer)	22	M	8:275
Newland, Jane	Leavenworth, Ward 3	38	F	10:221
Newland, Mary	" " "	15	F	10:228
Newlon, Anna NC	Breckenridge, Emporia (Farmer)	36	F	4:204
Newlon, Jacob J NC	" "	12	M	4:204
Newlon, James A. NC	" "	21	M	4:204
Newlon, Margaret	" "	38	F	4:196
Newlon, Mary E. NC	" "	15	F	4:204
Newman, Eliza	Jefferson, Ozawkie	16	F	5:103
Newman, Emily	" "	14	F	5:103
Newman, Hermon	" " (Farm Laborer)	21	M	5:103
Newman, J. T.	Arrap.;Tarryall,S.P.; Oregon Gulch	31	M	11:598
Newman, James	Coffey, Avon, Burlington (Farmer)	54	M	4:12
Newman, W. A.	Leav., Ft. Leav. P.O. (Clerk Q.M.D.)	44	M	10:317
Newman, Nancy	Jefferson, Ozawkie	17	F	5:103
Newman, Sarah	" "	48	F	5:103
Newman, Vincent	" " (Farmer)	52	M	5:103
Newton, Mary NC	Nemaha, Richmond, Seneca	33	F	3:101
Newton, Olive	Linn, Valley, Blooming Grove	5/12	M	7:48
Newton, Phineas	Atch., Kapioma, Muscotah (Farmer)	55	M	1:97
Newton, Thomas	Nemaha, Richmond, Seneca (Farmer)	64	M	3:101
Nichols, James L.	Leav., Ward 2 (Milling Business)	29	M	10:195
Nichols, Joseph	Jeff.,Grasshopper Falls (Millwright)	65	M	5:16
Nichols, T. C.	Arrapahoe, South Park	30	M	11:117
Nicholson, A. S.	" " "	27	M	11:122
Nicholson, G.	" " "	24	M	11:113
Nicholson, W.	Arrapahoe, Mountain City (Miner)	28	M	11:465
Nicholls, S. F.	Arrap., Quartz Valley (Quartz Mill)	45	M	11:494
Nickson, Israel	Allen, Iola P.O. (Farmer)	25	M	2:259
Nickson, Jemomilla	" " " (Farmer)	22	M	2:259
Nightengale, S.	Franklin, Ohio, Ohio City	5	F	8:226
Nightengale, W.	" " " "	6	M	8:226
Nilligan, Ellen	McGee, Brushville P.O. (Servant)	16	F	9:222
Niron, Martha NC	Douglas, Lawrence	33	F	6:224
Nixon, D. B. NC	Arrapahoe, Quartz Valley (Miner)	23	M	11:500
Noble, John D.	Shawnee, Soldier, Indianola (Farmer)	47	M	9:83
Nodine, Francis N.	McGee, Crawford Seminary P.O.(Farmer)	40	M	9:223
Noell, A. G.[1]	Coffey, Neosho, Burlington (Farmer)	30	M	4:75
Noell, Elisabeth[1]	Leavenworth, Ward 4	29	F	10:247
Noell, F. A.[1]	Coffey, Neosho, Burlington	30	M	4:75
Noell, John[1]	" " "	6	M	4:76
Noell, Julius H.[1]	" " " (Farmer)	32	M	4:75
Noell, Kaleb[1]	" " " (Farmer)	21	M	4:75
Noell, W. E.[1]	" " "	8	M	4:75
Noland, M. NC	Johnson, Monticello (Laborer)	28	M	6:81
Nolen, Frances NC	Atchison, Kapioma, Muscotah	51	M	1:96
Noll, Ariel NC	Bourbon, Mapleton P.O. (Farmer)	32	M	2:144
Noll, Malvina E. NC	" " " (Housewife)	30	F	2:144
Norman, Benj.	Brown, Claytonville, Robinson	20	M	3:40
Norman, John	" " "(Carpenter)	21	M	3:40
Norman, N. A.	" " "	47	F	3:40

[1]Spelled Noel in W.P.A. Index, but written Noell in Census records.
Arapahoe: spelled incorrectly with 2 r's in census and in this index also.

Name	Kansas: County; Township; P.O. Arap. Co.: Census Div. Not Township	age	Sex	Census V. Pg.
Norman, Theron	Brown, Claytonville, Robinson(Farmer)	52	M	3:40
North, E. C.	Arrapahoe, South Park	27	M	11:236
North, R. F.	Arrapahoe, South Park	20	M	11:132
Noudoyn, S.	Godfrey, Godfrey (Farmer)	38	M	9:185
Noudoyn, Susan	" "	35	F	9:185
Nounon, J. H.	Johnson, Shawnee (Lawyer)	26	M	6:31
Nown, J. F.	Leavenworth, Ward 1 (Clerk)	23	M	10:107
Noys, H.H.	Arrapahoe, South Park (Miner)	22	M	11:63
Nuckler, David	Leavenworth, Delaware (Farmer)	68	M	10:424
Nuckler, Easter NC	" "	58	F	10:424
Nudoyn, Elmira	Godfrey, Godfrey	38	F	9:185
Nudoyn, I.	" " (Farmer)	40	M	9:185
Nunch, Wm. F.	Leavenworth, 1st Ward (Clerk)	22	M	10:137
Nunger, Kate	Shawnee, Topeka	11	F	9:17
Nute, J.	Arrapahoe, South Park	28	M	11:234
Oathout, J.	" " "	22	M	11:156
Obrien, Wm.	" " "	28	M	11:150
Odem, W. W. SC	Arrapahoe, Russell Gulch	4	M	11:517
Oelrich, L. B.	Arrapahoe, South Park	32	M	11:219
Offrett, Wm.	Doniphan, White Cloud (Brick Mason)	26	M	1:439
Oglesby, Henry	Arrapahoe, South Park	34	M	11:128
Oglethorpe, L. L. NC	" " " (Miner)	30	M	11:15
O'Hara, Jennett	Bourbon, Marmaton P.O. (Weaver)	50	F	2:204
Olcott, A. J. NC	Arrapahoe, South Park	25	M	11:121
Older, C.	And., Washington, Garnett (Farmer)	48	M	7:255
Older, Mary	" " "	28	F	7:255
Oldham, F. SC	Douglas, Marion, Lawrence	66	F	6:403
Oliphant, Christiana	Leavenworth, Easton (Farmeress)	52	F	10:289
Oliver, Francis NC	Woodson, Liberty, Leroy (Farmer)	56	M	9:144
Oliver, John	Breckenridge, Emporia (Farmer)	54	M	4:189
Oliver, W.	Arrapahoe, South Park	38	M	11:9
Olney, E.	Johnson, Aubrey	26	F	6:38
O'Neil, D.	Douglas, Lecompton	6	M	6:355
O'Neil, J.	Arrapahoe, South Park	26	M	11:228
O'Neil, J.	Douglas, Lecompton	5	M	6:355
O'Neil, V.	" "	9	F	6:355
Oney, Eliza	Anderson, Washington, Garnett	37	F	7:254
Oney, James	" " "(Farmer)	51	M	7:254
Openchain, Bartlet	Marshall, Blue Rapids, Irving	33	M	3:210
Orcutt, A. C.	Arrapahoe, Denver (Trader)	25	M	11:413
Orcutt, D. B.	" " (Trader)	36	M	11:413
Orn, W.	Linn, Centerville, Keokuk(Shoemaker)	57	M	7:87
Orndorf, Joseph	Jeff.,Jeff.,Crooked Cr. (Farm Laborer)	30	M	5:26
Orndorf, Mandy	" " " "	25	F	5:26
Orr, Patrick R.	Leavenworth, Easton (Farmer)	52	M	10:304
Osborn, J. NC	Linn, Mound City (Farmer)	55	M	7:127
Osborne, Mathew SC	Anderson, Walker, Garnett (Farmer)	30	M	7:246
Osburn, H. P.	Woodson, Pleasant Grove (Farmer)	45	M	9:169
Osburn, Martha	Wood.,Greenfield,Pleasant Gr. (F.W.)	33	F	9:171
Osburn, Willie	Bourbon, Fort Scott P.O.	6	M	2:218
Oswalt, Mary	Jefferson, Grasshopper Falls	33	F	5:16
Otey, C. W.	Douglas, Lecompton (Clerk USDC)	29	M	6:350
Ott, M. T.	Johnson, Gardner	19	F	6:52
Ottmyer, J. P.	Arrapahoe, South Park	26	M	11:120
Overley, Sarah NC	Coffey, Neosho, Burlington	44	F	4:72
Overstolz, H.	Arrapahoe, South Park	22	M	11:108
Oviatt, O. G.	Arrap., Mountain City (Quartz Miller)	35	M	11:462
Ovoerk, J.	Johnson, Monticello (Carpenter)	30	M	6:80
Owen, Risden NC	Bourbon, Fort Scott P.O. (Farmer)	50	M	2:193
Owens, A.	John.; Oxf.; N.Santa Fe,Mo. (Farmer)	32	M	6:104
Owens, C.	" " " " " "	20	F	6:104

Arapahoe: spelled incorrectly with 2 r's in census and in this index also.

Name	Kansas: County; Township; P.O. Arap. Co.: Census Div. Not Township	Age	Sex	Census V Pg
Owens, Elisabeth G.	Leavenworth, Easton	32	F	10:284
Owens, H.	Johnson; Oxford; New Santa Fe, Mo.	6	M	6:104
Owens, J. A. SC	Atchison, Ward 3 (Physician)	25	M	1:56
Owens, S. SC	Johnson, Monticello	27	F	6:83
Owens, W NC	Johnson; Oxford, New Santa Fe, Mo.	24	F	6:104
Oxford, B. NC	Arrapahoe, South Park	18	M	11:61
Ozster, Phebe M.	Shawnee, Topeka (Seamstress)	30	F	9:6
Packard, N.	Arrapahoe, Mountain City	26	M	11:467
Page, Henry C. NC	Arrapahoe, South Park (Miner)	34	M	11:14
Page, James	Brown, Claytonv., Robinson (Farmer)	74	M	3:56
Page, James	Brown, Claytonville (Farmer)	43	M	3:55
Pagett, Rebecca	Douglas, Palmyra, Prairie City	30	F	6:297
Pain, M.	Doniphan, Center, Troy	51	F	1:261
Paine, Wm. NC	Doug., Lecompton, Big Sp. (Laborer)	32	M	6:366
Palfrey, C.	Arrapahoe, Valley of the Pl. (Miner)	34	M	11:774
Palmer, Charles	Don., Washington, Wathena (Farmer)	23	M	1:326
Palmer, E.	" " "	20	F	1:326
Palmer, J. H.	" " " (Farmer)	17	M	1:326
Palmer, J. M.	" " " (Farmer)	53	M	1:326
Palmer, Jesse	Arrapahoe, Denver (Miner)	33	M	11:398
Palmer, P. C.	Doniphan, Washington, Wathena	48	F	1:326
Palmer, R.	Douglas, Lecompton	15	M	6:354
Palmer, Robert	Leavenworth, Kickapoo	16	M	10:310
Pamplin, R.	Linn, Paris (Farmer)	60	M	7:129
Par, Alexander	Mars.,B. Rapids, Irving(Farm Laborer)	24	M	3:208
Pardee, C.	Frank.;Potta.;Walker,And.Co.(Farmer)	39	M	8:241
Parish, I. (or J.?)[1]	Johnson, Monticello (Farmer)	38	M	6:82
Parkens, Margaret	Linn, Valley, Blooming Grove	49	F	7:38
Parkens, Robertson	" " " "	15	M	7:38
Parker, C. NC	Doniphan, Iowa Point (Farmer)	31	M	1:435
Parker, C. S. NC	Brown, Irving, White Cloud (Farmer)	30	M	3:2
Parker, D.	Mor.,Clarks Cr.,Council Gr.(Farming)	35	M	4:280
Parker, D. A. [2],NC?	Douglas, Kanwaca, Lawrence	5	F	6:374
Parker, Elizabeth [2],NC?	" " "	30	F	6:374
Parker, Franklin	Mor., Clarks Cr.,Council Gr.(Farming)	19	M	4:280
Parker, Gains NC	Mars.,B.Rapids, Marysville (Farmer)	28	M	3:207
Parker, Jane	Morris, Clarks Creek, Council Grove	4	F	4:280
Parker, John [2],NC?	Douglas, Kanwaca, Lawrence	7	M	6:374
Parker, Martha NC	Doniphan, Iowa Point	50	F	1:432
Parker, Matilda	Morris, Clarks Creek, Council Grove	56	F	4:280
Parker, Patience NC	Allen, Humboldt P.O.	84	F	2:277
Parker, Rachel	Morris, Clarks Creek, Council Grove	22	F	4:280
Parker, S. NC	Doniphan, Iowa Point (Farmer)	24	M	1:432
Parker, Sarah NC	Breckenridge, Emporia	32	F	4:187
Parker, Shalet	Atchison, Ward 3	58	BF	1:32
Parker, Sop. NC	Doniphan, Iowa Point	20	F	1:432
Parker, T. W. J.	Don., Wayne, Doniphan (Farm Hand)	22	M	1:365
Parker, Thos.	Arrapahoe, South Park	35	M	11:126
Parker, W. R. NC	Doniphan, Iowa Point (Farmer)	59	M	1:432
Parker, Wm. NC	" " " (Farmer)	25	M	1:432
Parker, Wm.	Mor., Clarks Cr., Council Gr.(Farmer)	25	M	4:280
Parkinson, E. E.	Franklin, Centropolis, Minneola	8	M	8:211
Parkinson, J. E.	" " "	4	M	8:212
Parkinson, L.	" " "	9	F	8:211
Parkinson, M. E.	" " "	5	M	8:212
Parks, Frank SC	Atchison, Ward 3 (Boss Plasterer)	24	M	1:44
Parks, James NC	McGee, Osage Mission P.O. (Farmer)	45	M	9:234
Parks, Robert NC	Jackson, Douglas, Holton (Farmer)	42	M	5:173
Parks, S. A.	Franklin, Centropolis, Minneola	3	F	8:205

[1]See Isack Parrish, Dist. 17, p. 2, 1855 Census, age 30, emigrated from
  Missouri.

[2]W.P.A. indexer gave state of birth as N. C.?

  Arapahoe: spelled incorrectly with 2 r's in census and in this index also.

Name	Kansas: County; Township; P.O. Arap. Co.: Census Div. Not Township	Age	Sex	Census V. Pg.
Parks, William NC	McGee, Osage Mission P.O.	21	M	9:234
Parlin, Rich'd.	Arrapahoe, Valley of the Platte(Miner)	27	M	11:858
Parr, Alexander	Wash.,Mill Cr.,Marysv. (Farm Laborer)	26	M	3:267
Parrott, J. SC	Don., Wayne, Doniphan (Farm Hand)	25	M	1:369
Parrott, John SC	" " " (Farm Hand)	24	M	1:364
Parsely, Wm.	Jackson, Douglas, Holton (Farmer)	42	M	5:173
Parsons, James	Douglas, Wakarusa, Lawrence (Farmer)	61	M	6:255
Parsons, John NC	And., Town of Garnett (Blacksmith)	40	M	7:222
Parsons, Julias NC	" " " "	8	M	7:222
Parsons, M. S.	Arrapahoe, Valley of the Platte	26	M	11:833
Parsons, S. NC	Anderson, Town of Garnett	30	F	7:222
Parsons, William NC	" " " "	7	M	7:222
Pascal, Mary	Anderson, Washington, Garnett	24	F	7:255
Pate, Anderson	Atch.,Grasshopper, Kennekuk (Farmer)	49	M	1:92
Pate, Susan	" " "	72	F	1:91
Patrick, H.	Arrapahoe, South Clear Creek	28	M	11:750
Patrick, Harry G.	Bourbon, Dayton P.O. (Farmer)	40	M	2:147
Patrick, L.? A.	" " " (Housewife)	38	F	2:147
Patrick, Samuel J.	" " "	16	M	2:147
Patrick, William H.	" " "	18	M	2:147
Patten, Euphamia	McGee, Brushville P.O.	52	F	9:227
Patterson, A.	Arrapahoe, South Park (Miner)	39	M	11:26
Patterson, Alexander	Bourbon, Barnesville P.O. (Farmer)	56	M	2:179
Patterson, Anna R. J. NC	Bourbon, Dayton P.O. (Housewife)	19	F	2:156
Patterson, David S.D. NC	" " " (Farmer)	32	M	2:156
Patterson, W. C.	Arrapahoe, South Park	38	M	11:125
Pattison, R. C.	" " "	38	M	11:172
Pattneu, Harriet	Leavenworth, Ward 4	40	F	10:245
Pattneu, N. D.	" " " (Farmer)	38	M	10:245
Pattneu, Susan E.	" " "	16	F	10:245
Patton, J. H.	Nemaha, Clear Cr., Ash Pt. (Farmer)	38	M	3:90
Patton, W. S. T.	Arrapahoe, Denver	32	M	11:351
Paulk, Jane	Bourbon, Fort Scott P.O.(Housewife)	65	F	2:76
Paxton, J. D.	Doniphan, Highland (Minister-O.S.P.)	75	M	1:415
Payne, B.	Allen, Elizabeth Town P.O. (Farmer)	27	M	2:240
Payne, G.	Riley, Ogden P.O.	3	M	9:292
Payne, Henry T.	Breckenridge, Forest Hill (Farmer)	46?	M	4:183
Payne, James	Allen, Xenia P.O. (Farmer)	34	M	2:229
Payson, N.	Arrapahoe, South Park	30	M	11:124
Payton, R. G.	" " "	28	M	11:115
Peach, Jno. P.	" " "	22	M	11:43
Peacock, Elizabeth	Leavenworth, Alexandria, Easton	53	F	10:448
Peacock, Wm. S.	" " " " (Farmer)	53	M	10:448
Peading?, E.?	Arrapahoe, Denver	20	M	11:349
Pearson, E. NC	Doniphan, Iowa Point	37	F	1:434
Pearson, E. NC	" " "	10	M	1:434
Pearson, James NC	" " "	9	M	1:434
Pearson, Lucinda 1,NC	" " "	15	F	1:434
Pearson, Wm. NC	" " "	7	M	1:434
Peason, T. M.	Douglas, Kanwaca, Lawrence (Farmer)	42?	M	6:378
Peddle, A. C.	Arrapahoe, Denver (Trader)	33	M	11:367
Pedigo, M. A. NC	Doniphan, Washington, Elwood	37	F	1:331
Peege, J. A. NC	Coffey, Neosho, Burlington (Farmer)	67	M	4:70
Peer, A.	Douglas, Wakarusa, Lawrence	14	F	6:258
Pegg, M. A.	Arrapahoe, South Park	29	M	11:126
Pelear, A. NC	Douglas, Palmyra, Lawrence	38	F	6:268
Pemberton, R.	Leavenworth, Ward 4 (Carpenter)	67	M	10:270
Pendery, L.	Arrapahoe, South Park	26	M	11:226

1Original entry looks like Ludenia rather than Lucinda
  Arapahoe: spelled incorrectly with 2 r's in census and in this index also.

Name	Kansas: County; Township; P.O. Arap. Co.: Census Div. Not Township	Age	Sex	Census V.	Pg.
Pendleton, C.	Morris, Neosho, Council Grove	13	M	4:274	
Pendleton, Enoch	" " "	14	M	4:274	
Pennell, A.NC	Doniphan, Wolf River, Walnut Grove	18	BM	1:407	
Pennell, C.NC	" " " " "(Farmer)	27	BM	1:407	
Pennell, Chas.NC	" " " " "	16	BM	1:407	
Pennell, J. N.NC	" " " " "(Farmer)	24	BM	1:407	
Pennell, N.NC	" " " " "(Farmer)	46	BF	1:407	
Pennell, N. A.NC	" " " " "	20	BF	1:407	
Pennell, S.NC	" " " " "	24	BF	1:407	
Penturf, J.	Wood.,Verdigris,Pleasant Gr. (Farmer)	36	M	9:163	
Peoria, Mary J.	Lykins, Paola	17	F	8:39	
Percell, S.	Douglas, Kanwaca, Lawrence	29	M	6:376	
Perence, J.	Johnson, Aubrey (Farmer)	24	M	6:36	
Perkins, Albertha	Nemaha, Rock Creek, Albany	36	F	3:75	
Perkins, G. W.	Arrapahoe, Denver (Lawyer)	41	M	11:323	
Perkins, J.	Frank.,Centropolis,Minneola (Farmer)	18	M	8:215	
Perkins, M.	" " "	8	F	8:215	
Perkins, M. C.	" " "	12	M	8:215	
Perkins, Nancy	Marshall, Vermillion, Barrett Mills	38	F	3:234	
Perkins, R.	Franklin, Centropolis, Minneola	52	F	8:215	
Perkins, S.	" " "	14	M	8:215	
Perrill, J.	Osage, Ridgeway, Burlingame (Farmer)	54	M	8:336	
Perringer, Henry	Anderson, Walker, Garnett	23	M	7:246	
Perringer, John	" " " (Farmer)	33	M	7:246	
Perry, Sarah C.	Bourbon, Rockford P.O. (Housewife)	22	F	2:100	
Peterson, Daniel	Hunter, Eldorado, Chelsea(Blacksmith)	40	M	4:359	
Petticrew, James	Bourbon, Fort Scott P.O.	69		2:155	
Petts, Mary	Breckenridge, Forest Hill (Farmer)	56	F	4:182	
Peugh, M. M.NC	Lykins, Paola (Methodist Clergyman)	28	M	8:25	
Peyton, Dennis	Chase, Toledo (Farmer)	64	M	4:336	
Peyton, Homer	Arrapahoe, South Park	41	M	11:222	
Peyton, Jackson	Chase, Toledo	21	M	4:336	
Peyton, Louis	" " (House Carpenter)	35	M	4:336	
Peyton, Manda	" "	23	F	4:336	
Peyton, Martha	" "	19	F	4:336	
Peyton, Phillip	" " (Farmer)	26	M	4:336	
Peyton, Richard	Leavenworth, Ward 3 (Butcher)	29	M	10:198	
Peyton, Silas	Chase, Toledo	13	M	4:336	
Peyton, Thomas	" " (Farmer)	24	M	4:336	
Phenis, SabrahNC	Breckenridge, Pike, Plymouth	33	F	4:208	
Philips, I. W.	Arrapahoe, Denver (Confectionary)	24	M	11:347	
Philips, JoebNC	Jefferson, Ozawkie (Farm Laborer)	49	M	5:110	
Philips, JoelNC	Jefferson, Oskaloosa (Laborer)	49	M	5:133	
Phillips, Amos SC	Arrapahoe, Golden City (Miner)	36	M	11:448	
Phillips, Jas. A.NC	Lykins, Paola (Attorney)	24	M	8:29	
Phillips, M. M.NC	Woodson, Belmont	36	M	9:152	
Phillpot, Jno.SC	Arrapahoe, Golden City (Lawyer)	40	M	11:448	
Platt, Elizabeth	Brown, Locknow, Powhattan	35	F	3:67	
Picket, Alson G.NC	Breck., Pike, Plymouth (Farmer)	27	M	4:209	
Picket, Amos NC	" " " (F. Laborer)	28	M	4:214	
Picket, CynthiaNC	" " "	27	F	4:209	
Picket, John C.NC	" Emporia (Carpenter)	29	M	4:202	
Picket, PhebeNC	" "	60	F	4:202	
Pierce, Alex K.	Atchison, Center, Pardee (Farmer)	17	M	1:136	
Pierce, Casper	" " " (Farmer)	20	M	1:136	
Pierce, J. M.	" " "	46	M	1:137	
Pierce, JonathanNC	Breckenridge, Emporia (Farmer)	51	M	4:186	
Pierce, M. A.	Riley, Fort Riley P.O.	32	F	9:302	
Pierce, Martha Ann	Atchison, Center, Pardee	12	F	1:137	
Pierce, Sarah E.	" " "	14	F	1:137	
Pierce, W.NC	Douglas, Willow Springs (Farmer)	21	M	6:329	

Arapahoe: spelled incorrectly with 2 r's in census and in this index also.

Name	Kansas: County; Township; P.O. Arap. Co.: Census Div. Not Township	Age	Sex	Census V.: Pg.
Pierck, Andrew J.	McGee, Brushville P.O. (Farmer)	29	M	9:222
Pierson, F.	Arrapahoe, South Park	33	M	11:199
Pierson, John	Bourbon, Fort Scott P.O. (Farmer)	48	M	2:76
Piggott, William[NC]	Lyk.,Miami, New Lancaster (Farmer)	35	M	8:91
Pilcher, Isaac	Allen, Humboldt P.O. (Landlord)	56	M	2:292
Pile, E. A.[NC]	Johnson, McCamish, Hibbard	33	F	6:68
Piles, James S.	Atchison, Walnut, Sumner (Farmer)	32	M	1:172
Piles, Jim	Doniphan, White Cloud (Servant)	6	BM	1:438
Piles, Sarah	" " " (Servant)	24	BF	1:438
Pinkhard, Elias	Breckenridge, Forest Hill (Farmer)	48	M	4:182
Pirrcell, J. W.	Don., Wash., Wathena (Carpenter)	29	M	1:305
Pitman, J. S.[NC]	Arrapahoe, South Park	28	M	11:185
Pitman, William	Lykins, Osage, Osawatomie (Farmer)	49	M	8:77
Pitts, John[NC]	Jefferson, Oskaloosa (Farmer)	51	M	5:129
Pixley, P.[NG]	Arrapahoe, South Park	20	M	11:24
Plattenburg, Terry W.	Atchison, Ward 3 (Lumberman)	22	M	1:53
Plattenburg, P. D.	" " " (Teacher)	27	M	1:53
Pledget, T.[NC]	Linn, Mound City (Farmer)	50	M	7:119
Plotner, John H.	Atchison, Walnut, Sumner (Farmer)	34	M	1:175
Plum, A.?	Doniphan, Wayne, Doniphan (Farmer)	5	F	1:369
Plum, Aaron	" " " (Farmer)	41	M	1:369
Plum, Amanda	" " "	7	F	1:369
Plum, Caroline	" " "	1	F	1:369
Plum, Ellis	" " "	15	M	1:369
Plum, M.	" " "	10	F	1:369
Plum, M. E.	" " "	13	F	1:369
Plum, S.	" " "	39	F	1:369
Plum, S. P.?	" " "	2	M	1:369
Plum, W. J.	" " "	8	M	1:369
Plumer, John[NC]	Douglas, Marion, Lawrence (Farmer)	54	M	6:398
Plummer, A. J.	Arrapahoe, South Park	27	M	11:185
Plumnis, J. R.	Doniphan, Center, Troy (Farmer)	41	M	1:268
Plyley, James	Shaw., Soldier, Indiano.(Farm Laborer)	20	M	9:90
Plyley, Jane	" " " 40 or 48		F	9:90
Plyley, Josiah	" " " (Farm Laborer)	18	M	9:90
Plyley, Robt.	" " " (Farm Laborer)	24	M	9:90
Plyley, Samuel	" " " (Farm Laborer)	22	M	9:90
Poe, A. E.	Franklin, Ottawa, Hickory Creek	44	F	8:263
Poe, S. J.	Johnson, Union, Hibbard	10	F	6:13
Points, T. A.	Pottawatomie, Vienna, Louisville	48	F	5:253
Polly, J. H.	Arrapahoe, Nevada Gulch (Miner)	34	M	11:536
Pool, Benj.[NC]	Breckenridge, Forest Hill (Farmer)	73	M	4:183
Pool, R. B.	Arrapahoe, South Park	28	M	11:155
Pope, Lucy	Wyandotte, Quindaro	50	BF	10:50
Pope, Wiley[NC]	" " (Farmer)	60		10:50
Porsley, Wm. R.	Lykins, Osage, Osawatomie (Farmer)	49	M	8:78
Port, Arno	Linn, Potosi (Farmer)	51	M	7:77
Porter, A.[NC]	Arrapahoe, South Park	25	M	11:136
Porter, Francis	McGee, Crawford Seminary P.O.	42	F	9:225
Post, Armelia	Butler, Chelsea	22	F	4:342
Post, M. W.	Allen, Iola P.O. (Farmer)	27	M	2:262
Poston, Wm. A.	Doug., Willow Sp., McKinney (Farmer)	54	M	6:311
Poteet, Thomas	Atchison, Mt. Pleasant (Farmer)	61	BM	1:160
Potite, S.	Doniphan, Iowa Point (Farmer)	56	M	1:455
Potite, W.	Arrapahoe, Valley of the Platte	26	M	11:821
Potter, Lucy[NC]	Wyandotte, Wyandotte	40	F	10:40
Poulston, W. H.	Johnson, Shawnee (Laborer)	20	M	6:88
Powell, Alexander	Wyandotte, Wyandotte	10	M	10:39
Powell, Charity	" "	15	F	10:39
Powell, E.	Arrapahoe, California Gulch	37	M	11:282
Powell, Ellen	Wyandotte, Wyandotte	8	F	10:39

Arapahoe: spelled incorrectly with 2 r's in census and in this index also.

Name	Kansas: County; Township; P.O. Arap. Co.: Census Div. Not Township	Age	Sex	Census V. Pg.
Powell, Hannah	Leavenworth, Alexandria, Easton	38	F	10:456
Powell, J. S.(T.?S.)NC	Arrapahoe, California Gulch (Miner)	32	M	11:269
Powell, James	Wyandotte, Wyandotte	18	M	10:39
Powell, James H.	Leavenworth, Alexandria, Easton	15	M	10:456
Powell, Mary	Wyandotte, Wyandotte	48	F	10:39
Powell, Mary H.	Leavenworth, Alexandria, Easton	13	F	10:456
Powell, Richard	Wyandotte, Wyandotte	16	M	10:39
Powers, M.	Franklin, Centropolis, Minneola	2	M	8:210
Powers, Mary	Breckenridge, Fremont	24	F	4:166
Pragne, Mary C.NC	Allen, Humboldt P.O.	38	F	2:280
Prather, Albert	Douglas, Wakarusa, Lawrence	17	M	6:239
Prather, Elizabeth	" " "	21	F	6:239
Prather, Francis	" " "	18	F	6:239
Prather, L. A.	" " "	46	F	6:239
Prather, Mary	" " "	9	M	6:239
Prather, Nancy	" " "	17	F	6:239
Prather, Rachael	Greenwood, Eureka	20	F	9:178
Prathin, Francis SC	Leav., Stranger, Leavenworth City	74	F	10:476
Pratt, E.	Arrapahoe, South Park	35	M	11:193
Pratt, Geo.	" " " (Miner)	33	M	11:36
Pratt, J. O.	" " "	34	M	11:118
Preachet, DavidNC	Dickinson, Kansas Falls P.O.(Farmer)	34	M	4:307
Preachet, JamesNC	" " "! " (Farmer)	28	M	4:308
Preachet, MaryNC	" " " "	18	F	4:308
Prellican, Sarah	Leavenworth, Ward 1	62	F	10:114
Prentiss, Otis D.SC	Marshall, Marysville (Lawyer)	28	M	3:252
Prently, Isabella	Linn, Scott, Brooklyn	30	F	7:25
Prerost, ClaranceSC	Atchison, Ward 2 (Comm. Merc.)	24	M	1:33
Presnell, DanielNC	Atchison, Grasshopper, Kennekuk	3	M	1:89
Presnell, ElizahNC	" " " (Blacksmith)	28	M	1:89
Presnell, SarahNC	" " "	24	F	1:89
Prest, E.	Franklin, Peoria, Stanton	8	F	8:281
Prest, I.[2]	" " "	1	F	8:281
Prest, J.	" " "	4	M	8:281
Prest, M.	" " "	6	M	8:281
Prest, W.	" " "	10	M	8:281
Prest, W. H.	" " " (Landlord)	42	M	8:281
Prest, Wm.	" " "	5	M	8:281
Preston, W. E.	Arrapahoe, South Clear Creek	27	M	11:717
Price, H. R.	Arrapahoe, California Gulch (Miner)	27	M	11:291
Price, J. N.	Arrapahoe;Tarryall, South Park	23	M	11:609
Price, JosephNC	Anderson, Ozark, Garnett (Farmer)	46	M	7:249
Price, Martha B.NC	McGee, Osage Mission P.O.	36	F	9:236
Prichard, NelsonSC	Mad., Verdi., Madison Centre (Farmer)	40	M	4:246
Prichard, Rachael	Doniphan, Iowa Point	40	F	1:425
Priddy, Atha	Pottawatomie, St. George, Elden	36	F	5:267
Prince, C. P.	Arrapahoe, South Park	17	M	11:24
Prior, J.	Doniphan, Iowa Point	55	F	1:429
Pritchard, Charity[1],C	Atchison, Grasshopper, Kennekuk	26	F	1:90
Pritchard, Charles H. SC	Atchison, Ward 2 (Farmer)	18	M	1:33
Pritchard, ChristineSC	" " "	15	F	1:33
Pritchard, Ed. SC	" " " (Student Theology)	14	M	1:38
Pritchard, Edward C. SC	" " " (School Boy)	13	M	1:33
Pritchard, Louisa C. SC	" " "	50	F	1:33
Pritchett, E. SC	Lykins, Osawatomie	34	F	8:53
Privit, Wm. NC	Doniphan, Center, Troy (Farmer)	43	M	1:258
Proctor, A. C.	Arrapahoe, South Park	36	M	11:141
Proctor, D.	" " "	39	M	11:141

[1]Original census says "Carolina". [2]See p. 160: I. Prest, 38 F omitted.
Arapahoe: spelled incorrectly with 2 r's in census and in this index also.

Name	Kansas: County; Township; P.O. Arap. Co.: Census Div. Not Township	Age	Sex	Census V. Pg.
Proctor, Joseph NC	Shawnee, Topeka (Farmer)	72	M	9:21
Proctor, Lucy NC	" "	64	F	9:21
Proebustle, Matilda	Wyandotte, Wyandotte	31	F	10:39
Pronelfort, C.	Doniphan; Center, Lafayette; Troy	28	F	1:249
Pronelfort, Thos.	" " " "	6	M	1:249
Prosser, A.	Arrapahoe, South Park	37	M	11:183
Prouty, F.	" "	20	M	11:136
Prowl, Henry	Doniphan, Wolf River, Walnut Grove	6	M	1:409
Pruit, Mary A.	Leavenworth, Stranger, Leavenworth	19	F	10:460
Prum, Jno. D.	Arrapahoe;Tarryall,South Park (Miner)	25	M	11:601
Pry, C.	Doniphan, Wolf River, Walnut Grove	57	F	1:397
Pry, J.	" " " " "(Farmer)	68	M	1:397
Pry, John	" " " " "	20	M	1:397
Pry, S. E.	" " " " (Teacher)	24	F	1:397
Pry, T.	" " " " (Farm Hand)	19	M	1:397
Pry, Willet	" " " " (Farmer)	32	M	1:397
Pryor, R. B.	Arrapahoe, Golden City (Trader)	31	M	11:441
Puckett, N.	Douglas, Wakarusa, Lawrence	13	M	6:231
Puett, James NC	Anderson, Monroe, Garnett	12	M	7:215
Puett, John NC	" " " (Farmer)	21	M	7:214
Puett, Minerva NC	" " "	8	F	7:215
Puett, Nancy NC	" " "	16	F	7:214
Puett, Sarah NC	" " "	42	F	7:214
Puett, William NC	" " "	6	M	7:215
Puett, William NC	" " " (Farmer)	51	M	7:214
Puington, Jane NC	Douglas, Wakarusa, Lawrence	48	F	6:237
Pullman, Levi NC	Shawnee, Tecumseh (Farmer)	49	M	9:79
Purron, Alfred NC	Leav., Ft.Leavenworth P.O. (Waiter)	20	M	10:313
Putner, J. L. SC	Arrapahoe, South Park (Barber)	28	BM	11:8
Puycan, Samuel	Jackson, Holton	78	M	5:178
Pyde, Wm. NC	Jefferson, Oskaloosa (Farmer)	54	M	5:122
Quackenbush, Abrm.	Arrapahoe, South Clear Creek (Miner)	32	M	11:636
Quarles, Richard SC	Marshall, Marysville (Millwright)	25	M	3:255
Quiett, Hiram SC	Atchison, Center, Pardee	62	M	1:136
Quinett, S. F.	Arrapahoe, Quartz Valley (Saloon)	36	M	11:496
Race, Anna	Allen, Iola P.O. (Farmeress)	62	F	2:264
Radcliff, John	Marshall, Vermillion, Barrett Mills	5	M	3:228
Radcliff, John	" " " (Farmer)	32	M	3:228
Radcliff, Ugene	" " "	9	M	3:228
Rader, Chas.	Brown, Irving, Hiawatha	33	M	3:1
Rader, John	" " " (Farmer)	38	M	3:1
Rainwater, John NC	Breckenridge, Americus (Farmer)	53	M	4:225
Raley, E. W.	Arrapahoe, Denver (Merchant)	30	M	11:321
Ralph, C. M.	Arrapahoe, California Gulch (Miner)	29	M	11:280
Ralstan, Alex	Leavenworth, Kickapoo (Farmer)	30	M	10:323
Ralston, Martha E.	Leavenworth, Ward 4	26	F	10:276
Ralston, Mary E.	Leavenworth, Kickapoo	35	F	10:413
Ralston, Wilson	" " (Farmer)	35	M	10:413
Ramsey, J. F.	Arrapahoe, Valley of the Platte	29		11:783
Ramy, Frances	Allen, Iola P.O. (Servant)	80	F	2:271
Randal, C.	Franklin, Ohio, Sac and Fox Agency	10	F	8:224
Randal, E.	" " " " " "	8	F	8:224
Randal, H.	" " " " " "	11	M	8:224
Randall, D.	Arrapahoe, Denver (Doctor)	47	M	11:338
Randolph, E.	Johnson, Lexington	16	F	6:71
Randolph, G. NC	Riley, Randolph P.O. (Farmer)	64	M	9:299
Randolph, Sarah M.	Clay, Junction City P.O.	26	F	9:268
Randolph, Thos.	Arrapahoe, South Clear Creek (Miner)	25	M	11:756
Randolph, Wm.	" " "	21	M	11:669
Raney, Shanty NC	Leavenworth, Ward 3	35	BF	10:220

Omission: Pitter, W.; Arrapahoe, South Clear Creek; 38 M, 11:736
Arapahoe: spelled incorrectly with 2 r's in census and in this index also.

Name	Kansas: County; Township; P.O. Arap. Co.: Census Div. Not Township	Age	Sex	Census V.	Census Pg.
Ranis, Samuel	Marshall, Marysville (Master Mason)	30	M	3:254	
Rann, M. D.	Doniphan, Washington, Elwood	30	F	1:313	
Ransom, Elisabeth [SC]	Wyandotte, Wyandotte	54	F	10:37	
Ransom, John [NC]	" " (Farmer)	66	M	10:37	
Ransom, R. [NC]	Davis, Ft. Riley Res. (Lieut. USA)	32	M	9:358	
Rapp, Jas.	Arrapahoe, South Park (Miner)	27	M	11:27	
Ratcliff, J.	Johnson, Olathe (Farmer)	23	M	6:3	
Ratliff, E. [NC]	Davis, Ashland-Manhattan P.O.(Farmer)	50	M	9:353	
Ratliff, R.	Woodson, Eureka (Farmer)	48	M	9:181	
Ratliff, Sarah	Davis, Ashland-Manhattan P.O.	48	F	9:353	
Raught, Delia A. H.	Arrapahoe, Denver	22	F	11:324	
Ray, Andrew	Allen, Geneva P.O. (Farmer)	51	M	2:243	
Ray, John T.	Lykins,Richland,Marysville (Farmer)	32	M	8:21	
Ray, W.	Arrapahoe, Nevada Gulch (Merchant)	50	M	11:530	
Rayland, Anna	Anderson, Monroe, Garnett	50	F	7:218	
Raymond, N.	Arrapahoe, South Park	28	M	11:115	
Reans (Reams?), S.	Douglas, Palmyra, Prairie City	36	F	6:274	
Reap, Susana [NC]	Anderson, Monroe, Garnett	56	F	7:217	
Reaw, ? D. Miller	Arrapahoe, Denver (Law Student)	22	M	11:327	
Rebank, Wm.	Arrapahoe, South Park	29	M	11:249	
Rector, Jacob [NC]	Breckenridge, Forest Hill (Farmer)	50	M	4:175	
Rector, Martha [NC]	Atchison, Shannon, Atchison	58	F	1:75	
Redfenn, John [SC]	Lykins, Marysville, Lyons (Farmer)	63	M	8:131	
Redmond, Elvira	Leavenworth, Delaware	56	F	10:419	
Reece, A. M. [NC]	Atchison, Mt. Pleasant (Farmer)	47	M	1:155	
Reece, James M. [NC]	" " "	16	M	1:155	
Reece, Jennet [NC]	" " "	47	F	1:155	
Reece, Joel J. [NC]	" " "	17	M	1:155	
Reece, Mary K. [NC]	" " "	24	F	1:155	
Reece, Nancy J. [NC]	" " "	22	F	1:155	
Reece, Polly Ann [NC]	" " "	29	F	1:153	
Reece, Silas [NC]	" " " (Farmer)	37	M	1:153	
Reece, Sarah E. [NC]	" " "	19	F	1:155	
Reece, Wm. [NC]	Atchison, Grasshopper, Kennekuk	37	M	1:88	
Reece, Wm. D. [1,NC]	Atchison, Mt. Pleasant (Gold Seeker)	25	M	1:155	
Reed, A. J.	" " " (Farmer)	32	M	1:148	
Reed, C.	Franklin, Prairie, Stanton	58	F	8:282	
Reed, G. W.	" Peoria, " (Farmer)	49	M	8:279	
Reed, James	Douglas, Marion	44	M	6:395	
Reed, James	Lyk., Sugar Cr.,New Lancaster(Farmer)	24	M	8:98	
Reed, Jno. [NC]	Arrapahoe, Missouri City (Miner)	26	M	11:568	
Reed, Margarett	Lykins, Sugar Creek, New Lancaster	24	F	8:98	
Reed, N. C.	Franklin, Peoria, Peoria City	37	F	8:270	
Reed, R. R.	Franklin, Prairie, Stanton (Farmer)	56	M	8:282	
Reed, Simpson [NC]	Arrap., Spring Gulch (Miner)	40	M	11:539	
Reed, W. [SC]	Franklin, Ottawa, Hickory Creek	60	F	8:262	
Reed, W. [SC]	" " " " (Farmer)	57	M	8:262	
Reedy, Maria	Marshall, Blue Rapids	46	F	3:202	
Reehaid, A.	Linn, Valley, Blooming Gr. (Laborer)	20	M	7:38	
Rees, John	Don., Washington, Wathena (Farmer)	61	M	1:328	
Rees, R.	Don., Washington, Wathena	61	F	1:328	
Rees, Robt. [SC]	Arrapahoe, Golden City (Quartz Mill)	37	M	11:440	
Reese, Amos [2]	Leavenworth, Ward 2	66?	M	10:189	
Reese, R.	Arrapahoe, Nevada Gulch (Laborer)		M	11:502	
Reese, Rebecca [NC]	Breckenridge, Americus	66	F	4:217	
Reese, Robt. [SC]	Arrap.,Mt.Cy.,N.Cl.Cr. (Quartz Miller)	37	M	11:464	
Reese, Thomas	Breckenridge, Americus (Farmer)	80	M	4:217	
Reeser, Jacob [NC]	Atch., Grasshopper, Kennekuk (Farmer)	35	M	1:87	

[1]See A. C. Harrison, born in Virginia, "gold sacker" from Atchison.
[2]Nat. Archives Microfilm 1860 Census Kansas p. 101 (671), age clearly 60.

Arapahoe: spelled incorrectly with 2 r's in census and in this index also.

Name	Kansas: County; Township; P.O. Arap. Co.: Census Div. Not Township	Age	Sex	Census V. Pg.
Reeve, J. E.	Leavenworth, Ward 2 (Druggist)	19	F	10:156
Reeves, J. H.SC	Arrapahoe, Nevada Gulch (Miner)	22	M	11:533
Reezly, Solomon SC	Linn, Town of Paris (Merchant)	28	M	7:136
Register, Mathew A. NC	Leavenworth,Alexandria,Easton (Farmer)	28	M	10:447
Reice, Allen NC	Leavenworth, Ward 4 (Lawyer)	51	M	10:246
Reid, W. H.	Johnson, Lexington	6	M	6:74
Reniters, A.	Doniphan, Marion, Palermo (Teacher)	27	M	1:286
Renner, W. B.	Arrap.,Enterpr.Dist. (Quartz Miller)	22	M	11:492
Ressinger, Sarah	Douglas, Willow Springs	35	F	6:326
Reynolds, Adrian NC	Anderson, Washington, Garnett	18	M	7:253
Reynolds, E. A.	Arrapahoe, Quartz Valley (Miner)	36	M	11:496
Reynolds, Elizabeth NC	Anderson, Washington, Garnett	53	F	7:253
Reynolds, Ephraim NC	Chase, Falls, Cot.Falls (Farm Laborer)	32	M	4:330
Reynolds, Ephriam NC	Anderson, Washington, Garnett (Farmer)	30	M	7:253
Reynolds, Heber NC	" " " (Farmer)	30	M	7:251
Reynolds, James NC	" " " (Farmer)	27	M	7:253
Reynolds, Joseph B.	Atchison, Center, Pardee (M. D.)	50	M	1:132
Reynolds, Marcellus NC	Anderson, Washington, Garnett	16	M	7:253
Reynolds, Mary NC	" " "	30	F	7:251
Reynolds, Milford NC	" " "	11	M	7:253
Reynolds, Racheal NC	" " "	21	F	7:253
Reynolds, Rebecca NC	" " "	22	F	7:253
Reynolds, S. NC	Douglas, Clinton (Farmer)	31	M	6:409
Reynolds, S. E.	Franklin,Centropolis,Minneola	18	F	8:216
Reynolds, Spencer NC	Bourbon, Fort Scott P.O. (Farmer)	39	M	2:79
Reynolds, William NC	Anderson, Washington, Garnett	14	M	7:253
Reynolds, William NC	" " " (Farmer)	64	M	7:253
Rhodes, E.	Arrapahoe, South Clear Creek (Miner)	30	M	11:714
Rhodes, George	Douglas, Lawrence (Stage Driver)	28	M	6:208
Rhodes, H. G.	Arrapahoe, South Park	26	M	11:132
Rhotun, Elisha NC	Bourbon, Turkey Creek P.O. (Farmer)	59	M	2:113
Rhotun, Josiah	" " " "(Farm Laborer)	27	M	2:113
Rhotun, Matilda	" " " "(Housewife)	59	F	2:113
Rhymo, Wm.	Arrapahoe, Missouri City (Miner)	24	M	11:561
Rice, Benjamin B.	Bourbon, Dayton P.O. (Farmer)	69	M	2:157
Rice, C.	Douglas, Palmyra,Prairie City(Farmer)	35	M	6:275
Rice, Elizabeth NC	Lykins, Mound, Osawatomie	65	F	8:72
Rice, Hugh	Arrapahoe, Denver (Miner)	26	M	11:425
Rice, John	Bourbon, Xenia P.O. (Shoemaker)	45	M	2:130
Rice, Thomas NC	Lyk.,Mound,Osawat.,(Farmer-Merchant)	60	M	8:72
Rice, W. NC	Leavenworth, Easton	22	M	10:288
Rice, Wm.	Leavenworth, 1st Ward (Barber)	13	BM	10:137
Rich, Daniel NC	Breckenridge, Emporia (Farmer)	32	M	4:192
Rich, Hannah NC	" "	54	F	4:192
Rich, Lorenzo	Marshall, Marysville (Farmer)	22	M	3:243
Rich, Mary	Leavenworth, Fort Leavenworth P.O.	60	BF	10:313
Rich, Richard NC	Breckenridge, Emporia	59	M	4:192
Richards, Archibald NC	Brown, Locknow, Powhattan (Farmer)	25	M	3:64
Richards, Cyrus G.	Breck.,Cahola,Decorah (F. Laborer)	15	M	4:229
Richards, D. N. NC	Arrapahoe, Denver	24	M	11:385
Richards, David	Breckenridge, Cahola, Decorah(Farmer)	35	M	4:229
Richards, Francis M. NC	Lykins, Stanton (Farmer)	34	M	8:6
Richards, John	Breckenridge, Cahola, Decorah	8	M	4:229
Richards, R.	Doug., Wakarusa, Lawrence (Laborer)	23	M	6:257
Richards, Sandford	Breckenridge, Cahola, Decorah	4	M	4:229
Richardson, Chas.	Arrapahoe, Valley of the Platte	26	M	11:785
Richardson, Franklin NC	Cof.,Leroy,Burlington (Teamster)	25	M	4:18
Richardson, Henry NC	Bourbon, Fort Scott P.O. (Farmer)	26	M	2:93
Richardson, John NC	" " " (Farm Laborer)	20	M	2:93
Richardson, P.	Leavenworth, Fort Leavenworth P.O.	50	BM	10:318

Arapahoe: spelled incorrectly with 2 r's in census and in this index also.

Name	Kansas: County; Township; P.O. / Arap. Co.: Census Div. Not Township	Age	Sex	Census V:Pg
Richerson, Elizabeth	Linn, Mound City	37	F	7:123
Richie, Artesia	Jefferson, Ozawkie	40	F	5:105
Rickard, John G.	Allen, Humboldt P.O. (Farmer)	40	M	2:295
Riddle, G. W.NC	Douglas, Kanwaca, Lawrence (Farmer)	31	M	6:384
Riddle, Jefferson	Jefferson, Ozawkie (Farmer)	52	M	5:106
Riddy, Andrew J.	Wyandotte, Wyandotte (Farmer)	38	M	10:36
Riddy, Sarah J.	" "	34	F	10:36
Ridge, E. A.NC	Johnson, Spring Hill	10	F	6:47
Ridge, H.NC	" " "	55	F	6:47
Ridge, J.NC	" " "	25	F	6:47
Ridge, M.NC	" " " (Farmer)	55	M	6:47
Ridge, R. D.NC	" " " (Farmer)	21	M	6:47
Ridge, W.NC	" " " (Farmer)	24	M	6:47
Rigeons, JamesNC	Mor., Clarks Cr., Council Gr.(Farmer)	38	M	4:279
Rigney, M. C.	Arrapahoe, South Park	26	M	11:204
Riley, A. B.	Arrapahoe, Spring Gulch (Sheriff)	22	M	11:538
Riley, JohnNC	Linn, Scott, Brooklyn (Farmer)	73	M	7:26
Rinaggan, W.NC	Arrapahoe, South Park (Trader)	31		11:31
Ringerman, J.SC	Anderson, Washington, Garnett	49	F	7:251
Ringo, Martin	Atch., Shannon, Atchison (Laborer)	18	M	1:75
Rinker, LavinaNC	Breckenridge, Fremont	28	F	4:167
Rivers, Thos.	Arrapahoe, South Park	22	M	11:258
Roach, James N.	Bourbon, Fort Scott P.O. (Farmer)	40	M	2:222
Roads, Leander	Arrapahoe, Golden City (Miner)	45	M	11:454
Roake, Catharine	Leav., Alexandria, Easton	25	F	10:446
Roake, John N.	" " "(FarmerOverseer)	39	M	10:446
Robbins, A.	Franklin, Peoria, Stanton	2	F	8:281
Robbins, A.	" " "	7	F	8:281
Robbins, H.	" " "	4	M	8:281
Robelett, E. A.	Arrapahoe, Missouri City (Miner)	32	M	11:572
Robers, Sarah	Atchison, Ward 2	73	BF	1:32
Roberts, A.	Johnson, Olathe	4	F	6:1
Roberts, A. E.	" "	5	F	6:2
Roberts, B. F.	Franklin, Ottawa, Hickory Creek	7	M	8:265
Roberts, B. F.	Johnson, Olathe (Farmer)	20	M	6:1
Roberts, B. S.	" " (Landlord)	37	M	6:2
Roberts, C. D.	Douglas, Lecompton (Physician)	40	M	6:353
Roberts, C. D.	Franklin, Ottawa, Hickory Creek	8	F	8:265
Roberts, C. J.	Johnson, Olathe	18	F	6:1
Roberts, C. S.	Johnson, Monticello (Farmer)	50	M	6:80
Roberts, E.	Johnson, Olathe	12	M	6:2
Roberts, E.	Doniphan, Washington, Elwood	10	F	1:322
Roberts, E. A.	Franklin, Ottawa, Hickory Creek	11	M	8:265
Roberts, E. A.	Johnson, Olathe	8	F	6:1
Roberts, E. S.	" "	16	F	6:1
Roberts, G.	" "	7	M	6:2
Roberts, G. W.	" " (Farmer)	45	M	6:114
Roberts, G. W.	" "	10	M	6:1
Roberts, H.	Arrapahoe, South Park	25	M	11:121
Roberts, HannahNC	McGee, Medoc, Missouri P.O.	50	F	9:213
Roberts, J.	Johnson, Olathe	2	M	6:1
Roberts, J.	" " (Farmer)	47	M	6:1
Roberts, J. A.	" "	45	F	6:114
Roberts, J. G.NC	Arrapahoe, Denver	22	M	11:385
Roberts, JamesNC	Don., Washington, Whitehead (Farmer)	49	M	1:297
Roberts, Jesse?SC	Leavenworth, Kickapoo (Farmer)	47	M	10:408
Roberts, John	Butler, Chelsea (Farmer)	50	M	4:350
Roberts, L.	Johnson, Olathe	9	M	6:2
Roberts, L. D.	Arrapahoe, Missouri City (Miner)	21	M	11:564
Roberts, M.	Johnson, Olathe	26	F	6:1
Roberts, M.	Doniphan, Washington, Elwood	12	F	1:322

Arapahoe: spelled incorrectly with 2 r's in census and in this index also.

Name	Kansas: County; Township; P.O. / Arap. Co.: Census Div. Not Township	Age	Sex	Census V.:Pg.
Roberts, M.	Doniphan, Washington, Elwood	52	F	1:322
Roberts, M. A.	Johnson, Olathe	14	F	6:1
Roberts, M. E.	" "	6	F	6:1
Roberts, Nancy	Arrapahoe, Denver	32	F	11:343
Roberts, P. A.	Franklin, Ottawa, Hickory Creek	17	F	8:265
Roberts, R. J.	Johnson, Olathe	35	F	6:2
Roberts, Robert	Breckenridge, Fremont (Farmer)	35	M	4:168
Roberts, S. B.	Johnson, Olathe	14	F	6:1
Roberts, Thomas	Bourbon, Fort Scott P.O. (Land Agent)	32	M	2:221
Roberts, Victora	Doniphan, Washington, Elwood	21	F	1:322
Roberts, W. J.	Franklin, Ottawa, Hickory Creek	14	F	8:265
Roberts, William	Don., Washington, Elwood (Laborer)	16	M	1:322
Robertson, Elisa	Leavenworth, Ward 2	63	F	10:194
Robertson, H. G.	" " "	72	M	10:194
Robertson, Virginia	" " "	39	F	10:183
Robinson, Daniel[NC]	Bourbon, Fort Scott P.O.(FarmLaborer)	43	M	2:211
Robinson, Eleza	Woodson, Neosho Falls	35	F	9:135
Robinson, Green	Jeff., Jeff., Crooked Cr. (Farmer)	39	M	5:27
Robinson, I. H.[SC]	Arrapahoe, Russell Gulch (Miner)	23	M	11:517
Robinson, W.[SC]	" " " (Miner)	54	M	11:517
Robison, Ann H.[NC]	Bourbon, Fort Scott P.O. (Housewife)	39	BF	2:196
Robison, Garett	Bourbon, Marmaton P.O. (Farmer)	63	M	2:116
Robison, M.[NC]	Linn, Paris (M.E. Preacher)	50	M	7:157
Robison, Manford[NC]	Bourbon, Fort Scott P.O. (Farmer)	40	BM	2:196
Rock, Madison	Jack., Doug., Grassh. Falls (Farmer)	38	M	9:93
Rockwell, Martha E.	Lykins; Sugar Creek; West Point, Mo.	20	F	8:103
Rodabaugh, Jane	Atchison, Center, Pardee	46	F	1:124
Rodepes, S.	Don., Washington, Elwood (Laborer)	40	M	1:312
Rodgers, Elizabeth	Jeff., Jefferson, Winchester	17	F	5:44
Rodgers, George	Jeff., Jefferson, Winchester	12	M	5:44
Rodgers, John	Jeff., Jefferson, Winchester (Farmer)	40	M	5:44
Rodgers, Margaret	" " "	15	F	5:44
Rodgers, Mary	" " "	39	F	5:44
Rodgers, Virginia	" " "	9	F	5:44
Rodman, J.	Douglas, Eudora, Lawrence (Farmer)	52	M	6:344
Roe, Eliza	Morris, Grove, Council Grove	33	F	4:271
Roe, Jane	Bourbon, Xenia P.O. (Housewife	36	F	2:141
Roes, Hiram[NC]	Leav., Alexandria, Easton (Farmer)	30	M	10:445
Rogers, G. F.[NC]	Johnson, Lexington (Farmer)	28	M	6:75
Rogers, G. O.	Arrapahoe, South Park	25	M	11:203
Rogers, J.	Don., Burr Oak, Whitehead (Farmer)	40	M	1:341
Rogers, J. B. S.	Leavenworth, Ward 2 (Clerk)	24	M	10:195
Rogers, Jas.	Arrapahoe, Missouri City (Merchant)	50	M	11:561
Rogers, James	Doniphan, Burr Oak, Whitehead	14	M	1:341
Rogers, L.	" " "	30	F	1:341
Rogers, Nancy	Anderson, Jackson, Garnett	64	F	7:212
Rogers, Susan[NC]	Woodson, Belmont	64	F	9:151
Rogers, Thos.	Arrapahoe, South Park	30	M	11:194
Rogers, W.	Arrapahoe, Missouri City (Merchant)	19	M	11:561
Rogers, W.	Arrapahoe, South Park	35	M	11:169
Rogers, Z.? (or R.)[1,NC]	Johnson, Lexington (Farmer)	23	M	6:75
Rogers, Zeno[NC]	Douglas, Eudora (Farmer)	25	M	6:341
Rolin, A.[NC]	Doniphan, Wolf River, Walnut Grove	34	BM	1:407
Rolin, E. P.[NC]	" " " " "	10	BM	1:407
Rolin, Jane[NC]	" " " " "	8	BF	1:407
Rolin, Martha[NC]	" " " " "	30	BF	1:407
Rollice, Eliza[NC]	Atchison, Ward 2, Atchison	44	BF	1:37
Rollins, A.	Arrapahoe, South Park	28	M	11:218
Rollesson, Chas.	" " " (Miner)	29	M	11:45

[1]See 1855 Census, Dist. 16, p. 72, R. B. Rogers, age 21.

Arapahoe: spelled incorrectly with 2 r's in census and in this index also.

Name	Kansas: County; Township; P.O. Arap. Co.: Census Div. Not Township	Age	Sex	Census V. Pg.
Rolston, D.	Johnson, Shawnee (Farmer)	28	M	6:92
Rolston, F. R.	" "	35	F	6:92
Rolston, J. R.	" " (Farmer)	40	M	6:92
Ronie, Elisabeth	Leavenworth, Ward 3	57	F	10:218
Rooker, Emily[SC]	Arapahoe, Denver	40	F	11:369
Root, Caroline	Douglas, Palmyra, Baldwin	6	F	6:288
Root, James	" " " (Farmer)	30	M	6:288
Root, Mary A.	" " "	4	M	6:288
Root, Perlina	" " "	10	F	6:288
Rose, Fannie[NC]	Linn, Valley, Blooming Gr.	46	F	7:51
Rose, H.	" " " " (Farmer)	50	M	7:51
Rose, Julia (Julius?)	" " " " (Farmer)	23	F	7:51
Rose, Matilda	Lykins, Marysville, Spring Hill	51	F	8:128
Rose, P. H.	Johnson, Spring Hill (Farmer)	33	M	6:43
Rose, Peter W.	Lyk., Marysville, Spr. Hill (Farmer)	25	M	8:129
Rose, Saml. C.	" " " " (Farmer)	54	M	8:128
Rosenbarger, Emanuel	Atchison, Ward 2 (Clothier)	23	M	1:26
Ross, James	Linn, Scott,Twin Sprs.(Shingle Maker)	43	M	7:9
Ross, L.	Johnson, Shawnee	32	F	6:99
Roush, Caroline	Bourbon, Marmaton P.O. (Housewife)	25	F	2:102
Routh, Nancy V.	Leavenworth, Easton	24	F	10:285
Rowarek, P.	Linn, Valley, Blooming Gr.(Carpenter)	31	M	7:53
Rowley, C. S.	Arapahoe, South Park	40	M	11:124
Rowley, O. V.	" "	38	M	11:124
Royan, Mary	And., Wash., Garnett (Seamstress)	51	F	7:253
Royan, William[NC]	" " " (Farmer)	54	M	7:253
Royster, Ann	Jefferson, Oskaloosa	37	F	5:120
Ruggles, R. P.	Arapahoe, South Park (Miner)	37	M	11:18
Rulison, Jno.	" " "	23	M	11:214
Rumley, H. M.[NC]	And., Washington, Garnett (Farmer)	55	M	7:252
Rumpkin, H.	Arapahoe, South Park	44	M	11:170
Rumsey, O.	" " "	23	M	11:113
Rumsey, S. D.	Arapahoe, Valley of the Platte	26	M	11:820
Runage, E.	Arapahoe, South Clear Creek	30	M	11:709
Rupel, J. M.	Leavenworth, Ward 4	24	F	10:247
Rupell, J. W.[NC]	Leav., Alexandria, Easton (Shoemaker)	31	M	10:447
Rush, F.[1]	Frank.;Potta.;Walker, And.Co.	7	F	8:241
Rush, S. C.	Arapahoe, South Park	26	M	11:136
Rusman, George[NC]	Breck., Cahola, Americus (Farmer)	30	M	4:230
Russell, Allen	Arapahoe, Denver (Trader)	25	M	11:416
Russell, Gren[SC]	Arapahoe, Russell Gulch (Miner)	44	M	17:517
Russell, J.	Johnson, Olathe	25	F	6:115
Russell, Nancy	Douglas, Willow Springs (Farmer)	21	F	6:323
Russell, Sallisam	Arapahoe, Denver	29	F	11:319
Rutherford	Arapahoe, South Park	19	M	11:121
Rutherford, S.	Arapahoe, South Clear Creek (Miner)	28	M	11:753
Ryan, T. A.	Arapahoe, California Gulch (Miner)	22	M	11:271
Sabon, H. A.	Arapahoe, South Park	29	M	11:189
Saddler, James	Linn, Center., Oakwood (Carpenter)	51	M	7:93
Saddler, Lucinda	" " "	50	F	7:94
Sage, Ann	Doniphan, Washington, Elwood	19	F	1:321
Sage, Jas. B.	Lyk.; Sugar Cr.; West Pt.,Mo.(Farmer)	41	M	8:104
St. Clair, John	Potta., Blue, Manhattan (Farmer)	32	M	5:297
St. Clair, O. B.	Arapahoe, South Park (Miner)	34	M	11:73
Salisbury, Harriet Y.	Leav., Stranger, Leavenworth City	29	F	10:479
Salls, W.	Arapahoe, South Clear Creek (Miner)	35	M	11:767
Salmon, Joel	Arapahoe, South Park (Miner)	39	M	11:24
Sambeth, Mary	Linn, Valley, Blooming Grove	41	F	7:53
Samden, John	Coffey, Avon, Burlington (Farmer)	32	M	4:10
Sanderland, R. E.	Arapahoe, South Park	22	M	11:123

[1]M.Rush[NC] F 5, same address. Jno. Rush[NC] Arap., M 48, 11:342; see p.160.

Name	Kansas: County; Township; P.O. Arap. Co.: Census Div. Not Township	Age	Sex	Census V. Pg
Sanders, J. W.	Frank., Peoria, Stanton (Minister)	49	M	8:284
Sanders, Mary M.	Coffey, Avon, Burlington	32	F	4:9
Sanders, Patience[NC]	Nemaha, Richmond, Seneca	47	F	3:98
Sanders, W.[NC]	Allen, Humboldt P.O. (Farmer)	24	M	2:298
Sanders, Wm.	Arapahoe, South Park	26	M	11:166
Sanford, C.	Franklin, Ohio, Ohio City	4	M	8:229
Sanhem?, Wm.	Arapahoe, Golden City (Miner)	23	M	11:586
Saperite, A. N.[NC]	Coffey, Leroy (Carpenter)	28	M	4:29
Sarahass, Jno.	Arapahoe, South Park (Miner)	35	M	11:46
Saunders, Elisha	Atchison, Center, Pardee (Farmer)	65	M	1:136
Savory, Anett	Wyandotte, Wyandotte	6	F	10:42
Sawyer, Mary A.	Allen, Iola P.O.	24	F	2:256
Sayers, C. D.	Doniphan, White Cloud (Merchant)	22	M	1:437
Scaggs, Eleza	Doug., Willow Spr., McKinney	26	F	6:308
Scaggs, Francis	" " " "	22	F	6:295
Scaggs, J.	" " " " (Farmer)	57	M	6:295
Scaggs, James	" " " " (Farmer)	26	M	6:295
Scales, Elizabeth[NC]	Anderson, Washington, Garnett	55	F	7:254
Scarritt, Wm.	Arapahoe, South Park	38	M	11:229
Schayer, S.	Arapahoe, Denver (Hatter)	27	M	11:349
Schley, Winfield	" "	45	M	11:365
Schmitt, Thomas	Jackson, Holton	28	M	5:178
Schockleford, James	Wyandotte, Wyandotte	27	M	10:9
Schoen, Caroline[SC]	Bourbon, Marmaton P.O.	5	F	2:205
Schoen, Henry[SC]	" "	7	M	2:205
Schoen, Margaret[SC]	Bourbon, Pawnee P.O.	15	F	2:99
Schooler, J. B.	Arapahoe, Denver (Miner)	27		11:331
Schooley, J. B.	Arapahoe, California Gulch (Miner)	27	M	11:315
Schubert, Phoebe	Bourbon, Turkey Creek P.O.(Housewife)	23	F	2:107
Scott, A. G.	Arapahoe, South Park	27	M	11:210
Scott, D. W.	Davis, Ft.Riley Res. (Forage Master)	41	M	9:361
Scott, D. W.	Johnson, Shawnee (Physician)	27	M	6:31
Scott, J. B.	Coffey, Leroy	45	M	4:31
Scranton, J.	Arapahoe, South Park	35	M	11:184
Scroop, Levi	Arapahoe, California Gulch	29	M	11:284
Scrtchfeld, Edward	Mars., Vermil., B. Mills(Farm Laborer)	27	M	3:217
Scruggs, Jno. E.	Arapahoe, Missouri City (Miner)	26	M	11:558
Scynger, Scott	Douglas, Kanwaca, Lawrence (Farmer)	24	M	6:391
Seaman, Eliza	Bourbon, Mapleton P.O. (Housewife)	49	F	2:136
Seaman, William B.	Bourbon, Mapleton P.O. (Farmer)	53	M	2:136
Seamore, Nancy[NC]	Linn, Liberty, Centerville	20	F	7:3
Seamore, William	" " " (Farmer)	32	M	7:3
Seamore, William	" " " (Farmer)	32	M	7:3
Sears, Daniel	Wyandotte, Wyandotte (Laborer)	24	M	10:4
Seck, J. W.[NC]	Linn, Scott, Twin Springs (Carpenter)	45	M	7:21
Seck, James[NC]	" " " " (Farmer)	23	M	7:21
Seck, Jesse[NC]	" " " "	11	M	7:21
Seck, Lucinda[NC]	" " " "	44	F	7:21
Seck, Malinda[NC]	" " " "	20	F	7:21
Seck, Mar (Mary?) Ann[NC]	" " " "	16	F	7:21
Seck, Susan[NC]	" " " "	13	F	7:21
Sedford, Silas[NC]	Arapahoe, California Gulch	38	M	11:270
Segars, Elizabeth	Douglas, Lecompton, Big Springs	40	F	6:368
Self, T.	Johnson, Shawnee (Laborer)	36	M	6:28
Semans, W.	Leavenworth, Ward 3 (Lawyer)	59	M	10:215
Semaster, E.	Coffey, Avon, Burlington	26	M	4:12
Sencabaugh, Thos.	Arapahoe, South Park	28	M	11:253
Seratt, J.	Douglas, Kanwaca, Lawrence (Laborer)	23	M	6:391
Service, E.[SC]	Frank.;Potta.;Scipio (And. Co.)	32	F	8:238
Service, J. C.	" " " " "	3	M	8:238
Service, W. L.[SC]	" " " " " (Farmer)	35	M	8:238

Name	Kansas: County; Township; P.O. Arap. Co.: Census Div. Not Township	Age	Sex	Census V. : Pg
Severs, Isaac N.	Leavenworth, Ward 4	49	M	10:257
Severs, Martha	" " "	29	F	10:257
Seymore, Emilie	Arapahoe, Denver (Laundry)	25	BF	11:360
Seymour, E.	Osage, Ridgeway, Burlingame	18	F	8:335
Shafer, David	Breckenridge, Fremont (Farmer)	30	M	4:163
Shafer, Jno. M.	Arapahoe; Tarryall, South Park	29	M	11:611
Shaffer, Jno.	" " " "	24	M	11:620
Shaffer, Wm. M.	" " " " (Miner)	26	M	11:620
Shankel, Joab	Bourbon, Fort Scott P.O. (Farmer)	39	M	2:91
Shanks, C. C.	Arapahoe, Quartz Valley (Miner)	25	M	11:490
Shannon, Augustus A.	Leavenworth, Kickapoo (Farmer)	35	M	10:331
Shannon, F.	Johnson, Monticello (Farmer)	23	M	6:80
Shannon, J. C.	Arapahoe, South Clear Creek (Miner)	28	M	11:685
Shannon, M.	Johnson, Monticello (Farmer)	33	M	6:85
Shape, Annie	Leavenworth, 1st Ward	23	F	10:118
Sharp, A.	Arapahoe, South Park	20	M	11:31
Sharp, Emily	Woodson, Pleasant Grove (F. W.)	46	F	9:170
Sharp, George	Leav., Kickapoo (Justice of Peace)	46	M	10:324
Sharp, Martha	Doniphan, Washington, Wathena	37	F	1:302
Shave, E. P.	Arapahoe, Valley of the Platte	28	M	11:857
Shaw, A. A.	Doniphan, Wayne, Doniphan	13	M	1:369
Shaw, A. E.	" " "	16	M	1:369
Shaw, E.	" " "	38	F	1:369
Shaw, J.	" " " (Farmer)	38	M	1:369
Shaw, J. A.?	" " " (Farmer)	18	M	1:369
Shaw, J. G.	" Doniphan, Doniphan	24	M	1:382
Shaw, J. S.	Arapahoe, South Park	36	M	11:255
Shaw, Jesse L.	Doniphan, Wayne, Doniphan	8	M	1:369
Shaw, John	Coffey, Leroy, Burlington (Engineer)	36	M	4:21
Shaw, M. E.	Doniphan, Wayne, Doniphan	11	F	1:369
Shaw, S. (or L.?)	" " "	37	F	1:373
Shaw, T. H.	Arapahoe, South Park	26	M	11:194
Shaw, W. K.	Doniphan, Wayne, Doniphan (Farmer)	37	M	1:373
Shea, A.	Arapahoe, South Park	28	M	11:174
Shearer, David M.[NC]	Atchison, Grasshopper, Kennekuk	13	M	1:89
Shearer, Elbert W.[NC]	" " "	7	M	1:89
Shearer, Elizabeth[NC]	" " "	31	F	1:89
Shearer, James[NC]	" " " (Farmer)	19	M	1:89
Shearer, John D.[NC]	" " "	14	M	1:89
Shearer, Martha[NC]	" " "	54	F	1:89
Shearer, Martha C.[NC]	" " "	11	F	1:89
Shearer, Wm. M.[NC]	" " "	16	M	1:89
Sheets, Clabourne	" " " (Farmer)	19	M	1:92
Sheets, Isabella E.[NC]	" " "	12	F	1:92
Sheets, J. H.	Arapahoe, Valley of the Platte	31		11:783
Sheets, John[NC]	Atchison, Grasshopper,Kennekuk(Farmer)	37	M	1:92
Sheets, Lucy[NC]	" " "	33	F	1:92
Sheets, Luivilla[NC]	" " "	14	F	1:92
Shelby, T. S.	Arapahoe, Valley of the Platte	26	M	11:861
Sheldon, G. W.	Arapahoe, South Park	29	M	11:191
Shelly, M.	Douglas, Wakarusa, Lawrence (Farmer)	31	M	6:257
Shelton, M.[NC]	Franklin, Peoria, Peoria City	21	F	8:272
Shepherd, Elizabeth[NC]	Douglas, Wakarusa, Lawrence	65	F	6:245
Shepherd, Emily	Douglas, Willow Springs	44	F	6:323
Shepherd, J.	" " " (Farmer)	48	M	6:323
Shepherd, John	Douglas, Wakarusa, Lawrence (Farmer)	71	M	6:245
Sherrold, H. M.?[NC]	Frank.;Ottawa;Prairie City,Doug. Co.	23	M	8:258
Sherwood, T.[NC]	Riley, Ogden P.O. (Farmer)	44	M	9:288
Sherwood, Thos.	Arapahoe, South Park	36	M	11:128
Shewer, A.	Johnson, Gardner (Farmer)	19	M	6:55

Name	Kansas: County; Township; P.O. Arap. Co.: Census Div. Not Township	Age	Sex	Census V. Pg.
Shi, Miriam[NC]	McGee, Osage Mission P.O. (Farmer)	60	M	9:238
Shields, Daniel H.	Anderson, Reeder, Garnett (Farmer)	50	M	7:258
Shields, Margarett	Brown, Claytonville (Teacher)	19	M	3:39
Shields, S. C.	Brown, Claytonville (Farmer)	60	M	3:39
Shinn, E. J.	Arapahoe, Mountain City (Miner)	21	M	11:550
Ship, Charlott[NC]	Marshall, Blue Rapids, Irving	53	F	3:210
Shipment, J. W.	Don., Wash., Whitehead (Stonemason)	49	M	1:296
Shipment, R. L.	" " "	37	F	1:296
Shipment, W. T.	" " "	13	M	1:296
Shively, Elizabeth	Lykins, Paola	30	F	8:34
Shively, Theresa	" "	64	F	8:34
Shively, Wm. T.	" " (Farmer)	34	M	8:34
Shiverick, Wm.	Arapahoe, South Park	29	M	11:258
Shock, J. N.	Arapahoe, Valley of the Platte	27	M	11:819
Shockey, Eliza	Arapahoe, Arapahoe City	45	F	11:588
Shockey, Levi	" "	49	M	11:588
Shockley, Eliza J.	Breckenridge, Americus	23	F	4:222
Shoe, Elizabeth[NC]	Douglas, Palmyra, Prairie City	28	F	6:272
Shoe, S. T.[NC]	" " " " (Merchant)	37	M	6:271
Shoemaker, W.	Frank., Ohio, Ohio City (Physician)	39	F	8:234
Shoos,? S. A.	Arapahoe, Nevada Gulch (Miner)	21	M	11:529
Shores, R. A.[NC]	Frank.,Centrop.,Prairie City (Farmer)	32	M	8:219
Short, J. H.	Arapahoe, South Clear Creek	38	M	11:694
Short, Savila	Coffey, Avon, Burlington	32	F	4:12
Short, Warren H.[NC]	Allen, Geneva P.O. (Farmer)	32	M	2:255
Show, J.	Don., Wolf River, Walnut Gr. (Farmer)	40	M	1:399
Show, Mary	" " " " "	40	F	1:399
Show, S. W.	" " " " "	21	M	1:399
Shrader, N.	Johnson, Olathe	13	F	6:6
Shrimp, John K.	Atchison, Grasshopper, Kennekuk	?	M	1:86
Shuck, E. B. M.	Johnson; Oxford; New Santa Fe, Mo.	45	F	6:34
Shuck, L. A.	" " " " " "	19	F	6:34
Shuck, L. M.	" " " " " "	14	M	6:34
Shuck, M. E.	" " " " " "	8	F	6:34
Shuck, T. E.	" " " " " "	10	F	6:34
Shull, Lavinia[NC]	Coffey, Leroy, Burlington	43	F	4:25
Shulor, J.	Linn, Valley, Blooming Gr. (Farmer)	50	M	7:32
Shulor, Jane	" " " "	46	F	7:32
Shulter, Mary[NC]	Atchison, Shannon, Atchison	38	F	1:69
Shulter, John[NC]	" " "	7	M	1:69
Shulty, G. E.	Arapahoe, Nevada Gulch (Miner)	22	M	11:529
Shultz, Frances E.[NC]	Atchison, Center, Pardee (Farmer)	29	M	1:136
Shultz, Henry B.	Breck., Cahola, Americus (Farmer)	35	M	4:230
Shultz, J. E.	Arapahoe, South Clear Creek (Hotel)	42	M	11:644
Shultz, Jas. E.[NC]	Jefferson, Grasshopper Falls (Farmer)	32	M	5:23
Shuntz, D.	Frank., Ottawa, Prairie City,Doug.Co.	53	F	8:257
Shute, S. G.	Arapahoe, South Park	35	M	11:193
Shwappat, R.	Johnson, Shawnee	31	M	6:23
Sibert, George	Nemaha, Home, Centralia (Farmer)	31	M	3:128
Sibly, Robert	Marshall, Marysville (Millwright)	28	M	3:255
Sickels, James	Leavenworth, Easton (Laborer)	22	M	10:282
Sickes, Elizabeth	Douglas, Lecompton	68	F	6:369
Sigbert, J.	Atchison, Ward 2 (Policeman)	35	M	1:1
Sighman, J. W.	Arapahoe, Leavenworth Gulch (Miner)	48	M	11:555
Sikes, J. W.	Arapahoe, Valley of the Platte	35	M	11:859
Silver, W. C.	Arapahoe, Mountain City (Miner)	19	M	11:461
Simcock, G. M.	Morris, Grove, Council Gr. (Merchant)	30	M	4:270
Simmers, Ephraim[NG]	Cof., Leroy, Burlington (Carpenter)	35	M	4:24
Simmers, Polly[NC]	" " "	25	F	4:25
Simmons, Alpha[NC]	Jeff., Jeff., Crooked Cr. (Farmer)	49	M	5:28

Name	Kansas: County; Township; P.O. Arap. Co.: Census Div. Not Township	Age	Sex	Census V . Pg.
Simmons, Frances	Jeff., Jeff., Crooked Cr.	46	F	5:28
Simmons, Nancy L. NC	Atchison, Grasshopper, Kennekuk	29	F	1:89
Simmons, Sam'l.	Arapahoe, South Park	33	M	11:48
Simmons, T. W.	Arapahoe, Quartz Valley (Miner)	26	M	11:498
Simpson, J. H.	Arapahoe, California Gulch	28	M	11:292
Simpson, John	Bourbon, Fort Scott P.O. (Farmer)	68	M	2:198
Simpson, Nancy	Clay, Junction City P.O.	40	F	9:269
Simpson, Nancy J. NC	Atchison, Walnut, Sumner	35	F	1:172
Simpson, Sarah	Bourbon, Fort Scott P.O. (Housewife)	62	F	2:198
Sims, Charles	Lykins, Wea, Squiresville (Farmer)	43	M	8:113
Sims, John C. SC	Bourbon, Fort Scott P.O. (Attorney)	27	M	2:224
Singleton, O. SC	Arapahoe, Valley of the Platte (Miner)			11:778
Singleton, Samuel SC	Atchison, Walnut, Sumner (Farmer)	28	M	1:169
Sinnett, Jacob	Coffey, Leroy (Farmer)	60	M	4:28
Sitia, David	Wood., Liberty, Neosho Falls (Farmer)	68	M	9:143
Siria, Dorcas NC	" " " " (F.W.)	64	F	9:143
Sisson, L.	Arapahoe, South Park (Carpenter)	31	M	11:32
Sitt, Mary C.	Anderson, Town of Garnett	45	F	7:224
Sitton, J. T. SC	Arapahoe, Mountain City (Miner)	49	M	11:459
Skaggs, Andrew	Leav., Stranger, Leav. City (Farmer)	39	M	10:470
Skaggs, Elizabeth	" " " "	40	F	10:470
Skinner, J. W.	Arapahoe, Russell Gulch (Miner)	36	M	11:486
Slagle, Elizabeth	Brown, Claytonville, Robinson	48	F	3:47
Slagle, George	" " "	59	M	3:47
Slain, George	Jeff., Jeff., Crooked Cr. (Farmer)	27	M	5:39
Slain, Maria	" " " "	45	F	5:39
Slatter, Rachel NC	Bourbon, Turkey Creek P.O. (Housewife)	36	F	2:115
Slaughter, A.	Johnson, Lexington (Surveyor)	31	M	6:77
Slaughter, F.	" "	8	F	6:77
Slaughter, L. A.	" "	7	F	6:78
Slaughter, L. W.	" "	27	F	6:77
Slaughter,Lewis W.(orN?)	Leavenworth, Ward 2	20	M	10:146
Sleeper, Thos. SC	Arapahoe, South Clear Creek	35	M	11:766
Slocum, J.	Arapahoe, South Park	29	M	11:179
Smith, A.	John.; Oxf.; New Santa Fe,Mo.(Farmer)	40	M	6:106
Smith, A.	Franklin, Centropolis, Minneola	5	M	8:209
Smith, Abraham	Lykins, Paola (Saloon Keeper)	41	M	8:25
Smith, Baily SC	Leavenworth, Delaware (Farmer)	44	M	10:434
Smith, Benton	Douglas, Kanwaca, Lawrence (Farmer)	20	M	6:385
Smith, C. H.	Douglas, Wakarusa, Lawrence	45	F	6:235
Smith, Chas.	Arapahoe, California Gulch	22	M	11:281
Smith, Chas. W. NC	Coffey, Leroy, Burlington (Farmer)	54	M	4:27
Smith, Christopher	Chase, Cottonwood Falls (Farming)	29	M	4:320
Smith, Clark	Coffey, Neosho, Burlington (Farmer)	33	M	4:74
Smith, Conrad	Mars., Vermil.,Bar. M. (Day Laborer)	28	M	3:217
Smith, David	Woodson, Pleasant Grove (Farmer)	57	M	9:168
Smith, Dena	Leavenworth, Ward 3	70	BF	10:199
Smith, Dewitt	Arapahoe, California Gulch	24	M	11:282
Smith, E. NC	Linn, Scott, Twin Springs (Farmer)	47	M	7:10
Smith, Elijah	Bourbon, Fort Scott P.O. (Farmer)	35	M	2:88
Smith, Elizabeth	Leavenworth, 1st Ward	25	F	10:111
Smith, Fleming	Breckenridge, Americus (Farmer)	42	M	4:221
Smith, Francis	Linn, Valley, Blooming Grove	29	F	7:39
Smith, George F.	Douglas, Wakarusa, Lawrence (Farmer)	27	M	6:235
Smith, George H. NC	Don., Wolf River, Walnut Gr. (Farmer)	37	M	1:404
Smith, I.	Arapahoe, Denver (Miner)	31	M	11:323
Smith, J.	Johnson, Shawnee (Farmer)	36	M	6:25
Smith, J.	Frank., Ohio, Ohio City (Plasterer)	55	M	8:229
Smith, J.	Arapahoe, South Park (Miner)	26	M	11:28
Smith, J.	Douglas, Lecompton	8	M	6:358

Name	Kansas: County; Township; P.O. Arap. Co.: Census Div. Not Township	Age	Sex	Census V. . Pg.
Smith, J. C.	Arapahoe, Quartz Valley (Miner)	45	M	11:495
Smith, James	Bourbon, Fort Scott P.O. (Farmer)	30	M	2:154
Smith, Jas. J.NC	Lykins, Middle Cr., Paola (Laborer)	26	M	8:111
Smith, John E.	Bourbon, Fort Scott P.O.	6	M	2:88
Smith, M. E.	Doniphan, Wolf River, Walnut Grove	27	F	1:404
Smith, R.	Arapahoe, Golden City (Miner)	33	M	11:454
Smith, R. B.	Arapahoe, South Park	23	M	11:1
Smith, Rebecca	Leavenworth, Ward 2	26	F	10:151
Smith, Richard	" " " (Printer)	47	M	10:189
Smith, S.	Franklin, Centropolis, Minneola	24	F	8:209
Smith, Sarah	Douglas, Palmyra, Black Jack	18	F	6:289
Smith, SarahNC	Coffey, Leroy, Burlington	54	F	4:27
Smith, Sarah	Bourbon, Fort Scott P.O. (Housewife)	34	F	2:88
Smith, SusanaNC	Lykins, Miami, New Lancaster	29	F	8:88
Smith, Susanna	Jefferson, Ozawkie	51	F	5:100
Smith, T. B.	Arapahoe, Golden City (Miner)	30	M	11:456
Smith, Theodore G.	Wyandotte, Wyandotte	16	M	10:14
Smith, Thos. P.	Don., Lafayette Cent.,Troy(Shoemaker)	45	M	1:249
Smith, V.	Franklin, Centropolis, Minneola	2	F	;8:209
Smith, Virginia E.	Wyandotte, Wyandotte	14	F	10:14
Smith, W.	Frank., Centrop., Minneola (Farmer)	30	M	8:209
Smith, W. D.	Arapahoe; Tarryall, South Park	27	M	11:619
Smith, W. H.	Douglas, Lecompton	23	M	6:362
Smith, Wm.	Arapahoe, Denver (Çooking)	51	M	11:336
Smith, Wm.	Doniphan, Iowa Point (Blacksmith)	28	M	1:447
Smith, Wm.	And., Jackson, Garnett (Physician)	33	M	7:209
Smith, Wm. C.	Bourbon, Mapleton P.O. (Farmer)	70	M	2:132
Smith, William Ira	" " "	26	M	2:203
Smith, Wm. M.	Coffey, Neosho, Burlington (Farmer)	38	M	4:69
Smith, Wm. S.	Douglas, Lecompton (Blacksmith)	40	M	6:357
Smoker, Anson	Lykins, Osawatomie (Farmer)	48	M	8:68
Smoot, Luther R.	Leavenworth, Ward 2 (Banker)	37	M	10:146
Smoot, S. M.	Douglas, Lawrence	63	F	6:202
Smyth, Jno.1,Tn.	Arapahoe, Golden City (Miner)	30	M	11:446
Snively, David	Brown, Walnut Cr., Hamlin (Farmer)	25	M	3:28
Snodgrass, John	Don., Burr Oak, Whitehead (Laborer)	19	M	1:344
Snyder, J.	Arapahoe, South Clear Creek	31	M	11:641
Snyder, J.	Linn, Scott, Brooklyn (Farmer)	50	M	7:16
Snyder, J. B.	Arapahoe, Golden City (Carpenter)	36	M	11:451
Snyder, Margaret	Atchison, Shannon, Atchison		F	1:72
Snyder, Martha Ann	Atchison, Grasshopper, Kennekuk	20	F	1:91
Snyder, Solomon	Atchison, Center, Pardee	43	M	1:123
Soddefield, E.	Franklin, Peoria, Stanton (Farmer)	68	M	8:276
Sombeth, ElifasNC	Linn, Scott, Brooklyn	53	F	7:22
Sours, A.	Johnson, McCamish, Hibbard	18	F	6:65
Sours, A. E.	" " "	3	F	6:65
Sours, C.	" " "	16	F	6:65
Sours, C.	" " "	12	F	6:64
Sours, E.	" " "	10	F	6:64
Sours, F.	" " " (Farmer)	40	M	6:64
Sours, J.	" " "	42	F	6:65
Sours, M.	" " "	15	F	6:64
Sours, M. J.	" " "	6	F	6:64
Sours, N.	" " "	2	F	6:64
Sours, S.	" " "	4	M	6:64
Sours, P. E.	" " "	7	M	6:65
Sours, S.	" " "	41	F	6:64
Sours, S.	" " " (Farmer)	44	M	6:65

[1]Born in Tennessee.

Name	Kansas: County; Township; P.O. Arap. Co.: Census Div. Not Township	Age	Sex	Census V.	Census Pg.
Sours, S.	Johnson, McCamish, Hibbard	12	F	6:65	
Sours, T.	" " "	8	M	6:64	
Sours, T.	" " "	17	F	6:64	
Sours, W.	" " " (Farmer)	18	M	6:64	
Southard, Chas. W.NC	Leav., Stranger, Leav. City (Farmer)	33	M	10:476	
Southard, Daniel J.NC	Atchison, Mt. Pleasant	14	M	1:165	
Southard, E.NC	Arapahoe, Valley of the Platte	10 or 11		11:778	
Southard, JoelNC	Atchison, Mt. Pleasant (Farmer)	45	M	1:165	
Southard, Keziek M.NC	" " "	1	M	1:165	
Spahl, A. G.	Arapahoe, South Clear Creek	28	M	11:692	
Spain, JohnNC	Woodson, Liberty, Leroy (Farmer)	25	M	9:145	
Spain, R. N.	Douglas, Lawrence (Brickmaker)	27	M	6:222	
Sparkman, W.NC	Linn, Paris (Farmer)	48	M	7:129	
Sparks, J. J.	Doniphan, Iowa Point (Farmer)	23	M	1:423	
Sparks, L.	" " " (Farmer)	48	M	1:423	
Sparks, M.	" " " (Farmer)	27	M	1:423	
Sparks, M.	" " "	17	M	1:423	
Sparks, Mary	" " "	25	F	1:423	
Sparks, R.	" " "	12	M	1:423	
Sparks, Sarah	" " "	10	F	1:423	
Sparks, Simpson	" " "	15	M	1:423	
Sparlin, Rachel	Wyandotte, Wyandotte	30	F	10:2	
Sparr, A. J.	Frank., Centrop., Minneola (Farmer)	20	M	8:210	
Sparr, M.	" " "	24	F	8:210	
Spear, SamuelSC	Brown, Walnut Cr., Hamlin (Farmer)	44	M	3:27	
Speek, Sarah EllenNC	Atchison, Mt. Pleasant	29	F	1:158	
Spees, IsaacNC	Lykins, Wea, Paola	27	M	8:118	
Spees, LeannahNC	" " "	33	F	8:118	
Spees, PeterNC	" " " (Farmer)	36	M	8:118	
Spencer, A. M.	Doniphan, Wayne, Doniphan (Farmer)	60	M	1:366	
Spencer, D. C.NC	Linn, Mound City (Farmer)	26	M	7:119	
Spencer, E. A.	Doniphan, Wayne, Doniphan (Farmer)	31	M	1:376	
Spencer, Isaac	" " "	33	M	1:366	
Spencer, Lowis	Linn, Scott, Twin Springs	6	M	7:5	
Spencer, Mary	" " " "	24	F	7:5	
Spencer, Matilda	" " " "	13	F	7:5	
Spencer,J.?(or T? or O?)1	" " " " (Farmer)	36	M	7:5	
Spencer, Thomas SC	Frank.;Potta.;Scipio,And.Co.(Farmer)	60	M	8:237	
Spencer, Wm. L.	Doniphan, Wayne, Doniphan (Farmer)	39	M	1:393	
Sperlock, J.	Douglas, Lecompton	74	F	6:362	
Sperlock, M.NC	" " "	40	F	6:362	
Sperry, ElizaNC	Brown, Irving, Hiawatha	35	F	3:7	
Sperry, L.NC	" " "	6	M	3:7	
Spillman, N. I.NC	Woodson, Belmont (Farmer)	30	M	9:151	
Spooner, E. J.	Franklin, Centropolis, Minneola	23	F	8:216	
Spowl, Virg.	Doniphan, Wayne, Geary City	20	F	1:392	
Sprague, J. G.	Arapahoe, South Park	29	M	11:23	
Spratt, Ann	Leav., Stranger, Leavenworth City	60	F	10:464	
Spriggs, Sarah	Anderson, Monroe, Garnett	53	F	7:213	
Springfield, HenrySC	Arapahoe, Missouri City (Miner)		M	11:569	
Sprowle, Henry	Shawnee, Tecumseh	10	M	9:67	
Spurgeon, MaryNC	Breckenridge, Pike, Plymouth	70	F	4:209	
Spurgeon, SamuelNC	" " " (Farmer)	38	M	4:209	
Spurlock, Comfort	Jefferson, Oskaloosa	48	F	5:130	
Spurlock, Cyrus	" " (Farmer)	57	M	5:130	
Spurlock, D.	Linn, Valley, Blooming Gr. (Farmer)	53	M	7:32	
Spurlock, John	Jefferson, Oskaloosa (Farmer)	56	M	5:121	
Stack, James	Leavenworth, Easton (Farmer)	42	M	10:302	
Stagg, C.	Arapahoe, Valley of the Platte (Miner)			11:778	

1Occupation as carpenter rather than farmer given in original census.

Name	Kansas: County; Township; P.O. Arap. Co.: Census Div. Not Township	Age	Sex	Census V. Pg.
Stagg, Hugh	Atchison, Walnut, Sumner (Laborer)	38	M	1:169
Staley, A. NC	Coffey, Leroy, Burlington	38	F	4:22
Staley, James NC	" " "	39	M	4:22
Stall, A. M.	Arapahoe, South Clear Creek (Miner)	35	M	11:644
Stally, Edward NC	Breckenridge, Emporia (F. Laborer)	19	M	4:198
Stalwaker, Jesse	Linn, Centerville, Keokuk	13	M	7:84
Stalwaker, John	" " "	37	M	7:84
Stalwaker, Sarah	" " "	9	F	7:84
Stambaugh, J. W. R. NC	Arapahoe, Denver (Painter)	25	M	11:333
Stanly, R. P. NC	Johnson, Shawnee	42	F	6:91
Stanton, Betsy	Marshall, Vermillion, Barrett Mills	55	F	3:233
Stanton, F. P.	Douglas, Lecompton (Lawyer)	45	M	6:371
Stanton, Jane	" "	45	F	6:371
Staples, M.	" " (Teacher)	25	F	6:353
Starnes, Christina NC	Leavenworth, Delaware	44	F	10:431
Steele, Catharine	Shawnee, Topeka	45	F	9:15
Steele, Jno.	Arapahoe, California Gulch	30	M	11:284
Steele, John A.	Shawnee, Topeka (O.S.P. Clergyman; Teacher of Music)	56	M	9:15
Steele, Mary E.	Shawnee, Topeka	22	F	9:15
Stein, Susanah SC	Lykins, Miami, New Lancaster	63	F	8:92
Steinbury, Ard	Bourbon, Turkey Creek P.O.(Housewife)	25	F	2:107
Steinbury, Feurel	" " " "	4	M	2:107
Steinbury, Harriet	" " " "	13	F	2:107
Steinbury, Robert	" " " " (Farmer)	36	M	2:107
Stellwell, Wm.	Doniphan, Iowa Point (Carpenter)	50	M	1:419
Stephens, Jno. NC	Arapahoe, California Gulch	25	M	11:275
Stevens, E. A.	Arapahoe, South Clear Creek (Miner)	28	M	11:592
Stevens, Jas.	Arapahoe, Arapahoe City (Laborer)	24	M	11:587
Stevens, John A.	Atchison, Mt. Pleasant (Farmer)	51	M	1:149
Stevens, L. NC	Arapahoe, South Park (Surveyor)	38	M	11:7
Stevens, N. B.	Atchison, Ward 3 (Speculator)	48	M	1:47
Stevens, S. H.	Doniphan, Center, Troy	20	F	1:255
Stevenson, Charles	Shawnee, Monmouth, Tecumseh (Farmer)	42	M	9:63
Stevenson, Wm. SC	Anderson, Washington, Garnett (Farmer)	68	M	7:256
Stewart, A.	Johnson, Shawnee (Farmer)	46	M	6:88
Stewart, A. S.	Potta., Vienna, Louisville	24	F	5:245
Stewart, C. A.	" " " (Farmer)	30	M	5:245
Stewart, Catherine	Allen, Humboldt P.O.	47	F	2:279
Stewart, Elizabeth J. NC	Allen, Geneva P.O.	7	F	2:245
Stewart, Ezekial NC	" " " (Farmer)	30	M	2:245
Stewart, Henry NC	" " "	5	M	2:245
Stewart, J. C.	Arapahoe, Lake Gulch (Miner)	53	M	11:522
Stewart, John NC	Allen, Geneva P.O.	9	M	2:245
Stewart, Josiah SC	Bourbon, Fort Scott P.O. (Farmer)	53	M	2:153
Stewart, Margaret	Jefferson, Oskaloosa	30	F	5:121
Stewart, Martha M. NC	Allen, Geneva P.O.	28	F	2:245
Stewart, Mary Ann NC	" " "	6	F	2:245
Stewart, Thomas NC	Lyk.,Sugar Cr.,New Lancaster(Farmer)	62	M	8:99
Stewart, Virginia	Atchison, Shannon, Atchison	7	F	1:74
Stewart, William	Jefferson, Kaw, Kaw City (Farmer)	28	M	5:81
Stewart, William L.	Bourbon, Fort Scott P.O. (Plasterer)	31	M	2:223
Stice, J. NC	Johnson, Shawnee (Farmer)	36	M	6:90
Stife, E.	Osage, Ridgeway, Superior	54	F	8:358
Stife, L.	" " " (Farmer)	55	M	8:358
Stiges, Mary	Atchison, Mt. Pleasant	69	F	1:163
Stile, T. C.	Franklin, Centropolis, Minneola	27	M	8:205
Stiles, R. C.	Arapahoe, South Park	20	M	11:63
Stiles, Sally NC	McGee, Brushville P.O.	40	F	9:230
Stiles, William NC	" " " (Farmer)	80	M	9:230

Name	Kansas: County; Township; P.O. Arap. Co.: Census Div. Not Township	Age	Sex	Census V. Pg
Still, A.NC	Frank., Centrop.,Minneola (Physician)	64	M	8:205
Still, J. M.	Douglas, Wakarusa, Lawrence(Physician)	40	M	6:251
Still, Rhob	" " "	28	F	6:251
Still, W. P.	Franklin, Centropolis, Minneola	57	F	8:205
Stillhorn, J.	Arapahoe, South Park	29	M	11:137
Stillian, M	Cof., Avon, Burlington(Harness Maker)	29	M	4:16
Stock, Elizabeth	Wyandotte, Quindaro	32	F	10:55
Stockings, J.	Arapahoe, South Park	27	M	11:12
Stockmeyer, Wm.	" " "	24	M	11:129
Stockton, W.	Arapahoe, Valley of the Platte	27	M	11:817
Stolper, Robert E.SC	Leavenworth, Fort Leavenworth P.O.	7	M	10:320
Stone, B. L. G.	Allen, Geneva P.O. (Physician)	46	M	2:252
Stone, E.	Osage, Ridgeway, Superior	33	F	8:359
Stone, Elija	Arapahoe, South Park	26	M	11:148
Stone, Harriet	Bourbon, Xenia P.O. (Housewife)	30	F	2:130
Stone, Henry H.	Bourbon, Mapleton P.O. (Farmer)	57	M	2:138
Stone, James A.NC	Bourbon, Raysville P.O. (Farmer)	44	M	2:158
Stone, Martin	Bourbon, Xenia P.O.	11	M	2:130
Stone, S.	Arapahoe, South Park	26	M	11:123
Stone, WilliamNC	Bourbon, Raysville P.O. (Farmer)	46	M	2:168
Stonington, L. S.	Arapahoe, South Park	23	M	11:169
Stout, Addison NC	Breckenridge, Pike, Plymouth	4	M	4:213
Stout, Albert	Marshall, Blue Rapids, Marysville	12	M	3:207
Stout, Albert	" " " " (Farmer)	30	M	3:206
Stout, AsenathNC	Breckenridge, Pike, Plymouth	35	F	4:214
Stout, Cyrus NC	" " " (Farmer)	33	F	4:214
Stout, James NC	" " " (Farmer)	24	M	4:214
Stout, Joseph G. NC	" " "	4	M	4:214
Stout, Malon NC	" " " (Farmer)	29	M	4:213
Stout, Nancy NC	" " "	26	F	4:213
Stout, Nancy	Marshall, Blue Rapids, Marysville	30	F	3:206
Stout, Obed V. NC	Breckenridge, Pike, Plymouth	10	M	4:214
Stout, Peter	Marshall, Blue Rapids, Marysville	13	M	3:207
Stout, R.	Arapahoe, South Park	20	M	11:122
Stout, Sarah NC	Breckenridge, Pike, Plymouth	67	F	4:214
Stout, Susan NC	" " "	30	F	4:214
Stout, Thomas NC	" " "	6	M	4:214
Stover, Elizabeth	Breckenridge, Americus	24	F	4:227
Stover, Maria	" "	53	F	4:227
Stover, (?) W.	Arapahoe, Valley of the Platte	26	M	11:860
Stover, Wm.	Breckenridge, Americus (Farmer)	22	M	4:227
Stowe, Chas. E. NC	Arapahoe, Denver (Miner)	25	M	11:414
Strange, Calvin	Jeff., Jeff., Crooked Cr. (Laborer)	35	M	5:38
Strange, Charles	Doniphan, Washington, Wathena	15	M	1:329
Strange, E.	" " "	30	F	1:329
Strange, Haywood	" " "	8	M	1:329
Strange, P.	" " "	4	F	1:329
Strange, R.	" " "	11	F	1:329
Strange, R.	" " " (Farmer)	33	M	1:329
Strange, S.	" " " (Farmer)	59	M	1:329
Strange, Samuel	" " "	11	M	1:329
Strange, V.? NC	" " "	23	F	1:329
Strange, Wm. H.	" " "	13	M	1:329
Stranger, R.	Arapahoe, South Park	26	M	11:133
Striekler, James	Atchison, Lancaster (Farmer)	40	M	1:114
Strickler, Marshall	" "	12	M	1:114
Striekler, Martha Jane	" "	37	F	1:114
Striekler, Mary M.	" "	9	F	1:114
Striekler, Newman C.	" "	11	M	1:114
Strickler, Sarah E.	" "	9	F	1:114
Strickler, Sarah F.	" "	12	F	1:114

Name	Kansas: County; Township; P.O. Arap. Co.: Census Div. Not Township	Age	Sex	Census V. Pg.
Stricklin, S. Y. NC	Johnson, DeSota, Lexington (Grocer)	31	M	6:20
Stringfellow, B. F.	Atchison, Ward 2 (Attorney)	42	M	1:38
Strofford, J. NC	Frank., Centrop., Minneola (Farmer)	25	M	8:213
Strong, M. SC	Frank.;Potta.;Scipio, Anderson Co.	40	F	8:238
Strosmider, Elijah	Woodson, Owl Creek, Neosho Falls	21	M	9:149
Strosmider, J.	" " " " "(Farmer)	28	M	9:149
Stroud, James NC	Coffey, Leroy, Burlington (Farmer)	34	M	4:21
Stroud, James M. NC	" " " (Farmer)	24	M	4:21
Stroule, Dasilla	Arapahoe, Idahoe	35	F	11:593
Strumbo, James W.	Brown, Walnut Cr., Carson (Farmer)	40	M	3:29
Strumbo, Mary Ann	" " " "	38	F	3:29
Stuart, J. E. B. [1]	Davis, Ft. Riley Res. (Lieut. USA)	27	M	9:358
Stuck, J. C.	Johnson, Monticello (Farmer)	29	M	6:80
Stuck, Wm.	Arapahoe, South Clear Creek	26	M	11:704
Stuckman, E.	Arapahoe, South Park	24	M	11:182
Studebaker, Susanna	Douglas, Willow Springs	36	F	6:328
Stukesberry, Enoch	Jeff., Jeff., Winchester (Farmer)	60	M	5:42
Sturgis, D.	Arapahoe, South Park	25	M	11:171
Stutz, Rebecca NC	Atchison, Mt. Pleasant	55	F	1:157
Subtin, A. J.	Coffey, Neosho, Burlington (Farmer)	26	M	4:71
Subtin, Levi	" " " (Farmer)	39	M	4:71
Subtin, Sarah	" " "	39	F	4:71
Suddler, Charlotte	Douglas, Clinton	17	F	6:417
Sugar, James	Jeff., Ky., Oskaloosa (Farm Laborer)	18	M	5:64
Sullivan, Wm.	Arapahoe, South Park	34	M	11:131
Sumers, Hardin NC	Bourbon, Fort Scott P.O.	58	M	2:190
Summers, C. W.	Douglas, Lecompton (Clerk)	18	M	6:350
Sumpter, S. P. SC	Arapahoe,South Clear Cr.(Miner) 28or38		M	11:633
Sumpter, Thos. O. SC	Arapahoe, Valley of the Platte(Miner)	26	M	11:774
Suttle, John	Breckenridge, Emporia (Cab. Maker)	43	M	4:200
Sutton, D. W.	Coffey, Leroy (Miller)	44	M	4:33
Sutton, Lucinda NC	Douglas, Willow Springs, McKinney	40	F	6:308
Swain, Francis NC	Leavenworth, Alexandria, Easton	48	F	10:456
Swain, George NC	" " " (Farmer)	52	M	10:456
Swain, Mary B. NC	Douglas, Clinton	46	F	6:410
Swain, S. NC	" " (Farmer)	50?	M	6:410
Swank, B. V.	Franklin, Centropolis, Prairie City	4		8:219
Swank, W.	Franklin, Centropolis, Minneola	33	F	8:201
Swaringer, Elezabeth	Marshall, Marysville	9	F	3:251
Swaringer, Isabell	" "	7	F	3:252
Sweecer, Samuel	Coffey, Leroy, Burlington (Farmer)	27	M	4:24
Sweeny, Eliza Ann	Atchison, Shannon, Atchison	16	F	1:75
Sweeny, Mary E.	" " "	6	F	1:75
Sweeny, T. C.	Arapahoe, South Park	36	M	11:126
Sweitzer, J.	" " "	24	M	11:129
Sweney, Sarah	Atchison, Ward 3	18	F	1:61
Swift, John SC	Wash., Wash., Marysville (Surveyor)	27	M	3:259
Swift, Sarah SC	Leavenworth, Fort Leavenworth P.O.	26	F	10:318
Swisher, D.	Johnson, Lexington (Farmer)	28	M	6:77
Swisher, Frances H.	Breckenridge, Fremont	24	F	4:166
Swisher, Givens C.	Leavenworth, Kickapoo	12	M	10:329
Swisher, James H.	"	14	M	10:329
Swisher, Jane	Nemaha, Richmond, Seneca	38	F	3:105
Swisher, Melzo A.	Leavenworth, Kickapoo	5	M	10:329
Swisher, Peter	Nemaha, Richmond, Seneca (Farmer)	40	M	3:105
Swisher, Rhody	Leavenworth, Kickapoo	32	F	10:329
Swisher, Robert	" " (Farmer)	36	M	10:329
Swisher, Wm. B.	Breckenridge, Fremont (Physician)	34	M	4:166
Swisher, Zelfa V.	Leavenworth, Kickapoo	8	F	10:329
Sylvester, Elizath	Woodson, Verdigris, Belmont	22	F	9:162

[1] "Jeb" Stuart who became the beloved Confederate cavalry officer; see p. xxxi.

Name	Kansas: County; Township; P.O. Arap. Co.: Census Div. Not Township	Age	Sex	Census V. Pg.
Sylvester, Thomas	Woodson, Verdigris, Belmont (Farmer)	25	M	8:162
Symer, Wm. P.	Doniphan, Doniphan	31	M	1:383
Sypherd, Charles	Bourbon, Turkey Creek P.O.	18	M	2:122
Sypherd, Elizabeth	" " " " (Housewife)	45	F	2:122
Sypherd, John L.	" " " " (Farmer)	49	M	2:122
Talbot, Geo.	Arapahoe, South Park (Miner)	20	M	11:16
Tallock, L. SC	Riley, Manhattan-Henryville P.O.	38	F	9:311
Tamell, H.	Arapahoe, Valley of the Platte(Miner)	29	M	11:861
Tanner, B. R.	Arapahoe, Nevada Gulch (Miner)	31	M	11:521
Tappey, M.	Johnson, Olathe (Carpenter)	26	M	6:7
Tarbor, PeterNC	Arapahoe, Central City	28	M	11:509
Targold, A. F.	Arapahoe, South Clear Creek	36	M	11:694
Tarleton, O.SC	Arapahoe, Valley of the Platte	26	M	11:812
Tarr, Sam'l.	Arapahoe, South Clear Creek	24	M	11:751
Tarr, Washington	Atchison, Grasshopper, Kennekuk	24	M	1:86
Tasistu, G.	Arapahoe, South Park	34	M	11:190
Tate, Colly P.NC	Lykins, Wea, Paola	15	M	8:117
Tate, Edith	Leavenworth, Delaware, Delaware City	35	F	10:423
Tate, ErvinNC	Lykins, Wea, Paola	11	M	8:117
Tate, Lewis F.NC	" " "	13	M	8:117
Tate, Mary J.NC	" " "	9	F	8:117
Tate, Owen D.NC	" " " (Farmer)	45	M	8:117
Tate, SamuelNC	" " "	17	M	8:117
Tate, Solomon H.NC	" " "	4	M	8:117
Taugue, Sarah	Breckenridge, Americus	27	F	4:223
Taylor, A. E.	Johnson;Oxford;New Santa Fe, Mo.	9	F	6:110
Taylor, Armeta	Marshall, Vermillion, Barrett Mills	23	F	3:216
Taylor, F. J.	Johnson;Oxford;New Santa Fe, Mo.	12	F	6:110
Taylor, G.	Jefferson, Oskaloosa (Farmer)	33	M	5:121
Taylor, Goodwin	Lykins, Paola (Farmer)	54	M	8:26
Taylor, Isaac	Linn, Centerville, Keokuk (Farmer)	33	M	7:84
Taylor, J.	Doniphan, White Cloud (Cabinet Maker)	55	M	1:442
Taylor, James	Doniphan, Center, Troy (Farmer)	83	M	1:267
Taylor, JaneNC	Lykins, Paola	55	F	8:27
Taylor, John	Atchison, Ward 3 (Attorney)	50	M	1:57
Taylor, L. V.	Riley, Manhattan P.O.	29	F	9:281
Taylor, M. J.	Johnson;Oxford;New Santa Fe, Mo.	5	F	6:110
Taylor, N.	" " " " " "	26	F	6:110
Taylor, R. Z.	Davis, Kansas Falls P.O. (Merchant)	27	M	9:331
Taylor, Rachel	Jefferson, Oskaloosa	54	F	5:124
Taylor, Riley	Anderson, Walker, Garnett (Laborer)	22	M	7:244
Taylor, Rolly	Jefferson, Oskaloosa (Farmer)	60	M	5:124
Taylor, Susan	Doniphan, Iowa Point	22	F	1:452
Taylor, T.	John.;Oxf.;N.Santa Fe,Mo.(Carpenter)	45	M	6:110
Taylor, William	McGee, Fort Scott P.O. (Farmer)	53	M	9:206
Telford, S. V.NC	Arrap.,Tarryall,S.P.;Tarr.,Fair Play	23	M	11:616
Tengue, JacobNC	Bourbon, Turkey Creek P.O. (Farmer)	48	M	2:108
Tenison, Mary A.	" " " "(Housewife)	29	F	2:107
Tennaiw, J.NC	Arapahoe, South Park (Miner)	36	M	11:78
Tennyson, Scott	Arapahoe, Mountain City	9	M	11:468
Terrance, T. S.	Arapahoe, South Clear Creek	35	M	11:693
Terry, Sarah[1],NC?	Douglas, Lecompton	11	F	6:353
Terteet, H. A.SC	Arapahoe, Russell Gulch (Miner)	21	M	11:547
Tetens, P. S.	Douglas, Wakarusa	27	M	6:242
Teter, Lubar	Arapahoe, Central City (Miner)	53	M	11:579
Tharp, Anna E.	Lyk.;Sugar Cr.;West Pt.,Mo. (Farmer)	39	F	8:103
Tharp, Benj.	" " " " " " (Farmer)	66	M	8:104
Tharp, ElizabethNC	Lykins, Marysville, Paola (Widow)	69	F	8:124

[1]State of birth questioned because original entry was on wrong line.

Name	Kansas: County; Township; P.O. Arap. Co.: Census Div. Not Township	Age	Sex	Census V.: Pg.
Thayer, A. C.[NC]	Frank., Ottawa, Hickory Cr. (Farmer)	23	M	8:264
Thayer, B. M.[NC]	" " " " (Farmer)	49	M	8:264
Thayer, C.[NC]	" " " "	41	F	8:264
Thayer, C.[NC]	" " " "	17	F	8:264
Thayer, H. C.[NC]	" " " "	11	M	8:264
Thayer, M.[NC]	" " " "	13	F	8:264
Thayer, N.[NC]	" " " "	17	F	8:264
Thayer, P.[NC]	" " " "	7	F	8:264
Thayer, R. D.[NC]	" " " " (Farmer)	22	M	8:264
Thayer, R. K.[NC]	" " " "	9	M	8:264
Thayer, S. B.[NC]	" " " "	3	M	8:264
Thayer, W. D.[NC]	" " " " (Farmer)	20	M	8:264
Thenber, J. A.	Arapahoe, South Park	29	M	11:121
Terrell, Wm.	Leavenworth, Ward 2 (Barber)	19	BM	10:161
Thirston, Balis[SC]	Leav., Alexandria, Easton (Farmer)	32	M	10:455
Thomas, A.[NC]	Johnson, McCamish, Hibbard	36	F	6:59
Thomas, Able	Mars., Vermil., Barrett Mills(Farmer)	60	M	3:213
Thomas, Henderson[NC]	Butler, Chelsea (Farmer)	54	M	4:349
Thomas, J. F.	Arapahoe, Denver (Miner)	31	M	11:393
Thomas, Joseph[NC]	Leav., Alexandria, Easton (Farmer)	44	M	10:440
Thomas, Lewis[NC]	Linn, Potosi, Rovella (Farmer)	42	M	7:56
Thomas, Margaret[NC]	Butler, Chelsea	55	F	4:349
Thomas, Pressilla[NC]	Linn, Potosi, Rovella	40	F	7:56
Thomas, Samuel	Mars., Vermil., Barrett Mills(Farmer)	42	M	3:213
Thomas, Z. H.[NC]	Johnson, McCamish, Hibbard (Farmer)	34	M	6:59
Thompson, B. A.	Atchison, Mt. Pleasant (Farmer)	60	M	1:158
Thompson, C. P.	Doniphan, Washington, Whitehead	17	M	1:327
Thompson, Caroline T.	Leavenworth, Easton	37	F	10:300
Thompson, Chas. A.	Dickinson, Kansas Falls P.O.(Farmer)	28	M	4:304
Thompson, E.	Doniphan, Burr Oak, Whitehead	8	F	1:351
Thompson, Elisabeth	Leavenworth, Ward 3	37	F	10:213
Thompson, Eliza A.[NC]	Breckenridge, Emporia	32	F	4:204
Thompson, Geo.[NC]	Arapahoe; Tarryall, South Park	26	M	11:610
Thompson, George W.[NC]	Breckenridge, Emporia (Farmer)	34	M	4:204
Thompson, Henry S.	Arapahoe, South Park (Carpenter)	46	M	11:14
Thompson, J. M.	Don., Wash., Whitehead (Physician)	24	M	1:297
Thompson, John[NC]	Doniphan, Marion, Palermo (Farmer)	40	M	1:280
Thompson, L.	Riley, Manhattan-Henryville P.O.	63	F	9:311
Thompson, L.(or J?) M.	Doniphan, Washington, Whitehead	19	F	1:327
Thompson, Louisa	Lykins, Richland, Paola	33	F	8:15
Thompson, Mariah A.	Atchison, Mt. Pleasant	49	F	1:165
Thompson, Mary	Woodson, Verdigris, Belmont (F.W.)	23	F	9:159
Thompson, Mary	Marshall, Blue Rapids, Marysville	38	F	3:207
Thompson, Mary	Dickinson, Kansas Falls P.O.	28	F	4:304
Thompson, Mary[NC]	Doniphan, Marion, Palermo	38	F	1:280
Thompson, Mary J.	Leavenworth, Ward 3	11	F	10:213
Thompson, Rollins?	Doniphan, Wash., Whitehead (Farmer)	57	F	1:327
Thompson, R. C.	Leavenworth, Ward 3 (Merchant)	47	M	10:213
Thompson, Samuel	" " "	7	M	10:213
Thompson, Virginia	Doniphan, Center, Troy	21	F	1:266
Thompson, W.	Linn, Scott, Brooklyn (Carpenter)	35	M	7:15
Thompson, Waddy	Lykins, Richland, Paola (Trader)	32	M	8:15
Thompson, Wm. G.	Leavenworth, Ward 3	14	M	10:213
Thornbough, J. (or P.?)[1]	Franklin, Ottawa, Hickory Creek	8	M	8:261
Thornbough, S.[NC]	" " " "	43	F	8:261
Thornburgh, Wm.	Atchison, Ward 2 (Jeweler)	25	M	1:34
Thornsbury, Caroline	Morris, Neosho, Council Grove	22	F	4:275
Thornsbury, Elizabeth	" " " "	21	F	4:275
Thornsbury, Henry	" " " " (Farmer)	61	M	4:275

[1] State of birth may be Ia. rather than Va.

Name	Kansas: County; Township; P.O. Arap. Co.: Census Div. Not Township	Age	Sex	Census V.:Pg.
Thornsbury, Jackson	Morris, Neosho, Council Grove(Farmer)	18	M	4:275
Thornsbury, Nancy	" " " "	56	F	4:275
Thornsbury, Wm.	" " " "	13	M	4:275
Thorp, Emily[NC]	Leav., Stranger, Leavenworth City	36	F	10:474
Thorp, Josiah[NC]	" " " "	14	M	10:474
Thorp, Sarah J.	Allen, Elizabeth Town P.O.	32	F	2:239
Thorp, William[NC]	Leav., Stranger, Leav. City (Farmer)	33	M	10:474
Thrasher, Luther A.	Allen, Iola P.O. (Farmer)	25	M	2:269
Thrasher, William C.	" " " (Farmer)	30	M	2:249
Threewitt, Jas.	Lykins, Paola (Farmer)	27	M	8:41
Throckmoton, R.	Linn, Mound City (Farmer)	49	M	7:126
Throop, H. S.[NC]	Arapahoe, South Park (Miner)	47	M	11:62
Thurman, F. R.	Arapahoe, Spring Gulch (Miner)	52	M	11:539
Tier, A. W.	Don., Wash., Elwood (Carpenter)	28	M	1:337
Tileston, J.	Arapahoe, South Park	50	M	11:61
Tilghman, Amanda M.	Atchison, Mt. Pleasant	28	F	1:156
Tillinghust, H.	Arapahoe, South Park	43	M	11:174
Tilly, John H.	Bourbon, Barnesville P.O. (Physician)	31	M	2:169
Tilson, I. P.	Arapahoe, South Clear Creek	21	M	11:743
Tilton, S. D.[NC]	" " " " (Miner)	32	M	11:670
Timmons, J. R.	Don., Washington, Elwood (Teamster)	40	M	1:335
Tindal, D.	Don., Burr Oak, Whitehead (Farmer)	35	M	1:355
Tindal, P.	Don., Burr Oak, Whitehead (Farmer)	31	M	1:355
Tindal, W. H.	" " " " (Farmer)	40	M	1:355
Tindle, M.	" " " "	25	F	1:355
Tinner, Nathan	Arapahoe, South Park	31	M	11:197
Tippan, J. A.[1]	Franklin, Ottawa, Hickory Creek	3	F	8:264
Tittle, Anthony	Bourbon, Mapleton P.O. (Farmer)	53	M	2:132
Titus, Chas.	Arapahoe, Denver (Miner)	23	M	11:420
Toban, Fanny	Leavenworth, 1st Ward	32	F	10:114
Toban, Sarah	" " "	14	F	10:114
Tobey, N. C.	Arapahoe, South Park	27	M	11:23
Todd, John S.	Leavenworth, 1st Ward	4	M	10:111
Todd, Susan	" " " (Boarding House)	30	F	10:111
Todd, Thomas	" " "	6	M	10:111
Todd, Wm.	" " "	10	M	10:111
Todd, Wm. H.	Leavenworth, Ward 2 (Tinsmith)	21	M	10:164
Todhunter, L.	Douglas, Lecompton	22	F	6:370
Tolbert, James	Atchison, 1st Ward (Carpenter)	47	M	1:18
Toler, C.	Douglas, Lecompton	6	F	6:353
Toler, C. M.	" "	7	F	6:353
Toler, J.[NC]	Johnson, Monticello (Farmer)	63	M	6:83
Toler, N. S.?[NC]	" "	45	F	6:83
Toler, R.	Douglas, Lecompton	12	M	6:353
Tomer, Jno.	Arapahoe, South Park	26	M	11:251
Tomlinson, R.	Arapahoe, South Clear Creek	24	M	11:630
Tomlinson, S. C.[NC]	Arapahoe, South Park	26	M	11:128
Toney, W.	Cof., Calif., Burlington (Carpenter)	33	M	4:64
Tools, A. G.	Douglas, Palmyra, Baldwin (Farmer)	58	M	6:288
Torrance, R. C.	Arapahoe, South Clear Creek	32	M	11:655
Torrence, Jas.	Arapahoe, Quartz Valley	29	M	11:500
Total, Amelia[SC]	Shawnee, Tecumseh	18	F	9:69
Total, Henry[SC]	" " (Laborer)	21	M	9:69
Totton, Mary A.[NC]	Lykins, Osawatomie, Indianapolis	29	F	8:65
Totton, Nancy	Chase, Toledo	64	F	4:340
Towner, Jno.	Arapahoe, South Park	29	M	11:231
Towns, Jno. T.	Arapahoe, California Gulch	27	M	11:314
Townsend, A.	Arapahoe; Tarryall, South Park	21	M	11:614

[1]State of birth may be Ia. rather than Va.

Name	Kansas: County; Township; P.O. Arap. Co.: Census Div. Not Township	Age	Sex	Census V. Pg.
Townsend, Hannah	Leavenworth, 1st Ward	45	BF	10:116
Townsend, John T.	Lykins, Paola (Saloon Keeper)	28	M	8:25
Townsend, Lucy	Leavenworth, Ward 4	35	F	10:249
Townsend, M.	Douglas, Lecompton	34	BF	6:373
Townshend, Martha	Jefferson, Grasshopper Falls	35	BF	5:8
Townshend, Raney	" " "	60	BF	5:8
Tracher, E. J.	Frank., Potta., Shermanville	50	F	8:246
Tracher, M. M.	" " " (Teacher)	18	F	8:246
Trackwell, Wm.	Leav., Alexandria, Easton (Farmer)	58	M	10:454
Tracy, Anna	Bourbon, Marmaton P.O. (Housewife)	29	F	2:206
Trarke, D. S.	Arapahoe, Valley of the Platte	24	M	11:802
Traverse, F. G. W.	Brown, Locknon, Powhattan	15	M	3:63
Travis, C. A.	Douglas, Lecompton (Book Dealer)	27	M	6:350
Trescott, W. F.	Arapahoe, Valley of the Platte	24	M	11:810
Triggs, John	Breck., Pike, Plymouth (Farmer)	61	M	4:210
Triggs, Martha NC	" " "	39	F	4:210
Tritt, Anderson	Leavenworth, Alexandria, Easton	28	M	10:445
Tritt, Francis M.	" " "	22	F	10:445
Tritt, Perry B.	" " "	28	M	10:445
Tritt, Thomas	" " " (Farmer)	32	M	10:444
Trotter, Hanley B. NC	Bourbon, Turkey Creek P.O. (Farmer)	36	M	2:122
Trout, S. C.	Arapahoe, South Park	37	M	11:24
Trowbridge, Beal SC	Arapahoe, South Clear Creek (Miner)	27	M	11:686
Trowbridge, J. M.	Breckenridge, Forest Hill (Carpenter)	27	M	4:179
Troxel, Fredein	Lykins, Osawatomie (Farmer)	69	M	8:66
Truax, G.	Arapahoe, Lake Gulch (Merchant)	25	M	11:485
True, A. E.	Johnson, Olathe	53	F	6:3
Tucker, Arnold	Shawnee, Topeka (Laborer)	17	M	9:14
Tucker, Eliza	Linn, Mound City	33	F	7:111
Tucker, L. P.	" " " (Farmer)	45	F	7:111
Tuggel, John A.	Lykins, Marysville, Paola (Farmer)	48	M	8:125
Tull, Geo. R. NC	Lykins, Paola, Paola	23	M	8:41
Tulley, Philip	Arapahoe, South Park (Miner)	40	M	11:78
Turner, A.	Linn, Mound City	58	F	7:102
Turner, E. NC	Johnson, Gardner (Farmer)	37	M	6:50
Turner, G. G.	Arapahoe, Valley of the Platte	27	M	11:840
Turner, Grace	Nemaha, Rock Creek	50	F	3:80
Turner, H. C. NC	Johnson, Gardner	13	M	6:50
Turner, J. E. NC	" "	5	M	6:50
Turner, J. O. SC	Linn, Potosi (Farmer)	32	M	7:72
Turner, J. T. NC	Johnson, Gardner	8	M	6:50
Turner, M. J. NC	" "	12	F	6:50
Turner, R. NC	" "	10	F	6:50
Turner, R. A. SC	Arapahoe, Nevada Gulch (Miner)	23	M	11:533
Turner, R. N. NC	Johnson, Gardner	4	M	6:50
Turner, S. NC	" "	36	F	6:50
Turner, S. A. NC	" "	11	F	6:50
Tussman, W.	Franklin, Centropolis, Minneola	30	F	8:202
Tuttle, A. S. NC	Arapahoe, South Park	32	M	11:135
Tuttle, Abraham H.	Coffey, Burlington	16	M	4:43
Tuttle, John L.	Coffey, Burlington	11	M	4:43
Tuttle, William	" "	13	M	4:43
Tuttle, William NC	" " (Farmer)	29	M	4:43
Twidwell, William NC	Brown, Walnut Creek, Hamlin (Farmer)	38	M	3:32
Tyler, A.	Douglas, Lecompton	24	F	6:352
Undeler, Frances Carr	Wyandotte, Wyandotte (Laborer)	30	M	10:33
Underhill, Daniel NC	Linn, Liberty, Centerville (Farmer)	64	M	7:3
Underwood, J. NC	Don., Wolf River, Doniphan (Farmer)	60	M	1:396
Underwood, S. NC	Don., Wolf River, Doniphan	54	F	1:396
Urich, R.	Frank.,Prair.,Peoria City (Bricklayer)	29	M	8:268

Name	Kansas: County; Township; P.O. Arap. Co.: Census Div. Not Township	Age	Sex	Census V.:Pg.
Urich, W. F.	Frank., Prair., Peoria City	5	M	8:268
Vadeen, G.?	Doniphan, White Cloud (Farmer)	30	M	1:437
Vadeen, Wm. H.	" " " (Farmer)	35	M	1:437
Vail, Margret NC	Wyandotte, Wyandotte	34	F	10:42
Valle, Adolphus	Arapahoe, South Park (Miner)	40	M	11:68
Vallentine, J. P.	Arapahoe, Valley of the Platte	31	M	11:863
Van Blarcum, W.	Arapahoe, South Park	39	M	11:195
Vance, James	Dickinson, Kansas Falls P.O.(Laborer)	62	M	4:307
Vanderpool, Wm. NC	Davis,Ft.Riley,Ashland P.O.(Blacksmth)	52	M	9:352
Vanderslice, Eloana NC	Lykins, Osawatomie	60	F	8:63
Van Doren, T.	Arapahoe, South Clear Creek	24	M	11:730
Vandozen, John	Atch., Shannon, Atchison (Farmer)	27	M	1:76
Vandozen, Robert	" " " (Farmer)	25	M	1:76
Van Llyck, T.	Arapahoe, Valley of the Platte	27	M	11:824
Vannatta, Emma E.	Breckenridge, Waterloo	28	F	4:151
Vannory, Abraham NC	Atchison, Ward 1 (Carpenter)	39	M	1:19
Vanscoyee, Aaron	Anderson, Jackson, Garnett (Farmer)	56	M	7:208
Van Winkle, S.	Arapahoe, South Park	37	M	11:17
Vanzant, George C.	Douglas, Lecompton (Surveyor)	49	M	6:372
Varner, Charles NC	Jeff., Jeff., Crooked Cr.(FarmLaborer)	15	M	5:37
Varner, Joseph NC	" " " " (FarmLaborer)	18	M	5:37
Varner, Thomas NC	" " " " (Farmer)	44	M	5:37
Vaughan, Chas.	Arapahoe, South Park	33	M	11:263
Vaughan, J. C. SC	Leavenworth, Ward 4	54	M	10:256
Vaughn, Joseph NC	Brown, Irving, Hiawatha (Farmer)	49	M	3:7
Vaughn, Celia NC	" " "	3	F	3:7
Vaughn, Hewit NC	" " "	10	M	3:7
Vaught, Anthony SC	Wash., Wash., Marysville (Merchant)	36	M	3:259
Vaun, C. J.?	Otoe, Otoe, Chelsea	45	F	4:353
Veach, A.	Cof., Calif., Burlington (Farmer)	33	M	4:67
Veach, H.	Johnson, Gardner (Farmer)	35	M	6:56
Veach, R.	Cof., Calif., Burlington (Farmer)	22	M	4:67
Veatch, Hanson	Lykins, Osawatomie (Farmer)	43	M	8:55
Veatch, Sarah	" "	66	F	8:56
Vedder, C. H.	Arapahoe, South Park	25	M	11:136
Venable, D. SC	Arapahoe, Valley of the Platte			11:778
Venable, Hugh SC	Atchison, Ward 3 (Carpenter)	33	M	1:47
Venten, Felix	Allen, Humboldt P.O. (Blacksmith)	29	M	2:296
Verr, Blance A.	Anderson, Walker, Garnett (Farmer)	27	F	7:233
Verr, Hiram	" " "	16	M	7:233
Verr, Martha J.	" " "	18	F	7:233
Verr, Margaret	" " "	10	F	7:233
Verr, Mary C.	" " "	16	F	7:233
Verr, Phoebe	" " "	42	F	7:233
Verr, William	" " " (Farmer)	40	M	7:233
Verr, William	" " " (Farmer)	23	M	7:233
Vickers, William NC	Breckenridge, Waterloo (Stone Mason)	37	M	4:154
Vieus, Jemina	Bourbon, Fort Scott P.O.	15	F	2:90
Vinyard, Griffin	Atchison, Mt. Pleasant	30	M	1:159
Vitto, John NC	Coffey, Leroy, Burlington (Farmer)	53	M	4:20
Wabright, J.	Woodson, Eureka (Farmer)	40	M	9:181
Wade, Ellen	Doniphan, Iowa Point	6	F	1:459
Wade, Louisa	" " "	11	F	1:459
Wadkins, Eliza J. NC	Bourbon, Fort Scott P.O. (Housewife)	32	F	2:199
Wadkins, Mathew NC	" " " " (Farmer)	38	M	2:199
Wadkins, Morning	" " " "	16	F	2:199
Wadkins, Ruth	" " " "	10	F	2:199
Wadkins, Thomas	" " " "	14	M	2:199
Wadsworth, H.	Arapahoe, South Park (Ranch)	39	M	11:64
Wagman, James K.	Shawnee, Topeka (Farmer)	44	M	9:27

Name	Kansas: County; Township; P.O. Arap. Co.: Census Div. Not Township	Age	Sex	Census V.Pg.
Wagner, Harriett	Lykins, Marysville, Lyons (Widow)	55	F	8:120
Wagoner, Mary	Bourbon, Barnesville P.O.(Housekeeper)	51	F	2:180
Wain, Elizabeth[SC]	Linn, Mound City	50	F	7:127
Wakefield, J. A.[SC]	Douglas, Kanwaca, Lawrence (Farmer)	64	M	6:380
Wakefield, Joanna	Wyandotte, Wyandotte	33	F	10:14
Wakefield, Phyllis[1]	Leavenworth, Ward 3	58	BF	10:203
Waker, J.[NC]	Arapahoe, South Clear Creek (Miner)	25	M	11:754
Wakins, Washington	Marshall, Marysville (Master Mason)	25	M	3:254
Waldran, J.	Arapahoe, Valley of the Platte	24	M	11:818
Walker, A.[NC]	Linn, Centerville, Keokuk (Farmer)	50	M	7:83
Walker, A.	Doniphan, Marion, Palermo	27	F	1:277
Walker, Chas.[NC]	Linn, Centerville, Keokuk (Farmer)	16	M	7:84
Walker, Elizabeth[NC]	Linn, Centerville, Keokuk	7	F	7:84
Walker, Everett	Wyandotte, Wyandotte	7	M	10:36
Walker, G.	Arapahoe, South Park	27	M	11:219
Walker, Hannah	Wyandotte, Wyandotte	60	F	10:16
Walker, I.	Osage, Ridgeway, Burlingame	22	M	8:334
Walker, I.[2]	" " " (Farmer)	22	M	8:334
Walker, J.[NC]	Linn, Scott, Brooklyn (Farmer)	45	M	7:14
Walker, J.	Wood.,Verdigris,Pleasant Gr.(Farmer)	35	M	9:163
Walker, Jno.	Arapahoe, South Clear Creek (Miner)	25	M	11:592
Walker, John[NC]	Linn, Centerville, Keokuk	8	M	7:84
Walker, K.[NC]	Linn, Scott, Brooklyn	45	F	7:15
Walker, M.	Doniphan, Iowa Point (Farmer)	27	M	1:433
Walker, Margaret[NC]	Linn, Centerville, Keokuk	12	F	7:84
Wall, Margarett[NC]	Lykins, Wea, Paola	9	F	8:118
Walker, Martha[NC]	Linn, Centerville, Keokuk	14	F	7:84
Walker, Mary	Atchison, Mt. Pleasant	58	F	1:167
Walker, Nancy	Douglas, Lawrence	34	F	6:218
Walker, Samuel	Marshall, Blue Rapids (School Teacher)	75	M	3:201
Walker, Sarah[NC]	Linn, Centerville, Keokuk	17	F	7:83
Walker, Susan[NC]	" " "	40	F	7:83
Wall, Amanda R.[NC]	Lykins, Middle Creek, Jonesville	13	F	8:110
Wall, Francis	Jeff., Rock Cr.,Mt. Florence (Farmer)	24	M	5:89
Wall, John H.[NC]	Lykins, Middle Creek, Jonesville	18	M	8:110
Wall, Margarett C.[NC]	" " " "	10	F	8:110
Wall, Martha E.[NC]	Lykins, Middle Creek, Paola	20	F	8:109
Wall, Mary C.[NC]	" " " "	16	F	8:109
Wall, Nancy J.[NC]	" " " "	22	F	8:109
Wall, Rebecca[NC]	" " " "	45	F	8:109
Wall, Rich'd. M.	" " " " (Farmer)	48	M	8:109
Wall, Susan J.	Lykins, Middle Creek, Jonesville	8	F	8:110
Wallace, E.[NC]	Douglas, Lecompton, Lecompton	32	F	6:371
Wallace, G. W.	Johnson, Olathe (Shoemaker)	48	M	6:117
Wallace, J. A.[NC]	Douglas, Lecompton	15	M	6:371
Wallace, J. T.[NC]	" " (Farmer)	38	M	6:371
Wallace, James L.[NC]	Leav.,Stranger,Leav.(Farmer & Phys.)	48	M	10:461
Wallace, Mary	Leavenworth, Ward 4	35	F	10:274
Wallace, Nancy[NC]	Douglas, Lecompton	13	F	6:371
Wallace, S.[NC]	" "	9	F	6:371
Wallace, Susan[NC]	Shawnee, Soldier, Indianola	48	F	9:87
Wallace, Thos.[SC]	Arapahoe, Lake Gulch (Miner)	38	M	11:523
Waller, Augustine[NC]	Lykins, Wea, Paola	5	M	8:118
Waller, Catherinia[NC]	" " "	16	F	8:118
Waller, Eliza	Mars.,Vermil.,Barrett Mills(Farming)	43	F	3:216
Waller, Gaston[NC]	Lykins, Wea, Paola	17	M	8:118
Waller, Gilson W.	Pot.,Shannon,Manhatt.-Henryv.(Farmer)	24	M	5:302

[1]Spelled Fellis rather than Phyllis on original census record.
[2]State of birth looks more like Ia. or La. than Va.

Name	Kansas: County; Township; P.O. Arap. Co.: Census Div. Not Township	Age	Sex	Census V.	Pg.
Waller, Henry NC	Lykins, Wea, Paola (Farmer)	40	M	8:118	
Waller, Henry NC	" " "	6	M	8:118	
Waller, Julia B. NC	" " "	10	F	8:118	
Waller, Lewis NC	" " "	3	M	8:118	
Waller, Malinda E. NC	" " "	18	F	8:118	
Waller, Mary NC	" " "	26	F	8:118	
Waller, Nancy E. NC	" " "	18	F	8:118	
Waller, Rufus	Marshall, Vermillion, Barrett Mills	22	M	3:216	
Waller, S.	Riley, Fort Riley P.O. (Cook)	20	F	9:302	
Waller, Squire J. NC	Lykins, Wea, Paola	19	M	8:118	
Wallers, Jas.	Arapahoe, Russell Gulch (Miner)	40	M	11:543	
Walters, C. S.	Arapahoe, South Park	27	M	11:169	
Walters, I. M.	Franklin, Centropolis, Minneola	11	F	8:206	
Walters, James	Jackson, Douglas, Holton (Physician)	58	M	5:176	
Walters, M.	Douglas, Lecompton	24	F	6:369	
Walters, M. A.	Osage, Ridgeway, Burlingame	34	F	8:362	
Walters, M. E.	Franklin, Centropolis, Minneola	3	F	8:206	
Walters, P. R.	" " "	3	M	8:206	
Walters, S. J.	" " "	7	M	8:206	
Walters, W.	" " "	14	M	8:206	
Walthal, Jas. L.	Lykins, Mound, Osawatomie (Farmer)	31	M	8:73	
Waltin, Benjamin NC	Allen, Humboldt P.O. (Farmer)	30	M	2:298	
Waltin, Martha A. NC	" " "	25	F	2:298	
Wanless, John SC	Shaw.,Soldier,Indian.(Farm Laborer)	22	M	9:87	
Ward, Azor NC	Bourbon, Fort Scott P.O. (Farmer)	65	M	2:214	
Ward, David S.	Bourbon, Rockford P.O. (Farmer)	36	M	2:100	
Ward, F. W.	Arapahoe, South Park	32	M	11:117	
Ward, Hiram D.	Lykins, Paola (Land Agt.)	54	M	8:34	
Ward, Jane	Arapahoe, Denver	18	F	11:373	
Ward, Jonathan	Lykins, Marysville, Lyons (Farmer)	54	M	8:126	
Ward, Madison	Bourbon, Rockford P.O. (Farmer)	34	M	2:100	
Ward, Nancy NC	Douglass, Willow Springs	35	F	6:329	
Ware, H. M.	Leavenworth, Kickapoo (Farmer)	38	M	10:411	
Ware, R.	Arapahoe, South Park	38	M	11:127	
Warner, Mary	Allen, Geneva P.O.	24	F	2:253	
Warren, Isabe	Douglas, Wakarusa, Lawrence	63	F	6:240	
Warren, Nancy NC	Anderson, Walker, Garnett	55	F	7:238	
Warren, P.	Douglas, Wakarusa, Lawrence (Farmer)	61	M	6:240	
Warwick, P.	Arapahoe, South Park	35	M	11:134	
Washington, Mary NC	Anderson, Washington, Garnett	80	F	7:253	
Wasterson, John W.	Doug.,Palmyra,Prairie C.(Carpenter)	51	M	6:271	
Waters, Jno.	Arapahoe, South Park (Miner)	29	M	11:4	
Watkins, Catharine	Leavenworth, Easton	22	F	10:286	
Watkins, Fanny NC	Anderson, Jackson, Garnett	28	F	7:208	
Watkins, Margaret NC	Chase, Toledo	33	F	4:338	
Watkins, W. NC	Arapahoe, Russell Gulch (Chopery)	23	M	11:590	
Watson, C.	Douglas, Lecompton	50	F	6:354	
Watts, Ann	Morris, Neosho, Council Grove	30	F	4:275	
Watts, Hiram	" " " " (Farmer)	26	M	4:274	
Watts, P. M.?	Douglas, Kanwaca, Lawrence (Farmer)	44	M	6:386	
Watts, Rachel	" " "	33	F	6:386	
Way, Ann S. NC	Breckenridge, Emporia	23	F	4:202	
Way, Anthony NC	Leav., Alexandria, Easton (Farmer)	52	M	10:456	
Way, Arlando NC	Breckenridge, Pike, Plymouth	9	M	4:208	
Way, Charles P.	Atchison, Shannon, Atchison	7	M	1:79	
Way, Cicero NC	Breckenridge, Pike, Plymouth	7	M	4:208	
Way, George E.	Atchison, Shannon, Atchison	11	M	1:79	
Way, James O. NC	Breckenridge, Emporia (Carpenter)	27	M	4:202	
Way, James W.	Atchison, Shannon, Atchison	5	M	1:79	
Way, John R.	" " " (Blacksmith)	40	M	1:79	

Name	Kansas: County; Township; P.O. Arap. Co.: Census Div. Not Township	Age	Sex	Census V.	Census Pg.
Way, Margaret	Atchison, Shannon, Atchison	31	F	1:79	
Way, Mary	" " "	3	F	1:79	
Way, Sarah E.	" " "	9	F	1:79	
Weatherman, Julia	Linn, Centerville, Keokuk	15	F	7:87	
Weaver, George H.	Leavenworth, Ward 3 (Merchant)	41	M	10:215	
Webb, B.	John.;Oxford; New Santa Fe, Mo.	42	M	6:107	
Webb, J. A.	" " " " " "(Farmer)	44	M	6:107	
Webb, J. S.	" " " " " "	8	M	6:107	
Webb, James C.NC	Leavenworth, Easton (Farmer)	61	M	10:302	
Webb, MargaretNC	Coffey, Leroy	40	F	4:32	
Webb, Mary Elton	Atchison, Center, Pardee	47	F	1:136	
Webb, Nancy S.SC	Allen, Humboldt P.O.	50	F	2:286	
Webb, S. E.	Johnson; Oxford; New Santa Fe, Mo.	10	F	6:107	
Webb, SmithNC	Arapahoe, Denver	24	M	11:372	
Webb, W. H.	John.;Oxf.;New Santa Fe,Mo.(Farmer)	15	M	6:107	
Webber, J.	Arapahoe, Leavenworth Gulch (Miner)	47	M	11:556	
Webster, E.	Doniphan, Iowa Point	41	M	1:448	
Webster, G. W.	" " "	8	M	1:448	
Webster, J. W.	" " " (Miller)	38	M	1:448	
Webster, Jane	Coffey, California, Burlington	36	F	4:60	
Webster, L. C.	Doniphan, Iowa Point	5	F	1:448	
Webster, M. F.	" " "	3	F	1:448	
Wecherlock, Alice	Bourbon, Raysville P.O.	4/12	F	2:162	
Wecherlock, William	" " " (Carpenter)	22	M	2:162	
Weedon, Martha	Douglas, Wakarusa, Blanton	36	F	6:263	
Weer, E.	Johnson, Shawnee	91	F	6:94	
Weer, E.NC	" "	22	F	6:94	
Weer, S. M.NC	" "	23	F	6:29	
Weibly, Sophia	Hunter, Eldorado, Chelsea	44	F	4:361	
Weigh, Betsy	Woodson, Owl Cr., Neosho Falls (F.W.)	55	F	9:149	
Weil, G. M.	Arapahoe, Valley of the Platte(Trader)	35	M	11:816	
Weir, Henry	Arapahoe, South Park	26	M	11:118	
Welborn, Eliza G.NC	Wyandotte, Quindaro	38	F	10:60	
Welch, Andrew	Jeff., Grasshopper Falls (Shoemaker)	48	M	5:24	
Welch, H.NC	Franklin, Ohio, Ohio City (Farmer)	21	F	8:234	
Welch, John	Leavenworth, 1st Ward (Blacksmith)	51	BM	10:90	
Welch, L.	Franklin, Centropolis, Minneola	4	F	8:216	
Welch, M.	" " "	26	F	8:216	
Welch, S.	" " "	8	F	8:214	
Weld, D.NC	Franklin, Pottawat., Shermanville	34	F	8:247	
Weldon, S. W.	Arapahoe, Mountain City (Miner)		M	11:462	
Welkens, W.NC	Linn, Valley, Blooming Grove (Farmer)	45	M	7:30	
Weller, Sabina	Allen, Carlisle P.O.	32	F	2:236	
Welley, Elizabeth J.	Arapahoe, Central City	21	F	11:571	
Wells, B. J.	Doniphan, Wayne, Doniphan (Laborer)	30	M	1:365	
Wells, E. C.	Doug., Willow Spr., Brooklyn (Farmer)	23	M	6:322	
Wells, Emmett M.	Douglas, Willow Springs	24	M	6:328	
Wells, James M.	" " " (Farmer)	26	M	6:328	
Wells, John W.NC	Bourbon, Turkey Creek P.O. (Farmer)	32	M	2:114	
Wells, Joseph	Atch., Center, Pardee (Rev. Soldier)	100	M	1:136	
Wells, Lavina	Douglas, Willow Springs	44	F	6:328	
Wells, Martha	" " "	22	F	6:328	
Wells, Minerva	" " "	19	F	6:328	
Wells, RobertNC	Bourbon, Turkey Creek P.O. (Farmer)	26	M	2:107	
Wells, Robt.	Douglas, Willow Springs	15	M	6:328	
Wells, Samuel	" " "	17	M	6:328	
Wells, Wm. S.	" " " (Farmer)	48	W	6:328	
Welsh, John	Douglas, Wakarusa, Lawrence	79	M	6:261	
Welsh, M. H.	Arapahoe, South Park	42	M	11:224	
Werihtman, L.	Arapahoe, South Park	34	M	11:173	

Name	Kansas: County; Township; P.O. Arap. Co.: Census Div. Not Township	Age	Sex	Census V.:Pg.
Wesley, Henry	Arapahoe, South Park	24	M	11:223
West, J.	Nemaha, Granada, Eureka (Farmer)	33	M	3:115
West, Ralph SC	Wash., Wash.,Marysville (Merchant)	25	M	3:259
West, W. SC	Arapahoe; Tarryall, South Park (Miner)	26	M	11:604
West, W. T. NC	Osage, Ridgeway, Superior (Farmer)	30	M	8:349
West, Wm. S. NC	Arapahoe, Denver (Painter)	26	M	11:318
Westbrook, Florence	Leavenworth, 1st Ward	33	F	10:120
Westcott, N. P.	Arapahoe, South Park	45	M	11:124
Weston, Philo	Arapahoe, Denver (Plasterer)	38	M	11:325
Westover, J. W.	Arapahoe, South Park	23	M	11:130
Wever, P.	Franklin, Centropolis, Minneola	57	F	8:213
Whalars, Barnard	Leav., Stranger, Leavenworth City	15	M	10:480
Whalars, James	" " "	18	M	10:480
Whalen, Bernard	Leavenworth, Ward 4	15	M	10:254
Wharton, B. S.	Doniphan, Wayne, Doniphan (Farmer)	59	M	1:373
Wheat, B.	Coffey, Leroy, Burlington (Farmer)	52	M	4:19
Wheat, Charles W.	" " "	19	M	4:19
Wheat, George E.	" " "	11	M	4:19
Wheat, Henry C.	" " "	15	M	4:19
Wheat, John I.	" " " (Mail Contractor)	29	M	4:19
Wheat, Josephine	" " "	13	F	4:19
Wheat, Mary A.	" " "	6	F	4:19
Wheat, Rachael A.	" " "	46	F	4:19
Wheat, Robert C.	" " "	8	M	4:19
Wheat, Samuel H.	" " "	18	M	4:19
Wheeler, A.	Linn, Centerville	21	M	7:89
Wheeler, Cynthia NC	Breckenridge, Emporia	24	F	4:205
Wheeler, David NC	" "	20	M	4:205
Wheeler, David	Bourbon, Turkey Creek P.O. (Farmer)	51	M	2:122
Wheeler, Elias	Lykins, Osawatomie (Laborer)	37	M	8:50
Wheeler, Elizabeth	Lykins, Marysville, Lyons	23	F	8:120
Wheeler, Esther NC	Breckenridge, Emporia	47	F	4:205
Wheeler, Joab NC	" " (Farmer)	23	M	4:205
Wheeler, John NC	" "	13	M	4:205
Wheeler, Jonathan NC	" " (Farmer)	48	M	4:205
Wheeler, Julius NC	" "	17	M	4:205
Wheeler, Mary NC	" "	15	F	4:205
Wheeler, Mary NC	Bourbon, Marmaton P.O. (Housewife)	20	F	2:207
Wheeler, Pheobe	Bourbon, Turkey Creek P.O.(Housewife)	43	F	2:122
Wheeler, Sarah NC	Breckenridge, Emporia	10	F	4:206
Wheeler, Thomas	Lykins, Osawatomie (Laborer)	47	M	8:50
Wheeler, Virginia C.	Bourbon, Turkey Creek P.O.	18	F	2:122
Whelpley, J. S.	Arapahoe, South Park	45	M	11:122
Whelpley, R. P.	" " "	47	M	11:122
Whery, James	Greenwood, Eureka (Farmer)	39	M	9:176
Whery, Sharlott	" "	15	F	9:177
Wherry, Jno.	" " (Farmer)	31	M	9:177
Whitaker, J.	Johnson, Gardner (Farmer)	30	M	6:51
Whitcher, C.	Arapahoe, South Park	29	M	11:225
Whitcher, D. H.	Arapahoe, Mountain City (Butcher)	40	M	11:466
White, Angstine	Leav.; Alexandria, Easton (Farmer)	65	M	10:446
White, D. R. NC	Riley, Manhattan P.O. (Farmer)	30	M	9:310
White, F. NC	Don., Wolf River, Walnut Gr. (Farmer)	41	M	1:404
White, Isaac D.	Lykins; Sugar Creek; West Point, Mo.	7	M	8:101
White, J. NC	Riley, Manhattan P.O. (Farmer)	60	M	9:310
White, Jacob NC	Leav., Stranger, Leav. City (Farmer)	46	M	10:465
White, James	Lyk., Marysville, Spring Hill(Farmer)	52	M	8:129
White, James A.	Lykins; Sugar Creek; West Point, Mo.	9	M	8:101
White, John W.	" " " " " (Farmer)	35	M	8:100
White, Margarett SC	Lykins, Richland, Paola	89	F	8:23

Name	Kansas: County; Township; P.O. Arap. Co.: Census Div. Not Township	Age	Sex	Census V. Pg.
White, Martha SC	Douglas, Lecompton	34	M	6:353
White, Mary E.	Lykins; Sugar Creek; West Point, Mo.	33	F	8:101
White, N. NC	Riley, Manhattan-Henryv. P.O.(Farmer)	23	M	9:311
White, N.	Don., Wolf River, Walnut Gr. (Farmer)	31	M	1:398
White, Nancy NC	Riley, Manhattan P.O.	49	F	9:310
White, S. A.	Doniphan, Wolf River, Walnut Grove	30	F	1:398
White, S. H. NC	Douglas, Lecompton (Merchant)	28	M	6:353
White, Wm.	Atchison, Center, Pardee (Farmer)	41	M	1:119
Whited, Andrew J. NC	Allen, Carlisle P.O. (Carpenter)	27	M	2:238
Whitehair, Joseph	Jefferson, Jefferson, Crooked Creek	5	M	5:32
Whitehair, Louisa	" " " "	7	F	5:32
Whitehead, C. B.	Don., Washington, Whitehead (Farmer)	46	M	1:327
Whitehead, J. H.	Don., Wash., Bellemont (Hotel Keeper)	54	M	1:293
Whitehead, James R.	Leavenworth, 1st Ward(Clk.Dist.Court)	32	M	10:123
Whitehead, Lucy	Doniphan, Washington, Bellemont	50	F	1:293
Whitehead, M. A.	Doniphan, Washington, Whitehead	46	F	1:327
Whitehead, M. M.	" " "	9	F	1:327
Whitehead, Nannie	" " "	15	F	1:327
Whitehead, P. W.	" " "	14	M	1:327
Whitelock, Garnett	Allen, Iola P.O. (Farmer)	74	M	2:269
Whitelock, Lafayette	" " "	12	M	2:269
Whitelock, Thos. G.	" " " (Farmer)	72	M	2:269
Whiteman, J. S.	John.;Oxf.;New Santa Fe,Mo. (Farmer)	37	M	6:105
Whiteside, Letha	Potta.,Shannon,Henryville-Manhattan	31	F	5:301
Whiteside, Thomas SC	Leavenworth, Delaware (Physician)	23	F	10:312
Whiteside, Wm.	Arapahoe, South Park	26	M	11:203
Whitford, Mary J. NC	Lykins, Richland, Gardner	16	F	8:22
Whitney, C.	Franklin, Centropolis, Prairie City	11		8:219
Whitney, D.	Frank.,Peoria,Peoria City (Farmer)	38	M	8:273
Whitney, E.	Frank.,Centrop.,Prairie City (Farmer)	42		8:219
Whitney, E.	" " "	16		8:219
Whitney, G.	Frank., Peoria, Peoria City (Farmer)	17	M	8:274
Whitney, J.	" " " " (Farmer)	38	M	8:273
Whitney, J.	" " " " (Farmer)	34	M	8:274
Whitney, W. J.	Franklin, Centropolis, Prairie City	40		8:219
Whitsitt, Law.? NC	Morris, Grove, Council Gr.(Blacksmith)	42	M	4:266
Whittemon, J. M. NC	Arapahoe, South Clear Creek	32	M	11:631
Whutut, Ann	Doniphan, Washington, Whitehead	26	F	1:299
Wicker, Harmon A. NC	Lykins, Stanton (Blacksmith)	33	M	8:11
Wicklim, Andrew M.	Lykins, Wea, Squiresville	16	M	8:115
Wicklim, Austin G.	" " "	4	M	8:115
Wicklim, George	" " " (Farmer)	40	M	8:115
Wicklim, Giles A.	" " "	10	M	8:115
Wicklim, Julia A.	" " "	37	F	8:115
Wicklim, Loyd	" " "	8	M	8:115
Wicklim, Luginea	" " "	12	F	8:115
Widner, Henry	Atchison, Center, Pardee (Farmer)	39	M	1:121
Wikes, B. NC	Linn, Paris	59	F	7:133
Wikes, Felix NC	" " (Farmer)	27	M	7:133
Wikes, Henderson NC	" "	18	M	7:133
Wikes, William NC	" " (Farmer)	22	M	7:133
Wilan, Margaret	Allen, Iola P.O.	59	F	2:247
Wilbuforce, J.	Arapahoe, South Park	57	M	11:5
Wild, R. D.	Arapahoe, Valley of the Platte	31	M	11:861
Wilder, C.	Franklin, Centropolis, Minneola	14	M	8:212
Wilder, G. W.	" " "	9	M	8:213
Wilder, J. F.	" " "	11	M	8:213
Wildman, H. NC	Arapahoe, South Park	22	M	11:115
Wiley, D. A.	Wabaunsee, Zeandale	8	M	5:237
Wiley, J.	" "	29	F	5:237
Wiley, J. P.	Davis, Kansas Falls P.O. (Merchant)	40	M	9:331

Name	Kansas: County; Township; P.O. Arap. Co.: Census Div. Not Township	Age	Sex	Census V : Pg.
Wiley, Wm.	Wabaunsee, Zeandale (Farmer)	30	M	5:237
Wilhart, Emily M.	Pottawatomie,Shannon,Manhattan-Henryv.	26	F	5:302
Wilhite, Joshua	Breckenridge, Emporia (Farmer)	54	M	4:190
Wilhite, Virginia A.	" "	54	F	4:190
Wilhite, W. E.	Arapahoe, Missouri City (Miner)	27	M	11:551
Wilkenson, E. S.	Johnson, Olathe (Lawyer)	42	M	6:6
Wilkenson, J. M.	Arapahoe, Russell Gulch (Miner)	24	M	11:486
Wilkenson, Wm.	Arapahoe, Missouri City (Miner)	31	M	11:540
Wilkins, Elezabeth	Butler, Chelsea	27	F	4:342
Wilkinson, C̄. W.	Johnson, Olathe (Farmer)	31	M	6:120
Wilkison, Rachel	Douglas, Wakarusa, Lawrence	30	F	6:238
Willey, John W. NC	Bourbon, Xenia P.O. (Farmer)	44	M	2:141
Willey, Mary	Douglas, Eudora, Lawrence	42	F	6:347
William, S. SC	Frank.,Potta.,Shermanville (Farmer)	65	M	8:248
Williams, Amanda	Atchison, Ward 2	51	BF	1:32
Williams, Amo	Greenwood, Eureka, Pleasant Grove	2	F	9:184
Williams, Anna	Bourbon, Turkey Creek P.O.(Housewife)	23	F	2:115
Williams, B. W. NC	Leav.,Stranger,Leav. City (Farmer)	43	M	10:466
Williams, David S.	Arapahoe, South Park	34	M	11:139
Williams, Dick	Atchison, Ward 2 (Drayman)	51	BM	1:32
Williams, Disa	Douglas, Willow Springs, McKinney	23	F	6:311
Williams, E.	Doniphan, Center, Troy (Farmer)	50	M	1:267
Williams, E. Y.	Arapahoe, Denver (Carpenter)	60	M	11:344
Williams, Elizabeth	Linn, Valley, Blooming Grove	23	F	7:52
Williams, Frances NC	Atchison, Mt. Pleasant	19	F	1:153
Williams, J.	Don., Burr Oak, Whitehead (Farmer)	28	M	1:345
Williams, J.	" " " " (Farmer)	26	M	1:344
Williams, J. C.	Johnson, DeSota, Lexington (Miller)	30	M	6:19
Williams, J. H. NC	Arapahoe, Lake Gulch (Miner)	30	M	11:522
Williams, Losady NC	Lykins, Stanton	40	F	8:4
Williams, M. A.	Johnson, DeSota, Lexington (Miller)	36	M	6:19
Williams, M. J.	Doniphan, Center, Troy	21	F	1:268
Williams, Maria	Leavenworth, 1st Ward	24	F	10:90
Williams, Mary E. NC	Atchison, Mt. Pleasant	2/12	F	1:153
Williams, N.	Douglas, Willow Springs, McKinney	58	F	6:311
Williams, Nathan	Brown, Locknon, Eureka (Farmer)	46	M	3:62
Williams, Nilus	Leavenworth, Ward 4 (Trader)	40	M	10:255
Williams, Orrin NC	Lykins, Stanton (Farmer)	41	M	8:4
Williams, Robert	Leavenworth, 1st Ward	21	BM	10:137
Williams, S. A.	Arapahoe, Mountain City (Carpenter)	47	M	11:461
Williams, Samuel SC	Bourbon, Turkey Creek P.O. (Farmer)	55	M	2:110
Williams, Sarah	Butler, Chelsea	28	F	4:340
Williams, Sarah A.	Bourbon, Mapleton P.O. (Housewife)	22	F	2:137
Williams, Susan	Shawnee, Monmouth, Tecumseh	52	F	9:64
Williams, T.	Johnson, Olathe (Farmer)	40	M	6:114
Williams, T. W. NC	Coffey, Ottumwa, Burlington (Farmer)	31	M	4:50
Williams, Wm.	Doug., Willow Sp., McKinney (Farmer)	29	M	6:311
Williams, Wm. NC	Arapahoe, South Park	26	M	11:103
Williamson, Emily	Brown, Locknon, Powhattan	20	F	3:67
Williamson, L.	Mars., Blue Rap.,Marysv.(Day Laborer)	27	M	3:206
Williamson, Saml. N.R NC	Lykins, Paola (Saddler)	48	M	8:28
Williamson, W. W.	Frank.; Potta.;Walker, And.Co.(Farmer)	24	M	8:242
Williamson, William NG	Nemaha, Nemaha, Central City (Farmer)	48	M	3:85
Willington, Thomas	Linn, Mound City (Farmer)	66	M	7:114
Willis, Elizabeth NC	Brown, Claytonville	29	F	3:54
Willis, S.	Doniphan, Wayne, Doniphan	22	F	1:376
Wilmot, B. D.	Arapahoe, South Park	34	M	11:118
Wills, Malinda	Atchison, Grasshopper, Kennekuk	80	F	1:91
Wills, Sarah	Leavenworth, Kickapoo	54	F	10:406
Willson, Henry NC	Leav., Alexandria, Easton (Farmer)	45	M	10:456
Willson, Mary F.	" " "	44	F	10:456

Name	Kansas: County; Township; P.O. Arap. Co.: Census Div. Not Township	Age	Sex	Census V. Pg.
Wilmott, Seria	Leavenworth, Ward 3	19	F	10:199
Wilson, Alex	Arapahoe, South Park (Trader)	34	M	11:35
Wilson, Allen	Arapahoe, California Gulch (Miner)	25	M	11:267
Wilson, Allen	" " " (Miner)	25	M	11:316
Wilson, Allen	Potta.,St. George, Elden (Farmer)	25	M	5:267
Wilson, Anderson	Shawnee, Topeka (Farmer)	45	M	9:27
Wilson, Charles	Potta., St. George, Elden (Farmer)	18	M	5:267
Wilson, Chester	Arapahoe, South Park	30	M	11:127
Wilson, Christopher	Lykins, Middle Creek, Jonesville	14	M	8:106
Wilson, David	" " " "	8	M	8:106
Wilson, David	Coffey, Neosho, Burlington	3	M	4:76
Wilson, E.NC	Doniphan, Columbus City, Whitehead	50	F	1:358
Wilson, Eliza	Lykins, Middle Creek, Jonesville	15	F	8:106
Wilson, George	" " " "	5	M	8:106
Wilson, George	Coffey, Neosho, Burlington (Farmer)	30	M	4:76
Wilson, H.NC	Don., Columb., Whitehead (Merchant)	48	M	1:358
Wilson, J.NC	Arapahoe, Missouri City (Miner)	28	M	11:562
Wilson, J.NC	Franklin, Ohio, Ohio City (Farmer)	23	M	8:234
Wilson, J. L.	Arapahoe, Eureka Gulch (Carpenter)	26	M	11:511
Wilson, Jane	Lykins, Middle Creek, Jonesville	11	F	8:106
Wilson, Julia	Coffey, Neosho, Burlington	28	F	4:76
Wilson, Julia A.	Bourbon, Dayton P.O. (Housewife)	39	F	2:157
Wilson, Lou	Potta., St. George, Elden	20	F	5:267
Wilson, Lukins	Leavenworth, Ft. Leav. P.O.(Teamster)	40	M	10:317
Wilson, Malinda	Potta., St. George, Elden	14	F	5:267
Wilson, Margaret	" " " "	16	F	5:267
Wilson, Nancy	Shawnee, Topeka	40	F	9:27
Wilson, Robert	Leavenworth, Ward 1	25	M	10:123
Wilson, Sarah	Potta., St. George, Elden	49	F	5:267
Wilson, Susan	Lykins, Middle Creek, Jonesville	6	F	8:106
Wilson, Thomas	Potta., St. George, Elden (Farmer)	27	M	5:267
Wilson, W.NC	Franklin, Ohio, Ohio City	25	M	8:234
Wilson, William C.NC	Breck., Pike, Plymouth (Farmer)	23	M	4:210
Winburn, Thomas C.NC	Anderson, Monroe, Garnett	30	M	7:218
Winburn, W. G.NC	" " " (Farmer)	35	M	7:218
Windle, Susana	Bourbon, Xenia P.O. (Housewife)	30	F	2:127
Windsor, Charity	Leavenworth, Kickapoo	25	F	10:331
Windsor, Gazwell	Lykins, Paola (Carpenter)	50	M	8:31
Windsor, Thomas	Leavenworth, Kickapoo (Farmhand)	35	M	10:331
Winfield, D. I.	Davis, Ft. Riley P.O. (Farmhand)	19	M	9:348
Winfield, D. T.	" " " "	12	F	9:348
Winfield, E. D.	" " " "	17	F	9:348
Winfield, J. L.	" " " " (Farmer)	50	M	9:348
Winfield, Jas.	" " " "	15	M	9:348
Winfield, Louis	" " " " (Farmer)	21	M	9:348
Winfield, M. I.	" " " "	14	F	9:348
Winfield, M. W.	" " " "	45	F	9:348
Winfield, Zacloridge	" " " "	11	M	9:349
Wing, Jno.	Arapahoe, Denver (Banker)	26	M	11:351
Winghill, Wm. SC	Arapahoe, South Park (Miner)	33	M	11:16
Winkle, Fred	Atchison, Ward 2 (Saloon Keeper)	21	M	1:33
Winn, Derilla	Brown, Irving, Hiawatha (Farmer)	45	M	3:8
Winser, M.	Arapahoe, California Gulch	20	M	11:301
Winslow, O.	Arapahoe, Valley of the Platte	32	M	11:777
Winter, M. S.	Douglas, Eudora, Lawrence (Farmer)	25	M	6:347
Winter, Mary	" " "	2	F	6:347
Winters, H.	Arapahoe, Valley of the Platte	26	M	11:823
Wise, H. P.	Arapahoe, South Park	34	M	11:228
Wise, William H.NC	Allen, Carlisle P.O. (Farmer)	48	M	2:238
Withern, Samuel F.	Bourbon, Rockford P.O. (Farmer)	30	M	2:100

Name	Kansas: County; Township; P.O. Arap. Co.: Census Div. Not Township	Age	Sex	Census V. Pg.
Wood, Anna	Wyandotte, Wyandotte	24	F	10:46
Wood, Benjamin R.	Bourbon, Marmaton P.O. (Farmer)	24	M	2:117
Wolf, Alice	Leavenworth, Ward 3	4	F	10:232
Wolf, Charles	" " "	10	M	10:231
Wolf, Hiram	" " "	15	M	10:231
Wolf, Jane	" " "	36	F	10:231
Wolf, John	" " " (Farmer)	45	M	10:231
Wolf, John	" " "	11	M	10:231
Wolf, Mary	" " "	6	F	10:232
Wood, Adaline[NC]	Woodson, Belmont (F. W.)	18	F	9:150
Wood, Edward C.	Anderson, Monroe, Garnett	6	M	7:230
Wood, J.	Don., Wolf River, Walnut Gr.(Farmer)	65	M	1:407
Wood, John W.	Anderson, Monroe, Garnett (Carpenter)	31	M	7:229
Wood, Joseph	Morris, Neosho, Council Gr. (Farmer)	53	M	4:273
Wood, Joseph	Don., Washington, Bellemont (Surveyor)	24	M	1:294
Wood, Mary	Doniphan, Wolf River, Walnut Grove	38	F	1:407
Wood, Mary A.	Leavenworth, Ward 3	63	F	10:214
Wood, N.	Doniphan, Wolf River, Walnut Grove	60	M	1:407
Wood, Robt. G.[NC]	Leav.,Alexandria,Easton(M.D.&Farmer)	38	M	10:455
Wood, Sarah C.[NC]	Leavenworth, Alexandria, Easton	35	F	10:455
Wood, W.	Doniphan, Iowa Point (Farmer)	30	M	1:423
Wood, Wm.	Morris, Neosho, Council Gr. (Farmer)	47	M	4:276
Wood, William H.	Don., Washington, Bellemont (Lawyer)	26	M	1:294
Woodard, I. B.	Greenwood, Eureka (Minister)	29	M	9:178
Woodard, Mary	" "	27	F	9:178
Woode, Sylvester[NC]	Linn, Scott, Brooklyn (Farmer)	40	M	7:26
Woodland, D.	Douglas, Clinton (Farmer)	50	M	6:416
Woodland, Fanny	" "	48	F	6:416
Woods, James A.	Anderson, Monroe, Garnett (Farmer)	41	M	7:231
Woods, John[2],Ky.	Jefferson, Grasshopper Falls (Farmer)	22	M	5:18
Woodson, America	Leav., Kickapoo	35	F	10:310
Woodson, Daniel[1]	" " (Recorder Land Office)	36	M	10:310
Woodson, E.	Douglas, Lecompton	11	F	6:354
Woodson, Elizabeth	Leavenworth, Kickapoo	11	F	10:310
Woodson, Warren	" "	8	M	10:310
Woodward, Celina	Dickinson, Kansas Falls P.O.	30	F	4:305
Woodward, J.	Osage, Ridgeway, Superior (Farmer)	23	M	8:364
Woodward, James	Dickinson, Kansas Falls P.O.(Farmer)	27	M	4:305
Woodward, S.	Osage, Ridgeway, Superior (Farmer)	64	M	8:364
Woodward, Wm.	Dickinson, Kansas Falls P.O.(Farmer)	30	M	4:305
Woodworth, Geo.	Arapahoe, Valley of the Platte (Miner)	26	M	11:862
Woolston, R. V.	Arapahoe, South Park	23	M	11:116
Wooten, Richd.	Arapahoe, Denver (Trader)	42	M	11:363
Workman, Eunice[NC]	Arapahoe, Mountain City	21	F	11:476
Workman, Hannah	Atchison, Mt. Pleasant	71	F	1:162
World, M.	Leavenworth, Ward 2	19	F	10:163
Worley, Susannah	Clay, Junction City P.O. (Cook)	34	F	9:269
Worth, Henry S.	Arapahoe, South Park (Miner)	33	M	11:47
Worthington, W. E.	Arapahoe, South Clear Creek	29	M	11:749
Wough, E. W.	Douglas, Kanwaca, Lawrence (Farmer)	44	M	6:389
Wright, B. A.	Atchison, Ward 3	1	M	1:64
Wright, B. C.	" " " (Speculator)	33	M	1:64
Wright, Betsey[NC]	Coffey, Neosho, Burlington	34	F	4:76
Wright, C. W.	Arap.,Quartz Valley(Quartz&Saw Mill)	23	M	11:494
Wright, Clay H.	Atchison, Ward 2	28	M	1:3
Wright, Dan'l.	Jeff., Jeff., Crooked Cr. (Laborer)	40	M	5:38
Wright, J.	Osage, Ridgeway, Burlingame (Farmer)	28	M	8:353
Wright, L. E.	" " "	16	F	8:337

[1]See also 1855 Census, Dist. 17, p. 1.   [2]Born in Kentucky.

Name	Kansas: County; Township; P.O. Arap. Co.: Census Div. Not Township	Age	Sex	Census V: Pg
Wright, M.	Doniphan, Center, Troy	39	F	1:248
Wright, M. G.[2]	Osage, Ridgeway, Burlingame	13	F	8:337
Wright, Margaret A.	Atchison, Ward 3	24	F	1:64
Wright, Sarah	Breckenridge, Cahola, Americus	52	F	4:230
Wright, Wilson	Bourbon, Turkey Creek P.O. (Farmer)	41	M	2:108
Wyat, Augustus	Bourbon, Barnesville P.O. (Farmer)	27	M	2:178
Wyatt, C.[NC]	Johnson; Oxford; New Santa Fe, Mo.	11	M	6:105
Wyatt, E.[NC]	" " " " " "	34	F	6:105
Wyatt, H.[NC]	" " " " " (Farmer)	18	M	6:105
Wyatt, J. W.[NC]	" " " " " (Farmer)	20	M	6:105
Wyatt, K.[NC]	" " " " " (Farmer)	14	M	6:105
Wyatt, L.[NC]	" " " " " (Farmer)	45	M	6:105
Wyatt, L. H.[NC]	" " " " "	10	M	6:105
Wyatt, T. J.[NC]	" " " " "	15	F	6:105
Wyatt, W.[NC]	" " "" " " (Farmer)	24	M	6:109
Wykirst, Alex	Doniphan, Burr Oak, Whitehead	5	M	1:344
Wykirst, H. C.	" " " " (Farmer)	27	M	1:344
Wykirst, M. J.	" " " "	25	F	1:344
Wykirst, T.	" " " " (Farmer)	18	M	1:344
Wykirst, Thomas B.	" " " " (Farmer)	20	M	1:344
Wykirst, William	" " " " (Farmer)	25	M	1:344
Wykort, H.	" " " "	35	F	1:348
Wykort, H. R.	" " " "	8	F	1:348
Wykort, M. J.	" " " "	12	F	1:348
Wykort, R.	" " " " (Farmer)	36	M	1:348
Wykort, S. A.	" " " "	9	F	1:348
Wynne, E. A.[NC]	Doniphan, Center, Troy	43	F	1:261
Wynne, M.	" " " (Blacksmith)	71	M	1:261
Yates, Ira G.	Jeff., Jeff., Winchester (Farmer)	39	M	5:43
Yates, Joan	" " "	37	F	5:43
Yates, Wm.	Douglas, Kanwaca, Lawrence	6	M	6:385
York, Alexander[NC]	Jefferson, Ozawkie (Farmer)	24	M	5:101
York, Lodiska[NC]	" "	18	F	5:101
York, Rachel[NC]	" "	14	F	5:101
York, Robert[NC]	" "	12	M	5:101
Young, Allen T.	Atchison, Center, Pardee (Farmer)	51	M	1:139
Young, Calver	Linn, Scott, Twin Springs	9	M	7:5
Young, F.	Doniphan, Iowa Point (Carpenter)	30	M	1:422
Young, J. C.	Arapahoe, South Clear Creek	33	M	11:751
Young, Susan	Linn, Scott, Twin Springs	29	F	7:5
Young, Wm. G.	Nem., Red Vermillion, America (Farmer)	51	M	3:137
Youngman, Ellen	Wyandotte, Quindaro	53	F	10:56
Zane, Noah E.	" "	47	M	10:65
Zelpha, Jane[NC]	Linn, Scott	13	F	7:21
Zelpha, Tide[NC]	" "	9	M	7:21
Zimmerman, Geo. E.	Allen, Humboldt P.O. (Physician)	40	M	2:289
Zomes, J.[1]	Frank., Centrop., Minneola (Farmer)	18	M	8:206
Zomes, O.[1]	" " "	1	M	8:206
Zuis, William	Allen (Farmer)	22	M	2:234

Addendum

Name		Age	Sex	Census V: Pg
Lock, Sarah	Bourbon, Mapleton P.O.	15	F	2:148
Pitter, W.	Arapahoe, South Clear Creek	38	M	11:736
Prest, I.[NC]	Franklin, Peoria, Stanton	38	F	8:281
Rush, Jno.[NC]	Arapahoe, Denver (Farmer)	48	M	11:342
Rush, M.	Frank.; Potta.; Walker, Anderson Co.	5	F	8:241

[1] Surname possibly Zomes, but looks more like Znnes or Znnis; birthplace may be Ill. or Ia. rather than Va.

[2] Birth state may be La. rather than Va.

APPENDIX

Jeffrey Dickinson Manning and his brother, Brown Rothwell Manning, my grandsons,
join a Wagons' Ho trip through Gove County, Kansas

Analysis of Occupations of Settlers From the Four Selected States

3569 Settlers From The Four States Reported as Employed Out of 9358 Total

Total	Born	Reported Employed	Farmers	Miners	Suppliers	Builders	Arti-sans	Sub-totals
4355	Va.	1682	1024	172+	71	84	67	1418
3382	Tenn.	1129	793	96+	34	27	34	984
1364	N. C.	611	451	49+	15	21	13	549
257	S. C.	147	66	35+	6	9	8	124
9358	4 States	3569	2334	352+	126	141	122	3075

An examination of the number employed in comparison to the total population from each of the states shows about one-third of those from Tennessee and Virginia and more than half of those from the Carolinas are gainfully employed. This may reflect the difference in the emigration pattern from the states. It may be that those from the Carolinas were later emigrants and had not brought large established families with them as had the Virginians and Tennesseans. Also a careful study of the original census might show a larger proportion of single settlers from the Carolinas thus accounting for the higher proportion of employed persons.

In 1860 the entire country was largely rural, so that it is not surprising that Kansas Territory with its fertile valleys and productive grasslands attracted many farmers. The early discovery of gold in Colorado had stimulated emigration which accounts for the large number of miners. Of the 3569 employed persons 2334 were engaged in farming, roughly two-thirds. Incomplete returns of the miners' make this column of figures of no real value.

The overwhelming proportion of the employed, six-sevenths, were found in the five groups: farming, mining, supplying needs, building trades, and the artisans. The next group includes many of the professionals and so-called white-collar workers.

Born In	Reported Employed	Lawyers	Court Offic.	Physi-cians	Minis-ters	Teach-ers	Speculators Bankers
Va.	1682	30	1	28	17	19	6
Tenn.	1129	7	6	8	9	5	-
N. C.	611	5	-	7	4	3	-
S. C.	147	5	-	7	2	-	-
Four states	3569	47	7	50	32	27	6

Almost five per cent of the settlers from South Carolina were in this group of professionals and almost ten per cent of her total employed persons. South Carolina furnished about the same number of physicians as Tennessee. Tennessee was generally low in this entire professional group.

Suppliers: merchants, traders, grocers, butchers, bakers, warehousemen.
Builders: carpenters, masons, plasterers, painters, shingle-makers.
Artisans and artists: blacksmiths, wagonmakers, wheelwrights, machinists, engineers, millers, saw, grist and quartz millers, millwrights; cabinet and chair makers, silversmiths, artists, spinners and weavers, potters, saddlers, harness makers, gunsmiths, tinsmiths.

Physicians

Born in Tennessee

Alfred M. H. Bills, age 36; Bourbon, Fort Scott P. O.	2:189
James Carter, age 30; Coffey, Leroy, Leroy P.O.	4:29
J. Cursac, age 54; Franklin, Peoria, Peoria City P. O.	8:269
George A. Cutter, age 29; Coffey, Leroy, Leroy P. O.	4:31
R. H. Herchford, age 27; Doniphan, Wayne, Doniphan	1:363
O. S. Laws, age 33; Johnson, McCamish, Hibbard P. O.	6:65
J. Lee, age 36; Doniphan, Iowa Point, Iowa Pt. P. O.	1:447
J. M. Lewis, age 30; Douglas, Lawrence, Lawrence P. O.	6:208
Nathaniel Rowen, age 22; Leav., Stranger, Leav. City (also farmer)	10:466
A. T. Still, age 35; Douglas, Centropolis	6:265

Born in Virginia

S. R. Anderson, age 36; Nemaha, Capioma, Pleasant Springs	3:109
J. G. Barton, age 28; Johnson, Olathe, Olathe P. O.	6:4
J. H. Beam, age 28; Arapahoe, Mountain City, Mt. City P. O.	11:462
Samuel K. Collin, age 46; Allen, Iola P. O.	2:270
A. R. Earl, age 38; Atchison, Walnut, Sumner P. O.	1:175
John W. Fackler, age 44; Leavenworth, Ward 2, Leavenworth	10:194
P. C. Fergason, age 46; Doniphan, Marion, Palermo P. O.	1:281
James Grass, age 37; Linn, Valley, Blooming Grove	7:30
Jacob Harmon, age 56; Arapahoe, Denver, Denver P. O.	11:352
H. H. Hudnal, age 47; Doniphan, Doniphan, Doniphan P. O.	1:386
J. E. McGinnis, age 54; Madison, Hartford, Hartford P. O.	4:234
S. D. Mann, age 30; Linn, Valley, Blooming Grove	7:30
B. Means, Student of Medicine, age 33; Douglas, Lawrence P. O.	6:206
Creswell Moore, age 35; Lykins, Marysville, Lyons P. O.	8:120
G. R. Muzum, age 30; Doniphan, Iowa Point, Iowa Point P. O.	1:430
J. H. Myres, age 32; Coffey, Leroy, Leroy P. O.	4:30
D. Randolph, age 47; Arapahoe, Denver, Denver P. O.	11:338
Joseph B. Reynolds, age 50; Atchison, Center, Pardee	1:132
C. D. Roberts, age 40; Douglas, Lecompton, Lecompton P. O.	6:353
D. W. Scott, age 27; Johnson, Shawnee, Shawnee P. O.	6:31
W. Shoemaker, age 39; Franklin, Ohio, Ohio City	8:234
Wm. Smith, age 33; Anderson, Jackson, Garnett	7:209
J. M. Still, age 40; Douglas, Wakarusa, Lawrence P. O.	6:251
B. L. G. Stone, age 46; Allen, Geneva P. O.	2:252
Wm. B. Swisher, age 34; Breckinridge, Fremont, Fremont P. O.	4:166
J. M. Thompson, age 24; Doniphan, Washington, Whitehead P. O.	1:297
John H. Tilly, age 31; Bourbon, Barnesville P. O.	2:169
George E. Zimmerman, age 40; Allen, Humboldt P. O.	2:289

Born in North Carolina

John Balfour, age 43; Linn, Scott, Brooklyn P. O.	7:15
Henry P. C. Harris, age 33; Leav., Kickapoo (also farmer)	10:414
Edward Kennedy, age 28; Jefferson, Kaw, Kaw City P. O.	5:90
S. D. Moore, age 53; Atchison, Center, Pardee P. O.	1:132
A. Still, age 64; Franklin, Centropolis, Minneola P. O.	8:205
James L. Wallace, age 48; Leav., Stranger, Leav. City (also farmer)	10:461
Robert G. Wood, age 38; Leav., Alexandria, Easton (also farmer)	10:455

Born in South Carolina

T. Brockett, age 67; Linn, Valley, Blooming Grove P. O.	7:33
S. Harris, age 25; Johnson, Monticello, Monticello P. O.	6:83
T. A. Lasey, age 23; Atchison, Mt. Pleasant, Mt. Pleasant P. O.	1:150
M. Mills, Surgeon, USA, age 48; Davis, Ft. Riley Reserve	9:359
J. A. Owens, age 25; Atchison, Ward 3, Atchison P. O.	1:56
James Walters, age 58; Jackson, Douglas, Holton P. O.	5:176
Thomas Whiteside, age 23; Leavenworth, Delaware, Delaware City	10:312

Veterinarian

Born in Tennessee

George Fisher, Horse Doctor, age 28; Arapahoe, Denver	11:350

Teachers

Born in Tennessee
Ebenezer Bearden, age 32; Linn, Paris, Paris   7:146
Jesse Lewis, age 19; Linn, Scott, Brooklyn   7:27
Eli Murphy, age 36; Doniphan, Center, Troy   1:266
M. Toler, age 24; female; Johnson, Monticello, Monticello   6:83
Abijah H. Warden, age 24; Linn, Potosi, Rovella   7:59

Born in Virginia
Fanny Brown, age 22; Linn, Potosi, Rovella   7:55
Harrison Brown, age 25; Linn, Potosi, Rovella   7:55
M. Cuningham, age 20; female; Johnson, Lexington, Lexington   6:71
R. A. Deckerson, age 22; female; Doniphan, Iowa Point, Iowa Point   1:426
James Dickenson, Teacher C.S., age 29; Brown, Claytonville, Robinson   3:59
John Dickenson, age 50; Brown, Claytonville, Robinson   3:41
A. C. Harrison, age 33; Arapahoe, Denver, Denver   11:320
Cordelia Kinison, age 21; Linn, Potosi, Potosi   7:78
W. P. Leech, age 21; Woodson, Pleasant Grove, Pleasant Grove   9:169
C. E. Longerbone, age 28; female; Brown, Walnut Creek, Hamlin   3:33
S. E. Pry, age 24, female; Doniphan, Wolf River, Walnut Grove   1:397
A. Reniters, age 27; Doniphan, Marion, Palermo   1:286
Margarett Shields, age 19; Brown, Claytonville, Claytonville   3:39
M. Staples, age 25, female; Douglas, Lecompton, Lecompton   6:353
Mary E. Steele, Teacher of Music, age 22; Shawnee, Topeka, Topeka   9:15
M. M. Tracher, age 18, female; Franklin, Pottawatomie, Shermanville   8:246
Samuel Waller, age 75; Marshall, Blue Rapids, Blue Rapids   3:201

Born in North Carolina
David Manlove, age 64; Bourbon, Fort Scott   2:220
Andrew Moody, age 40; Woodson, Neosho Falls, Neosho Falls   9:136
P. D. Plattenburg, age 27; Atchison, Ward 3, Atchison   1:53

Editors, Printers, Book Dealers

Born in Tennessee
J. W. Stile, age 24, editor; Franklin, Centropolis, Minneola   8:205

Born in Virginia
J. M. Geffin, age 26, editor; Johnson, Olathe, Olathe   6:4
J. Lyman, age 50, editor; Linn, Mound City, Mound City   7:104

C. I. Clark, age 17, book dealer; Arapahoe, Denver, Denver   11:334
C. A. Travis, age 27, book dealer; Douglas, Lecompton, Lecompton   6:350

Richard Smith, age 47, printer; Leavenworth, Ward 2, Leavenworth   10:189

Born in South Carolina
W. W. Herbert, age 32, lawyer-editor; Davis, Kansas Falls P. O.   9:331

Ministers

Methodist

Born in Tennessee
W. Craig, age 50; Woodson, Verdigris, Pleasant Grove   9:161
Elam Herrington, age 34; Jefferson, Oskaloosa, Oskaloosa   5:117
Raidiford Tenison, age 55; Bourbon, Marmaton P. O.   2:106
F. M. Williams, age 35; Atchison, Walnut, Sumner; (M.E. South)   1:179

Born in Virginia
William Barret, age 55; Wyandotte, Wyandotte, Wyandotte   10:20
Samuel Beaser, age 40; Bourbon, Ft. Scott P. O.   2:90
B. F. Browman, age 37; Doniphan, Washington, Wathena   1:329
Vincent N. James, age 32; Atchison, Center, Pardee (C.M.E. Church S.)   1:140
Chas. Jordon, age 69; Shawnee, Tecumseh, Tecumseh   9:71
J. W. Maddox, age 51; Breckinridge, Forest Hill, Forest Hill   4:174

Born in North Carolina
W. N. Hamby, age 45; Anderson, Washington, Garnett   7:252
M. M. Peugh, age 28; Lykins, Paola, Paola   8:25
M. Robinson, age 50; Linn, Paris, Paris   7:157

Presbyterian

Born in Tennessee
D. G. Davis, age 28; U.P. Min. and farmer; Johnson, McCamish, Hibbard   6:62
Joseph B. Lowrance, age 37; Cumberland Min. Lykins, Paola, Paola   8:36

Born in Virginia
J. D. Paxton, age 75; O.S.P. Min.; Doniphan, Highland, Highland   1:415
John A. Steele, age 56; O.S.P. Min.; Shawnee, Topeka, Topeka   9:15

Protestant Episcopal

Born in Virginia
Charles M. Callaway, age 32; P.E. Min.; Shawnee, Topeka, Topeka   9:1
Jno. H. Drummond, age 45; P.E. Clrgm.; Lykins, Marysville, Spring Hill   8:129

Baptist

Born in Virginia
James Hummer, age 37; Lykins, Marysville, Lyons   8:120

Congregational

Born in South Carolina
J. D. Liggett, age 38; Leavenworth, Ward 3, Leavenworth   10:226

Universalist (Probably)

Born in Tennessee
D. Campbell, age 40; Universal Min.; Johnson, Shawnee, Shawnee   6:87

B. F. Minister

Born in Virginia
L. A. Alderson, age 48; Atchison, Ward 3, Atchison   1:64

Church Affiliation Not Given

Born in Tennessee
C. R. Rice, age 27; Johnson, Shawnee, Shawnee   6:24
A. M. Wilson, age 57; Franklin, Peoria, Peoria City   8:271

Born in Virginia
Wm. Buffington, age 33; Atchison, Walnut, Sumner   1:177
Robert O. Burky, age 38; Bourbon, Ft. Scott P. O.   2:90
Henry Craig, age 30; Morris, Grove, Council Grove   4:272
J. W. Sanders, age 49; Franklin, Peoria, Stanton   8:284
I. B. Woodard, age 29; Greenwood, Eureka, Eureka   9:178

Born in North Carolina
W. Moore, age 55; Franklin; Ottawa; Prairie City, Douglas Co.   8:253

Born in South Carolina
Ed. Pritchard, age 14; Student of Th.; Atchison, Ward 2, Atchison   1:38

Artists and Craftsmen

Artists

Born in Virginia
Adison D. Dixon, age 30; Atchison, 1st Ward, Atchison   1:19

Cabinet Makers

Born in Tennessee
Joseph N. Brown, age 26; Lykins, Marysville, Lyons   8:119
Stephen G. Euback, age 56; Bourbon, Raysville P. O.   2:158
Born in Virginia
A. Davis, age 30; Coffey, Leroy, Leroy   4:33
John Suttle, age 43; Breckinridge, Emporia, Emporia   4:200
J. Taylor, age 55; Doniphan, White Cloud, White Cloud   1:442

C. Makers

Born in Virginia
George Fenton, age 29; Linn, Mound City, Mound City   7:106
J. T. Lynch, age 32; Douglas, Palmyra, McKinney   6:304

Chairmakers

Born in Virginia
F. Barnes, age 43; Franklin, Centropolis, Minneola   8:201
A. P. Gandy, age 35; Chase, Falls, Cottonwood Falls   4:322

Silversmiths

Born in Tennessee
W. D. Brown, age 37; Doniphan, Iowa Point, Iowa Point   1:446
Born in North Carolina
P. H. Hunt, age 30; Breckinridge, Emporia, Emporia   4:201

Jewelers

Born in Virginia
Wm. Thornburgh, age 25; Atchison, Ward 2, Atchison   1:34

Spinners and Weavers

Born in Tennessee
Ruth Sampless, Weaver, age 38; Jefferson, Kentucky, Oskaloosa   5:75
Eleanor Scott, Spinner and weaver, age 48; Jefferson, Oskaloosa   5:127
Born in Virginia
Elizabeth Caldwell, Weaver, age 48; Jefferson, Kentucky, Oskaloosa   5:74
Jennett O'Hara, Weaver, age 50; Bourbon, Marmaton P. O.   2:204
Born in North Carolina
B. Burris, Weaver and spinner, female age 49; Jeff., Ozawkie, Ozawkie   5:103

Potters

Born in Virginia
John Cochrane, age 26; Jefferson, Oscaloosa, Oscaloosa   5:117
William Cochrane, age 29; Jefferson, Oskaloosa, Oskaloosa   5:117

1860 Settlers Engaged in Public Service

Born in Virginia
Saml. Arney, age 21, postmaster; Anderson, Washington, Garnett   7:255
T. J. Baker, age 27, postmaster; Wyandotte, Wyandotte, Wyandotte   10:44

A. Kyton, age 34, mail contractor; Doniphan, Iowa Point, Iowa Point   1:450
John I. Wheat, age 29, mail contractor; Coffey, Leroy, Burlington   4:19

I. E. Ficklin, age 20, express agent; Arapahoe, Denver, Denver   11:328

James Bentley, age 30, express rider; Nemaha, Richmond, Seneca   3:94

George Rhodes, age 28, stage driver; Douglas, Lawrence, Lawrence   6:208

Government Agents

Born in Tennessee
M. M. Campbell, age 49; Agent A.B.S.; Atchison, Center, Pardee P. O.   1:124
S. B. Garrett, age 38; Reg. Land Office; Davis, Junction City P. O.   9:335

Born in Virginia
Thomas Roberts, age 32; Land Agent; Bourbon, Fort Scott P. O.   2:221
Hiram D. Ward, age 54; Land Agent; Lykins, Paola, Paola   8:34

Born in South Carolina
Thomas Killick, age 27; General Agent; Leavenworth, Kickapoo P. O.   10:327

Surveyors

Born in Virginia
Gusland C. Hubbard, age 59; Surveyor; Atchison, 1st Ward, Atchison   1:15
George C. Vanzant, age 49; Surveyor; Douglas, Lecompton, Lecompton   6:372
Joseph Wood, age 24, Surveyor; Doniphan, Washington, Bellemont   1:294

Born in North Carolina
L. Stevens, age 38; Surveyor; Arapahoe, South Park   11:7

Born in South Carolina
John Swift, age 27, Surveyor; Washington, Washington, Marysville   3:259

Army Service Personnel

Born in Tennessee
J. B. McIntyre, age 26; Lieut. USA; Davis, Ft. Riley Reserve   9:358

Born in Virginia
W. A. Newman, age 44; Clerk QMD; Leavenworth, Fort Leavenworth   10:317
D. W. Scott, age 41; Forage Master; Davis, Ft. Riley Reserve   9:361
J. E. B. Stuart, age 27; Lieut. USA; Ft. Riley Reserve   9:358

Born in North Carolina
J. G. Martin, age 41; Brevt. Maj. USA; Davis, Ft. Riley Reserve   9:359
R. Ransom, age 32; Lieut. USA; Davis, Ft. Riley Reserve   9:358

Born in South Carolina
M. Mills, age 48; Surgeon, USA; Davis, Ft. Riley Reserve   9:359

Lawyers

Born in Tennessee

O. A. Barrett, age 25; Douglas, Lawrence, Lawrence	6:217
James Campbell, age 36; Johnson, Olathe, Olathe	6:1
Isaac Freeman, age 22; Linn, Paris, Paris	7:148
John Martin, age 26; Shawnee, Tecumseh, Tecumseh	9:68
Ricd. W. Massey, age 36; Lykins, Stanton, Stanton	8:11
Edward W. White, age 36; Lykins, Paola, Paola	8:28
T. B. Wright, age 29; Arapahoe, Denver	11:429

Born in Virginia

A. I. Baker, age 36; Breckinridge, Agnes City Township & P. O.	4:146
P. C. Cobell, age 26; Douglas, Lecompton Township & P. O.	6:350
Joseph Cochrane, age 27; Jefferson, Oskaloosa Township & P. O.	5:117
J. F. Cooper, age 24; Davis, Kansas Falls P. O.	9:331
A. S. Devenney, age 26; Johnson, Olathe, Olathe	6:2
H. F. Green, age 34; Leavenworth, Ward 3, Leavenworth	10:222
Junius Hartford, age 28; Atchison, Ward 2, Atchison	1:33
T. T. Haverhill, age 28; Arapahoe, Denver	11:411
A. Hud, age 37; Doniphan, Center, Troy	1:241
J. W.? Jenkins, age 24; Douglas, Lawrence	6:217
James Jones, age 32; Jefferson, Kaw, Kaw City	5:85
Wm. Kimberlan, age 29; Arapahoe, Mountain City	11:472
George W. M. Lane, age 30; Leavenworth, Ward 4, Leavenworth	10:268
. . . Litchfield, age 25; Arapahoe, Denver	11:351
E. M. Lowe, age 27; Leavenworth, Ward 2, Leavenworth	10:146
James B. Lowry, age 39; Anderson, Reeder, Garnett	7:258
J. H. McDowell, age 35; Leavenworth, Ward 4, Leavenworth	10:281
B. D. Mareman, age 40; Doniphan, Iowa Point P. O.	1:437
W. A. Markham, age 31; Doniphan, Iowa Point P. O.	1:447
G. Mock, age 24; Doniphan, White Cloud P. O.	1:442
G. W. Mock, age 19; Doniphan, White Cloud P. O.	1:442
M. S. Mock, age 21; Doniphan, White Cloud P. O.	1:442
J. H. Nounon, age 26; Johnson, Shawnee P. O.	6:31
G. W. Perkins, age 41; Arapahoe, Denver, Denver	11:323
D. Miller Reaw, Law Student, age 22; Arapahoe, Denver	11:327
W. Semans, age 59; Leavenworth, Ward 3, Leavenworth	10:215
F. P. Stanton, age 45; Douglas, Lecompton, Lecompton	6:371
B. F. Stringfellow, age 42; Atchison, Ward 2, Atchison	1:38
John Taylor, age 50; Atchison, Ward 3, Atchison	1:57
E. S. Wilkenson, age 42; Johnson, Olathe, Olathe	6:6

Born in North Carolina

Walter Allen, age 26; Jefferson, Oskaloosa Township & P. O.	5:109
A. F. Clewell, age 26; Arap.; Tarryall South Park; T'all-Fair Play	11:616
W. A. Johnston, age 29; Anderson, Town of Garnett	7:224
Jas. A. Phillips, age 24; Lykins, Paola P. O.	8:29
Allen Reice, age 51; Leavenworth, Ward 4, Leavenworth	10:246

Born in South Carolina

Joseph P. Carr, age 28; Atchison, Ward 2, Atchison	1:33
W. W. Herbert, Lawyer-Editor, age 32; Davis, Kansas Falls P. O.	9:331
Jno. Phillpot, age 40; Arapahoe, Golden City	11:448
Otis D. Prentiss, age 28; Marshall, Marysville Township & P. O.	3:252
John C. Sims, age 27; Bourbon, Fort Scott P. O.	2:224

Bankers and Speculators

Born in Virginia

C. Lewin, Banker, age 23; Doniphan, Iowa Point, Iowa Point	1:446
Luther R. Smoot, Banker, age 37; Leavenworth, Ward 2, Leavenworth	10:146
Jno. Wing, Banker, age 26; Arapahoe, Denver	11:351
C. E. Cooley, Speculator, age 25; Arapahoe, Denver	11:336
N. B. Stevens, Speculator, age 48; Atchison, Ward 3, Atchison	1:47
B. C. Wright, Speculator, age 33; Atchison, Ward 3, Atchison	1:64

Government, Judicial, and Law Enforcement Officers
Living in Kansas Territory in 1860

Judges
Born in Tennessee
J. Y. Campbell, Probate Judge, age 45; Anderson, Town of Garnett   7:221

Clerk of District Court
J. A. Burton, age 35; Leavenworth, Ward 2, Leavenworth   10:191

Recorders
Samuel C. Greene, age 41; Arapahoe, Denver, Denver   11:408
P. C. Sameburner, age 54; Arapahoe, Denver, Denver   11:408
J. B. Tenny, age 46; Arapahoe, Denver, Denver   11:402

Clerk of District Court
Born in Virginia
C. W. Otey, age 29; Douglas, Lecompton Township and P. O.   6:350
James R. Whitehead, age 32; Leavenworth, 1st Ward, Leavenworth   10:123

Justices of the Peace
Robt. B. Highley, age 51; Lykins, Paola Township and P. O.   8:26
William Mahon, age 61; Coffey, Leroy, Burlington P. O.   4:19
George Sharp, age 46; Leavenworth, Kickapoo Township and P. O.   10:324

Sheriffs
Born in Tennessee
Albert Dillomer, age 50; Arapahoe, Quartz Valley   11:490

Born in Virginia
Jno. H. Kehler, age 31; Arapahoe, Mountain City   11:469
A. B. Riley, age 22; Arapahoe, Spring Gulch   11:538

Constables
Born in Tennessee
S. C. Houston, age 24; Johnson, Shawnee Township and P. O.   6:25

Born in Virginia
John P. Madox, age 26; Lykins, Paola Township and P. O.   8:36

Born in North Carolina
John W. Buchanan, age 29; Bourbon, Ft. Scott P. O.   2:223
Philip Copple, age 44; Linn, Paris Township and P. O.   7:148

Policeman
Born in Virginia
J. Sigbert, age 35; Atchison, Ward 2, Atchison   1:1

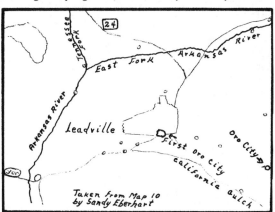

Taken from Map 10
by Sandy Eberhart

Comparing 1860 Census Subdivisions with Place Names on 1890 Kansas Maps

In the Foreword on page xvii, the population returns of the 1860 K. T. Census are given by counties for Kansas proper and by census divisions for the "Arapahoe" or "Colorado" area. These tabulations came from the Government Printing Office publication Population of the United States in 1860, Table 2, p. 162 (Kansas proper) and Table 3, p. 548 (Territory of Colorado). A detailed analysis of the population by census subdivisions for each county is given in Table 3, pages 163, 164, and 165 for Kansas proper. These subdivisions are townships and post offices for the most part, but sometimes with just one given or just the name of the county given in sparsely settled areas such as Godfroy. Only 27 of the 41 counties of Kansas proper are included in this detailed tabulation. The footnote on page 165 states: No return of subdivisions for 14 counties--Allen, Bourbon, Butler, Clay, Davis, Dickinson, Dorn, Godfrey, Hunter, Marion, McGhee, Otoe, Riley, and Wilson. The subdivisions for these missing counties have been obtained from the original census records for inclusion on the following pages. A sample of the available tabulation is given below from page 165 of the publication just cited. No comparable breakdown of the "Colorado" divisions has been found.

| City, town | County | White | | | Free Colored | | | Aggregate |
		M	F	Total	M	F	Total	
Monmouth	Shawnee Co.	150	160	310	-	-	-	310
Soldier	do	192	157	349	-	-	-	349
Tecumseh	do	345	314	659	4	4	8	667
Topeka	do	453	306	759	-	-	-	759
Williamsport	do	93	100	193	-	-	-	193

Identification of the subdivisions of Kansas proper in relation to post offices (extracting material from Kansas Post Offices) or in relation to townships (extracting material from Huling's "List of Townships") has been assembled in the following pages. Some notes of caution in using this material taken from the introduction to Kansas Post Offices are given below.

Page v. Official post office dates and spellings sometimes do not reflect actual dates and spellings, and discrepancies between federal and local records are not unusual.

Page vi. Some post offices were known locally by other names than those listed; no branch post offices were listed, and other offices may have operated before or after the dates shown.

Page vi. County designations of early post offices may not always be accurate because early surveying was inaccurate, county lines were ill-defined, and location of post offices before the county was organized was sometimes only approximate. Because of this a few offices may be listed under counties in which their sites are not to be found today.

Comparing 1860 Census Subdivisions with Place Names on Admire's 1890 Maps

    To aid in location 1860 census subdivisions small county maps, original-
ly published in Admire's 1890 Handbook, have been placed below near the
counties and subdivision listings which are underlined for easy identification.
The maps have been enlarged but not uniformly so; for example Leavenworth
County has been enlarged greatly out of proportion to the other counties in
order to achieve some degree of legibility.

    The census subdivisions, townships and post offices, are listed below
in the order they appear in the hand-written census books. The information
on the post offices includes the dates only on those established after the
1860 census; the others were established prior to that time.

WASHINGTON - Mill Creek township
Washington township (P.O. est. 1861)

Washington.

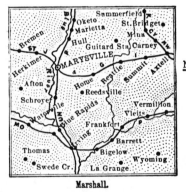

Marshall.

MARSHALL - Blue Rapids township & P. O.
    Guitard township (P. O. Guittard Station
       est. 1861)
    Marysville township & P. O.
    Vermillion township (Vermillion City P.O.)

CLAY - Junction City (P.O. in Davis Co.)
    Fort Riley (P.O. in Davis Co.)

Clay.

Abbreviations for Railroads on Admire's Maps

AT&SF: Atchison, Topeka & Santa Fe
B&MR: Burlington & Missouri River
Bur&Nor: Burlington & Northern
KCNW: Kansas City North Western
MP: Missouri Pacific
UP: Union Pacific

CRI&P: Chicago, Rock Island & Pacific
KCFS&M: Kansas City, Ft. Scott & Memphis
LK&W: Leavenworth, Kansas and Western
LT&SW: Leavenworth, Topeka & Southwestern
MK&T: Missouri, Kansas and Texas "Katy"
StJ&GRI: St. Joseph & Grand Island
StL&SF: St. Louis & San Francisco

Comparison of 1860 Subdivisions with Place Names on Admire's 1890 Maps

NEMAHA - Capioma township & P. O.
  Clear Creek township (P.O. est. 1870; P.O. formerly at Ash Point)
  Grenada township
  Home township (P.O. est. Marshall Co. 1874)
  Nemaha township
  Red Vermillion township
  Richmond township (P.O. 1855-1859)
  Rock Creek township

Nemaha.

BROWN - Claytonville P.O.
  Irving township
  Lochnin
  Walnut Creek

Brown.

JACKSON - Douglas township
  Franklin township & P.O.
  Holton P. O.
  Jefferson township

Jackson.

RILEY - Town of Manhattan,
        Manhattan P.O.
  Ogden township & P.O.
  Ogden-Manhattan
  Henryville P.O.
  Randolph P.O.

Riley.

Pottawatomie.

Geary. (Davis)

POTTAWATOMIE - Blue township
  Rockingham
  Shannon township (There was a Shannon P.O. in
    Riley Co. 1855-58)
  Saint George township (P.O. est. 9/1860;
    formerly at Eldon)
  Vienna township (P.O. est. 1862)

DAVIS - Kansas Falls P.O.(P.O. est. in Riley Co.)
  Junction City P.O.(P.O. est. in Riley Co.)
  Fort Riley P.O. (P.O. formerly at Pawnee)
  Ashland (now a township in Riley Co.)
  Fort Riley Reserve, Ft. Riley P.O.

Comparison of 1860 Subdivisions with Place Names on Admire's 1890 Maps

LEAVENWORTH - Alexandria township & P. O.
  Delaware township (Delaware City P. O.)
  Easton township & P. O.
  Ft. Leavenworth P.O. (formerly Cantonment Leavenworth)
  Kickapoo township (Kickapoo City P. O.)
  Leavenworth (Leavenworth City P. O.)
  Stranger township (P. O. est. 1867; P.O. name changed
    to Linwood 1877)

Leavenworth.

WYANDOT(T)
WYANDOTTE - Quindaro township & P. O.
  Wyandotte (Wyandott)
  township & P.O. (P.O.
  name changed to Kansas
  City in 1887)

Wyandotte.

Jefferson

JEFFERSON - Grasshopper Falls P.O. (P.O. name changed
  to Sautrell Falls, then to Valley Falls)
  Jefferson township (Jefferson P. O., Doug. Co. est.
    1865, name changed to North Lawrence 1872)
  Kaw township (Kaw City P. O.)
  Kentucky township
  Ozawkie township & P. O.
  Oskaloosa township & P. O.
  Rock Creek township (P. O. est. 1872; had been at
    Cook's Ford since 1865)

Doniphan.

DONIPHAN - Burr Oak township
  Center township
  Elwood P. O.
  Iowa Point P. O. (Iowa is a modern township)
  Marion township
  Washington township
  Wayne township
  Wolf River township (P. O. est. 1865;
    P. O. name formerly Ridge Farm; est.
    Normanville 1862)

Atchison.

ATCHISON - Atchison P. O.
  Center township
  Grasshopper township
  Kappaoma (Kapioma) township
  Lancaster township & P. O.
  Mt. Pleasant township & P. O. (P. O. moved to
    Locust Grove; later to Potter)
  Shannon township (P. O. est. 1882)
  Walnut township

Comparison of 1860 Subdivisions with Place Names on Admire's 1890 Maps

Douglas

DOUGLAS - <u>Clinton</u> township & P.O. (P.O. formerly
     named Bloomington)
<u>Eudora</u> township & P.O.
<u>Kanwaca</u> township & P.O.
<u>Lawrence</u> P.O.
<u>Lecompton</u> township & P.O.
<u>Marion</u> t'ship (P.O. name changed to Globe 1881)
<u>Palmyra</u> township & P.O. (P.O. name changed to
     Baldwin City 1862)
<u>Wakarusa</u> township & P.O.
<u>Willow Springs</u> township (P.O. 1861; P.O. for-
     formerly named Davis and briefly named Akron
     in 1870)

Johnson.

Franklin.

Miami. (Lykins)

JOHNSON - <u>Olathe</u> township & P.O.
   <u>Aubrey</u> township & P.O.
   <u>Spring Hill</u> township & P.O.
   <u>Gardner</u> (seen as Gardiner often) township & P.O.
   <u>Lexington</u> township & P.O. [P.O. moved to De Sota (DeSota) 1863]
   <u>DeSota</u> (P.O. est. 1863, from Lexington)
   <u>Monticello</u> township & P.O.
   <u>Shawnee</u> township & P.O.
   <u>McCammish</u> township
   <u>Oxford</u> township
   <u>Union</u>
FRANKLIN - <u>Centropolis</u> t'ship [P.O. 1863, formerly at Minneola (St. Bernard)]
   <u>Ohio</u> township (Ohio City P.O. moved to Princeton 1870)
   <u>Ottawa</u> township (Ottawa Creek P.O. moved to Ottawa 1864)
   <u>Peoria</u> township & P.O.
   <u>Pottawatomie</u> township (P.O. in Coffey Co. est. 1882)

LYKINS - <u>Marysville</u> township
   <u>Miami</u> township (Miami Village P.O.)
   <u>Middle Creek</u> township
   <u>Mound</u> township (Mound Creek P.O. est. 1876 may have been in same area)
   <u>Osage</u> township (P.O. est. 1864; moved to Fontania 1869; name changed to
     Fontana)
   <u>Osawatomie</u> township & P.O.
   <u>Paola</u> township & P.O. (P.O. formerly at Paola Village)
   <u>Richland</u> township
   <u>Stanton</u> township & P.O.
   <u>Sugar Creek</u> township (Sugar P.O. est. 1885 may have been in same area)
   <u>Wea</u> township (P.O. est. 1867)

Comparison of 1860 Subdivisions with Place Names on Admire's 1890 Maps

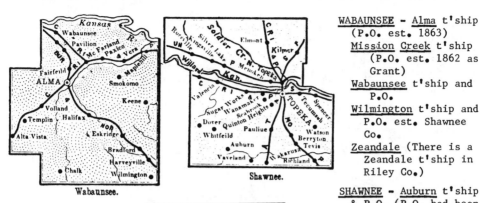

Wabaunsee.   Shawnee.

WABAUNSEE - Alma t'ship
  (P.O. est. 1863)
  Mission Creek t'ship
    (P.O. est. 1862 as
    Grant)
  Wabaunsee t'ship and
    P.O.
  Wilmington t'ship and
    P.O. est. Shawnee
    Co.
  Zeandale (There is a
    Zeandale t'ship in
    Riley Co.)

SHAWNEE - Auburn t'ship
  & P.O. (P.O. had been
    called Brownsville)
  Monmouth township
  Soldier township
  Tecumseh township &
    P.O.
  Topeka t'ship & P.O.
  Williamsport t'ship &
    P.O. (P.O. moved to
    Wakarusa in 1863)

Lyon.
(Breckinridge)

Osage.

OSAGE - Ridgeway township &
  P.O. (formerly est. in Elk
  Creek, Shawnee Co.)

BRECKINRIDGE - Agnes City P. O.
  Americus P. O. (P.O. formerly named Orleans and
    briefly (1864-66) called Sheridan)
  Cahola (P.O. at one time in Morris Co.; est. 1879,
    Chase Co.)
  Emporia township & P.O. (P.O. moved from Columbia)
  Forest Hill P. O.
  Fremont township & P. O.
  Pike township (Pike P. O. in Wabaunsee Co., est.
    1883; formerly named Albion)
  Waterloo township & P. O.

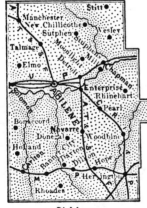

Dickinson.

Morris.

DICKINSON - Kansas Falls (P.O. Davis
  Co.; est. in Riley Co.; now in
  Geary Co.)

MORRIS - Clarke's Creek township
  Grove
  Neosho township

Comparison of 1860 Subdivisions with Place Names on Admire's 1890 Maps

MARION - Marion (Cottonwood Falls P.O.,
   Chase Co.; est. in Wise Co.)

Marion.

CHASE - Bazaar township & P.O.
   Cottonwood township (P.O. est. 1871;
      named Strong P.O. 1881)
   Diamond Creek township
   Falls township (Cottonwood Falls P.O.)
   Toledo township & P.O.

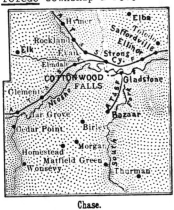

Chase.

GREENWOOD - Eureka township & P.O.
   Greenfield (P.O. Elk Co., est. in Howard Co. 1870)
   Pleasant Grove township & P.O. (moved to Toronto,
      Woodson Co. 1870)

BUTLER - Toledo (Toledo township & P.O. in Chase Co.)
   Chelsea township & P.O.
   Chelsea township, Eureka P.O. in Greenwood Co.

OTOE - Otoe, Chelsea (Chelsea P.O., Butler Co.)

HUNTER - Eldorado (Eldorado township, Butler Co.)
   Chelsea (Chelsea P.O., Butler Co.)

GODFREY (GODFROY)

Greenwood
↓

Elk (N. part of Godfrey)

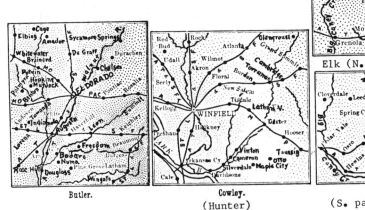

Butler.   Cowley.   Chantauqua.
                         (Hunter)   (S. part of Godfrey)

Comparison of 1860 Subdivisions with Place Names on Admire's 1890 Maps

COFFEY - Avon township (P. O. est. 1865)
  Burlington township & P. O. (P. O. formerly at Hampden)
  California township
  Leroy (Le Roy) township & P. O.
  Neosho township (Neosho City P. O.)
  Ottumwa township & P. O.
  Pottawatomie township (P. O. est. 1882)

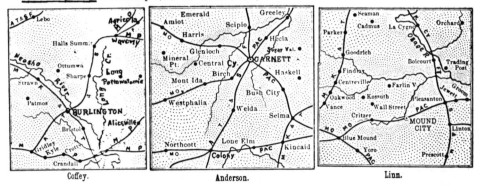

Coffey.   Anderson.   Linn.

ANDERSON - Jackson township (Jackson P.O., Linn Co.)
  Monroe
  Ozark (P. O. est. 1862; had been in Allen Co.; moved to Kincaid 1885)
  Reeder township (P. O. est. 1882)
  Walker township & P. O. (P. O. name changed to Mt. Gilead 1861; moved to
    Greeley 1866)
  Washington township

LINN - Centerville township (Centreville) & P. O.
  Liberty township
  Mound City township & P. O. (formerly named Sugar Mound P. O.)
  Paris township & P. O.
  Potosi (formerly Hillsborough) township & P.O.(P.O. moved to Pleasanton
    in 1869)
  Scott township
  Valley township

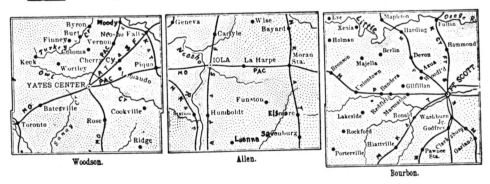

Woodson.   Allen.   Bourbon.

WOODSON - Belmont township & P. O.
  Liberty township (P. O. est. 1867)

McGEE - Ft. Scott P.O. est. 1843; attached to Bates Co., Mo.
  Brushville P.O.
    Crawford Seminary P.O. serviced through Missouri 1848-1863; may be
      in Crawford township; there is also a Crawford township in Craw.Co.
  Medoc, Mo. (probably post office serving census area)

Comparison of 1860 Subdivisions with Place Names on Admire's 1890 Maps

ALLEN - Xenia P. O., Bourbon Co. (moved from Peru, Allen Co.)
   Elizabethtown P. O. Anderson Co.
   Iola P. O. (moved from Cofachiqui
   Carlisle (Carlyle spelling seen more often) P. O. (moved from Florence)
   Geneva P. O.
   Humboldt P. O. (tabulation of additional Humboldt area residents mixed
      with Dorn Co. in separate census book)
   Turkey Creek P. O., Bourbon Co.; name changed to Uniontown 3/10/1873

BOURBON - Fort Scott P. O. est. 3/3/1843 (attached to Bates Co., Mo., for
            administrative purposes before the establishment of K. T.)
   Wheeling, Mo. P. O.
   Pawnee township & P. O. (moved to Hiattville 1872)
   Rockford P. O.
   Marmaton (Marmiton) township & P. O.
   Turkey Creek P. O. (P. O. name changed to Uniontown 1873)
   Dayton P. O.
   Xenia P. O. (P. O. moved from Peru, Allen Co.)
   Mapleton P. O.
   Rayville (Raysville) P. O. est. 3/29/1860; (P.O. moved from Osage; and
      previously at Carbondale)
   Barnesville P. O.

WILSON - Wilson (Belmont P. O., Woodson Co.)

DORN - Osage Catholic Mission (Catholic Mission P. O. name changed to Osage
   Mission 1868, and to Saint Paul P. O. in 1895 Neosho Co.)

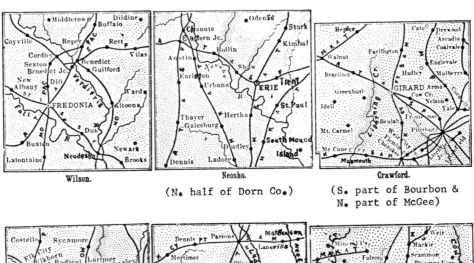

Wilson.

Neosho.

(N. half of Dorn Co.)

Crawford.

(S. part of Bourbon &
N. part of McGee)

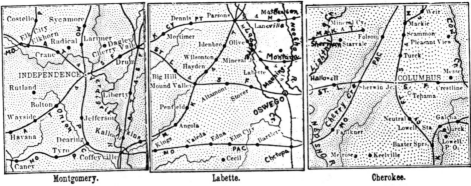

Montgomery.

(S. part of Wilson)

Labette.

(S. Half of Dorn)

Cherokee.

(McGee)

Andreas' Map of Eastern Kansas in November, 1854, Showing Boundaries of
First Election Districts Established, Places of Voting, etc.

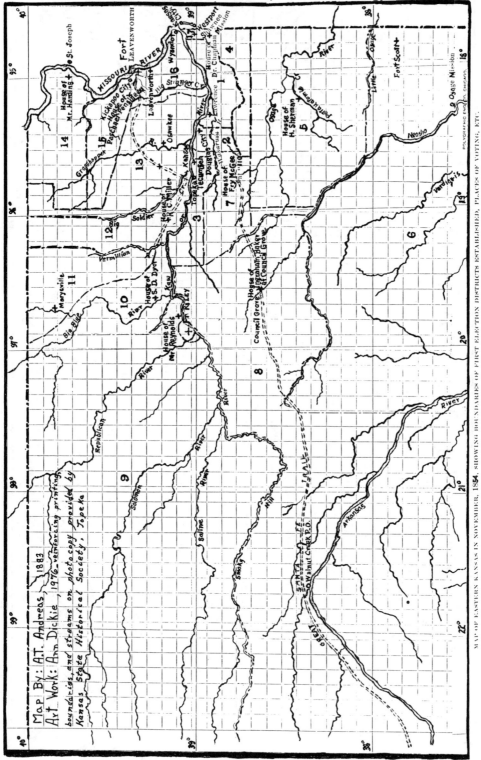

MAP OF EASTERN KANSAS IN NOVEMBER, 1854, SHOWING BOUNDARIES OF FIRST ELECTION DISTRICTS ESTABLISHED, PLACES OF VOTING, ETC.

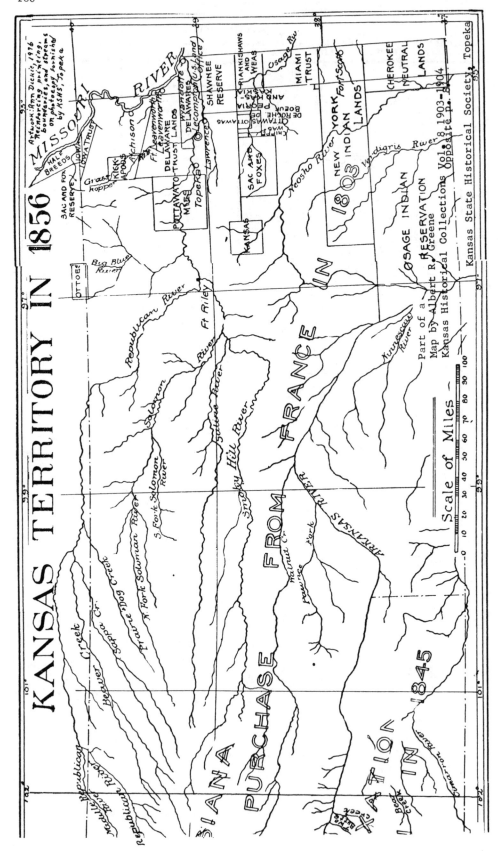

KANSAS TERRITORY IN 1856

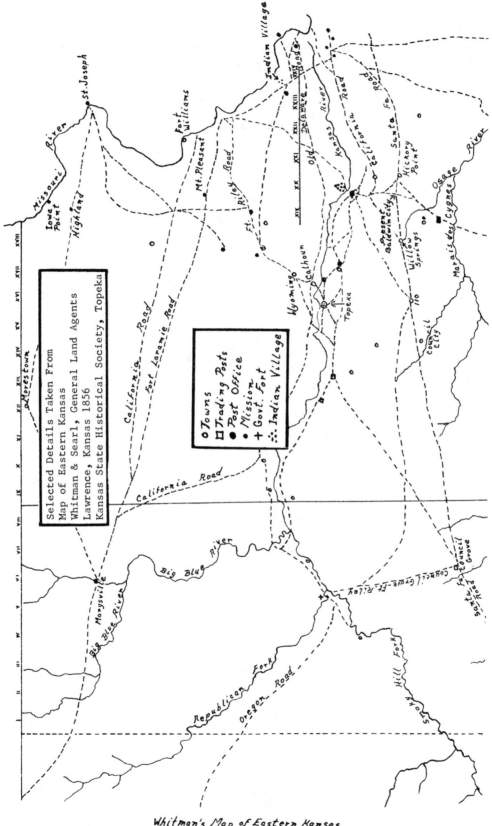

Whitman's Map of Eastern Kansas

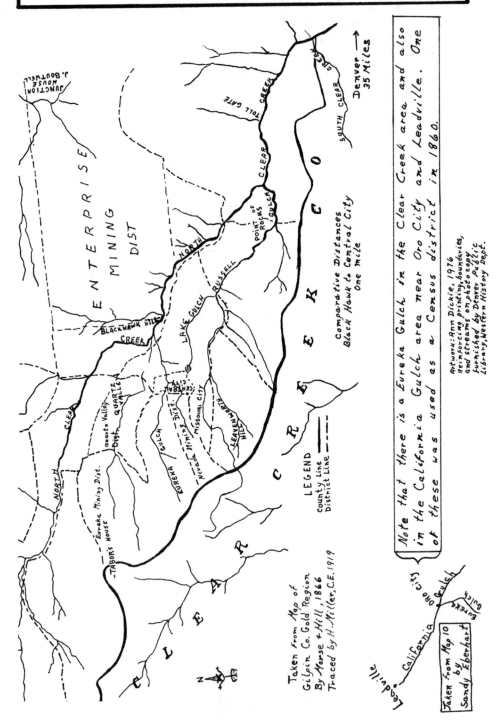

1860 Census Districts

| Central City | Enterprise District | Lake Gulch | Quartz Valley |
| Clear Creek | Eureka Gulch | Missouri City | Russell's Gulch |

Selective Maps Showing Census Districts in Colorado Area

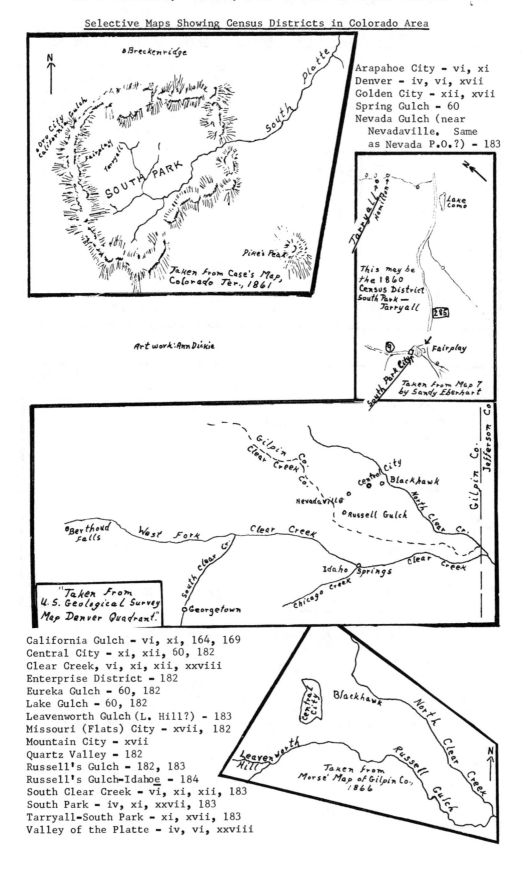

Arapahoe City - vi, xi
Denver - iv, vi, xvii
Golden City - xii, xvii
Spring Gulch - 60
Nevada Gulch (near
   Nevadaville. Same
   as Nevada P.O.?) - 183

Maps Showing Selected Extinct or Obscure Places, Landmarks as
Well as Other Identifications Needed for Orientation in the Colorado Area

Art Work: Ann Dickie

Arkansas River: East Fork, Tennessee Fk., 169
Clear Creek West Fork to Berthoud Falls, xi
Surveyors' Lines: Base Line; Eighth Guide
   Meridian West of 6th Prin. Mer., xxviii
Trails: Arkansas River, Cherokee, L.&P.P.
   Express, Santa Fe, Taos, vi
   Smoky Hill, vi, vii

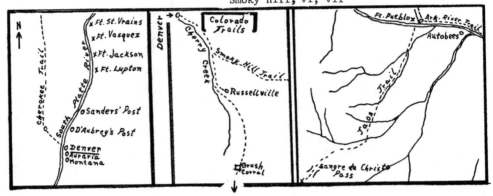

Ft. Pueblo

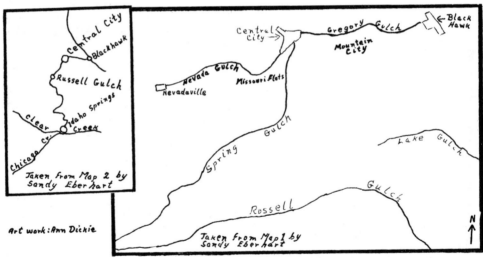

Art work: Ann Dickie

An Annotated List of Works Cited

Andreas, A. T., *History of the State of Kansas*, Chicago 1883; being reprinted
1976 by the Atchison County Historical Society.

Bauer, Ozment, and Willard, *Colorado Postal History: The Post Offices*
(Crete, Neb.: J-B Publishing Co., 1971)

Baughman, Robert, *Kansas Post Offices* (Topeka: Kansas State Historical
Society, 1961)

Eberhart, Perry, *Guide to the Colorado Ghost Towns and Mining Camps* (Denver:
Alan Swallow, 2679 S. York St., 1959)

Everton, George B., Sr., *Handy Book For Genealogists* (Logan, Utah: The
Everton Publishers, Inc., 1971)

Gill, Helen G., "The Establishment of Counties in Kansas," *Kansas Historical
Collections*, Vol. 8.

Government Printing Office, Washington, D. C.: *Population of the United
States in 1860, Compiled From the Original Returns of the Eighth Census.*

  The History and Growth of the United States Census, prepared by the
  Bureau of Labor for the Senate Committee on the Census, 1900.

  Preliminary Report on the Eighth Census, Ex. Dec. No. 116, House of
  Representatives, 1862, pp. 130-131.

  Federal Population Census 1790-1890 (Microfilm), National Archives and
  Records Services, Publication Catalog No. 71-3, 1971, p. 29.

Hafen, Leroy R., ed., *Colorado Gold Rush: Contemporary Letters and Reports,
1858-1859* (Glendale, Calif.: Arthur H. Clark Co., 1941)

Huling, A. S., Compiler, "Index to Townships in Kansas." (Topeka: 11-page
mimeo. and a 28-page typed copy in Kansas State Hist. Society Library)

Isely and Richards, *The Story of Kansas*, (Topeka: Kansas State Board of
Education, 1953)

Jackson, Clarence S., *Picture Maker of the Old West: William Henry Jackson*
(New York: Charles Scribner's Sons, 1947)

Kansas State Historical Society, Topeka
  History of Kansas Newspapers: 1854-1916
  "Kansas Dead Town File", compiled by Mrs. F. C. Montgomery.

Kansas Historical Collections
  Vol. 7, "Origin of County Names," pp. 472-474.
      8, "Early Kansas Counties," p. 89.
      8, "Map of Kansas, 1855," p. 450.
     37, "Bypaths of Kansas History," p. 451.

Prentis, Noble L., *History of Kansas* (Winfield: E. P. Greer Publisher, 1899)
  Description of counties: origin of name; county seat; date of organization;
  maps of counties showing towns, streams, roads, R.R., military reservations,
  etc. Maps taken from Admire's *Political Handbook of Kansas*, Crane & Co.,
  Topeka.

Richmond, Robert W., *Kansas: A Land of Contrasts* (St. Charles, Mo.: Forum
Press, 1974)

Rydjord, John, *Kansas Place-Names* (Norman: University of Oklahoma Press, 1972)

Topeka Daily Capital, January 30, and *Topeka Journal*, January 27, 1961.
  Write-up of program and other activities of the State of Kansas Centennial
  celebration.

Whittemore, Margaret, *Historic Kansas: A Centenary Sketchbook*. (Lawrence:
The University of Kansas Press, 1954)

Williams, Albert N., *Rocky Mountain Country* (New York: Duell, Sloan & Pearce,
1950) American Folkways Series, Erskine Caldwell, Editor.

Zornow, William Frank, *Kansas: A History of the Jayhawk State* (Norman:
University of Oklahoma Press, 1971)

Maps Used

The maps listed below were reproduced in whole or in part in this volume; to increase legibility, a great deal of detail was generally omitted. The complete citation for the source of each map is given in the Bibliography.

Andreas' "Map of Eastern Kansas in November, 1854: first election districts"

Bauer's "Colorado Territorial Counties, November 1, 1861"

Sonny Eberhart's maps in Perry Eberhart's Guide to Colorado Ghost Towns

Kansas State Historical Society:
Map by Gunn and Mitchell, Lecompton, K.T., 1861
"Map of Eastern Kansas" by Whitman & Searl, general land agents, Lawrence Kansas, 1856, pub. by J. P. Jewett & Co., Boston
Greene's "Kansas Territory in 1856, Kansas Historical Collections, Vol. 8

Colorado State Historical and Natural History Society:
"Colorado Territory, Compiled from Government Maps & Actual Surveys, 1861," Francis M. Case, Sur. Genl. Co. Ty. (Map No. 55)

Denver Public Library, Western History Department:
Morse & Hill's "Gilpin County, Colorado, 1866," traced by H. Miller, 1918
"Famous Central City Gold District"

Mitchell's "Map of Kansas, 1861" in Bauman's Kansas in Maps, 1961

Everton's "State of Colorado"

Gill's "Early Kansas Counties"

Ackerson's "The Gold Region" in Hafen's Colorado Gold Rush, p. 389.

"Jackson's West" in Picture Maker of the Old West by Clarence S. Jackson

Admire's county maps of Kansas in Prentis' History of Kansas

Richmond's "Historic Roads and Trails" from Kansas: A Land of Contrasts

Williams' "Early Rocky Mountain Trails" from Rocky Mountain Country

"Western United States," U. S. Geological Survey, Denver Quadrant, NJ 13-2

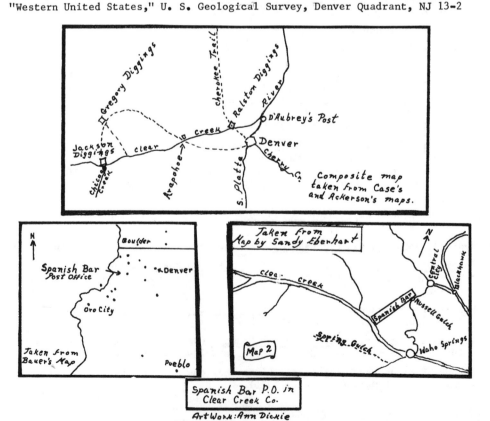

Composite map taken from Case's and Ackerson's maps.

Spanish Bar P.O. in Clear Creek Co.

ArtWork: Ann Dickie

Sources of Relevant Maps

Annual Report of the Kansas State Board of Agriculture, Topeka: beginning in 1874 county maps were included, showing township names and boundaries, cities and towns, railroads, government and railroad lands, location of school buildings; also short history of county and analysis of population by place of birth. A sample map is shown here, Cherokee Co.; its parent county, McGee, had the following census subdivisions in 1860: Fort Scott, Medoc, Mo. (settlers south of Fort Scott on or near military road); Brushville, Crawford Seminary, and Osage (Catholic) Mission, now re-named St. Paul, Neosho Co.

Cherokee County, 1875: A Sample Map from the Annual Reports

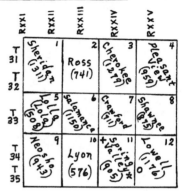

Towns in each township in Cherokee County
1. Sherman City, New Memphis, Fruitland
2. Millersburg 3. Coalfield 4. Neutral City, Pleasant View 5. Bero
6. Columbus 7. _ _ _ 8. Brownsville
9. _ _ _ _ 10. Favor and Reelville
11. Brush Creek and Baxter Springs
12. _ _ _ _ The xerox copy of the map is dark and very hard to read; there may be towns other than those tabulated.

+ Brush Creek *Baxter Springs (Population, 1059) o Approximate location of Crawford (Methodist) Seminary

Library of Congress maps showing 1860 place names in Colorado
Ebert's maps under the direction of Gov. Wm. Gilpin:
"Central Gold Region" pub. by Jacob Monk, Phila., 1862 shows Arapahoe City, Golden Gate, Jefferson, Mt. Vernon, Nevada, Spanish Bar in Lake Co., etc.
"Central Gold Region" pub. by Colton & Co., N. Y., 1866; some additional place names shown are Huntsville, Oro City, and Tarryall.
A similar map pub. by Schuchman, Pittsburgh, Pa., taken from the original field notes by O. B. Gunn, Wyandott, K.T., 1859 shows additionally Auraria and Montana.
A sectional & topographical map pub. by Colton, 1871, showing additionally Spanish Bar in Clear Creek County

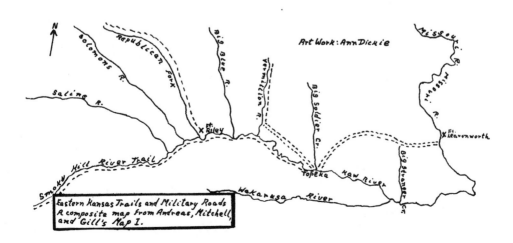